UNIBANCO GUIDES
NORTHEAST BRAZIL

ABOUT THIS GUIDEBOOK

The *Northeast Brazil Guide* describes attractions, hotels, restaurants, and other establishments and services that a team of reporters hand-picked in the course of much research and travel. No compensation of any kind was accepted from the establishments mentioned, and the guidebook's sponsor exercised no editorial input or influence.

We assigned restaurants to price categories based on the price of each eatery's most popular menu item plus a 10% service fee, which is the size of a standard tip in Brazil. Hotels' price categories are based on the daily rate for a double-occupancy room.

Addresses, phone numbers, business hours and prices came from the establishments themselves, and the *Guide*'s researchers verified these data. The publisher is not responsible for any inaccuracies or changes that occurred after the publication date (December 2006). Business hours and service prices often change between high and low tourism seasons and should be confirmed in advance whenever possible.

Before traveling along a given route, visitors are advised to consult the Highway Patrol (refer to Useful Information on page number 443) for information on road conditions and tolls.

Collaborators

Jarbas Vasconcelos, Joaquim Falcão, José Eduardo Agualusa, Josimar Melo, Robert Betenson, Walter Salles, Xico Sá

Sponsors

2006

BEĨ
Rua Dr. Renato Paes de Barros, 717, 4º andar
CEP 04530-001 Itaim-Bibi São Paulo SP
Tel.: (11) 3089-8855 Fax: (11) 3089-8899
www.bei.com.br bei@bei.com.br

UNIBANCO GUIDES
NORTHEAST BRAZIL

BEĩ

All rights reserved by BEĨ

Conception, editorial coordination,
cover, graphic design, and layout
BEĨ

Editing
BEĨ

Desktop Publishing
BEĨ

Project Consultant and Editor
Ben Harder

Associate Editors
Teresa Elsey, Ankur Ghosh,
Carolyn Gramling, Matthew Kinsey,
Laura Martin, and Jenny Pegg

Translation
Daniela Travaglini and Lynne Reay Pereira

Translation Coordination
Gaída Duque Estrada

Proofreading
Ben Harder

Cover Illustration
Marcelo Fernandes and Pedro Kastro

Photography Coordinator
Solange A. Barreira

Maps
Luiz Fernando Martini

BEĨ Team:
EDITORIAL STAFF: Ana Luisa Martins,
Fabiana Pereira, Laura Aguiar,
Marcelo Pen, and Solange A. Barreira

TRAINEE: Ana Carolina Higa

DESIGN AND LAYOUT: Alexandre Costa,
Américo Freiria, and Yumi Saneshigue

DESIGN AND LAYOUT ASSISTANTS:
Paulo Albergaria and Rosilene de Andrade

GRAPHIC PRODUCTION: Luis Alvim

ADMINISTRATIVE STAFF: Ana Paula Guerra,
Gabriella Guimarães, and Gercílio Correa

MARKETING: Midori Yamamoto

SALES: Ana Maria Capuano,
Cristiane Pedro, and
Fernanda Gomensoro

Image Digitalization and Processing
Pancrom

Printing
Pancrom

Dados Internacionais de Catalogação na Publicação (CIP)
(Câmara Brasileira do Livro, SP, Brasil)

Northeast Brazil Guides Unibanco / [Conception, editorial coordination,
cover, graphic design and layout BEĨ; translation Daniela Travaglini,
Lynne Reay Pereira ; maps Luiz Fernando Martini]. — São Paulo :
BEĨ Comunicação, 2006.

Título original: Guia Unibanco Nordeste
Vários colaboradores.
ISBN 85-86518-82-4

1. Nordeste – Descrição e viagem – Guias
2. Turismo – Nordeste I. Fernandes, Marcelo.
II. Kastro, Pedro. III. Martini, Luiz Fernando.

06-9551   CDD-918.13

Índice para catálogo sistemático:
1. Nordeste: Guias turísticos   918.13

Summary

How to use this guidebook	7
Glossary	8
Why visit the Northeast	12
An Africa that Worked Out, by José Eduardo Agualusa	14

Introduction

History	16
The Sertão, Then and Now, by Xico Sá	24
Music	26
Cousine	32
Mixed Flavors, Welcoming Food, by Josimar Melo	38
Folk Arts	40
Fine Arts	44
Architecture	49
Literature	53
Geography, Ecology and Ecotourism	55

Bahia — 60

Salvador	62
Neighborhoods and Beaches	62
Lower City	64
Upper City	66
Pelourinho	66
Neighborhoods from Centro to Barra	76
City Beaches	82
Bonfim and Ribeira	84
Rio Vermelho	86
Todos os Santos Bay	88
Recôncavo Baiano	90
Cachoeira	90
Santo Amaro da Purificação	93
The North Coast	94
Estrada do Coco	94
Linha Verde	97
Dendê Coast	99
Morro de São Paulo	99
Boipeba Island	102
Maraú Peninsula and Camamu Bay	104
Cacau Coast	107
Ilhéus	107
Historical Center	107
Itacaré	110
Canavieiras	113
Discovery Coast	115
Porto Seguro	115
Arraial d'Ajuda	118
Trancoso	122
Around Trancoso	123
Caraíva	124
Santa Cruz Cabrália	126
Santo André	127
Whale Coast	128
Cumuruxatiba and Ponta do Corumbau	128
Caravelas and Alcobaça	130
Abrolhos	132
Diving Spots in the Abrolhos Archipelago and Sorrounding Areas	133
The Backlands and the River	134
Juazeiro	134
Canudos State Park	135
Paulo Afonso	137
Chapada Diamantina	139
Lençóis	139
Chapada Diamantina National Park	142
Hiking Trails	142
Andaraí	144
Mucugê	144
Igatu	146
Capão Valley (Caeté-Açu)	146
Jacobina	148
Morro do Chapéu	148
Rio de Contas	149

Sergipe — 152

Aracaju	154
Laranjeiras	157
São Cristóvão	159
Canindé do São Francisco	160

Alagoas — 162

Maceió	164
Lace Makers and other Artists	168
The South Coast	169
Marechal Deodoro	169
Barra de São Miguel	170
The North Coast	172
Barra de Santo Antônio	172
São Miguel dos Milagres	174
Japaratinga	175
Maragogi	175
Mouth of the São Francisco River	176
Penedo	176
Piranhas	179
Piaçabuçu	180

Summary

"Barren Lives" or the Redefinition of Northeast Brazil In the Films of Nelson Pereira dos Santos, by Walter Salles 182

Pernambuco 184

Recife 186
Historical Center 188
Santo Antônio, São José and Boa Vista 193
Sorrounding Areas 199
The World According to Pernambuco, by Jarbas Vasconcelos 202
Olinda 204
Five Good Reasons to Love Olinda, by Joaquim Falcão 212
The South Coast 214
Santo Agostinho Cape 214
Porto de Galinhas 214
Tamandaré 217
North of Recife 218
Itamaracá Island 218
Igarassu 220
Zona da Mata 221
Tracunhaém 221
Vicência 222
Lagoa do Carro 222
Carpina 223
Fernando de Noronha 224
The Agreste Region 230
Caruaru 230
Bezerros 232
Gravatá 234
Garanhuns 234
Fazenda Nova 235
Sertão 236
Serra Talhada 236
Triunfo 238
Petrolina 240

Paraíba 242

João Pessoa 244
The Coast 250
Inland 254
Campina Grande 254
Cabaceiras 256
Ingá 258
Areia 258
Sousa 259

Rio Grande do Norte 260

Natal 262
The South Coast 272
Pipa 274
The North Coast 277
Inland 281

Ceará 284

Fortaleza 286
Beach Neighborhoods 286
The City Center 288
Off the Beaten Track 291
The East Coast 294
Aquiraz 297
Cascavel and Beberibe 299
Canoa Quebrada 300
The West Coast 302
Cumbuco 304
Jericoacoara 304
Camocim 308
The Mountains 310
Sobral 310
Ubajara 311
Sertão 314
Juazeiro do Norte 314
Crato 316
Around Crato 317

Piauí 318

Teresina 320
Sete Cidades
    National Park 323
Oeiras 326
São Raimundo Nonato 326
Serra da Capivara
    National Park 327
Parnaíba River Delta 331
Caju Island 333

Maranhão 334

São Luís 336
Alcântara 346
Lençóis Maranhenses 350
Barreirinhas 351
Santo Amaro do Maranhão 354
Simple Pleasures in Lençóis, by Robert Betenson 356

Hotels, Restaurants and Services 358

Useful Information 443

Consulates in the Northeast 446

Embassis in Brasília 446

Acknowledgements 448

Photo Credits 448

How to Use This Guidebook

The *Northeast Brazil Guide* offers readers suggestions for touring the region and provides essential information for understanding its culture and its natural attractions. The guide is divided into three sections.

The **Introduction** is a series of explanatory articles on history, music, cuisine, folk art, fine art, architecture, literature, and geography,

The **Destinations** section has nine chapters, one for each state in the region: Bahia, Sergipe, Alagoas, Pernambuco, Paraíba, Rio Grande do Norte, Ceará, Piauí and Maranhão. These chapters cover a wide range of destinations and attractions, catering to as many interests as possible.

Throughout the guidebook, there are **boxes containing additional information** on many sights and attractions. Particularly pleasant hotels and restaurants are highlighted in boxes labeled **Our Recommendation**. And scattered throughout the book, **signed essays** by writers, journalists, researchers, and experts dig into subjects that are of special relevance to Brazil and that, without the right guidebook, many visitors would miss.

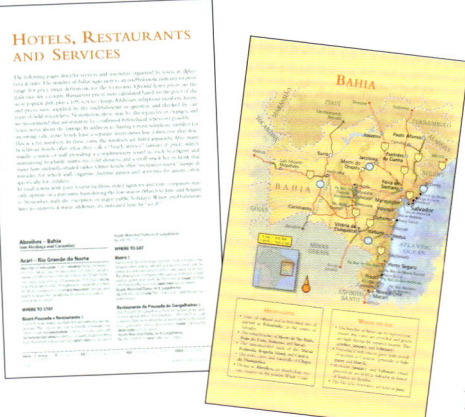

The final section, **Hotels, Restaurants, and Services**, lists establishments that we consider most suitable for and most appealing to foreign visitors. Towns and cities appear in alphabetical order, and under each community's heading, recommended businesses are listed. This section also gives additional useful information, such as distances between destinations, tips on how to get around using the Brazilian highway system, and lists of agencies, guides, telephone codes, and other essentials.

Portuguese Glossary and Phrasebook

Directions
Direita [jee-RAY-ta] – Right
Esquerda [esh-CARE-dah] – Left
Reto [REH-to] – Straight
Vire [VEER-ee] – Turn
Norte [NOR-chee] – North
Sul [SOOL] – South
Leste [LES-chee] – East
Oeste [oo-ES-chee] – West
Aberto [ah-BEAR-too] – Open
Fechado [feh-SHA-doo] – Closed

Transportation
Aeroporto [er-oo-POUR-too] – Airport
Barco [BAHR-koo] – Boat
Bilhete [bil-YEH-chee] – Ticket (for transportation)
Carro [CA-hoo] – Car
Estação [es-ta-SAOW] – Station
Horário [oh-RA-ree-oo] – Schedule
Ônibus [OH-knee-boos] – Bus
Rodoviária (Rod.) [ho-do-vee-AH-ri-a] – Bus station
Trem [TRAYM] – Train

Practicalities
Banco [BAHN-koo] – Bank
Caixa automático [KAI-sha oh-toe-MA-chee-ko] – ATM
Câmbio [KAHM-bee-oo] – Currency exchange
Correio [koh-HAY-oh] – Post office
Drogaria [droh-gah-REE-ah], Farmácia [far-MAH-see-ah] – Pharmacy
Hospital [os-pee-TAW] – Hospital
Livraria [leev-rah-REE-ah] – Bookstore
Loja [LOH-zha] – Store
Médico [MEH-dee-koo] – Doctor
Polícia [poh-LEE-see-ah] – Police
Real [hay-OW] – The Brazilian currency; plural: reais [hay-EYES])
Troco [TROH-koo] – Change

Around Town
Avenida (Av.) [ah-veh-KNEE-da] – Avenue
Bairro [BYE-hoe] – District/suburb
Capela [ca-PEH-la] – Chapel
Casa [KAH-za] – House
Catedral [cah-teh-DROW] – Cathedral
Centro [SEN-chroo] – Center; downtown
Edifício [eh-dee-FEE-see-oo] – Building
Feira [FAY-ra] – Fair
Igreja (Ig.) [ee-GRAY-jah] – Church
Jardim (Jd.) [zhar-DEEM] – Garden
Largo (Lgo.) [LAR-goo] – Plaza
Mercado [mer-KAH-doo] – Market
Museu [moo-SEH-OO] – Museum
Parque [PAR-key] – Park
Ponte [PAHN-chee] – Bridge
Praça (Pça.) [PRAH-shah] – Square
Praia [PRY-ah] – Beach
Rua (R.) [HOO-ah] – Street

In the Countryside
Cachoeira [ka-show-AY-rah] – Waterfall
Caverna [kah-VARE-nah] – Cave
Estrada [ess-TRA-dah] – Road
Fazenda [fa-ZEN-dah] – Farm
Floresta [flo-RES-tah] – Forest
Garganta [gar-GAHN-ta] – Gorge
Gruta [GREW-ta] – Cave
Ilha [EEL-ya] – Island
Lagoa [lah-GO-ah] – Lake
Lago [LAH-goo] – Lake
Mata [MAH-ta] – Forest
Mirante [me-RAHN-chee] – Lookout
Morro [MOE-hoo] – Hill
Parque – Park (Pq. Est. denotes an *estadual* or state park; Pq. Fl. a *florestal* or forest park)
Pico [PEE-koo] – Peak
Ribeirão [hee-bay-RAOW] – Brook
Rio [HEE-oo] – River
Rodovia (Rod.) [hoe-doe-VEE-ah] – Highway
Serra [SEH-ha] – Mountain range or continuous hills
Trilha [TREAL-ya] – Trail
Vale [VAH-leh] – Valley
Via [VEE-ah] – Highway

Accommodations
Albergue [all-BEAR-ge] – Hostel
Banheiro [bahn-YAY-roo] – Bathroom
Cama [KAH-ma] – Bed
Cuarto [KWAR-too] – Room
Pousada [poo-ZAH-da] – Guesthouse

Food and Drink
Água [AH-gwa] – Water
Bebida [beh-BEE-dah] – Drink

Bife [BEE-fee] – Steak
Cachaça [ka-SHAH-sah] – Traditional Brazilian white rum, made from sugar cane
Café-da-manhã [kah-FAY da mon-YA] – Breakfast
Caipirinha [kay-pee-REEN-ya] – The most famous Brazilian cocktail, made of cachaça, lime, sugar and ice. Try one with "cachaça envelhecida" (aged cachaça).
Camarão [kah-ma-RAOW] – Shrimp
Cardápio [car-DAH-pee-oo] – Menu
Carne [CAR-knee] – Meat
Carne de porco [CAR-knee jee POUR-koo] – Pork
Cerveja [sare-VAY-ja], chopp [SHOP] – Beer
Churrascaria [chew-hoss-ka-REE-ah] – All-you-can-eat barbeque restaurant
Comida [koo-MEE-dah] – Food
Conta [CONE-tah] – Bill
Frango [FRAN-goo] – Chicken
Lanchonete [lawn-choh-NEH-chee] – Lunch counter, snack bar
Massas [MAH-sauce] – Pasta
Pão [POW] – Bread
Peixe [PAY-shee] – Fish
Prato [PRAH-too] – Plate
Queijo [KAY-jew] – Cheese
Refrigerante [he-free-jer-ON-chee] – Soft drink
Restaurante [hess-tow-RAHN-chee] – Restaurant
Sobremesa [soh-bray-MAY-za] – Dessert
Sorvete [sore-VEH-chee] – Ice cream
Suco [SOO-koo] – Juice

Nightlife
Bar – Bar
Barraca [ba-HA-ka] – Beach shack bar
Boate [BWA-chee] – Nightclub
Teatro [tay-AHT-roo] – Theatre

Key Words and Phrases

Hello – Oi, Olá (informal) [OY, oh-LAH]
Good morning – Bom dia [bome JEE-ah]
Good afternoon – Boa tarde [bwa TAR-jee]
Good evening – Boa noite [bwa NOY-chee]
Goodbye – Tchau [CHOW]
Please – Por favor [pour fah-VOAR]
Thank you (very much) – (Muito) obrigado [MOO-EE-toh oh-bree-GAH-doe] is what men say. Women say: (Muito) obrigada
Yes – Sim [SEEM]
No – Não [NOW]
Today – Hoje [OH-jee]
Tomorrow – Amanhã [ah-mahn-YA]
My name is… – Meu nome é… [may-oo KNOW-me EH]
What's your name? – Qual é seu nome? [k-wow EH say-oo KNOW-me]
I'm sick/hurt – Estou doente/com dor [ess-TOH doe-EN-chee/comb DOOR]
Where is….? – Onde fica….? [OWN-jee FEE-ka]
I need help – Preciso de ajuda [preh-SEE-zoo jee ah-JEW-dah]
I don't speak Portuguese – Não falo português. [NOW FAH-loo pour-chew-GAYss]
How much (is this)? – Quanto custa? [KWAN-too KOOS-tah]
I'd like… – Gostaria… [goes-ta-REE-ia]
Help – Ajuda [ah-JEW-dah]

Numbers
0: zero [say-roo]
1: um [OOM]
2: dois [DOYCE]
3: três [TRACE]
4: quatro [KWAH-troo]
5: cinco [SEEN-koo]
6: seis [SAYS]
7: sete [SHE-chee]
8: oito [OY-two]
9: nove [NOH-vee]
10: dez [DAYS]
20: vinte [VEEN-chee]
30: trinta [TREEN-ta]
40: quarenta [kwah-REN-ta]
50: cinqüenta [seen-KWAIN-ta]
100: cem [SAME]
200: duzentos [doo-ZEN-toos]
500: quinhentos [keen-YAYN-toos]
1000: mil [MEW]

Days
Monday – Segunda-feira (Seg.) [seh-GOON-dah FAY-rah]
Tuesday – Terça-feira (Ter.) [TARE-sah]
Wednesday – Quarta-feira (Qua.) [KWAR-tah]
Thursday – Quinta-feira (Qui.) [KEEN-tah]
Friday – Sexta-feira (Sex.) [SAYSH-tah]
Saturday – Sábado (Sáb.) [SAH-ba-doo]
Sunday – Domingo (Dom.) [doh-MEAN-goo]

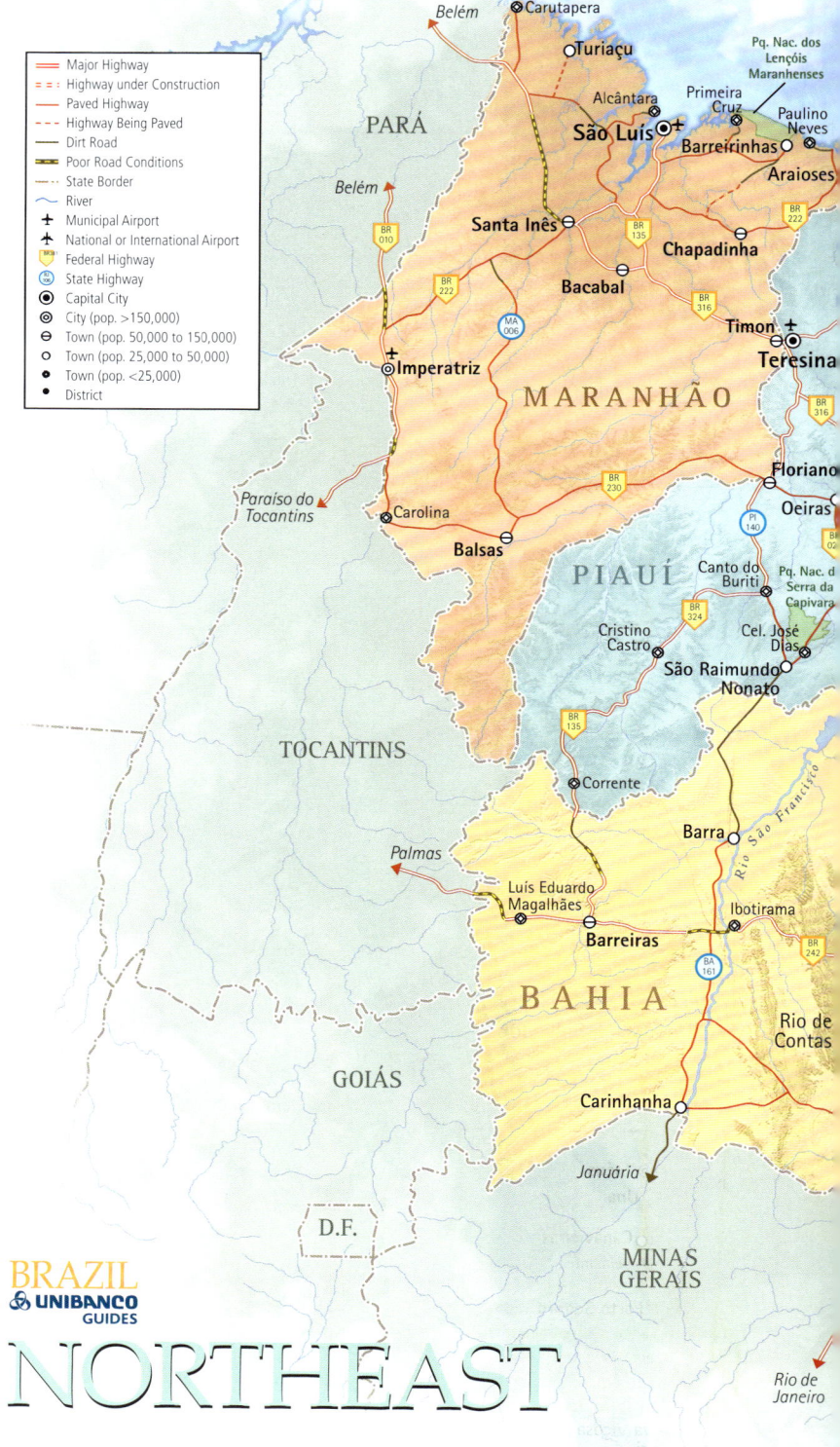

Why Visit the Northeast?

The Northeast is Brazil's most-visited region, and the foundation of its popularity is no mystery. Every twist of its long and sinuous coastline reveals a distinct tropical paradise, complete with blue ocean, white sands, and palm trees. And sun. Plenty of sun. Every day.

A crenellated façade house in Rio Grande do Norte

The irresistible scenery is by itself worth the journey, but the Northeast offers much more than a string of stunning beaches. History runs deep in this region, where European ships first landed in Brazil, and signs of the past are everywhere: baroque churches rise among modern buildings in both state capitals and quiet village squares, ancient fortresses seem to still guard the coast against forgotten foes, and ubiquitous two-story houses recall the domestic lives and labors of past residents.

Towering dunes at Jericoacoara beach

Another past, a time even more remote, also lives on in the Northeast. The region's prehistory reveals itself in the cave drawings in the Capivara Mountains, in Piauí, and in the fossils found in Santana do Cariri, in Ceará. One can also glimpse the past in Sete Cidades, in Piauí, where over millions of years the wind has sculpted colossal rock formations. These and many other archeological and geological curiosities lie scattered through the backlands, or *sertão*.

Unspoilt landscape in Fernando de Noronha

In the *sertão*'s vastness lies another Northeast, a counterpoint to the carefree tourism of sun and sea. Here travel is still arduous, as it was for the continent's earliest pioneers, the landscape is arid, and luxury is absent. But those patient enough to brave the hardships of rocky roads and sparse, uncomfortable lodgings will be rewarded with a rare insight into rich and unique cultures. Charming handicrafts, swinging festivities, and authentic street markets overflow with enticing sights, smells, and experiences.

Some places belong to Mother Nature. In the center of the region's southernmost state, Bahia, the region known as Chapada Diamantina draws a growing number of comfort-seekers to its natural attractions, including waterfalls, rivers, and caves that contain shockingly blue pools. Tourism has injected new economic viability into the region's small towns, which sprang up during the diamond boom of the 18th century. In Lençóis Maranhenses, another block of nature that's far to the north, the tourism industry is not as well-developed. Here, visitors must have an adventurous spirit to enjoy what is in store. The scenery displays rare beauty. White dunes, swept continually by the wind, form and reform, blue and green lakes, winding rivers and small fishing villages hide among these shifting mountains of sand. The people who live here tell stories of whole towns being swallowed by the sands, of ghost ships being buried in the dunes, and of voices and lights that can only be seen when the moon is full.

Valleys and mountains in Chapada Diamantina

The Northeast offers all kinds of pleasures. *Afoxé* and *maracatu* drums and carnivals fuel pleasures for the body and soul and take form in music and dance. Northeastern tables also offer up pleasurably delicacies always complementing the region's ubiquitous tapioca. And, of course, the simplest pleasure of all is the sensory feast of the coast. The ocean and palm trees dance before the eyes, warm sand shifts underfoot, and the plentiful hot sun beams down.

Placid lagoons in Lençóis Maranhenses

An Africa that Worked Out

The Northeast of Brazil, especially Salvador, in Bahia, has become something of a happy Africa in recent decades. It is Africa as Africa could be. It is an Africa that works, despite the terrible crime that marked its origin – slavery.

It is this transplanted sapling from Africa that has borne much splendid fruit for South America's largest cultural melting pot. *Capoeira*, Brazil's unique martial art. *Candomblé*, the African-derived religious rituals. Carnival, the sweat-soaked samba parades and celebrations before Lent. Samba, the rhythmic dance. The novels of Jorge Amado. *Maracatu, trio elétrico*, Caetano Veloso, and Gilberto Gil. Add to these cultural manifestations and icons of art the delicacies that Bahian women make and sell on almost every street corner. The cultural face that Brazil shows to the world is largely the face of the Northeast, and that face is, at its roots, an African face.

The first time that I, a son of Africa, visited the historical town of Olinda, I felt as if I had gone back to the best days of my childhood. There I was, in the Northeast of Brazil. Yet it was just as if I was walking through Benguela, in Angola, peeking past adobe walls into spacious backyards, or evesdropping on the idle chat of the people who lounged in chairs on the sidewalk. Many of the people in Olinda had the same peaceful air, the same joy, even the same faces as others I had known as a boy, in the most racial mixed of all the cities on Africa's West Coast.

In the region's everyday speech, I also found many words that came directly from Kimbundu. That bright, round, musical language that, although in decline, is still spoken in and around the capital of Angola. I heard words like *camundongo* (mouse), *calango* (lizard), *cafuné* (the act of stroking someone's hair), *cafuzo* (a person who's a mixture of Indian and black), *cabaça* (a type of vessel), and *liamba* (marijuana). Most of these words have kept their original meaning. Others from Kimbundu are spoken even in Portugal itself, as well as in Brazil's evolved version of that tongue, but most Portuguese are less aware than Brazilians that they use these borrowed terms to communicate – terms like *carimbo* (rubber stamp), *minhoca* (earthworm), *cambada* (a group of people or objects) or *cachimbo* (pipe).

The truth is that not only men and women were brought over on the slave ships, but also ancient gods – *Xangô, Ogum, Iemanjá*, among many others – as well as languages, culinaries secrets, sexual techniques, ornaments, sacred objects, and even a variety of plants and animals. I was once surprised to find, in a small village in the countryside of Pernambuco, an enormous *imbondeiro*, or baobab (*Adansonia digitata*), which is a majestic tree with an extremely thick trunk. I have seen many schools and barbershops in Angola that stand in the shadows of such trees. As for the *imbondeiro* I found in Pernambuco, it provided shelter for a small repair shop.

In many of the languages spoken along the West Coast of Africa, the word "sea" is the same as "death": *calunga*. The word evokes for me the suffering of the men, women and children who were stolen from their African villages, chained, and thrown into dark holds on terrifying ships. The long, painful journey to the New World must have seemed like death itself. And to come out in the light, on the far side of the ocean, must have been like being reborn. Separated from their families and homelands, they swiftly assumed new identities. They forged their blood, their languages, and their beliefs into the extraordinary melting pot called Brazil.

In the same way that mixing primary colors together can create more complex hues, new rhythms are also born from combining older ones. That can be said for religions, flavors, and everything that has come into being beneath the Northeast's shining sun. Of course, the region has retained, here and there, some rich and virtually untouched cultural treasures, such as rituals and religious practices from Nigeria or Benin. But it has simultaneously generated new practices through its fusion of African, European, and indigenous traditions.

Brazil, as a collective experiment in integration, is the future of the world

José Eduardo Agualusa,
Angolan journalist and writer, author of Nação Crioula (Creole) *and* O Vendedor de Passados (The Book of Chameleons/ The Man Who Sold Pasts), *among other books*

Porto de Salvador by Pierre Verger

History

Before it became the cradle of Brazilian popular culture, the Northeast developed as a powerful colonial economy based on its once-thriving sugar industry. The region, now among the nation's poorest, still bears the marks of its past, even as it seeks a new ticket to the future.

The notion that Northeast Brazil is a united cultural and geographical entity is recent, but the entwined roots of this diverse region are as old as the continent's European and African settlement. It was not until 1970 that the Brazilian government actually drew it up as it stands today, with nine separate states. Through the early years of the Brazilian Republic in the 19th century, the "top" portion of the country, including the Amazon region, was simply referred to as the North, with no attempt to organize or unite the region's many diverse cultures and traditions. Efforts to divide the area into discrete geographical compartments first began in the last century, as part of the push to industrialize the more rural northern territories.

Early Settlements

Most historical accounts agree that it was on northeastern soil that the Old World first encountered the land that would become Brazil: First contact occurred in 1500, when Pedro Álvares Cabral's fleet of Portuguese ships dropped anchor off the shores of what is today Porto Seguro, in the state of Bahia.

Much to the disappointment of the new arrivals, the place where they had disembarked lacked the rare spices and precious metals they had set out from Portugal to find. The area did have an abundance of other natural resources, however, particularly brazilwood, which yielded a textile dye then popular in Europe. Still, though they often visited the coast in search of this wood, it took nearly 30 years for the Portuguese to truly begin settling the region. In the meantime, Brazil's shores began to attract smugglers, pirates, and adventurers from various distant lands.

By 1534, the Portuguese had put down permanent roots in Brazil. They had divided the land into large, hereditary tracts called *capitanias*, or captaincies. The captaincy system was a bureaucratic failure,

Desembarque de Cabral em Porto Seguro (Cabral lands in Porto Seguro), by Oscar Pereira da Silva, Paulista Museum

and only two captaincies, Pernambuco and São Vicente, truly prospered – owing mainly to the sugarcane crops they cultivated. In 1548, an official government was put in place. The first governor, Tomé de Sousa, arrived from Portugal the following year to set up the colony's administrative center at Vila do Pereira, a village settled in an area we know today as Salvador's Porto da Barra. The colony's main exports were brazilwood and sugar. To cultivate these crops, the government turned to enslaving the indigenous Tupinambás. Though some members of this group fled inland, many fell into slavery, converted to Catholicism, and labored for generations on the plantations and in the sugar mills. With the aid of this free labor, the sugar industry gradually supplanted brazilwood collection as the economic mainstay of the new colony.

The Sugar Era

Though it's difficult to pinpoint the exact moment when sugarcane reached Brazil, by the late 1500s it was already growing in abundance. It would be the colony's economical pillar for the next several centuries. Sugarcane plantations spread all along the Northeast coast, with Pernambuco and Bahia emerging as the most important producers thanks to their fertile land, their ports at Recife and Salvador, respectively, and their relative proximity to Europe.

The sugar industry became the most dynamic enterprise in the colony on the basis of large estates, monoculture, and a heavy reliance first on a native enslaved workforce and later on slaves from Africa. Colonial society revolved around the sugar mill and the huge, surrounding plantations. The master and his family lived in the *casa grande* (great house) and the slaves in the *senzala* (slave quarters). The relationship between these two *loci* defined the society of the sugar era. Salvador was the main center for the sale of slaves, who came mostly from Guinea, the Gold Coast, and Benin. The city remained as such until the beginning of the 18th century, when sugar declined in prominence and Rio de Janeiro, which is closer to the gold mines of Minas Gerais, in the country's Southeast, became the center of the slave trade. In spite of that shift, the Northeast remains home to the highest concentration of black people in Brazil, and it is still the region where African and Afro-Brazilian traditions are best preserved and celebrated.

European Invasions

Soon after the Portuguese initially settled near Salvador in the 1500s, they set out from their captaincie to plant townships all along the northern coast of Bahia. Their degree of success varied from place to place, in large parts because of resistance by indigenous inhabitants and invasions by other Europeans.

Since the first years after Cabral's arrival in the Northeast, the French had occupied the territory that now comprises the states of Sergipe, Paraíba, Alagoas, and Rio Grande do Norte. In 1612, the French briefly seized Maranhão from the Portuguese and founded São Luís. The Portuguese regained the area three years later, and the Portuguese Crown promptly encouraged colonists from the Azores to settle the volatile region in order to ensure its stability under their flag. The Crown thus created and directly administered the provinces of Maranhão and Grão-Pará.

The profitable sugar industry drew the attention of more than just the Portuguese and the French. In 1624, the Dutch West India Company attacked the Portuguese settlement at Salvador, but were promptly defeated. Six years later, however, they made a more successful attempt at Pernambuco, conquering Recife by 1637 and continuing on to take Filipéia (now João Pessoa), Fortaleza, and São Luís by 1644.

The Dutch "Golden Age"

The seven years' struggle between the Dutch and the Portuguese for control of Pernambuco was tumultuous, a period of rebellion and all-out war. Nevertheless, the era of Dutch occupation that followed stands in the popular imagination as a golden age – a fabled, almost mythic time. Immediately upon his arrival as governor of Recife in

1637, the Dutch Count Maurits of Nassau set a policy of religious tolerance – there were two synagogues in Recife – as well as one of reconciliation with the remaining Portuguese residents. He also brought scientists from Europe to study the topography and diseases of the tropical region, and encouraged artists such as Frans Post, Albert Eckhout, and Zacharias Wagener to draw inspiration from native flora and fauna and from scenes of colonial life.

Count Nassau returned to Europe in 1644, after the twin blow of sugar being devalued in the international market and him having disputes with the Dutch West India Company. The following year the Portuguese expelled the Dutch, who took with them sugarcane cuttings that they promptly planted in their colonies in the Antilles. Portugal had finally regained Pernambuco, but in doing so it had lost its monopoly over the sugar trade forever.

Beyond Sugar

Though sugar was at first the focus of the economy in the Northeast, other crops came to play more important roles as time passed. Tobacco was the major crop in the Recôncavo area of Bahia. Slave traders used it extensively as currency in Africa, and the highest-quality varieties were exported to Europe. Livestock breeding, initially developed to provide animal traction for operating the sugar mills,

Engenho (Plantation), oil on wood, by Frans Post, Ricardo Brennard Institute

soon moved to the open countryside. Colonial administrators encouraged such husbandry because it facilitated settlement of the vast, outlying flatlands of the Northeast's interior. Indeed, the state of Piauí is the only one to have been settled first in the countryside – by cattlemen from Bahia – and only later along the coast. Ever since the initial Portuguese settlements in the 1500s, farmers had cultivated cotton alongside sugar, but the former didn't truly flourish until the 18th century. By that time, a decrease in sugar exports and the start of the Industrial Revolution in England, drove upward both the supply and the demand for cotton. When North American cotton production screeched to a halt during the American Civil War, Brazilian production boomed, particularly in the state of Maranhão.

Rebellions and Uprisings

The Northeast was wise to cultivate crops other than sugar, as the outlook for the sugar trade grew dim by the start of the 18th century. Competition with the Antilles had led to a decline in profits, and the discovery of gold in Minas Gerais had shifted the economic axis of the colony to the southeast. Economic instability spawned several rebellions against the Portuguese Crown. One of the first such protests occurred in 1684, in Maranhão, in an upheaval known as Revolta dos Beckman – a protest against slavery, trade regulations, and the commercial monopoly held by the Companhia de Comércio do Maranhão (Maranhão Trading Company). A sugar crisis also triggered the Guerra dos Mascates (Merchants' War; 1710-1712), a conflict between the debt-ridden rural aristocracy of Olinda and the newly rich merchants (*mascates*) of Recife.

Talk of liberation and republican ideals, which were sweeping through the United States and France in the late 1700s, also influenced the colonists in Brazil. In 1798, the so-called Conjuração dos Alfaiates (Tailors' Revolt) in Bahia gained the support of the general population. It was the first time that social unrest had been tied to a movement for independence. In 1817, the Revolução Pernambucana rebellion spread from Recife out to the backlands of the Northeast state. It brought disparate groups – landowners, tradesmen, military, judges and priests – together for the first time in a struggle for independence and republican rule of the Northeast.

Following the Brazilian Proclamation of Independence on September 7, 1822, violent social unrest continued – particularly in Bahia – until July 2, 1823. That's when the colonists defeated a final Portuguese stronghold in the Recôncavo area. (Even today, Bahia's capital, Salvador, celebrates Victory Day more racuously than it celebrates Brazil's official Independence Day holiday.) In 1824, the Portuguese emperor Dom Pedro I dissolved the Constituent Assembly, which was a vestige of colonial rule, and proclaimed a royal republic under a new Brazilian Constitution. This reignited the republican fervor in Pernambuco, which joined with Paraíba, Rio Grande do Norte, and Ceará to form the Confederação do Equador (Confederation of the Equator). This homegrown attempt at independence was short-lived; Portugal thwarted it within four months.

Independence-seekers rebelled across the country throughout the 19th century. Their revolts reflected widespread discontent with Portuguese rule at all levels of society. In Pernambuco, the Guerra dos Cabanos (1832-1835) mobilized small landowners, indigenous peoples, and slaves in a religiously motivated struggle. In Salvador, tradesmen and middle-class workers formed a republican movement known as Sabinada (1837-1838), which was violently suppressed. In Maranhão, the Balaiada Revolt (1838-1841) rallied mestizos. And the Revolução Praieira (1848), in Pernambuco, was a political battle between the urban, liberal middle-class and the conservative rural landowners.

Meanwhile, the conditions of slaves throughout the Northeast were becoming increasingly unbearable, and slave revolts were common, particularly in the Recôncavo area. Significant among these was the Revolta dos Malês (Muslim Insurrection) of 1835, in Salvador. Abolitionism gained favor with Brazilians during this period, both because of the bracing effects of the uprisings and thanks to the work of some influential anti-slavery campaigners. Ceará abolished slavery in 1884, four years before a national edict, the Lei Áurea, or Golden Rule, banned slavery throughout Brazil.

COLONELS AND BANDITS

During the First Republic new forms of social unrest arose. Principal among this was the practice of political extortion known as *coronelismo*. To elect candidates who served their interests, so-called "colonels" – really civilian members of the rural landowners elite of Brazil's interior – traded physical protection, jobs, schooling, and medication in exchange for the votes of the poor. Violence was a common tool of these renegade colonels, and thuggish bodyguards (*jagunços*) enforced their demands. Indeed, a dispute among colonels ended in the 1930 assassination of João Pessoa, governor of Paraíba. That event triggered the revolution that ultimately brought President Getúlio Vargas, the controversial nacionalist leader, to power.

During the period that saw the colonels engaged in their political machinations, a separate threat to social order dominated the region's politically disempowered: Heavily-armed bandits called *cangaceiros* pillaged the villages of the Northeast through the 1940s. Despite their destructive nature, the bandits' nomadic lifestyle and flair for challenging authority gave them a romantic aura in the public imagination. That aura lives on in such legendary figures as Lampião, the most famous *cangaceiro*. Known for years for his wily and spectacular escapes from death, Lampião was finally ambushed and killed by state police in 1938 at Angicos, Sergipe. He perished with his female companion, Maria Bonita, and many of his men. Corisco, his successor and the last of the *cangaceiros*, was captured and killed two years later.

The Canudos War

The Canudos War (1896-1897) was perhaps the first major upheaval event to wrack the newborn Brazilian Republic (1889). What at first looked like a simple religious conflict between rural workers and small landowners in Bahia escalated into a violent campaign between the government and the civilians and became known as Guerra dos Canudos. The war takes its name from the town of Canudos, which Antônio Conselheiro (Anthony the Counselor) founded as a religious settlement in 1893. "The Counselor," an itinerant religious mystic from Ceará who favored the monarchy, cultivated rumors that his followers were planning to invade a neighboring town. Government troops arrived to stop him – but, astonishingly, the trained soldiers were defeated. Two additional, heavily armed government forces in the area also failed. The army's humiliation at the hands of what was considered a fringe group quickly brought the conflict to the forefront of national news. Finally, in October 1897, after more than three full months of fighting, a government army of 8,000 succeeded in destroying the village and executing everyone captured alive.

New Directions

The colonial sugar trade was both a blessing and a curse for the Northeast. One the one hand, it assured the region's economic prosperity at the time and helped unify and cultivate its unique, still-prized culture. But on the other, the plantation system bred social problems that have plagued the region throughout its history. Even though it has

Canudos surrenders, October 2, 1897

moved past the growing pains of the First Republic years – the era of corrupt *coronéis* and marauding bandits – the Northeast still faces difficult challenges. Marked by extreme poverty and prone to long periods of drought, the region suffered from constant emigration throughout the 20th century. The rise of the rubber industry in Amazônia, in the North, drew laborers from the Northeast, particularly during the major droughts of 1877 and 1915. More recently, *nordestinos* have left for the industrial cities of the Southeast and the Central West, particularly during the mid-century construction of the new capital in Brasília. Once the most populous region in Brazil, the Northeast is home today to just 30 percent of the country's population.

Despite the bleak economic outlook for the region, the Northeast is still the center of several important industries, including oil, textiles, and mining and metallurgy. In the São Francisco River Valley, the city of Petrolina has developed a unique and well-irrigated fruit-growing industry. Much of the region's once-rural population has urbanized, and the cities – particularly along the coast – are becoming major metropolitan centers. It is these pulsing foci of creativity that, in a sense, produce the region's most important product: The Northeast's cultural output – including its literature, music, fine arts, and cinema – exerts tremendous influence on the entire country. Caught between material poverty and metaphysical riches, between the archaic and the modern, the Northeast faces its challenges head-on as it writes its own history.

The *Sertão*, Then and Now

Hit the road – but be careful! Not just with the winding, pothole-riddled byways of the Northeast's vast *sertão* (rural backlands), but with your own mental image of what the backcountry is. If as you head inland into the Northeast you expect a simple, small-town paradise, or a place frozen in time – perhaps akin to Macondo, the magical village imagined by Gabriel García Márquez – you might be in for a shock. Thankfully, it is precisely in the shock of clashing expectations that you will find all the best and richest things the region has to offer today.

So yes, you'll still see plenty of *vaqueiros,* cowboys – one of the region's most traditional, iconic characters – but today they herd their cattle and goats atop zooming motorbikes. The small towns and villages in the Northeast are crawling with these bikes, both for personal transport and in the ubiquitous "moto-taxis." The horse, donkey, and mule are being replaced. Indeed, moto-taxi drivers have become such popular figures in the region that they are frequently the subject of pop songs, portrayed in sappy verses that picture them as ardent ladies' men – sort of rustic Don Juans.

Modernity has truly arrived in the backlands, even in the humblest of cottages. Satellite dishes embellish the rooftops of every home-sweet-home. The traditional image of the *sertanejos* (backlanders) as naïve yokels – immortalized by the Brazilian born writer Monteiro Lobato in his fictional character Jeca Tatu – is long gone. The *sertanejo* of today is, above all else, a hip individual. But, contrary to what cynics may say, this doesn't mean the end of cherished regional culture and customs. The backland spirit remains as powerful as ever.

Take, for example, the fabled but long-forgotten *violeiro* (guitar player), a legacy of Brazil's Iberian past. He has never been so fashionable. He lives on, takes inspiration from his modern setting, singing about the latest trends and fashions, news, TV sex, the drama of the soaps – all brought to him via satellite TV! While traveling in the *sertão,* you'll probably chance upon a guitar festival. These are epic duels where *violeiros* trade off improvised verses (called *repente*s) on a subject chosen on the spot by a jury. If you hear of such an event nearby, don't miss it. You may even have the chance to hear Oliveira de Panelas, one of the best *repentistas* of all time, improvising rhymes about globalization, George W. Bush's war in Iraq, or another of his favorite topics.

In short, leave behind any preconceptions you have of the Northeast of yore, and enter into a great journey with the mindset of a journalist or documentarian. Venture into the region with no prejudice or stereotypes. The worst traveler is the one who leaves their neck of the woods with their mind already made up about what they find.

Also, don't spend all your time on the beaches. Go deeper, enrich your journey, turn away from the beachside paradises and the well-worn tourist trail. A night in the backlands is something to treasure for the rest of your life, like a classic scene from a great movie – say, Marcelo Gomes's *Cinemas, Aspirinas e Urubus* (Cinemas, Aspirins, and Vultures). The arid scenery takes on a whitish hue; owls screech in the vast night air; there might be music in the distance, but the dominant sound is contemplative silent, a moonlit nothingness.

A trip "out West" should impart a sense of how calm, how almost Zen-like, the pace of life in the backlands can be. Locals are efficient communicators. A few sentences speak volumes; sometimes just a twitch of the lips is worth a thousand words. Ask anyone whether something is far off or near, and they might just purse their lips, as if to say, "It's right there." Then you end up walking 'til you drop! But the people here are not all silent types. Another typical backland character, richly portrayed in the region's *cordel* literature, is part Don Quixote, and partly his companion Sancho. This type is a crazy dreamer, an anti-hero, and a joker who hustles and uses his wits to survive.

You will find these characters and more in "Jualina," the main metropolis of the backlands. This urban center actually comprises two cities: Juazeiro (in Bahia) and Petrolina (in Pernambuco). The São Francisco River has divided these twin cities since birth. Or, head to Juazeiro do Norte and neighboring Barbalha and Crato in Ceará, known as "the Mecca of Cariri". There, you will find gardens at a crossroads where all the aspects of the Northeast meet. The modern walk hand-in-hand with the messianic. This is the homeland of Padre Cícero, a priest who attained sainthood by popular vote!

So, hit the road, and welcome to a country that no longer fits its own stereotypes. Don't complain about the changes. The culture is evolving, and that makes Northeast both self-contradictory and thrilling. The convergence of old traditions and new ways makes the region stronger, and it will fortify your travels as well.

To travel, after all, is to lose sight of the past.

Xico Sá,
journalist and writer born in Crato, Ceará, author of Modos de Macho & Modinhas de Fêmea, Nova Geografia da Fome (*with U. Dettmar*), A Divina Comédia da Fama *and* Catecismo de Devoções, Intimidades & Pornografias

The drums of Olodum bring beats to the streets of Salvador during Carnival

Music

The rhythms, themes, and creativity of the Northeast – and their continual interplay of tradition and innovation – compose the musical backdrop of Brazilian culture.

Of all the regions of Brazil, the Northeast most conscientiously preserves its musical traditions. Indian, African, and Iberian influences merge in hundreds of different northeastern rhythms. African roots underlie the *candomblé* drums and *capoeira* dances so abundant in Bahia. The thrumming guitars and improvised verses called *repentes*, a classical feature of backlands culture, are inherited from the Iberian Peninsula and influenced the Moors. By contrast, indigenous people of the Northeast's Pernambuco state introduced the choreographic style called the *caboclinhos*. In this art form, popular at Carnival, dancers dress as Indians. And the *zambê*, a circle dance in which the participants invite each other to dance "navel to navel" or *umbigadas*, came to Rio Grande do Norte from Angola. Popular festivities featuring these and other musical traditions are plentiful in the Northeast throughout the year, and they rise to a crescendo during Carnival and June festivities.

Ijexá, Frevo, and *Maracatu*

The states of Bahia and Pernambuco represent the main centers of Carnival in the Northeast. In Bahia's capital, Salvador, tourism has made Carnival a profitable show. *Axé* music, which is a fusion of traditional regional rhythms and commercial pop born in the 1980s, is ever-present at Carnival celebrations. Song-blaring trucks called *trios elétricos* blast the music through the streets as dancers crowd around. The city also showcases several traditional forms of African music, such as the Afro-Brazilian Carnival groups known as *afoxés* and *blocos afro.* The first *afoxés* appeared in the late 19th century, such as the famous Filhos de Gandhy (Sons of Gandhi). This group shuffles along the streets of Salvador, dragging their sandals to the *Candomblé*-associated sound of *ijexás,* and saluting African divinities called *orixás* in their ancestral tongue, Yoruba. Despite their ties to the past, the *blocos afro* appeared only in the 1970s. One such group, Ilê Aiyê, affirms black culture and racial identity by accepting as members only people of African descent.

In Pernambuco, Carnival is a more spontaneous celebration. *Frevo* and *maracatu* are the main beats supporting a variety of dances, such as *coco* circle dances and *caboclinhos*. *Frevo* can be traced back to the late 19th century and probably derives from polka and military marches. It's characterized by an unmistakably frenzied beat and a continuous whirl of arms and legs. Drums, rattles, and *gonguês*, which are percussion instruments similar to cowbells, drive *maracatu*, which involves carefully rehearsed and coordinated group performances. Dressed in colorful costumes, the members of a *maracatu* group, or *nações* (nation), follow a richly embellished, pole-mounted doll called the *calunga*. Seu Salusiano, the founder of the group Piaba de Ouro (Golden Piaba Fish) in Pernambuco, has promoted a variation called *maracatu rural*, which some hold to be more faithful to the style's African roots.

During Carnival, *frevo* bands spread their vibrant brass music throughout Olinda and Recife and join forces with the *maracatu nações*. Since the 1960s, Recife has celebrated the Noite dos Tambores Silenciosos (Night of the Silent Drums) at midnight on the Sunday of Carnival. The drummers and a crowd gather in the courtyard in front of Nossa Senhora do Terço Church, in the old part of town, and hold a moment of silence to honor the Africans once enslaved there. Many hours of music follow this pause. All the *nações* from Pernambuco come together for this annual event, including some of Brazil's longest-running music groups, such as Elefante (Elephant, founded in 1800), Leão Coroado (Crowned Lion, 1863) and Estrela Brilhante (Shining Star, 1910).

In the Bellows of the Accordion

Like percussion instruments, the accordion (or *sanfona*) plays an essential role in the music of the Northeast. The *pé-de-bode* (goat-foot) squeezebox – a popular 8-bass accordion – predominates in *forró*, a dance fuelled by the fusion of rhythms such as *baião*, *coco*, *xaxado* and *xote*. With the *zabumba* drum and the triangle, it forms the basic trio for this so-called "dance with no etiquette." *Forró* has evolved from popular local form of entertainment into a nationwide musical genre, due primarily to mass migrations of people from the Northeast to the cultural and economic powerhouse of Southeast Brazil.

By the time of his death in 1989, Luís Gonzaga was the king of *baião*, a musical style that he spent his life promoting. Born in Exu, in the backlands of Pernambuco, Gonzaga became a household name in the 1940s while performing in Rio de Janeiro. He befriended many illustrious northeasterners such as singer Marinês, the accordion play-

Caboclos-de-lança, typical characters of the *maracatu rural* performance

ers Sivuca and Dominguinhos, and fellow musician Jackson do Pandeiro. Born to an extremely poor family in Paraíba, Jackson and his parents couldn't afford to buy him an accordian, so he instead became a master of his instrument, a type of tambourine called the *pandeiro*.

Forró accompanies an annual mainstay of the Northeast's cultural: the *festas juninas* (the June festivals). These popular church celebrations mark the feast days for Saint Anthony, Saint John, and Saint Peter, and they take place throughout Brazil. In the Northeast, though, the festivities draw huge crowds, and the parties last for many days. In June, the whole region teems with dances and food. Caruaru, in Pernambuco, and Campina Grande, in Paraíba, compete every year for the title of best *festa junina*, and each attracts up to 150,000 visitors a day.

Other Sounds

While Luís Gonzaga was introducing Brazil to the sounds of the backlands, Bahia's Dorival Caymmi garnered fame as one of the country's greatest musicians and *sambistas*. Samba was born in Bahia, then brought to Rio de Janeiro by northeastern immigrants who settled on the outskirts of Rio. In 2005, Unesco proclaimed the *samba de roda*, which originated in the Recôncavo area, to be a Masterpiece of the Oral and Intangible Heritage of Humanity.

At the end of the 1950s, *bossa-nova* arose in Rio de Janeiro. Its elaborate guitar instrumentation and its intimate atmospherics contrasted with the overblown style that had previously pervaded Brazilian popular music. Despite *bossa-nova*'s Rio roots, the greatest symbol of this distinctly genre was to be a Bahian-born talent, João Gilberto.

Throughout the politically charged years of the 1960s, popular music festivals rocked the Brazilian cultural scene. The festivals served as a vehicle for young artists' voices during the military dictatorship that took power in 1964. There, Geraldo Vandré of Paraíba performed famous politically-inspired songs, and Bahians Caetano Veloso and Gilberto Gil, whose impact on Brazilian music would be felt for years to come, also performed. In 1968, the pair kicked off the *Tropicália* movement alongside Bahians Tom Zé and Capinam, and singers Maria Bethânia and Gal Costa. The movement challenged stereotypes of what constitutes good and bad taste and integrated foreign influences and regional sounds. In the same decade, multi-instrumentalist Hermeto Paschoal, from Alagoas, and his group Quarteto Novo began combining the regional rhythms of *baião* and *xaxado* with contemporary jazz harmonies. Moacir Santos, who was born in the backlands of Pernambuco, released his first album in 1965. He has since built an internationally acclaimed career as a conductor, composer, and musical arranger.

From the Northeast to the World

Since the 1970s, northeastern artists have dominated the Brazilian recording industry. An enormous roster of singers and composers – with varying allegiance to the traditional rhythms of their home region – have achieved nationwide success, such as Djavan, Belchior, Fagner, Raul Seixas, Elba Ramalho, Zé Ramalho, Nando Cordel, and Alceu Valença.

Traditional northeastern rhythms have also reached nationwide audiences. The Banda de Pífanos de Caruaru, founded in 1924 in the backlands of Alagoas, recorded its unique sound for the first time in 1972. A *banda de pífanos* is a traditional band with several wind instruments and a simple percussion set. At the end of the decade, avant-garde percussionist Naná Vasconcelos conquered audiences of the United States, Europe, and Japan during a critically acclaimed tour.

In the 1980s, Salvador's *bloco afro* Olodum became a national sensation, and Timbalada, a percussion band led by composer Carlinhos Brown, followed suit. The genre known as *axé* music has taken several singers to the top of the Brazilian charts, including Margareth Menezes, Daniela Mercury and Ivete Sangalo. Throughout the 1990s, singer, composer and arranger Lenine gained popularity in Brazil and Europe. With a missionary's zeal for spreading the Northeast's music,

Antônio Nóbrega – a dancer, musician and scholar of regional culture – researches and promotes the rich cultural heritage of the Northeast.

Electric Guitars and Samplers

The youngest generation of musicians has turned out just as creative as its predecessors. Zeca Baleiro and Rita Ribeiro successfully combined the folklore of their native Maranhão with electronic pop. The bands Mestre Ambrósio and Cordel do Fogo Encantado mix popular poetry with the rhythms of the backlands. The exotic drums of *tore*, for example, infuse the music with a syncopated, African-style beat. Similarly, Chico César, from Paraíba, has repeatedly hit the charts.

The Northeast's vitality and talent is most on display during the region's annual musical festivals. Percussionists from all over the world have convened at Percpan (World Percussion Panorama), in Salvador, since 1994. Abril Pro Rock and Rec Beat, both held in Recife, were founded respectively in 1993 and 1995. Each of these annual festivals brought attention to the movement known as *mangue beat* (literally, the beat of the mangrove swamp). The music, an unlikely combination of soul, funk, hip hop and *maracatu,* is the brainchild of Chico Science and his band Nação Zumbi. The last several Abril Pro Rock festivals hosted performances by two important new representatives of the regional scene: Pitty and DJ Dolores. Pitty, a rocker from Bahia, bucks current trends in favoring heavy guitars. DJ Dolores, from Sergipe – has toured the world playing his unique mix of electronics, street sounds, and traditional rhythms of his homeland.

State Origin of the Northeastern Rhythms and Sounds

Bahia – *candomblé, axé, samba-de-roda, capoeira, samba reggae, ijexá, afoxé*

Sergipe – *reisado, guerreiro, coco-de-roda, bacamarteiro*

Alagoas – *coco-de-roda, guerreiro, chegança, pagode alagoano* (regional variation), *baianá, masseira, boi de maragogi, pagode de viola, martelo agalopado, roda de valsar*

Pernambuco – *maracatu baque solto, maracatu baque virado, caboclinhos, cavalo marinho, candomblé, frevo, coco, ciranda, repente*

Paraíba – *ciranda, nau catarineta, coco-de-roda, baião*

Rio Grande do Norte – *coco-de-roda, zambê*

Ceará – *reisado, guerreiro, maracatu, maneiro pau*

Piauí – *reisado, coco-de-roda*

Maranhão – *tambor de crioula, boi de pindaré, boi de matraca, boi de orquestra, boi de costa de mão, tambor de mina, reggae maranhense*

Beiju molhado

Caruru

Moqueca de camarão

Acarajé

Buchada

Baião-de-dois

Cuisine

The food of the Northeast will surprise and delight even the most jaded traveler's palate. Its combination of European, African, and indigenous influences takes advantage of an extraordinary wealth of local seasonings and ingredients.

The food of the Northeast is plentiful and varied. The fruits of land and sea could provide an abundance on their own. Chef after chef has creatively incorporated this wealth of natural ingredients into recipes and ideas inspired by numerous European cultures – notably, the Portuguese, French, and Dutch – as well as by Africans and native Indians. An underlying trait of many of the region's specialities is that they require much time and dedication to prepare. As the Brazilian sociologist Gilberto Freyre put it: "Only the large amount of leisure time enjoyed by rich ladies, and the ready labor of black slaves and maids, can explain the rigid demands of certain recipes belonging to the mansions and great houses of the old established families."

Some formerly localized dishes are now common across the Northeast. Breakfast often means tapioca or *mungunzá* (cornmeal and milk) puddings with coconut, sweet potatoes, strips of sun-dried beef (known as *carne de sol*), clarified butter, and coffee sweetened with hard brown sugar. For lunch – the biggest meal of the day – you will find *feijão-de-corda* (black-eyed peas), stews of *bode* (goat) and *cabrito* (kid), and preparations of sheep and pig innards, alongside seafood dishes like the signature *moqueca de peixe* (fish stew), soft crab and pumpkin with dried shrimp, with a starter of oysters and mussels. For supper, typically a light meal, you'll enjoy tapioca, roasted cheese curds, yams, and coffee. Dessert comes in many variations, but common to nearly all of them is the use of sugar (a taste inherited from Europe), coconut (from Africa) and manioc (native to Brazil). This irresistible union of social and culinary traditions can be enjoyed in such delights as *cocada* (coconut candy), *bolinho-de-estudante* (deep-fried tapioca cakes dusted with sugar and cinnamon), and *beiju* (manioc starch pancakes) with coconut.

Juices and Compotes

Fruits that don't grow elsewhere in the country flourish in the Northeast's lush forests and arid soil. These include the acerola, cashew, *cajá*, star fruit, *graviola, pitanga,* and tamarind, and they all can be enjoyed in refreshing drinks, ice cream, or compotes – or eaten simply as they are. The popularity of fruit on the northeastern menu is actually a recent phenomenon. In the 1940s, esteemed foreign guests complained to the manager of the Grand Hotel in Recife about the absence of local fruits served for dessert.

There are some ingredients and culinary traditions, however, that do not cross state borders. For example, *dendê* palm oil, which is very popular along the coast of Bahia, is not used in Sergipe. The *babassu* oil of Maranhão disappears once you reach the twisting, turning roads of Piauí, where a more typical dish is lime compote. That fruity concoction, like many northeastern recipes, require lengthy preparation time. It is meticulously steeped and prepared over 24 hours.

Vatapá

IMPORTED INGREDIENTS

The Northeast's checkered sociopolitical history has played a major role in shaping the region's cuisine. In addition to sugar cultivation, the Portuguese conquerors introduced exotic fruits (like coconuts, mangos, jackfruit, and bananas), rice, and malagueta peppers, all of which became fixtures of the agricultural and culinary landscape of the Northeast. The strong flavors now popular in the region first found their way into dishes prepared by slaves from Africa. The *dendê* palm tree, originally from Angola, was cultivated around the city of Salvador, the center of slave trade at the time. The oil from this tree, used to fry *acarajé* (black-eyed pea fritters, a traditional religious offering), gradually replaced European olive oil in the plantation kitchens – a case of the masters acquiring the habits of their slaves. An eclectic example that not even labels such as "black food" or "*Candomblé* food" managed to hold back the delight.

Typical Regional Dishes

Certain ingredients are present in dishes prepared throughout the Northeast's nine states. The main one is manioc, a root vegetable cultivated first by the native Indians. It is called *macaxeira* or *aipim* in the Northeast and appears in both sweet and savory dishes. Shrimp, fish, and lobster are eaten all along the coast, while sun-dried beef and jerky and goat tripe and innards dominate the farmlands of the *sertão* (backlands). The following is a sampling of popular regional dishes. Those with no indication of origin are eaten throughout the Northeast.

Common Ingredients

Dendê oil: extracted from the fruit of the *dendê* palm, which originated in Africa
Carimã: fermented manioc paste
Feijão-de-corda: black-eyed peas, either shelled and in the pod
Manteiga-de-garrafa: clarified butter that has been skimmed off boiling cream and remains liquid at room temperature
Queijo-de-coalho: dry, white curd cheese, lightly salted
Queijo-manteiga: soft cream cheese
Rapadura: brown sugar cubes
Tapioca: flour obtained by heating manioc starch

Some Common Dishes

Abará (Bahia): ground black-eyed peas steamed in banana leaves
Acarajé (Bahia): black-eyed pea fritters, fried in *dendê* oil
Arroz-de-cuxá (Maranhão): rice with sorrel leaves, sesame seeds, manioc flour and seasonings
Arroz-de-hauçá (Bahia): white rice with beef jerky and smoked shrimp
Arroz-de-leite (Sergipe): rice boiled in milk and salt
Baião-de-dois (Piauí and Ceará): black-eyed peas with rice, and beef jerky with rice
Beiju (Bahia): tapioca pancakes
Beiju de folha (Bahia): tapioca steamed in banana leaves
Bobó de camarão (Bahia): shrimp in manioc stew
Capote (Piauí): Guinea fowl with rice
Carne de bode: sun-dried goat meat
Carne de sol: Salted beef cured in the sun until it reaches a jerky-like consistency
Caruru (Bahia and Sergipe): okra cooked in *dendê* oil with shrimp, fish and seasonings
Chambaril (Paraíba): beef shank
Cozido pernambucano (Pernambuco): stewed beef and vegetables
Efó (Bahia): dried shrimp with *taioba* (a spinach-like leaf), peanuts and cashew nuts
Feijoada: beef jerky in a bean broth to which pork loin and other cuts of pork, sausage, back bacon, and spare ribs have been added. Northeast variation: kidney beans instead of black beans, cooked with vegetables like pumpkin and cabbage, in the manner of a Portuguese stew

Galinha à cabidela: chicken stew enriched with chicken blood
Mão-de-vaca: beef marrow-bone
Maria-isabel (Piauí): sun-dried beef with rice
Paçoca: beef jerky fried in fat and ground up with manioc flour in a mortar
Panelada: beef innards with flour-thickened sauce
Rubacão (Paraíba): a stew of rice, beans and cheese with sun-dried meat or shrimp
Sarapatel (Pernambuco): pig's intestines and liver stewed in thickened blood
Vatapá (Bahia): a stew of fish or chicken with shrimp, coconut milk, *dendê* oil, cashews and peanuts
Xinxim de galinha (Bahia): well-seasoned chicken pieces with shrimp, *dendê* oil, cashews and peanuts

Sweets

Bolo Sousa Leão (Pernambuco): cake of fermented manioc flour, eggs, butter and coconut milk
Bolo-de-rolo (Pernambuco): guava jellyroll
Cartola: fried banana and cream cheese
Doce de espécie (Maranhão): small coconut cakes
Grude (Ceará): dessert of manioc starch and coconut
Queijada: coconut cookies
Quindim de Iaiá (Bahia): coconut-and-egg dessert

Cartola

Cuisine

Dendê

Jambo

Açaí

Araçá

Mangaba

Serigüela

Graviola

CUISINE

Cajá

Juá

Pitanga

Cacao beans

Cashew

Pinha

Mixed Flavors, Welcoming Food

Being a displaced northeasterner – I was born in the Boa Viagem neighborhood of Recife, but moved to south Brazil at age two – I pay great attention to details every time I go back to this home I hardly knew. Since I work as a food critic, the welcoming food of the Northeast particularly fascinates me.

However, my obsession with food is nothing new. I have vivid childhood memories of watching my father in the kitchen on weekends in São Paulo. A native of Paraíba who grew up in Bom Jardim, Pernambuco, my father took great pleasure in cooking at home on Sundays. Dressed only in shorts, he'd sip a *cachaça* or scotch while he prepared lunch for a medley of people. On any given Sunday, our guests might include *bossa nova* singers, veteran politicians, the managing director of *Le Monde* (when he was on holiday in Brazil), a Dominican friar who was later exiled, a famous local writer… all gathered together from the corners of the globe, and all enjoyed the food of the Northeast. A common sight at our lunch table was a version of the classic Brazilian stew, *feijoada,* that amazed people from other parts of the country: My dad made it with kidney beans instead of black beans, and he cooked it with vegetables like pumpkin and cabbage, as if it were a Portuguese stew.

A simple observation about the food of the Northeast has always struck me. Though the region is closely associated with the sea, its food cannot be summed up in the fish dishes of the coastal states. For even in coastal cities, fish is not a daily staple, and beans, manioc, rice, and beef are eaten more frequently. This is not to say that the backlands dominate the diet of the Northeast, either. Rather, diversity reigns. Between the coast and the backlands, between one state and another, lies great culinary wealth waiting to be discovered by anyone who enjoys eating well.

A good example is *carne de sol*, which is of great historical importance in the diet of the local population, not to mention the whole of Brazil. This kind of meat – salted, sun-dried beef – is prepared differently in the Northeast than in the rest of the country. The beef jerky of the South is dry and stiff, and great for stewing with beans or shredding and frying with onion. By contrast, that of the Northeast, though similarly easy to prepare, is less salty, more delicate and succulent, and can be used like fresh meat: It is delicious when grilled or lightly fried in clarified butter. And even within the Northeast, beef (and other local staples like manioc flour and red chili pepper) varies in style and preparation from state to state, as those who have tried the *carnes* of Picuí, Paraíba, or Seridó can attest.

A trip through the backlands will lead you to strange and unfamiliar delights. Try *queijo coalho,* which are cheese curds, or goat (usually the kid or baby goat, *cabrito*), whether it be stewed meat or the famous *buchada* (tripe and innards). Look for chicken prepared with its own blood (*galinha à cabidela*) or instead with okra. Try sun-dried beef with pumpkin or *escondidinho* (layers of sun-dried beef and manioc purée). Taste *baião-de-dois* (a rice-and-beans dish that has varying ingredients). All these and more will tantalize your palate in the Northeast.

Seafood is also popular, and it gains a special flavor if it's enjoyed while one is gazing at the ocean, lulled by the breeze. Dishes can be as simple as *caldinho de sururu* (shellfish broth) or *casquinha de carangueijo* (stuffed crab in its shell), or served in more complex preparations. Even the interior states have seafood dishes to call their own, such as *arroz-de-cuxá* from Maranhão, in which the sweetness of shrimp is balanced by the acidity of sorrel. A popular repast for travelers is a picnic on the beach, sipping a *caipirinha* or a fruit cocktail made from good local *cachaça*. From the vendors that roam the sands, you can buy shrimp or grilled cheese curds on sticks that have been cooked on charcoal burners. Afterwards, you'll be hopeless to resist local desserts from *mungunzá*, to manioc pudding, to the jellyroll on which people from Pernambuco pride themselves, to the simple caramels called *alfenims*.

To savor the flavors of the Northeast is to dive into the cultural syncretism that brought Portuguese, Dutch, French, and African elements to the region and added them to the foods of the native Indians. From the many problems of the region's history – predatory colonization, the enslaving of natives and Africans, the agricultural practices that devastated the Atlantic forest – has arisen a richness of mixed flavors, unforgettable to those who pass through this region even once.

Josimar Melo
Pernambuco native and food critic for the newspaper Folha de São Paulo, *director of the site* Basílico *and author of* Guia Josimar Melo de São Paulo

Caranguejada

Sururu

Jelly roll

Cocada

Folk Arts

The folk art of the Northeast, while rooted deeply in tradition, continually develops new expressive techniques and materials. Its unquenchable capacity for reinvention is a tribute to the vitality of Brazilian culture.

The arts and crafts of the Northeast are varied, reflecting the region's size and diversity, yet similar forms and styles exist, with slight variations, throughout the region. Lacework, for example, is found along the entire northeastern coast and in parts of the backlands, particularly in the towns along the São Francisco River. Women work with needles or bobbins, using cushions or wooden frames as support, to produce fine lacework like that brought to the colony by the first Europeans. Their handiwork produces finery with such colorful names as *labirinto* (labyrinth), *boa-noite* (a common flower, but also "goodnight"), *filé* (filet), and *redendê* (from the Norwegian *hardanger)*. This fine work isn't found only in small towns – it dresses the fashionistas of the Brazilian state capitals, too.

Group Work, Individual Artists' Work

Some handicrafts result from collective effort and cannot be attributed to a single artist, while others bear the mark of an individual artisan. The masks, costumes, and embroidered clothes worn during Carnival, the *bumba-meu-boi,* and *folias-de-reis* festivities; the clothes and objects used in Afro-Brazilian rituals; and the puppets known as *mamulengos* are generally made by anonymous artists.

In Caruaru, in rural Pernambuco, however, the clay figurines typical of the region owe much to the unique style and expression of the artist Vitalino Pereira dos Santos (1909–1963). His portrayals of everyday country

Clay figurines by Carmélia Rodrigues da Silva

life brought him numerous followers and earned him the title *Mestre* (Master). Today his children and grandchildren continue his work, and Unesco has named his neighborhood, Alto do Moura, the Americas' principal center for figurative art.

Nearby, in the forest region of Pernambuco, more than half the town of Tracunhaém earns its income from ceramics production. The ceramics depict sacred and solemn themes, as seen in the saints made by Maria Amélia and Zezinho and in the magnificent lions of Mestre Nuca (1937–2004).

Cordel Literature

Perhaps nothing is more typical of the region's folk art than *cordel* literature, which consists of printed booklets sold in the streets and markets of the backlands. Woodcut prints decorate the covers and illustrate the text, which may address any imaginable theme – from romance and folklore to social and political criticism. Bezerros, in Pernambuco, next to Caruaru, has been called "the capital of *cordel*" and is home to some of its most famous producers, including octogenarian J. Borges, who is a poet, singer, and illustrator. The *cordel* tradition also survives in Ceará, in the town of Juazeiro do Norte, where the legendary sculptor Mestre Noza (1897–1984) lived.

Wood Crafts

Traditional regional woodwork is often connected to religious imagery. In Cachoeira, in the Recôncavo Baiano area, Boaventura da Silva Filho (1932–1992) – known as Louco ("madman") – achieved fame by sculpting elongated figures of Catholic saints and African Candomblé divinities called *orixás*. As is customary, Louco passed on his craft to his family and pupils, and today religious pieces are produced there by Louco Filho ("madman's son"), Doidão ("crackpot"), Dory, and Mimo. In Triunfo, a town in Pernambuco, Chico Santeiro carves statues of saints and the Virgin Mary and dresses them opulently. In Acari, Rio Grande do Norte, Ambrósio Córdula carves saints, nativity scenes, and angels.

Some local styles of woodworking are on the wane, including votive offerings, which were an 18th-century tradition. For example, painted boards depicting scenes of miraculous cures, once popular, are no longer produced. The *salas de milagres* (miracle rooms) of certain churches, sanctuaries, and pilgrimage centers contain wooden replicas of body parts that worshipers once sculpted to express divine gratitude for granted favors; these too are no longer in production. The artist Aberaldo, from Ilha do Ferro, in Alagoas state, created a new style of votive offerings, giving them color and converting them into decorative objects.

The famous, grotesque gargoyle heads called *carrancas*, used by boatmen along the São Francisco River to ward off evil spirits, are reminders of the area's superstitious heritage. In Santa Maria das Vitórias, Bahia, Francisco Biquiba dy Lafuente Guarani (1884–1987) carved some of the best examples of this form. In the 1960s, a nationwide *carranca* craze led to mass production of less-striking copies all along the river, particularly in Petrolina.

Wood is also a raw material of everyday objects such as furniture and toys. In Acari, Manuel Jerônimo Filho makes marvelous toy trucks. In Maranhão, Nhozinho (1904–1974) carved soft *buriti* palm into small figures meant to represent local personages and characters from the *bumba-meu-boi* festivities. His work can be seen in the museum named after him in São Luís. Palm trees provide raw material for other artisans in the backlands and on the coast. People of the Parnaíba delta, in Piauí, use fibers from the *carnaúba* palm to make baskets and decorative objects. Artisans from coastal Alagoas make mats, bags, and hats using straw from the *ouricuri* palm.

Between Tradition and the Marketplace

Folk art is both a cultural artifact and a source of income for artists. These craftspeople balance faithful reproduction of traditional styles with their desire to discover new techniques and employ materials. Crafts pass from generation to generation, adapting along the way to changing tastes and new circumstances. In Acari, scrap metal from cars is turned into figurines and toys by Dimauri Lima de Souza. In Ceará, the sand used to create landscapes in small bottles, once collected from the multi-colored Majorlândia dunes, now receives artificial dyes. In Santana do Cariri, in the backlands of Ceará, the government encourages people to reproduce replicas of fossil remains in order to prevent the illicit sale of the local archaeological heritage. It is just one more way that the myriad items of northeastern arts and crafts – cloths, hammocks, miniatures, toys, drawings, votive offerings, saddles, leatherwork, ornaments, and utensils – have been recreated and reinterpreted.

Folk Arts

Clay figurine

Wood figurine by Aberaldo

Wood figurine by Nino

A Mulher Misteriosa, woodcut print by J. Borges

FINE ARTS

In the Northeast, European influences dating back to colonial times have shaped an artistic tradition into something that is uniquely Brazilian.

The first representations of the Northeast Brazilian landscape were the works of European artists who accompanied Count Maurits of Nassau during the Dutch occupation of Pernambuco (1630-1654). Frans Post painted landscapes of sugar plantations and fortresses, while Albert Eckhout depicted animals, plants, and people on huge canvases. Zacharias Waneger, Nassau's clerk and an amateur artist, drew the fauna and flora of the new Dutch territories in minute detail.

Although Dutch Calvinists were the first artists to represent Northeast Brazil, Portuguese Catholics created the works that would characterize the first centuries of the colony. The religious orders that traveled to the region and the laymen they hired to decorate their churches left a significant artistic heritage. The first sculptors of religious images in Bahia were the Benedictine monk Agostinho da Piedade (1580-1661) and his student Agostinho de Jesus (1600-1661). As sugar barons became wealthier, building new churches or enlarging and renovating the old, Jesuits and Franciscans also became formidable sculptors along the 17th century. In time, artists born in the colony, often those of mixed blood, took over carving and painting the glories of God. João de Deus Sepúlveda of Pernambuco, a mulatto, painted, among other things, the ceiling of São Pedro dos Clérigos Church in Recife during the second half of the 18th century.

Whatever the background of the artists, they found it necessary to adapt Portuguese traditions to the resources available in the colony. Lacking marble for sculptures, for example, they developed intricate wood carving techniques instead. Francisco das Chargas, known as Cabra, was one of the most skilled carvers. Little is known about him, except that he was a mulatto from Salvador. In 1758, commissioned by the Third Order of Carmel, he carved a magnificent statue of the dead Christ, *Cristo Morto*, with rubies representing drops of blood. Manuel Inácio da Costa (1763-1857), also from Salvador, is considered the greatest sculptor of the era.

His legacy includes the statue of São Pedro de Alcântara in São Francisco Church.

The Bahia School of Painting

The late 18th and early 19th centuries witnessed growing influence of the Escola Baiana de Pintura. This artistic school emphasized European techniques and influences. Its greatest proponent, José Joaquim da Rocha (1737-1807), was a Brazilian who had learned his craft in Lisbon. Upon returning to Salvador, he became the most sought-after painter of his time. He is particularly renowned for his work on the nave ceiling of Conceição da Glória Church. Rocha trained numerous apprentices, including José Teófilo de Jesus (1758-1847), who also studied in Europe. Jesus is known for his decorative work in churches, but he was also a portrait painter. Antônio Franco Velasco (1780-1833), also of the Escola Baiana, painted the nave ceiling of Nosso Senhor do Bonfim Church, among others, and became famous for his portraits.

Academicism

In the 19th century, painting branched off from architecture and religious worship and became a discipline in its own right. Brazilian art continued to reflect European trends, as it had since the early days of the colony. Artists at the Academy of Fine Arts in Rio de Janeiro often pursued studies abroad. Far from rejecting their own country, however, they were searching for new ways of portraying Brazil.

Paraíba native Pedro Américo (1843-1905) painted what has become the archetypical depiction of the proclamation of independence. The painting, *Independência ou Morte* (Independence or Death), is an image familiar to every Brazilian and can be seen in the Paulista Museum (also known as the Ipiranga Museum) in São Paulo. In *Último Tamoio* (The Last Tamoio Indian), Rodolfo Amoedo (1857-1941) of Bahia created a persisting image of the Indian, a national symbol. Telles Júnior (1851-1914), a native of Pernambuco, studied in Europe and used what he learned there to portray the Northeast. Other significant artists of this period are Arsênio Silva (1833-1883) from Pernambuco, who introduced the use of gouache to Brazil, and Rosalvo Ribeiro (1867-1915), from Alagoas, who specialized in military scenes.

The adaptation of European styles and techniques to Brazilian themes continued into the second decade of the 20th century, when

Fine Arts

Zona Operária (Working-Class Suburbs), by Cícero Dias. Watercolor and ink on paper, 1928

Farol da Barra, by Pancetti. Oil on canvas, 1954

Brazilian artists joined the modernist movement. The two greatest Brazilian painters of the time, both from Pernambuco, took their crafts abroad. In Paris, Vicente do Rego Monteiro (1899-1970) perfected a style influenced by native ceramics. Cícero Dias (1907-2003), who at the end of the 1920s painted Surrealism-inspired watercolors in the hues and themes of his native Recife, spent most of his life in Europe.

The Northeast not only exported artists, but also received artistic émigrés from abroad – particularly artists who were enchanted by its landscapes. José Pancetti (1902 -1958), born in São Paulo to an Italian family, settled in Salvador in the early 1950s, where he produced some of his best seascapes. During the same period, the Argentinean known universally by his nickname, Carybé (1911-1997), recorded cultural aspects of Bahia in paintings and drawings bearing his unmistakable stamp.

New Directions

Between 1940 and 1950, the visual arts underwent a phase of effervescent renewal. Salvadorean artists participating in this movement include Carybé; Genaro de Carvalho (1922-1971), known for his tapestries; the painter Jenner Augusto (1923), from Sergipe; and the sculptor Mário Cravo (1923). The Sociedade Cearense de Artes Plásticas (Ceará Fine Arts Society), created in 1943, produced such famous names as Aldemir Martins (1922-2006), Sérvulo Esmeraldo (1929–), Raimundo Cela (1890-1954), and Antônio Bandeira (1922-1967), the great abstract artist. In Recife, the Ateliê Coletivo da Sociedade de Arte Moderna (Studio Collective of Modern Art) was formed in 1948. Its main descendent is Gilvan Samico (1928–), a painter and woodcut print artist who renewed the northeastern literary tradition of *cordel*. João Câmara Filho (1944–) was also part of this studio. A native of Paraíba, he later depicted scenes of the Brazilian military dictatorship in dense, somber colors.

The interchange between external influences and local references continues today. The constructivism of Rubem Valentim (1926-1991), from Salvador, used *candomblé* symbols. Francisco Brennand (1927–) of Recife creates sculptures using techniques from the European ceramic tradition. Frans Krajcberg (1921–), born in Poland, lives in the south of Bahia and uses roots, trunks, and calcified liana vine in sculptures that unite artistic research and ecological militancy. Leonilson (1957-1993), a one-name wonder from Ceará, worked in São Paulo, creating drawings, paintings, and embroidery.

Artworks native to the northeastern region or connected to its culture include the woodcut prints of Guita Charifker (1936–); the photographs of Pierre Verger (1902-1996), Mário Cravo Neto (1947–), and Christian Cravo (1974–); the African-inspired sculptures of Agnaldo dos Santos (1926-1962) and Emanoel Araújo (1940-); and many more like the work of Antonio Dias (1944–) installation pieces using many mediuns such as text, video, and photography, Gil Vicente (1958–), Sebastião Pedrosa, from Recife, and Marepe, from Bahia (1970–), who exhibits installations and paintings in galleries in São Paulo and Rio de Janeiro . The art of the Northeast has come to encompass many artists working in diverse media.

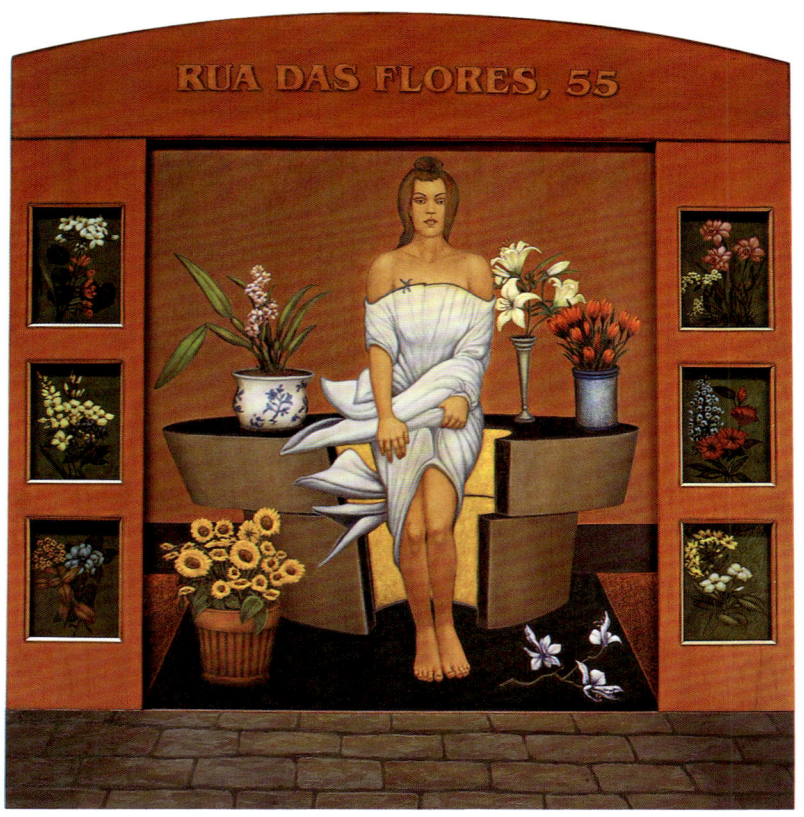

Rua das Flores, 55, by João Câmara. Oil on canvas and wood, 1999

Architecture

Over five centuries, the architecture of the Northeast has evolved from baroque excess, through Jesuit asuterity, to rational modern design.

"On the balconies of the town houses / in old São Salvador / there are memories of maidens / from the times of the emperor," sang the Bahian native, composer and singer Dorival Caymmi in the early 1940s. These memory-laden homes still stand in the city center and constitute one of the most magnificent architectural ensembles in the country. Salvador's houses are not an isolated architectural treasure; they are a small part of the vast architectural heritage developed through the centuries in the Northeast.

The region is also home to a large number of fortresses, which were built to repel attacks of pirates and invading armies (there were originally 15 such fortresses in Salvador's Todos os Santos Bay alone). The Northeast's greatest architectural inheritance, however, is its collection of churches. The majority line the coast and were commissioned by clergy who accompanied the colonists, particularly Jesuits. The Jesuit Society of Jesus oversaw a particularly intense campaign to spread its particular brand of Catholicism, but the group was expelled from Brazil in 1759. The colony's art and architecture nonetheless continued to manifest what is called the Jesuit style, which the urbanist that designed Brasília, architect Lucio Costa, describes as "more renaissance, more restrained, more ordered and reserved, and imbued with the severe spirit of th e Counter-Reformation." Churches built in the 16th, 17th, and early 18th centuries are simple in design, generally rectangular, and have sober, bare façades. It is often the case that the interiors display the ornamental exuberance typical of the baroque style – as if, embodying the ideals of the Society of Jesus, the virtues of the spirit were valued over outward appearance.

Churches and Forts

Although religious architecture of the Northeast retained many of its original characteristics down through the centuries, it also underwent certain transformations. For example, the simple frontispiece of the 17th century church evolved into façades flanked by bell towers in the 18th century. Altarpieces also became more heavily decorated, with reliefs of sculpted hardwood covered in gold leaf. The same church may have evidence of several styles, a result of constant renovations by the rich land owners known as the sugar barons as they prospered.

A fundamental component of colonial church decoration is ceiling painting. The illusionist perspective techniques developed by Italians in the 17th century were picked up by Brazilian artists in the early-to-mid 18th century. The nave ceilings of the churches of São Pedro dos Clérigos in Recife and Nossa Senhora da Conceição da Praia in Salvador are home to excellent examples of this technique. The latter's ceiling was painted by José Joaquim da Rocha, one of the great names of the Brazilian baroque period.

Finally, it is worth highlighting the extensive use of decorative tiles, which were brought from Portugal from the 18th century onward to decorate building exteriors, tower cupolas (such as that of the Franciscan convent in João Pessoa, Paraíba's state capital), cloisters, and sacristies – it is interesting to note that these areas, normally restricted to use by clergy, may have received such luxurious decoration due to the fact that members of the local aristocracy also used to meet there. The magnificent sacristy of the Basílica de Salvador Cathedral in Bahia's capital, encrusted with tortoiseshell and ivory, is a fine example of such private opulence.

Sacristy of Basílica Cathedral, in Salvador

From Farmstead to Townhouse

The region's economic dependence on sugar cultivation guided its architectural development. Rural landowners tended to build complexes that included a main house, where the owners lived, a chapel, *senzala* (slave quarters), and an *engenho* (sugar mill) with its machinery. As sugar production flourished, buildings became more and more luxurious. Mud and plaster were replaced by brick or stone; the unadorned, single-level home was replaced by the *solar* (manor). Solar do Unhão in Salvador, Bahia, built for Judge Pedro Unhão Castelo Branco in the 17th century, is an example of refinement and practical functionality: The complex has warehouses and quays (docks) in addition to the main house, slave quarters, and chapel. In 1962, the property was restored by architect Lina Bo Bardi and today houses the Museu de Arte Moderna (Museum of Modern Art).

In the early years of the colony every aspect of the sugar plantation owner's life revolved around the borders of his property. Towns were little more than trading posts and administration centers; town dwellings were small and unimpressive. When the process of urbanization accelerated at the beginning of the 19th century, more opulent buildings began to appear, like the *sobrados* (two-storey town houses with balconies that were built for the elite). In São Luís, the state capital of Maranhão (where wealth came from cotton rather than sugar), house façades were tiled like the churches in Pernambuco and Bahia. In the whole Northeast, as was true elsewhere in the colony, two-storey homes often served a dual function for small retailers, who ran their businesses on the ground floor and lived on the upper floor.

In the semi-arid northeastern rural area where cattle-raising was the way of life, houses were largely simple, unadorned, brick or stone buildings with porches or verandas that served as living rooms as well.

Other Influences

By the 1840s and 50s, newly independent Brazil was creating a fresh national image by consciously turning its back on its colonial, baroque past. In 1840 alone, Recife gained tree-lined streets, a coach-based public transportation system, and piped water. The town's Campo das Princesas Palace (1840), Santa Isabel Theater (1850), and Liceu de Artes e Ofícios (School of Arts and Crafts, 1880) rose from the ground in succession. Other cities were revitalized, as well, and many state capitals were moved from their former colonial sites: the capital of Piauí moved from Oeiras to Teresina in 1852, and the capital of Sergipe moved from São

Architecture

Cristóvão to Aracaju in 1855. This impulse for change continued into the early 20th century, when, inspired by the example of Rio de Janeiro, Recife established an urban sanitation program and remodeled many city buildings in addition to demolishing most of the old Bairro do Recife neighborhood. Other state capitals, such as João Pessoa and Salvador, followed suit. The 1970s saw the creation of revitalization projects to rescue historic colonial city centers, including São Luís and Salvador.

The modern architecture that flourished in Brazil between the 1930s and 1960s was introduced to Recife by the Brazilian architect Acácio Gil Borsoi and the Portuguese architect Delfim Amorim. The movement these two men founded became known as the Recife School of Architecture, and its influence spread throughout the Northeast. Among the architects who introduced new elements to the region's landscape, the names Luís Nunes, Mário Russo, Mário Láscio, Carlos Alberto Carneiro da Cunha, and Liberal de Castro figure prominently.

In the backlands and city outskirts you can often find small, colorful, low-income homes with decorated turrets – dwellings that somehow managed to combine Jesuit austerity, baroque excess, and modern rationality. It's a spontaneous architecture, bright and expressive, just like the region's culture.

House with turrets, interior of Ceará

Inside Reis Magos Fort, Natal

Recife's historic town center

Sobrado, interior of Ceará

Literature

The writing of the Northeast has always exhibited great energy. Its most unique phenomenon is what's called *cordel* literature, which consists of booklets printed from blocks of carved wood. In the area of traditional literature, the novels of Jorge Amado have garnered acclaim in Brazil and abroad.

In the 17th century, Bahian poet Gregório de Mattos, a well-educated man of refined culture, developed a reputation for implacably satirical poetry, which he wielded against the powerful. His literary contribution, which includes lyrical and religious poetry, would be just the first in a series of locally inspired writings that the Northeast would endow to Brazil.

Gonçalves Dias of Maranhão and Castro Alves of Bahia defined Brazilian poetry during the mid-19th century. Among the romantics of the 19th century, José de Alencar stands out. He had a systematic "literary project" that included the cultivation of the "Brazilian language". That mission led him to incorporate into his novels a variety of Brazilian themes, including native peoples, local history, and urban life in the Northeast.

Around that time, a popular regional form of poetry separately began to take shape. With the help of private printing shops, which began to sprout up in the 1930s, this form eventually grew into the formidable cultural phenomenon known as *cordel* literature. *Cordel* would establish the reputations of many poets, including Aderaldo Ferreira de Araújo, also known as Cego (Blind) Aderaldo, and Antonio Gonçalves Silva, otherwise known as Patativa do Assaré.

The Northeast inspired the naturalist movement that developed in Brazil on the eve of the 20th century. Aluísio de Azevedo distinguished himself as the movement's greatest novelist with *O Mulato* (1881, *The Mulatto*) and especially with *O Cortiço* (1890, *A Brazilian Tenement*).

The novelists' accomplishments set the stage for the true blossoming of Brazilian literature, in which fiction took a regional focus, especially in the Northeast, and reached the pinnacle of its excellence. The best-known 20th-century representatives of the northeastern genre are José Américo de Almeida, Rachel de Queiroz, and José

An iluminogravura by Ariano Suassuna for his poem *Soneto de Babilônia e Sertão* (detail)

Lins do Rego. The last wrote *Menino de Engenho* (1932, *Plantation Boy*). Graciliano Ramos, whose masterpieces include *São Bernardo* (1934, published in English with the same title) and *Vidas Secas* (1938, *Barren Lives*), reached beyond the confines of regionalism touching on universal literary realms.

Then there's Jorge Amado, who during his career published more than thirty books, some of which were translated into dozens of languages. Amado's 1933 *Cacau* was the first Bahian theme novel. In the 1970s and 80s, João Ubaldo Ribeiro of Bahia published *Sargento Getúlio* (*Sergeant Getulio*) and *Viva o Povo Brasileiro* (*An Invincible Memory*). In his novel *Avalovara* (1973, also published in English), Osman Lins of Pernambuco experimented with a complex, original structure. Ariano Suassuna of Paraíba, considered one of Brazil's greatest living playwrights, made his debut in narrative prose in 1971.

Like the region's literature, northeastern poetry has made strides toward maturity. This can be seen in the work of Manuel Bandeira of Pernambuco, who brought together aesthetic freedom and metaphysical reflection. At the same time, Jorge de Lima of Alagoas worked in epic dimensions. By cultivating what he called "objective" poetry, João Cabral de Melo Neto elevated social criticism and denunciation of inequity to an art, and, surprisingly, did so while adhering to rigorous, traditional lyrical structure. The same care is visible in the work of Ferreira Gullar, who, while in political exile during the military dictatorship, penned *Poema Sujo* in 1976. With a rare mastery of verse, he evokes his native São Luís, in Maranhão. The passion of Gullar's longing for his home continue the tradition of his intellectual predecessors and their powerful emotions for Brazil's great Northeast.

Geography, Ecology, and Ecotourism

The vast Northeast region is home to a variety of landscapes and ecosystems. The backlands' forests, mountain ranges, and cliffs lie inlands of 3,500 kilometers of scenic coastline and some of the finest beaches in the country.

Nine Brazilian states comprise the Northeast. Starting from the south with Bahia, and moving north along the coast, are the states of Sergipe, Alagoas, Pernambuco, Paraíba, and Rio Grande do Norte. The last borders the ocean to the east and north, as the coastline pivots. Moving west along Brazil's northern coast from Rio Grande do Norte, we have Ceará, Piauí, and Maranhão. Together, these states cover nearly 1.5 million square kilometers (580,000 square miles), or nearly 20% of the country. The Northeast is larger than Portugal, Spain, France, and Germany combined. It's not surprising, then, that the region is home to diverse landscapes and climates, from mild green forests to arid backlands, from dramatic mountain ranges to warm, gorgeous beaches, and from stark cliffs to gentle pools of crystal-clear water. These areas host a variety of flora and fauna and provide visitors with a wide range of leisure options.

Forest and Semi-Arid Lands

The Northeast has four climate sub-regions and numerous diverse, transitional landscapes, including those known as the *zona da mata*, the *agreste*, and the *caatinga*. The *zona da mata* is a forested strip with a tropical climate, abundant rains, and fertile soil. It is a thin strip at most 200 kilometers (125 miles) wide and runs along the coastline all the way from Rio Grande do Norte to southern Bahia. The area still retains some of its original landscape, known as Atlantic forest, even though logging practices that began in colonial times have dramatically reduced the forest's area. Clearance occurred first as colonists exploited the land's brazilwood, and later as farmers created open spaces for cultivating sugarcane and cacao. More recently, the cellulose industry and uncontrolled urbanization have scarred the land. In the remaining forests and other surviving green areas, animals such as the golden-lion tamarin, muriqui, otter, giant armadillo, and the jaguar live under continual threat of extinction.

Inland from the *zona da mata* lies a semi-arid region known as the *agreste*. This area is characterized by a patchwork of wet, swampy areas and dry areas. Rainfall can vary dramatically over relatively small distances. In areas where it rains regularly, families practice subsistence farming. In dry stretches, most raise livestock instead. The *agreste* region contains the greatest concentration of goats in the country.

CAATINGA AND PALM GROVES

The dry section of the *agreste* transitions into *caatinga*, a type of ecosystem found only in Brazil. It exists in all the Northeastern states except Sergipe. In the *caatinga* there are two seasons: rainy and dry. The word *caatinga* means "white forest" in the native Tupi-Guarani language. It's an apt description for the landscape during the dry season, when the dried-out soil cracks and leaves disappear, giving tree and shrub trunks a grayish color. But the barren-looking *caatinga* conceals rich biodiversity, including cacti like the *mandacaru* and *xiquexique*, palm cactus, piassaba palm trees, aveloz, shrubs (including the castor oil plant), and hardwood trees like brauna and tonka. During the rainy season, vegetation bursts forth in many hues. One of the most common *caatinga* trees is the *juazeiro*, the only evergreen species in the area. The area's many indigenous animal include the rock cavy, guinea pig, opossum, brocket deer, and the common marmoset, as well as various lizards, snakes, and birds. Bird watchers may catch a glimpse of picui ground-doves, scaly-headed parrots, caracaras, and picazuro pigeons.

Halfway into the state of Piauí, the Northeast's landscape shifts again. All the way to the state's border with Maranhão, groves of palm trees known as *cocais* are common sights. This is the mid-Northeast, a transitional vegetation belt that marks the border between the backlands and the Equatorial Amazon region. Palm trees, including *buriti*, *oiticica*, *carnauba*, and *babassu*, thrive in the humid climate, and grow larger the closer they are to the Amazon. Oil and wax from these palms have various industrial uses, especially in the manufacture of cosmetics. Birds of the region include rails, tinamous, vultures, hawks, and macaws. Marsupials, bats, predatory mammals, reptiles, and a rat known as the *rato-do-mato* are also frequent sights.

RIVER AND SEA

Two mighty rivers run through the Northeast: the São Francisco and the Parnaíba. Smaller rivers tend to disappear during the dry season and thus play a less significant role in local life.

Geography, Ecology, and Ecotourism

Manatee, Paraíba

King vulture, *caatinga*

Crab, Fernando de Noronha

Brown booby, Abrolhos

Mandacaru cactus, *caatinga*

Bromeliad, Chapada Diamantina

Mangrove swamp, Bahia

Palm groves, Maranhão

Caatinga, a uniquely Brazilian ecosystem

The São Francisco River — affectionately known by the people who live along its banks as Velho Chico ("Old Chico") — begins to the south, in the state of Minas Gerais, and traverses the driest parts of the Northeast as it flows through Bahia, Pernambuco, Alagoas, and Sergipe. The Brazilian government has long toyed with the idea of diverting some of its waters to the driest surrounding areas, but the plan had fallen in and out of favor for many years with no decisive action taken. In 2000 the government once more began to push the project forward amid intense controversy. Hydroelectric plants harness the river's tremendous power at Sobradinho, Xingó, and Paulo Afonso.

The Parnaíba River flows through Ceará, Piauí, and Maranhão. Its mouth, which marks the border between the last two states, forms the Parnaíba Delta, the largest salt-water delta in the Americas. Seventy percent of the delta is considered part of Maranhão, which has recently cultivated an ecotourism industry focused on this important conservation area.

The Northeast possesses one-third of Brazil's coastline, a total of about 3,500 kilometers (2,200 miles) of beaches. Tourists flock to the sands, lured by idyllic images. The reefs, lagoons, cliffs, dunes, lakes, fens, and mangrove swamps serve as habitats for several animal species, including turtles, manatees, crabs, lobsters, and abundant fishes that are critical to the survival of local communities.

Thanks to the Northeast's cultural and geographical variety, it's easy to see why each visit here is full of surprises and discoveries.

Where to Find Adventure

Canyoning – Chapada Diamantina (BAHIA)

Mountain Climbing – Capivara Range (PIAUÍ), Lençóis (BAHIA), Paulo Afonso (BAHIA)

Kitesurfing – Itacaré (BAHIA), Jericoacoara (CEARÁ), Natal (RIO GRANDE DO NORTE), Parnaíba Delta (PARAÍBA), São Miguel do Gostoso (RIO GRANDE DO NORTE), Touros (RIO GRANDE DO NORTE)

Diving – Abrolhos (BAHIA, photo), Alcobaça (BAHIA), Arraial d'Ajuda (BAHIA), Barra de Jacuípe (BAHIA), Barra Grande (BAHIA), Barreirinhas (MARANHÃO), Cabo de Santo Agostinho (PERNAMBUCO), Cairu (BAHIA), Caraíva (BAHIA), Caravelas (BAHIA), Cumuruxatiba (BAHIA), Fernando de Noronha (PERNAMBUCO), Jericoacoara (CEARÁ), Jijoca de Jericoacoara (CEARÁ), João Pessoa (PERNAMBUCO), Outeiro Village (BAHIA); Paripueira (ALAGOAS), Pirangi (RIO GRANDE DO NORTE), Ponta do Corumbau (BAHIA), Prado (BAHIA), Santa Cruz Cabrália (BAHIA), Todos os Santos Bay (BAHIA), Touros (RIO GRANDE DO NORTE), Trancoso (BAHIA), coral reefs along the southern Pernambuco state coastline

Mountain Biking – Capivara Range (PIAUÍ), Chapada Diamantina (BAHIA), Crato (CEARÁ), Prado-Arraial d'Ajuda (BAHIA)

Off-Roading – Boipeba Island (BAHIA), Chapada Diamantina (BAHIA), Itacaré (BAHIA), Lençóis Maranhenses (MARANHÃO); coastal regions of Ceará and Rio Grande do Norte

Rafting – Itacaré (BAHIA), Nilo Peçanha (BAHIA)

Rappeling/Cascading – Camamu (BAHIA), Chapada Diamantina (BAHIA), Itacaré (BAHIA), Ituberá (BAHIA), Paulo Afonso (BAHIA), Serra Talhada (PERNAMBUCO), Triunfo (PERNAMBUCO)

Surfing – Aquiraz (CEARÁ), Arembepe (BAHIA), Barra de Mamanguape (PERNAMBUCO), Barra de São Miguel (ALAGOAS), Belmonte (BAHIA), Boipeba Island (BAHIA), Fernando de Noronha (PERNAMBUCO), Fortaleza (CEARÁ), Ilhéus (BAHIA), Itacaré (BAHIA), Ituberá (BAHIA), Jericoacoara (CEARÁ), João Pessoa (PERNAMBUCO), Maceió (ALAGOAS), Praia do Francês (ALAGOAS), Morro de São Paulo (BAHIA), Natal (RIO GRANDE DO NORTE), Pipa (RIO GRANDE DO NORTE), Porto de Galinhas (PERNAMBUCO), Salvador (BAHIA), Santa Cruz Cabrália (BAHIA), Santo André (BAHIA); coral reefs along the southern Pernambuco state coastline

Trekking – Capivara Range (PIAUÍ), Chapada Diamantina (BAHIA), Fernando de Noronha (PERNAMBUCO), Lençóis Maranhenses (MARANHÃO), Mucugê (BAHIA), Paulo Afonso (BAHIA), Rio de Contas (BAHIA)

Sailing – Arraial d'Ajuda (BAHIA), Fernando de Noronha (PERNAMBUCO), Jijoca de Jericoacoara (CEARÁ), Praia do Francês (ALAGOAS)

Windsurfing – Arraial d'Ajuda (BAHIA), Jericoacoara (CEARÁ), Jijoca de Jericoacoara (CEARÁ), Praia do Forte (BAHIA), São Miguel do Gostoso (RIO GRANDE DO NORTE)

BAHIA

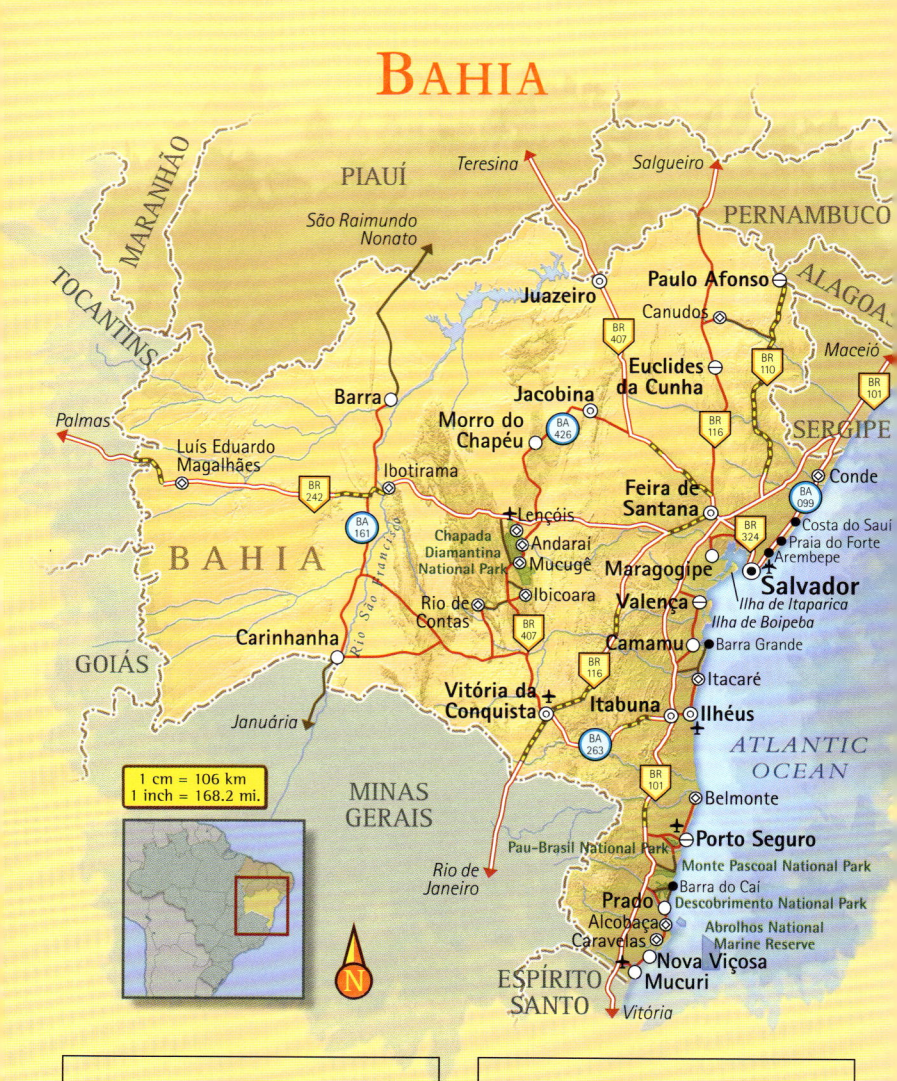

Scale: 1 cm = 106 km; 1 inch = 168.2 mi.

Highlights

- Tours of cultural and architectural sites of interest in **Pelourinho**, in the center of Salvador.
- The urban beaches of **Morro de São Paulo, Praia do Forte, Trancoso**, and **Itacaré**.
- The untrammeled sands of the **Maraú Peninsula, Boipeba Island**, and **Caraíva**.
- The treks, caves, and waterfalls of **Chapada Diamantina**.
- Diving in **Abrolhos**, an island-chain marine reserve on the pristine Whale Coast.

When to go

- The beaches of Bahia can be enjoyed year-round. But cities are crowded and prices are high during the summer months (**December, January**, and **February**).
- Everyone is welcome to party with crowds of revelers at Carnival, (generally in **February** and **March**).
- Between **January** and **February** ritual processions are held in Salvador in honor of Senhor do Bonfim.
- The São João festivities, are held in **June**.

Bahia

The history of Bahia is in some ways the history of Brazil. It was here, in what is now the town of Porto Seguro, that a squadron commanded by the Portuguese navigator Pedro Álvares Cabral came ashore in 1500, a historical event that marked the discovery of the new land. Less than fifty years later, construction of the colony's first capital began on that same ground. Though it would be centuries before the Brazilian nation would be realized, the first stone in its foundation was laid. In addition to major African cultural influences, traces of the Portuguese presence are still visible in Bahia's forts, churches, farms, and sugar plantations. Throughout the 16th and 17th centuries Bahia was the center of the colony's slave-trade; by the end of the 19th century, however, it was at the forefront of the abolitionist movement. Today, no Brazilian state has a larger black population, nor preserves its African legacy with such intensity and pride.

The best place to start getting to know Bahia is in its capital city, Salvador, whose cultural vibrancy distinguishes it from other state capitals. It is a good point of departure for the wide variety of beaches that dot the state's coastline – from the gentle waves and comfortable tourist facilities of Praia do Forte in the north to the turquoise waters of the Abrolhos archipelago, a diving destination, in the south. There is more to Bahia than its coastline, however. Visitors who venture to the inland region of Chapada Diamantina will be rewarded with some of the country's finest scenery and a chance to experience the rich culture of the *sertão* backlands.

Baianas on their way to the stair-washing ceremony at Nosso Senhor do Bonfim Basilica

SALVADOR

Salvador was chosen as Brazil's earliest capital for its attractive geographical attributes. Seventy meter (230 foot) bluffs divide the upper and lower parts of the city, which are known as Cidade Alta and Cidade Baixa, respectively. From the heights of Cidade Alta the entire Baía de Todos os Santos (All Saints Bay) can be seen, making it impossible for ships to approach unnoticed, a feature that was particularly attractive to its 16th century founders. An ancient fault line, the Falha Geológica de Salvador, is responsible for the "two-story" topography of the city. Urban planning here took after that in the similarly hilly terrain of Lisbon and Porto. The city's commercial center radiates outward from the port, while the upper level is largely comprised of residential, administrative, and religious buildings. This division is fundamental to understanding the

SALVADOR'S NEIGHBORHOODS AND BEACHES

Bonfim
The outside steps of the Church of Bonfim are the site of the famous stair-washing ceremony known as Lavagem do Bonfim. On the third Thursday in January hundreds of local women, known as baianas, don traditional white dresses and perform the ritual of religious syncretism, which blends Catholic and African traditions. Over ten thousand spectators gather to watch the ceremony, dance, eat, and enjoy musical performances.

Tororó
Dique do Tororó, one of the city's largest parks, offers several leisure options. Next door is the Bahia Soccer Club's Fonte Nova Stadium.

Cabula
The Cabula neighborhood is home to several Candomblé terreiros (temples). It is located on the outskirts of the city, on the way to the airport.

Abaeté
Visitors flock to the dunes of Parque da Lagoa park and the waters of Lagoa do Abaeté lagoon.

Campo Grande
Home of Dois de Julho Square, where Bahian Independence is commemorated every year at the base of the Caboclo statue.

Barra
The most popular, lively tourist spot on the coast. Visitors come to enjoy and explore the beach, fort, lighthouse, and shopping mall. During Carnival, Barra serves as the starting point for the *trio elétrico* that the famous Bahian musician Dodô performs on.

Ondina
An extension of Barra beach and the finishing point for Dodô's *trio elétrico* procession.

dynamics of Salvador today: the Pelourinho District, which is part of Cidade Alta, has more than eight hundred 17th and 18th-century dwellings, most of which have been restored or are in the process of restoration. Cidade Alta is also home to some of the most important churches in Salvador.

In Cidade Baixa you can visit all fifteen forts that once protected the colonial capital from seaborne threats. There are also hotels, a variety of businesses, buzzing nightlife destinations, marinas dotted with pleasure boats, and 30 kilometers (19 miles) of city beaches. Some of Salvador's most exciting attractions are found on the bay between the Bonfim and Barra neighborhoods. The few locals who speak English are often more than happy to offer suggestions and provide insider perspective. Note that it's not safe to walk around Cidade Baixa, or any poorly lit area, at night. Instead, take a taxi between establishments and your hotel.

Pelourinho
Cultural heart of the city and host to many musical performances, *capoeira* demonstrations, and *trio elétricos* (large trucks with huge amplifiers and stages). Pelourinho even has its own neighborhood *trio elétrico* called Batatinha.

Piatã
A palm-fringed beach with calm waters. The Placafor stretch is popular for water sports.

Itapuã
Far from the city center, like neighboring Stella Maris and Flamengo, it has the best facilities of any beach in Salvador.

Praia de Armação
The Aeroclube Plaza Show, a waterfront shopping mall with shops, restaurants, bars, and performance space, is Praia de Armação's main draw.

Rio Vermelho
Rio Vermelho's vibrant nightlife attracts locals and tourists alike. The neighborhood is also home to a popular market where you can buy delicious regional dishes.

TRIOS ELÉTRICOS ROUTES
- Avenida Circuit
- Barra/Ondina Circuit
- Batatinha Circuit

Lower City

❶ Modelo Market

The busy Mercado Modelo is popular among tourists for its arts and crafts products, and is worth a visit if only to look at the picturesque, old building that houses it. Its location in the center of Cidade Baixa, makes it easy to find. *Capoeira* demonstrations frequently take place behind the market. In front is one of the symbols of Salvador, the Fonte de Oxalá (Oxalá's Fountain) sculpture by Mário Cravo Junior of the African deity Oxalá. There are two traditional restaurants on the second floor of the market: Camafeu de Oxóssi and Maria de São Pedro, both of which sell local dishes.
Praça Visconde de Cairu, 250, Comércio, tel. (71) 3241-2893. Mon – Sat, 9am – 7pm; Sun and holidays, 9am – 2pm.

❷ Nossa Senhora da Conceição da Praia Church

Nestled at the foot of the steep bluff that separates Cidade Alta from Cidade Baixa, the Igreja Nossa Senhora da Conceição da Praia has great symbolic value for the people of Bahia. Spacious and naturally well lit, it was built in the second half of the 18th century on the site where the first chapel in Salvador was erected in 1549. Work on the new church began in Alentejo, Portugal, where limestone blocks were cut, numbered, and shipped to the colony. The highlight of the interior is the nave ceiling, which was painted sometime around 1774 by José Joaquim da Rocha (1737-1807), one of the great names in Brazilian baroque artistry. The annual Conceição da Praia festivities take place here on December 8th and mark the beginning of a cycle of religious ceremonies and festivities that extend through the summer and culminate in Carnival.
Largo da Conceição da Praia, no #, Comércio, tel. (71) 3242-0545. Tue – Fri, 7am – 11:30am and 3pm – 5pm; Sat, Sun and Mon – 7am – 11:30am.

View of Cidade Alta, with Mercado Modelo (left) and Elevador Lacerda (background)

❸ Solar do Unhão

It is worth setting aside an entire afternoon to visit this magnificent stone mansion overlooking Todos os Santos Bay. Built in the 17th century for Judge Pedro Unhão Castelo Branco, it was later used for commerce. Visitors are welcome to roam the premises and explore the main house, slave quarters, chapel, and warehouses, as well as the quays that served as a point of departure for sugar produced in Recôncavo. The building was restored in 1962 and today is home to the **Museu de Arte Moderna** (Modern Art Museum, also known as MAM), whose collection includes nearly a thousand works by popular Brazilian artists such as Tarsila do Amaral, Portinari, and Di Cavalcanti. The garden has been reinvented as the **Parque das Esculturas** (Sculpture Park), with pieces by Carybé, Mário Cravo, Rubem Valentim, and other recognized artists. There is a bar on the pier with outdoor tables and occasional live music. For many, the greatest attraction here is the magnificent sunset view.
Avenida do Contorno, no #, Comércio. Solar do Unhão: tel. (71) 3117-6131. Thu – Sun, 1pm – 7pm; bar and restaurant: tel. 3329-5551. Mon – Sat, noon – midnight.

A sculpture by Mário Cravo Junior in Cidade Baixa

Getting from the Upper City to the Lower City

The physical separation of Salvador's two halves has long been an obstacle to the movement of people and goods. In the 16th century Cidade Alta and Cidade Baixa were connected by the "priests' hoist," a crane built by the Jesuits. In the 19th century the hoist was replaced by the Elevador Lacerda elevator and the Plano Inclinado Gonçalves funicular railway. These, along with the steep alleyway (*ladeira*) known as **Ladeira da Misericórdia**, are the three options for moving between the two city levels.

Elevador Lacerda
The opening of the first elevator in 1873 had an enormous impact on city life. Designed by engineer Antônio Lacerda, the modern-day elevator connects Praça Tomé de Souza Square, in the upper city, with Praça Visconde de Cairu Square, in the lower city. The 23-second trip costs five *centavos*. In 1930, when a second tower was build, the elevator was decorated in the art-deco style that it retains today. The elevator's four cabins transport between 27,000 and 35,000 people per day in the high season (December to February). There is a tourist information desk in the lower elevator building. The nighttime lighting system makes the elevator a highlight of the evening cityscape.
Cidade Alta: Praça Tomé de Souza, no #; Cidade Baixa: Praça Visconde de Cairu, no #, tel. (71) 3243-4030, 3322-7049. Daily, 24 hours a day.

Plano Inclinado Gonçalves
The funicular railway has two tram-like carriages that can transport up to 11,000 people a day in the high season. It is the best way to get from the Pelourinho neighborhood to the lower city because the station is conveniently located behind the basilica in Praça da Sé Square. It costs the same five centavos as the Elevador Lacerda, and the trip, which lasts less than a minute, affords a panoramic view of Todos os Santos Bay.
Cidade Alta: Praça Ramos de Queirós, Praça da Sé, no #; Cidade Baixa: Rua Guindaste dos Padres, no #, tel. (71) 3322-6894. Mon – Fri, 7am – 7pm; Sat, 7am – 1pm. Closed on holidays.

Upper City

❹ Tomé de Souza Square or Municipal Square

Praça Tomé de Souza, the oldest square in the city, is a true mosaic of styles. The early 20th century Palácio Rio Branco sits next to the ultra-modern Palácio Tomé de Souza, built in 1986 to be Salvador's City Hall. Nearby, the old Paço Municipal building, with its Tuscan arches and columns, contrasts with the art deco façade of the Elevador Lacerda tower, and traces of old tram tracks share space with the large number of parked cars that make life difficult for visitors.

❺ Sé Square

Only hints of the foundation of the 16th century Igreja da Sé church remain. In 1930, the church and an entire block of 17th, 18th, and 19th century houses were demolished to make way for a new electric tramline, forming what is today Praça da Sé. Between 1950 and 1980 the square functioned as the city's main bus terminal. By then in a dilapidated state, it underwent a long process of renovation and today is a worthwhile destination for anyone visiting the city's historical center. The *Cruz Caída* (*Fallen Cross*) monument, by Mário Cravo, that stands in the square was erected in memory of Father Antônio Vieira, a Jesuit who preached in the Igreja da Sé in the 17th century. Vieira, a man of deep conviction, gained fame for his anti-slavery sermons and writings.

Pelourinho

No other place in Salvador pulses like Pelourinho. Its streets and squares, lined by historic, brightly colored houses, constantly buzz with the comings and goings of Brazilians and foreign tourists alike. They are all here to enjoy Pelourinho's noteworthy cultural offerings, art shops, bars, and restaurants. Declared a World Heritage Cultural Site by Unesco in 1985, the heart of the old center, **Largo do Pelourinho** square, has nearly eight hundred homes from the 17th, 18th, and 19th centuries. Renovations of the historic houses have been underway since 1992, and thus far over five hundred dwellings have been restored. Up until the 19th century, the square held a whipping post (*pelourinho*) that was used for criminals and rebel slaves. Take a leisurely stroll up and down the *ladeiras* (steep alleyways) around the square and let yourself be surprised: along the alleyway that leads to **Forte de Santo Antônio Além do Carmo** fort, built in the 17th century, you will pass by **Largo Teresa Batista** and **Largo Quincas Berro d'Água** squares (where there are frequent shows, *capoeira*, and percussion performances). On Ladeira do Carmo you will come across the beautiful **Igreja do Santíssimo Sacramento do Passo** church, built in 1737 (but closed to visitors for now). A word of warning: don't attempt to reach Pelourinho by car as there is nowhere to park, and many streets are closed to traffic. Also, look after your personal belongings. Pelourinho, though heavily policed, attracts pick-pockets.

❻ Terreiro de Jesus square

The original settlement of Salvador developed inside walls that

Salvador

PILAR

SAÚDE

PELOURINHO
- Senac
- Uauá
- A Cubana
- Jardim das Delícias
- Maria Mata Mouro

COMÉRCIO
- PÇA. INGLATERRA
- PÇA. CONDE DOS ARCOS
- A Cubana
- PÇA. TOMÉ DE SOUZA
- PÇA. VISC. DE CAIRU
- PÇA. DOS VETERANOS

S. PEDRO
- PÇA. DA BARROQUINHA
- LGO. DE S. BENTO

SALVADOR

STA. TERESA

PÇA. DA PIEDADE

TODOS OS SANTOS BAY

Streets:
- R. DA NORUEGA
- R. DA ESPANHA
- AV. DA FRANÇA
- R. MIGUEL CALMON
- AV. ESTADOS UNIDOS
- R. CONS. LAFAYETE
- LAD. DO CARMO
- AV. DR. JOSÉ JOAQUIM SEABRA
- LD. DA SAÚDE
- R. MQ. DE BARBACENA
- R. PEDRO JULIO BARBUDA
- R. DO GENIPAPEIRO
- LGO. DO CAIS DO OURO
- LGO. DO PELOURINHO
- LD. DO FERRÃO
- R. GREGÓRIO DE MATOS
- R. ALFREDO DE BRITO
- R. DAS LARANJEIRAS
- LD. DA ORDEM 3ª DE S. FRANCISCO
- LD. DA PRATA
- R. FONTE NOVA DO DESTERRO
- LG. CRUZEIRO DE S. FRANCISCO
- R. CORPO SANTO
- R. DA MISERICÓRDIA
- R. TIRA CHAPÉU
- LD. DA PRAÇA
- R. S. FRANCISCO
- R. DE SANTANA
- LD. DO DESTERRO
- R. BÉLGICA
- R. CONCEIÇÃO DA PRAIA
- AV. DAS NAUS
- R. DA JUDA
- R. JOSÉ GONÇALVES
- R. DO TESOURO
- R. RUI BARBOSA
- R. DO GRAVATÁ
- R. DO SATÉLITE
- R. DO TINGUI
- R. DA INDEPENDÊNCIA
- R. DA PALMA
- LD. DO BAIGAL
- R. DA CASTANHEDA
- R. ENG. ALCIONE
- R. DA MOURARIA
- R. CHILE
- R. DO PARAGO
- AV. SETE DE SETEMBRO
- R. LUIS MURAT
- R. DA PREGUIÇA
- R. CARLOS GOMES
- AV. JOANA ANGÉLICA
- AV. LAFAIETE COUTINHO (AV. CONTORNO)
- R. DO SODRÉ
- R. VISC. DE MAUA
- R. DO CABEÇA
- R. GABRIEL SOARES
- TR. GABRIEL SOARES
- R. PEDRO AUTRAN
- R. DO SATÉLITE
- R. DIREITA DA PIEDADE

N ↙

encompassed the area between what are now called Castro Alves Square and Municipal Square. With the growth of sugarcane cultivation the settlement spread beyond the walls, giving rise to Terreiro de Jesus Square, which is also known as Praça Quinze de Novembro. It is home to the old Igreja do Colégio de Jesus church, now a basilica. Near the 19th-century French iron fountain are two other noteworthy churches: 18th-century **Ordem Terceira de São Domingos de Gusmão** and 19th-century **São Pedro dos Clérigos**.

7 BASÍLICA CATHEDRAL

Colégio de Jesus church is where the impassioned and politically engaged Jesuit priest Father Antônio Vieira delivered some of his most important sermons. The Jesuits built it between 1657 and 1672 to replace the parish's original, 16th-century wattle-and-daub house of worship. Its distinctive limestone walls came to Brazil as ballast on Portuguese ships. The twin tower Portuguese façade is a blend of the Jesuit architectural tradition and unique spiral scrollwork, while the interior combines baroque and rococo styles. It is well worth taking a close look at the reliquary busts on the altar, the paintings on copper in the sacristy, and the lovely jacaranda chest encrusted with ivory, bone, and tortoiseshell.

Praça Quinze de Novembro, no #, Terreiro de Jesus, Pelourinho, tel. (71) 3321-4573. Mon – Sat, 8:30am – 11:30am and 1:30pm – 5:30pm; Sun, 9am – 6pm.

8 AFRO-BRAZILIAN MUSEUM AND MUSEUM OF ARCHAEOLOGY AND ETHNOLOGY

Both museums are housed in an early 19th century building that originally served as headquarters for the first medical school in Brazil. The Museu Afro-Brasileiro collection includes maps of slave traffic routes, a beautiful collection of African *orixás*

An exquisite nave ceiling is the highlight of São Domingo de Gusmão Church

statues, and 27 carved cedar panels depicting Candomblé rituals and dieties. The **Museu de Arqueologia e Etnologia** has a small but well-organized collection of archaeological material from sites in Bahia, as well as indigenous artifacts and paintings and photographs of the local indigenous population.
Praça Quinze de Novembro, no # (the old Medical school), Terreiro de Jesus, Pelourinho, tel. 71/3321-2013. Mon – Fri, 9am – 6pm; Sat and Sun, 10am – 5pm.

❾ ORDEM TERCEIRA DE SÃO DOMINGOS DE GUSMÃO CHURCH

Visitors to 18th century Igreja da Ordem Terceira de São Domingos de Gusmão must be sure to see the nave ceiling, where José Joaquim da Rocha created an allegorical depiction of São Domingo's entry into heaven. Da Rocha also painted the murals that decorate the main reception room. The church façade has rococo lines but the original carvings inside were replaced by neo-classical works.
Praça Quinze de Novembro, no #,

The opulence of São Francisco Church

Terreiro de Jesus, Pelourinho, tel. (71) 3242-4185. Mon – Fri, 8:30am – noon and 2pm – 6pm; Sun, 8am – 10am.

❿ SÃO FRANCISCO CHURCH AND CONVENT

The Igreja and Convento de São Francisco, built between 1686 and 1750,

---

PIERRE VERGER'S LEGACY

French photographer and cultural anthropologist **Pierre Verger**, an important figure in the academic study of Afro-Brazilian culture in Bahia, was born in Paris in 1902. In 1932, at the age of thirty, he decided to become a photographer and set off to explore and photograph the world. Fourteen years later he landed in Bahia. He was introduced to Candomblé, began to study it, and moved to Africa soon thereafter. In 1953, aged 51, he became a *babalaô*, or *pai-de-santo* (high priest), receiving the name Fatumbi ("reborn").

His books exploring the culture and religion of the Yoruba peoples and their descendants, both in Africa and Brazil, are required reading for anyone who would like to gain an understanding of the subject. Originally self-taught, Verger later received a PhD in Ethnology from the Sorbonne. He died in Salvador in 1996, leaving behind a photographic collection of inestimable value. A small part of his work can be seen at the **Galeria Fundação Pierre Verger** gallery (*Rua da Misericórdia, 9, Pelourinho; tel. 71/ 3321-2341; Mon – Sat, 8am – 8pm; Sun and holidays, 8am – 3pm*), which holds periodic exhibitions and sells books, CDs, posters, shirts, and other items. Some distance from Pelourinho, the house where Verger lived is now headquarters for the **Fundação Pierre Verger** foundation (*Ladeira da Vila América, 6, Engenho Velho de Brotas; tel. 71/3261-7453, 3261-1695. High season: 9am – 9pm; sun and holidays, 9am – 5pm; low season: Mon – Sat, 8am – 8pm*). Researchers can access his library and collection of 62,000 pictures.

is one of the most extraordinary baroque churches in the world and is the most opulent in Brazil. Eight hundred kilos (1,765 pounds) of gold were used to gild the woodcarvings inside. In Portugal, only the Franciscan Church in Porto has comparable carvings. In addition to the omnipresent gold decorations, the blue tiles in the church and cloisters depicting scenes from the life of Saint Francis of Assisi are outstanding. Look to one of the side altars for the mournful statue of São Pedro de Alcântara. On the ground floor of the cloisters are tiled murals inspired by Flemish drawings. The Latin quotations on the tiles are from Horace, a rare example of classical influence in a Brazilian Catholic church.
Praça Anchieta, no #, Pelourinho, tel. (71) 3322-6430. Mon – Sat, 8am – 5:30pm; Sun, 8am – 4pm.

⓫ Ordem Terceira de São Francisco Church

Igreja da Ordem Terceira de São Francisco and its neighbor, Igreja and Convento de São Francisco, comprise the most impressive architectural ensemble in the city. The façade of the Igreja da Ordem Terceira de São Francisco, the only one of its kind in Brazil, is made entirely of limestone and sandstone carved in the plateresque baroque style (an ornate style popular in 15th and 16th century Spain). Most of the tiled murals inside portray scenes of Lisbon before the earthquake of 1755. They also depict the wedding festivities of Dom José, son of the Portuguese monarch Dom João V. The church remains open during restoration work that began in 2005.
Rua da Ordem Terceira (formerly Inácio Accioli), no #, Pelourinho, tel. (71) 3321-6968. Daily, 8am – 5pm.

⓬ Udo Knoff Museum of Tiles and Ceramics

The Udo Knoff Museum showcases sections of façades from mansions in Salvador and elsewhere in Brazil, as well as Portugal, France, Holland, England, and Italy. Some date back to the 16th century. The collection, unique in Latin America, is the fruit of thirty years of research by the German ceramic artist Udo Knoff, who lived in Salvador from 1950 until his death in 1994. The Museu Udo Knoff de Azulejaria e Cerâmica also offers ceramics workshops, with lessons in restoration and visits to other museums, galleries, and potteries.
Rua Frei Vicente, 3, Pelourinho, tel. (71) 3117-6388. Tue – Sat, 1pm – 6pm.

⓭ Jorge Amado House and Foundation

A stop at Fundação Casa de Jorge Amado is a must for admirers of the popular Bahia writer. Foreign visitors who've never heard of him will at least gain an appreciation for how revered this creative genius is in his native land. The museum hosts workshops, courses, and cultural events, and the collection includes videos, photographs, and awards that the writer received during his career. There is a snack bar and a small gift store that sells his books.
Largo do Pelourinho, no #, Pelourinho, tel. (71) 3321-0070. Mon – Sat, 9am – 6pm.

⓮ City Museum

The Museu da Cidade houses statues, votive offerings, paintings, tapestries, and sculptures by local artists, as well as an exhibit on the Candomblé religion. One room is dedicated to the poet Castro Alves, another to

traditional *bruxas de pano* (rag witch dolls). There is a collection of *caboclo* and *cabocla* figure replicas. The characters, which represent the fight and reconciliation between Brazil and Portugal, respectively, have been used since the 19th century in the traditional celebration of Bahia independence.
Praça José de Alencar, 3, Largo. do Pelourinho, tel. (71) 3321-0070. Mon – Fri, 9am – 6pm.

15 Nossa Senhora do Rosário dos Pretos Church

Every Tuesday at 6pm a different kind of Mass is the center of attention in Largo do Pelourinho. Hymns with African rhythms, accompanied by percussion instruments, fill Igreja Nossa Senhora do Rosário dos Pretos in one of the greatest expressions of syncretism in Bahia. Senhora do Rosário dos Pretos was the patron saint of slaves, and the church was built by members of the *Irmandade de Nossa Senhora dos Homens Pretos do Pelourinho*, a local brotherhood of men of African descent. It took almost the entire 18th century to complete the church, since the slaves could only work on the building during their rare time off.
Praça José de Alencar, no #, Pelourinho, tel. (71) 3326-9701. Mon – Fri, 8:30am – 6pm; Sat and Sun, 8:30am – 3pm.

16 Abelardo Rodrigues Museum

One of the most valuable collections of sacred art in the country can be seen in the Museu Abelardo Rodrigues in Solar do Ferrão. The museum is located in a beautiful 17th century mansion that formerly served as a Jesuit seminary. The collection includes statues, drawings, and hand-crafted items of precious metal, wood,

Nossa Senhora do Rosário dos Pretos Church

soapstone, and clay from as far away as Europe and the Far East.
Rua Gregório de Matos, 45, Pelourinho, tel. (71) 3117-6381. Tue – Sat, 1pm – 6pm.

17 Tempostal Museum

The "postcard temple" was born of one man's passion for collecting postcards.

Our Recommendation

🍴 The **Paraíso Tropical** restaurant in the Cabula neighborhood puts a new twist on old Brazilian recipes by making imaginative substitutions for key ingredients: *dendê* palm oil has been replaced by *dendê* fruit juice, coconut milk by coconut pulp and water, lemon by *biribiri* (a sour fruit), and coriander by lime leaves. The result is delicate, delicious food. The restaurant atmosphere is reminiscent of a farm (roosters crow in the background), and the windows of the simple, open dining area peer out at the level of the treetops. *Rua Edgar Loureiro, 98-B, Cabula, tel. (71) 3384-7464. Mon – Sat, 11am – 11pm; Sun, 11am – 10pm.*

Additional information on page 358.

Antônio Marcelino do Nascimento first began collecting in the 1940s, and today the collection of small rectangles sends visitors on a voyage through time, bearing witness to the many transformations undergone by Salvador and other Brazilian cities. There is, for example, a 1898 postcard of the first version of the Elevador Lacerda. The Museu Tempostal collection was

THE BIRTHPLACE OF *CAPOEIRA*

Culturally emblematic and a genuinely Brazilian sport, *capoeira* is a mixture of martial arts, dance, and ritual developed by African slaves in Brazil sometime in the late 18th or early 19th century. The unique combination of *ginga* (a rhythmic dance step), evasive ducks, and clever blows was particularly popular in Bahia, Rio de Janeiro, and Pernambuco. The movements are always accompanied by litanies (chants) and instruments like the *berimbau* (a single string percussion instrument), the *pandeiro* (a kind of tambourine), and the *atabaque* drum. Despite a sweeping ban by the government in 1890, *capoeira* thrived in secret. In 1932, Manuel dos Reis Machado, known as Mestre Bimba, founded the Centro de Cultura Física center in Salvador. The school allowed him to circumvent the government's prohibition. Mestre Bimba incorporated new techniques, including movements adapted from other martial arts. In 1937 he gave a special performance for President Getúlio Vargas, who was so impressed with the "true national sport" that he revoked the ban. In 1942, the Centro Esportivo de Capoeira Angola sports center was set up by Vicente Ferreira Pastinha, known as Mestre Pastinha, who promoted a slower style of *capoeira* more similar to that practiced by slaves. Today, both styles are popular. Bimba's son, *Mestre* Nenel, founded the **Fundação Mestre Bimba**, which supports the **Escola de Capoeira Filhos de Bimba** school (*Rua Gregório de Matos, 51, basement, Pelourinho; tel. 71/3322-5082*). Open performances (which allow visiting *capoeira* enthusiasts to participate) are held on Saturdays at 11am. The building that used to be the Centro de Cultura Física is now the **Associação de Capoeira Mestre Bimba** (*Rua das Laranjeiras, 1, Pelourinho; tel. 71/3322-0639*), which holds exhibitions on Tuesdays, Fridays, and Saturdays at 7pm, and open performances on Thursdays at 8pm. *Mestres* João Pequeno and Morais, who were Pastinha's apprentices when they were young, have turned Forte Santo Antônio Além do Carmo fort into a *capoeira* center. João Pequeno's **Centro Esportivo de Capoeira Angola** is on the ground floor and holds exhibitions on Tuesdays, Thursdays, and Saturdays at 7:30pm and on Sundays at 5pm. **Grupo de Capoeira Angola Pelourinho** (GCAP) occupies the upper floor and gives exhibitions on Saturdays at 7pm (*Forte da Capoeira, Largo de Santo Antônio Além do Carmo, no #, Santo Antônio; tel. 71/3321-7587*).

Pelourinho's old colonial buildings

acquired by the state of Bahia in the 1990s and contains more than 35,000 postcards and photographs.
Rua Gregório de Matos, 33, Pelourinho, tel. (71) 3117-6383. Tue – Sat, 1pm – 6pm.

18 ORDEM TERCEIRA DO CARMO CHURCH

A steep side street leads to Ordem Terceira do Carmo church. The building was rebuilt in the rococo style in the early 19th century after a fire damaged the church in 1786. It is currently in a poor state of repair. The church is certainly worth a visit, however, if only to see the magnificent statue of *Senhor Morto* (the Dead Lord), which was carved in cedar in 1730 by Francisco Xavier Chagas, known as Cabra. Hundreds of small rubies were used to create the effect of blood streaming from his wounds, a fairly common technique in 18th and 19th century Portuguese-Brazilian statues. The Igreja da Ordem Terceira do Carmo is part of an architectural ensemble that includes Nossa Senhora do Carmo Church and also a convent of the same name, which has been converted into a hotel. Nossa Senhora do Carmo's interior is ornamented with lovely silver and jacaranda pieces. The structure is currently undergoing restoration.
Largo do Carmo, no #, Pelourinho. Mon – Sat, 8am – noon and 2pm – 6pm.

OUR RECOMMENDATION

The **Convento do Carmo** convent, which served as military headquarters for the Dutch in 1642, is today one of the largest luxury hotels in Brazil. Its 17th and 18th century architectural characteristics have been well-preserved. The hotel restaurant, Restaurante Conventual, is open to visitors and guests alike. It's worth taking a moment to admire the ceiling, altar, floor, and tiles in the main lobby. *Rua do Carmo, 1, Pelourinho, Santo Antônio, tel. (71) 3327-8400.*

Additional information on page 358.

Exu  Ogum  Xangô  Logunedé  Iemanjá

CANDOMBLÉ AND CATHOLICISM

Oxalá and Iemanjá are deities as familiar to people from Bahia as Jesus Christ and the Virgin Mary are to the rest of Brazil, the largest Catholic country on the planet. Candomblé temples, known as *terreiros*, are around every corner: there are an estimated two thousand *terreiros* in Salvador (as compared to approximately 280 Catholic churches). Candomblé is descended from a religion practiced in Africa. Forced to convert to Catholicism, African slaves managed to keep their religious traditions alive in secret by associating their deities – the orixás, which represent forces of nature – with Catholic saints. In this way, Iemanjá, queen of the sea, became identified with Nossa Senhora da Conceição (Our Lady of the Immaculate Conception), Oxalá, the god of creation, with Jesus, and Iansã, the queen of lightning, with Saint Barbara. Such combination of religious traditions is known as syncretism, and it was a strategy that allowed the slaves to successfully maintain their culture. The annual festival in honor of Nosso Senhor de Bonfim (see page 84) is an excellent example of a spiritual celebration during which Christian and Candomblé practitioners unite in prayer. Led by *mães-de-santo*, also known as *ialorixás* (priestesses), Candomblé *ter-*

Oxumaré

Euá  Oxaguiã  Omolu  Oxalufã  Oxum

Nanã Buruku  Iansã  Obá  Ossain  Oxóssi

reiros are attended by initiated members, though some are open to the public. One of the most famous *terreiros* is **Terreiro do Gantois** (*Rua Alto do Gantois, 23, Federação; tel. 71/3331-9231*). It is open to visitors on Sunday nights between the end of September and the beginning of December, but is only open to non-initiates on specific dates during the rest of the year. A National Heritage Site, **Terreiro da Casa Branca** (*Avenida Vasco da Gama, 463, Vasco da Gama; tel. 71/3335-3100*) was founded in 1830 and is the oldest Candomblé temple in the country. The most important building in the temple complex is the *Casa Branca* (White House), where rituals are held. Nearby are residences for the *filhos-de-santo* (priest-mediums). On the outskirts of the city is another National Heritage site, **Terreiro Ilê Axé Opô Afonjá** (*Rua Direita de São Gonçalo do Retiro, 557, Cabula; tel. 71/3384-5229*). The Ilê Axé Opô Afonjá terreiro complex consists of a library, a school, several houses dedicated to different *orixás*, a museum with exhibits on the history of the *terreiro* and the Yoruba religious tradition, and the residence of the *ialorixá*. The *terreiro* is open daily in the months of September, October, and November from noon onward.

African Heritage

Pelourinho's African heritage is celebrated and cultivated by organizations like **Casa do Benim** (*Rua Padre Agostinho Gomes, 17, Pelourinho; tel. 71/3241-5679; Mon – Fri, noon – 6pm*). Casa do Benim's headquarters house a collection of objects from Benin made from gourds, wood, and bronze. The similarities between Bahia and Benin, a country in West Africa, are explored in the photographs of Pierre Verger, which are on permanent exhibit. *Atabaque* drum and dance courses are also taught here. **Casa da Nigéria** (*Rua Alfredo de Brito, 26, Pelourinho; tel. 71/3241-3667; Mon – Fri, 10am – 1pm and 2pm – 6pm*) offers similar exhibits of artifacts, photographs, and paintings, as well as a Yoruba language course. A kind of unofficial Jamaican embassy, the multifunctional **Quilombo do Pelô** (*Rua Alfredo de Brito, 13, Pelourinho; tel. 71/3322-4374; restaurant: daily, 9am – midnight*) building houses a show and exhibition area, gift store, restaurant, and guesthouse. The restaurant serves popular Jamaican dishes, including chicken with curry or spicy jerk sauce, as well as traditional breakfasts of fruit and steamed root vegetables. Jamaican music lovers flock to **Praça do Reggae** (*Largo do Pelourinho, 22, 24, and 26; tel. 71/3117-6451, 3241-3625; Daily, 6pm – until the last customer leaves*), where Carnival *bloco* shows and rehearsals are held September through March. Despite the name, Praça do Reggae also showcases other types of music, including soul, funk, and hip hop. It also hosts film series every Wednesday and offers *capoeira* and African dance workshops between April and June.

Lovers of African rhythms will enjoy visiting the **Ateliê Percussivo Mestre Lua** craft workshop (*Rua Inácio Accioli, 3, formerly da Ordem Terceira, Pelourinho; tel. 71/3488-3600; Mon – Fri, 9am – 7pm; Sat, 9am – 3pm*), where "Brazilian" instruments like the single-string percussion instrument known as the *berimbau*, the *atabaque* drum, and the *pandeiro* (an instrument similar to a tambourine) live side-by-side with "African" instruments like the djum-djum, djembe, and saba drums. Lua's followers play, sing, and perform *capoeira* on Sundays at 8pm in Terreiro de Jesus Square.

Neighborhoods from Centro to Barra

Praça Castro Alves offers a view that takes in the whole sweep of Brazilian architectural and cultural history. The building that today houses the **Federação Baiana de Futebol** (Bahia Soccer Federation) was formerly the **Teatro São João**, one of the first theaters in the Brazilian colony. To the right of the square, a steep street teeming with street vendors leads to a 17th-century church, the **Igreja da Barroquinha**, which was damaged by fire in 1983. Now undergoing restoration, it will eventually house a cultural center. Near the church are busts of the Bahian musicians Dodô and Osmar, who invented the *trio elétrico*. Also in the vicinity is **Igreja da Ajuda**, a church built to replace Salvador's second chapel. Overlooking the sea is the **Conjunto Cultural da Caixa Econômica Federal** building. In the 18th century the premises served as a Jesuit rallying point and the placewhere Father Antônio Vieira used to give his polemical sermons. In the mid-20th century, it served as a refuge for widows and later served as a newspaper's headquarters for decades.

Dique do Tororó park

Dique do Tororó park is a sports complex and leisure center with jogging paths, rowing lanes, fishing decks, moorings for small boats, a children's playground, and a stage for shows. Around the lake are eight statues of *orixás* by the sculptor Tati Moreno. In the early hours of February 2nd, before the Iemanjá festivities begin, followers of Candomblé make offerings here to Oxum, the goddess of fresh water. Dique do Tororó is next door to the Otávio Mangabeira soccer stadium, also known as Fonte Nova. Traffic in the area can be very heavy when there is a game. *Avenida Vasco da Gama, no #, Engenho Velho de Brotas, tel. (71) 3382-0847.*

19 Castro Alves Square

"The square belongs to the people / just as the sky belongs to the condor," wrote the Bahian poet Castro Alves (1847-1871). The square named in his honor really does belong to the people: it is at the heart of Salvador Carnival celebrations. Praça Castro Alves square was constructed in the 16th century on marshland. The city's *pelourinho* (whipping post) stood on the early square, as did the gates of the first city walls. The square affords a magnificent view of Todos os Santos Bay.

20 São Bento Monastery

Founded by Benedictine monks in 1582, the monastery was one of the first in the Americas. The original building has been altered through the centuries, though modifications have generally stayed true to a design developed by Brother Macário de São João at the end of the 17th century. About thirty monks live a cloistered life here. Mass is performed daily, and Gregorian chants can be heard on Sundays in the monastery's church, the sober Basílica de São Sebastião. The museum in the upper part of the church houses more than two thousand pieces of religious art, furniture, paintings, and hand-crafted items made of precious metal. Among these are important works by Brother Agostinho de Piedade (1580-1661), one of the first sculptors of religious subjects in Brazil, and works by painter José Joaquim da Rocha. Mosteiro de São Bento also has a splendid library with some very rare books and documents. *Largo de São Bento, 1, Centro, tel. (71) 2106-5200. Mon – Fri, 9am – 11:30am and 1pm – 4:30pm. Mass: Mon – Fri, 7am and 6:20pm; Sat, 7am; Sun, 10am (with Gregorian chants).*

Dique do Tororó park's leisure facilities and homages to orixás

㉑ BAHIA MUSEUM OF SACRED ART

The Museu de Arte Sacra da Bahia is in a 17th-century complex that used to be the Santa Teresa de Ávila Church and Convent. The museum contains one of the most important collections of religious art in Brazil. Highlights include a 17th century ivory statue of Christ nailed to a delicately carved jacaranda cross, an enormous sacristy chest, and the silver chapel altar. The view of Todos os Santos Bay from the museum courtyard is magnificent. A word of warning: Ladeira da Preguiça, one of the roads used to access the museum, is not safe; it's better to take the longer route via Largo Dois de Julho square.

Rua do Sodré, 276, Dois de Julho, tel. (71) 3243-6511. Mon – Fri, 11:30am – 5:30pm.

㉒ PIEDADE SQUARE

The garden around Nossa Senhora da Piedade Church and Convent, a neoclassical building with gilt friezes and Corinthian columns, creates a harmonious image when paired with the 250-meter railings by the artist Carybé.

NEW BOOKS, USED BOOKS

If you are visiting the area around Castro Alves Square, heading towards Pelourinho, the stores selling new and second-hand books are a must. The traditional **Livraria Brandão** bookstore (*Rua Rui Barbosa, 15, Centro, tel. 71/ 3243-5383; Mon – Fri, 8am – 6pm; Sat, 8am – 2pm*), has around three hundred thousand volumes, many rare and out of print, some English editions. In the second-hand store **O Berinjela** (*Travessa. da Ajuda, 1, store #2, Centro, tel. 71/3322-0247; Mon – Fri, 9am – 6:30pm; Sat, 9am – 2pm*), customers are greeted with coffee, vegetarian savories and cakes. Their stock includes LPs, CDs and comic books. The store holds monthly rock concerts with local bands. **Espaço do Autor Baiano** (*Rua Gregório de Matos, 43, Pelourinho, tel. 71/3266-1426; Mon and Wed – Fri, 10am – 7pm; Tue 10am – 6pm; Sat, 9am – 1pm*), maintained by the NGO *Viva o Livro* which was set up in 2001, is a cultural center for the development of reading habits and a showcase for new writers.

㉓ GABINETE PORTUGUÊS LIBRARY

The Gabinete Português de Leitura's 22,000 volumes of Portuguese and Brazilian literature are housed in an imposing 1917 manuelino-style building. In its collection is an important set of historical documents. The Centro de Estudos Portugueses, a research center that holds exhibitions and cultural events, is also in the building.
Praça da Piedade, no #, São Pedro, tel. (71) 3329-5758. Mon – Fri, 9am – noon and 2pm – 5:30pm.

㉔ HENRIQUETA CATHARINO MUSEUM

The museum collection includes the dress worn by Princess Isabel for the ceremony in which she became Regent of Brazil, as well as a collection of clothes that belonged to female slaves. Fifteen thousand other items are housed here as well, including furniture, porcelain, works of art, a collection of small shrines, and delicate miniature reproductions of church altars dating back to the 19th century. The mansion that houses the museum was built between 1937 and 1939 by educator Henriqueta Catharino to be the Instituto Feminino da Bahia, an institution dedicated to the education of women.
Rua Monsenhor Flaviano, 2, Politeama de Cima, tel. (71) 3329-5522. Tue – Fri, 10am – noon and 1pm – 6pm; Sat, 2pm – 6pm.

㉕ BAHIA ART MUSEUM

The Museu de Arte da Bahia, founded in 1918, is the oldest museum in the state. In its collection are 16th and 17th century religious statues, furniture, silverware, and porcelain, as well as works by José Joaquim da Rocha, José Teófilo de Jesus, and Rodrigues Nunes, masters of the Bahia school of painting. The museum is in the Palácio da Vitória, a large, neocolonial palace. The *palácio*, in turn, emerged in 1925 from a renovation and repurposing of the old Solar Cerqueira Lima, where balls and soirées were thrown by nobility during the reign of the Portuguese Empire in the 19th century.
Avenida 7 de Setembro, 2340, Corredor da Vitória, tel. (71) 3117-6902. Thu – Fri, 2pm – 7pm; Sat and Sun, 2:30pm – 6:30pm.

ART GALLERIES AND STUDIOS

Salvador is home to a thriving arts community. **Paulo Darzé Galeria de Arte** (*Rua Doutor Chrysippo de Aguiar, 8, Corredor da Vitória; tel. 71/3267-0930; Mon – Fri, 9am – 7pm; Sat, 9am – 1pm*) showcases contemporary artwork such as the oil canvasses of the esteemed Caetano Dias and Siron Franco and the photographs of Mário Cravo Neto and Christian Cravo. Sculptures and drawings are also on display. The gallery has a café and bookshop. **Oxum Casa de Arte** (*Avenida Sete de Setembro, 3026, Ladeira da Barra; tel. 71/3336-9774; Mon – Fri, 9am – noon and 2pm – 7pm; Sat, 9am – 1pm*) specializes in paintings and illustrations by Carybé and is run by his widow, Nancy Bernabó. The gallery also carries work by other artists. The Brazilian painters Di Cavalcanti, Portinari, and Pancetti make up most of the collection at **Roberto Alban Galeria de Arte** (*Praça. dos Tupinambás, 2, store #12, Comércio; tel. 71/3243-3982; Mon – Fri, noon – 7pm and 8:30pm – 11pm; Sat, 8:30pm – midnight*), which holds an auction every November. In addition to galleries, it is possible to familiarize yourself with the work of artists and artisans in Salvador by visiting their studios. The most famous of these is the studio of painter, sculptor, and potter **Bel Borba** (*Rua Luís Viana, 14, Pelourinho; tel. 71/3243-9370; Mon – Fri, 9am – 6pm*). **Reinaldo Eckenberger** (*Rua do Passo, 68, Carmo; tel. 71/3241-5456, call ahead for an appointment*) makes figurines and tiles decorated with imaginative designs.

㉖ CARLOS COSTA PINTO MUSEUM
The Carlos Costa Pinto Museum explores the lifestyles of the Brazilian elite from the 17th century to the 20th century. More than 3,000 pieces of silverware, crystal, paintings, porcelain, and furniture are on display, including fine examples of Brazilian paintings from the 19th century. Of particular interest is the collection of the gold and silver trinkets and charms worn by slave girls. The museum also contains the pleasant **Café Balangadan**.
Avenida 7 de Setembro, 2490, Corredor da Vitória, tel. (71) 3336-6081. Daily (except Tue and Sun), 2:30pm – 7:45pm.

SHOPPING

Pelourinho provides plenty of shopping options. At **Didara** (*Rua Gregório de Matos, 20, store #4; tel. 71/3321-9428; Mon – Fri, 10am – 10pm; Sat, 10am – 6pm; Sun, 10am – 4pm*), textile designer Goya Lopes creates clothing and household items with Afro-Brazilian motifs. **Vill'axé Show Room** (*Rua das Laranjeiras, 9; tel. 71/3321-1650; Mon – Sat, 9:30am – 8:30pm; Sun, 9am – 3pm*) sells cotton clothing with silkscreen-printed designs taken from regional culture, including saints and *orixás*. Inspired by the mythologies of diverse cultures, **Marcia Ganem** (*Rua das Laranjeiras, 10; tel. 71/3322-0234; Mon – Sat, 10am – 8pm*) makes clothing with polyamide fiber and also sells accessories made of the same fiber and semi-precious stones. Among the very Brazilian decorative objects at **Coisas da Terra** (*Rua Maciel de Baixo, 19; tel. 71/3322-9322; Mon – Fri, 10am – 7pm; Sat, 10am – 6pm*) are ceramics from south Bahia, including flowers, fruits, and animals made by Selma Calheiras.

MAUÁ INSTITUTE
The best place to purchase arts and crafts in Salvador is at the Instituto Mauá. It sells pieces from handicraft communities around the state, including wood and coconut crafts from Rio de Contas, ceramics from Maragogipinho, basketwork from Massarandupió, and hammocks from Paulo Afonso. There are two stores, a larger store in Barra (*Praça Azevedo Fernandes, 2; tel. 71/3116-6196; Mon and Sat, 10am – 6pm; Thu – Fri, 9am – 6pm*), and a smaller store in Pelourinho (*Rua Gregório de Matos, 27; tel. 71/3116-6712; Mon and Sat, 10am – 6pm; Tue – Fri, 9am – 6pm*).

Figurine for sale at the Mauá Institute

SHOPPING MALLS
Those who prefer to shop in air-conditioned comfort can head for the sophisticated **Shopping Iguatemi** mall (*Avenida Tancredo Neves, 148, Pituba; tel. 71/4002-3003; Mon – Sat, 9am – 10pm; Sun, 3pm – 9pm*). **Shopping Barra** (*Avenida Centenário, 2992; tel. 71/2108-8222; Mon – Fri, 9am – 10pm; Sat, 9am – 9pm; Sun, 3pm – 9pm*), only one block from Barra beach, is more relaxed. Near Armação beach, the **Aeroclube Plaza Show** (*Avenida Otávio Mangabeira, 6000, Boca do Rio; tel. 71/3462-8000; stores: Mon – Sun, noon – 11pm; bars and restaurants: daily, noon – 1am*) is a single-storey, open-air shopping center with more leisure and restaurant options.

CARNIVAL

Two million people crowd the streets of Salvador during the city's Carnival, one of the biggest in the country. Here, the celebration is unlike those in Rio de Janeiro and São Paulo, which are samba school parades, or those of Olinda (in Pernambuco) and Ouro Preto (in Minas Gerais), in which revelers follow small *blocos* (carnival groups) playing *frevo* or *marchinhas* (Brazilian martial music). Carnival in Bahia draws throngs of dancing celebrants who accompany large trucks with huge amplifiers and movable stages known as *trios elétricos*. Popular groups sit on the trucks and play *axé* music, a style that mixes *frevo* with pop.

The *trio elétrico* was born in 1950, when guitarist Afonso Antônio do Nascimento, also known as Dodô, and *cavaquinho* (small four string guitar, like the ukelele) player Osmar Álvares de Macedo, known as Osmar, installed two loudspeakers in an old truck, jumped in the back, and drove around playing their instruments and "electrifying" the city during Carnival. The duo was enormously popular. These days, there are three Carnival routes: **Avenida**, which runs from Campo Grande to Castro Alves Square and then to the end of Rua Carlos Gomes road; **Barra/Ondina**, which begins at the Farol da Barra lighthouse and ends at nearby Ondina beach; and **Batatinha**, which cuts through Pelourinho. In the early hours of Ash Wednesday morning, the great meeting of the *trios elétricos* occurs in Castro Alves Square and in Barra, near the lighthouse. To participate in Carnival celebrations in Salvador you must be prepared for significant pushing and shoving and busy, dirty public toilets. The most fun is to be had inside the roped-off area around each truck, and getting that close requires buying a ticket package. (The package includes a colorful tabard-style T-shirt, or "*abadá*" that serves as a visual ticket that is associated with a particular *bloco*.) From within the ropes, you'll be able to see the band close up and will generally have access to a bar, toilets, and medical facilities. Outside

A *trio elétrico* draws a crowd during Salvador's Carnival, the world's largest such celebration

Dressed in blue and white, the Sons of Gandhy honor the Candomblé deities called *orixás*

these areas the heaving crowds can be dangerous. VIPs enjoy the festivities from the top of support vehicles or from viewing boxes scattered throughout the city. An important tip: the most sought-after *abadás*, such as Camaleão, usually sell out the first day tickets go on sale (Ash Wednesday of the previous year) so planning ahead is crucial.

For Camaleão, Araketu, Daniela Mercury, and Timbalada reservations, contact Central do Carnaval, tel. (71) 3535-3000, or log onto www.centraldocarnaval.com.br. For Ivete Sangalo, contact Axemix, tel. (71) 3281-0400, or log onto www.axemix.com.br.

CARNIVAL STREET GROUPS

Salvador's *blocos* animate the city year-round on the streets and in their studios. The **Filhos de Ghandy** (*Rua Gregório de Matos, 53, Pelourinho; tel. 71/3321-7073*), founded in 1949 in honor of Mahatma Gandhi, parade dressed in white and performing *afoxé*, a rhythm closely related to traditional Candomblé music and played in honor of deities known as *orixás*. The group rehearses on Sundays at 4pm in their Pelourinho studio. Formed seven years ago by worshippers at the Ilê Axé Oyá Candomblé temple, **Cortejo Afro** (*Rua da Ordem Terceira, formerly Inácio Accioli, 27, Pelourinho; tel. 71/9134-2751*) rehearses at 9pm every Monday from October through to Carnival in Praça Teresa Batista square. The internationally famous **Olodum** (*Rua Gregório de Matos, 22, Pelourinho; tel. 71/3321-5010*) was established in 1979 and performs on Tuesdays in Teresa Batista Square at 8:30pm, joined by a guest band at 10pm. The group runs the **Centro de Memória Olodum** museum and the **Escola Criativa Olodum** school for underprivileged children. Located far from the town center, the **Ilê Aiyê** studio (*Rua do Curuzu, 228, Liberdade; tel. 71/3256-1013*) annually excites revelers along Ladeira do Curuzu street on its way to Campo Grande. Rehearsals are held on Saturdays at 10pm in their cultural center, **Centro Cultural Senzala do Barro Preto**.

City Beaches

Barra

Barra is the birthplace of the city of Salvador, which began as a small village established around the cove where the sea meets the bay. Originally known as Velha, or Pereira, it was a center for the brazilwood and sugarcane trade and headquarters. In 1549, Governor-General Tomé de Sousa landed at this small cove to establish a seat of colonial power, and transfered the colonial center of administration to Cidade Alta, the upper city.

Nowadays **Praia da Barra** is the busiest part of the capital and during Carnival serves as the meeting point for several *trios elétricos*. Strolling past its hotels, bars, and restaurants is particularly agreeable at sunset. Barra is a good point of departure for exploration of the city's beaches (*see map on pages 62-63*). **Forte de Santo Antônio** fort separates Barra from the calm waters of **Praia do Porto**, and the choppier waters of **Praia do Farol**, which are more suitable for surfing. The decagon-shaped fort was the first in Brazil; construction began in 1534. The fort is home to a nautical museum, the **Museu Náutico** (*Largo do Farol da Barra, no #, Barra; tel. 71/3331-8039; Tue – Sun, 8am – 7pm*), which exhibits maps, navigational equipment, models of old ships, and caravels. It also has a café, which is open from 8am to 11pm. **Farol da Barra,** a lighthouse built in 1698, stands near the fort. It is still functioning, though closed to visitors.

Ondina and Rio Vermelho

Just past Praia da Barra beach, the Ondina beach shoreline alternates between rough sea and stretches of calm waters created by natural pools surrounded by rocks. It is the second in a series of ten city beaches that become less polluted as you go north. Rio Vermelho's beaches, which are

The lighthouse at Santo Antônio Fort, a historic landmark on Barra

To the north of Salvador, the famous Itapuã Lighthouse stands on a popular white sand beach

just north of Ondina, are not suitable for bathing and serve as ports for local fishermen.

PIATÃ, ITAPUÃ, AND ABAETÉ

The tranquil **Praia de Piatã** on the north coast is dotted with *barracas* (beach huts), bars, and restaurants. Good tourist facilities are also available. This is particularly true, as well, in Itapuã (27 kilometers, 17 miles, from the city center), a fishing village made legendary through poetic songs. White sand and coconut palms surround *barracas* serving food and drink. There is also a base nearby for Projeto Tamar, where visitors can learn about the organization's work to protect turtles. Lovely **Farol de Itapuã** lighthouse towers above the beach's white sands, but access is restricted. Near Itapuã, the dark waters of the protected **Lagoa do Abaeté** lagoon contrast with the whiteness of the dunes and the colors of the surrounding vegetation.

STELLA MARIS, FLAMENGO, AND ALELUIA BEACHES

Reefs at these beaches create large waves at high tide and natural pools at low tide, making **Stella Maris** attractive to surfers and bathers alike. During the summer months some *barracas* are open into the night. **Praia do Flamengo**, 3 kilometers (2 miles) north of Stella Maris, has maintained its unspoiled beauty. With its strong waves, the next beach, **Aleluia**, is a favorite of young people and is home to the popular **Barraca do Lôro** (*Avenida Praia do Flamengo, no #; tel. 71/3374-7509; daily, 8am – 5pm*), which has another branch in Catussaba beach (*Rua do Camping, no #; tel. 71/3374-0767; daily, 8am – 6pm*).

A GOOD BAHIAN CIGAR

Tabacaria Corona, a tobacconist's that also sells imported cigars, has five stores. The main one is in the **Aeroclube Plaza Show** shopping mall (*Avenida Otávio Mangabeira, 6000, Boca do Rio; tel. 71/3461-0549; daily, 10am – 2pm*). In Pelourinho, the **Tabacaria Rosa do Prado Cigar Shop** (*Rua da Ordem Terceira, formerly Inácio Accioli, 5, Pelourinho; tel. 71/3322-1258; daily, 9:30am – 7pm*) sells only local cigars, despite its English name. In the historic town center, **Tabacaria CGC** (*Rua do Bispo, 5, Praça da Sé; tel. 71/3322-7817; Mon – Fri, 9am – 7pm; Sat and Sun. 10am – 2:30pm*) has a special area for customers to enjoy a cigar or sip coffee.

Bonfim and Ribeira

The shores of Todos os Santos Bay that stretch from Elevador Lacerda 8 kilometers (5 miles) to the north of *Cidade Baixa* offer interesting sights. This walk is usually most interesting during the Bonfim procession in January. Exploring by car or bus allows more time at each stop.

Nosso Senhor do Bonfim Basilica

One of the greatest celebrations of syncretism in Bahia – the stair washing ceremony – is celebrated here at the Basílica de Nosso Senhor do Bonfim, which is as sacred to Catholics as it is to Candomblé followers, who worship *Oxalá*, the god of creation. Completed in 1772, the church's rococo façade is covered with 19th century Portuguese tiles; the interior architecture is largely neo-classical in style. It's particularly worth seeing the nave ceiling, the sacristy murals, and the side nave aisle paintings. On the high altar is an impressive statue of Christ brought from Portugal in the mid-18th century. Every year, on the second Thursday after Epiphany, the Nosso Senhor do Bonfim ceremony is held in the church. It is estimated that nearly one million people participate in the procession that leaves Nossa Senhora da Conceição Church at 10am that day and winds its way toward Bonfim. Five hundred Bahian women, dressed in traditional white, bless the crowds by sprinkling them with the scented water they carry in jugs on their heads. At the end of the ceremony, the first ten steps of the church stairs are ritually purified with scented water, flowers, and herbs. Afterward, prayers give way to less sacred celebrations that include music and feasting on the streets. The festival is approximately two hundred years old, as is the tradition of tying *fitinha*s *do Senhor Bonfim* (festival ribbons) around the wrist or to the church railings, making three wishes in the process, one for each knot. The wishes are granted, they say, when the ribbons come untied naturally.
Largo do Bonfim, no #, tel. (71) 3312-4512. Tue – Sun, 6am – 11:30am and 1:30pm – 6pm.

Situated 300 meters from the beach, São Marcelo Fort took its current form in 1690

SÃO JOAQUIM MARKET

Live goats and chickens, medicinal herbs, Candomblé objects… everything is sold at the São Joaquim market, the most authentic of the forty or so open-air markets in Salvador. The noise of the animals mixes with the cries of 7,000 vendors who showcase their wares in a labyrinth of stalls. Visiting such a market is a rare experience, and anyone wanting to live it should go in the morning, when it is cleaner, and the fruits and vegetables are fresher. While in the area, take the opportunity to visit nearby **Mercado de Ouro** (*Rua Torquato Bahia, 84, Comércio*), the so-called gold market, also home to **Juarez Restaurante**, famous for its traditional filet mignon. *Market: Avenida Oscar Portes, no #, Calçada, tel. (71) 3314-6096/9133-3488. Mon – Sat, 5am – 7pm; Sun, 5am – 2pm.*

FORTS

Forte de Monte Serrat was built to prevent ships from entering the port of Salvador. Due to its strategic position at the northern city limits, it complemented the protection afforded by **Forte de Santo Antônio da Barra** (*see Praia da Barra page 82*), at the southern end of the city. But it was only after expulsion of the Dutch by the Portuguese that most of the fifteen forts in Salvador were constructed. Centuries later, the wonderful view of the bay remains largely the same, but the **Forte de Monte Serrat** today houses the **Museu da Armaria** (*Rua Santa Rita Durão, no #, Monte Serrat; tel. 71/3313-7339, 3311-9418; Daily, 9am – 5pm*), a museum of weapons from colonial times to today. **Forte de São Diogo**, built between 1625 and 1634, is also on Porto da Barra beach (*Rua do Forte de São Diogo, no #, Porto da Barra; tel. 71/3264-3195; Tue – Sun, 9:30am – noon and 1:30pm – 5:30pm*). Today visitors look at models of the forts of Salvador and watch a video in Portuguese, English, and Spanish that explains the role these forts played in coastal defense. Every day at noon the fort fires its cannon. Originally built of wood on a sandbank 300 meters (980 feet) out into the bay, **Forte de São Marcelo** (*Avenida da França, no #, Comércio, Centro Náutico da Bahia; tel. 71/8882-8776; Tue – Sun, 9am – 6pm in January only, English speaking guides*) was rebuilt in stone in 1624 and given

---

ICE CREAM TO BATTLE THE HEAT

Watching the sunset from Ponta do Humaitá point is usually best paired with a trip to **Sorveteria da Ribeira** (*Praça. General Osório, 87, Ribeira; tel. 71/3316-5451; Sun – Thu, 10am – 11pm; Fri and Sat, 10am – midnight*), an excellent ice cream shop located in front of the beach of the same name. The outdoor tables are crowded in summer. Among the fifty flavors available, the most unusual are *mangaba* and *cajá*, which are made from local fruits. **Le Glacier Laporte**'s (*Largo do Cruzeiro de São Francisco, 21, Pelourinho; tel. 71/3266-3649; daily, 10am – 9pm*) forty flavors include pepper with nutmeg and orange chocolate. The oldest ice-cream parlor in Salvador, **A Cubana** (*Rua Alfredo de Brito, 12, Pelourinho; tel. 71/3321-6162; Sun – Thu, 9am – 10pm; Fri and Sat, 9am – midnight; also at Praça Tomé de Souza, 1, upper part of Elevador Lacerda, tel. 71/3322-7000; Mon and Wed, 9am – 10pm; Tue, Thu, Fri, Sat and Sun, 9am – midnight*) is also a good place from which to watch the sunset. A Cubana serves regional fruit flavors like *graviola* and *cupuaçu* paired with their exclusive chocolate nut cake. On the beach, **Sorvete da Barra** (*Rua Belo Horizonte, 102, Jardim Brasil; tel. 71/3264-6552; daily, 8am – 10:30pm*), serves coconut and *pitanga* ice cream, among others.

its current, circular form in the course of subsequent construction in 1690. "Forte do Mar" ("Fort of the Sea"), as Forte de São Marcelo is called, can be reached only by boat, which depart from Centro Náutica da Bahia (The Bahia Nautical Center). English-speaking guides are available at the fort.

SISTER DULCE MEMORIAL
Irmã Dulce (1914-2003), a nun, was nominated for the Nobel Peace Prize for her humanitarian work. Visitors come to view photographs and personal objects. *Avenida Bonfim, 161, Roma, tel. (71) 3310-1115. Tue – Sat, 10am – 5pm; Sun, 10am – 3pm.*

RIO VERMELHO

Visitors flock to Rio Vermelho for its *acarajé* stalls (the most traditional in the city) and lively nightlife. It's also pleasant to stand on Rio Vermelho Beach, whose deep, rocky waters are stirred by the comings and goings of fishing boats. Nearby on the same sands, a small, discreet, white house with a blue door and windows – the colors being those of the African sea goddess Iemanjá *(page 74)* – and an area for offerings hints that this neighborhood is a center for the popular Iemanjá festivities. To earn the sea goddess's lifesaving protection, fisherman offer her flowers, perfume, and other sundries that might be favored by a fickle woman.

RIO VERMELHO MARKET
At the end of the day, locals and tourists alike congregate in Largo da Mariquita square at the Mercado do Rio Vermelho market *(daily, 24 hours a day)*. It's a perfect spot for watching the sunset, chatting, enjoying a cold beer, and savoring tasty snacks from one of the approximately 30 stalls. It tends to get busier after 2am, and the revelry often continues till dawn. The **Boteco do França** bar *(Rua Borges dos Reis, 24-A, Rio Vermelho; tel. 71/3334-2734; Tue – Sun, noon – until the last customer leaves)*, also in Largo da Mariquita square, has good music and excellent food.
Market: Rua Odelom Santos, no #, near Largo da Mariquita. Daily, 24 hours a day.

IEMANJÁ FESTIVITIES AND *FEIJOADA*
Every year on February 2nd, Rio Vermelho beach is taken over by thousands of the faithful. Dressed in white, they chant, dance, and make offerings of perfumes, flowers, and mirrors to the goddess of the seas, Iemanjá. Festa de Iemanjá culminates in a ritual where a boat is set out to sea carrying a statue of the goddess, followed by dozens of rafts, launches, and sailboats. After gifts have been thrown into the waters, the boats return to the beach and the *trios elétricos* create a Carnival-like atmosphere. Another festival custom is *feijoada de Iemanjá*

A stall sells *acarajés* and other Bahian snacks

Rio Vermelho Beach fills with flowers and other offerings for the Iemanjá festivities

(black beans with pork), which can be eaten in the neighborhood's restaurants. On the festival day **Dinha do Acarajé** (*Largo de Santana, no #, Rio Vermelho; tel. 71/3334-0525/3334-1703; Mon – Fri, 4:30pm – midnight; Sat and Sun, 11am – midnight*) serves all you can eat for a fixed price. **Feijoada da Dadá** (*Rua Frei Vicente, 5, Pelourinho; tel. 71/3321-9642; daily, 11:30am – midnight*), a restaurant in the Pestana Hotel, celebrates a week in advance.

THE BAIANAS WHO MAKE ACARAJÉ

Rio Vermelho is well known for having the best *acarajé* makers in the city: **Regina**, **Cira**, and **Dinha**. *Acarajé* is a small cake made with a paste of cooked black-eyed peas that is stuffed with *vatapá* and shrimp and fried in *dendê* palm oil. The women selling them on the street are unmistakable: they wear traditional full skirts, blouses, and turbans of white. Necklaces and bracelets adorn their necks and wrists. These adornments represent and honor Candomblé deities. The turban is symbolic of Arab influence in North Africa, while the white clothes represent the rough cloth worn by slaves. The *acarajé*, as well as several other traditional foods, including *vatapá* and *caruru*, which the Brazilian government recently recognized as masterpieces of "intangible" cultural heritage.

PITUAÇU AND MÁRIO CRAVO SCULPTURE PARK

Situated near the shoreline, **Parque Metropolitano do Pituaçu** is one of the largest green spaces in Salvador. Vegetation reminiscent of Atlantic forest covers its 1,050 hectares, and the park is crisscrossed by 15 kilometers (9 miles) of bike lanes shaded by cashew trees, *dendê*, and coconut palms. Pedal boats can be rented to explore the park's lake. The park contains the **Espaço Mário Cravo** gallery, where a thousand sculptures donated to the state by the Bahian artist are exhibited. Cravo is most famed for his giant depictions of African dieties.

Park: Avenida Otávio Mangabeira, no #, Pituaçu, tel. (71) 3363-5859. Daily, 8am – 5pm. Espaço Mário Cravo: Jardim Iracema, no #, Portal de Pituaçu, tel. (71) 3363-4054. Daily, 8am – noon and 1:30pm – 6pm.

TODOS OS SANTOS BAY

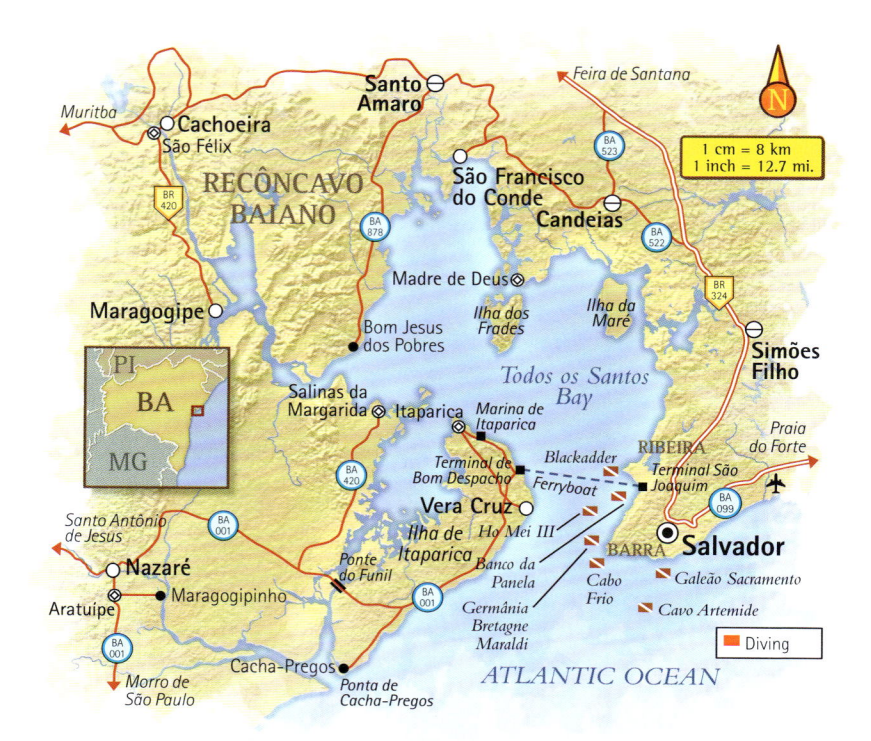

Todos os Santos Bay, the largest bay in Brazil, is a popular destination among sailing enthusiasts. Boat trips regularly depart from Salvador and the other cities in the Recôncavo Baiano area. Salvador, considered by some the best base in the Northeast for water sports tourism, regularly hosts international regattas. The Mar Grande–Salvador Crossing Race is held here every December, when dozens of competitors plunge into the water to swim the 12 kilometers from Itaparica Island to Barra Beach. Itaparica, Ilha dos Frades, Ilha da Maré, and other islands in the bay can be reached by public catamarans and ferries that depart from São Joaquim terminal (*next to the market of the same name; Avenida Oscar Pontes, 1051, Água de Menino; tel: 71/3327-2530; ferryboat: daily, 5am – 11:30pm and catamarã: daily, 8am – 6pm*). Visitors can also sign up for a tour (*All Tour: tel. 71/3254-1020; L. R. Turismo: tel. 71/3241-1526*) at the Centro Náutico (*tel. 71/3242-4366*) in front of Mercado Modelo. The third option is to hire a boat with crew, which can also be arranged at Centro Náutico. Baía de Todos os Santos is one of the best places in Brazil for diving: the average water temperature is 26°C (79°F) and visibility is as great as 20 meters. In addition to the teeming marine life of the reefs, there are about forty sunken ships under the waters of the bay. Fifteen of them can be reached by boat from Barra Beach. Particularly worth visiting is the Portuguese command vessel *Sacramento*, which sank in 1668 to a depth of 30 meters (100 feet), and the 180-meter-long (590 feet) Greek cargo ship *Cavo Artemide*. The *Germânia* and the *Bretagne*, both of which sank in 19th century, are 150 meters (490 feet) from Praia do Farol beach in only 8 meters (26 feet) of water and can be reached by swimmers. Some agencies organize night trips (*Dive Bahia: Avenida Sete de Setembro, 3809, Porto da Barra; tel. 71/3264-3820; Bahia Scub: Avenida Contorno, 1010, store # 12, Comércio; tel. 71/3321-0156*).

The homage paid to Iemanjá in the Rio Vermelho neighborhood annually on February 2 (*see Rio Vermelho page 86*) is not the only religious boat procession in Salvador. Continuing a tradition that began in the 18th century, on the morning of the first day of the new year dozens of small boats take to the bay's waters in honor of **Bom Jesus dos Navegantes** (Jesus, protector of sailors). The retinue congregates at Nossa Senhora da Conceição da Praia Church, in the Comércio neighborhood, and processes to Nossa Senhora da Boa Viagem Church, in the neighborhood of Barra.

Itaparica Island

Ilha de Itaparica offers a tranquil atmosphere and a beautiful view of the city, and is only 20 minutes by catamaran or 50 minutes by ferry. The island is divided into two municipalities, **Vera Cruz** and **Itaparica**. The Vera Cruz coast, which faces Salvador, is known for its natural beauty. Visitors usually come ashore at **Mar Grande** and make their way to the quieter beaches of **Barra do Gil**, **Penha**, and **Conceição**, which are nonetheless dotted with resorts, summer condos, and guesthouses. The Itaparica municipality is home to some photogenic historical sites and the Bom Despacho ferry terminal. There are several pleasant squares in the town center. **Sete de Janeiro** Square commemorates the events of January 7, when regional troops resisted the Portuguese in the War of Independence. There is also a fort, old homes, and other historic buildings, including the **Igreja de São Lourenço**, built in 1610. **Praça da Quitanda**, a square full of bars and restaurants with outdoor tables, is a lovely place to sit and enjoy the sunset. On weekends there are long lines for the ferry to Itaparica. The island can also be reached by car, via a bridge near the town of Nazaré das Farinhas. From Salvador, go west on the BR-324 highway and then take BR-101 south through Nazaré das Farinhas. The 292-kilometer (181-mile) drive is only worth the effort, if you are planning on visiting the south coast as well.

Caxixis Market Fair in Nazaré

If you are on Itaparica Island during Holy Week, it's worth going to the town of Cacha-Pregos and finding a spot on a boat to Feira dos Caxixis de Nazaré. That fair is held in Nazaré, a 16th-century town in Recôncavo Baiano. Market vendors sell distinctive ceramics from Maragogipinho, located 10 kilometers (6 miles) from Nazaré on the banks of the Rio Jaguaripe River. Red clay is used to make vases, water jugs, decorative objects, and caxixis, miniatures popular with children. There are no hotels, but anyone wishing to stay overnight can do so in neighboring Santo Antônio de Jesus, 32 kilometers (20 miles) away. If you are coming from Salvador, you can skip the boat trip and simply drive 216 kilometers (134 miles) southwest along BR-324 to reach Nazaré.

RECÔNCAVO BAIANO

The Recôncavo Baiano region encompasses 33 municipalities in the area surrounding Todos os Santos Bay. The town of Cachoeira, on the west bank of the Rio Paraguaçu river, is home to many important examples of colonial baroque architecture. Across the river from Cachoeira is São Felix; the two towns are connected by the Ponte Dom Pedro II bridge. Both towns are approximately 116 kilometers (72 miles) from Salvador. Among the symbols of their former status as economic powers are its churches. **Igreja Matriz de Nossa Senhora do Rosário** (*Rua Ana Nery, no #; currently being restored*) was built between 1693 and 1754. Take a moment to look at the tiled murals in the main chapel and the fine nave ceiling. Besides the 18th-century **Igreja de Nossa Senhora da Conceição do Monte** (*Largo do Monte, no #*), attractions include the **Casa de Oração (House of Prayers)**, which is also known as Igreja de Nossa Senhora do Carmo, and the **Igreja da Ordem Terceira do Carmo** (*Rua Inocêncio Boaventura, no #. Mon – Fri, 9am – 5pm; Sat and Sun, 9am – 1pm*), which was built in 1778 and is currently under restoration. Tobacco became a lucrative agricultural enterprise in neighboring São Félix. The *baiana* known as **Nega** sets up stall in the square every afternoon to sell her famous *abarás* and *acarajés*. São Félix and Cachoeira can be explored on foot in two days.

CACHOEIRA

TOWN COUNCIL CHAMBER AND PRISON

The town council chamber and prison building was constructed between 1698 and 1712 and was last renovated in 1789. In 1822 it served as the seat of the Bahia state government; today it houses the Town Council Chamber and the Museu dos Escravos (Slave Museum). Notice the robust walls made of stone and whale-oil mortar: they were built to withstand frequent

Dom Pedro II Bridge reflects the economic vitality of Cachoeira and São Felix during the 19th century

flooding of the Paraguaçu River.
Praça da Aclamação, no #, Centro, tel. (75) 3425-1018. Daily, 8am – 6pm.

Cachoeria Regional Museum (IPHAN Museum)

The Museu Regional de Cachoeira, located in a lovely house built in the 1720s, exhibits furniture from the 17th, 18th, and 19th centuries, as well as a large collection of documents, photographs, books, and newspapers connected to the town's history. As you enter, notice the mark on the left-hand wall, near the stairs; it illustrates the level reached by river waters during the last flood in 1989.
Praça da Aclamação, 4, Centro, tel. (75) 3425-1123. Mon – Fri, 8am – noon and 2pm – 5pm; Sat and Sun, 8am – noon.

Boa Morte Sisterhood

The Irmandade da Boa Morte (The Sisterhood of the Good Death) was established nearly 250 years ago by freed female slaves. It is one of the few confraternities in the Americas devoted to final days of Our Lady. It brings together women over the age of fifty for the traditional Nossa Senhora da Boa Morte festivities, which take place in the sisterhood's headquarters on August 13th, 14th, and 15th. Celebrations include processions, samba, *capoeira* performances, and an abundance of local dishes, including *feijoada, vatapá, caruru, cozido* (a meat and vegetable stew), and *maniçoba* (manioc leaves with pork and sausage). The event is one of the main draws around the world for self-consciously "black tourism" and every year it attracts visitors from Africa and the United States. The sisterhood's buildings house a memorial to Our Lady, a colonial style chapel, and an exhibition room.
Rua Treze de Maio, 32, Centro, tel. (75) 3425-1468, 9965-6195. Tue – Fri, 10am – 6pm; Sat, 10am – 5pm.

Santa Casa da Misericórdia Hospital

The façade of the early 18th century São João de Deus Hospital building is an imposing presence in the Cachoeira town square. The Igreja do Hospital São João de Deus church is annexed to the hospital.
Praça Doutor Aristides Milton, no #, Centro, tel. (75) 3425-1019.

Dannemann Factory and Cultural Center

The **Fábrica de Charutos Dannemann** is visible from Cachoeira on the other side of the Paraguaçu River. The factory can be reached by crossing the 365-meter (1,200-foot) Ponte Dom Pedro II bridge by car or on foot, but walkers should be extremely careful of vehicles on the bridge and the poor state of the iron structure. For many years the west bank of the river held large warehouses that stored tobacco grown in the Recôncavo Bahiano region. These fertile lands attracted German cigar-maker Gerhard Dannemann to the region and motivated him to build his factory, today the only one in the city. More than 25,000 cigars are produced every month, and tourists are allowed to watch the cigar rolling, which is, by tradition, exclusively women's work. The **Centro Cultural Dannemann**, a cultural center installed in the factory's old main building, holds the **Bienal de Artes do Recôncavo** (a biennial arts festival that runs from November of each even-numbered year through the following January) and the **Festival de Filarmônicas** (a music festival that is also held every other year, in November and the first week of December).
Avenida Salvador Pinto, 29, Centro, São Félix, tel. (75) 3425-2208. Tue – Sat, 8am – 5pm; Sun, 1pm – 5pm (cultural center only).

Nossa Senhora d'Ajuda Chapel

Capela de Nossa Senhora d'Ajuda, the oldest chapel in the city, was built between 1595 and 1606. Simple and unadorned, it honors Our Lady of Ajuda, the patron saint of sugarcane plantations. Slaves revered her and used to place her statue on the chapel steps to calm the waters of the Paraguaçu River during flood season. The **Festa de Nossa Senhora d'Ajuda** festivities, held at the beginning of November, include a ritual washing of the stairs, as well as masses, *capoeira* and samba performances, and traditional *afoxé* presentations, which include music-accompanied parades of African-style dancers.
Largo d'Ajuda, no #, tel. (75) 3425-3179. Mon – Fri, 8am – noon and 2pm – 5pm.

Studios

The streets of Cachoeira are home to artists and artisans who find their inspiration in Recôncavo. In the 1960s, **Louco** created statues of *orixás* and Catholic saints from wood. After his death his son **Louco Filho** (*Rua Treze de Maio, 18, Centro; tel. 75/9988-6509; daily, 8am – 10pm*) continued his work and has trained his own students, including **Fory** (*Rua Treze de Maio, 31; tel. 75/3425-1142, 9991-9732; daily, 8am – noon and 1pm – 6pm*), **Dory** (*Praça Ivone Bessa Ramos, 13; daily, 7am – 7pm*), **Mimo** (*Rua Manoel Paulo Filho, 1; tel. 75/3425-3127, 9982-9896; daily, 8am – 7pm*) and **Doidão** (*Rua Ana Nery, 42, tel. 75/3425-2764, 9982-4004; daily, 9am – 6pm*). African culture is also the subject of woodcut prints by **Davi Rodrigues** (*Rua J.J. Seabra, 68, Centro; tel. 75/3425-2686, 9126-4515; daily, 8am – noon and 2pm – 5pm*). Examples of these artists' work can be seen at **Café Pouso da Palavra**, a pleasant bookstore and art gallery (*Praça da Aclamação, 8, Centro; tel. 75/3425-1604; Tue – Thu, 10am – 5pm, Fri – Mon, 9am – 10pm*).

Boat Trips on the Paraguaçu River

Boat trips on the Paraguaçu are typically long (up to three hours) and often tiring. The boats depart from the Cachoeira port quays (*tel. 75/9191-7082, ask to speak to Bim*). The first site on your tour will be the old **Engenho Vitória** sugarcane plantation; it's best to pass on this optional stop as the ill-kept buildings are more beautiful from afar than close up. Further on, is **Igreja de Santo Antônio** church in the village of **São Francisco do Paraguaçu**. The mid-17th century church is beautiful. São Francisco do Paraguaçu can also be reached by heading west along highway BA-026 toward the town of Santo Amaro; it is 47 kilometers (29 miles) from Cachoeria, 22 of them on dirt road.

Hansen Bahia Foundation and Museum

The 1830 *sobrado* houses a collection of nearly 13,000 pieces associated with the German artist Karl Heinz Hansen, known locally as Hansen Bahia. Hansen embraced Brazil with such devotion that he changed his name to honor the state that was the central theme of his vast number of works. He died in 1978, and bequeathed most of his work to cities of Cachoeira and São Félix. In the Fundação e Museu Hansen Bahia, the most impressive examples of his work are the woodcut prints entitled O *impressor e a musa* (*The Printer and the Muse*), and the untranslated series *Flor de São Miguel*. The house where he lived in São Félix is now a museum that preserves his furniture and other possessions and educates visitors about his life's work.
Foundation: Rua Treze de Maio, 13, Cachoeira, tel. (75) 3425-1453. Hansen Bahia's house: Ladeira de Santa Bárbara, no #, São Félix. Tue – Fri, 9am – 5pm; Sat, Sun and holidays, 9am – 2pm.

Santo Amaro da Purificação

Santo Amaro da Purificação still bears traces of the prosperity that made its name known in the days of the sugar barons. The historical **Casa de Câmara e Cadeia (**Council Chamber and Prison) and the **Convento dos Humildes** convent, both built in colonial style during the 18th century, are surrounded by modern commercial buildings. The town comes alive during the first two weeks of May for **Bembé do Mercado** festivities. The *samba de roda*, popular at that festival, is a performance of music and dance that originated here. If you are traveling toward Cachoeira and São Félix along BR-324, Santo Amaro lies on the way, 70 kilometers (44 miles) southwest from Salvador.

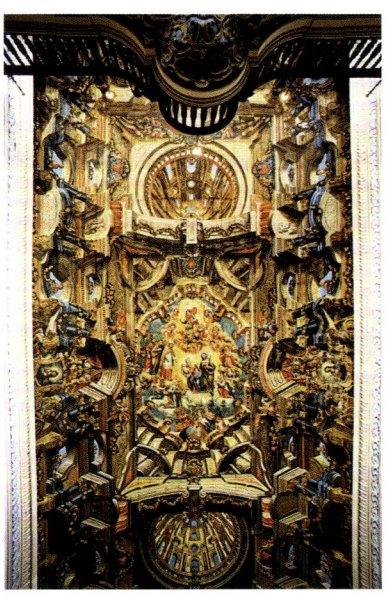

The ceiling of Santo Amaro da Purificação Church

Bembé do Mercado

The Bembé do Mercado festival celebrates the signing of the Lei Áurea, which officially abolished slavery on May 13, 1888. According to legend, on the first anniversary of the signing, former slaves flocked to **Praça do Mercado** square to celebrate. Instead of speeches, all that could be heard was the beat of *bembé,* a drum whose name is a distortion of *candomblé*. On the following day offerings were made to the goddess Iemanjá. Since then, the ritual has been repeated on the first fortnight in May. Today, the celebration includes music and traditional dances like the *maculelê*, *capoeira*, and *samba de roda*.

Nossa Senhora da Purificação Church

The imposing baroque façade of the Igreja Matriz de Nossa Senhora da Purificação hints at the ornate interior and its seven altars. The nave and sacristy walls are covered with Portuguese tiles and the ceiling painting depicts the purification of Mary. Between January 23rd and February 2nd celebrations, masses, and processions associated with the Nossa Senhora da Purificação festivities bring the town alive with sound and color. *Praça da Purificação, no #, Centro; tel. (75) 3241-1172. Mon – Fri, 8am – noon and 2pm – 5pm; Sat, 8am – noon.*

São Francisco do Conde

The small village of São Francisco do Conde, 66 kilometers (41 miles) from Salvador, was founded in 1697 around the **Igreja e Convento de Santo Antônio** church and convent. Last renovated in the early 18th century, the church is in dire need of restoration but is still worth a visit. The central nave is decorated with Portuguese tiles, and the sacristy and altar depict scenes from the Bible and the life of Saint Anthony.

Barra do Jacuípe, just off the Coconut Highway, is a perfect setting for water sports

THE NORTH COAST

Charming villages, beaches cut by rivulets, wind-blown coconut trees. The beauty of the stretch of coast between Salvador and the border with Sergipe is irresistible. The area is easily accessible on the well-maintained BA-099 state highway, which runs for 230 kilometers (143 miles) along the coast. The first 84 kilometers (52 miles) of the BA-099 are known as the **Estrada do Coco** (Coconut Highway). Past Praia do Forte the next 146 kilometers (91 miles) of highway is known as the **Linha Verde** (Green Line) in recognition of its environmentally-friendly construction. Many Salvador residents have summer homes in the area, which includes the townships of **Mata de São João, Camaçari** (an important petrochemical center), and **Conde**. Although the north coast is a relatively short drive from the capital, making day trips possible, the natural scenery makes a longer stay worthwhile.

ESTRADA DO COCO

AREMBEPE

In the 1970s Arembepe was a favorite haunt of Raul Seixas, Janis Joplin, and hordes of young people. Today it still serves as an alternative to more conventional tourist destinations. The village clings to its hippie roots amid dunes, sandbars, and natural pools, only a short walk from the sea. Buildings today are brick but their roofs are still thatched and a community of approximately fifty still lives without electricity or running water. In the town center locals sell crafts in the market. **Projeto Tamar** is based in Arembepe and allows visitors to observe the work being done to protect marine turtles for free and without too many other tourists around (a similar opportunity is available in neighboring Praia do Forte, but it is not free). There are two nice beaches near Arembepe: **Barra do Jacuípe**, which is an ideal destination for water sports, and

SERGIPE

Mangue Seco
This town at the mouth of the Real River borders the state of Sergipe.

Sítio do Conde
Starting point for anyone going south to Barra do Itariri, or north to Barra do Itapicuru.

Massarandupió
Near dunes and a fishing village, a nudist beach.

Imbassai
It is necessary to cross the wooden foot bridges over the Barroso River, which runs parallel to the sea, to reach the beaches and clear waters.

Praia do Forte
Praia do Forte's beaches and calm seas make it an ideal destination for snorkeling. Bars and restaurants liven up the weekends.

Porto Sauípe
This beach at the mouth of Sauípe River has rocky, unsafe waters; swim at low tide only.

Itacimirim
Praia da Espera beach marks the end of Brazilian adventurer Amyr Klink's 1984 trans-Atlantic crossing by rowboat.

Arembepe
A magnet for hippies, this village is close to beaches with natural pools (Arembepe and Piruí) and surfing (d'Aldeia). It serves as an alternative to more conventional tourist destinations.

Locations on map: Aracaju, Mangue Seco, Indiaroba, Coqueiro, Costa Azul, Barra do Itapicuru, Jandaira, Siribinha, Sítio do Conde, Conde, Rio Real, Rio Itapicuru, Rio Itariri, Linha Verde, Barra do Itariri, Baixio, Subaúma, Massarandupió, Porto do Sauípe, Costa do Sauípe, Imbassai de Santo Antônio, Praia do Forte, Itacimirim, Guarajuba, Barra do Jacuípe, Arembepe, de Jauá, Pojuca, Mata de São João, Dias d'Ávila, São Sebastião do Passé, Camaçari, Candeias, Simões Filho, Madre de Deus, Lauro de Freitas, Feira de Santana, Salvador, Rio Pojuca, Estrada do Coco, Todos os Santos Bay, Itaparica Island, Atlantic Ocean

BR 101 · BA 233 · BA 400 · BA 099 · BR 110 · BR 324

1 cm = 11 km
1 inch = 17.46 mi.

N

Itacimirim, where the Pojuca River enters the sea. The seafood restaurant **Mar Aberto** (*additional information on page 358*) is usually the first stop for anyone heading north. Arembepe is 40 kilometers (25 miles) north of Salvador.

Praia do Forte

A base for exploration of Bahia's north coast, the town of Praia do Forte, 91 kilometers (57 miles) from Salvador maintains fishing village traditions side-by-side with the sophisticated craft and clothing stores that have sprung up to cater to tourists. Neither cars nor apartment buildings are allowed in the town center. The bars and restaurants create a lively atmosphere, particularly on weekends. The Praia do Forte EcoResort is a favorite among water-sports enthusiasts, particularly windsurfers. The resort's 14 kilometers (9 miles) of clear coastal waters also attract snorkelers. Praia do Forte is nationally known as the headquarters for Brazil's largest sea turtle protection program, **Projeto Tamar**. The project has been working to protect turtles along 8,000 kilometers (5,000 miles) of Brazilian coastline since 1980. The headquarters complex includes a visitors center where tourists can view turtles and incubating eggs, watch an educational video, browse the gift store, and relax in the bar and restaurant. Between December and February, the Tamar team organizes night trips to observe turtles laying eggs in the sand (*Avenida Farol Garcia d'Ávila, no #, Praia do Forte; tel. 71/3676-1045; daily, 9am – 6pm*). Another popular activity in Praia do Forte is whale-watching. Trips supervised by biologists from the **Instituto Baleia Jubarte** (Humpback Whale Institute) are available July through October (*tel. 71/3676-1463, 8827-9037*). The trips can be arranged by Centrotur (*tel. 71/3676-1091*). Part of the proceeds from these trips benefit the Institute, which runs a research base, visitors center, and souvenir shop in Praia do Forte. The **Reserva de Preservação Ambiental Sapiranga**

The ruins of Garcia d'Ávila castle rise from a small hill

(*Estrada do Coco, km 52, Praia do Forte; tel. 71/3676-0211, 9968-1007; daily, 9am – 5pm*), an environmental organization run by the Fundação Garcia d'Ávila Foundation, maintains a variety of trails for hikers, cyclists, and horseback riders. Some routes are accessible to jeeps and quadricycles, both of which can be rented here. It is also possible to swim in the rapids of the Pojuca River, surrounded by Atlantic forest. Observing local wildlife, including the marmoset, the three-toed sloth, and the blue-fronted Amazon parrot, is much more interesting when accompanied by guides from the community. Local agencies provide hotels in the area with lists of available guides.

In addition to ecological excursions, it is interesting to visit the old **Castelo Garcia d'Ávila**, also known as Casa do Torre, the "towered house" (*Rua do Castelo, no #, accessed by 2.5 km of dirt road; take the turnoff next to the exit for Praia do Forte; tel. 71/3676-1073; Tue – Sun, 9am – 6pm*). What remains of the castle has been beautifully restored and rises majestically from the top of a small hill at the end of a steep but fairly obvious dirt path. The castle, built between 1551 and 1564, is one of the earliest stone buildings in Brazil and is the only Portuguese building in the country with the characteristics of a medieval military fortress. It served as the residence of royal dignitary Garcia d'Ávila and his descendents for ten generations and used to be the heart of a sizeable *sesmaria* (a tract of land awarded by the Portuguese Crown). The medieval atmosphere inside the castle is palpable thanks to poor lighting and the thick stone walls. A three-year effort restored the castle's lovely chapel to its present state, which is thought to look very much as it did 1551. There is a small archaeological museum in the castle that displays colonial objects found during excavations.

Linha Verde

Imbassaí

Imbassaí, 75 kilometers (47 miles) north of Salvador, is a small village with dirt roads and charming accommodations. A local highlight is adjacent Imbassaí beach. The Barroso River meets the sea here, and vacationers congregate at this point to enjoy both fresh and salt water and sit on kiosk chairs. The beach is accessed by bridges that span the river. Tourists staying in Imbassaí can also visit the **Cachoeira de Dona Zilda** waterfall or take a boat trip on the river; hotels will provide interested guests with logistical details. Neighboring **Praia de Santo Antônio** beach is a 5-kilometer (3-mile) hike along the shore (anyone approaching from Costa do Sauípe to the south walks only half this distance). The easiest way to reach the beach, however, is by the paved road that leads to the village of Vila do Diogo, just 1 km from the beach.

Costa do Sauípe

The largest tourist complex in the Northeast is on Praia do Porto Sauípe, a beach 105 kilometers (65 miles) north from Salvador. It is comprised of five large hotels and six mid-sized guesthouses. Leisure options are numerous and include horseback riding, a golf course, tennis courts, and a water sports center. The pools and private beach can be used by non-guests, if they

Mangue Seco offers tranquility and spectacular scenery

pay a day-use fee. The beach, however, is very stony and leaves much to be desired: the dunes of nearby Imbassaí and Santo Antônio are more attractive.

Massarandupió

Protected by dunes and coconut groves, Massarandupió, 123 kilometers (76 miles) from Salvador, is one of the many nudist beach in Bahia. To access the beach, drivers must navigate a pot-hole-ridden 10-kilometer (6-mile) dirt road near Porto Saupe that marks the beginning of the coastline highway called the Linha Verde. Men are not allowed without a female companion.

Sítio do Conde

Sítio do Conde is a major tourist area north of Costa do Sauípe, nearly 202 kilometers (126 miles) from Salvador. Visitors will find themselves with no shortage of accommodations and restaurants to choose from. Two rivers, the Itariri and the Itapicuru, define the limits of the most pleasant stretches of Sítio do Conde's tranquil beaches. In **Barra do Itariri**, 13 kilometers (8 miles) to the south, visitors are forced to make a "difficult" choice between swimming in fresh water in the river, or in salt water, in the sea, a dilemma that also confronts visitors to the north of Barra do Itariri among the dunes of **Barra do Itapicuru**. Near the fishing village of **Siribinha**, 16 kilometers (10 miles) north of Sítio do Conde, thrill seekers slide down the 30-meter (100-foot) **Cavalo Ruço** dune into the Piranji River.

Mangue Seco

On the banks of the Rio Real, the river that separates the states of Bahia and Sergipe, the northernmost beach of the Linha Verde highway lies hidden 77 kilometers (48 miles) north of Sítio do Conde and 246 kilometers (153 miles) north of Salvador. Between the river and the sea dunes stretch up to 30 meters (100 feet) toward the sky. To best enjoy Mangue Seco's peace and tranquility, take SE-318 highway to Pontal, which is over the state border in Sergipe, and then rent a boat there for a 15-minute ride in the direction of the sea. Visitors can also rent a buggy in Mangue Seco and use it to explore the mouth of the Rio Real, the village of Coqueiro, and Costa Azul beach.

DENDÊ COAST

MORRO DE SÃO PAULO

Morro de São Paulo is the most popular destination on the dendê palm–fringed coastline, called the Costa do Dendê, that stretches from Valença to Itacaré. Some 248 kilometers (154 miles) from Salvador, Morro is on the island of Ilha de Tinharé, which, along with 22 other islands, makes up **Cairu**, Brazil's only archipelago-based municipality. Rainforest, lowlands, dunes, mangrove, swamps, and beautiful beaches with reefs and crystalclear pools compose the scenary. Founded in the 16th century as a sleepy fishing village, Morro is now a much livelier spot, rustic yet sophisticated, a study in contrasts. Its car-free streets are filled with sophisticated stores, bars and restaurants tucked in among food and craft stalls, and a mix of young travelers search for everything from wild nightlife to some rest and relaxation at the quieter guesthouses on Quarta Praia. There are no streets, just alleys, only some four-wheel drives and tractors are used to access the more remote locations. Main access to Tinharé and Morro is via Valença, a colonial town on the banks of the Una River. You can leave your car at the port in a rented space (keep your keys with you), then hop in a boat for the one-and-a-half-hour crossing. Boats also make the two-hour trip directly from Salvador's Mercado Modelo (several companies operate here). Two air-taxi companies, Addey Táxi-Aéreo (tel. 71/3377-1993) and Aero Star Táxi-Aéreo (tel. 71/3377-4406), make the trip in just 30 minutes.

Morro de São Paulo: a car-free but lively village

Ponta da Pedra
String of small, rocky beaches, mostly unfrequented.

Praia do Forte
Small beach with many natural pools, accessible only at low tide, and then only from the nearby ruins of an old fort.

1 cm = 5.8 km
1 inch = 9.2 mi.

Ponta da Pedra do Forte
Morro do Farol
Primeira Praia
Gamboa
Morro de São Paulo
Segunda Praia
Ilha da Saudade
Terceira Praia
Quarta Praia
do Encanto (Quinta Praia)

Primeira Praia
First Beach (Morro's main beaches are numbered, not named). Built up with food stalls and basic services, this is the only beach suitable for surfing. Great view of Morro do Farol hill.

Segunda Praia
The most popular beach for visitors is backed by houses and guesthouses, and features natural pools at low tide.

ATLANTIC OCEAN

Canal de Taperoá
Valença
Rio Guarapuá
Cairu
Ilha de Tinharé
Rio Cairu
Ilha de Cairu
Taperoá
Torrinhas
Rio do Inferno
do Pontal
Boca da Barra
Velha Boipeba
Tassimirim
de Cueira
Ilha de Boipeba
de Moreré
Bainema
Nilo Peçanha
Cova da Onça
Ponta dos Castelhanos

Terceira Praia
Full of guesthouses, in front of Caitá Island, with coral reefs. Ideal for divers.

Quarta Praia
The longest and least-visited beach has coral reefs and natural pools.

Praia do Encanto (Quinta Praia)
Landscape dominated by mangrove swamps. The sand disappears at high tide.

Salvador
Camamu

> ### ZAMBIAPUNGA AND CARETAS FESTIVALS
>
> In **Nilo Peçanha**, 30 kilometers (18 miles) from Valença, in the early hours of November 1st (All Saints' Day), masked men dressed in colorful costumes dance in the streets and play drums, *cuícas* (friction drums), and even tools such as hoes. This is *zambiapunga*, a folk festival brought to Bahia by slaves from Africa in the 18th century. A similar celebration takes place in Cairu on October 8th and 9th, and is called *caretas*. Both festivities begin with a firework display at 5am.

The Tourist District

The steep street up from the docks takes visitors to the **Portaló**, a 16th-century stone archway leading directly to the **Igreja de Nossa Senhora da Luz** church (built 1855) and **Praça Aureliano de Lima** square. The square sits on **Rua Caminho da Praia**, the main access road to the beach and the center of town (with stores, restaurants, guesthouses and tour agencies). Nearby **Rua Fonte Grande** (named for the fountain built in 1746 to collect water for early settlers) leads to the quiet village of **Gamboa**, the deserted, calm **Praia da Ponta da Pedra** beach, and steps up to **Campo da Mangaba**, which offers a lovely view of Segunda and Terceira beaches. The main means of transport in town are tractors and modified trucks called *jardineiras* Porters can help with baggage, but it's best to agree on a price in advance.

Morro Lighthouse and Tapirandu Fort

On the hill topped by the Farol do Morro de São Paulo lighthouse, you can also see the Fortaleza do Tapirandu, a fort now in ruins. Built in 1630 by Portuguese colonists, the fortified walls were added in 1728 and extend out for 678 meters (2,225 feet). The lighthouse itself dates from 1835. To reach it, follow the path that begins beside Nossa Senhora da Luz church. The ten-minute trip up the hill is well worth it for the breathtaking view of the coast and crystalline waters, in picturesque contrast to the ruins and old buildings of town. Adventure-seekers can try the zip-line (*tel. 75/3652-1219, 8805-9796; daily, 10am – 6pm*), which starts from 57 meters above sea level with a 340-meter (1,115 feet) glide down to Primeira Praia.

Boat Trips

One option for exploring the area around Morro is a boat daytrip around Tinharé Island. Boats leave from Segunda Praia and head for the natural pools in **Garupuá** village, all great for diving. Next up is **Ilha de Boipeba**. More rustic and primitive, this island has trees, mangrove swamps and beaches with pristine blue water that can be also admired from the trails on foot or horseback. Next stop is at **Praia de Moreré**, with its wide diversity of marine wildlife. Then comes **Praia Boca da Barra**. A stop here usually lasts three hours – plenty of time to enjoy the calm waters, *afoxé* and reggae music, and snacks from the *barracas*. It's a quick walk to the crystal-clear waters of **Tassimirim** from here as well. From Boipeba, the tour heads down the **Rio do Inferno** to the town of **Cairu** and its baroque-style **Convento de Santo Antônio** (*tel. 75/3653-2118; daily, 9am – 11am and 1pm – 6pm*), built in 1654 using Portuguese tiles. Note that swimwear is not allowed in the convent. The tour finishes at the **Cairu River Estuary** before returning to Morro de São Paulo in the late afternoon. *Contact: Itha do Mar, tel. (75) 3652-1104, fax 3652-1225.*

Nightlife

The bars and nightclubs in Morro de São Paulo buzz on weekends and during the holiday season. The fun begins in the small village square and along the narrow streets of Caminho da Praia and Fonte Grande, where visitors and locals gather to discuss the best parties that night, usually somewhere among **Segunda Praia**'s popular bars. Some visitors don't even make plans, choosing to enjoy the music and fruit cocktails served on the cool, calm beaches all night.

Boipeba Island

South of Ilha de Tinharé, the island of Ilha de Boipeba ("flat snake" in the indigenous Tupi-Guarani language) is so rich in natural beauty it is a protected state nature reserve, home to dunes, mangrove swamps, and coastal vegetation (*restinga*), and ringed by coral reefs. As in Morro de São Paulo, there are no cars on the streets. Unlike its neighbor, however, it remains largely undeveloped, welcoming visitors but never losing sight of its environmental and cultural treasures. The reefs have plenty of lobsters and seafood, local fishermen serves up fresh appetizers for visitors.

The best route to Boipeba (accessible only by boat or plane) is on the Rio do Inferno by motorboat from Torrinhas, in Cairu; it's a 30-minute trip. Another boat option is to cross from Valença (four hours by boat or one hour by motorboat), or from Morro de São Paulo (two hours by motorboat). There are also direct flights (35 minutes) from Salvador.

View of Moreré, with Bainema in the background

Coral reefs encircling Boipeba

Velha Boipeba

The main village on the island, known as Velha Boipeba, is where most locals live and where visitors get most simple services. Founded in the 16th century, the village is centered on **Praça de Santo Antônio** and its simple **Igreja do Divino Espírito Santo**, dating from the 17th century. In early June, the streets come alive with colorful flags, countless food and drink stalls, and *forró* bands for the **Festa do Glorioso Divino Espírito Santo** (Holy Spirit festivities), the island's patron and protector.

The Beaches, on Foot or by Boat

Boipeba has almost 20 kilometers of beaches, most of them quiet, with calm seas. Coral reefs abound on some stretches, and conditions allow surfing in many places. The most popular beach is **Boca da Barra**, with plenty of snack and drink kiosks to satisfy visitors from Morro. A 30-minute walk south brings you to **Tassimirim,** an extensive beach framed by luxuriant vegetation and coconut groves. Farther on is deserted **Praia de Cueira**, with its four kilometers of coconut groves. Turtles lay their eggs in the **Cueira** and **Tassimirim** beaches. Separated from Cueira by an easily-crossed river is **Moreré**, a small fishing village famous for the shrimp *moqueca* and plantains served at the **Mar e Coco restaurant**. The beautiful beach has warn clear water and coral pools forming natural aquariums. **Bainema** comes next, where, with luck, visitors can watch dragnet fishing, followed by **Ponta dos Castelhanos**. At the extreme south of the island and difficult to reach is **Cova da Onça**, a cove at the mouth of the Rio dos Patos. Walking from Boca da Barra to Ponta dos Castelhanos takes about three and a half hours, though boats can be hired at Boca to make the trip in half the time. It is also possible to reach Moreré directly from Boca da Barra via an 800-meter trail over the hill that separates the two beaches.

Diving and Snorkeling

Protected by a barrier of coral reefs, Tinharé and Boipeba islands are ideal spots for both free and scuba-diving. On Boipeba, the natural pools at Moreré and Tassimirim are ideal for snorkeling, as is the beach at Ponta dos Castelhanos, where you can go by boat to see *Madre de Dios*, a colonial-era Spanish shipwreck. In Morro de São Paulo, tour agencies hold "baptism" dives for virgin divers. There are other points for more experienced divers, such as the coral reefs in **Itatiba** and **Itatimirim**, at a depth of about 25 meters (82 feet).
Contact: Companhia do Mergulho, tel. (75) 3652-1200, fax 3653-7127, Morro de São Paulo.

Maraú Peninsula and Camamu Bay

Off in an untouched corner of Bahia is the **Península de Maraú** ("dawn sunlight," a name of indigenous origin) and its islands, beaches facing the open sea and the bay, lagoons, dunes, rivers, and mangrove swamps. Departures to the area are from **Camamu**, a town 335 kilometers (208 miles) from Salvador. Boats leave every hour from the port, which also takes in the catches from the fishing communities scattered throughout the island and islets of **Baía de Camamu**. The crossing takes an hour and a half to reach the village of **Barra Grande**. Bathed in calm, fresh waters which result from the meeting of the sea and the Maraú River, this village of sandy streets has become more and more popular with Brazilian and foreign visitors, who can find good guesthouse and restaurant facilities there. The land route to Maraú is accessible only to 4×4 vehicles, coming from Itacaré or Ubaitaba, which are 56 and 90 kilometers (35 and 56 miles) respectively from Barra Grande.

Taipus de Fora

This beach is famous for its multi-hued sea water (courtesy of vivid barrier reefs) and the natural pools teeming with marine life trapped at low tide (also an ideal time for free-diving). The area is home to the beachfront shacks, called *barracas*, **Das Meninas, Do Francês** and **Do Gaúcho.** They offer masks and snorkels for hire alongside their selection of seafood dishes. Modified pick-up trucks called *jardineiras* make regular trips between Barra Grande and Taipus de Fora.

A Trip around the Peninsula

Jardineiras (pick-up trucks) are the best means of transport on the Península de Maraú. Trips can be

Boat trips around Camamu Bay reveal the community's devotion to environmental conservation

Três Coqueiros
Beach with strong waves accessible on foot from Barra Grande. Near Ponta do Mutá, where the waters of the sea and Maraú River meet.

Barra Grande
With its calm seas, this fishing village attracts more and more visitors and new residents each year.

Taipus de Fora
Coral reefs and natural pools are the attraction here.

Cajaíba
A village with boat-building traditions.

Lagoa Azul
This tree-fringed lagoon is named for its vivid shades of blue (azul).

Cassange
Quiet and deserted, with stretches suitable for water sports. A sandbank forms Lagoa do Cassange, a lagoon good for swimming.

Saquaíra and Algodões
This stretch of coast is lined with coconut palms plus a few summerhouses and fishing villages.

Cachoeira do Tremembé
A small waterfall about 30 meters wide.

1 cm = 2.8 km
1 inch = 4.4 mi.

arranged in Barra Grande, with the route and price fixed on departure. The most well-traveled itinerary begins at Taipus de Fora and the small **Lagoa Azul**, where the clear waters reportedly have cosmetic properties. Next is **Lagoa e Praia do Cassange**, a lagoon and beach with calm, dark waters. From the top of the nearby **Morro da Bela Vista** (also known as "Morro do Celular" or Cellphone Hill since it's the only place to pick up a telephone signal), you can see the striking color contrast between the lagoon and the sea waters at Cassange. A big surprise here is Gidésio, storyteller extraordinaire, with his seafood *pastéis* (fried pasties) and juice of *gaiteira*, a fruit from the northeastern backlands. From here you can choose between the seaside villages of Saquaíra or Algodões, or head for Morro do Farol de Taipus, a hill with a panoramic view of the sunset over the peninsula.

Camamu Bay

A boat trip around the islands in Baía de Camamu reveals the region's commitment to preserving natural beauty and traditional culture and fishing ways. Setting out from Barra Grande, the first stop is **Ilha da Pedra Furada**, an island dotted with beaches and mangrove swamps, that has a great view of Ponta do Mutá. The boat yards on the waterfront of **Cajaíba** are the next stop, and a great place to learn about the fishermen's long tradition of boat building. **Cachoeira de Tremembé**, a waterfall with a drop of about 5 meters, appears after a motorboat trip of around one and a half hours. Notice the peace and quiet in **Maraú,** with its brightly colored houses, some built in the mid-19th century. The village affords a lovely view of the small port, the market and the estuary. Nearby **Ilha do Sapinho** is home to **Restaurante do Jorge**, which serves food cooked in the family kitchen. The last two stops are **Ilha do Goió**, with its semi-deserted beaches, and **Campinho**, a village with an abandoned pier, good for fishing. The return trip to Barra Grande is often illuminated by the setting sun. Whether by boat or motorboat, the trips leave from the ports in Camamu, Jobel (in Saquaíra village) or Barra Grande, and the route can be arranged in advance.

Camamu and Valença

The small town of **Camamu** was once the second largest city in Bahia. Now it is best known as the launching point for trips to nearby Ituberá, which is home to one of the most beautiful waterfalls on the Brazilian coast, the **Cachoeira da Pancada Grande**. Visitors can cross the wooden bridge to the 40-meter drop, and follow the 300 steps to the summit. The waterfall is also a good spot for rappelling and cascading, both of which can be organized through agencies in the town such as Ativa Rafting (*tel. 73/3257-2079*). The same group also organize whitewater rafting trips on the Rio das Almas in the neighboring town of Nilo Peçanha.

Valença, 30 kilometers from Nilo Peçanha and the gateway to Morro de São Paulo, is a pleasant town dating from the second half of the 18th century. Among the old houses and historical buildings is the **Igreja de Nossa Senhora do Amparo**, a church built in 1757 on top of a hill that overlooks the Una River estuary.

Cacau Coast

Ilhéus

The stretch of coast known as the Costa de Cacau led the world in cacao production at the beginning of the 20th century. Its largest city, Ilhéus, however, earned its fame in literature. The writer Jorge Amado (1912-2001) set some of his most popular novels here, including *Gabriela Cravo e Canela* (*Gabriela, Clove and Cinnamon*). Ilhéus is 462 kilometers (287 miles) south of Salvador, 65 kilometers (40 miles) south from Itacaré and 110 kilometers (68 miles) north from Canavieiras on the BA-001 highway. But the town's attractions are not merely literary: good hotels and guesthouses provide access to historical buildings, inviting beaches, and Atlantic forest. Ilhéus was founded in the early years of the colony, a result of the sugar boom. The historic chapel from this time, **Capela do Rio do Engenho de Sant'Ana,** pre-dates 1550 and is Ilhéus's oldest surviving building. Most of the buildings in the town's historic center, however, date from the early-20th-century cacao boom.

Historical Center

1. Vesúvio
2. Teatro Municipal
3. Casa de Cultura Jorge Amado
4. Casa dos Artistas
5. Associação Comercial
6. Palácio Paranaguá
7. Rua Antônio Lavigne
8. Igreja matriz de São Jorge dos Ilhéus
9. Palacete Misael Tavares
10. Casa de Tonico Bastos
11. Catedral de São Sebastião
12. Ilhéus Hotel
13. Antigo Porto
14. Bataclan

Jorge Amado

Brazil's most popular modern writer was born in 1912 near Ilhéus, on Fazenda Aurícidia, a farm in Itabuna. Jorge Amado grew up on his father's cacao plantation and watched as the cacao industry came to replace the sugar industry. The conflicts he witnessed between planters and exporters would become themes in his works. A militant communist, Amado was arrested four times and lived in exile in Uruguay, France, and Czechoslovakia.

Amado's works include 25 novels, two volumes of memoirs, two biographies, two children's books, and innumerable short stories and poems, which have been translated into 50-some languages. The writer received honors in Brazil and worldwide, among them a place in the Brazilian Academy of Letters and an honorary doctorate from Lumiére University in Lyons, France. He also was awarded Candomblé's highest honor, that of *Oba Orolu*, bestowed by the temple Axé Opô Afonjá *terreiro*. Jorge Amado died on August 6, 2001 in Salvador and his ashes were scattered around the mango tree at his house in Salvador's Rio Vermelho neighborhood.

A walk around the center of Ilhéus is an introduction to the life and works of Jorge Amado. **Vesúvio**, a bar that figures in the plot of *Gabriela Cravo e Canela*, opened in 1920 and still serves chilled *chope* (draft beer) at sidewalk tables. Close by is the **Teatro Municipal**, the former Ilhéus Cine-Theater (built 1932), whose matinees the writer frequented. Nearby buildings all date from the golden age of cacao: the **Casa dos Artistas** arts center, built at the end of the 19th century, the **Associação Comercial** (Trade Association) from 1932, and the **Palácio Paranaguá** (today the City Hall) from 1907. **Rua Antônio Lavigne** was specially paved with English cobblestones for the wedding of the daughter of local *coronel* (rich, influential landowner) Misael Tavares, one of the region's most powerful cacao barons. His house, a 1922 mansion on the same street, is known as **Palacete Misael Tavares**. The street leads to **Igreja Matriz de São Jorge dos Ilhéus** church, originally built in the 16th century. The house known as **Casa de Tonico Bastos,** named for a womanizing character from Jorge Amado's works, is near **Catedral de São Sebastião**, a cathedral built in eclectic style between 1930 and 1967. Other attractions include the **Ilhéus Hotel,** built in the 1920s and home to one of the Northeast's first elevators, the **Antigo Porto** (old port), and the traditional nightclub **Bataclan**, immortalized in *Gabriela* and once frequented by cacao barons. Young guides who work in **Praça da Matriz de São Sebastião** square are happy to lead tours of the town center.

Jorge Amado's House and Cultural Center

A lucky 1920 lottery ticket allowed Jorge Amado's father, *coronel* João Amado de Farias, to build this 582-square-meter (6,264-square-foot) mansion with 5-meter (16-foot) ceilings, a jacaranda floor, and an English tiled veranda. In this house, Jorge Amado wrote his first novel, *O País do Carnaval*, which was published in Rio de Janeiro in 1931. Guided tours of the Casa de Cultura Jorge Amado see Amado's bedroom, which today displays covers from his books, as well as old photographs and personal objects.
Rua Jorge Amado, 21, Centro Histórico, tel. (73) 3634-8986. High season: Sat, 9am – 13h; low season: Mon – Fri, 9am – noon and 2pm – 6pm.

Cacao Plantations

Some cacao plantations offer guided tours, but they must be arranged in advance. Cacao trees are small and grow in the shade of other trees, including some of the tallest Atlantic forest species, making the plantations pleasantly scenic. At **Fazenda Primavera** *(BR-415 highway, also known as Rodovia Ilhéus–Itabuna, Km 20, tel. 73/3613-7817, 9983-7627; Mon – Fri, 9am – 2pm; Sat, 9am – schedule in advance)* and **Fazenda Yrerê** *(Rodovia Ilhéus–Itabuna highway, Km 11, tel. 73/3656-5054; schedule in advance)*, visitors walk through the plantations, seeing the production process from fruit harvest to separation of pulp from seeds. A tasting session usually follows the tour.

Beaches South of Ilhéus

A favorite of the cacao barons back in the day, the long **Praia dos Milionários** (Millionaires' Beach) boasts kiosks and freshwater showers and is the town's most popular beach. The next beach, **Cururupe**, known for its strong waves and mangroves, has a checkered past: it's said that the Portuguese wiped out an entire village of Tupiquinin Indians here in 1559. The Olivença district, 16 kilometers (10 miles) from Ilhéus, is home to the beaches most popular with surfers. **Praia de Back Door** (named after the famous surf beach on Oahu, Hawaii) hops with bars and restaurants, as does neighboring **Batuba**. After **Canabrava** and its large hotels, the road veers toward the mountains, making it difficult to reach the quiet coconut palm–fringed beaches **Acuípe** and **Itapororoca**.

Una Eco-Park

A fine example of the Atlantic forest's rich biodiversity, **Ecoparque do Una**, 45 kilometers (28 miles) from Ilhéus, is home to centuries-old trees and numerous animal species in 383 hectares (946 acres) of virgin forest. The Reserva Particular de Proteção Natural is a private nature reserve that accepts groups of up to 15 people. Along a 2-kilometer (about 1-mile) trail, visitors can see golden-lion tamarins (the park's symbol) or yellow-breasted capuchin monkeys, as

The coast to the south of Ilhéus: a string of well-developed beaches

well as watch rubber tapping in a rubber tree plantation. Bridges suspended 100 meters (328 feet) in the air, running through the treetops, afford a spectacularly unique view of the forest.

BA-001 highway, also known as Rodovia Ilhéus–Canavieiras, Km 45. Tel. (73) 3633-1121. High season, Tue – Sat, 9am – 2pm (tours every hour); low season: Thu – Sat, 9am, 10am and 1pm. Visits require advance arrangements (up to 15 people).

ITACARÉ

The Rio de Contas flows here from Chapada Diamantina, and standing at the river's mouth is **Itacaré,** the surfer's paradise of the Bahian coast. The town's name means "winding river of stones" in indigenous Tupi-Guarani language. Four hundred forty kilometers (273 miles) from Salvador and 65 kilometers (41 miles) from Ilhéus, the town offers 15 beaches framed by rugged coastline and forested hills criss-crossed by trails, rivers, and waterfalls. The mountainous landscape is vastly different from that of most of the Northeast. The exuberant outdoors, designated an environmentally protected area, also attracts rappelers, rafters, cascaders, and canopy climbers. The arrival of adventure sports has quickly changed the tenor of this old fishing village where Jesuits built the **Capela de São Miguel** chapel in 1731. The guesthouses and bars, which play everything from *forró* to electronic music, are concentrated on beaches in the town center. For a quieter visit, head for the less populated beaches to the south, accessible only by trails.

DISTANT BEACHES
The locals call the beaches far from Itacaré village *praias de fora* (out-of-town beaches). The nearest is the tiny but beautiful **Prainha**, which sits on private property but can be accessed, for a fee, through a condominium. It can also be reached by trail from Praia da Ribeira, but because robberies have occurred along the trail, that route is not recommended. Access to the lovely **Praia de São José** and neighboring **Jeribucaçu** also comes at a price, but all three of these beaches offer good surfing. **Engenhoca** and **Havaizinho** are accessible by dirt road from Itacaré. The first is sometimes nearly deserted: though there are some tapioca and coconut juice sellers, it's advisable to bring your own water and snacks. Havaizinho, 20 minutes away by foot, promises good surfing waves and a lookout point. **Itacarezinho** is the only area beach with seafront bars and restaurants. Access the beach through the restaurant of the same name or take a 30-minute walk from the road.

TIJUÍPE WATERFALL
A 10-minute walk from Praia de Itacarezinho leads to Cachoeira do Tijuípe, on the Tijuípe River. Its 4-meter (13-foot) drop forms icy freshwater pools excellent for swimming. A restaurant serves as a base for the area. Drive to Km 43 on the Rodovia Ilhéus-Itacaré highway.

CANOE TRIPS
From the mouth of the Rio de Contas, at Coroinha Beach, simple canoe tours head approximately 6 kilometers (almost 4 miles) upriver to

Praia do Pontal
This beach at the mouth of the Rio de Contas has an extensive spread of sand, though it's significantly reduced at high tide.

Praia da Coroinha
The kiosks make this the most commercialized beach in Itacaré. It is not suitable for swimming.

Praia da Concha
Offers an excellent view of the sunset and lively nightlife.

Praia do Resende
Not very crowded, this beach has coconut palms on the sand and Atlantic forest on its slopes. Good for surfing and swimming, but watch out for the rocks.

Praia de Tiririca
The main surfing beach in Itacaré is trendy and has comfortable guesthouses.

Praia da Costa
A small patch of sand with medium-sized waves, it's less popular than neighboring Tiririca.

Praia da Ribeira
The last of the city beaches offers natural pools formed by springs that flow down the slopes.

Prainha
A small cove of pale sand surrounded by Atlantic forest.

Praia de São José
A larger cove offering green slopes.

Jeribucaçu
Deserted, diverse terrain: concentrations of trees and swamps as well as creeks, reefs, and coconut groves.

Engenhoca
The green sea contrasts with the pale sand, and the surfing's good.

Havaizinho
An extremely rocky beach, not recommended for swimming.

Itacarezinho
An expansive beach, good for strolling, swimming, and surfing.

1 cm = 1.3 km
1 inch = 2 mi.

Cachoeira do Cleandro. The trip itself is more appealing than the waterfall: gray river dolphins come to the estuary in search of food and the route winds through twisted mangrove roots inhabited by crabs, including the tiny *aratu*, which are visible at low tide. The waterfall has two 5-meter (16-foot) cascades, but rocks make it unsuitable for swimming. Stop by the simple **Bar e Restaurante Manguezal** and try the tasty seafood, served under the trees. If your return trip coincides with sunset, you're in for a treat: seen from a canoe in the middle of the Rio de Contas, it's unforgettable.
Contact: NV Turismo, tel. (73) 3251-2039, 9199-2272; Itacaré Ecoturismo, tel. (73) 3251-3666; Eco Trip, tel. (73) 3251-2191, 9975-1114.

Rafting on the Contas River
The swift **Rio de Contas** is one of Brazil's best for rafting. Trips leave from **Taboquinhas**, a village 28 kilometers (17 miles) north of Itacaré on a dirt road. The class 3 and 4 rapids are excellent on this stretch of the river. Lifeguards and specialist guides ensure the safety of those participating. If rafting hasn't tired you out, try a spot of rappelling or cascading at **Cachoeira do Noré**, a waterfall boasting an 18-meter (59-foot) drop. Two instructors accompany each descent.
Contact: NV Turismo, tel. (73) 3251-2039, 9199-2272; Itacaré Ecoturismo, tel. (73) 3251-3666; Eco Trip, tel. (73) 3251-2191, 9975-1114.

Off-road to Maraú
A round trip of 114 kilometers (71 miles) on sandy, pot-holed roads takes the adventurous to the beach at **Taipus de Fora** on the **Maraú peninsula**. But a swim in the **Lagoa do Cassange** lagoon, the view from the **Morro do Celular** and **Morro do Farol** hills, and the natural pools on the beach at Taipus de Fora more than make up for the effort expended by the journey, which begins in Itacaré at 7:30am.
Contact: Caminho da Terra, tel. (73) 3251-3053; NV Turismo, tel. (73) 3251-2039, 9199-2272.

Canopy Climbing at Ribeira Beach
The canopy climbing circuit at **Praia da Ribeira**, the farthest beach in central Itacaré, is considered moderately difficult. An area of about 5,000 square meters (54,000 square feet) of Atlantic forest offers 17 different kinds of adventure activities, including a zipline and suspended rope bridges. The aerial course is more than 200 meters (656 feet) long, with a maximum height of 10 meters (32 feet).
Contact: Conduru Ecoturismo, tel. (73) 3251-3089.

Surfing in Itacaré
Itacaré was an isolated fishing village until the 1990s, when it was discovered by surfers such as Alfio Lagnado, from São Paulo, who taught locals the sport and spread the gospel about surfing to the rest of the country. In 1998, the opening of a paved road, the Estrada-Parque (BA-001 highway), made access to the region even easier. Today, the area is most crowded in July, when the ocean swell from the south and southeast peaks. **Praia dos Corais**, a beach that can be reached by the rocks at the end of Praia da Concha, is the only vertical reef break in Itacaré; the rest are on sandy-

Itacaré: a paradise of surfing, adventure sports, and tranquil beaches

bottomed beachs. **Praia do Pontal** greets some of the country's longest waves, while **Tirica,** where waves break near the sand, has Itacaré's highest surf. Tirica is part of Super Surf, the Brazilian surfing circuit, and hosts state and local championships.

Estrada-Parque Highway

The 72-kilometer (44-mile) stretch of BA-001 highway that connects Ilhéus to Itacaré, passing through Uruçuca, is called **Estrada-Parque**. The highway cuts through the state nature reserve, Itacaré–Serra Grande, which protects a precious stretch of Atlantic forest. In a single hectare (two and a half acres), 456 tree species have been identified – a world record. Built in 1998, the Estrada-Parque is Brazil's first environmentally friendly highway. Every 100 meters (328 feet), subterranean tunnels have been provided to allow animals, such as the crabs common in the mangrove swamps, to cross the road. It's worth taking the highway during the day to stop at the **Mirante de Serra Grande** and **Mirante de Camboinha**, lookout points showcasing the green shades of the Atlantic forest and the sea. For the first 9 kilometers (5 miles) from Ilhéus and the first 6 kilometers (4 miles) from Itacaré, the road has a cycle lane.

Canavieiras

Surrounded by mangrove swamps, Atlantic rainforest and beaches, Canavieiras is home to a wealth of marine life, earning the nickname "crab capital". The southern limit of the Costa do Cacau coast, it's 113 kilometers (70 miles) from Ilhéus and 505 kilometers (313 miles) from Salvador. The Portuguese founded a village here in the mid-18th century.

Canavieiras developed around the Vieira family's sugarcane plantation. At the end of the 19th century, however, the sugarcane industry was supplanted by the cacao boom. Today, colonial houses coexist with buildings dating from the heyday of cacao, including the **Biblioteca Municipal** library (1900) and the former home of the old **Philarmônica Lyra do Commércio** orchestra (1894), both in **Praça da Bandeira** square.

Atalaia Island
Ilha de Atalaia, an 18-kilometer-long (11-mile-long) island connected to Canavieiras by bridge, is bordered by sea and swamp. **Atalaia** is a pleasant fishing village of just over fifty houses clustered around a small chapel and a soccer field. Local women, as they have for generations, catch small crabs (*aratus*) in the muddy swamps. They whistle to attract the crabs and then capture them with bamboo sticks. The **Festa de Louvor a Santo Antônio**, a celebration held from June 1st to 13th, is the highlight of the year in Atalaia. After each day's Catholic mass, people young and old congregate in the church square to dance *forró*. Atalaia's most popular beaches are **Praia da Costa** and **Praia de Atalaia**, both which offer calm seas and seafood stands. To the south, **Barra de Atalaia**, at the mouth of the **Rio Pardo**, is almost deserted, as is **Praia da Costa Norte**. **Praia do Albino**, at the mouth of the Rio Patipe, offers strolls along the sandbanks between river and sea. Access the beach either by dirt road (12 kilometers, or 7 miles, from the bridge) or by boat, a trip you'll need to arrange in advance.
Contact: Marina Canes, tel. (73) 3284-3735.

Barra Velha Beach
Praia de Barra Velha, which stands among mangrove swamps, coconut groves, and white sand, is a quiet island beach, home to just a few straw fishing huts. The beach is virtually deserted because access depends on a dirt road and ferryboat crossing. By car, access is via the BA-001 highway, 16 kilometers (10 miles) north of Canavieiras. It's also possible to arrive by ferry or boat. The one-and-a-half-hour crossing from Atalaia Island passes the mangrove swamps of the Patipe River. At low tide, patches of dark mud considered by locals to have aphrodisiac qualities appear. Bring your own water and snacks on the trip.
Contact: Marina Canes, tel. (73) 3284-3735.

Blue Marlin Fishing
Canavieiras offers one of the Atlantic's best sites for blue marlin fishing. **Royal Charlotte,** a sandbank 126 kilometers (70 nautical miles) from the coast, also attracts white marlin, tuna, mackerel, and dorado. The blue marlin, a difficult catch sought-after by deep-sea fishing enthusiasts, visits the Brazilian coast in summer (November to January), when the waters of the northeastern coast are warm and clear. It can measure up to 4 meters (13 feet) and weigh as much as 500 kilograms (1,100 pounds). They have blue backs and silver underbellies. Before being hauled aboard, the swift fish fight tirelessly. As marlin flesh has no commercial value, the fish are returned live to the ocean after being caught.
Contact: Artmarina, tel. (73) 3284-1262.

Discovery Coast

Porto Seguro

Porto Seguro is the base for exploring the Costa do Descobrimento (Discovery Coast), the strip of shore that covers Arraial d'Ajuda, Trancoso, Espelho, Curuípe, and Caraíva. The northern part of the coast includes Santa Cruz Cabrália and Santo André. Founded in 1526 and declared a National Heritage Site, Porto Seguro was the first town where the Portuguese set foot on the lands that would become Brazil. Traces of early colonization can be seen throughout the region. The town has suffered a renewed colonization of sorts since the 1980s, in part because it is one of the favorite tourist destinations offered by big tour operators. During the high season (July, the New Year period, and Carnival season in February or March), the town is transformed. The beaches and bars are crowded and barracas with *axé* and *forró* dance-music shows spring up everywhere. Porto Seguro offers good tourist services and facilities, including an airport and various banks and hotels. The community is 723 kilometers (455 miles) south from Salvador; from the latter, take either the BA-324 or BR-101 highways to Eunápolis and then the BR-367 highway to Porto Seguro. Coming from the south, Porto Seguro stands 600 kilometers (373 miles) north from Vitória (Espírito Santo's state capital). Take the BR-101 highway north to Eunápolis and then the aforementioned stretch of BR-367.

Historical Center

The small and well-preserved Cidade Histórica offers a two-hour self-guided tour the first constructions from the beginning of the official history of Brazil. The tour, which explores Misericórdia Square, begins at the oldest monument in the country, the **Marco da Posse**. This marble block is engraved with the seal of the Portuguese crown and the cross of the

Old colonial houses abound in Porto Seguro

Order of Christ, the organization that financed the Portuguese sea explorations. The simple **Igreja de Nossa Senhora da Peña** church (*Praça Pero de Campos Tourinho, no #, tel. 73/3288-6363; daily (except Wed), 9am – 5pm*), built in 1535, and renovated in the 18th century, contains the oldest statue of Saint Francis of Assisi in the country. The **Museu de Porto Seguro** has multi-media rooms and a small collection of indigenous crafts. The museum is inside an 18th-century building, which used to be the Casa de Câmara e Cadeia (Council Chamber and Prison) (*Praça Pero Campos Tourinho, no #, tel. 73/3288-5182; daily, 9am – 5pm*). The oldest church in Brazil, **Igreja de Nossa Senhora da Misericórdia** (*Praça da Misericórdia, no #, tel. 73/3288-0828; Sat – Thu, 9:30am – 1:30pm and 2:30pm – 5pm*), was built in 1526 and today houses the **Museu de Arte Sacra**, a museum of religious art. Its most important pieces include a ruby-encrusted statue of Jesus carrying the cross, and a life-size statue of Christ crucified. Both pieces date from the late 16th century. The **Igreja de São Benedito** (*Rua Doutor Antônio Ricaldi, no #*), a church built by the Jesuits, probably in 1549, stands beside the ruins of the **Colégio dos Jesuítas** (Jesuit College), built in 1551. While walking past the colonial houses, visitors can enjoy *capoeira* performances and take in wonderful view of the coast – the sunset is particularly lovely.

Beaches and Kiosks

The *barracas* (kiosks) are the main attraction on the beaches of Porto Seguro, and in their way, they are true entertainment complexes. Functioning not only as restaurants and snack bars, they also offer gym and dance classes (*lambada* and *lambaeróbica*, a combination of aerobics and lambada), music shows (*forró* and *axé*) Internet access, and water sports. The trendiest *barracas* are **Axé Moi, Tôa-Tôa,** and **Gaúcho,** on **Praia de Taperapuã**, and **Barramares** on **Praia do Rio dos Mangues**. Nighttime entertainment rotates among the main *barracas*. As a result, there are new options every day. In the high season, the entertainment is almost uninterrupted, with shows beginning at 3am and going on until sunrise. **Mundaí, Itacimirim**, and **Curuípe**, which has natural pools at low tide, are quieter beaches. **Praia Ponta Grande** and **Praia do Mutá**, the last two beaches in Porto Seguro are the most peaceful and solitary.

Passarela do Álcool

This street is an open shopping mall, with stores, restaurants, bars, and stalls selling cachaça (sugarcane rum), pepper sauce, the coconut dessert called *cocada*, and craftwork, including items made by Pataxó Indians. Brightly colored stalls sell *capeta* – a popular drink from Porto Seguro, made with fruits, vodka or cachaça, powdered guaraná, and cinnamon. Hold your ground against the pushy waiters.
Avenida Portugal, no #, Centro.

Discovery Era Memorial

Built on Praia de Curuípe, the Memorial da Época do Descobrimento is known for its replica of Pedro Álvares Cabral's flagship. Mestre Quincas, a well-known local artist, created the replica. A tour of the cabin and holds reveals the fragility of the original ship.
Avenida Beira-Mar, 800, Orla Norte, tel. (73) 3268-2586. High season, daily, 8:30am – 6pm; low season, Mon – Sat, 8:30am – 12:30pm and 1:30pm – 5pm.

Parque do Descobrimento recreates the city as it was in the 16th century

RECIFE DE FORA REEF MARINE PARK

One of the largest coral formations in the world, Recife de Fora holds a wide diversity of marine life. A dive beneath the water reveals a variety of coral reefs, fish, mollusks, and turtles. Tourist agencies in Porto Seguro offer two-hour schooner cruises that leave each morning around low time. Cruises are also available in Arraial d'Ajuda, where they leave from the ferryboat terminal. If you plan to walk on the coral, take training shoes. Snorkel and goggles can be rented on the boat.

Contact: Pataxó Turismo, tel. (73) 3288-1256, 3288-2507, 9979-5597; Yes Tour Receptivo, tel. (73) 3288-3363/ 3288-1644.

ILHA DOS AQUÁRIOS

This four-aquarium complex is on **Ilha do Pacuio**, a river island on the Rio Buranhém, which separates Porto Seguro from Arraial d'Ajuda. The largest aquarium holds 220,000 liters (58,000 gallons) of water and features fish such as sharks and moray eels. The other three reproduce the typical marine habitat found around Porto Seguro, which includes coral, brightly colored fish, and sponges. In addition to the aquariums, Ilha dos Aquários is part of a leisure complex with a swimming pool, volleyball courts, a food court, art gallery, and bromeliad and orchid vivarium. Its animated nightlife features live music performances aimed mainly at the younger set.

Ilha do Pacuio, tel. (73) 3575-1031, 3288-3166. Reach it on Companhia do Mar's ferry, Praça dos Pataxós, 16, tel. (73) 3288-2107. Fri, 10pm – 7am; high season: Fri and Sun, 10pm – 7am.

VERA CRUZ NATURE RESERVE

Located between Porto Seguro and Eunápolis, Reserva Particular do Patrimônio Natural, covers 60 square kilometers and is home to about 250 bird species and 40 mammalian species. Some of these birds and mammals, as well as approximately 50 species of amphibians and 60 species of reptiles, are threatened with extinction. The private reserve offers a brief presentation and a guided walk, which takes you across bridges suspended among imposing brazilwood and jacaranda trees. Visits must be arranged in advance.

BR-367 highway (towards Eunápolis), Km 37, tel. (73) 3166-1535/9985-1808. Mon – Fri, 8am – 5pm.

Colored Cliffs mark the coast of Arraial d'Ajuda

Arraial d'Ajuda

The district of Arraial d'Ajuda, 4 kilometers (2 miles) south of Porto Seguro, was founded by the Jesuits in the mid-16th century. Today's cosmopolitan atmosphere contrasts with what remains of the old colonial village. The cobbled streets are narrow and winding, with lighting at night often provided by candles. Today, these old streets are home to stores, cafés, and studios, most located on and around **Estrada de Mucugê** road. **Rua da Broadway** is a trendy nightspot, but it is slowly losing ground to the large beach *barracas*. Restaurants usually open in the middle of the afternoon, as tourists tend to sleep late and enjoy the beach in the afternoon; shopping is done at night. Arraial's charming accommodations and culinary variety attract mostly families and couples. To get here from Porto Seguro, either take the direct, 10-minute ferry ride (and expect crowds in high season) or drive the long way around: Halfway back toward Eunápolis, turn left onto BA-001. This roundabout route is 60 kilometers (37 miles) in all.

Beaches

Arraial has beaches for those looking for a lively spot as well as for those in search of peace and quiet. **Apaga-Fogo** and **Araçaípe,** two beaches near the Porto Seguro ferry, have been taken over by hotels and guesthouses. Natural pools form at low tide among the coral reefs, making these beaches ideal for calm snorkeling that's unimpeded by ocean swells. **Mucugê**, the next beach, is the busiest in Arraial. Always crowded with tourists and beach vendors, its kiosks rent out water-sports equipment. With its strong waves and low-tide natural pools, Mucugê is the stage for nighttime luaus and raves. Similar parties occur on the neighboring beach, **Praia do Parracho,** with its shows, New Year celebrations, dance lessons, and *capoeira* and *lambada* performances. Tourists can rent kayaks, sailboats, and diving equipment from the enormous kiosks on the beach. **Pitinga** is a little less crowded than other beaches, and has a few kiosks and charming guesthouses. Pitinga's sand is powdery and the water is good for swimming, especially at low tide. Further ahead is **Lagoa Azul,** a dried-up pool enclosed by high, multi-colored cliffs. The more isolated **Taípe** has a more rugged landscape with its tall cream and blue-colored cliff walls and its strong waves. Taípe attracts turtles at egg-laying time and is suitable for fly-fishing. Its cabanas have restaurants and stores. It's possible to walk along almost all the beaches, starting from Mucugê in Arraial to Trancoso village (about 12 kilometers, 7 miles), and crossing the **Rio da Barra**, which meets the sea on a deserted beach of the same name. We recommend starting an hour before low tide and returning by bus or car.

PARTYING AT THE KIOSKS AT NIGHT

Like Porto Seguro, Arraial was a pioneer in axé music. At any given time during the day, axé can be heard over loudspeakers on the beach, but at night electronic music takes hold. In the early hours during the summer months, foreign DJs spin at raves for a young crowd on Praia do Parracho. Luaus are standard fare in Arraial, and the best ones take place in the moonlight in barracas such as **Magnólia, Wind Point Parracho** and **Cabana Grande** – all of which are on Praia do Parracho. The beach at Mucugê also hosts parties.

AJUDA SQUARE

Largo d'Ajuda is the historic center of Arraial d'Ajuda and is recognized and protected by Brazilian's heritage agency, Iphan. It includes the small, unadorned **Igreja Matriz de Nossa Senhora d'Ajuda**, built between 1549 and 1551, which affords a view of the Costa do Descobrimento. Simple houses encircle the Praça da Matriz square. Most of them have been turned into stores, studios, bakeries, and snack bars. Across from Praça da Matriz, is the famous **Rua da Broadway**. Largo d'Ajuda fills with pilgrims during the August 15th festivities in honor of Nossa Senhora d'Ajuda, patron and protector of the town.

MUCUGÊ ROAD

Estrada do Mucugê is the main connection between the center of Arraial and Praia do Mucugê. Numerous kombi vans provide transportation along this road. A huge concentration of businesses on the road and surrounding streets ply many trades: clothing and decoration shops, boutiques, cafés, Internet cafés, restaurants, and guesthouses, as well as tourist agencies and car rental companies. During the summer high season cars are not allowed between 6pm and dawn.

STUDIOS

Several artists live in Arraial, offering a variety of work in their studios,

---

OUR RECOMMENDATION

🍴 **Rosa dos Ventos** is a restaurant near the historical center. Filled with works by local artists, its extensive menu includes seafood and a variety of meat dishes. Rosa dos Ventos uses ingredients from its own garden and orchard, favoring seasonings, fruits and greens in season. (*Alameda dos Flamboyants, 24, Centro, tel. 73/3375-1271.*)

A charming guesthouse, **Pousada Pitinga**, is on the beach of the same name. Its colorful cabins with verandas, hammocks, and a sea-view, are all decorated with local arts and crafts. Pousada Pitinga also offers a mini-spa, mini-library, amphitheater, and restaurant at the water's edge. (*Estrada da Pitinga, 1633, Praia da Pitinga, tel. 73/3575-1067.*)

Additional information on page 358.

Mucugê, next to Arraial d'Ajuda

workshops, and stores. **Ateliê de Batik Gal Sarmento** (*Rua Nova, 203, tel. 73/3575-1857. High season, daily, 9am – noon; 3pm – 10pm; low season: daily, 4pm – 9pm*) features objet d'art, canvasses, and fabrics with indigenous motifs designed by owner Gal Sarmento. Geraldo Casado creates figurative paintings inspired by indigenous culture; both his abstract and hyper-realistic paintings are for sale at **Arraial d'Arte** (*Rua do Mucugê, 250, store # 8, tel. 73/3575-3022; Mon – Sat, 4pm – 11pm*) and in his studio (*Estrada da Balsa, 1446, Apaga Fogo, tel. 73/3575-3031; Mon – Sat, 9am – 7pm*). Established by the artist Keko, the **Centro Cultural Arraial d'Ajuda** houses an art gallery and a drawing, painting, and sculpting school. In the first two weeks of December it hosts the arts festival, Cultura Mix, which brings together artists from the region for exhibitions and music and theater presentations (*Praça Brigadeiro Eduardo Gomes, 136, tel. 73/3575-1852; Mon – Sat, 5pm – 8pm*). Oil or acrylic paintings with a variety of motifs by Fátima Medeiros are sold at **Ateliê Estrela do Mar Café e Doceria** (*Praça Brigadeiro Eduardo Gomes, 35-F, tel. 73/3575-3576; daily 3pm – 10pm*), where Zenália sells popular sweet delicacies.

Capoeira Sul da Bahia Cultural Center

Internationally famous performer Mestre Railson established capoeira, a martial-arts-mimicking dance form, in his birthplace of Arraial. The Espaço Cultural Capoeira Sul da Bahia is part of the Associação de Capoeira Sul da Bahia (South Bahia Capoeira Association) which trains teachers to promote the sport in other countries. On Saturday at 8pm the school offers capoeira presentations to the public. Members also perform at the beach kiosks, nightclubs, and at some hotels in the region.
Rua da Capoeira, no #, tel. (73) 3575-2981, 3575-3194. Mon – Fri, 9am – 2pm and 4pm – 10pm; Sat, 5pm – 10pm.

Water Park

Arraial d'Ajuda Eco Parque (formerly Paradise Water Park) is in a 60,000-square-meter area (650,000 square feet) of Atlantic forest on Praia d'Ajuda (also called Praia de Coqueiros, do Delegado, and dos Pescadores). It has a swimming pool with waves, an artificial river, and water slides. The complex offers all-day tickets (10am – 5pm for R$ 35.00) and is a good option for families. In summer, live music can be heard from a stage in front of the wave pool.
Estrada do Arraial d'Ajuda, Km 4.5, tel. (73) 3575-8600. Days of operation vary by season.

Belmonte
Close-to-deserted beaches seem to float on sea water that's darkened by inflowing fresh water. Between January and September, when the level of the Jequitinonha River is low, the sea water is clearer.

Santo André
Quiet, sparsely populated, with wide, flat beaches. Its fresh water is from the João de Tiba River, and its salt water is from the sea.

Porto Seguro
Beaches with mostly calm waters offer the tourist a wealth of activities and a very lively atmosphere. The last two beaches, Ponta Grande and Mutá, are quieter.

Arraial d'Ajuda
Calm seas as a result of the reefs that create natural pools at low tide. Tourists flock to the beaches for their beauty and services such as kiosks, bars, and restaurants.

Trancoso
Beaches surrounded by mangrove swamp and the Trancoso River have extensive stretches of sand, accessible on foot, by horse, bicycle, or boat. The beach at Ponta de Itapororoca is suitable for fishing. Praia dos Coqueiros is the departure point for boat trips. Deserted areas of Praia dos Nativos, the nearest beach to the village, have been effectively given over to nudists.

Espelho and Curuípe
Separated by the creek Riacho do Espelho, these beaches have cliffs, coconut groves, natural pools, and seas with crystal clear waters. One of the most beautiful stretches of coast in Bahia.

Caraíva
Long strips of soft sand and slightly rougher seas. Several deserted beaches, mostly in coves protected by reefs. There are also stretches with coral, coconut groves, and cliffs. The clear waters here are perfect for diving.

1 cm = 8 km
1 inch = 12.7 mi.

Just of Espelho beach, colorful reef fish await

Trancoso

The colonial town of Trancoso first gained popularity in the 1970s, as a haven for hippies and free spirits. These days, however, it is synonymous with high fashion and sophistication, and it features innumerable designer boutiques set in the midst of simple, unadorned architecture. The town has maintained the shape of Jesuit villages. The heart of Trancoso is **Quadrado**, a picturesque area of restaurants, bars, shops, and guesthouses encircled by well-preserved old houses that line a large unpaved square lacking streetlights. On top of the cliff, Quadrado bustles with travelers even into the evening hours, when candles cast flickering shadows onto the dim, starlit streets and all types of music – from jazz to *forró* – fill the air. Among the architectural remnants of colonization is the 18th-century **Igreja de São João Batista**, built on the site of a ruined Jesuit convent and noteworthy for its spare architectural style, pink limestone, and wood details. The city's most popular festival is the Festa de São Sebastião which draws the faithful every year on January 20th to its processions, music, fireworks, and dancing.

Our Recommendation

On the water's edge, near the Trancoso River, is **Pousada Estrela d'Água**, a guesthouse offering spacious rooms and chalets set in a garden. The pool and communal areas have ocean views. (*Estrada Arraial d'Ajuda, no #, 1.5 km from Trancoso, tel. 73/3668-1030*). The well-equipped rooms of **Pousada El Gordo**, near the church in the Quadrado, accommodate up to four people each and offer sea or garden views and access to a pool. There is a bar and lively restaurant serving a variety of dishes. (*Praça São João, 7, Quadrado, tel. 73/3668-1193.*)

Additional information on page 358.

AROUND TRANCOSO

The southern portion of Bahia (running from Taípe to Caraíva) is ideal for outdoor activities on both land and water – everything from horseback riding, cycling, 4×4 driving and quadricycling to schooner or motorboat trips, coral diving, and river kayaking. The largely deserted beaches welcome walkers. The **Vale dos Búfalos**, a majestic valley with lush vegetation, features some 4,000 buffalo and several bird species. The **Estrada dos Macacos** road cuts through farmland, rivers, and Atlantic forest inhabited by monkeys, while visitors to **Estrada da Sapiara** will see manioc flourmills and coconut plantations. Tours are offered by agencies in Porto Seguro, Arraial, and Trancoso.

Contact: In Trancoso, Latitude 16 Expedições, tel. (73) 3668-2260, 8803-0016.

CURUÍPE AND ESPELHO BEACHES

These two *praias* – virtually indistinguishable and separated only by a small creek, Riacho do Espelho – feature charming restaurants and guesthouses set in a dramatic landscape of cliffs, coconut groves, and natural pools. The hammocks, lounge chairs, and sofas scattered along the sand give these beaches a cozy atmosphere. Espelho ("mirror") owes its name to the time of morning when low tide perfectly reflects the blue sky. The front gate of the Outeiro das Brisas Condominium controls vehicle access from Trancoso (only guests are allowed in the condominium area), but both beaches can also be reached by boat or motorboat from Trancoso or Caraíva. At low tide, head just north of Curuípe to the small, unsophisticated **Praia dos Amores** ("Lovers Beach"), for its natural pools and cliffs, which entice honeymooners.

Art and Fashion

Trancoso has a good selection of ceramics, decorative objects, and antiques. **Bel Prisco** (*Praça São João, no #, Galeria Quadrado 4, tel. 73/3668-2203*) sells household ceramics. **Cerâmica Calazans** (*Praça São João, no #, tel. 73/3668-1112; Mon – Fri, 9am – noon and 2pm – 9pm; Sat, 4pm – 10pm*) sells light fixtures, paintings, and colorful photo frames made by artisans at Fazenda Calá farm. Crafts from Africa and South America can be found at **Baobab** (*Rua Carlos Alberto Parracho, 130, store #2, tel. 73/3668-1901; Mon – Fri, 4pm – 10pm*). **Cheia de Graça** (*Praça São João, 333, tel. 73/3668-1492. High season, 3pm – 11pm; low season: daily, 4pm – 11pm*) sells mobiles, lamps, and cushions, as well as items made from straw and seeds by artist Laila Assef. **Pindorama** (*Rua do Telégrafo, 10, Shopping Canto Verde, store #8, tel. 73/3668-1277; high season: daily, 10am – 11pm; low season: 4pm – 11pm*) has baskets, sculptures, indigenous art, woodcut prints, embroidery, and lace. **Etnia** (*Praça São João, no #, tel. 73/3668-1137; high season: daily, 5pm – midnight; low season: 4:30pm – 10:30pm*) sells furniture from many different parts of the world. **Casa do Bosque** (*Bosque, no #, Quadrado, tel. 73/3668-2054; Daily, 5pm – 10pm*) sells antiques, folk art, and furniture from Minas Gerais, a state to the south.

Trancoso is a fashion hotspot, with branches of many famous designer boutiques from Rio and São Paulo. These include **Richards** (*Praça São João, no #*) and **Salinas** (*Praça São João, no #, tel. 73/3668-1461; High season: daily, 4pm – midnight; low season: daily, 3pm – 11pm*), **Maria Cristina Maguy** (*Praça São João, no #; daily, 4pm – 11pm*), **Marisa Ribeiro** (*Praça São João, 120, tel. 73/3668-1026. High season, daily, 4pm – midnight; low season: Mon – Sat, 4pm – 10pm*), and **Lenny** (*Praça São João, no #, Galeria do Quadrado 4, tel. 73/3668-1908. High season: daily, 4pm – midnight; low season: daily, 4pm – 11pm*).

Outeiro Village

The cliffside Vila do Outeiro has exclusive guesthouses, restaurants, and the residential condominium Outeiro das Brisas. Its unspoilt beach is lined with coconut trees, while the clear sea is excellent for diving. The difficulty of access, which is controlled by the condominium, guarantees peace and quiet in both village and beach. To get there from Porto Seguro by car, take BA-001 highway to the Trancoso intersection, then follow the curvy dirt road towards Caraíva until you reach Outeiro.

Archaeological Museum and Golf Courses

The **Terravista Golf Course** complex, between Taípe and Rio da Barra beaches, is part golf course and part archaeological site. Excavations made for the construction of the course revealed household objects, ceramics, and tools of the Aratu and Tupi-Guaraní Indian tribes, all now on display at the museum. Terravista is one of the best places in the Northeast to play golf. It has an 18-hole course, four of which are seaside, as well as golf instructors and equipment for hire.

Caraíva

This quiet, scenic fishing village has sandy beaches, coconut groves, and rivers but neither nighttime electricity (the generators switch off at 10pm), nor cars (they are not allowed), nor paved streets. One explanation for the town's idyllic state of preservation is its remoteness: It is accessible by motorboat from Trancoso only in the height of summer. The rest of the year the trip entails taking the Monte Pascoal exit (Km 753) off the BR-101 highway, following a dirt road for 43 kilometers, then crossing the Rio Caraíva by canoe. The canoe trips must be negotiated with the local fishermen who own the boats. If you make the trek, take in the town at sunset, sitting in the pleasant bar called **Boteco do Pará.** The bar's owner, Pará, is also a canoeist and offers long boat trips to beaches such as Espelho, Curuípe or to Ponta do Curumbau village. Also recommended is the traditional, lively *forró* dancing that fills the main street, Rua do Rio, as well as Rua do Ouriço and Rua do Pelé, and runs until the early hours on the weekends. On the immense, unspoilt beaches of soft sand, the liveliest spots during the day are the two bars, **Bar da Praia** and **Coco Brasil.** We recommend the restaurant at **Pousada da Lagoa,** a guesthouse surrounded by extensive gardens and featuring paintings and sculptures. A late afternoon spent here is quite pleasant. In the main square, near the tiny **Igreja de São Sebastião,** you can hire *bugueiros* (buggy drivers) for a trip on the dunes or a visit to **Barra Velha,** where Pataxó Indians live.

Monte Pascoal

Reaching the historic mountain Monte Pascoal – the first piece of Brazilian soil seen by Europeans on Cabral's expedition from Portugal – requires determination and stamina. The route there passes through typical coastal vegetation (*restinga*), flood zones, and thick mangrove swamps. Motorboats from Caraíva run along the Caraíva and Benício rivers, as do buggies on the beach, but the last stretch of the trip requires taking a 4×4 to the foot of the mountain. The 1.5-kilometer hike to the summit, at an altitude of 536 meters (1,760 feet), is scenic – with leafy trees, bromeliads, lovely lookouts, and rich bird life. But it is also quite difficult. Monte Pascoal presides over the **Parque Nacional de Monte Pascoal,** a national park of 14,480 hectares (35,780 acres) of Atlantic forest

Monte Pascoal: Atlantic forest covers the first place seen by Portuguese voyager Cabral

and beaches that also includes the **Reserva Indígena de Barra Velha**.

Barra Velha Indian Reservation

The Pataxó Indians of Barra Velha preserve their traditional folkways and share them willingly with visitors. They put on presentations of dance and song and demonstrate rituals, games, and martial arts. They also sell arts and crafts made of wood, coconut, and seeds. Arrange a trip in advance with one of the local tour agencies in Arraial d'Ajuda or Porto Seguro. The trip from Caraíva involves riding horseback or going by buggy.

Santa Cruz Cabrália

The history of Santa Cruz Cabrália (which lies between Porto Seguro and Belmonte), is tied to the early days of colonial exploration. The first Catholic mass on Brazilian soil took place on the small island of Coroa Vermelha, on April 26th, 1500. In an open-air amphitheater, locals commemorate the event on each anniversary, and a steel cross stands on the spot where the Portuguese and Indians first met. The town's small historical center stands atop the cliffs in Cidade Alta, the town's highest neighborhood, overlooking the coast. Buildings in the church square include **Igreja de Nossa Senhora da Conceição** (*Tue – Sun, 8am – 5pm*), built in the 18th century to replace an original church from 1630; the **Casa de Câmera e Cadeia** (Council Chamber and Prison); and the **first cemetery**. The lower part of town, Cidade Baixa, centers around Praça Pedro Álvares Cabral, a plaza. The 30-some kilometers of neighboring beaches are not very beautiful, however, and muddy river waters darken the sea.

Jaqueira Indian Reservation

The Pataxó Indians on the Reserva da Jaqueira, en route to Coroa Vermelha, present dances, games, bow and arrow and hunting techniques, and information about village life to visitors. A visit to the reservation lasts three hours and includes a tour of village huts, and demonstrations of traditional cooking, manioc-flour preparation, and the cultivation of medicinal herbs. Some tours include a meal prepared by the Indians – fish baked in leaves and *cauim*, an alcoholic drink made from manioc root. Native craftwork can be purchased at the end of the tour.

Contact: Pataxó Turismo, in Porto Seguro, tel. (73) 3288-1256, 3288-2507.

Boat Trips and Diving

A schooner trip on the region's biggest river, the Rio João de Tiba, starts with a visit to **Ilha do Sol**. That island is popular as a river swimming spot and as a destination for buying sweets. Confectioner Mara hand-makes about sixty different delicacies, most of which are coconut-based. Some tour agencies include in their trip a mud bath in the island's swamps. From there, the next

Pataxó craftwork in Santa Cruz Cabrália

stop is **Parque Marinho de Coroa Alta**, a diving area with more than ten types of reefs; at low tide, natural pools form that are up to 1.5 meters deep and suitable for snorkeling. The park – a formation of sand and crumbling coral reefs that does not become immersed at high tide – owes its name to its crown (*coroa*) shape. Occasionally, tours stop at **Fazenda da Mãe Teresa**, a farm full of coconut groves, cashew trees, and a pineapple plantation. The farm has trails, a lagoon, and a restaurant to satisfy any carnivore.
Contact: In Cabrália: *Navegação Cabrália, tel. (73) 3282-1050; Taípe Turismo, tel. (73) 3288-1127, 3288-3127; Paraíso, tel. (73) 3575-1844. In Porto Seguro: Yes Tour Receptivo, tel. (73) 3288-3363, 3288-3432.*

Santo André

This town covers a vast 13-square-kilometer area of coastal plain, lined with coconut groves and both saltwater beaches and freshwater beaches (those facing the Rio João Tiba). Sparsely populated and absent of raucuous nightlife, Santo André is a place of rest and retreat. The ten-minute ferry crossing over the João de Tiba River from Cabrália heads north up the coast, ending at the unspoilt beaches of **Santo Antônio** and **Guaiú,** the latter popular with surfers. In neighboring **Mojiquiçaba** you will find the simple beachfront Bar Lamarão, which is popular with surfers and famous for its delicious crab *pastéis* (fried pasties). This should be seasoned with a strong, homemade pepper sauce.

Our Recommendation

🍽 The beachfront **Restaurante Maria Nilza**, in a simple thatched hut with benches and straw mats, makes a perfect spot for admiring the sunset or the limitless view of the horizon. Maria Nilza herself carefully prepares appetizers, *moquecas*, vatapá stews, and fried fish on a wood-burning stove. The restaurant is in Guaiú, a district of Santa Cruz Cabrália, on the road to Belmonte. (*Rua da Praia, 380, Guaiú, tel. 73/3671-2047, 9985-4215; daily 9:30am – 5pm.*)

Additional information on page 358.

Belmonte

Sleepy Belmonte (56 kilometers north of Santo André) used to be one of the five biggest cacao producers in Brazil. Today, the economy is much less robust, with locals making their livings off fishing and the cultivation of coconuts, papayas, black pepper, and piassava palms. Economic decline has not interfered with the charm of the old town, however: the wide streets, grand squares and bandstands, and ornately decorated façades of the buildings are well worth a stroll. One of the town's gems is the 35-meter high **lighthouse**, built in 1800. The sea at Belmonte is brownish because of the rivers that empty into it, among them the Rio Jetiquinonha, which is beautiful at sunset. The city has no official guesthouse accommodations nor sophisticated restaurants, but good, simple meals are available at **Restaurante do Diogo**, which serves *moquecas* and *guaiamun* crabs. Take the opportunity to get to know the work of **Dona Dagmar**, a local artisan who makes ceramics in her backyard with the help of some of her twenty children. The small local orchestras known as *filarmônicas* perform on special occasions just as they have done since the 19th century. Try catching them, for example, during the **Festival de Retreta** – or simply in a local house during a birthday celebration.

Cumuruxatiba's pier recalls the sand-mining era

WHALE COAST

CUMURUXATIBA AND PONTA DO CORUMBAU

The long stretch of coast from Caraíva to Mucuri – including the Abrolhos archipelago – is known as the Costa das Baleias (Whale Coast). The name refers to the humpback whales that swim these waters in the Brazilian winter and spring. Cumuruxatiba, the best place to enjoy the region's beauty, is a simple fishing village set in a dramatic landscape of colorful cliffs, diverse vegetation, long beaches, and rocky islands that are perfect for reef diving. The village is accessible by boat or dirt road, whether coming from Porto Seguro in the north (along the BR-101 highway) or from Prado or Caravelas in the south. Originally inhabited by the indigenous Pataxós Indians, Cumuru – as the peaceful village is affectionately called – is now an ideal refuge for anyone seeking seclusion without forgoing comfort. Many of the welcoming hotels and guesthouses in Cumuru offer tours and water-sports equipment for guests, and the whole area is ideal for walking, horseback riding, cycling, sailing, and buggy-riding. You can watch the humpback whales from July to November, their breeding

OUR RECOMMENDATION

🍽 The simple, spacious restaurant **Mama África** offers great vegetarian dishes and excellent desserts, as well as different cachaças from the state of Minas Gerais. Good options include the sweet-and-sour shrimp and the cod gratin. The owners, Angola-born Dolores and her Swiss husband Walter, enjoy chatting with customers, and the couple hosts local events in the high season (*Alameda Roberto Pompeu, 4, Rio do Peixe Grande, 3 km from the center of Cumuruxatiba, tel. 73/3573-1274; daily, 4pm – 11pm; in the low season, arrangements must be made in advance*).

Additional information on page 358.

season. At low tide, especially during the full moon and new moon, the sea recedes considerably, creating striking patterns on the sand. On the beach near the center of the village, a pier projecting into the sea evokes the sand mining that it was constructed for in the 1960s.

Ponta do Corumbau

To the north of Cumuru, near the Pataxós and Itacolomi reefs, is one of the most beautiful and isolated beaches in the region. Ponta do Corumbau is a small, one-kilometer peninsula, surrounded by mangrove swamps and bisected by a river. You can reach it by motorboat or boat, or in a 4×4 (take BR-489 highway, followed by a dirt road trek to Vila Corumbau). The beach's sole *barraca*, Sol e Vida, is owned by the fisherman Ariovaldo, who offers boat rides and seafood meals. Other options for food are the high-quality resort restaurants or meals served by locals in their homes.

Barra do Caí Beach

This deserted beach, crossed by the Caí River, offers a privileged view of Monte Pascoal. That mountain is a landmark for fishermen. A cross marks the spot on the beach where the native Indians first encountered Cabral's Portuguese expedition, come ashore to take on fresh water. The beach offers a few *barracas*, as well as Restaurante da Glória, open only in the high season. Apart from these, the only attractions on land are a townhouse and a small chapel.

Boat Trips

Boat trips from Cumuru usually involve either diving or whalewatching. The top diving spot is Ponta do Corumbau, as the Carapeba reefs there are ideal for snorkeling. Biologist-led whalewatching tours (which run only from July to November, during the mating season) usually last two

Ponta do Corumbau, a lovely, isolated point

Prado and Beco das Garrafas

The town of Prado has the best tourist infrastructure between Caraíva and Caravelas. In the colorful town center is **Beco das Garrafas**, an alley filled with small restaurants popular with travelers – something you won't find in neighboring Alcobaça and Caravelas, farther to the south. The area here has a stunning 84 kilometers (52 miles) of beaches, but the sea's brown waters make most less inviting. Visitors are better served strolling along the beautiful mangrove-fringed Rio Jucuruçu. Prado is also the starting point for many boat trips in the area. A good time to visit Prado is either during Carnival or on June 29th, when the city holds festivities honoring Saint Peter, the patron saint of fishermen.

hours. Passengers also get to hear the humpback whales "singing" to each other through a device called a hydrophone. Other options include speedboat rides to the towns of Corumbau and Caraíva, and to the beaches of Curuípe and Praia do Espelho. Those who prefer not to use organized tour operators can hire the popular guide Mestre Antônio Carlos (who pioneered the local boat-tour business) and choose a personalized route with his guidance.
Contact: *Aquamar, Cumuruxatiba beach, tel. (73) 3573-1360. Mestre Antônio Carlos, tel. (73) 3573-1127.*

Trekking and Horseback Riding

One of the most interesting treks in the region is the long walk from Cumuru to Porto Seguro, guided by the experienced veteran Hélio Nativa (*tel. 73/8803-7724*). There are also easier, shorter treks that can run as far as Caraíva (around 42 kilometers), returning by boat or car (*Aquamar, Cumuruxatiba beach, tel. 73/3573-1360*). Those up for an eight-day trek can try the fascinating but demanding walk from Prado north to Porto Seguro, which passes farms, beaches, stunning cliffs, palm trees, and mangroves (*guide Pradinho, in Prado, tel. 73/8811-3886, 3298-1514*). Horseback-riding trips include either a ride through the woods (*guides Andréa and Alexandre, tel. 73/3573-1184*) or one by the cliffs and along the shore (*Aquamar, Cumuruxatiba beach, tel. 73/3573-1360*). The rides range from 4 to 9 kilometers in length.

Caravelas and Alcobaça

Caravelas is the main gateway to the Abrolhos archipelago. It offers much better tour agencies and hotels than the poorly-developed Alcobaça, which is the other main gateway to the region. The beaches in both towns – as well as in neighboring **Mucuri** and **Nova Viçosa** – are not the most attractive in the region; rivers darken their waters. The main attraction in Caravelas is its historical center (dating from its founding in 1503), which is easily explored on foot. Some of the colonial houses along **Rua Barão do Rio Branco** and **Rua Sete de Setembro** still have their original Portuguese-tiled façades. Unfortunately, the baroque **Igreja Matriz de Santo Antônio**, built in the 18th century, has lost its original features and preserves only a few statues from the period. Also worth a visit is the port

Humpback whales cruise the tranquil waters of Abrolhos

in the neighboring town of Ponta da Areia. This important late-19th and early-20th-century center for coffee exportation declined in power with the closing of the coffee-ferrying Bahia–Minas Railroad in 1961. Despite being in Bahia – where Carnaval usually means *trios elétricos* and *axé* music – Caravelas maintains a tradition of samba school parades during Carnival, as is more popular in the Southeast. The artist Frans Krajcberg has lived in Nova Viçosa since 1982, and he uses material he collects in the mangroves and woods in his creations.

IBAMA VISITORS' CENTER
A model of a 17-meter (56-feet) humpback whale is the main attraction in the Centro de Visitantes do Ibama. Ibama is the acronym for the Brazilian Institute of Environment and Renewable Natural Resources, and the center offers photographic exhibitions and houses an environment-focused library, as well as holding folkloric performances and workshops. There are attentive guides to answer visitors' questions about the group and their work.
Contact: Praia do Quitongo, no #, Caravelas, tel. (73) 3297-1111. Thu – Sun, 8am – noon and 2pm – 7pm.

HUMPBACK WHALE INSTITUTE
The Instituto Baleia Jubarte is a NGO created in 1996 to promote environmental education and to protect the Abrolhos National Marine Reserve. Biologists from the institute, who accompany every boat that enters the reserve, give visitors lectures. The group aims to educate the community on the environment and monitor the whale population. The institute also holds exhibitions and sells whale-themed videos and souvenirs.
Contact: Rua Barão do Rio Branco, 26, tel. (73) 3297-1240; Mon – Fri, 8am – noon and 2pm – 6pm; Sat 8:30am – noon.

ABROLHOS

The **Parque Nacional Marinho dos Abrolhos** (Abrolhos National Marine Reserve) is 70 kilometers (44 miles) from Caravelas, and the trip between the two places takes 2 hours by motorboat, 3 hours by catamaran, or 7 hours by sailboat. The park encompasses the **Arquipélago dos Abrolhos**, formed by five islands – Redonda, Guarita, Sueste, Siriba, and Santa Bárbara. The largest of the islands, Santa Bárbara has clear waters that allow diving and snorkeling in water that averages 24°C (75°F). Underwater visibility can reach up to 20 meters (68 feet) from May to September. Charles Darwin and Jacques Cousteau visited Abrolhos and its menagerie of terrestrial and marine animals, including coral reefs and *atobá* birds (boobies). Humpback whales, the park's greatest attraction, are in the area from July to November. The probability of seeing a whale during this time is high enough that tour groups offer partial refunds for visitors who don't spot any. Tours last 1 or 2 days and include a visit to Siriba, the only island where docking is permitted. Reservations for high season must be made well in advance, as the government agency Ibama limits the number of visitors per day. Depending on weather conditions, which are often poor during July and August, the Navy may not give permission for boats to leave the coast. September and October are optimal times to visit, with good weather and excellent halewatching. During low season boat trips require a minimum of ten passengers.

Contact: *Abrolhos Embarcações, tel. (73) 3297-1172.*

THE HUMPBACK WHALE'S MIGRATION ROUTE

Humpback whales can extend up to 16 meters (52 feet) in length and weigh up to 40 tons. They migrate from the tip of North America (their main feeding grounds) to the clear warm waters off the south of Bahia to mate and calve. Humpbacks can be spotted at little as an hour's boat ride from the Bahia coast, where males and females meet over a symphony of mating calls. Biologists from the Humpback Whale Institute have been recording this music through hydrophones for the past half decade, and they have noticed changes in these "cries" with each mating season.

Shallow waters are a hallmark of Abrolhos

Diving Spots in the Abrolhos Archipelago and Surrounding Areas

Siriba Island
Siriba's tongue-shaped underwater reef shelf teems with fish.

Siriba Caves
Underwater caves on Siriba Island reach up to 30 meters (98 feet) in length and 13 meters (43 feet) deep.

Sueste Island
The mushroom-shaped coral formations (chapeirões) found here range from 4 to 7 meters (13 to 23 feet) high. Alert divers can spot groupers up to 25 kilos (55 pounds) inside the coral's labyrinths, which were created when the tops of the formations fused together.

Parcel de Abrolhos Reefs
The chapeirões here are similar to those off Sueste's coast, but reach a height of 16 to 20 meters (52 to 66 feet).

Rosalinda Wreck
The Rosalinda, sunk in 1955, is 102 meters (335 feet) long. Though its bow breaks the surface, the ship's stern is 20 meters (66 feet) down.

Fringing Reef
The fringing reef around Santa Bárbara island forms a plateau 3 meters (10 feet) below the water's surface. Sea turtles often sleep among the coral, and people can dive to as much as 8 meters.

Redonda Reefs
This is a good place to spot sea turtles that have come ashore to lay their eggs.

Atabá and Califórnia Reefs
The chapeirões here reach heights of 20 to 27 meters (66 to 89 feet). Reefs up to 38 meters (125 feet) feature long columns of chapeirões yet to develop their characteristic mushroom shape.

Timbebas Reef
One of the most beautiful coral formations in the area; the waters of Timbebas have 10 to 20 meters (33 to 66 feet) of visibility and are perfect for snorkeling.

Guaratiba Reefs
Shoals of sea turtles frequent this diving spot.

Cassumba Island
Ilha da Cassumba features sprawling trails and a large mangrove swamp on area of 100 square kilometers (40 square miles).

THE BACKLANDS AND THE RIVER

Sertão, or backlands, is the term used for the vast semi-arid hinterland of the Northeast that extends north from the state of Minas Gerais. The drought-prone area is heavily symbolic to Brazilians, as it is an immense, inhospitable land far removed from the countries urban, globalized metropolises. The Bahian backlands bordering the **Rio São Francisco** and Pernambuco illustrate this contrast: The landscape is rough, the roads precarious, and the villages impoverished. Plenty of activity exists, however, in the cities of **Juazeiro** and **Paulo Afonso**, in the havens of colorful landscape at the west and east ends of the semicircle drawn by the river. The journey beyond these cities is an arduous one, recommended only for the adventurous. But those willing to face the potholed, deserted roads of the backlands can visit the **Parque Estadual de Canudos**. That state park honors the memory of the most tragic uprising in Brazilian history, which Antônio Conselheiro led in the late 19th century *(see page 135)*. **Euclides da Cunha**, a town 70 kilometers (43 miles) from the park, offers the best accommodation in the area.

JUAZEIRO

Travel to Juazeiro by boat, or cross the Ponte Eurico Gaspar Dutra bridge from Petrolina, on the north side of the Rio São Francisco, in Pernambuco. Among the city's main attractions is the **Ilha do Fogo**, one of the most beautiful islands along the river. A single 20-meter-high

Restaurants and bars line the Juazeiro riverfront

rock rests in the center of the island. Juazeiro's nightlife is abundant: A string of bars, restaurants, and nightclubs lines the shore of the river. In addition to serving as a gateway for visitors, the modern airport in nearby Petrolina funnels Juazeiro's products, such as tropical fruits, to international markets. Despite modern conveniences, this Bahian city upholds tradition, including the festivities of **Bom Jesus dos Navegantes**, a river procession dating back to 1750, and **Reis de Boi**, a local variation of *bumba-meu-boi* – a street performance that combines theater, music, and dance. During **Semana Santa** (Holy Week) celebrations, throngs of penitent worshipers practice self-flagellation along the city's streets. The **São João** festivities in June are among the liveliest in the Northeast. Ten private boats make the 5-minute crossing from Petrolina to Juazeiro daily, starting at 6am and running until 6:30pm. On weekends, travelers can hire boats to visit islands along the São Francisco River. This service is available beginning at 9:30am at the Orla Hotel (*Rua Rui Barbosa, 18, Centro, tel. 74/3611-9179*).

RODEADOURO ISLAND

Beaches, soccer fields, volleyball courts, and a camping area adorn the 1-kilometer length of Ilha de Rodeadouro, which lies about an hour by boat from Juazeiro. The *Nina* makes a stop here on Sundays, and the boat also stops at **Ilha do Maroto** and **Ilha do Massangano**. An onboard restaurant and live music provide entertainment during the trip.
Contact: Luís, of the Nina, *tel. (87) 3864-7909.*

SOBRADINHO DAM

The **Sobradinho** river dam, 60 kilometers (37 miles) west of Juazeiro, offers a beautiful view of the reservoir, which is the twelfth-largest in the world. The Sobradinho Lock allows for passage from the São Francisco River to the port of Petrolina. The boat *Nina* usually sails through the lock on the last Sunday of the month. Daytrips throughout the weekshould be arranged in advance.
Contact: Luís, of the Nina, *tel. (87) 3864-7909.*

OUR RECOMMENDATION

🍽 Dona Maria at **Restaurante Maria do Peixe** has been attracting people from the Juazeiro region with her *surubim* fish dishes for thirty years. The restaurant's only cook, she serves sun-dried beef and other regional dishes. Her flawless cuisine draws a mixed clientele of artists, politicians, businessmen, and tourists (*Quadra C, 19, Castelo Branco, tel. 74/3611-3043; Mon – Fri, 11am – 9pm; Sat and Sun, 11am – 4pm*).

Additional information on page 358.

CANUDOS STATE PARK

Euclides da Cunha described the 1960s flood of **Canudos** village in his book *Os Sertões* (published in English as *Rebellion in the Backlands*). The town's ruins can still be seen in times of drought. The Canudos of today, with a population of 5,000, shows just a few traces of the past. One of them is the **Memorial Antônio Conselheiro** (*Avenida Juscelino*

Kubitschek, no #, Centro, tel. 75/3494-2000; Mon – Fri, 8am – noon and 2pm – 6pm; Sat, 9am – noon and 3pm – 5pm; Sun, by advance arrangement only.), a museum filled with remnants of the Canudos War, from ammunition to combatants' skulls. To trace Antônio Conselheiro's steps (see box below), drive 11 kilometers (7 miles) to **Parque Estadual de Canudos** (BR-235, no #, tel. 75/3494-2000). Find accommodation in Euclides da Cunha, a 70-kilometer (44-mile) drive across the arid, stunted forest of the *caatinga*. Markers indicate where combat occurred. Among the battlefield are the **Vale da Morte** (Valley of Death), containing the remains of soldiers who died in combat, the **Fazenda Velha** (Old Farm), previously an army headquarters, and **Alto do Mário**, a hill offering panoramic views of the area. Guided tours can be arranged at Memorial Antônio Conselheiro or through the Department of Tourism (*Secretaria de Educação e Turismo de Canudos, tel. 75/3494-2165*).

EUCLIDES DA CUNHA

In the late 19th century, the village of Cumbe served as headquarters for the government troops who fought in the Canudos War. Today the renamed Euclides da Cunha boasts a population of 30,000 people and draws the region's greatest volume of tourist traffic. On Saturdays a century-old fair sets up downtown, offering everything from leather goods to food and clothes. The central square still exhibits a wartime cannon, which Conselheiro's followers nicknamed the *matadeira* (killing machine). The 230-kilometer (143-mile) drive to Euclides da Cunha from Juazeiro takes about five hours. Though the first 50 kilometers (31 miles) along the BR-314 highway towards Salvador are fairly smooth, the road can be treacherous after the intersection at Filadélfia. There are no rest areas or service stations between that intersection and Monte Santo, about 36 kilometers (22 miles) outside of Euclides da Cunha.

THE CANUDOS WAR

During the first years of the Brazilian Republic, the religious leader Antônio Conselheiro ("Antônio the Counselor") came to political prominence in the *sertão*. He preached of better days for the backlands and advocated the eradication of poverty. A supporter of the Monarchy, Conselheiro brought together 8,000 people in the village of Canudos to create his own religious enclave, known as the "Belo Monte Empire." In 1896, the federal government sent a small task force to suppress what to them seemed a minor uprising of religious fanatics and monarchists. To the government's surprise, the rebels defeated the military force, as well as two subsequent government expeditionary forces of 600 and 1,300 men, respectively. The final strike by government troops came in October 1897, when 6,000 soldiers arrived in Canudos; 4,000 of the troops died in combat before their forces overwhelmed Antonio's defenders. After the bloody battle, the Republican troops finally burned down the village; 800 captured backlanders were cruelly beheaded in retaliation for what the government saw as humiliating defeats, and Conselheiro also perished. Euclides da Cunha brilliantly describes this massacre in one of the masterpieces of Brazilian literature: *Os Sertões* (*Rebellion in the Backlands*). In the 1980s, Peruvian novelist Mario Vargas Llosa revisited the morbid episode in *The War of the End of the World*.

Paulo Afonso

An exuberant green city full of gardens, Paulo Afonso comes as a surprise in the arid landscape of the *sertão*. Even more surprising is the city's main attraction, a hydroelectric power station that lives in perfect aesthetic harmony with the surrounding rock formations, canyons, and 80-meter (262-foot) waterfalls of the São Francisco River. A popular destination for ecotourism and adventure-sports enthusiasts, Paulo Afonso is on Bahia's borders with Pernambuco, Sergipe, and Alagoas. Though it lies 460 kilometers (286 miles)north from Salvador, it has decent tourist services. The major obstacle to enjoying a visit is the difficulty of access: The roads to Paulo Afonso are precarious, and flights to the airport are infrequent.

The São Francisco Hydroelectric Company

The city of Paulo Afonso arose around the **Companhia Hidrelétrica de São Francisco** (Chesf), a complex of four power plants that supplies electricity to the entire Northeast. The basic tour of the plant lasts four hours. Cars take visitors to **three powerplants**, where elevators lead to views of the machinery at work inside the enormous rocks, and then to **Angiquinhos**, the first powerplant in the Northeast, which was built in 1913. The tour ends with a cable-car ride over the São Francisco River. From the cable car you can see such sights as: the **Furna dos Morcegos** (bat cave), the purported hideout of Lampião and his bandit gang; the **Cachoeira de Paulo Afonso** waterfall; and the spectacular **São Francisco River canyon** (*see page 160*).
An alternate tour begins at the church by the entrance to Chesf and continues to **plant 4**, with side visits to the subterranean galleries and turbines. After this is a stop at the

The rock formations of Paulo Afonso are perfect for adventure sports fans

Anfiteatro de Pedra (Stone Amphitheater), which is set in the rock walls of the canyon. From there visitors can walk to the Furna dos Morcegos cave. This is the route favored by hikers, though it is more demanding due to the extreme heat and slippery rocks.
Contact: Rua do Triunfo, 170, Alves de Souza, tel. (75) 3282-2203. Mon – Fri, 7:30am – 11:30am and 1:30 pm – 5:30 pm; visits must be arranged in advance.

Paulo Afonso Artisan Association

The craft fair held by the Associação Pauloafonsina de Artesãos, in the center of Paulo Afonso, offers the region's best handicrafts. Embroidery, lace, needlework locally known as *fuxico*: flower appliqués made from left over scraps of material, rag dolls, wood sculpting, fine marquetry, and many others crafts sell for prices that are much more attractive than those found in larger cities.
Contact: Avenida Getúlio Vargas, 60, Centro, tel. (75) 3282-5538. Mon – Fri, 9am – 6pm; Sat, 8am – 6pm; Sun, 8am – 1pm; low season: close on Tue.

Raso da Catarina Nature Reserve

The Estação Ecológica Raso da Catarina covers approximately 100,000 hectares (250,000 acres), encompassing the municipalities of Canudos, Glória, Macucurê, and Paulo Afonso. This region is one of the driest areas on the planet, though some small, hearty bushes cling tenaciously to the parched soil. Catarina is the world's only *caatinga* reserve, and it contains unusual vegetation such as shrubs, bromeliads, and cacti like the *xiquexique* and *mandacaru*. The major attraction on the reserve is the 12-kilometer-long **Baixa do Chico**, a canyon with huge sandstone walls and impressive rock formations. One formation, which resembles a statue of a saint, draws throngs of the faithful every year. Twelve Pancararé Indian families live in a village on the reserve; visitors to the village require a permit from **Funai**, the Brazilian Indian Protection Agency (*Rua Floriano Peixoto, 855, Centro, tel. 75/3281-3782; Mon – Fri, 8am – noon and 2pm – 6pm*). Visitors are also asked to donate basic provisions to the community. Tour operators usually supply the necessary documentation, and it takes no more than a week to obtain the necessary permit. To get to the indigenous reserve, drive to Juá village, which is 40 kilometers (25 miles) from Paulo Afonso, and then continue 30 kilometers along a track that leads to the native reservation. From this point, if you wish, you must continue on foot for about 8 hours, a trip recommended only for experienced hikers.
Contact: Ageturb, tel. (75) 3281-2757.

Umbuzeiro Range

Near the village of **Riacho**, 50 kilometers (31 miles) from Paulo Afonso via the BR-110 highway, sits the Serra do Umbuzeiro mountain range, with its cliff walls rising up to 400 meters (1,300 feet). The range features rock paintings and typical *caatinga* vegetation, and is a very popular destination for rappelling and rock climbing. Hawks and reptiles populate the area, and the top of the hills affords a panoramic view of the region – one can see as far as Juazeiro.
Contact: Ageturb tourist agency, tel. (75) 3281-2757.

The astonishing play of light and color on the surface of Poço Encantado

CHAPADA DIAMANTINA

Deep in the heart of Bahia, the Chapada Diamantina (Diamond Highlands) and its Sincorá mountain range have long been a popular destination for travelers. Adventurous types are drawn by the region's challenging hikes, climbs, mountain biking, and rappeling, as well as growing ecotourism opportunities. The area also attracts those who just want to admire nature, be it the beautiful sunset from atop **Morro do Pai Inácio** hill in Lençóis, a majestic waterfall like **Fumaça**, or the play of light on the **Poço Encantado** pond. Cultural traditions are also an attraction here, including the memorable, candle-lit Corpus Christi procession that takes place in **Rio de Contas** on the first Thursday that falls 60 days after Easter. Though named for the diamond boom that sprung up here in the 19th century, the region no longer has active mining. It has been banned since 1985. These days, nature is Chapada Diamantina's true gem. Traveling to Chapada Diamantina by car (via the potholed, poorly-marked BR-242 highway) requires patience and careful attention. The airport in Lençóis receives regular flights from Salvador and São Paulo.

LENÇÓIS

Lençóis, about 425 kilometers (264 miles) west from Salvador, is the perfect base for exploring Chapada Diamantina. Its colonial houses and rosy stone sidewalks – well-preserved despite the legions of travelers who descend on the city every year – make this charming, simple town an attraction in itself. Founded as a small village in 1856, Lençóis grew to become the third largest city in Bahia and home to the French vice consulate thanks to the diamond boom and trade with Europe. Great food and music abound in Lençóis. Try to catch the city orchestra at the Mercado Municipal. Gorgeous scenery is also abundant in the surrounding caves and waterfalls. Pictures of this panoramic landscape are on

TORRINHA, PRATINHA, AND LAPA DOCE CAVES

The town of **Iraquara**, about 82 kilometers (51 miles) north of Lençóis, deserves its nickname, "the town of caves." One cave, the **Gruta de Torrinha**, features rare aragonite "flowers," which are coral-like rock formations. Inside the **Gruta da Pratinha** is an underground stream suitable for diving and snorkeling (if wearing a life vest) and home to 24 uniquely identified species of fish. Two of the species are specially adapted to live in perpetual darkness; the rest are restricted to the naturally illuminated areas. Near Pratinha is the **Gruta Azul** (Blue Grotto), where the sunlight creates beautiful blue color effects when reflected in the cave's stream. The **Lapa Doce** cave has a spacious tunnel, which is some 40 meters (131 feet) high and 850 meters (2,800 feet) long, and contains many stalactites and stalagmites.
Contact: Associação dos Condutores de Visitantes de Lençóis (Acvl), tel. (75) 3334-1425; Terra Chapada Expedições, tel. (75) 3334-1304.

permanent exhibition at environmentalist-photographer **Calil Neto**'s gallery (*Praça Horácio de Matos, 82, Centro, tel. 75/3334-1950; Mon – Sat, 8am – 2pm and 5pm – 11pm*). To get to Lençóis from Salvador, take BR-324 to Feira de Santana, then BR-116 onto BR-242. That last highway leads into the city. When turning on to BR-242 from BR-116, look to the right side of the road. The turnoff is surrounded by gas stations and not well marked.

SERRANO AREA AND SOSSEGO WATERFALL

This stretch of the Lençóis River is named Serrano (from the mountains). Guided tours usually take visitors first to the **Salão de Areias**, whose sandstone rock formations local artisans mine to create multicolored landscapes in small bottles. The next stops are the waterfalls known as **Cachoeirinha** (6 meters) and **Cachoeira Primavera** (9 meters), followed by the **Poço Halley** pool.

The landscape surrounding Cachoeira do Sossego rewards those who struggle to reach the place

South of Lençóis is the pink-walled **Cachoeira do Sossego** (a 15-meter waterfall), one of the greatest attractions in the region. En route to Sossego is the **Ribeirão do Meio**, a natural waterslide. The hike there is not easy: after 6 kilometers (3.7 miles) of trails, there are 2 kilometers of climbing over a rocky riverbed. The large, deep pool at the bottom of the waterfall is good for diving and swimming. Besides the river, waterfalls, and cave pools, there are attractions for climbers as well.
Contact: Associação dos Condutores de Visitantes de Lençóis (Acvl), tel. (75) 3334-1425; Terra Chapada Expedições, tel. (75) 3334-1304.

Pai Inácio Hill

Morro do Pai Inácio offers a panoramic view of Chapada Diamantina. The 30-minute walk up this 1,170-meter-high hill features lovely vegetation. At the foot of the hill is the **Orquidário Pai Inácio** nursery, home to hundreds of orchid species. According to local legend, the slave Pai Inácio fled up this hill and escaped his pursuers by jumping off and floating safely to the ground with an umbrella. Travelers interested in rappelling and zip-lining (flying fox) can visit **Cachoeira** waterfall and **Poço do Diabo** pool, on the **Rio Mucugezinho** river. They're just a 10-minute drive from the hill.
Contact: Associação dos Condutores de Visitantes de Lençóis (Acvl), tel. (75) 3334-1425; Terra Chapada Expedições, tel. (75) 3334-1304.

Lapão Cave

With a 50-meter (164-foot) wide entrance and depth of 1 kilometer, the Gruta do Lapão is one of the largest quartzite caves in the country. Since quartz, which is one of the hardest of the common minerals, rarely forms caves, its abundance here is quite unusual. Instead of stalactites and stalagmites (which are created by water action on limestone), the cave interior features a floor of loose quartzite tiles, which make interesting sounds under travelers' feet. Farther inside the cave this strange symphony gives way to the thundering sound of the river's flowing water. Visits to the cave last about four and a half hours roundtrip. It's advisable to take water, snacks, insect repellent, a flashlight, and an oil lamp. But at some point on the way, turn off your lights for a few minutes and savor in silence the cave's absolute darkness.
Contact: Associação dos Condutores de Visitantes de Lençóis (Acvl), tel. (75) 3334-1425; Terra Chapada Expedições, tel. (75) 3334-1304.

Crystal-Blue Pools

When the light is right, the **Poço Encantado**, in the town of Itaetê, about 160 kilometers (100 miles) from Lençóis, contains extraordinarily blue water. The pool lies in an area of carbonate rocks. This geological formation is prone to water infiltration and, therefore, to the formation of caves and subterranean tunnels. The waters have a prism-like effect on sunlight entering the cave between April and September, which gives the pool its name, "enchanted well". To reach the blue pool, make the exhausting descent down a 90 meters (295 feet) of steep steps and trails. Although, swimming in the pool has been banned, it is still worth the hike to see it.

Smaller and shallower than Poço Encantado, **Poço Azul** is in Nova Redenção, 67 kilometers (42 miles) from Andaraí. Swimming is also prohibited here. The best time of the year to go is between February and October.
Contact: Associação dos Condutores de Visitantes de Andaraí (Acva), tel. (75) 3335-2255.

CHAPADA DIAMANTINA NATIONAL PARK

The Parque Nacional da Chapada Diamantina seems like an island. Dirt roads and trails surround its rivers, mountains, and woods, and the BA-142 state highway is the only road that runs through it. With 152,000 hectares (375,600 acres) that encompass the municipalities of Lençóis, Andaraí, Mucugê, and Palmeiras, the park is often confused with the Sincorá Range. There are ton of options for **hiking** and **adventure sports** – and the landscape is stunning.
Contact: Pé no Mato, tel. (75) 3344-1105; Terra Chapada Expedições, tel. (75) 3334-1304.

HIKING TRAILS

Pai Inácio Hill–Capão
From the top of Morro do Pai Inácio you can see Morro do Camelo to the north. To the south, a string of fields and valleys leads to the foot of Morrão – this is where the trail begins. An excellent choice for a medium-difficulty hike through breathtaking scenery, the trek is about 30 kilometers (19 miles) long – 25 kilometers on foot and 5 kilometers by car. It can take all day to get to Capão, but if you decide to visit Conceição dos Gatos by car, it will only take five hours to reach the village.

Lençóis–Capão
This medium-difficulty hike takes about five hours. The trail passes the foot of Morrão ("large hill") and winds along several rivers, which make for excellent swimming spots.

Morrão
You can reach the hill by any of several trails, including the ones listed above, those departing from the Pai Inácio Hill-Capão, and those leaving from the valley or from the village of Conceição dos Gatos. Once at the foot of the hill, you can reach the top within 90 minutes. It's a steep ascent – at some points it'll seem like you are climbing, rather than hiking – but the view from the top and the hill's beautiful terrain make it worth the effort.

Igatu–Andaraí
This easy, four-hour trail doesn't demand much from its hikers. From the central square pass the Igreja de São Sebastião and the cemetery and follow the left bank of the Rio Xique-Xique. Mining activity has significantly altered the landscape along the trail. The hills overlook the region's cacti, xiquexique, and the beaches on the Rio Paraguaçu at the foot of the hills.

Paty Valley
This is a long and demanding trail, but with multiple starting and stopping points, you can choose to walk a shorter stretch. Located within the heart of the Sincorá Range, the deep Vale do Paty is surrounded by beautiful hills and majestic walls. The most commonly used trails within the valley start at either Capão, in the north, at Guinévillage, in the west, or at Andaraí, in the east. A less traveled trail starts at Mucugê in the south.

Lençóis–Fumaça Waterfall
You'll have to be in excellent shape to reach the breathtaking Cachoeira da Fumaça (see page 147). There are two ways to get there: a three-day hike from Lençóis or a day-long drive from Capão. The three-day hike starts at the bottom of the waterfall, climbs to the top, and finishes at the Capão Valley. Driving straight to Capão – 50 kilometers (31 miles) on paved roads and 22 kilometers (14 miles) on dirt roads – leaves you with a 6-kilometer (4-mile) walk up a steep slope to the top of the waterfall, and brings you back to Capão on the same day.

ADVENTURE SPORTS

Trekking is not the only option for adventure sports buffs in Chapada Diamantina. Many of the hiking trails double as trails for mountain biking. In Lençóis, guides and tour operators lead various activities like climbing, rappelling, and canyoning at **Morro do Camelo** (250 meters, 820 feet) and **Pai Inácio** (150 meters, 490 feet). Other attractions include: **Gruta do Lapão** cave (55 meters, 180 feet), which offers those activities as well as bungee jumping and "cave jumping" (bungee jumping at the mouth of the cave); **Cachoeira do Mosquito** waterfall (two cascades, respectively 35 and 50 meters, or 115 and 165 feet high); and north of Chapada Diamantina, near **Morro do Chapéu** hill, 350 kilometers (217 miles) from Lençóis. Transportation is included for the locales that are farther away: **Gruta dos Brejões** cave (a depth of 123 meters, 404 feet); **Serra dos Brejões** range (170 meters, 560 feet); and **Cachoeira do Buracão** waterfall (100 meters, 330 feet), in Ibicoara, 230 kilometers (143 miles) from Lençóis. *Contact: Nativos da Chapada, tel. (75) 3334-1314; Andrenalina, tel. (75) 3334-1689.* Mountain biking: *Contact: Rony Aleixo, tel. (75) 3334-1700.*

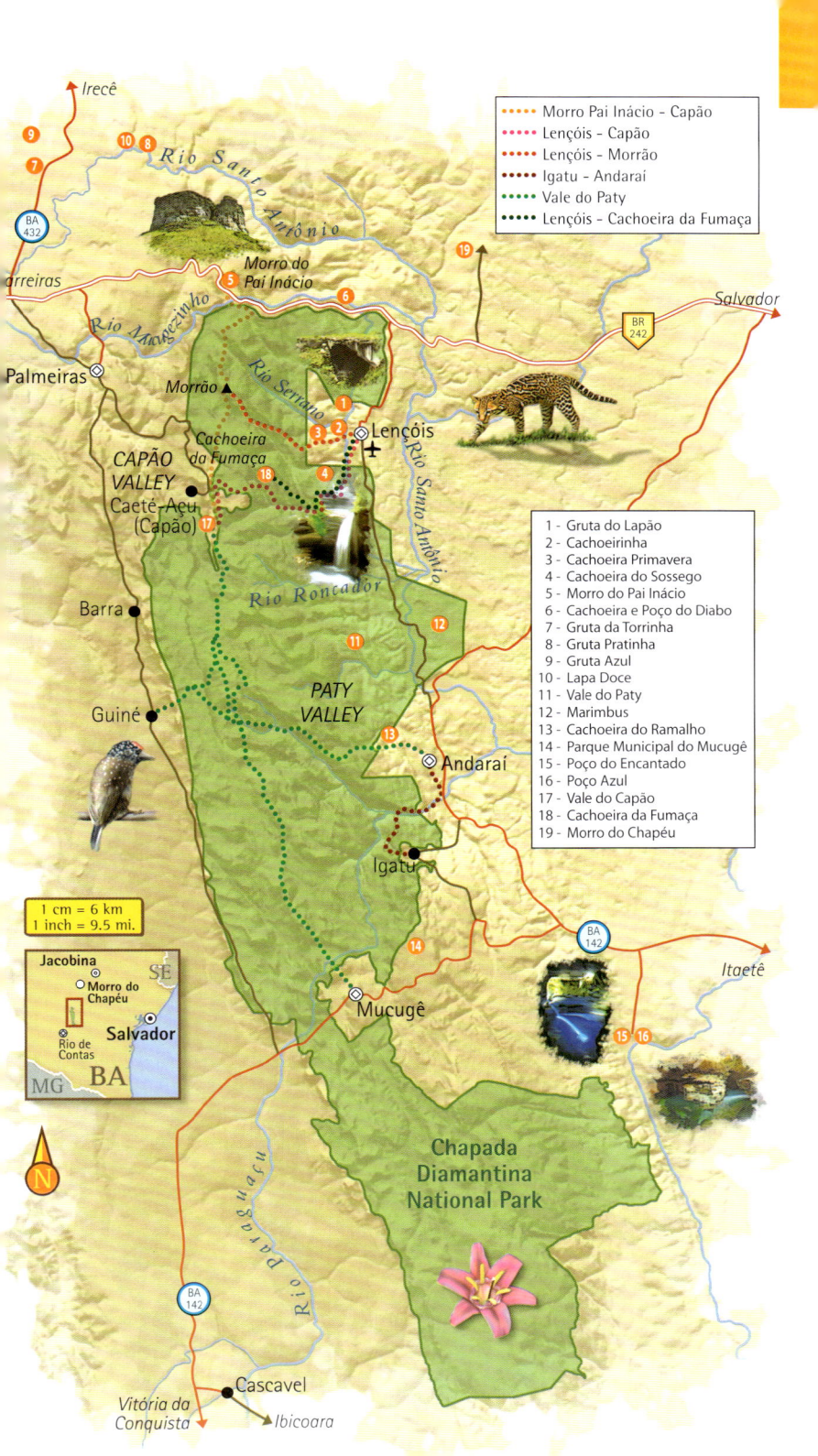

- Morro Pai Inácio – Capão
- Lençóis – Capão
- Lençóis – Morrão
- Igatu – Andaraí
- Vale do Paty
- Lençóis – Cachoeira da Fumaça

1 - Gruta do Lapão
2 - Cachoeirinha
3 - Cachoeira Primavera
4 - Cachoeira do Sossego
5 - Morro do Pai Inácio
6 - Cachoeira e Poço do Diabo
7 - Gruta da Torrinha
8 - Gruta Pratinha
9 - Gruta Azul
10 - Lapa Doce
11 - Vale do Paty
12 - Marimbus
13 - Cachoeira do Ramalho
14 - Parque Municipal do Mucugê
15 - Poço do Encantado
16 - Poço Azul
17 - Vale do Capão
18 - Cachoeira da Fumaça
19 - Morro do Chapéu

1 cm = 6 km
1 inch = 9.5 mi.

Chapada Diamantina National Park

Paty Valley: untouchable backlands

ANDARAÍ

Andaraí, 100 kilometers (62 miles) south from Lençóis on the BA-142 highway, is a town frozen in time: people seem to live here just as they did during the diamond-mining era. Sitting on the eastern edges of the Sincorá Range, Andaraí leads a simpler existence than Mucugê and Lençóis, and, as a result, tourist services are limited. The town is one of the gateways to **Vale do Paty** and its well-trodden hiking trails. Other attractions around Andaraí include the **Marimbus** wetlands, the **Roncador** and **Garapa** rivers, and the **Ramalho** waterfall, with its 90-meter (295-foot) drop.

MARIMBUS
Where the Santo Antônio River meets the plains at the foot of the Sincorá Range, are several flooded areas: the Marimbus wetlands. A canoe is the best vehicle for taking in this region, which is also known as "*O pantanal da Chapada*" (the Chapada wetlands, in contrast to the vast Pantanal wetlands farther south). The fauna and flora of the wetlands are some of the main highlights of the area, which a huge variety of birds and fish, anacondas, caimans, *pacas*, and tapirs, as well as a remarkable set of water lilies.
Contact: Associação dos Condutores de Visitantes de Andaraí (ACVA), tel. (75) 3335-2255.

MUCUGÊ

The small town of Mucugê, 134 kilometers (83 miles) south from Lençóis on the BA-142 highway, has a pleasant climate and an average temperature of 19°C (66°F). Iphan, the National Institute for Artistic and Historical Heritage, protects its well-preserved historical center. The **City**

Hall, the **Matriz de Santa Isabel** and **Santo Antônio** churches, and the striking **Byzantine cemetery**, with its white gravestones, are among the many buildings built during the 19th century.

Mucugê City Park

The Parque Municipal de Mucugê opened in 1999, and its main attraction is the **Projeto Sempre-Viva**. The *sempre-viva* ("everlastings") flower has been an important source of income for the people in the Chapada Diamantina since the end of the diamond boom. As a result, the beautiful flower has become an endangered species; Ibama banned the buying and selling of the flower in 1985. The park is currently in the process of studying the pollination process in an effort to develop new cultivation technologies. The hope is that these new technologies will make *sempre-vivas* commercially viable in the future, thereby increasing revenue to the town. In the park, trails lead to the waterfalls of Piabinhas, Tiburtino and Andorinhas, as well as to the researchers' lodgings and lab, and a snack bar and gift shop.

BA-142 highway, Km 96, towards Andaraí, 4 kilometers (2.5 miles) from Mucugê, tel. (75) 3338-2156. Daily, 8:30am – 6pm.

Ibicoara

Ibicoara, 202 kilometers (126 miles) south from Lençóis, owes its tourism industry to the **Cachoeira do Buracão** and **Cachoeira da Fumacinha**. The former, a waterfall with an 85-meter (280-foot) drop and several swimming pools, is one of the greatest natural attractions in the Chapada Diamantina. It is on private property in a canyon, in the south end of the park, so you will need to hire a guide for the 1-hour drive and 30-minute walk to the waterfall. Cachoeira da Fumacinha, with its 100-meter (330-foot) cascade, is a demanding, 8-hour walk. This rocky route becomes very slippery when it rains; it follows a river at the bottom of a deep canyon for most of the way, so there is a high risk of falling.

Contact: Associação dos Condutores de Visitantes do Vale do Capão (ACVVC), tel. (75) 3344-1087; Pé no Mato, tel. (75) 3344-1105.

Igatu

This largely abandoned hilltop town stands on rocks covered by only a thin layer of soil. With no easy access to mud and clay, builders used stone for most of the buildings. The district was founded between 1844 and 1846, and it once was one of the most important mining centers in the Chapada Diamantina. Some estimates place its population at 10,000 during the diamond boom, but today there are just over 350 people who call Igatu home. Still, many of the old houses are well preserved, making the town an intriguing, almost magical place to visit. Formerly known as Xique-Xique, Igatu is only 14 kilometers (9 miles) away south from Andaraí along the BA-142 highway. At either Km 52 or Km 82 turn off onto the dirt road and drive west an additional 6 kilometer (4 mile).

Arte & Memória Gallery

The Galeria Arte & Memória opened in 2002 in a house styled after the town's lovely old stone buildings. The gallery offers temporary exhibitions of fine arts and photography, as well as a café, which may serve the best cappuccino in the Chapada Diamantina. Near the gallery's outside entrance, the Museu do Garimpeiro (Prospector's Museum) features a small collection of objects found in the old mines.
Rua Luís dos Santos, no #, tel. (75) 3335-2510. Tue – Sun, 9am – 6pm.

Caim Ramp

Rampa do Caim trail ends at a point overlooking the entire Chapada Diamantina. Despite the long, 10-kilometer (6-mile) climb, the hike is not very demanding. Trail guides usually take visitors to two different lookout points; one offers views of the **Paraguaçu canyon**, and the other of the **Paty river** and **valley**. The ascent takes about two and a half hours and the return a little less time. A longer and more demanding hike down to the bottom involves heading towards the Cânion do Paraguaçu and walking 13 kilometers (8 miles) on the banks of the river until you reach the BA-142 highway, near Andaraí. From there you will have to arrange for transportation back to Igatu.
Contact: *Associação dos Condutores de Visitantes de Andaraí (ACVA), tel. (75) 3335-2255.*

Amarildo's Place

Amarildo dos Santos, the living "database" of the town, owns a curious shop near the central square in Igatu. Not only is Amarildo the repository of an endless amount of information about Igatu and its residents, but he also sells local history books that he wrote and illustrated. Amarildo's shop features an impressive magazine collection, although the periodicals are entirely in Portuguese, and a small tourist information center. His hospitality knows no bounds: he has been known to welcome visitors to his famous house, which is located in the same building as the shop.
Rua Sete de Setembro, no #. Daily, no fixed hours.

Capão Valley (Caeté-Açu)

The Capão river flows from the south of the Vale do Capão to the north. The valley is on the northwest border of the park, 70 kilometers (43 miles) west from Lençóis; it's accessible from the highway, Estrada Palmeiras–Caeté-Açu, through 18 kilometers (11 miles) of dirt road. Over the last three decades, the valley has received an influx of new residents who are drawn to its natural beauty. Tourism is flourishing, with backpackers flocking here for the beautiful waterfalls, peace, and tranquility. This is where the main trail begins, leading to the highest waterfall in Brazil, with a drop of 340 meters (1,115 feet).

Fumaça Waterfall

The Cachoeira da Fumaça, discovered only in the 1960s, is the most popular attraction in the Chapada Diamantina. There are two ways to get there: a 6-kilometer hike, or a three-day hike from Lençóis (*see page 139*). The 6-kilometer (4-mile) hike takes you 2 kilometers up a steep slope to the top of the canyon, offering a wonderful view of the waterfall. The more challenging, three-day hike is worth the effort when you reach the waterfall: The reason for the name "*fumaça*" (smoke) becomes evident once you see the smoke-like effect coming from the spray of the water. During the busiest season, some locals sell home-made cakes and juice to the hikers.

Contact: Associação dos Condutores de Visitantes do Vale do Capão (ACVVC), tel. (75) 3344-1087; Pé no Mato, tel. (75) 3344-1105; Terra Chapada Expedições, tel. (75) 3334-1304.

Fumaça Waterwall: spray drenches the rock face

Jacobina

Upon first glance, Jacobina, 283 kilometers (176 miles) north from Lençóis, seems as if it has been fashioned whole and deliberately plopped down in a deep valley surrounded by majestic peaks. The town has its share of historical buildings, like the **Igreja Matriz de Santo Antônio** and the now-closed **Clube Aurora** – the club where the first *micareta* bands played. *Micaretas,* Carnival-like festivities occurring outside of the Carnival season, primarily in the Northeast, are rumored to have been created in Jacobina. From Feira de Santana, Jacobina is accessible by the BR-324 highway nothwest.

Waterfalls

There are hundreds of waterfalls within a short distance of Jacobina. The best-known ones lie near Itaitu village, 9 kilometers (5.6 miles) from the Jacobina exit on the BR-324 highway. Those familiar with the plunging waterfalls in the Chapada Diamantina, which spill from huge vertical walls into cavernous canyons, will be surprised by the difference here: waterfalls around Jacobina cascade down steep bedrock into deep rivers. A 20-minute hike through hundreds of babassu palms leads to **Véu de Noiva** (35 meters, 115 feet), located in the middle of lush rainforest. Like many waterfalls in the area, the **Cachoeira do Piancó** (20 meters, 66 feet) is only accessible by crossing private property. To reach its swimming pools, you must go first by car, then continue on foot for 15 minutes. **Cachoeira das Arapongas** has a series of cascades averaging 6 meters (20 feet) long, and several diving pools, like the **Poço da Geladeira**. Access to the waterfall is limited, however, so you should try to arrange a visit in advance.
Contact: Associação Regional de Monitores de Atrativos Turísticos (Armat), tel. (74) 3621-6872, 9961-1148.

Morro do Chapéu

Near the town of Morro do Chapéu, 172 kilometers (107 miles) north of Lençóis, is the **Cachoeira do Ferro Doido**. The waterfall, recognized as a state natural monument, sometimes dries up between December to February, so you may want to go there during the wetter months. The waterfall, **Gruta dos Brejões** cave, and **Vila do Ventura**, a village that once was a major diamond center are the region's must-see attractions. Morro do Chapéu is accessible from Rodovia do Feijão on the BA-052 highway, coming from Feira de Santana; it can also be reached by the BR-122 highway, coming from BR-242.

Ventura Village

This ghost village in Morro do Chapéu, is home to the **Estrada do Ouro** (Gold Road) connecting the Chapada Diamantina to Minas Gerais. The road, planned route for horseback trips and pilgrimages, is a linchpin in a regional revitalization project. Other attractions around Vila do Ventura include many archeological sites, the former **Sítio de Igrejinha**, now known as **Cidade das Pedras** (City of Stones), and the **Cachoeira do Ventura** also known as **Cachoeira do André Mocó**. Most of the archeological sites are caves with ancient paintings on the rock walls. In the Cidade das Pedras, rock formations come together to resemble a city. The best time to see the falls is during the rainy season, between November and March, as they are dry during the rest of the year. With a guide's assistance, you can visit the village and its surroundings within a day; the local tourist office (*tel. 74/3653-1826*) can recommend a good guide.

Brejões Cave

When you reach the mouth of Gruta dos Brejões, in Morro do Chapéu, it is easy to see why the cave has become well-known. At 106 meters (348 feet) high and 7.8 kilometers (4.8 miles) long, its size alone is impressive. But that's not all: it has a river running through it, several tunnels and underground galleries. Moreover, the surrounding area contains a selection of unusual flora and fauna, including rare species like the black-chested buzzard-eagle and the broad-snouted caiman. For more information, contact the tourist office (*tel. 74/3653-1826*).

Rio de Contas

Rio de Contas, 225 kilometers (140 miles) south of Lençóis, is one of the most important historical towns in Bahia, with many of its buildings protected by Iphan. The first inhabitants of the area are said to have been the survivors of a slave ship that reportedly sunk off the coast near the mouth of the Contas River during the 17th or 18th century. The fugitives might have followed the river up to a secluded location around its source, near the modern town and settled the area. The town's architecture is extremely well-preserved, due to the the efforts of the local community, and the work of projeto Monumenta, a conservation project supported by the Department of Culture. Rio de Contas is home to the highest peaks in the Northeast. The beautiful **Pico das Almas**, 1958 meters (6,424 feet) high, probably stages the most moving Corpus

Tiny Rio das Contas has preserved its architectural heritage

Christi celebrations in the region, which usually occur in June. The best way to reach Rio de Contas is by the BA-142 highway, from Barra da Estiva to Tanhaçu, then following the BR-030 highway to Brumado. From Brumado, take the BA-148 highway to Livramento de Nossa Senhora, which leads to Rio de Contas. There are a few more beautiful, shorter routes: from the BA-142 highway heading towards Juciape, you can get to Rio de Contas through Marcolino Moura; or take the not-so-well-maintained dirt road from BR-242 to the BA-148 highway, heading towards Piatã and Abaíra, and passing by João Corrêa, Juciape, and Marcolino Moura.

The Town Center and Its Surroundings

Those interested in the cultural history of the Chapada Diamantina should be sure to visit the center of Rio das Contas and some of its neighboring villages. In the town center, its main buildings, protected by Iphan, include the 18th-century **Casa de Câmara e Cadeia** (Council Chamber and Prison), which currently serves as the town's courthouse, and the 19th-century **Town Hall** and **Teatro São Carlos**, a theater. In **Bananal** and **Barra**, two communities of runaway slaves' descendents make their livings off of the exhausted land. In spite of their hardships, they fervently preserve some traditional dances, songs, and prayers of the past. As you go farther towards Morro do Bittencourt hill (1,500 meters, 4,920 feet), the landscape changes: near the village of **Mato Grosso**, farming fields stretch from the backyards of houses to the hills. Coffee, corn, chayote, and other vegetables grow within the simple irrigation systems, terraces, and stone walls. For the most part, this is pesticide-free, organic agriculture. Mato Grosso is an old settlement of Santo Antônio de Mato Grosso – settled mainly by the Portuguese, it grew into a village by 1718. Be sure to check out some of the houses' beautiful gardens. From atop Bittencourt Hill you have an almost 360-degree view of the area; we recommend hiring a guide to get to the top.

Contact: Associação dos Condutores de Visitantes de Rio de Contas (Acvrc), tel.

Corpus Christi by Candlelight

The Corpus Christi celebration is very important to the residents of Rio de Contas. Locals often paint their houses in the weeks that precede the holiday. The holiday itself falls on the first Thursday that comes at least 60 days after Easter, which will be May 22 in 2008 but is in early June in most upcoming years. On Wednesday, the eve of the festivities, children cover the sidewalks with white paintings and everybody decorates their houses with small candle lanterns. All of the house plants are placed outside, transforming the town into a huge, illuminated garden. The street lamps are turned off, one by one, and the whole town of Rio de Contas is visible only by the flickering light of the lanterns. A procession then winds through the streets, accompanied by the town orchestra, which plays marching music and leads the faithful to the church. There, they celebrate the Corpus Christi Eve mass for hours. The next day, the children's sidewalk paintings are covered with brightly colored sawdust, rice husks, and other materials – the streets appear to be covered with colorful carpets. Throughout the day there are several masses, and festivities take over the town; throngs of people from the region and the obligatory crowd of tourists stream through the streets.

Pico das Almas trail runs through verdant vegetation

(77) 3475-2430; *Pouso dos Creoulos*, tel. (77) 3475-2018.

Waterfalls

The area around Rio de Contas boasts several waterfalls, though they are hardly the region's main attraction. The **Cachoeira do Rio Brumado**, located next to the road to Livramento de Nossa Senhora, 9 kilometers (5.6 miles) to the south, is a well-known waterfall. Standing 70 meters (230 feet) high, it takes about 30 minutes to walk to the top.
Contact: *Associação dos Condutores de Visitantes de Rio de Contas (Acvrc)*, tel. (77) 3475-2430; *Pouso dos Creoulos*, tel. (77) 3475-2018.

Mountain Ranges

The highest hills in the Northeast are found around Rio de Contas. **Serra do Barbado**, at 2,033 meters (6,670 feet) high, claims the honor of the tallest peak, followed by Pico do Itobira, 1,970 meters (6,460 feet) high. However, **Pico das Almas**, 1,958 meters (6,424 feet) high, is the most well-known, with its beautiful rock formations and more than 1,200 species of plants. It takes an entire day to climb Pico das Almas, with more than 17 kilometers (11 miles) along a dirt road, followed by a 3-hour hike to the top. This hike is difficult: be sure to hire a guide and bring snacks, water, and warm coats. Other peaks are just as challenging to summit: it takes 4 hours of demanding hiking to reach the **Pico do Itobira**, and, the most distant of all, **Pico do Barbado** is a 7-hour hike on a challenging hilly trail.
Contact: *Associação dos Condutores de Visitantes de Rio de Contas (Avrc)*, tel. (77) 3475-2430; *Pouso dos Creoulos*, tel. (77) 3475-2018.

Vaccaro Farm

The famous organic *cachaça* "Serra das Almas" is grown right on this farm. In order to get certification as an organic product, the sugarcane crops as well as the employees' working conditions must adhere to rigorous regulation. Anyone interested in seeing the production process at Fazenda Vaccaro should arrange in advance for a guided tour.
Contact: *Associação dos Condutores de Visitantes de Rio de Contas (ACVRC)*, tel. (77) 3475-2430; *Pouso dos Creoulos*, tel. (77) 3475-2018.

SERGIPE

1 cm = 20 km
1 inch = 31.7 mi.

Highlights

- Atalaia beach, Aracaju's most fashionable.
- Catamaran and schooner trips through the São Francisco River canyon, departing from Canindé.
- The historic city center and Sacred Art Museum in São Cristóvão.
- The beautiful 16th-century architecture of Laranjeiras.

When to Go

- Avoid the rainy season (April to July) to enjoy the beaches and trips on the São Francisco River.
- In January, for the folklore performances at Laranjeiras's Encontro Cultural festival.
- In June, for the Forró Caju festival, especially on the 24th for St. John's Day festivities.

SERGIPE

The smallest Brazilian state may also boast small prices, but its store of natural beauty and historic treasures bump it up significantly in the rankings. In the column for natural attractions, suffice it to mention the canyon of the São Francisco River, also called "Old Chico," in Canindé de São Francisco. It's the fifth largest canyon in the world and the most navigable. As for historical attractions, former state capital São Cristóvão, founded in the late 16th century, preserves a beautiful architectural heritage and folklore-inspired festivals. The *reisado*, a dramatic dance originating in late 19th-century Catholic traditions, is but one example of its rich legacy. Aracaju, home to the state government since 1855, caters to all tastes and boast the lively nightlife, bars, and restaurants of the Atalaia beachfront as well as the rich collections of the Memorial de Sergipe museum. Arts and crafts made by local artisans fill regional markets. Forró Caju, held in Aracaju in June, is a two-week music festival that attracts thousands. Laranjeiras, near the state capital, is home to Nossa Senhora da Conceição church (1743), one of Sergipe's most historically and religiously significant monuments.

Sergipe, which parted politically from the captaincy of Bahia in 1823, was home to some of the indigenous peoples most resistant to 16th-century colonization. "Cirizipe" or "Cerigipe" means "crab sting" in Tupi-Guarani and was the name of an indigenous leader who fought the Portuguese.

Explore the magnificent São Francisco Canyon by motorboat, catamaran, or schooner.

ARACAJU

Founded in 1855, Aracaju, replaced São Cristóvão as the capital of the then-province. Sitting on the banks of the Rio Sergipe, it beckons visitors to about 30 kilometers (19 miles) of beachfront and warm, calm waters. The major historic monuments are concentrated in the city center, with **Praça Fausto Cardoso** square at its heart. Also among them is **Palácio Olímpio Campos** palace (1863), the old government seat. Outside this area, don't miss the **Colina de Santo Antônio**, the hill that was home to Aracaju's first urban settlement. From the top, you can see nearly the entire city as well as the estuary of the state's namesake river. Also visit the new **Orla de Atalaia**, a 4-kilometer (2.5-mile) beachfront buzzing with *barracas*, bars, and restaurants. The **Mercado Municipal** and numerous other sites vend arts and crafts. Feeling festive? In June, the thirteen-day **Forró Caju** festival, held in **Praça Hilton Lopes**, draws thousands to the square. Beach bunnies will find that the state's best—and even Mangue Seco in neighboring Bahia—are just a daytrip from Aracaju. Many visitors go as far as Mangue Seco in Bahia.

ATALAIA AND ARUANA BEACHES
Aracaju really has only one beach, though it goes by many names. The trendiest stretch is **Praia de Atalaia**, where an attractively built-up shoreline offers a coconut-shaded promenade, a bike path, sports facilities, a playground, event areas, and tourist information kiosks. The wide strip of sand allows pleasant swimming at any point. The next stretch is called **Praia de Aruana**, and it has the ever-lively **Passarela do Caranguejo**, a row of restaurants and *barracas* specializing in *caranguejo* (freshwater crab). Praia de Aruana also boasts the **Oceanário de Aracaju** *(Avenida Santos Dumont, no #, Atalaia beachfront, tel. 79/3243-3214, 3243-6126; Tue – Fri, 2pm –8pm; Sat, Sun, and holidays, 9am – 9pm; in Jan. daily, 9am – 10pm)*, an oceanarium maintained by Projeto Tamar (a group

Praia de Pirambu, a stretch of coast that hosts a Projeto Tamar base.

dedicated to the protection of sea turtles). Opened in 2002, the oceanarium occupies a 1,100-square-meter (11,840-square-foot) turtle-shaped building. Its 18 aquariums and two tanks are home to 60 species of turtles, fish, and seahorses. The freshwater species come from the Rio São Francisco, while the saltwater creatures are collected from all over the region. The oceanarium has its own restaurant, bar, and 40-seat auditorium. **Projeto Tamar**'s Sergipe site is on Praia de Pirambu, a beach 30 kilometers (19 miles) from Aracaju. *(Reserva Biológica de Santa Isabel, no #, zona rural (rural area), tel. 79/3276-1201/3276-1217/9148-0106. Mon – Sat, 8am – 5pm.)* Call to arrange visits in advance.

SERGIPE MEMORIAL

The exhibits in the 13-room Memorial de Sergipe illuminate Sergipe's social and cultural history. Established by Tiradentes University (UNIT) in 1994, the museum is near the city center. Its first rooms trace the history of the state chronologically. Later rooms are devoted to arts and crafts and religious statuary. Don't miss the pieces resembling the *cangaceiro* Lampião or the weapons used by police to kill him in 1938 at Grota do Angico, a farm in the interior of Sergipe. The Rosa Moreira Faria room exhibits works by that artist, who painted a history of the state on porcelain. Visits, led by a UNIT guide, last about an hour.
Avenida Beira-Mar, 626, 13 de Julho neighborhood, tel. (79) 3211-3579. Mon, 2pm – 6pm, Tue – Sat, 9am – 6pm.

OUR RECOMMENDATION

Initially a *forró* club, **Cariri** reopened as a restaurant in the same place on the Passarela do Caranguejo in 2000. Today it hosts the region's best traditional *forró*. (Called *pé-de-serra*, literally "foot-of-the-mountain," the music is usually played by a trio of accordion, triangle, and *zabumba* drum.) Menu specialties include *camarão ao cariri* (house-style shrimp) and grilled goat. Fine jets of water sprayed intermittently from the roof keep the atmosphere cool. *(Avenida Santos Dumont, no #, Passarela do Caranguejo, Atalaia beachfront, tel. 79/3243-1379/3243-5370. Daily, 10am – until the last customer leaves)*

Additional information on page 358.

Green turtles, a species common on the Sergipe coast

SERGIPE ANTHROPOLOGICAL MUSEUM

The Museu do Homen Sergipano, founded in 1996, exhibits archaeological objects, documents, and photographs. Maintained by the Federal University of Sergipe, it is housed in an early 20th-century building in the city center. Besides its permanent collection, the museum hosts temporary exhibitions and a library. Guided weekend tours in English can be arranged.
Rua Estância, 228, Centro, tel. (79) 3211-5798. Mon – Fri, 8am – noon and 2pm – 5:30pm.

ARTS AND CRAFTS MARKETS

Sergipe's artisans craft a diversity of sculptures, basketry, woven goods, embroidery, and lace. In Aracaju, get an introduction to their wares at the **Museu do Artesanato**, a museum that displays a variety of pieces in clay and wood and hosts stores offering bedcovers, tablecloths, women's clothing, and other products *(Praça Olímpio Campos, formerly Rua 24 Horas, no #, Centro, tel. 79/3214-6834; museum: Mon – Fri, 7am – 6pm; stores: Mon – Sat, 9am – 6pm).* At the **Mercado Municipal Antônio Franco**, you'll find craft items from all over the state *(Rua José do Prado Franco, no #; Mon – Sat, 6am – 6pm; Sun, 6am – 1pm).* For the most sophisticated works, visit the **Centro de Arte e Cultura de Sergipe**, on the beachfront at Atalaia. This cultural center's collection of fine regional work is all for sale. Pride of place is given to the work of José Roberto de Freitas, also known as Beto Pezão (Big Foot), who makes clay figurines with enormous feet. Also prominent are the miniature works of Cícero Alves dos Santos, who is known as Véio (Old Man). Véio holds the Guinness record for the world's smallest wooden sculpture, less than 1 millimeter in each dimension. You lose it, you buy it. *(Avenida Santos Dumont, no #, Atalaia beachfront, tel. 79/3255-1413. Mon – Thu, 10am – 10pm; Fri – Sat, 10am – 11pm; Sun and holidays, 4pm – 10pm.)*

LARANJEIRAS

Laranjeiras, 23 kilometers (14 miles) from Aracaju, was founded in 1594. In 1701, the Jesuits left their mark, building the **Capela de Santo Antônio** and the first residence of the order, known as the **Retiro** (Retreat). The chapel and the Retiro, both protected by Iphan, are about a kilometer from the town center. Though the buildings are on private property, visits are possible if arranged 48 hours in advance. *(Fazenda Brandão, no #, zona rural (rural area). Arrange visits by calling Maísse Gama at 79/3280-1172.)* The **Igreja de Nossa Senhora da Conceição de Camandaroba**, a church dating from 1743, is also protected. *(Rua da Comandaroba, no #, zona rural (rural area), about 1 kilometer from the town center. Tue – Fri, 10am – 5pm; Sat – Sun, 1pm – 5pm.)* One of the state's most valuable cultural monuments, it may be the last Jesuit construction in Sergipe, as the Order of Jesus was expelled from the colony in 1759. Notice the rich stone carvings in the entrance doorway. To visit the church, contact the Secretaria de Cultura e Turismo (Department of Culture and Tourism), which can arrange an English-speaking guide for visitors. The department's staff can also set up visits to the **Igreja Matriz Sagrado Coração de Jesus** *(Praça da Matriz, no #, tel. 79/3281-1033; Mon – Fri, 9am – noon and 2:30pm – 5pm; Sat, 9am – noon; Sun, 6:30am – 10:30am)*, in the center of Laranjeiras. Opened in 1790, the church retains its original form, despite many renovations since. The **Igreja do Bom Jesus dos Navegantes** *(Rodovia Walter Franco, no #, at the town entrance; Tue – Sun, 10am – noon and 2pm - 5pm)* opened to the faithful in 1905. The church is perched high on a hill, offering visitors a panoramic view of the town and the Rio Cotinguiba

Laranjeiras, founded in the 16th century, holds onto a valued heritage

Historic buildings in Matriz do Sagrado Coração de Jesus Square, in Laranjeiras

river. As the church is quite removed from the town center, it's best to ask the Secretaria de Cultura e Turismo to arrange a time for your visit and recommend a guide to accompany you. Laranjeiras offers a pair of interesting museums. The collections of the **Museu Afro-Brasileiro** *(Rua José do Prado Franco, 70, tel. 79/3281-2418; Tue – Fri, 10am – 5pm; Sat, Sun, and holidays, 1pm – 5pm)* bear witness to the history of Brazilian black culture. The rooms of the imposing building explore specific themes, such as the sugarcane industry or the mistreatment of slaves. A second floor area is dedicated to religion. Guided tours are available. A notable attraction of the **Museu de Arte Sacra** *(Praça Doutor Heráclito Diniz Gonçalves, 39, tel. 79/3281-2486; Tue – Fri, 10am – 5pm; Sat – Sun, 1pm – 5pm)* is a 17th-century gilded German harmonium. The aged instrument still can summon some sounds. The museum accommodates disabled visitors.

REGIONAL EVENTS

Laranjeiras is famous for its festivals. For thirty years it has been the stage for the **Encontro Cultural**, the most important cultural event of its kind in the state, which occurs in January. During the festival, the city presents its unique folklore to the public in a series of celebrations. The **taieira**, held on January 6, the Feast of the Epiphany, honors the black Catholic saints Nossa Senhora do Rosário and São Benedito in an example of the vibrant syncretism between Catholicism and African-cult celebrations. The spectacle of **Lambe-Sujo** and **Caboclinho**, a dramatic dance dating to the time of runaway slaves, enacts a symbolic battle between black and Indian fighters. On the second Sunday in October, the two groups parade in the streets to the accompaniment of percussion instruments such as the *timbau, cuíca* (friction drum), *caceteira,* and *tabaque.*

São Cristóvão

This former capital of Sergipe dates to 1590 and is one of the oldest cities in Brazil. The government agency Iphan has protected it as a culturally significant site since 1939. São Cristóvão, like Salvador, developed on the Portuguese model, divided between a *cidade alta* (upper city), the seat of civil and religious power, and a *cidade baixa* (lower city), the site of the port and home to poorer residents. Today, the well-preserved town center offers historic sights along level streets. A guide is not necessary, but those offering their services in Praça de São Francisco square (in front of the Museu de Arte Sacra) are generally well informed. Be sure to agree on a price before setting out with a guide. Tasty regional cuisine is on offer at **Solar de Parati**, in Matriz Square, while the nearby **Casa da Queijada** serves delicious small coconut cakes *(queijadinhas)*. São Cristóvão is 23 kilometers (14 miles) from Aracaju along the SE-004 highway, known as Rodovia João Bebe Água.

Museums

With a collection of about 500 pieces, the **Museu de Arte Sacra de São Cristóvão** *(Praça de São Francisco, no #, no telephone; Tue – Sun, 9:30 am – 5:30pm)*, opened in 1974, is one of Brazil's three most important museums of sacred art. (The other two are in São Paulo and Bahia.) Construction on the Franciscan convent that now contains the museum began in 1657 but took until 1726 to finish. Among the museum's 17th-century gems are: the Trono do Santíssimo (Throne of the Most Holy), in cedar and gold leaf, and two ivory crucifixes. The **Museu Histórico de Sergipe** *(Praça São Francisco, no #, tel. 79/3261-1435; Tue – Sun, 1pm – 5pm)*, in the same square, offers chronological sequences of furniture, decorative objects, and religious garments. The museum is housed in an 18th-century palace, originally the provincial president's residence.

Churches

Of all the monuments protected by Iphan in Sergipe, the **Matriz de Nossa Senhora da Vitória** *(Praça da Matriz, no #, tel. 79/3261-1605; Mon, 8am – 10:30 am; Tue – Fri, 8am – 11am and 2pm – 4:30pm; Sat, 2pm – 4:30pm)* is the oldest. Originally built by the Jesuits in the first half of the 17th century, the church was damaged in the war against the Dutch, then almost completely rebuilt. At Praça do Carmo, workmen began the architectural ensemble formed by the **Igreja de Nossa Senhora do Carmo** *(daily, 8am – 11am and 2pm – 5pm)*, the **Igreja da Ordem Terceira** *(daily 8am – 11:30am and 2pm – 5pm)*, and the **Convento** at the end of the 17th century, but construction took nearly a century to finish. Every year, the faithful carry the statue of Senhor dos Passos (Christ carrying the Cross) during the Holy Week procession. **Igreja Nossa Senhora do Amparo** *(Travessa do Amparo, no #, formerly Rua das Flores; Tue – Fri, 8am – 11:30am and 2pm – 5pm)* is said to have been built by the Dutch invaders. For a time, an old black brotherhood, the Irmandade de Amparo dos Homens Pardos, maintained the structure. When the brotherhood stopped functioning in 1902, upkeep of the church passed to the parish priest of São Cristóvão.

Folklore Groups
Caceteira, one of the city's ten folklore groups, is a main attraction in São Cristóvão. Group members dance all night to the rhythm of *samba-de-coco*, which is marked by call-and-response vocals, clapping, and foot-stomping, and accompanied by percussion instruments. In the morning, the performers search for a flagpole where prizes have been hung, a northeastern folk tradition. Performances take place during the Christmas season, as well as in June and throughout the year on certain floating dates. *(Casa do Folklore Zeca de Norberto, Praça da Matriz, no #. Tue – Sun, 8am – noon and 2pm – 5pm.)*

Canindé do São Francisco

This town lies 198 kilometers (123 miles) from Aracaju, at the borders of Sergipe, Alagoas, and Bahia, and is the main departure point for boat trips through the **São Francisco River canyon**. The **lookout point at the Xingó hydroelectric plant** and the **Museu Arqueológico**, with its prehistoric human remain, are worth a visit. **Grota do Angico**, where police killed the infamous bandit *cangaceiro* Lampião, is also in Canindé, though the best way to get there is via Piranhas, on the opposite bank of the river, in Alagoas *(see page 179)*.

The São Francisco River Canyon
The 65-million-year-old **Cânion do Rio São Francisco** is said to be the world's fifth largest canyon and is its most navigable. Catamaran and schooner trips through the canyon are Canindé's biggest attractions, and motorboat trips are also available. No matter how you do it, the trip takes about 3 hours. After the first hour, tours stop for 40 minutes at **Paraíso do Talhado**, a stretch of the canyon that looks like an enormous swimming pool and is good for diving and canoeing. The trip continues past beautiful rock formations, including **Pedra do Gavião** and **Pedra do Japonês**, and to **Morro dos Macacos** hill. When choosing which trip to take, note that schooners offer shelter from the unrelenting sun, while catamarans provide "natural swimming pools": a kind of net dropped into the river to allow swimming during the trip. *Contact: MS-TUR, tel. (79) 9972-1320, (82) 9986-2038. Nine departures daily (including all three types of craft) between 8am and 3pm. Make reservations in advance.*

Xingó Hydroelectric Plant
A guided tour of this plant, 5 kilometers (3 miles) from Piranhas, which is across the state border in Alagoas, includes an impressive view from the lookout point. Anyone traveling between Paulo Afonso, Bahia, and Piranhas should stop and take advantage of the good services and clean facilities. The highlight of the visitor center is a wooden model of the plant. The plant also offers immaculate gardens punctuated by rock sculptures.

Xingó Archeological Museum
The Museu de Arqueologia de Xingó

The Xingó Hydroelectric Plant offers guided tours

(MAX) houses Latin America's largest collection of prehistoric human skeletons. The oldest dates to 7,000 B.C. The museum's nearly 200 artifacts come from archaeological sites in Justino and São José. Arranged in six rooms, the collection includes tools, necklaces, and domestic utensils. Some of the ceramic items are more than 11,000 years old. A 15-minute video describes the excavations and the restoration work done in the museum. Opened in 2000, MAX is part of the Federal University of Sergipe and operates in partnership with the hydroelectric plant. Surprisingly, only a few dozen people visit the museum on a typical day.
Rodovia Canindé–Piranhas, tel. (79) 3212-6453. Wed – Sun, 9:30am – 4:30pm.

GROTA DO ANGICO

On July 18, 1938, at the farm known as Fazenda Angicos, police ambushed and killed Virgulino Ferreira da Silva (the infamous bandit known as Lampião), his wife (Maria Gomes de Oliveira, known as Maria Bonita), and nine other *cangaceiros* or bandits. To get to the farm, take a motorboat or catamaran from Piranhas. Boats dock at Angicos's only restaurant. From there, you'll walk to the scene of the slaughter – a cave, or rather a cavity in a large rock. Wear lightweight clothing, shoes, sunglasses, and a hat, and carry water and insect repellent. During the 4-hour trip, the guide will reconstruct the events of the deadly day in a moving tale that moves some visitors to pray for the victims when they reach the cave. Two crosses inscribed with the names of those who died have been erected in the *cangaceiros*'s honor. Guided tours require a minimum of fifteen people and must be booked in advance.
Contact: *MS-TUR, tel. (82) 9986-2038. Departures from Xingó Park Hotel, tel. (79) 3346-1245.*

ALAGOAS

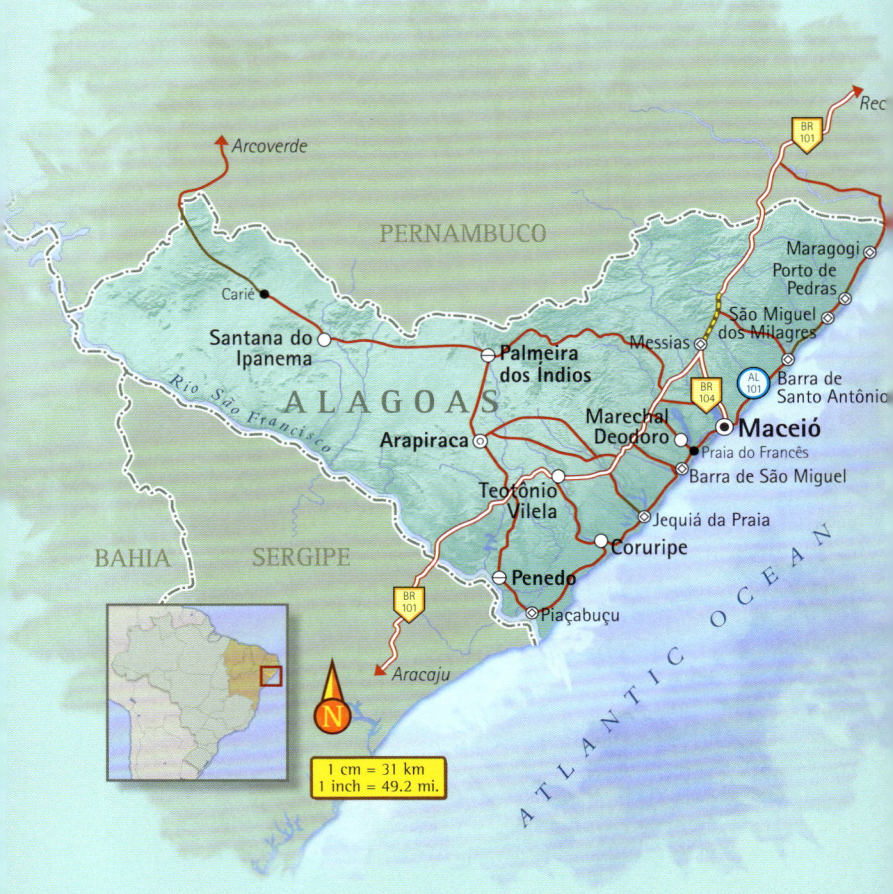

Highlights

- Raft trips to the natural pools in **Pajuçara** and schooner trips to the **Lagoa Mundaú** and **Lagoa Manguaba** lagoons.
- The beaches of **Praia do Francês** in Marechal Deodoro and **Praia do Gunga** in Barra de São Miguel.
- The **Rota Ecológica**, a road that links fourteen beaches along the coast between Barra do Camaragibe and Japaratinga.
- The traditional lace crafts of **Pontal da Barra**.
- The 18th-century architecture of **Penedo**.

When to Go

- In **summer**, for the best beach weather – perfect for driving the Rota Ecológica ("Ecological Route"), 40 kilometers (25mi.) of astonishing landscape, part of the coral reef itinerary.
- In **April**, to see the Festival de Tradições Populares folk celebrations in Penedo, on the banks of the São Francisco River.
- In **June**, to enjoy the lively São João festivities in Maceió.
- In **November**, for the Maceió Fest, an electrifying out-of-season Carnival.

ALAGOAS

Alagoas occupies the inverted triangle of land between the Rio São Francisco and the Atlantic Ocean. The state is home to some of the Northeast's most popular aquatic destinations; even the name Alagoas (*lagoas* means lagoons) hints at its myriad watery attractions. No wander that some of the most popular destinations of the Northeast are in this state. In its capital, Maceió, tourists will be enchanted by a sea that looks like a watercolor painting in shades of green. Beaches are the big draw of the town, whether it's the green sea of Praia de Pajuçara or the lively beachfront *barraca* (kiosk) scene at Praia de Ponta Verde. Apart from clear seas, pristine sands and majestic coconut groves, tourists have at their disposal a large number of hotels, restaurants, and *barracas* (kiosks) with live music, which make Ponta Verde beach the liveliest spot on the city coast. Away from Maceió, visitors have more surprises in store. Jet ski and surfing enthusiasts should not miss the former provincial capital of Marechal Deodoro, particularly the popular surfing and sailing beach Praia do Francês. Maragogi, in the far north of the state, is known for its *galés* (large natural pools). And Piaçabuçu, just to the south, is best known as the site of the dramatic "meeting of the waters," where the mighty São Francisco river flows into the sea.

Carro Quebrado beach, in Barra de Santo Antônio

ALAGOAS

MACEIÓ

First-time visitors to Maceió are immediately struck by the beauty of the surrounding waters – the brilliant, vivid green of the ocean and the **Lagoa Mundaú** lagoon. Among the city's many spectacular beaches are **Praia de Pajuçara**, famous for its natural pools, and **Praia do Francês**, in Marechal Deodoro, with calm seas on one side and strong surfing waves on the other.

The native Tupi-Guaraní tribe first named the region *maçayó* or *maçaio-k*, which means "covering the marsh." The Portuguese colonists who settled here in 1815 adopted this name, as well, and kept it when the town became the state capital in 1839.

In addition to its own beachfront attractions, Maceió serves as a base for day trips to towns like **Barra de São Miguel** (40 kilometers, 25 miles), **Maragogi** (130 kilometers, 81 miles), and **Penedo** (160 kilometers, 99 miles), all must-sees for visitors.

CITY BEACHES

Pajuçara (2 kilometers from the city center), with its calm, reef-protected waters, is the best known of Maceió's beaches. At low tide, *jangadas* (rafts) depart from Pajuçara for trips to the natural pools. Farther out from the center (4 kilometers) is vibrant **Ponta Verde**, a pristine, clear beach covered in coconut trees. **Jatiúca,** 6 kilometers from the center, is a popular location for surfing championships, and the site of the Lampião bar (famous for its all-night *forró* dances). With its strong waves and submerged reefs, **Cruz das Almas** (8 kilometers from the center) is another surfers' favorite. Pajuçara and Jatiúca both have showers and jogging/bike paths.

Highlights
1. Bairro Jaraguá
2. Museu Théo Brandão
3. Museu de Artes Pierre Chalita
4. Teatro Teodoro

Arts and Crafts
1. Núcleo Artesanal do Pontal da Barra
2. Pavilhão do Artesanato
3. Armazém do Sebrae
4. Ateliê Viver de Arte

Boats on the famous natural pools at Pajuçara, on Maceió's coast

Pajuçara's Arts and Crafts Market

The traditional Feirinha de Artesanato de Pajuçara began as a small, outdoor artisan market. In 2002, it was covered over and became a major marketplace, with around two hundred stalls selling a variety of crafts. The busiest time to go is late afternoon, when there are also *forró* shows. The market is held daily near the departure point of the *jangadas* (rafts) headed for the natural pools.
Rua Doutor Antônio Gouveia, no #, Pajuçara Beach; daily, 10am – 10pm.

Schooner Trips

The most popular boat-tour itinerary in Maceió visits 9 of the 32 islands in the Lagoa Mundaú and Lagoa Manguaba lagoons. Several boats make this two-hour trip, leaving daily from Pontal da Barra at 9:30am and 3:30pm. The undisputed highlight of each tour is a visit to the dazzling point where the waters of the lagoons and sea meet. Also popular are the interesting stories about the islands that guides share along the way. For example, **Ilha do Fogo**

> ### Local Delicacies
>
> The women who sell *tapioca* on the beaches of Maceió are legendary among locals and travelers alike. *Tapioca* is a wafer-thin pancake made of manioc flour, and is a legacy of the region's indigenous cuisine. Today it comes with both sweet and savory fillings. The most traditional preparation is with grated coconut and cheese, though some vendors sell more elaborate versions like fried banana and *brigadeiro* (chocolate and condensed milk). Stalls usually set up shop after 5pm on the beaches of Pajuçara, Jatiúca, and Ponta Verde. The best (and friendliest) seller in all of Maceió is **Irmã**, who can be found at Ponta Verde beach on most days.

An island in the Manguaba Lagoon, best visited on a schooner trip

("Drunk's Island") earned its name from the tipsy workers at the *cachaça* distillery that once operated there.
Contact: Edvantur, tel. (82) 9976-2189, 3351-9067. Daily, 9am; noon and 1pm.

CATAMARAN TRIPS TO PARIPUEIRA
The longest coral reef in the country starts at **Praia Paripueira**, 32 kilometers from Maceió. At low tide, you can walk almost a kilometer out to sea with the water coming up only as far as your knees. Biologists accompany the catamaran trips to the reefs, which last about two hours (including a stop for diving). Tickets for the trips are sold at Restaurante Mar e Cia. Always confirm departure times with the restaurant, as they vary depending on the tides.
Contact: Mar e Cia, tel. (82) 3293-1983, 3293-2031.

JARAGUÁ NEIGHBORHOOD
Near both the city center and Praia de Pajuçara, Jaraguá was for centuries the most important neighborhood in Maceió. The area first rose to prominence in the 1500s as a stop for ships on the brazilwood trade route. Growth continued with the sugar trade, and by the 19th century the neighborhood was full of large townhouses and luxury goods stores. Jaraguá eventually fell to disrepair as a result of economic decline, and became a seedy red-light district. Thankfully, since 1995, a well-organized project has taken major steps to revive the neighborhood. The government declared it a National Historic Site, and tourists have begun to visit the area. The old townhouses and

warehouses are now popular bars and nightclubs. One of Jaraguá's landmarks is the neoclassical **Associação Comercial de Alagoas** building, built in 1926 by designer José Paulino de Albuquerque Lins. Echoing its architectural style is the **Museu da Imagem e do Som de Alagoas** (also known as **Misa**), an image and sound museum. The building dates from 1869, and it housed the city's old Customs and Excise building. Today Misa hosts both permanent exhibits and a rotating roster of live events in its upstairs auditorium.

THÉO BRANDÃO MUSEUM

The Customs and Excise Tax building is also home to the Museu Théo Brandão, a museum dedicated to folk culture and traditions. Local doctor and folklore specialist Théo Brandão (1907-1981) donated most of the pieces in the collection, which focuses on folk art and clothing from the Northeast, as well as other regions of Brazil and even Spain and Portugal. There are several outstanding examples of local artwork, including the anthropomorphic clay jugs made by Júlio Rufino and the ceramics of Mestres Vitalino and Nô Caboclo. An auditorium in the museum features folklore presentations every Thursday at 7pm.
Avenida da Paz, 1490, tel. (82) 3221-2651. Tue – Fri, 9am – 5pm; Sat and Sun, 2pm – 5pm.

PIERRE CHALITA ART MUSEUM

The Museu de Artes Pierre Chalita has more than 3,000 works in its exhibits, including paintings, silverware, and furniture, with a focus on the 18th, 19th, and 20th centuries. The basement features works by modern Brazilian painters. Baroque objects occupy the first floor. The second floor is dedicated to paintings by the artist who gave his name to the museum.
Praça Marechal Floriano Peixoto, 44, Centro, tel. (82) 3223-4298. Mon – Fri, 8am – noon and 2pm – 5:30pm.

DEODORO THEATER

A centerpiece of the region's cultural landscape since its inauguration in 1910, the Teatro Deodoro continues to produce plays and concerts. The theater is named for Alagoas-born Deodoro da Fonseca, military commander who became Brazil's first president. The ornate interior has velvet seats and bronze detailing on the ceiling.
Praça Marechal Deodoro, no #, Centro, tel. (82) 3315-5651. Mon – Fri, 8am – 2pm.

OUR RECOMMENDATION

🍽 **Wanchaco** restaurant serves authentic Peruvian dishes of fresh fish and seafood. Some items, like the Andean fruit jellies, are imported from Peru. A highlight of the menu is the Japanese-influenced grilled fish and shrimp in sweet and sour ginger sauce. *(Rua São Francisco de Assis, 93, Jatiúca, tel. 82/3377-6114/ 3377-6024; Mon – Thu, noon – 3pm and 7pm – 11:30pm; Fri, noon – 4pm and 7pm – 12:30am; Sat, 7pm – 2am).*

Divina Gula specializes in the cuisine of Minas Gerais, including *tutu à mineira* (bean purée) and homemade *cachaças*. Alagoas is represented in seafood dishes like the shrimp with soy sauce, ginger, lime mayonnaise, and herbs. *(Rua Engenheiro Paulo Brandão Nogueira, 85, Jatiúca, tel. 82/3235-1016/3235-1262; Tue – Sun, noon – until the last customer leaves).*

Additional information on page 358.

LACE MAKERS AND OTHER ARTISTS

Some of Maceió's most talented folk artists sell their wares at the craft market **Mercado de Artesanato da Pajuçara** *(Rua Melo Morais, 617, Levada; Mon – Fri, 8am – 6pm; Sat, 8am – noon)*. The **Núcleo Artesanal** handcraft center in Pontal da Barra features more than 250 stores and studios. This is one of the best spots in Alagoas for traditional *filé* lacework, in which *rendeiras* (lacemakers) weave fine, colored threads into intricate patterns supposedly inspired by fishermen's nets. The **Pavilhão do Artesanato** *(Avenida Silvio Viana, 1447 – formerly Doutor Antônio Gouveia –, Ponta Verde, tel. 82/3231-3901; daily, 10am – 10pm)* looks like a shopping mall, the pavilion has around 150 craft stores, a food court, and an Internet café.

The market is an excellent place to browse items made of *ouricuri* palm straw (from the town of Coruripe, in Alagoas), as well as pieces from other states in the Northeast.

If you visit just one place, make it the **Armazém do Sebrae**, a warehouse in Jaguaré *(Avenida da Paz, 878, tel. 82/3223-8200; Mon – Fri, 9am – 6pm; Sat, 9am – 2pm)*, where you'll find lace, embroidery, sculptures, mats, and bedcovers. The **Ateliê Viver de Arte** studio *(Rua Manuel Maia Nobre, 257, Farol, tel. 82/3223-5257; Mon – Fri, 8am – 6pm; Sat, 8am – noon)*, run by sisters Rosa Maria Piatti and Ana Maria, features painted ceramics, bags, and home furnishings.

Folk art from Alagoas

ZUMBI DOS PALMARES

The state of Alagoas was the site of the greatest slave revolt in Brazil's history. The leader of the revolt was Zumbi, a slave of Angolan descent born in 1655 in Palmares, about 70 kilometers from Maceió. Baptized as Francisco and raised by Father Antônio Melo, Zumbi learned Latin and served as an altar boy as a child. At fifteen he ran away from his protector and took the Bantu name he is known by today. When he returned to his native Palmares years later, Zumbi joined a rapidly growing community of *quilombos* (settlements of escaped slaves), named União dos Palmares. Its members strived to keep traditional African culture and folkways alive. As the community grew (reaching 30,000 members at its peak), it survived by raising animals and crops on small farm plots. The news of slaves living in freedom and subsisting on their own land drew the attention of nearby farmers, who joined with the colonial government to send troops into Palmares. Surprisingly, the armed men of the *quilombos* handily defeated the government's troops for decades. The men of the *quilombos* were victorious until 1694, when Zumbi was wounded and the Palmares community was destroyed. Zumbi returned a year later at the head of the army, but was soon betrayed by one of his commanders and captured by the government. He was executed in Viçosa on November 20th 1695, and his head was displayed in the public square of Recife as an example for other slaves thinking of defying their masters. The date of his execution is now celebrated in Brazil as the *Dia da Consciência Negra* (Black Awareness Day).

Trendy Praia do Francês, named in remembrance of invasions by the French in colonial times

South Coast

Marechal Deodoro

The Portuguese first settled what is now the town of Marechal Deodoro in the 16th century; the original village was called Santa Maria Madalena da Lagoa do Sul. From the very beginning the town was subject to attacks by French troops, who hoped to gain a colonial foothold in the area. Despite the invasions, the town grew and prospered through the time of the sugar boom in Brazil during the 17th century, even serving as the provincial capital of Alagoas until 1839. After the beginning of the First Republic era in the early 20th century, the town changed its name to honor its most illustrious son, the military commander (Marechal) Deodoro. Deodoro officially proclaimed the First Republic in Brazil, in 1889, and served as its first president. Today Marechal Deodoro is filled with traces of its colorful past. The city's historic center, protected by Iphan (the Institute for National Artistic and Historical Heritage), features colonial houses, baroque churches, and neo-classical buildings. City Hall is in the luxurious **Palácio Provincial** *(Rua Doutor Tavares Bastos, no #, Centro, tel. 82/3263-2600, 3263-2601, Secretaria de Cultura e Turismo; Mon – Fri, 7am – 2pm)*, the palace once housed the provincial government. The town does not attract visitors solely on account of its cultural heritage, however. It is also blessed by nature; a regional highlight is beautiful **Praia do Francês**, a beach whose name evokes the French invasions of early colonial times.

Franciscan Complex (Sacred Art Museum)

The **Igreja Santa Maria Madalena** and **Convento Franciscano** are two of the most precious architectural treasures in all of Alagoas. This single church and convent complex was built between 1684 and 1723. The buildings' baroque façades stand out against the simple old colonial homes

that surround them. The interiors are equally ornate, particularly the baroque carvings in the convent and José Elói's elaborate ceiling paintings in the church. The **Museu de Arte Sacra do Estado** has been a part of the complex since 1984. The museum's collection includes some 200 sacred items from the 17th through 19th centuries, including sculptures, paintings, furniture, jewelry, and liturgical objects. The statue of Nossa Senhora do Ó dates from the 17th century and is a highlight of the collection. From the same period is a crown belonging to the city's patron and protector, Nossa Senhora da Conceição. The crown is still used to this day in the city's annual Epiphany processions. Guides from City Hall, some of them English-speaking, lead tours of the museum.
Praça João XXIII, no #, Centro, tel. (82) 3263-1623. Daily, 9am – 5pm.

Marechal Deodoro's House

The house of Manuel Deodoro da Fonseca (1827-1892) is one of the city's most popular attractions. Though the building is a National Historical Monument, nothing remains of its original 18th-century architecture except for the façade. The collection of paintings and furniture from Deodoro's time helps visitors imagine daily life in the Proclamation of the Republic era. Displays also feature Deodoro's various personal effects.
Rua Marechal Deodoro, no #, Centro, tel. (82) 3263-2608 (Secretaria de Cultura e Turismo). Daily, 8am – 5pm.

Francês Beach

The blue-green waters and fine white sands of Praia do Francês are eight kilometers from Marechal Deodoro. A five-kilometer strip of reefs just offshore creates a calm natural pool good for sailing, jet skiing, and banana boating. Other stretches of the beach are much choppier, with stronger waves, making them popular among surfers. The beachfront scene is always busy, as the shore is crowded with bars and restaurants.

Massagueira

The Massagueira district is 10 kilometers from Marechal Deodoro, on the shores of **Lagoa Manguaba** lagoon. This simple fishing village is best known for its bars, which serve delicious seafood dishes of shrimp, crab, and *sururu* (a type of shellfish). *Broas* (corn cakes), meringues, and manioc cake are also popular, as are the coconut desserts sold along the road leading to the village.

Barra de São Miguel

In 1556, Brazil's first bishop was eaten by Caeté Indians on a beach in this district, 33 kilometers from Maceió and 17 kilometers from Marechal Deodoro. São Miguel has thankfully moved past this cannibalistic tragedy, and is now the most popular seaside resort in Alagoas. The area also hosts the Northeast's annual surfing championship, the **Campeonato Nordestino de Surfe**. There are two beaches available to visitors: the calm, reef-protected waters of Niquim beach, and the stronger currents of São Miguel beach, which is very popular with surfers. Both spots have reasonable hotel facilities. The area serves as a hub for excursions to **Praia do Gunga** and **Praia de Barra do Jequiá**, as well as the **Dunas de Marapé** dunes.

Praia do Francês
This pale, white beach offers visitors calm waters and natural pools on one side, and strong waves for surfing on the other.

Barra de São Miguel
A lively, urban beach with fine, white sand, calm seas, and natural swimming pools at low tide.

Praia do Gunga
A grove-blanketed beach where the Lagoa do Roteiro lagoon meets the sea. The beach offers many activities for travelers, including water sports equipment for hire.

Praia da Lagoa Azeda
This wild, cliff-fronted beach has coarse sand and no real facilities for travelers.

Barra do Jequiá
A wide strip of pale sand and crystal-clear waters, accessible only by foot. Boats to the Marapé dunes depart from here.

Praia do Pituba
Great for fishing, with white sand and rough seas. To reach the beach without crossing private property, go first to neighboring Praia da Lagoa do Pau beach.

Praia da Lagoa do Pau
A popular swimming beach, with rough seas, strong waves, and coarse, yellow sand. This beach is the point where the Rio Pau empties into the sea.

1 cm = 3.4 km
1 inch = 5.3 mi.

Gunga Beach

This large, isolated beach is covered in coconut groves, with the sea on one side and the freshwater Lagoa do Roteiro lagoon on the other. Unfortunately, only patrons of the Enseada Hotel (and their guests) can access the beach by land. Those who are not guests of the Enseada must hire a boat or schooner to make the 20-minute trip from the docks at Barra de São Miguel. At the docks you may also hire boats for trips to the mangrove forests along the Niquim River.

Barra do Jequiá Beach and Marapé Dunes

There are two major attractions in **Jequiá da Praia**, 68 kilometers (42 miles) south from Maceió and 35 kilometers (22 miles) south from Barra de São Miguel. The first is Praia de Barra do Jequiá, with its brilliant white sands and crystal clear waters at the mouth of the Jequiá River. The other attraction is the resort complex at Dunas de Marapé. This cluster of guesthouses, restaurants, and kiosks faces scenic dunes and cliffs. *Jangadas* (rafts) from the beach make frequent trips across the Rio Jequiá to Marapé. *Secretaria de Esportes e Turismo de Jequiá da Praia (Sports and Tourism Department), tel. 82/3276-5235.*

Straw Art

Many travelers come to Coruripe, 57 kilometers (35 miles) south from Barra de São Miguel and 85 kilometers (53 miles) from Maceió, for its 30 kilometers of beautiful beaches. But beaches are not the area's only attraction. The nearby village of **Pontal do Coruripe**, about 10 kilometers from the town center, features handicrafts made from the fronds of *ouricuri* palms. Local artisans sell tablemats, bags, and many other pieces woven from this traditional material. *Associação das Artesãs do Pontal de Coruripe, Rua Grande, no #, tel. (82) 3273-7215.*

North Coast

Barra de Santo Antônio

Barra de Santo Antônio, 44 kilometers (27 miles) north from Maceió, grew out of a 17th-century Dutch village. The town is split by the Rio Santo Antônio, with government offices and tourist services on the right bank and attractions on the left. Left bank sights include historic buildings, such as **Igreja de Nossa Senhora da Conceição** church, and natural wonders like **Ilha da Croa** island. The town is famous for its Carnival and *festas juninas,* São João festivities. Additional merry-making occurs in September welcoming the summer season. And in January townsfolk honor their patron saint, Saint Sebastian. **Praia de Carro Quebrado** beach, surrounded by many-colored cliffs, is considered one of the Northeast's splendors.

Croa Island

Ilha da Croa is hardly an accurate name; the "island" is actually a peninsula peppered with natural pools and defined by a line of reefs. The peninsula stretches into the water near the town's historic district. A car ferry and several passenger boats are available for those who want to make the 5-minute trip across.

PERNAMBUCO

Maragogi
Maragogi's soft, white sands and calm, blue seas grow lively in summer. At low tide natural pools, called galés, appear.

São Bento
The waters are as quiet as the beach's sleepy fishing village. In the rainy season, the Maragogi River darkens the seawater.

Japaratinga
Japaratinga's dark blue seas, colorful cliffs, and coconut groves have been carefully preserved.

Barreiras do Boqueirão
Rough seas lap this beach of coconut groves. The sand is fine-grained along some stretches and coarse and pebbly along others.

Praia de Porto de Pedras
Reefs, calm seas, a narrow strip of white sand, and mangroves cluster around the mouth of the Manguaba River.

Lages
An isolated beach on a coconut farm, surrounded by calm seas and an extensive stretch of coarse sand and reefs.

Patacho
Reach this beach by dirt road through coconut groves. Its narrow strip of coarse sand and calm, reef-speckled seas are in an environmentally protected area.

Tatuamunha
A deserted stretch of fine sand and coconut trees. The waters are clear and calm with numerous reefs. Manatees swim in the Tatuamunha River.

Praia do Marceneiro
Near São Miguel dos Milagres village, this long strip of sand is covered with dense coconut groves and is ideal for walking. Gentle waves roll over its reef barrier.

Praia da Barra do Camaragibe
Calm, multi-hued seas lap the beach's coarse sand, and locals trap fish nearby.

Praia da Pedra do Cebola
Rough seas meet fine, pale sand at this isolated beach, which can be reached by foot from Carro Quebrado beach.

Carro Quebrado
Carro Quebrado is deserted and difficult to reach, but lined with colorful cliffs. In the high season barracas (kiosks) dot the beach.

Praia de Tabuba
Located at the mouth of the Sapucaí River, Praia de Tabuba beach's natural pools teem with colorful fish during low tide.

1 cm = 5.5 km
1 inch = 8.7 mi.

Quiet Praia do Morro is easy to get to from the town of Carro Quebrado

Carro Quebrado

To visit the town's best-known beach, cross the Santo Antônio River to Croa Island. From there, follow 6 kilometers (4 miles) of unsigned, coconut tree–lined dirt road to the beach. Local kids are happy to serve as guides as long as they're rewarded with a bit of change. It's a good idea to let one just in your car and show the way. The beach's striking sand cliffs shade from deep purple to beige. If time (ample) and tides (low) allow, consider extending your trip to the cliffs and clear waters of **Praia do Morro** and **Praia da Pedra do Cebola**.

Tabuba Beach

Praia de Tabuba, 4 kilometers (2.5 miles) from Barra de Santo Antônio, is situated at the mouth of the Sapucaí River. Natural pools and exceptionally clear water await visitors. The soft, brilliant white sand is perfect for sunbathing. On clear days, sailing rafts called *jangada* depart from the beach to take visitors for a pleasant spin.

São Miguel dos Milagres

The history of tiny São Miguel dos Milagres, 108 kilometers (67 miles) north from Maceió, is cloaked in legend. It is said that a fisherman found a statue of São Miguel Arcanjo (Saint Michael the Archangel), which cured him of a serious illness. True or not, the fact remains that the old settlement of Nossa Senhora, originally a center of anti-Dutch resistance, became a village at the beginning of the 19th century, taking the name of its patron saint. Today its quiet pace is complemented by its beautiful beaches and calm, crystal-clear waters. *Jangadas* glide by in a picture of unfaltering tranquility. **Praia de Porto de Pedras** is 15 kilometers (9 miles) from the center of São Miguel dos Milagres. Other nearby beaches worth visiting include **Tatuamunha**, **Patacho**, and **Lages**.

JAPARATINGA

This town, 115 kilometers (71 miles) north from Maceió and near the city of Maragogi, boasts spectacular beaches. **Barreiras do Boqueirão** is the last beach of the **Rota Ecológica** (Ecological Route), which also includes São Miguel dos Milagres, Porto de Pedras, and Passo de Camaragibe. Freshwater springs line the road leading to coconut-fringed Barreiras do Boqueirão, earning the beach the nickname Praia das Bicas ("Spring Beach"). When the weather is hot, the springs can be extremely crowded.

MARAGOGI

Postcard-perfect Maragogi is halfway between Recife and Maceió, 130 kilometers (81 miles) from both. After Maceió, it's Alagoas' most popular tourist destination. At the center of the Costa dos Corais ("Coral Coast"), the city is draped with beaches, coconut trees, and coral reefs. It takes its name from the river that borders it, but before 1892 it was also called "Gamela" and "Isabel." Though noted for its resistance to the Dutch occupation, the town today is renowned for its warm hospitality toward all visitors (even those of Dutch ancestry). Daytrippers head for the *galés* (natural pools) and to São Bento village to try the local specialty, *bolo de goma* (cornstarch cookies).

BEACHES

Lively **Praia de Maragogi** is hemmed in by hotels, guesthouses, restaurants, and craft stores. Sun-worshipping throngs soak up the natural beauty and take boat trips from the shore. If you'd prefer quiet, head 4 kilometers (2.5 miles) toward Recife to **Praia de São Bento**. It's the first beach you see after crossing the Rio Salgado, which separates Japaratinga from Maragogi. Tranquil **Peroba**, 12 kilometers (7 miles) from Maragogi, entices visitors to kick back amid coconut trees, natural pools, and intensely blue waters. On the border with Pernambuco, the beach lacks for bars and restaurants, but is home to an increasing number of guesthouses.

TRIPS TO THE GALÉS

Alagoas's signature natural pools, the *galés*, are 6 kilometers (4 miles) from the coast by motorboat or catamaran. The pools are known for their uniquely large size. Their crystal-clear waters reflect white coral-speckled sand and teem with fish. Feed the fish only with food approved by Ibama (the Brazilian Institute of Environment and Renewable Natural Resources), which young boys sell on the beach.

CORNSTARCH COOKIES

São Bento village is the capital of *bolo de goma* (cornstarch cookies), a traditional treat similar to the *sequilhos* eaten in the south of Brazil. Guesthouses, bars, and shops display bags of the little shell-shaped temptations. Entire families are often dedicated to the production of this delicacy, whose origins date to the Dutch invasion.

On the banks of the São Francisco River, Penedo preserves a precious architectural heritage

Mouth of the São Francisco River

Penedo

Founded in 1565, Penedo is an important page in Brazil's colonial history. Built on the banks of the Rio São Francisco, it's home to an enviable collection of architecture. Particular gems include 19th-century **Teatro Sete de Setembro** theater and three 18th-century churches, **Igreja de Nossa Senhora da Corrente**, **Igreja de São Gonçalo Garcia dos Homens Pardos**, and **Igreja de Nossa Senhora dos Anjos**. The **Marituba do Peixe** floodplains, just 20 kilometers (12 miles) from the city, are a worthwhile side trip. Penedo is accessed from Maceió by taking the well-paved AL-101 highway 168 kilometers (104 miles) south. If you're coming from Aracaju, take the BR-101 highway north to the junction near Nascença, then the SE-304 to Neópolis, 35 kilometers (22 miles) away on the state border. From there a ferry runs to Penedo, across the São Francisco River, every thirty minutes.

Churches

The lengthy construction of **Igreja de Nossa Senhora da Corrente** (*Praça 12 de Abril, no #, Centro; Tue – Sun, 8am – 5pm*) was begun in 1764 and finished some 125 years later. The simple façade of this masterpiece of Brazilian rococo belies its rich interior. The high altar is adorned with gold leaf and pink and blue marble framed by Portuguese tiles. Equally astonishing are the pulpit carvings, the nave ceiling painted by Libório Lazdro Lial Afes of Pernambuco (who also worked on several of Penedo's other religious buildings), and the 19th-century English floor tiles. A recent restoration was funded by Programa Monumenta, supported by the Department of Culture. The church is said to have hidden runaway slaves behind a false door in the side altar (to the left as you look into the church from the entrance). More rapidly constructed was the **Igreja de São Gonçalo Garcia dos Homens Pardos** *(Avenida Floriano Peixoto, no #, Centro; Tue – Sat, 8am – 5pm; Sun, 9am – 4pm)*, which opened its doors in 1759, a mere year after the ground was broken. It's known for its 19th-century neo-gothic bell towers. Construction on the **Catedral de Nossa Senhora do Rosário** *(Praça Barão de Penedo, 1, Centro, tel. 82/3551-2686; daily, 8am – 5pm)* began in 1690. The façade was demolished in 1815 and replaced by the current one, which has beautiful stained glass windows. Built by the Franciscans between the 17th and 18th centuries, the complex of **Igreja de Nossa Senhora dos Anjos** and the **Convento de São Francisco** *(Praça Frei Camilo de Lelis, no #, Centro; Tue – Fri, 8am – 11am and 2pm – 5pm; Sat – Sun, 8am – 11am)* is one of Alagoas's most important architectural sites. The church and convent were built in the Portuguese baroque style. Their sober exteriors contrast with the rich rococo carvings inside. Look for the optical illusion in the church's distinctive ceiling painting by Libório Lazdro Lial Afes.

Paço Imperial Museum

Ever since it hosted Dom Pedro II and his retinue in 1859, this 18th-century town house has been known as Paço Imperial ("Imperial Palace"). The institution collects 18th- and 19th-century religious art, furniture, and decorative objects, all donations from local families. Opened in 1971, the museum was an initiative of then-mayor Raimundo Marinho. From the second floor visitors can enjoy views of the São Francisco River. A giant canvas by Francisco Lopes Ruiz's portrays the emperor who made the building famous.
Praça 12 de Abril, 9, Centro, tel. (82) 3551-2498. Tue – Sat, 11am – 5pm; Sun, 8am – noon.

The high altar of Nossa Senhora da Corrente church is a rococo masterpiece

Sete de Setembro Theater

The Teatro Sete de Setembro is home to the Filarmônica Imperial de Penedo (Penedo's Imperial Phillarmonic), established in 1865. Construction began in 1881, and the theater was inaugurated three years later on Independence Day, September 7 ("*sete de setembro*"). The neo-classical design is the work of Italian architect Luiz Lucariny. Four ceramic statues high on the façade represent the muses of poetry, music, dance, and painting. The theater was restored in the 1980s. In July and August it hosts the Festival de Férias no Teatro drama festival.
Avenida Floriano Peixoto, no #. Daily, 8am – 5pm.

Casa do Penedo Museum

The nine rooms of this museum read like a city résumé. Collections include artifacts of illustrious local families, photographs, and historical documents. The Casa do Penedo Foundation restores and preserves old newspapers and books and supports local writers. Guided tours of the museum can be arranged.
Rua João Pessoa, 126, Centro, tel. (82) 3551-5443. Tue – Sun, 8am – noon and 2pm – 6pm.

Trips to Marituba do Peixe

Marituba is 20 kilometers (12 miles) east from Penedo, between Penedo and Piaçabuçu. This "Pantanal of Alagoas" is known for its large floodplains with navigable canals. A canoe trip through the canals lasts about an hour. Local guides (found at Penedo's only tour agency, listed below, or in front of Igreja da Nossa Senhora da Corrente) will help you hire a canoeist. Marituba's other attraction is Casa da Farinha, an old-fashioned flour mill still grinding with its original wooden mechanism. Straw crafts are common in Penedo; women frequently sell bags, hats, and baskets from their doorsteps.
Contact: *Associação de Condutores em Turismo de Penedo (Acontur), tel. (82) 9936-4770; Secretaria de Cultura e Turismo, tel. (82) 3551-2727.*

Penedo's colorful houses reveal traces of colonial Brazil

While in charming Piranhas, be sure not to miss the Museum of Banditry

Piranhas

Brightly colored historic houses line the banks of the Rio São Francisco in this charming colonial city. Dom Pedro II was enchanted by the town and spent some time here – wagging tongues say a local noblewoman enchanted him, as well. Piranhas is also the acknowledged capital of *cangaço* (backland banditry). For all its fame, however, the town was never actually attacked by the *cangaceiro* Lampião. The bandit king spared the city because its single entrance could easily have left the bandits surrounded, and because he was devoted to the Virgin Mary, the city's patron and protector. The city would not spare Lampião, however. Troops from the town left to capture the *cangaceiro* and his band and returned with eleven heads to exhibit in the public square. Among these were Lampião's and that of his wife, Maria Bonita. Though the gruesome evidence eventually made its way to Bahia, Piranhas was where the historic photographs were taken. Bone up on the history of *cangaço* at the Museu do Sertão, one of the city's few attractions.

Sertão Museum
The city's neo-classical municipal railway station building has housed the Museu de Sertão since 1983. One room exhibits material related to the navigation of the Rio São Francisco, northeastern folk culture, and the railroad that passes through town. The second room houses pulpits, shrines, and other religious items. The third room has an extensive collection of *cangaço* artifacts, from personal items belonging to Lampião and his band, to the 1930s posters offering a reward for his capture, dead or alive. One of the museum staff, Josias Valão dos Santos, is an

The scenery surrounding the mouth of the Rio São Francisco invites a trip by boat or buggy

attraction in and of himself: he had the dubious honor of arranging the heads of the dead bandits on the steps of city hall. He'll eagerly tell curious visitors the story, as well as those of his many other backland adventures.

Antigo prédio da estação ferroviária de Piranhas (the old Piranhas railway station building). Daily, 8am – 5:30pm.

PIAÇABUÇU

Piaçabuçu sits on the left bank of the Rio São Francisco, its main attraction. The town is very close to the river's mouth, and a boat or buggy trip to the spot where Old Chico's waters meet the sea is a must. Visitors should also try to visit **Praia do Pontal do Peba**, a beach famed for its shrimp fishing. Piaçabuçu is 138 kilometers (86 miles) south from Maceió by the AL-101 highway, and 26 kilometers (16 miles) east from Penedo along a good paved road.

MOUTH OF THE SÃO FRANCISCO RIVER

There are several departure points for boat trips on the last 13 kilometers (8 miles) of the Rio São Francisco, most of them near roadside bars along the road to Piaçabuçu. You can also prevail upon the boatmen who work in the city's quays. Tours normally take around two and a half hours round trip by fishing boat. You'll pass mangroves and dunes and make a stop near the river mouth so you can walk to where the waters meet, an environmentally protected area. Buggy trips will also take you there: tours last approximately three hours and cover 21 kilometers (13 miles). They cruise around Pontal do Peba beach, cross farms to the dunes, and then drop off visitors for the walk to the river's mouth. Instead of walking to the river's mouth, the more adventurous can go the last 3 to 5 kilometers

(about 2 to 3 miles) attached to a buggy-pulled parachute.
Contact: *Delta 1, tel. (82) 3552-1226, 9918-6991.*

PONTAL DO PEBA BEACH

Praia do Pontal do Peba is a 23-kilometer (14-mile) beach, 13 kilometers (8 miles) from the center of Piaçabuçu. The beach's fine, compact sand is backed by dunes, and the sands and waters draw sea turtles to lay their eggs and shrimp fishermen to ply their trade. Fishing is good, especially bait-casting. The beach can get crowded, particularly in areas where guesthouses and restaurants vie for space with fishermen's houses and summer homes.
Contact: *Mercator, tel. (82) 3557-1217, 3557-1363.*

ALONG THE WINDING SÃO FRANCISCO RIVER

The Rio São Francisco is born in Minas Gerais's Serra da Canastra mountain range. It then flows toward the Northeast, watering the otherwise dry land of four states. Its winding 3000-kilometer (1,850-mile) course divides Bahia from Pernambuco and Sergipe from Alagoas, then empties into the sea. The river flows through almost 500 municipalities, and, since 1847, towns not so lucky to sit along its banks have campaigned for the river's route to be diverted to cure their water shortages. Diversion projects are shelved and re-opened intermittently, always amid huge controversy. In Bahia, Old Chico slakes the thirst of Bom Jesus da Lapa, Barra, and Juazeiro, towns fervently devoted to the saint for whom the river is named. The river's current of mysticism is also evident in the *carrancas* – grotesque gargoyles placed on boat bows to ward off evil spirits. But modern technology has its place on the river, as well: Brazil's first hydroelectric plant, Angiquinho, was constructed on the Rio São Francisco in 1913. Today, the river is dammed at Sobradinho, Paulo Afonso, and Xingó, in Alagoas. In Petrolina, Pernambuco, the river irrigates fruit crops. Its potential for tourism, however, is only exploited in Canindé do São Francisco, Sergipe, and Piranhas, as well as in Penedo, Alagoas, at the scenic merging of its waters with the Atlantic Ocean.

"Barren Lives," or The Redefinition of Northeast Brazil in the Films of Nelson Pereira dos Santos

One of Brazil's most extraordinary films took five years to make. In 1958, Nelson Pereira dos Santos began to adapt Graciliano Ramos' classic book *Vidas Secas* (*Barren Lives*) for the screen. This story of northeastern Brazil grapples with drought, the accumulation of land by the wealthy, and the resulting tension between economic classes.

Nelson dos Santos chose Juazeiro, in the backlands of Bahia, as the setting for his film. But on Carnival Sunday in 1960, just as the first shot was being prepared, a downpour began. The rain continued for days, then weeks. The director who had revolutionized Brazilian cinema with *Rio 40 Degrees* (*Rio 40 Graus*) had been outmatched by a sullen sky.

The backlands turned into a sea. The filming of *Vidas Secas* was suspended, and for lack of another project, Nelson Pereira dos Santos decided to make a film from scratch. He would be the director and main actor. Thus did he create the film *Mandacaru Vermelho*, a masterpiece about a bloody family dispute that leads, on the spot of the violence, to the growth of a red mandacaru tree.

Three years later, Nelson returned to the northeastern backlands to attempt once more to film *Vidas Secas*. He brought with him Luís Carlos Barreto, a young photographer influenced by Henri Cartier-Bresson's work with direct, unfiltered light. The director imagined that this light could represent the blinding sun of the Northeast, the heat of the *caatinga* region, and the *seca* (drought) itself. He refused to beautify the Brazilian backlands, distancing himself from the elaborate photography of Mexico's Gabriel Figueroa. With *Vidas Secas*, dos Santos opened a chapter of Brazilian film in which cinematic image acquired a sensory quality. What was felt became more important than what was said.

The setting for the film also changed. The director this time chose to film in Palmeira dos Índios, Graciliano Ramos' setting for *Vidas Secas*. He hired an assistant, Jofre Soares, who would become one of the main actors in the film and eventually a star of Brazilian cinema. Jofre helped Nelson choose the local cast, including the excellent actors who play the boys Genival and Gilvan. Other actors came from Rio de Janeiro. The role of Sinhá Vitória was played by Maria Ribeiro, an old friend of the director and an employee of the Líder film laboratory. Átila Iório played the role of Fabiano.

The film's depiction of the exodus of Fabiano and Sinhá Vitória's family demonstrates why Nelson Pereira dos Santos is the acknowledged master of the last fifty years of Brazilian cinema. Each of his images seems essential to the story. There is nothing superfluous. Additionally, *Vidas Secas* is an entirely faithful adaptation of the novel. The film is as dense and spare as the book. Every moment, every silence, and every gesture is meaningful.

Extraordinary though it is, *Vidas Secas* had a very short run in cinemas. It was shown for only two weeks in Rio de Janeiro's Metro theaters, a chain owned by the American company Metro-Goldwyn-Mayer. A boycott that caused Brazilian movies to suffer in foreign distribution further limited the film's audience.

In that era, countries were responsible for choosing a film to represent their nation at the Cannes Film Festival. For 1963, the Brazilian government selected *Black God, White Devil* (*Deus e o Diabo na Terra do Sol*) by Glauber Rocha. However, in an unusual move, *Vidas Secas* was chosen by the festival for the official competition despite not having been officially nominated by Brazil. After Cannes, the film was applauded by the public and praised by critics.

More than forty-two years after its premiere, *Vidas Secas* has stood the test of time and remains more relevant than ever. *Vidas Secas* is more than great: it is a film that continues to inspire the whole of Brazilian cinema.

Walter Salles
Director of Foreign Land (Terra Estrangeira),
Central Station (Central do Brasil), Behind the Sun (Abril Despedaçado),
and The Motorcycle Diaries (Diários de Motocicleta).

After the rain, green sprouts rise from the parched earth of the backlands

PERNAMBUCO

One glance at a map of Pernambuco is enough to notice how different the state is. A narrow strip of land with only 187 kilometers (116 miles) of coastline, Pernambuco extends for 724 kilometers (450 miles) into the *sertão*. It was on this very stretch of coast that Portuguese nobleman Duarte Coelho landed in 1535 to assume the captaincy Dom João III conferred upon him. Future colonizers found a shore protected by reefs, which explains why the Indians nicknamed this land "Paranampuca" (Sea that Breaks on Rocks), a name that ultimately prevailed over the official Nova Lusitânia. The best way to familiarize oneself with Pernambuco is to begin in Recife and Olinda, twin colonial cities that offer the most historical insight into the region. Both preserve traces of their colonial history in their monuments and extraordinarily rich culture, and both share unique Carnival traditions: The *maracatu*, *caboclinhos*, and *frevo* groups, a mix of Portuguese, African and Indian cultures, originally practiced their arts on Pernambuco's sugarcane plantations. Starting out from Recife, follow the coast, where beaches with calm, warm waters appear amidst summer houses and sophisticated hotels. It's about 535 kilometers (332 miles) east from here to the beautiful archipelago of Fernando de Noronha. For a deeper knowledge of regional culture, visit the Zona da Mata, birthplace of the *maracatu rural* folk dance. Authentic native handicrafts are available in the nearby *agreste* region, as well as the semi-arid *sertão*, whose lands hide a harsh beauty.

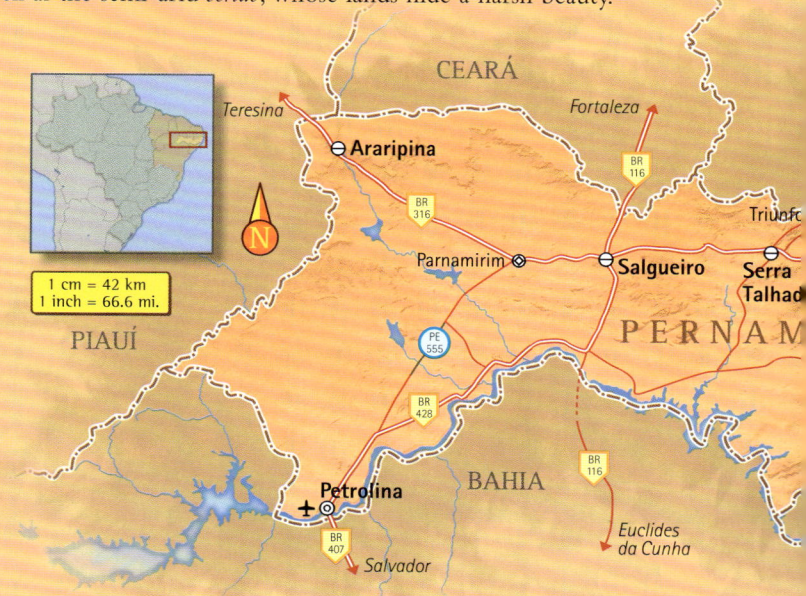

1 cm = 42 km.
1 inch = 66.6 mi.

Neo-classical buildings on Rua da Aurora, in the center of Recife

Highlights

- Explore the cultural routes and architecture of **Recife** and **Olinda**.
- Witness the natural beauty of **Cabo de Santo Agostinho** coast and **Tamandaré**.
- Marvel at an underwater paradise just off **Fernando de Noronha** island.
- See first-hand the traditional folklore and handicrafts of the **Zona da Mata** region.
- Follow the wine route of the *sertão* and check out ceramics from **Caruaru**, in the semi-arid *agreste* region.

When to go

- Summer brings crowds and higher prices to Pernambuco beaches, as well as Fernando de Noronha island and the surrounding archipelago. But pleasant temperatures make these areas accessible any time of year.
- Between **February** and **March**, the festivities of Carnival combine fun and folklore.
- In **June**, São João festivities bring fairs and bonfires to towns in the *agreste* and *sertão* regions.

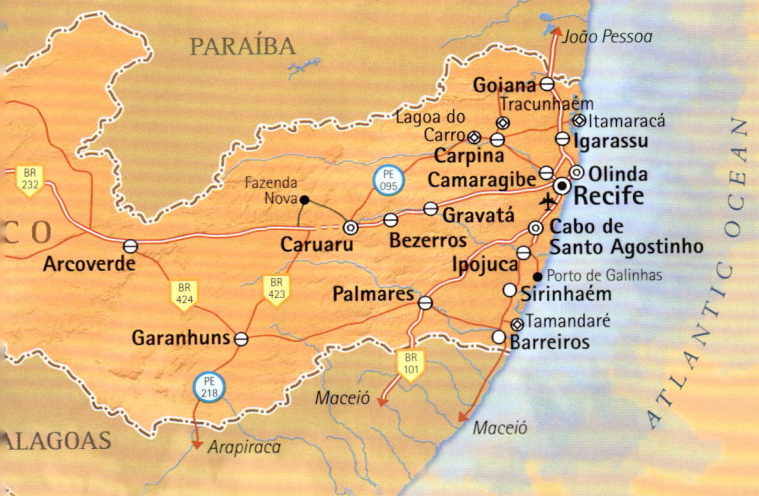

PERNAMBUCO

RECIFE

Born on the quays out of a natural anchorage spot, Recife began to expand beyond its coastal borders in 1537, giving rise to the modern-day neighborhoods of **Santo Antônio** and **São José**. In 1630, when the Dutch invaded the state, enslaved workforces operated 121 sugarcane plantations. The plantations along the Capibaribe River gave rise to such neighborhoods as Graças, Madalena, and Casa Forte. Becoming familiar with the history of Recife is best accomplished through guided tours, where you'll learn of its evolution from marshland – the Rio Capibaribe flows through the city – to the commercial center it is today. It also means enjoying the sun on the city beaches and those in the surrounding area, extending for 20 kilometers (12 miles) from **Maria Farinha** to **Candeias**. The best accommodation and services can be found in **Boa Viagem**, in the neighborhood of the same name. The neighboring cities, so close they can be reached in a few minutes from the city center, complement what the capital has to offer. The best views of Recife are those from lookout points in **Olinda**, just 7 kilometers (4 miles) to the north. Locals frequent Olinda bars, popular spots in Boa Viagem, and the neighborhood of Recife in equal measure.

For an idea of monthly events in Recife, consult the *Agenda Cultural*, a small booklet available from the

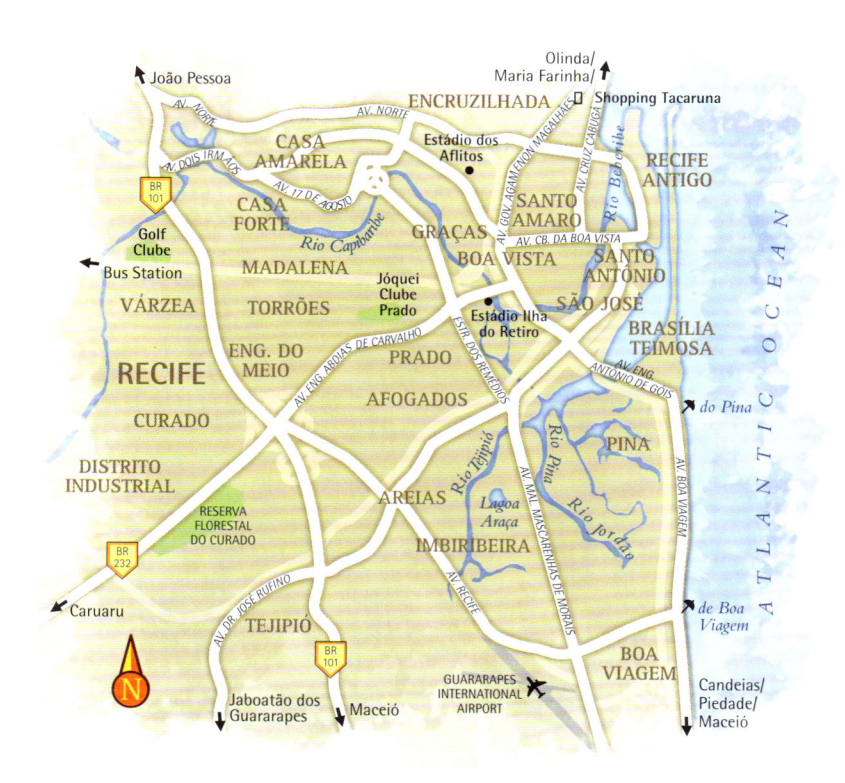

Boa Viagem beachfront and reef barrier

Centro de Informações Turísticas tourist center (*Rua da Guia, no #, tel. 81/3224-2361; Mon – Sat, 9am – 11pm; Sun, 9am – 10pm*). South of the capital is the metropolitan **Jaboatão dos Guararapes**. In addition to its upstanding seafront hotels, the city is home to **Igreja de Nossa Senhora dos Prazeres dos Montes Guararapes**. The church was built in 1782 on the site where Northeast colonists expelled the Dutch in 1654.

CITY BEACHES

Locals and visitors alike frequent the sands of **Pina** and **Boa Viagem**, as well as the neighboring **Piedade** and **Candeias** beaches in Jaboatão dos Guararapes. Boa Viagem leads the pack as best area beach, with a promenade featuring jogging paths and good eateries and restroom facilities. Young people congregate between Rua Félix de Brito and Rua Antônio Falcão, in front of the Acaiaca building. Pay attention to signs indicating where shark attacks occur, and remember surfing is prohibited. Our advice is to enjoy the sea only at low tide, and never cross the reef barrier.

TRIPS ON THE CAPIBARIBE RIVER

Catamaran trips down the Rio Capibaribe offer an unusual and thorough tour of central Recife areas. Boats embark at **Forte das Cinco**

SHARKS IN RECIFE

Swimming and surfing can be dangerous sports at the Pina and Boa Viagem beaches of Recife, and at Piedade and Candeias in Jaboatão dos Guararapes. Data from the Federal Rural University of Pernambuco lists 44 attacks by bull sharks (*Carcharhinus leucas*) and tiger sharks (*Galeocerdo cuvieri*) since 1992. Thirteen attacks were fatal. Most attacks occur on Boa Viagem beach, which experts attribute to an ecological imbalance caused by construction of the Suape port in the 1980s. Danger zones are marked along the shoreline. Swimming is permitted during low tide and in the more shallow inland pools, but forbidden beyond the protective reefs.

Pontas and pass through the neighborhoods of Recife's origin, from **Ilha de Santo Antônio** and **Ilha de São José** islands to **Boa Vista**. You'll pass under the **Ponte Maurício de Nassau** and **Ponte Buarque de Macedo,** bridges restored at the beginning of the 20th century. The trip continues past the **Paço Alfândega** monument, erected in 1826, and the 18th-century **Igreja da Madre de Deus** church, skirting the **Praça da República** square until the Rio Capibaribe intersectsthe **Rio Beberibe**. The tour ends at **Casa da Cultura** cultural center, among the multicolored houses of **Rua da Aurora**.
Contact: Catamarã Tours, tel. (81) 3424-2845, 9973-4077.

Forts

Forte do Brum rests at the entrance to the port of Recife (*Praça Comunidade Luso-Brasileira, no #, Recife Antigo, tel. 81/3224-4620; Tue – Fri, 9am – 4:30pm; Sat and Sun, 2pm – 5pm*). The Portuguese completed this structure of wattle and daub in 1629, only to see it stormed by the Dutch one year later. Following the invaders' expulsion in 1654, the fortress was rebuilt of stone. Dutch military erected their **Forte de São Tiago das Cinco Pontas** (*Praça Cinco Pontas, no #, São José, tel. 81/3224-8492; Tue – Fri, 9am – 6pm; Sat and Sun, 1pm – 5pm*), originally named Forte Frederik Hendrik, upon invading Brazil in 1630. Following Portuguese victory years later, locals rebuilt the then-demolished fort in stone, with a chapel dedicated to São Tiago. The nearby Museu da Cidade archives an interesting collection of antiquated Recife maps and photographs.

Historical Center

Recife's historical center, also called the Bairro de Recife or Recife Antigo, lies along a narrow strip of land between the Capibaribe River and the Atlantic Ocean. A total of 39 bridges cross the many canals and form a tropical Venice. A journey on foot is still the best bet for exploring the many influences of Recife's historical center, including several examples of Dutch and French architecture along with a blend of modern interventions. The Dutch presence in the city is strong, and of the urban development at the beginning of the 20th century, gave the Recife a French touch. This is where you will find **Porto do Recife**, a port never without the whistle of a departing ship, besides all the forts, colonial mansions, museums, and churchs. Take your time and enjoy the ice cream parlors and restaurants, and try fruit juices and coconut milk, which venders sell at almost every corner.

Marco Zero

Officially named Praça Barão do Rio Branco, Marco Zero (Ground Zero) marks the intersection of three major boulevards: Marquês de Olinda, Rio Branco, and Barbosa Lima Avenues. The roundabout offers a good vantage point for viewing the sea from amid the hustle and bustle of the city. These 20th-century avenues are laid out in a Parisian urban-planning style.
Notable sites surrounding the square include the **Instituto Cultural Bandepe** cultural art center, built in 1914 and restored in 2002, a cultural center that holds seasonal art

Pernambuco

1 - Parque das Esculturas
2 - Marco Zero
3 - Rua do Bom Jesus e Sinagoga Kahal Zur Israel
4 - Paço Alfândega, igreja da Madre de Deus e Chanteclair
5 - Capela Dourada
6 - Praça da República
7 - Mercado de São José
8 - Rua da Aurora
9 - Casa da Cultura
10 - Igreja N. S. da Conceição dos Militares
11 - Igreja Matriz de Santo Antônio
12 - Basílica de N. S. do Carmo
13 - Pátio de São Pedro
14 - Pátio do Terço

exhibitions; the **Associação Comercial do Recife** (trade association), from 1915, and the **Bolsa de Valores** stock exchange building, established 1912. Celebrated surrealist (and local artist) Cícero Dias (1907-2003) painted the square's wind rose.

SCULPTURE PARK

The Parque das Esculturas is a permanent exhibition of sculptures by local painter and sculptor Francisco Brennand. His 32-meter (105-foot)-high **Coluna de Cristal** (Crystal Column) rises above the other artworks. Along the day the park is accessible by boat from Marco Zero, it was built on a reef opposite to the site. Another way to get there is by car from the **Brasília Teimosa** neighborhood. Beside the park the **Casa de Banho** (*Arrecifes do Porto de Recife, Km 1, no #, Brasília Teimosa, tel. 81/3075-8776, 3467-9951; Wed and Thu, 11am – 5pm; Fri – Sun, 11am – 7pm*) bar offers a picturesque view of Recife, better yet when served with a cold beer and *caldinho de sururu* (shellfish broth). The bar's name (Bathhouse) refers to the community clubs of yesteryear, where locals swam together among the reefs.

BOM JESUS STREET

During the Dutch occupation of Recife (1630-1654), the trade concetrated center Rua do Bom Jesus was known as **Rua dos Judeus** (Jew Street). The end of Dutch occupation also marked the end of religious tolerance. Today, the street displays an eclectic style of well-preserved colorful buildings with balconies and protective turrets, accented by the occasional restaurant or bar with sidewalk tables. **Empório Bom Jesus** (*#183-A, tel. 81/3424-7474; Mon – Thu, 9am – 6pm; Fri, 9am – 8pm; Sun, 4pm – 9pm*) sells tapioca and *bolo-de-rolo* (jelly rolls) alongside Brazilian handicrafts. **Galerias** (*#35, tel. 81/3424-9371; Mon – Sat, 6am – midnight; Sun, 3pm – 11pm*), serves a traditional malted milk. The collection at **Ranulpho Galeria de Arte** (*#125, ground floor, tel. 81/3225-0068; Mon – Fri, 10am – 7pm*) encompasses works by Volpi, Siron Franco, and Lula Cardoso Ayres. The gallery also exhibits ruins of a stone wall the Dutch built to protect the city. On Sunday afternoons Rua do Bom Jesus is home to a bustling market with scores of stalls that offer an array of goods, from clothes to home décor to biscuits and cakes.

Palas Atena (Pallas Athena), by Francisco Brennand

KAHAL ZUR ISRAEL SYNAGOGUE

The first synagogue in the Americas was rediscovered after detailed archaeological work in the 18th century. Closed down in 1654 and recently restored in 2002, it serves as a memorial to the Jewish presence in Pernambuco during the Dutch occupation. Visitors to the Sinagoga Kahal Zur Israel – "Rock of Israel" – will observe the synagogue's walls as intact as they were when the building closed in 1654. Also note the *mikvê*, a kind of pool used for Jewish purification rituals.
Rua do Bom Jesus, 197 and 203, Recife Antigo, tel. (81) 3224-2128. Tue – Fri, 9am – 5pm; Sun, 3pm – 7pm.

Malakoff Tower Observatory

Temporary art and photography exhibitions occupy three floors of the Observatório Cultural Torre Malakoff, but the real treat of this 19th-century tower is the view from the top. On one side, the masts of ships at anchor form a screen against the backdrop of the horizon. On the other, old buildings rise from the city's historic center. A telescope is available for stargazers whose sights aim a bit more heavenly than the Recife seaside. Great to visit on a full moon evening.
Praça do Arsenal, no #, Recife Antigo, tel. (81) 3424-8704. Tue – Sun, 3pm – 8pm.

Apolo Theater

Joaquim Lopes de Barros Cabral Teive (1816-1892) designed the limestone façade carved in Portugal, triangular lintels, and curved balconies of the Teatro Apolo, a fine example of 19th-century architecture. Shortly after the theater opened in 1846, competition with the neighboring Teatro Santa Isabel in 1850 caused Apolo owners to shut its doors. It served as a warehouse for more than a century. Now restored, the theater houses one of the most comfortable cinemas and show venues in Recife.
Rua do Apolo, 121, Recife Antigo, tel. (81) 3224-1114. Mon – Fri, 8am – noon and 2pm – 6pm. Opening times vary by show.

Malakoff Tower, the venue for moonlit nights

The Jewish Presence in Dutch Brazil

Portuguese Sephardic Jews and Ashkenazi Jews moved here from Poland and Germany to escape the Inquisition, and they welcomed the arrival of the Dutch in Recife in 1630. Count Maurits of Nassau, the Calvinist governor of Dutch Brazil, established considerable religious tolerance in the colony, in accordance with the values of The Dutch West India Company. Jews engaged in trade on Rua do Bom Jesus (then the Rua dos Judeus), where the Zur Israel Synagogue was built in 1636. Portuguese Rabbi Isaac Aboab da Fonseca arrived to preside over the temple in 1641. It was Fonseca who, while in Recife, wrote the first piece of Hebrew literature in the Americas. His poem, "Mi Kamókha" (Who Is like Thee), tells of the Insurreição Pernambucana (a Portuguese campaign to regain Brazilian territory) and the dire poverty the Jewish community faced when the Portuguese expelled the Dutch. More than 400 Jews returned to Holland following expulsion of Dutch troops from Brazil in 1654. Twenty-three of them fled to New Amsterdam, the future New York City. There they formed the colonies' first Jewish community. Rabbi Fonseca moved to Amsterdam and opened a Portuguese synagogue in 1675.

Carnival in Recife

Carnival on the streets of Recife is one of the most democratic and diverse parties in the country. It begins a week before the actual holiday, when *frevo* and *maracatu* groups hold open rehearsals in clubs or even on the streets. The **Bloco da Saudade** carnival group has brought new life to old traditions with its women's choir and *pau e corda* orchestra (featuring string and woodwind instruments) since 1974, hosting very nostalgic, lively Carnival dances every year. On Carnival Friday in Recife more than 400 percussionists from 11 *maracatu* musical groups (called *nações*) in Recife play side by side under percussionist Naná Vasconcelos' direction. Rehearsals for the opening ceremony of Carnival festivities can be attended during the whole previous week at the city's Marco Zero. Saturday morning brings **Galo da Madrugada**, when more than two million people take over the streets of Santo Antônio, São José, and Boa Vista. The Galo is the largest, if not the most crowded, street Carnival group in the world. Several Recife hotspots keep the party alive from Saturday onward. **Pátio de São Pedro** courtyard presents traditional song and dance such as *coco de roda*, *afoxé*, *ciranda,* and *frevo*. The **Cais da Alfândega** quays become a stage for the **Rec Beat** festival, featuring popular names from the Brazilian rock and electronic scenes. Among the performances are musicians involved with the *mangue beat* movement, a combination of regional and imported rhythms originally developed by Chico Science (1966-1997) and his Nação Zumbi. Samba school parades march down **Avenida Guararapes.** On Monday **Pátio do Terço** hosts **Noite dos Tambores Silenciosos** (Night of the Silent Drums; *see page 198*). **Praça do Arsenal**, in Recife, is the departure point for many *blocos* (groups) representing traditions such as *maracatu*, *caboclinhos*, and the powerful, infectious rhythm of *frevo*. A program of Carnival events is released in advance every year and available at tourist information offices in Recife.

Madre Deus Cathedral

Priests from the Congregation of the Oratory (called Oratorians) completed work on the Igreja Concatedral da Madre Deus in 1720. Its original design being from 1679 though. Now a National Heritage Site, the cathedral comprises a nave and six side chapels.

Excited crowds celebrate day and night during Recife's street Carnival

Fire damage destroyed the 18th-century baroque ceiling carvings in 1970, but IPHAN, a government institution, has since restored them. The sacristy's Estremoz marble font is one of the finest in Brazil.
Rua da Alfândega (Rua da Madre Deus), no #, Recife Antigo, tel. (81) 3224-5587. Tue – Fri, 8am – noon and 2pm – 5pm; Sat, 8am –11am; Sun, 8am – noon.

PAÇO ALFÂNDEGA SHOPPING MALL
Originally built on the Capibaribe River to house Oratorians, the Paço Alfândega is now a National Heritage Site. It became the Pernambuco Customs building in 1826, and opened as a shopping mall at the end of 2003, after careful restoration work. Forty-six stores keep the mall chock-full of designer labels, including **Fause Haten** and **Herchcovitch**. **Ana Paes** sells clothes trimmed with hand-crafted lace and *fuxico* (flower appliqués made from leftover scraps of material). The highlight of the ground floor is the bookshop **Livraria Cultura** and, on the third floor, **Espaço Cultural Banco do Brasil** cultural center hosts regular film screenings.
Rua da Alfândega, 35, Bairro de Recife, tel. (81) 3419-7500. Mon – Sat, 10am – 10pm; Sun, noon – 9pm.

SANTO ANTÔNIO, SÃO JOSÉ AND BOA VISTA

Founded in the mid-17th century, the Santo Antônio, São José, and Boa Vista neighborhoods are home to important architecture, including the buildings that first formed Praça da República square and Pátio de São Pedro courtyard. Most of Recife's historical churches are also here, such as the **Igreja do Divino Espírito Santo** of 1641. Long walks are a great way to explore the narrow streets and of these neighborhoods and their Capibaribe River views. **Mercado de São José**, the city's trading post beside the **Basílica de Nossa Senhora da Penha** church (1880-1920), bustles with the liveliness and cheer of the Recife people.

República Square

Formerly on the grounds of Count Maurits of Nassau's gardens, the park at Praça da República covers 23,000 square meters (250,000 square feet). The state's government offices at **Palácio do Campo das Princesas** (1840) surround the square. The **Palácio do Campo das Princesas** (1840), **Teatro Santa Isabel** (1850), **Palácio da Justiça** (1928), and the **Liceu de Artes e Oficios** (1880), architectual gems inspired by French neo-classicism, complete the scene. French naturalist Emile Bérenger designed the park's gardens in 1875. Brazilian landscape artist Roberto Burle Max remodeled the square just 60 years later. An enormous African baoab tree (*Adansonia digitata*) looms impressively over the square, though the date of its planting remains unknown.

Santa Isabel Theater

French engineer Louis Léger Vauthier designed the classic pink façade and distinct archways of Teatro Santa Isabel. Destroyed by fire in 1869, this National Heritage Site received a full-blown restoration that included columns and iron parapets. A statue of the architect Vauthier stands at the building's entrance.
Praça da República, no #, Santo Antônio, tel. (81) 3232-2939. Schedule in advance.

Aurora Street

Formerly a marshland along the left bank of the Capibaribe River, the Rua da Aurora faces east, and gets its name from the first rays of the rising sun that grace the street at dawn (*aurora*). On the opposite bank is Rua do Sol, bathed in sunlight at dusk. The engineer who designed the nearby **Secretaria de Segurança Pública** (Department of Public Safety), former residence of the Count of Boa Vista, in 1842 also lent his hands to construction of the Santa Isabel Theater. Another institution of note is the **Ginásio Pernambucano**, built in 1885 and now the oldest operating school in the state. The 1920s witnessed the construction of the city's first apartment buildings, including **Montreal, Capibaribe** and **Iemanjá**.

MAMAM (Museum of Modern Art)

Housed in a charming manor on the Rua da Aurora, the collection at Museu de Arte Moderna Aloísio Magalhães (MAMAM) comprises nine hundred works and includes pieces by the likes of Alex Flemming, João Câmara, Francisco Brennand. Local artist Aloísio de Magalhães (1927-1982) lent his talent to the lobby's tiled mural – and earned himself a permanent place in the museum.
Rua da Aurora, 265, Boa Vista, tel. (81) 3232-1694. Tue and Thu – Sun, noon – 6pm; Wed, 8am – 6pm.

> ### Our Recommendation
>
> 🍽 Despite having changed owners several times since opening in 1882, **Leite** restaurant remains in Portuguese hands. Brazil has a visible influence on the international menu. A favorite haunt of politicians and businessmen alike, Leite reputedly serves the best *cartola* (fried banana and cheese sprinkled with sugar and cinnamon) in Recife. *Praça Joaquim Nabuco, 147, Santo Antônio, tel. (81) 3224-7977. Sun – Fri, 11am – 4pm.*
>
> *Additional information on page 358.*

The impressive Santa Isabel Theater has stood since Brazil's imperial era

SÃO LUIZ MOVIE THEATER

Cine São Luiz is the oldest movie theater in Recife. Outfitted with 1,200 seats, the main auditorium features stained-glass panels on either side of the silver screen. The large iron and glass doors at the theater's entrance remain intact from its opening in 1952, reminiscent of a time when evening dress for filmgoers was mandatory. A lobby mural by native Recife painter Lula Cardoso Ayres (1910-1987) welcomes visitors.
Rua da Aurora, 175, Boa Vista, tel. (81) 3207-3000. Opening hours vary according to the current program.

CASA DA CULTURA

After authorities decommissioned the Casa de Detenção de Recife (Recife's prison) in 1973, local merchants converted the penitentiary's 156 cells into this arts and crafts center. Ceramics from Alto do Moura, embroidery from Passira, clay pieces from Tracunhaém, and out-of-print books are among the good for sale.
Rua Floriano Peixoto, no #, São José, tel. (81) 3224-2850. Mon – Fri, 9am – 7pm; Sat, 9am – 6pm; Sun, 9am – 2pm.

RECIFE'S MARKETS

Markets in Recife are a synthesis of the flavors, smells, and colors of Pernambuco. Though French engineer Victor Lieutier designed **Mercado de São José** (*Praça Dom Vital, no #, São José, tel. 81/3424-2322, 3424-8221; Mon – Sat, 6am – 5:30pm; Sun, 6am – noon*) after traditional Parisian markets, its 46 pavilions sell authentic Pernambucan cuisine. You'll also find statues depicting *Orixás* of the *Xangô* (as *Candomblé* is called in Recife). In addition, you can find arts and crafts from the Zona da Mata, *agreste* and *sertão* regions of Pernambuco, including traditional toys, straw baskets, hammocks, and embroidered tablecloths. While the Mercado de São José attracts customers from around the globe, **Mercado de Casa**

Amarela (*Estrada do Arraial, 4000, Casa Amarela, tel. 81/3441-7998*) and **Mercado da Madalena** (*Rua Real da Torre, no #, Madalena, tel. 81/3227-6280 (public phone); Mon – Sat, 5am – 6m; Sun, 5am – 1pm*) draw a more local, low-profile crowd. Mercado de Casa Amarela is the second iron structure built in Recife. In 1930 the market was dismantled and moved from Caxangá to its present site. The Mercado da Madalena, formerly known as Mercado Bacurau because its bars honored patrons until the early morning hours (the bacurau is a nocturnal bird), is still the haunt of the city's bohemians, when its bars serve hot *macaxeira* (manioc) with chicken stew or roasted cheese as an end-of-the-night breakfast.

Nossa Senhora da Conceição dos Militares Church

Its lone bell tower goes almost unnoticed amidst the neon signs of the most commercial street in Recife. The real wealth of this church, however, is hidden inside: a statue of Nossa Senhora da Conceição (Our Lady of the Immaculate Conception), rests on an altar of rococo carvings in white and gold. Paintings of the Virgin Mary cover the ceiling, one of which portrays her pregnant and surrounded by angels. A mural above the choir depicts the Batalha dos Guararapes battle between Dutch and Portuguese forces in 1648. This National Heritage Site, was built in the 18th century by the Irmandade dos Sargentos e Soldados do Terço da Infantaria da Guarnição de Recife, a local military brotherhood.
Rua Nova, 309, Santo Antônio, tel. (81) 3224-3106. Mon, Tue, Thu and Fri, 8am – noon and 2pm – 4pm; Sat and Sun, 8am – noon (closed on Wed).

Nossa Senhora do Carmo Basilica and Convent

Highlights of the 18th-century Basílica and Convento de Nossa Senhora do Carmo include the main chapel ceiling painted in blue and gold, completed in 1767, and the altar, where the same colors are applied to rococo carvings. The high ceilings create space for the balconies with their ornate balustrades, which encircle the whole nave; the balconies themselves contain paintings with richly carved borders. Built on the former site of the Palácio Boa Vista, the **Igreja de Santa Teresa da Ordem Terceira do Carmo** features a rococo frontispiece that dates back to 1803 and a ceiling divided in 40 gilded tiles, each depicting a scene from the life of Saint Teresa.
Avenida Dantas Barreto, no #, Santo Antônio, tel. (81) 3224-3341. Mon, 6am – 5pm; Tue – Fri, 6am – 7pm; Sat, 6am – 1pm; Sun, 8am – 1pm and 6pm – 8pm.

Matriz de Santo Antônio Church

Those hoping to escape the bustle of Praça da Independência can seek solitude at this nearby cathedral, also called Santíssimo Sacramento. Built between 1753 and 1790, the church combines baroque touches with elements introduced in later renovations, such as the 19th-century ceiling painting by Sebastião da Silva Tavares.
Praça da Independência, Santo Antônio, tel. (81) 3224-5076. Mon – Fri, 7am – noon and 2pm – 6pm; Sat, 4pm – 7pm; Sun, 7am – noon and 4pm – 7pm.

Gold Chapel

The greatest example of baroque architecture in Recife is the richly decorated, 18th-century Capela Dourada. Gold leaf adorns the altar, walls, and ceiling. Now a National Heritage Site belonging to the **Convento Franciscano**, the complex also includes the **Igreja de Santo Antônio** church and the old Hospital dos Terceiros Franciscanos. The nearby **Museu Franciscano de Arte Sacra** exhibits religious art from the 18th century.

Rua do Imperador Dom Pedro II, no #, Santo Antônio, tel. (81) 3224-0530. Mon – Fri, 8am – 11:30am and 2pm – 5pm; Sat, 8am – 11:30am.

São Pedro Courtyard

Rows of colorful, turreted houses form the Pátio de São Pedro, one of few courtyards reminiscent of colonial Brazil. The striking stone façade of the **Concatedral de São Pedro dos Clérigos** dominates the square, which is a National Heritage Site. Today, bars and restaurants occupy the old one- and two-storied houses. **Buraquinho** *(#28, tel. 81/3224-3765; Mon, 11am – 4pm; Tue – Sat, 11am – 9pm)* serves traditional northeastern dishes and **Casa do Carnaval** *(#52, tel. 81/3224-2739; Mon, Wed, and Thu, 9am – 6pm; Tue and Fri, 9am – 10pm; closed on Sat)* explores the study of regional folklore. On Tuesday nights, Pátio de São Pedro becomes a stage for **Terça-feira Negra**, a musical event promoting Afro-Brazilian culture.

Rosário dos Pretos Church

Built between 1739 and 1777 as a place of worship for slaves, the Igreja do Rosário dos Pretos is predominantly rococo in style. The entire church is protected by the historic preservation group Iphan. The façade is decorated with stone

Gilded carvings in the baroque Capela Dourada

Pátio de São Pedro faces the stone façade of Concatedral de São Pedro dos Clérigos

carving of exceptional quality. The highlight of the interior is a fine statue of the Virgin, most likely dating from the 18th century. The church is best known in Recife as the departure point for the traditional *Cortejo do Rei do Congo* (Royal Procession of the King of Congo). This ritual procession originated with slaves brought from Africa to work on sugar plantations in colonial-era Pernambuco. The creation of the procession and its attendant rituals mark the origin of the *maracatu* tradition in Recife.

Rua Estreita do Rosário, no #, Santo Antônio, tel. (81) 3224-3929. Mon – Fri, 9am – 5pm; Sun, 7am – 9am.

Night of the Silent Drums

Every year on the Monday of Carnaval, throngs of *maracatu* groups and other celebrants gather in the courtyard of the 18th-century Igreja da Nossa Senhora do Terço to pay tribute to blacks who died in the days of slavery. They pound away on their drums all day and all night, with one exception. At midnight, all the drums stop and the lights are turned off, as the crowd observes a moment of silence to symbolically commemorate the colonial-era prohibition against African cultural and religious practices. This tradition is known as *maracatu-nação* to differentiate Recife's customs from the rural practice of *maracatu* that originated in the Zona da Mata area. Though locals have only gathered to celebrate this specific event since 1968, the tradition of *maracatu-nação* can be traced back to 1650. Another aspect of the tradition is meant to enact through music and dance the coronation ceremony of an African king and queen. Ironically, however, the accompanying procession more closely matches European royal traditions. The procession is also known as the *Cortejo do Rei do Congo* (Royal Procession of the King of Congo) because a majority of the slaves that were brought to Brazil came from the Congo.

Surrounding Areas

The neighborhoods farther from the center (and coast) of Recife are traditionally called "*arredores*" (surrounding areas), though they are still part of the city. These developed from farms and sugar plantation lands along the Capibaribe River, which still preserve a country atmosphere as in the **Poço na Panela** and **Apipucos** neighborhoods. Here visitors will find some of Recife's most important museums, such as the **Museu do Homem do Nordeste** (Museum of Northeastern People). Nearby Várzea boasts **Oficina Francisco Brennand**, a pottery workshop in the former São João sugar plantation.

Pasárgada Museum
Writer Manuel Bandeira (1886-1968) spent his childhood in this house. An exhibit of the poet's personal possessions is available for perusal. The museum's name refers to one of his most famous poems. Pasárgada is a virtual kingdom, where the poet could do everything he couldn't do in real life. There is also a bookshop on site.
Rua da União, 263, Boa Vista, tel. (81) 3134-3013. Mon – Fri, 8am – 6pm.

State Museum
The Baron of Beberibe's family owned this 19th-century mansion prior to its preservation as a national treasure. Though the museum is currently under renovation, most of its collection has been transferred to the Espaço Cícero Dias annex, opened in 2003. Chinese and English porcelain, 17th- and 18th-century furniture, paintings by Telles Júnior, and ritual Candomblé objects are among the objects on display.
Avenida Rui Barbosa, 960, Graças, tel. (81) 3427-9322. Tue – Fri, 10am – 5pm; Sat and Sun, 2pm – 5pm.

Poço da Panela
Nineteenth-century buildings line the cobblestone streets of this neighborhood, built on the former grounds of the Casa Forte sugar plantation along the Capibaribe River. Dating back to 1772, the Igreja de Nossa Senhora da Saúde church (*Rua Real do Poço, no #*), stands out amidst Imperial palms. Cold beer and cheese sandwiches are made to order at **Mercearia do Vital**, right on the church square, where sidewalk tables offer a calm respite to match your surroundings.

Jaqueira Park
Formerly a farm on the banks of the Capibaribe River, the charming Parque da Jaqueira is among the city's most enchanting places. Jackfruit, olive, and *jambo* trees ornament the 1-kilometer (0.6-mile) jogging path that skirts the park, which also features designated areas for cycling and roller-skating and a children's playground. An 18th-century chapel dedicated to Nossa Senhora da Conçeição (Our Lady of the Immaculate Conception) but known as the Capela da Jaqueira,

---

Our Recommendation

🍽 Recife delicatessen **Casa dos Frios**, has been dishing out its acclaimed *bolo-de-rolo* (jelly rolls) and *bolo Sousa Leão* cakes since 1957. The two cake recipes that are exclusive to Recife. *(Avenida Rui Barbosa, 412, Graças; tel. 81/3421-1259. Mon – Wed, 8am – 7pm; Thu – Sat, 8m – 8pm; Sun, 8am – 1pm).*

Additional information on page 358.

shares the premises, and houses murals depicting the story of Saint Joseph. The chapel's altarpiece and pulpit have gold covered rococo carvings. Roberto Burle Marx designed a garden to enhance the park, now a National Heritage Site, in 1970.
Avenida Rui Barbosa, no #, Jaqueira, tel. (81) 3447-8025. Daily, 5am – 10pm.

Art Galleries
Two galleries in Recife offer visitors a view of the contemporary art production in Pernambuco.
Galeria Amparo 60 (*Avenida Domingos Ferreira, 92, Boa Viagem, tel. 81/3325-4728; Mon – Fri, 9am – 6pm; Sat, 10am – 1pm*) exhibits works by some of the most reputable contemporary artists in Recife and Olinda, such as Christina Machado, Rinaldo, José Patrício, and Paulo Meira. **Galeria Mariana Moura** (*Avenida Rui Barbosa, 735, Graças, tel. 81/3421-3725; Mon – Fri, 10am – 7pm; closed on Sat*), showcases talent from Marcelo Silveira, Gil Vicente, Alexandre Nóbrega, and Janine Toledo, among others.

Francisco Brennand Ceramics Factory
The Brennand family turned this former colonial sugar plantation into a ceramics factory in 1971. Artist Francisco Brennand presides over the grounds, magically landscaped with sculptures, gardens, lakes with black swans. Roberto Burle Marx designed the square that separates Brennand's workshop from the Accademia, an area dedicated to Francisco's permanent collection of paintings and drawings. Visits may be arranged in advance and will take a whole afternoon. A pleasant café with a small store complements the visit.
Propriedade Santos Cosme e Damião, no #, access via Avenida Caxangá, Várzea, tel. (81) 3271-2466. Mon – Thu, 8am – 5pm; Fri, 8am – 4pm.

Jaqueira Park offers leisure opportunities on the banks of the Capibaribe River

SCIENCE AND ART IN DUTCH BRAZIL

Count Maurits of Nassau arrived in Recife in 1637, accompanied by an entourage of 46 scholars that included, among others, naturalists Georg Marcgrave and Willem Piso. While Marcgrave compiled the first compendiums of the fauna and flora of the new continent, painters Frans Post (1612-1680) and Albert Eckhout (1610-1665) recorded the landscape and inhabitants of Pernambuco in minute detail, especially the Indians and black slaves. The efforts of Nassau's group resulted in an unprecedented historic and scientific heritage. Eckhout left a collection of eight huge paintings of Brazilian peoples, several smaller oils-on-canvas, watercolors, and drawings of plants. Post's oil depictions of Frederik Hendrik Fort, renamed the Cinco Pontas Fort can be found at the Ricardo Brennand Institute.

THE RICARDO BRENNAND INSTITUTE

Francisco's cousin, Ricardo Brennand, opened his eponymous learning center, the Instituto Ricardo Brennand, in 2002. The two Gothic buildings look like a medieval castle. It houses the Institute's Castelo (castle), Pinacoteca (art gallery), and Biblioteca (library). The exceptional collection comprises valuable paintings, maps, manuscripts, books, and coins produced over the 24 years the Dutch occupied the Northeast. Among the highlights are 17 canvasses by Frans Post, including a depiction of the Frederik Hendrik Fort of 1630, and a trove of medieval arms and armor.
Alameda Antônio Brennand, no #, Várzea, tel. (81) 2121-0352. Tue – Sun, 1pm – 5pm.

MUSEUM OF NORTHEASTERN PEOPLES

The Museu do Homem do Nordeste offers an excellent opportunity to learn the origins of northeastern culture. Owned by the Fundação Joaquim Nabuco foundation and operated since 1979, the museum is divided into three exhibits: "Açúcar" (Sugar) illustrates the historical and technological aspects of sugarcane cultivation; "Oh de Casa!" (Anyone Home?), showcases decorative and utilitarian objects essential to life in the Northeast; and "Antropologia" (Anthropology) features articles inspired by folklore and religion. The museum is currently closed due to restoration work begun in 2005. No fixed date has been set for its reopening.
Avenida 17 de Agosto, 2187, Casa Forte, tel. (81) 3073-6332. Tue – Sun, 8am – 5pm.

GILBERTO FREYRE FOUNDATION

The controversial anthropologist Gilberto Freyre published 89 books in his lifetime about Brazilian and northeastern society. The author of the 1933 classic *Casa-Grande & Senzala* (published in English as *The Masters and the Slaves*), today in its 50th edition, lived and wrote in this house, which he nicknamed Vivenda Santo Antônio de Apipucos. The Fundação Gilberto Freyre library shelves titles from an array of topics and features distinct Portuguese tiled murals.
Rua Dois Irmãos, 320, Apipucos, tel. (81) 3441-1733. Mon – Fri, 9am – 5pm.

The World According to Pernambuco

You may have heard that Pernambucans are immodest. Well, modesty aside, Pernambuco is the richest and most culturally diverse state in Brazil. Our cultural spectrum is a gift, a calling, which appears in our music and literature, and displays a unique dimension in the fine arts.

Wherever you travel on this long stretch of land that unfolds from the Atlantic westward to the backlands, you won't find a piece of art untouched by nature. Even works that incorporate synthetic materials possess an essence of the earth, much like the art that the ancient masters created. Traditional art is powerful in Pernambuco, always alive and fresh, constantly reinventing itself. For example, the clay figurines from Alto do Moura, made famous by Vitalino Pereira dos Santos, come from a long tradition that continues with the work of Manuel Eudócio, a contemporary of the *mestre* (master) from Caruaru. Sculptor Ana das Carrancas, from Petrolina, was recently honored with the Ordem do Mérito Cultural (Order of Cultural Merit), a distinction awarded by the Ministry of Culture. The list goes on, becoming longer with the addition of each new generation, as storied artisan families put new hands to old traditions.

My admiration for folk art grew in strength and scope during the late 1960s, when my involvement in party politics gave me the opportunity to travel around Pernambuco. I was able to meet some of the greatest artisans of the time, and so my old passion, which had started at the street markets in Zona da Mata, where I was born and raised, grew bigger. The small clay animal figurines inspired by the work of Mestre Vitalino kindled that passion in me. During these long trips around Pernambuco's backlands, I saw for the first time the religious statues of Ibimirim, and Petrolina's famed *carrancas* – grotesque gargoyles placed on boat bows to ward off evil spirits.

What were toys for a boy turned into a grown man's indulgence. Folk art is ultimately one of the most gratifying ways to discover what has been called "the soul of Pernambuco." This soul is a mixture of various cultures from at least three continents: America, Africa, and Europe. It can sometimes be all smiles, and at other times, it conveys a heartbreaking sadness.

Some people might ask me whether, after almost forty years on this earth, it is still possible for me to be surprised by the folk art produced in Pernambuco. Of course! Today, the influences are even more varied than in the past. Media has broadened the artists' repertoire of themes. They are no longer limited to portraying life in their hometown.

The sacred and the profane, however, continue to walk hand in hand, as is evident during the patron-saint festivities held in countless Brazilian towns. The influence of so-called highbrow culture over folk art has also grown considerably, making it more difficult to tell the two apart. In the last few years, many folk art representatives have showcased their work in some of the most important galleries and cultural centers in Brazil. This is only natural for the country that introduced such folk talents as Cícero Dias and Vicente do Rego Monteiro to the international art world.

It is also only natural for Pernambuco's artists to record, in their unique way, the beauty of this region, which has touched artists worldwide over the last four centuries. The Spanish, Portuguese, Dutch, Germans, British, French – all of them left Pernambuco convinced that the natural wealth seen here was unrivaled.

Our sun, our sea, and our nature – coastal or inland – offer a singular blend of lights, colors, and sensations. Recife and Olinda require no introduction, but for anyone coming to Pernambuco, these twin cities offer just a taste of the artistic wealth that flourishes from the coast to the backlands and the borders at the far ends of the state.

In the state capital, Recife, there are plenty of places where a visitor can experience some of this wealth. A place to start is Mercado de São José, which offers a suitable window into Pernambuco's way of life. At this market, in the Santo Antônio neighborhood, Pernambuco will seduce your eyes, nose, and palate. In Olinda, the locale of choice for many artists' studios, folk art can be found at Portal das Artes and Ateliê da Barbearia. If you have the time, don't miss the Centro de Artesanato de Pernambuco, an arts-and-crafts center in Bezerros.

If the above evidence has not refuted, in every mind, the notion that the people of Pernambuco have pretentious delusions of grandeur, it is worth mentioning that Unesco has recognized Alto do Moura as the greatest center of representational art in the Americas.

Jarbas Vasconcelos
Governor of Pernambuco
and collector of Brazilian folk art

This woodcut print by J. Borges depicts a psychoanalyst and his patient

Olinda

One of the most important historical cities in Brazil, Olinda also plays host to one of the liveliest Carnival celebrations in the country. This city of old colonial buildings is home to friars and nuns, wild merrymakers, fast-talking young guides, artists, and folk musicians. Tourists come here for the city's beautiful views of the sea, coconut groves. The state capital, Recife, only 7 kilometers (4 miles) to the north, is visible from various lookout points. Olinda was founded by the Portuguese nobleman Duarte Coelho in 1535, sacked and burned by the Dutch in 1631, and rebuilt during the Restauração Pernambucana (restoration period) in 1654. Today, the city is divided into two areas: the Cidade Baixa (lower city) and the Cidade Alta (upper city). Cidade Baixa, the flat region by the sea, is home to many people working in nearby Recife; Cidade Alta, the historical section, is a Unesco World Heritage Site. Despite Unesco's protection, Olinda still suffers from the effects of unauthorized construction, poorly planned urban growth in the surrounding neighborhoods, and the daily threat of the advancing sea. A walk through Olinda's steep streets requires stamina and a little patience – guides and street vendors loudly hassle passersby. Tourists flock to the city's crowded beaches and take long walks along the popular promenade.

1. Museu de Arte Sacra de Pernambuco
2. Catedral da Sé
3. Igreja e Mosteiro de São Bento
4. Igreja de N. S. da Misericórdia
5. Igreja de N. S. da Graça e Seminário de Olinda
6. Conjunto do Convento de São Francisco
7. Igreja e Convento de N. S. da Conceição
8. Igreja de N. S. do Monte

Olinda's Cidade Alta, a Unesco World Heritage Site

LOOKOUT POINTS

Mirantes are everywhere in Olinda. The two most popular *mirantes*, accessible on foot from the sloping street called Ladeira da Misericórdia, are the benches in front of **Igreja de Nossa Senhora da Misericórdia** church and **Alto da Sé**. The latter site, where the Sé Cathedral stands, is the highest point in Olinda. Be sure to walk backward up the steep street in order to take in the view as it gradually unfold beneath you. Ladeira da Sé, another street that leads up to the *mirantes*, is not as steep, but it lacks some of the charm of Ladeira da Misericórdia. The Igreja de Nossa Senhora da Misericórdia church stands at the top of Ladeira da Misericórdia. From the curved benches at the front of the church, visitors can see the famous four corners of Olinda – the point where the four main town roads cross – as well as houses surrounded by tall coconut palms and leafy mango trees, church towers, the sea, the Capibaribe River, and, farther off, the port city of Recife. The Sé Cathedral, set on the Alto da Sé, is one block away. From the Alto da Sé, you can get the best views of neighboring Recife and the roofs of the old houses and churches of the Cidade Alta. If possible, watch the sunset from here and try the popular crispy tapioca or roasted cheese on a skewer from the Alto da Sé street market.

OUR RECOMMENDATION

🍽 Tiny **Bodega de Véio**, a grocery store-cum-bar, serves its cold cuts sliced to order and its beer cold. It attracts a varied clientele and tends to become crowded by the end of the afternoon (*Rua do Amparo, 212, Carmo, tel. (81) 3429-0185; Mon – Sat, 8am – 11pm; Sun, 8am – 2pm*).

At the **Oficina do Sabor** restaurant, chef César Santos's popular dishes include tasty fried beef jerky served with manioc purée and pumpkin *farofa* (seasoned manioc rough flour) or shrimp-stuffed pumpkin with pitanga fruit or mango sauce. The restaurant provides patrons with a lovely view of Olinda alongside its tasty dishes (*Rua do Amparo, 335, Cidade Alta, tel. 81/ 3429-3331; Tue – Thu, noon – 4pm and 6pm – midnight; Fri, noon – 4pm and 6pm – 1am; Sat, noon – 1am; Sun, noon – 5pm*).

Additional information on page 358.

Giant dolls parade through Olinda on the Tuesday that's the last day of Carnival

Amparo Street

Rua do Amparo is an old street lined with studios, museums, and stores. **Iza do Amparo** (*#159, Amparo, tel. 81/3429-2357; daily, 10am – 10pm*) sells painted tablecloths and bedcovers, as well as acrylic canvasses. The **Vilanova** studio (*#224, Amparo, tel. 81/3439-7629, 9972-9162; daily, 8am – 8pm*) primarily showcases oil paintings with folklore themes, while urban and historical scenes fill the creative panels of **Tereza Costa Rego**'s studio (*#242, Amparo, tel. 81/3429-2008; visits must be arranged in advance*). The utilitarian ceramics of **Betty Gattis** and the multi-colored canvasses of **Jairo Arcoverde** are on display at **BG/JA** (*#135, Amparo, tel. 81/3429-3479; Mon – Sat, 9:30am – 9:30pm; Sun, 9:30am – 5pm*). **Roberto Lúcio** uses a combination of wood, leather, steel, rags, and photographs to create his rich panels, while his daughter **Marina Mendonça** makes ceramics; both work out of the same private studio (*#293, Amparo, tel. 81/3494-2292, 3429-2141, 8847-9150; visits must be arranged in advance*).

Markets

Mercado da Ribeira (*Rua Bernardo Vieira de Melo, no #, Varadouro, tel. 81/3429-7706; daily, 9am – 6pm*) is home to 16 stalls that sell handcrafts and local art. **Mercado Eufrásio Barbosa** (*Avenida Sigismundo Gonçalves, no #, Varadouro, tel. 81/3439-2911; Mon – Sat, 9am – 6pm*), located at the entrance to the town, features craft stalls, snack bars, and stores selling every type of food imaginable. A 250-seat theater, also on the market's premises, is home to the *maracatu* dance-and-percussion group **Nação Pernambuco**, and opens on weekends for local performances.

Pernambuco Sacred Art Museum

Located in Alto da Sé, this 16th-century building has served as the Town

Council building, a bishop's residence, a school, an army headquarters, and a convent. The collection at the Museu de Arte Sacra includes colonial paintings created by native Indians in Jesuit workshops in Bogotá, Cuzco, La Paz, Quito, and other colonial cities. The collection also showcases folk artists' wood, clay, and plaster sculptures, as well as a room of old maps and a detailed inventory of Olinda's monuments.
Rua Bispo Coutinho, 726, Alto da Sé, tel. (81) 3429-0032. Mon – Fri, 9am – 12:30pm.

Masks and Dolls

Mestre Julião's brightly colored paper mâché masks depict devils, animals with prominent horns, and human faces with exaggerated features. Widely worn throughout Olinda's Carnival, the masks are available for sale at **Ateliê Julião das Máscaras** (*Avenida Joaquim Nabuco, 1102, Varadouro, tel. 81/3439-5439/9129-6318; daily, 2pm – 8pm*). Giant dolls (bonecos) that stand approximately 3.6 meters (11.8 feet) tall and weigh up to 50 kilos (110 pounds) are another Olinda Carnival tradition. Produced mainly by the artist **Silvio Botelho**. The dolls cost around R$3,000, or about US$1,400. Botelho's studio (*Rua do Amparo, 45, Carmo, tel. 81/3439-2443/9966-3344; Mon – Sat, 8am – noon and 2pm – 6pm*) is open to the public. The **Museu do Mamulengo** (*Rua do Amparo, 59, Amparo, tel. 81/3439-3495*) has a collection of more than 700 dolls, but structural problems within the building have kept the museum closed with no date set for reopening.

Carnival on the Streets of Olinda

Samba schools, *maracatu* dancers and musicians, and a number of other groups draw an annual crowd of two million revelers to the steep, narrow streets of Olinda's Cidade Alta. The city hall has divided the town into "theme areas" (*frevo, maracatu*) that vary from year to year. The truly impressive variety of traditions and cross-cultural influences present at carnival are best demonstrated by its musical and dancing groups' offerings, which include *caboclinhos* (dancers and players that show off indigenous traditions), *Afoxés* (Candomblé), *ursos* ("bears," whose style is inspired by European gypsy traditions), and the *blocos* and *troças* that follow the *bonecos* (giant dolls) along the streets. The partying continues around the clock, with an estimated 350 groups – each with its own orchestra, themes, colors, and audience – parading by. Each group holds a separate parade. Perennial performance groups include: Pitombeira dos Quatro Cantos, Elefante, Vassourinhas, Lenhadores, Grêmio Lítero Recreativo Eu Acho é Pouco, Enquanto Isso na Sala de Justiça, and Bacalhau do Batata, whose parade marks the end of the festivities on Ash Wednesday. On Monday, the *maracatu* groups meet in the Cidade Tabajara neighborhood before parading through the steep streets. The creative costumes of the various groups are always a highlight of the festivities: performers wear papier-mâché masks from Julião das Máscaras's studio, as well as homemade outfits representing everyone from super-heroes to international public figures. The *bonecos* also attract a fair amount of attention; one of the *bonecos*, the Homem da Meia-Noite ("Midnight Man"), has been kicking off the festivities at midnight on Saturday since its creation in 1932. A large number of *bonecos* gather on Tuesday, during the traditional Encontro dos Bonecos. Several other older members of the *bonecos* "family" can be seen parading to the sound of *frevo* orchestras: Mulher do Meio-Dia ("Mid-day Woman"), created in 1967, Filho do Homem da Meia-Noite ("Son of the Midnight Man"), from 1980, and Menino and Menina da Tarde ("Afternoon Boy and Girl"), from 1974. A complete schedule of performances is usually available two weeks before Carnival in hotels, guesthouses, restaurants, and public places.

Brazilian Fiddle House

Mestre Salustiano, also known as Mestre Salu, is a local with deep knowledge of regional folk culture. This is his workshop, the Casa da Rabeca do Brasil. Mastre Salu's father, Manuel Salustiano Soares, was the founder of the *maracatu* group known as Maracatu Piaba de Ouro (Golden Piaba Fish). Mestre Salu has been at the forefront of the movement to preserve several culturally significant rhythms and dances, including a variation on *maracatu* known as *maracatu rural*, or *maracatu de baque-solto*, *caboclinhos* (a performance of indigenous origin), and circle dances like *coco* and *ciranda*. Every year during Carnival, he presides over a meeting of Olinda's *maracatu* groups, bringing together the slow, rhythmic percussion of the urban *maracatu* style, also called *maracatu de baque-virado*, and the fast-tempo orchestras of the *maracatu rural*. Casa da Rabeca also runs a year-round program featuring popular artists, most of whom perform the traditional style of *forró* known as *pé-de-serra* (usually played by an accordion, triangle, and *zabumba* drum trio), and the improvised verses of the *repentistas*. The fiddle-playing *repentistas* are like cowboy-poets, or backland rappers, who improvise lyrics on the spot as they voice their feelings about personal tribulations or current events. *Rua Curupira, 125, Cidade Tabajara, tel. (81) 3371-8246. Shows on Sat, 8pm; Sun, 5pm.*

São Bento Monastery and Church

With its heavy jacaranda doors, fine, gilded cedar carvings on the high altar, and intricate ceiling paintings depicting the life of São Bento, the Igreja de São

---

The Olinda Art Circuit

Art studios line the streets of Olinda. Some have fixed visiting hours, while others require pre-arranged appointments. Particularly worth a visit are the studios of **João Câmara**, a painter from Paraíba and master of magic realism (*Rua das Pernambucanas, 420, tel. 81/3222-1563; call ahead*) and watercolorist **Guita Charifker** (*Rua Saldanha Marinho, 206, tel. 81/3429-1758*). An Olinda painter and former sailor, **J. Calazans** describes his paintings, with their heavy strokes and strong colors, as "neo-primitive" (*Ladeira da Misericórdia, 155, 1ª floor, Alto da Sé, tel. 81/3439-7756, 9192-3793; daily, 9am – 8pm; summer (Dec.-Feb.), until 10pm*). **Roberto Lúcio**, from Paraíba, is an important contemporary artist who creates unique panels and installations using a variety of different materials (*Rua do Amparo, 293, 1ˢᵗ floor, tel. 81/3429-2141; call ahead*). **Tereza Costa Rego**'s wood panels depict historical scenes, like old nightclubs on the quays of the port of Recife (*Rua do Amparo, 242, tel. 81/3429-2008*). Olinda and northeastern culture inspire the naïf oil paintings of **Gina** (*Rua Henrique Dias, 145, tel. 81/3493-5060*). **José Cláudio** covers his figurative canvasses with colorful, generous brush strokes (*Rua Geraldo Silva, 185, tel. 81/3429-3595*). **Luciano Pinheiro** creates multi-colored, abstract paintings (*Rua Bispo Coutinho, 828, tel. 81/3429-0232*). **Marianne Perretti**, a Frenchwoman who has settled in Pernambuco, makes beautiful stained glass (*Rua Coronel Joaquim Cavalcanti, 511, tel. 81/3429-1308*). The incredibly detailed carvings of **Gilvan Samico** made him one of the greatest names in woodcut prints in Brazil. A reserved man, he prefers to work behind closed doors (*tel. 81/9113-3998/9673-0035; ask for Joseane*). Works by these artists, as well as others, are showcased at the annual **Olinda Arte em Toda Parte**, an arts festival that takes place in late November and early December. During the festival artists across Olinda open their studio doors and increase their production (*information center: Ladeira da Misericórdia, 86, Carmo, tel. 81/3429-1750*).

Baroque art in the sacristy of São Bento Church dates from 1599

Bento is one of the richest churches in Olinda. The sandstone columns supporting the heavy choir and the finely carved pulpit and refined sacristy set it apart from other churches. The church and monastery were constructed in the late 16th century in a predominantly baroque style. One of the country's first law schools opened here in the 19th century and operated under the auspices of the church. On Sundays at 10am, monks open the church doors and accompany mass with Gregorian chants.
Rua de São Bento, no #, Varadouro, tel. (81) 3429-3288. Church: daily, 8am – 11am and 2pm – 5pm. Monastery: Mon – Sat, 8am – 11am and 2pm – 5pm.

NOSSA SENHORA DA GRAÇA CHURCH AND OLINDA SEMINARY
Duarte Coelho ordered the construction of the chapel in 1552, and immediately turned it over to the Jesuits. From here the Jesuits worked to convert the local native population and developed plans for the Real Colégio de Olinda (Olinda Royal College), which was constructed in 1575. Burned by the Dutch, restoration of the Igreja de Nossa Senhora da Graça began in 1660. The Arquidiocesano School, the Faculty of Architecture, and the School of Agronomy have all resided in the Royal College at some point. The Seminário da Arquidiocese seminary functions out of the chapel today. Despite many renovations, the complex is a rare example of 16th-century architecture: The side altars in the church contain the oldest stone constructions in Brazil. Visits are restricted to certain areas and visitors must be accompanied by a pre-arranged guide.
Rua Bispo Coutinho, no #, Carmo, tel. (81) 3429-0627. Mon – Fri, 2:30pm – 4pm. Mar – Jun and Aug – Nov only.

SÃO FRANCISCO CONVENT COMPLEX
The Franciscans began construction on the Convento de São Francisco in 1585 and gradually extended its boundaries. The complex, consisting of the Igreja de Nossa Senhora das Neves church, the Capela de São Roque chapel, and

Nossa Senhora das Neves Church, part of the São Francisco Convent complex

the convent, was damaged during the Dutch invasion and renovated in the 17th century. The chapter room in the convent cloisters, the only surviving room from the original convent, catches your eye with its blue, yellow, and red Portuguese tiles. These tiles extend throughout the church, convent corridors, and the chapel. Highlights inside the church include its impressive paneled ceiling, with 18th-century paintings depicting the Holy Family, and tiled murals showing the life of the Virgin and the circumcision of Jesus. The sacristy at the back of the church is worth a peek; it contains a sumptuously carved jacaranda chest. The chapel connected to the church also displays finely detailed carvings.
Rua São Francisco, 280, Carmo, tel. (81) 3429-0517. Mon – Fri, 7am – noon and 2pm – 5pm; Sat, 7am – noon.

Nossa Senhora da Conceição Church and Convent

Built in 1585, this building was a shelter for homeless women in the 16th century. After the Dutch burned the church to the ground, it was rebuilt in 1675 and turned into a convent. Currently in the care of the Sisters of Saint Dorothy, it now only opens to the public on Sunday mornings for nine o'clock mass. Highlights of the church include its ceiling paintings, which depict the life of the Virgin, and the gold and polychrome statue of Nossa Senhora da Conceição (Our Lady of the Immaculate Conception), with its silver crown.
Largo da Misericórdia, no #, Alto da Sé, tel. (81) 3429-3108. Tue and Thu, 5:30pm; Fri, 6:30am; and Sun, 9am.

Nossa Senhora do Monte Church

Igreja de Nossa Senhora do Monte was built in 1540 in an isolated location 55 meters (180 feet) above sea level. Today, 30 Benedictine sisters live here. The church is known for its distinctive architectural elements: a stone arch around the entrance door and a simple interior with no ceiling and exposed beams. The stark altar contains a statue of São Bento (Saint Benedict). Try to visit the church at five o'clock, when the nuns sing and sell their traditional *bricelets* (wafer-thin layers of pastry, folded to form a puff-pastry biscuit) at the side door. The Swiss recipe has become almost sacred

due to the nuns' exceptional pastry-making skills. If you miss the five o'clock window, be assured that the biscuits can also be ordered by phone.
Praça Nossa Senhora do Monte, no #, Bultrins, tel. (81) 3429-0317. Daily, 8:30am – 11am and 2:30pm – 5pm.

NOSSA SENHORA DA MISERICÓRDIA CHURCH

Also known as Igreja de Nossa Senhora da Luz, this church was built in 1540. Burned down during the Dutch invasion, it was restored soon after the Dutch were expelled. Today, Benedictine sisters look after the church and sing daily at 6pm mass. Highlights include the Dom João V carvings on the pulpit and altar, the ceiling panels illustrating the life of the Virgin Mary, the Portuguese stone baptismal font, and the lovely view of Olinda from the churchyard.
Largo da Misericórdia, no #, Alto da Sé, tel. (81) 3429-2922. Daily 8am – noon and 2pm –5pm.

SÉ CATHEDRAL

The most important church in Olinda, the Catedral da Sé, or Igreja de São Salvador do Mundo has passed through many construction phases. The first small, wattle-and-daub building dates from 1540. The year 1584 saw the construction of a whitewashed stone church; the Dutch later pulled it down and it was rebuilt in 1656. After extensive restoration work throughout the 20th century, further renovations recovered the original 16th-century design. Drawings and photographs exhibited on the side of the church capture each stage of construction and renovation. The 17th-century tiled murals inside the church and the views of Olinda and Recife (*see page 205*) from outside the church are worth a look.
Rua Bispo Coutinho, no #, Alto da Sé, tel. (81) 3271-4270. Tue – Sun, 8am – noon and 2pm – 5pm.

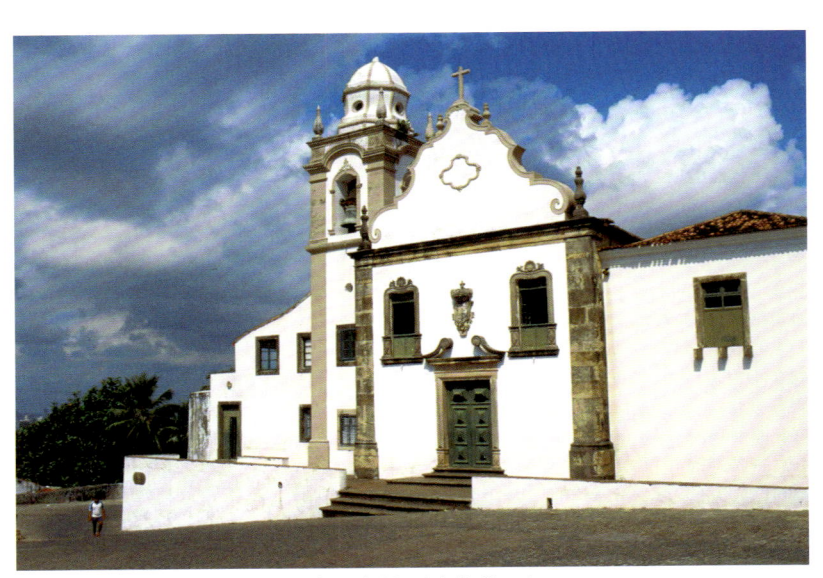

Benedictine nuns look after Nossa Senhora da Misericórdia Church

Five Good Reasons to Love Olinda

1. *Olinda é só para os olhos, não se apalpa, é só desejo.*
Ninguém diz: é lá que eu moro.
Diz somente: é lá que eu vejo.
(Olinda is for the eyes only, you can't touch it, it's pure yearning.
(Nobody says: it's where I live.
(They just say: it's where I see.) Carlos Pena Filho

According to legend, upon arriving here in the early 1500s, Duarte Coelho, captain of the Pernambuco, gazed upon the landscape and exclaimed: "Oh, what a beautiful place to build a village!" His words in Portuguese – "oh, linda" meaning "oh, beautiful" – inspired the name of the town. If you go up Alto da Sé you will see that, contrary to what its stark, treeless streets suggest, Olinda is extremely green. The town was divided into lots 7 meters (23 feet) wide by 70 meters (230 feet) long; rows of historical façades line the streets and protect large, hidden gardens of mango, bread-fruit, and banana trees. Stay a little longer in Alto da Sé, and you will understand what makes Olinda a Unesco World Heritage Site. Here in Olinda, Portuguese colonization and tropical greenery blend harmoniously. The immensity of the Atlantic, with its hues of blue and green, surrounds the hills and churches of the city. Across a strip of ocean, Recife beckons. Olinda sees the world and blends into the horizon. Olinda is sight.

2. *Olinda, quero cantar a ti esta canção,*
Teus coqueirais, o teu sol, o teu mar
Faz vibrar meu coração
De amor a sonhar, minha Olinda sem igual,
Salve o teu Carnaval!
(Olinda, I want to sing this song for you,
(Your coconut groves, your sun, your sea
(Make my heart beat faster
(Dreaming of love, my peerless Olinda,
(Long live your Carnival!)
Clídio Nigro e Clóvis Vieira

There are two major Carnival groups: *Elefante* and *Pitombeira*. The lyrics of *Pitombeira*'s anthem claim that without *Pitombeira* there is no Carnival. But it was *Elefante*'s lyrics (above) that became the official anthem of Olinda's Carnival, where everything turns into the rhythm of *frevo*. Carnival begins one week early in Olinda. That Saturday night, the extended party begins with the procession of one of the giant dolls. As the phrase goes, "Here comes the Midnight Man, roaming around the streets, his costume is white and green, to celebrate Carnival." Behind him, thousands of wild revelers sing and dance to the frantic *frevo* rhythm, rejoicing in life. Each of the dozens of groups, ranging from the irreverent *Ceroula* to the yellow-and-red *Eu Acho É Pouco*, has its own anthem. You can join any of them for free, so long as you sing and dance the *frevo*, keeping the beat. After Carnival, Olinda is still full of music. On Fridays, there are evening street serenades and a deafening *maracatu* at Mercado Varadouro market. During the week, there are Banda Henrique Dias rehearsals and Gregorian chants. Every day at noon, the bells of the fascinating São Bento Monastery carillon – the best in Brazil – toll endlessly. Olinda is song and dance.

3. If you can sing Olinda, you can just as well paint her coconut trees, her sun, her sea, to make the "heart beat faster." There is no such thing as an Olinda school of art or an Olinda movement. And yet, in everything in Olinda there is art. There is no distinctive style, theme, or concept; light is the main element. Artists don't paint landscapes here – they paint its light, its brightness, and its vivacity ("viva the city"). Its distinctive features revolve around its diversity, freedom, and multiplicity of styles. Its artists sometimes disagree or argue, but every year in late November, the town becomes an enormous communal art studio with the arrival of *Arte em Toda Parte*, and artists put aside their differences to exchange ideas with one another. This convergence of artists is one of Olinda's greatest assets. More than 200 artists open their studios and homes to the public each year; the city is truly a haven and an inspiration for art.

4. Olinda has stubbornly survived over 400 years of hardships. Pirates looted it, but the city survived. The Dutch laid siege and set it ablaze in the 16th century, but the city survived. It fought the Mascates War, battled Recife, and suffered economic collapse, political disgrace, and anti-historic modernism, and still the city survived. In the past, its population consisted of members of the rural aristocracy; today, striving artists and retired city workers call it home. Architecturally, it is a huge mess. There is no predominant style; Olinda has them all. You may find a 19th-century townhouse right next to a 17th-century home. There are no luxury mansions with countless doors and windows. There are no palaces. Almost every façade blends centuries together, a result of the endless phases of renovation. Olinda's architectural diversity is unique and individualistic. High-rise buildings are banned. Its churches have remained strong, and hold on to their gilded rococo and tiles – Franciscan on one side, Benedictine on the other. Its streets need to be paved. It is polluted. The street lights are archaic. But Olinda endures.

5. Don't leave without going back to Alto da Sé – to sit at a *tapioca* kiosk at sunset, admiring the view, sipping a cold beer, and enjoying roasted curd cheese and coconut *tapioca*. The simple, country cheese has taken the nation (and even cosmopolitan Ipanema beach) by storm. The tapioca of Olinda has found its way to the best restaurants in Brazil, revamped, sweet or savory, in the hands of young chefs. But you can also find it in Beco das Garrafas alley, where a man sits selling *cuscuz* (tapioca and coconut cake) and *pamonha* (corn and milk paste wrapped in corn husks). Restaurants become true flavor workshops, offering *moranga de camarão* (shrimp baked in pumpkin), and serving traditional Brazilian dishes such as *galinha de cabidela* (chicken stew enriched with its own blood), strong *sarapatel* (stewed pig's tripe and liver enriched with thickened blood), and piles of manioc root covered in sun-dried beef. But whatever and wherever you eat, don't leave Olinda without making a toast to life. Stop by the tiny bar on Rua do Amparo to order the famous "Pau de Índio" (Indian's Spear, a brand of *cachaça*), an eau de vie, a brandy, or a good old *cachaça*. Olinda is also food and drink.

Long live Olinda!

Joaquim Falcão

A part time resident of Olinda, Joaquim has worked at Fundação Gilberto Freyre, Fundação Joaquim Nabuco, and Fundação Pró-Memória. He is the vice-president of the Instituto Itaú Cultural and a dean of Fundação Getúlio Vargas Law School in Rio de Janeiro

The South Coast

The Costa Sul (South Coast) encompasses all of Pernambuco's beaches from Recife to Maceió, extending from Cabo de Santo Agostinho beach (home to the port of Suape) to Tamandaré, near Alagoas. This stretch of coast is often referred as the **Costa dos Arrecifes** (Reef Coast) for its abundance of coral reefs. Most of the beaches are within a two-hour trip from Recife along PE-060, with the farthest beach roughly 100 kilometers (60 miles) away. To reach Cabo de Santo Agostinho's best beaches, including Gaibu, Calhetas, Pedra do Xaréu, and Camboa, drive along PE-028. From Porto de Galinhas, take PE-038 to visit Muro Alto, Praia do Cupe, Praia da Vila, and Maracaípe beaches. To get to Tamandaré's best beaches, Carneiros and Tamandaré, take PE-076. Alternatively, try beach-hopping near the hotels, restaurants, and resorts of Cabo de Santo Agostinho or Porto de Galinhas. In addition to its often-crowded beaches, the Costa dos Arrecifes offers quiet retreats and such activities as reef-pool diving, walks, dune buggy trips, surfing, and water sports.

Santo Agostinho Cape

About 33 kilometers (20 miles) from Recife, Cabo de Santo Agostinho is the easternmost point in Pernambuco. It was a point of reference for the first European ships that arrived in the country and in the 17th century its fort resisted the Duch invasion. Spanish navigator Vicente Pinzón is said to have landed here in January 1500, three months before Cabral arrived in Bahia and "discovered" Brazil. A bust in Praça Vicente Pinzón honors this early arrival. As the military ruins on the beaches attest, the first colonial settlement witnessed clashes between Indians, the Portuguese, and the Dutch for control of this strategic cape locale. The city grew to prominence in the sugar era, and the surrounding landscape is still dotted with plantations. Chief among these is the Massangana, once home to abolitionist Joaquim Nabuco and now a cultural center. **Vila de Nazaré,** the highest point in Cabo de Santo Agostinho, boasts the tiny 16th-century church **Igreja de Nossa Senhora de Nazaré** as well as the ruins of a 17th-century Carmelite convent.

Porto de Galinhas

The most popular beach destination in Pernambuco was once a busy port of entry for slave ships. When ships continued to unload here illegally (after slavery was outlawed), they referred to their cargo as *galinhas d'Angola* (guinea fowl), thus earning the port its name. The area was a sleepy fishing village until the 1970s, when its beaches and warm waters began to attract hordes of visitors. Travelers looking to venture beyond the beach can enjoy surfing, exploring in buggies, chartering *jangadas* (rafts) to dive sites at natural pools and coral reefs, and hiking through mangrove forests. At night, you can check out the bars, restaurants, and shops of Rua da Esperança and Praça das Piscinas

Pedra do Xaréu
A fishing village with a rocky beach, blue sea, and a few simple barracas. Best reached by car from Calhetas.

Gaibu
White sands border dangerous waters, while the rocky south side offers lovely views. Amenities include hotels, bars, and restaurants.

Calhetas
A favorite spot of surfers and divers, home to the popular Bar do Arthur. Cross over the rocks at Gaibu and follow the steep trail down to the beach.

Gamboa
At the mouth of the Ipojuca River, with calm waters and mangroves. Accessible by a dirt road from Porto de Galinhas.

Muro Alto
This enormous natural pool takes its name (High Wall) from the cliffs and coral reefs that surround it. The calm waters are good for sailing and water sports.

Praia do Cupe
Surrounded by coconut groves and Atlantic forest, with strong waves (especially between March and December). The water is calmer and forms natural pools in the beach's western, or left-hand, corner.

Praia da Vila
This fashionable spot gets very crowded in summer. Traditional rafts ferry visitors from the beach near the village to the natural pools.

Maracaípe
Coarse sand and good waves make this beach ideal for surfing – it's even on the Brazilian and international surf circuits. Nightlife centers on the sandy streets of Vila de Todos os Santos.

Carneiros
A 5-kilometers stretch of coconut groves, pale sand, and reef walls near the mouth of the Formoso River. Accessible by a dirt road across private property.

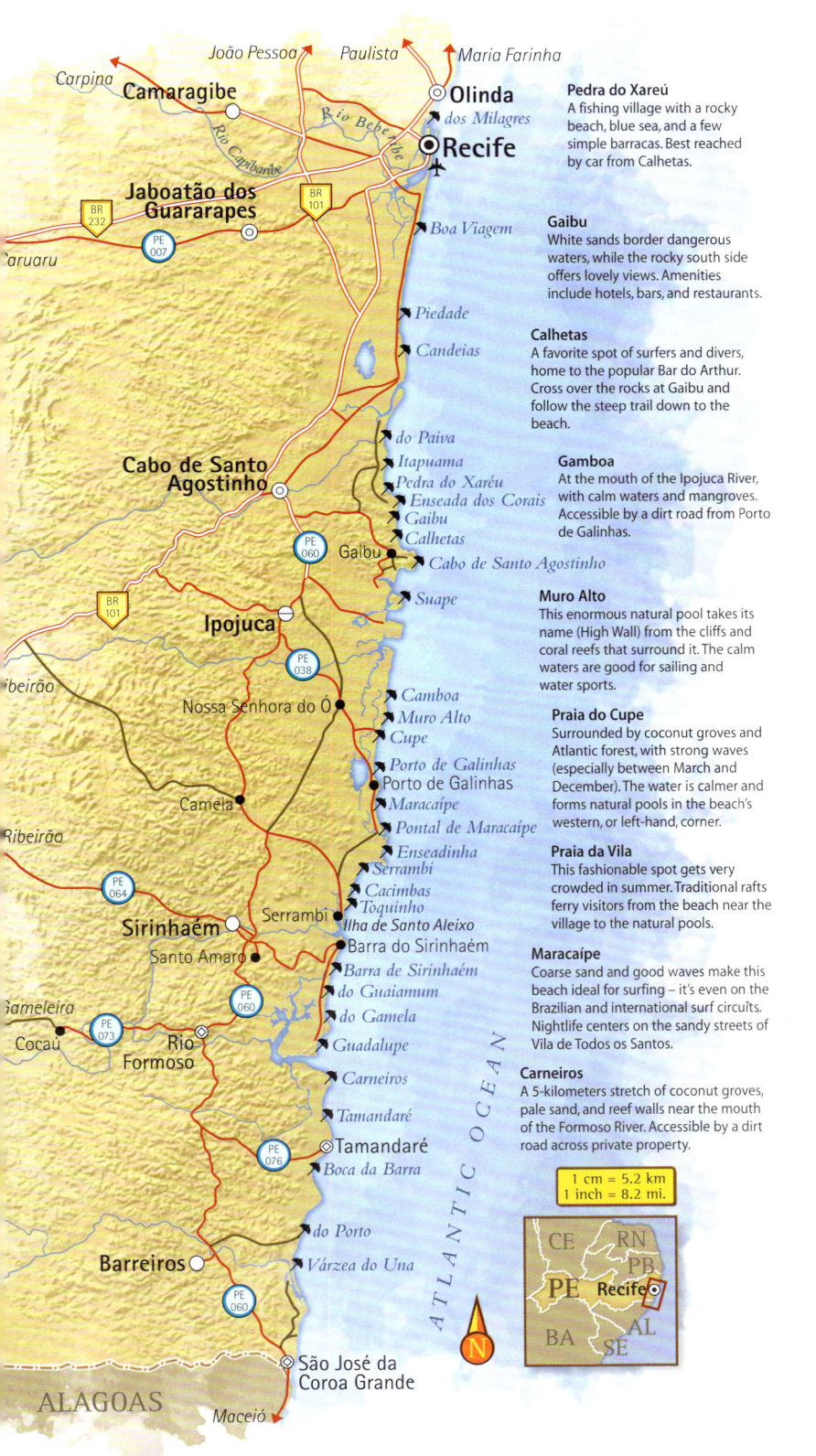

1 cm = 5.2 km
1 inch = 8.2 mi.

Naturais, a lively square by the sea. Porto de Galinhas is 60 kilometers (37 miles) from Recife along clearly marked roads. To get there, take BR-101 toward the south coast, then the PE-060 from Cabo de Santo Agostinho to Ipojuca. From there, take the PE-038 to Nossa Senhora do Ó, and connect to PE-09.

Boat Trips on the Maracaípe River

The Rio Maracaípe is actually an arm of the sea. The mangroves on its banks form a rare seahorse habitat that is protected and monitored by the Hippocampus Project. Rafts from Pontal de Maracaípe depart from Boca na Botija restaurant for 40-minute trips to the area. Numerous ocean species reproduce in the river before returning to sea, among them crabs, oysters, and even rays. The "floating restaurants," which sit atop rafts, are great spots to enjoy a fresh lunch of fried fish, salad, crab broth, coconut juice, and beer. ***Contact****: Lourivaldo (Nino), tel. (81) 9187-6943.*

Buggy Trips

Delightful half- and full-day buggy trips run from Praia da Vila to the beaches north and south of Porto de Galinhas. Visitors *can* rent and drive dune buggies themselves, but hiring a driver is recommended; drivers are more adept at fixing buggies stuck in the sand, and are better at navigating through detours that may be necessary in bad weather. The trip known as *ponta a ponta*, offered by the local buggy association (*tel. 81/3552-1930*), lasts two and a half hours and drives from Muro Alto beach to Maracaípe (with the option to continue on to Serrambi). Other trips run to the beaches of Cabo de Santo Agostinho to the north and to Carneiros in the extreme south.

Porto de Galinhas: rafts ferry visitors to the natural pools

Natural Pools

Rafts to the natural pools depart Praia da Vila at low tide. Once you're at the pools, you can snorkel and feed the fish with the urchins supplied by the raftsmen. You can also explore the coral pools by foot, but wear shoes to protect your feet from the sea urchins that feed there.

Santo Aleixo Island

Boats run from Praia do Vila to tiny Ilha de Santo Aleixo, near Serrambi beach. The trip includes a 1-hour stop on the island for taking a stroll around or snorkeling in the ocean pools. After stopping at Santo Aleixo, the boat continues on to Carneiros beach, in Tamandaré, where it makes a stop for lunch and a swim in the calm waters. A raft ferries visitors from Praia do Vila to the 25-person boat, which departs around 8:30am and returns around 5pm. **Contact:** *Topázio Passeios de Barco, tel. (81) 3552-1710, 9107-6405.*

Nightlife

Porto de Galinhas has nightlife that caters to all tastes, from funk, pop, rock, and electronic music, to local styles such as *forró*, *axé*, and MPB (Música Popular Brasileira). In high season, the different venues in town take turns supplying the entertainment, with each spot responsible for a specific type of music one night a week. The hotspot **Palhoção** features traditional *forró* on weekends. Young audiences dance until dawn at the raves and local rock shows held most nights at the beach at Maracaípe.

Our Recommendation

Sommerville Beach Resort on Muro Alto Beach offers a variety of leisure options. The comfortable rooms have Internet access, and the large complex features two restaurants and an excellently-equipped gym (*Rodovia PE-09, Praia de Muro Alto, tel. 81/3302-5555*).

Fashionable **Beijupirá** serves up wonderful fish dishes in pleasing surroundings. The traditional beef jerky dishes are worth a taste as well (*Rua Beijupirá, no #, tel. 81/3552-2354*).

Additional information on page 358.

Tamandaré

Tamandaré's 16 beautiful kilometers of beaches lie along a pure blue sea, and are generally less crowded than those in Porto de Galinhas (though facilities such as hotels and restaurants are better in Galinhas). The town's six beaches are Boca da Barra, Baía de Tamandaré, Pontal do Lira, Praia de Tamandaré (the most popular), Campas, and Carneiros. Carneiros is particularly beautiful and relatively non-commercial. Tamandaré is in a federally protected conservation area, near one of the region's largest swaths of Atlantic forest, the **Reserva Biológica de Saltinho**. A major attraction of the reserve is Cachoeira da Bulha, a 10-meter (33-foot) waterfall. Among Tamandaré's historical attractions are **Capela de Santo Inácio**, a chapel built in 1780, and **Forte de Santo Inácio**, a fort dating from 1691. A bust of naval hero Admiral Tamandaré, the father of the Brazilian navy, stands guard over this town where he spent a short time.

To reach Tamandaré from Recife, take PE-060 to PE-076 highways.

North of Recife

Itamaracá Island

Ilha da Itamaracá has a variety of attractions to complement a trip to neighboring Igarassu (*see page 220*). The island is home to the restored **Forte Orange**, a four-bastioned fort built by the Dutch in 1631 and later captured by the Portuguese. It was the Portuguese who renamed it the Fortaleza de Santa Cruz de Itamaracá and built it up to its present, robust state. The 16th-century chapel and small museum on-site display weapons, cannon balls, and porcelain from the era of the fort's initial construction (*Sítio Histórico Forte Orange, no #, Forte Orange, tel. 81/3544-1646; Mon – Sat, 9am – 5pm; Sun and holidays, 8am – 5pm*). The ocenarium at the **Ecoparque Peixe-Boi & Cia** features nine manatees (*Trichechus manatus*), as well as lectures on the animal by local biology and oceanography students. Ibama (the Brazilian Institute of Environment and Renewable Natural Resources) also hosts Projeto Peixe-Boi, a private manatee rehabilitation unit on-site that cares for beached manatee calves and releases them back into the wild. The oceanarium also has a projection room screening documentaries, a gift shop, and a snack bar (*Estrada do Forte Orange, no #, Forte Orange, tel. 81/3544-1056; Tue – Sun, 10am – 4pm; Jan. daily, 10am – 4pm*). To see Forte Orange from the vantage point of the original 16th-century explorers, take a small motorboat to **Coroa do Avião**, a tiny island just off the coast that is also home to several bars (*Praia do Forte Orange; daily, 8:30am – 5pm*). Itamaracá's cultural center is **Estrela de Lia**, founded by folk artist Lia de Itamaracá. Its main focus is preserving and celebrating the local *ciranda* music and circle dance traditions. The center

Tiny Coroa do Avião Island affords a sea view of Forte Orange

organizes occasional *ciranda* performances on a covered open-air stage on Jaguaribe beach, led by Lia or a special guest (such as Selma do Coco and Mestre Salustiano). The nearby bar offers a delicious lime juice with *capim-santo* (lemongrass), made by Zeza. Be sure to confirm that there will be a performance before making plans (*Rua Benigno Galvão, 15 and 16, tel. 81/3539-0619; Sat, 9pm*).

The 16th-century village of **Vila Velha,** once a colonial administrative headquarters, is now a collection of simple brick houses near the old **Igreja de Nossa Senhora da Conceição** (*Rua João Paulo II, no #, tel. 81/3543-0569; daily, 7:30am – 5pm*) and Igreja de Nossa Senhora dos Pretos. The elevated site offers a view of the sea, the Canal de Santa Cruz, and Coroa do Avião island. In colonial days, the site also provided a strategic lookout for enemy attacks, though it was no protection against Dutch troops who invaded in 1631, overtaking the city and christening it

Cannon at the historic Forte Orange

Cidade Schoppe (*Exit between Km 9 and Km 10 on the Estrada Recife–Itamaracá road*).

Ilha da Itamaracá is 50 kilometers (31 miles) north of Recife; take the BR-101 highway towards Paraíba, then go east on PE-35.

IGARASSU

Tiny Igarassu founded in 1535 is a National Heritage Site. The town boasts several well-preserved 18th- and 19th-century buildings, among them the art museum **Pinacoteca do Convento Franciscano Santo Antônio de Igarassu** (*Rua Barbosa Lima, no #, tel. 81/3543-0481; daily 8am – 5pm*). One of the highlights of this collection is the set of 24 oil paintings on wood panels, dating from 17th- and 18th-century, all of which depict religious figures and historical scenes from the region. One such panel shows a 1685 outbreak of yellow fever that devastated Recife and other nearby cities, supposedly passing over Igarassu thanks to the protection of its patron saints Cosmas and Damian. Igarassu has had a church honoring its two patron saints since its founding in 1535. Though the original wattle and daub **Igreja de São Cosme e São Damião** was destroyed by the Dutch in 1634, it was rebuilt in 1654, and later altered to incorporate baroque architectural elements. Unfortunately, the striking painted murals are almost entirely gone from the interior today; thankfully the side of the church offers a lovely view of the rooftops of Igarassu (*Rua Frei Caneca, 56, Centro, tel. 81/3543-0518; Mon – Fri, 8am – noon and 2pm – 5pm; Sat, 8am – 11am; Sun, 7am – 7pm*). The stone **Igreja de Santo Antônio**, inside the Franciscan convent, is the best preserved of the town's churches. Built in 1588, it was pillaged in the disputes between the Dutch and Portuguese, but subsequently renovated. The high altar is gold-painted cedar, done in a baroque style. Tiled murals on the side walls depict Saint Anthony's many miracles and holy visions. The sacristy contains a solid wood chest from the 1700s, with a stone font. To reach Igarassu, follow BR-101 north from Recife for 30 kilometers (19 miles).

Santo Antônio Church and Convent (left), with São Cosme e São Damião Church in the background.

Goiana

Goiana was a medium-sized town that gained prosperity in the sugar boom years. The town was founded by the Portuguese in the mid-16th century and soon taken by the Dutch. It was the setting for a legendary battle that was the first ever fought entirely by women in Brazil; the female colonists in town took up arms against the Dutch invaders and succeeded in driving them back. The town was the first in the country to abolish slavery, which it did before the national abolition edict came into effect.

The **Igreja de Nossa Senhora do Rosário dos Homens Pretos** (*Secretaria de Turismo, Rua do Rosário, no #, Centro, tel. 81/3626-0171); Mon – Fri, 8am – 5pm*) is Goiana's most important church. It houses the **Museu de Arte Sacra**, with its rich collection of 17th- and 18th-century statues. The church was originally built in the 1500s, with baroque features added in the next century. The highlights of the museum's holdings are the statues of the Virgin, Nossa Senhora do Amparo, and Nossa Senhora do Leite. For years the Catholic Church refused to accept or display the statue of the Senhora do Leite (Lady of Milk), as it shows the Virgin Mary's exposed breast.

Goiana is 60 kilometers (37 miles) northwest of Recife, along the BR-101.

Zona da Mata

Tracunhaém

The town of Tracunhaém takes its name, which means "dish of ants," from a legend that claims that the local Indians escaped from the Portuguese invaders by climbing into the Serra de Trapoá range – which resembled a container full of insects. Ceramics are Tracunhaém's other indigenous inheritance. The old potteries are now modern studios – such as those of famous artisans Nuca and Zezinho. The Centro de Produção Artesanal is a good starting point for learning about local ceramics. Tracunhaém is 63 kilometers (39 miles) northwest of Recife. Take the BR-232 west from Recife towards Caruaru, and turn north when you reach the intersection with BR-408. Both roads have poor signage.

Studios

Manuel Borges da Silva, known as **Nuca**, is famed for several ceramic creations, among them lions with curly manes and a doll figure known as Dondoca. His studio (*Rua Manoel Pereira de Morais, 118*) keeps with the town's tradition of supporting entire families through the ceramics production trade. Ceramics is also a family affair at **Ateliê Zezinho** (*Avenida Desembargador Carlos Vaz, 110, Centro, tel. 81/3646-1215; daily, 7am – 6pm*), where José Joaquim da Silva produces life-sized statues of saints. Saints are also the specialty of **Ateliê Maria Amélia** (*Praça Costa Azevedo, 76, tel. 81/3646-1778*), the studio that sells the work of Maria Amélia da Silva. At Christmastime, pieces from Tracunhaém command very high prices in Recife's top shopping malls.

Craft Production Center

The Centro de Produção Artesanal brings together those apprentice and professional ceramicists who do not have their own studios. The center sells the work of its 45 participants as well as holding arts and crafts courses for the public.

Praça Costa de Azevedo, no #; Mon – Fri, 9am – 6pm.

VICÊNCIA

Vicência grew out of an old rural property, and, until 1891, was but a small district of the neighboring town of Nazaré da Mata. Vicência features more than fifty sugarcane plantations, with architectural styles that span the entire tradition of northeastern architecture. Many of these plantations are still in operation, offering visitors both a chance to experience history and a chance to sample various types of *cachaças*, all distilled in small mills on-site at the plantations.
Vicência is 87 kilometers (54 miles) northwest of Recife, along the PE-74.

POÇO COMPRIDO PLANTATION MILL

This mill is the only 18th-century building of its type left in the entire state. The chapel annexed to the main house, the external staircase, and the absence of an internal courtyard are all characteristic of the architectural style of that period. In the 19th century, the mill hosted meetings of separatists such as Frei Caneca, one of the leaders of the Confederation of the Equator (1824). Protected by Iphan and recently restored, Poço Comprido now functions as a museum. Its collection features photographs of sugarcane plantations and mills in Pernambuco, some of which are no longer in existence.
Vila Murupé, Vicência, accessible by the BR-407 and PE-074 highways, tel. (81) 3641-1635, 9902-1227. Tue – Sun, 9am – 5pm.

THE CITY OF EMBROIDERY

Passira, 90 kilometers (56 miles) northwest of Recife makes its living from embroidery – so much so that it has earned the nickname "The City of Embroidery." Everywhere in town – on sidewalks, in front of houses, in stores, on small farms – you'll see women chatting and stitching, while men sell the finished tablecloths, sheets, shirts, and other linens. The women show and sell their work at the Feira do Bordado (Embroidery Fair), which runs in October (*Rua da Matriz, no #, information: Secretaria de Cultura, tel. 81/3651-1073*).

LAGOA DO CARRO

Meaning "Ox Cart Lake," the origin of the town's name is as straightforward as they come: Years ago, an ox-cart is said to have fallen into a nearby lake. The town is known for its rug makers. The town is also known for its Museu da Cachaça, with a world record number of *cachaças* on display. Lagoa do Carro is 61 kilometers (38 miles) northwest of Recife; continue 10 kilometers (6 miles) past the Carpina intersection on the PE-90.

NEEDLEPOINT

The **Associação de Tapeceiras de Lagoa do Carro** is an organization of some one hundred craftswomen famed for their needlework. A large warehouse that features their wares sits by the side of the PE-90 (*Km 8 on PE-90, tel. 81/3261-8848; Mon – Sat, 8am – noon and 2pm –5:30pm*). The store **Marina Artesanato** (*Km 8 on PE-90, tel. 81/3621-8375; daily, 7am – 5pm*) also sells work by several of the artisans. The rug makers of Lagoa de Carro formed the **Cooperativa Arte Nossa** (*Km 8 on PE-90, tel. 81/3621-8238; daily 8am – 5pm*), a co-operative which now has 25 branches. In conjunction with the Association, the Cooperative acts as an intermediary

Cachaça Museum

Browsing in a Brasília supermarket in 1986, José Moisés de Moura was so impressed by the variety of *cachaças*. He bought twenty labels that were available, beginning the collection that now comprises the Museu da Cachaça. Opened in 1998, the museum's vast assortment of liquors earned a mention in the Guinness Book of World Records as "the greatest collector of *cachaças* in the world." In early 2005, the museum held 7,310 labels. These include varieties from every state in Brazil, as well as *cachaças* from 20 other countries. The museum reserves two bottles of each variety for its collection and offers the rest for tasting and selling. *Chácara Girassol, no #, Zona Rural, tel. (81) 3621-8208. Daily, 9am – 5pm.*

CARPINA

Carpina is the self-styled capital of the Zona da Mata. Its most cherished local tradition is a style of puppet theater using dolls known as **mamulengos** – a name derived from *mão* (hand) and *molenga* (loose). Carpina is also known for its Vaquejada (a kind of rodeo), its São João festivities, and its donkey races. The famed Cavalgada horseback riding event is held on the surrounding sugarcane plantations. Carpina is 9 kilometers (6 miles) south of Tracunhaém and 49 kilometers (30 miles) northwest of Recife, reached on the BR-408 highway heading toward Caruaru.

Puppet Makers

Much of Carpina's fame as the "Puppet City" comes from the work of Antônio Elias da Silva, known as Saúba. His pieces can be seen in the Museu do Mamulengo in Olinda as well as the Museu do Homem do Nordeste in Recife. Other notable *mamulengueiros* (puppet-makers) are Adel, Bibil, Pindoca, and Miro, who sell their work in the city and to hotels throughout the Northeast and Southeast of Brazil. Like many crafts, puppet-making often supports entire families.

Bulls, Donkeys, and Horses

To win the **Vaquejada** competition held every May in Carpina, a horseman must bring down a bull by pulling on its tail. The Vaquejada competition attracts a more affluent crowd than the *corrida de jegues* (donkey race), which the town holds every September. In November, some six hundred horsemen ride in the **Cavalgada**. They spend an entire day riding among the sugarcane plantations. It is a tradition that the plantation owners take turns supplying the riders with lunch every year.

A *mamulengo* puppet, a typical Carpina craft

ÁGUA DOCE SUGARCANE PLANTATION MILL

You can see every stage of traditional, small-scale *cachaça* production here, from the selecting of the sugarcane to the bottling of the finished product. In between, you'll learn how the drink is prepared in a copper still and aged in oak barrels. At Engenho Água Doce, the sugarcane is pesticide-free and crushed within 24 hours of being cut. Tours end with a *cachaça* tasting session. *Rodovia PE-074, Km 10, Vicência, tel. (81) 3641-1257, 9936-5169. Daily, 7am – 11am and 1pm – 5pm.*

NAZARÉ DA MATA

The municipality of Nazaré da Mata has is famed for its dedication to **maracatu rural**. This 19th-century dance style is a fusion of several dance traditions of indigenous, African, and Portuguese (specifically Catholic) origin: the most obvious influences are from *bumba-meu-boi, pastoril, cavalo-marinho, caboclinho,* and *folia-de-reis.* Today the town's eighteen dance groups (some with up to 200 members each) still blend the region's music, dance, costumes, and characters. The orchestra that accompanies the dancers features many percussion instruments – *zabumba,* bass, and snare drums, *cuícas, gonguês* (cow bells), and *ganzá* shakers – as well as trumpets, clarinets, and trombones. The group leader, called *mestre,* animates each performance by delivering improvised verses. This folk tradition is best enjoyed during Carnival or at the Encontro de Maracatus, held annually near the end of November in the town's central square. At other times of the year, you'll find *maracatu* groups giving presentations at events organized by City Hall *(information: Secretaria de Cultura, tel. 81/3633-1888, 8718-2018).* Nazaré da Mata is 65 kilometers (40 miles) northwest of Recife along BR-408.

FERNANDO DE NORONHA

"This is heaven," wrote Amerigo Vespucci in 1503 upon arriving on the shores of the Fernando de Noronha Archipelago. The Italian explorer was part of an exploratory Portuguese expedition led by Gonçalo Coelho and financed by the nobleman Fernão de Loronha. In the five hundred years that followed, the breathtaking natural beauty of this isolated archipelago inspired similar awe and fascination in successive waves of invaders from Portugal (beginning in 1503), the Netherlands (1629), and France (1736), and continues to inspire tourists and Brazilians alike today. The 15-kilometer long, 3.5-kilometer-wide string of 21 islands that comprise Fernando de Noronha Archipelago float far out in the Atlantic off the coast of Brazil, 350 kilometers (220 miles) east of Natal and 550 kilometers (340 miles) east of Recife. In the 18th century, a prison was built on the largest island, which is also called Fernando de Noronha. The island's and archipelago's namesake is a corruption of the name of the nobleman who was granted the territory by the crown. In 1988, 85% of the island became a National Marine Reserve, and in 2001, Unesco declared it a World Heritage site. As such, the number of visitors to the island is now limited. Each

LOOKOUT POINTS

1 - Baía do Sancho
2 - Baía dos Golfinhos
3 - Ponta das Caracas
4 - Boldró
5 - Buraco da Raquel
6 - Leão
7 - Baía dos Porcos

Diving

1 cm = 2.8 km
1 inch = 4.4 mi.

Pontal do Norte
Cordilheiras — *Macaxeira*
Cabeço das Cordas
Buraco do Inferno
Cação
Cagarras Funda
Ilha da Rata
Cagarras Rasa
Ressurreta
Buraco das Cabras
Meio Island
Meio Island
Sela Gineta Island — *Sela Gineta*
Rasa Island
São José Island
Cuscuz Island
Viuvinha Island
Ponta de Santo Antônio (Air France)
Pedras Secas I
Buraco da Raquel
Pedras Secas II
Porto de Santo Antônio
Cabeço da Caieira
Naufrágio do Porto de Santo Antônio (Porto)
Enseada da Caieira
Pontinha
do Cachorro
Morro do Francês
Morro de Fora
Morro de Fora
Vila dos Remédios
Vila do Trinta
do Meio
Ponta da Pedra Alta
da Conceição
Frade Island
Frade Island
BR 363
Morro do Pico
da Atalaia
Morro do Espinhaço
do Boldró
Airport
Ponta do Espinhaço
do Americano
do Bode
da Quixaba
Ovos Island
Trinta Réis Island
Cacimba do Padre
Ovos Island
Laje Dois Irmãos
Morro Dois Irmãos
Morro Boa Vista
Cabeluda Island
Baía dos Porcos
Baía do Sueste
Chapéu de Sueste Island
Baía do Sancho
Fernando de Noronha Island
Cabeço Submarino
Ponta das Caracas
Corveta Ipiranga V17
Iuias
Ponta das Caracas
Baía dos Golfinhos
do Leão
Naufrágio do Leão
Morro da Viúva
Morro do Leão

INNER SEA

OUTER SEA

RN
PB
PE
Recife

HIKING TRAILS

- Costa Esmeralda (Boldró-Cacimba do Padre)
- Capim-Açu (Quixaba-Praia do Leão)
- Atalaia (Sueste-Atalaia)
- Costa Azul (Centro-Boldró)
- Dos Golfinhos (Sancho-Mirante dos Golfinhos)
- Do Farol (Sancho-Ponta da Sapata)
- Pontinha-Pedra Alta (Atalaia-Caieira)
- Porto (Caieira-Buraco da Raquel)
- Jardim Elizabeth (Porto-Praia do Cachorro)

Cavernas da Sapata
Ponta Capim Açu
Cabeço da Sapata
Ponta do Barro Vermelho
Ponta da Sapata

Praia do Leão, a bird sanctuary where sea turtles also lay their eggs

visitor is also required to pay a hefty environmental protection fee; the amount is determined by the length of their stay (a week is typical). There are two daily flights to Fernando de Noronha from Natal or from Recife; travelers can also reach the islands on one of the cruise ships (like the *Pacific*) that stop at the islands between October and February (*contact: CVC, tel. 11/2191-8410*).

> ### SHARK CULT
>
> Unlike sharks off the coast of Recife, the sharks of Fernando de Noronha are docile. Reports of attacks on divers are rare on the island, as there is an abundance of food available to the sharks. Near the port, the **Museu dos Tubarões** (Shark Museum) displays enormous jawbones and dorsal fins. The museum restaurant offers dishes prepared with a signature creation known as *tubalhau* (salted shark meat), which is cured from non-endangered species caught off the mainland. *Avenida Joaquim Ferreira Gomes, 40, Vila do Porto, tel. (81) 3619-1365. Mon – Sat, 8:30am – 6:30 pm; Sun, noon – 6pm.*

Once on the island, favored modes of transportation are buses (which every half hour run around the island, starting from vila dos Remédios, the main village center), rented motorcycles, and rented buggies. The main road across the island is BR-363 highway, the shortest federal highway in the country at only 6.8 kilometers (4 miles) long. There is only one bank and no currency exchange bureau on the island. As prices at local markets are high, it is better to bring any provisions you might need with you from the mainland.

REMÉDIOS

Vila dos Remédios is the island's main urban center. It sprang up in the late 1700s around the **Igreja de Nossa Senhora dos Remédios** (*Terminal Turístico do Cachorro, no #, Jardim Elisabeth; daily, 8:30am – 7pm; Sun, mass at 8pm*), still the center of town and now an Iphan-protected historical site. Every year on August 29th, the church hosts a lively festival honoring the Virgin Mary, patron and protector of the village. Year-round, locals and visitors alike gather at the stores, cafés, and bars surrounding the church, like the popular **Bar do Cachorro** (*Terminal Turístico do Cachorro, no #, Jardim Elizabeth, tel. 81/3619-0165; Mon – Sat, noon – until the last customer leaves*). Behind the church are the ruins of the **Fortaleza de Nossa Senhora dos Remédios**, one of ten coastal fortifications built by the Portuguese in the 18th century. Other notable buildings in the village include the **Palácio de São Miguel** palace (*Rua São Miguel, no #, 81/3619-1378; Mon – Fri, 8:30am – noon and 2pm – 6pm*), Noronha's administrative center, and the **Memorial Noronhense** (*Sítio Histórico do Cachorro, no #, tel. 81/3619-0010; Mon – Fri, 8am – noon and 2pm – 6pm*), a museum chronicling the archipelago's history.

Though Remédios is small, it has adequate facilities for travelers, including ten restaurants and roughly 105 guesthouses, which are local residences that rent rooms to travelers.

SURFING, FISHING, AND SAILING CALENDAR

The waves create the most tubular shapes in November and April, making those months the best for **surfing** on the beaches facing the mainland (*mar de dentro*), especially Praia do Boldró and Cacimba do Padre. January brings national and international surfing championships to the island (*Associação de Surfe de Fernando de Noronha, Rua Inês Cordeiro, 9, Floresta Velha, tel. 81/3619-1324*).

August draws **fishing** enthusiasts with the Torneio de Pesca Oceânica, a nation deep-sea fishing tournament. Angling is allowed year-round, but only outside the limits of the special Marine Reserve area. Fishermen report catching barracudas, marlins, and sailfish on the island (*Squalo Pesca Esportiva e Passeios, Rua Padre Gurgel, 4040, Boldró, tel. 81/9606-3292; daily, 8am – 8pm*). The two Regatas Oceânicas Internacionais (international **sailing** regattas), Recife–Noronha and Noronha–Natal, are held here every September (*Cabanga Iate Clube de Recife, Avenida Engenheiro José Esteleta, no #, Cabanga, tel. 81/3428-4277; Tue – Sun, 8am – 6pm; Iate Clube de Natal, Rua Coronel Flamínio, no #, Santos Reis, tel. 84/3202-4402/3202-7676; Tue – Sun, 8am – 10pm*).

Beaches

Along much of Noronha's coastline you can see cliffs ringed by rocky beaches, the result of years of coral, shell, and volcanic rock sedimentation. The portion of the island closest to the Brazilian mainland is referred to as "*mar de dentro*" (inner sea), while the easternmost reaches are known as "*mar de fora*" (outer sea). The eleven beaches on the *mar de dentro* side are better protected from ocean winds, meaning their waters are calmer and better for snorkeling. Among the most popular of these beaches is **Baía do Sancho**. Sea turtles come ashore at Sancho to lay their eggs, so access is restricted from 6pm to 6am in hatching season (January to July). Also popular on the *mar de dentro* side of the island are: **Baía dos Porcos**, where reefs form natural pools teeming with fish; **Praia do Cachorro** and **Praia do Meio**, the busier beaches closest to Remédios; and **Praia de Santo Antônio**, where divers can visit the wreckage of the Greek ship *Eleani Sthathos*.

On the *mar de fora* side of the island is **Praia do Atalaia**, with its sea full of colorful fish. Access is restricted to 100 visitors per day. Groups of 25 are admitted every 20 minutes beginning at low tide. The long **Praia do Leão** beach faces Ilha da Viuvinha island. Swimming can be dangerous here at high tide because of the rocky shoreline. Leão is a bird sanctuary and sea turtle hatching ground, so access is restricted as at Baía do Sancho. **Baía do Sueste** is home to the ruins of the Forte de São Joaquim. The beach is accessible by the island's only paved road.

Snorkeling and "Planasub"

The beauty of the underwater life surrounding Noronha makes masks and snorkels essential travel gear. Sancho Bay and the beaches of Atalaia, Boldró, and Conceição are some of the best snorkeling spots on the island. The so-called "planasub" is another popular option for wildlife viewing. Invented in Noronha in 1997 by fishing engineer Leonardo Bertrand, this transparent acrylic board is used by snorkelers being pulled along by a motorboat through the water, acting as a support while still allowing unobstructed views. Planasub trips usually last for one hour, pulling visitors across the water for roughly 4 kilometers.

Contact: Museu dos Tubarões e Embarcação Golfinho, tel. (81) 3619-1365.

Deep-Sea Diving

A favorite destination for scuba divers, the waters of Fernando de Noronha boast a wealth of marine life, with countless species of fish, sharks, rays, and eels darting among colorful coral formations. There are 16 diving spots to choose from on Noronha, all with

Reefs form natural pools at Baía dos Porcos

crystal-clear waters and all with underwater visibility of around 50 meters (165 feet). Certified divers have the option of diving down 63 meters (207 feet). Children aged 10 years and older can take 30-minute, 15-meter (50-foot) dives accompanied by an instructor.
Contact: Águas Claras, tel. (81) 3619-1225; Atlantis Divers, tel. (81) 3619-1371; Noronha Divers, tel. (81) 3619-1112.

BOAT TRIPS

Boat trips are an excellent way to see the unique and colorful landscape of the archipelago for yourself. Boats make the 3-hour trip around the island daily, leaving from Praia do Porto up the west coast of the Fernando de Noronha island, to Ponta da Sapata. Trips depart both early in the morning and in the afternoon. Guides point out the most interesting spots and offer a detailed history of the region. The undisputed highlight of the trip is Baía dos Golfinhos (Dolphin Bay), where spinner dolphins (*Stenella longirostris*) usually make an appearance.
Contact: Barco Naonda, tel. (81) 3619-1307; Associação de Barcos de Turismo, tel. (81) 3619-1360, 3619-1977.

KAYAKING ALONG THE COAST

Travelers also have the option of taking guided two-person kayak tours to Cacimba do Padre, at the limits of the Marine Reserve (a roughly 2-hour trip). Thankfully, a motorboat tows the kayaks behind it on the return journey to Vila dos Remédios, so there's no need to paddle upwind.
Contact: Remos da Ilha, tel. (81) 3619-1914, 9994-7890.

TAMAR PROJECT

Dedicated to the protection of sea turtles, **Projeto Tamar** is one of the most successful environmental initiatives in Brazil. The Tamar team gives lectures on everything from turtles to dolphins every day at 9pm at the Centro de Turismo do Projeto Tamar (Tamar Project visitors center) and the **Centro de Visitantes do Parque Nacional Marinho** (National Marine Reserve Visitors Center) both coordinate special events and lead guided tours of the turtle hatchings.
Contact: Alameda Boldró, no #, Boldró, tel. (81) 3619-1174. Daily, 8am – 10 pm.

HIKING TRAILS

There are nine main hiking and biking trails on Fernando de Noronha, offering visitors access to the island's 16 unrestricted beaches and seven lookout points. **Costa Esmeralda** (3 kilometers long), runs from Boldró to Cacimba do Padre beaches, and is one of the most popular treks on the island. **Capim-Açu** (10 kilometers) is the island's longest trail, crossing from Quixaba to Praia do Leão beaches. **Atalaia** starts at Sueste and crosses the only island mangrove swamp in the Atlantic. **Costa Azul** (2 kilometers), accessible only at low tide, starts at the center of the village of Remedios, passes Morro do Pico hill, and ends at the Mirante do Boldró lookout. **Trilha dos Golfinhos** (2 kilometers) starts at the Mirante do Sancho and passes the ruins of São João Batista and the Morro dos Dois Irmãos hill en route to the 70-meter-high Mirante dos Golfinhos. **Trilha do Farol** is just 2.5 kilometers long but very steep, rising sharply up from Sancho Bay to Mirante do Farol at Ponta da Sapata. **Pontinha-Pedra Alta** (3 kilometers) runs from Atalaia to Caieira beach. **Porto,** a very short trail near the port, runs from Caieira to Buraco da Raquel. **Jardim Elizabeth** follows the Estrada Velha do Porto road to Praia do Cachorro.

THE AGRESTE REGION

CARUARU

Considered the capital of the *agreste* region, Caruaru is 132 kilometers (82 miles) west from Recife. Every June 24, the city seems to compete with Campina Grande (in Paraíba) to hold the largest **Festa de São João** in Brazil. Though Campina draws more people, the festivities last longer in Caruaru, where they begin the first weekend in June and end nearly one month later. The celebration is headquartered at **Pátio de Eventos Luiz Lua Gonzaga**, an exterior portico of the Espaço Cultural Tancredo Neves. Every year during the festival, this cultural center features an exhibit known as Vila do Forró, a reproduction of a typical Brazilian country village. The festival brings *quadrilha* dancers, guitarists, and *repentistas* (improvisational musical poets) out into the streets to perform alongside groups of marching *bacamarteiros*. The latter get their name from the wide-barreled traditional firearms (*bacamartes*) they carry while parading to the rhythm of the *xaxado* music being played by small bands of accordions, triangles, *zabumba* drums, and *pífanos* (flutes).

Caruaru also has attractions for those visiting during the other 11 months of the year. The town is home to the biggest street market in the Northeast, the **Caruaru Market**. Also worth a visit is the **Museu Casa do Mestre Vitalino** museum, which honors the town's most illustrious son. To reach Caruaru from Recife, head west on BR-232, a rare, well-maintained, two-lane highway. From Campina Grande, take BR-104 going south.

CARUARU MARKET

Set up in the more than 150,000 square meters (1,615,000 square feet) of the Parque 18 de Maio, this is the largest market in the Northeast. Shoppers will find stalls here featuring everything

Quadrilha dancing during Caruaru's June festivities

Catimbau National Park

Opened to visitors in 2002, this virtually untouched and undeveloped park lies in the Vale do Catimbau valley, surrounded by the mountain ranges of Buíque. The park is approximately 25 kilometers (16 miles) southwest of Arcoverde. The terrain runs from semi-arid *agreste* to *sertão*, encompassing *caatinga*, Atlantic forest, rocky woodland, and *cerrado*. This diverse landscape supports about 150 bird species, including the hooded siskin, a native of the Northeast. The park's greatest attraction is its unusual rock formations. Rock walls take on unusual shapes and are naturally colored in vivid reds, yellows, and blues, the result of weather change and erosion over time. Catimbau is also the second largest archaeological park in the country, on account of the prehistoric paintings and engravings that adorn the rocks. The chief excavation site in the park is at Alcobaça. You can refresh yourself and top off your canteens at **Paraíso Selvagem**, a spring with natural pools for bathing. You can explore Catimbau's 62,300 hectares (154,000 acres) on foot or by 4×4 vehicle. You must be accompanied by a guide (English speakers available) from the Catimbau Guide Association. To get to the park from Recife, head west on BR-232 to Arcoverde, then south on the PE-076 highway to Buíque. Both roads are in very poor condition.
Contact: Associação de Guias do Catimbau, tel. (87) 3816-3052.

---

from artisans to faith healers, medicinal herbs to electronic goods. It's a good idea to shop around before you buy, since prices differ significantly from one stall to the next. On Saturdays the market sells only food and crafts, and gets so crowded that it is difficult to move around. Monday brings the **Feira da Sulanca** (a local term for clothes made by small manufacturers), when retailers from other cities visit in search of inexpensive merchandise to sell in their own stores.
Parque 18 de Maio, no #, Centro. Mon – Sat, 7am – 5:30pm; Sun, no fixed time.

Alto do Moura

Caruaru's highest concentration of craft studios is in the **Alto do Moura** neighborhood, 7 kilometers (4 miles) from the center of Caruaru. One of the studios belongs to Severino Vitalino, son of ceramics master **Mestre Vitalino** (Vitalino Pereira da Silva, 1909-1963), a legend of Brazilian folk art. Since 1971, Severino has run the **Museu Casa do Mestre Vitalino** (*Rua Mestre Vitalino, no #, tel. 81/3722-0397; Mon –Sat, 8am – noon and 2pm – 5pm; Sun, 8am – noon*), a museum dedicated to his father and housed in the home the artist built for himself in 1959. The museum features examples of the master's work (none are for sale) as well as his personal items. Down the road from the museum you'll find the workshops of several other artisans, most notably **Luiz Galdino** (*Rua Mestre Vitalino, 455, tel. 81/3722-0369; daily 8am – 5pm*), **Manuel Eudócio** (*Rua Mestre Vitalino, 151, tel. 81/3722-7732; Mon – Fri, 8am – noon and 2pm – 6pm; Sat, 9am – 6pm*) and **Família Zé Caboclo** (*Rua Mestre Vitalino, 66, tel. 81/3722-2379/3722-0374; Mon – Sat, 8am – 6pm; Sun, 8am – noon*).

Clay Museum and Forró Museum

The **Espaço Cultural Tancredo Neves** cultural center was opened in 1988. The center houses the city's two most important museums: the Museu do Barro Zé Caboclo, and the Museu do Forró Luiz Gonzaga.

The **Museu do Barro Zé Caboclo** is on the first floor, block B, of the complex. It features some 2,300 clay pieces. Exhibits are divided into five areas. The Sala Ceramistas do Alto do Moura (Alto do Moura Ceramists' Room) displays the work of all the major local artists, with the exception of Mestre Vitalino, whose 67 pieces get their own room. Among the Vitalino holdings is *O Homem e o Gato Maracajá* (The Man and the Wildcat), considered the artist's first important work in clay. The Coleção Abelardo Rodrigues displays works from other important folk art centers in the Northeast, including Tracunhaém, Petrolina, and Goiana. The museum also has a contemporary art gallery and a space for temporary exhibitions.

The **Museu do Forró Luiz Gonzaga** is on the ground floor of the same block. The museum takes its name from Luiz Gonzaga, the first musician to bring local *forró* music to audiences outside of the *sertão*. The museum's extensive collection of Gonzaga's instruments, clothes, and records is spread over three rooms. There is also an entire room dedicated to the festivities held every June in the "Capital of Forró," as Caruaru is known.

An annex of the Tancredo Neves center houses **Espaço Elba Ramalho**, which displays the clothes and personal effects of *forró* singer Elba Ramalho, who, though born in Paraíba, is now an icon of *forró* in Caruaru.

Praça Coronel José Vasconcellos, 100, block B, Centro, tel. (81) 3701-1533. Tue – Sat, 8am – 5pm; Sun, 9am – 1pm.

Clay folk art

Bom Jesus Hill

Caruaru sprang up around the 630-meter (2,070-feet) high Morro do Bom Jesus hill. The chapel at the top of the hill was originally named Capela do Socorro, but was renamed the Capela do Bom Jesus by the local Diocese. The lookout points on the hill offer sweeping views of the Caruaru Market and Maurício de Nassau, the city's nicest neighborhood.

Bezerros

Bezerros is best known for its woodcut prints and Carnaval *papangus* (papier mâché masks). The town is 27 kilometers east of Caruaru and 20 kilometers west of Gravatá, at Km 107 on BR-232. It is worth a visit to Bezerros to see the studios of the artisans who specialize in these traditional craft forms, such as woodcut master J. Borges and papier mâché artist Lula Vassoureiro. Also worthwhile is the headquarters of the **Associação dos Artesãos**, which sells a wide variety of pieces. A trip up to **Serra Negra** affords excellent views and an opportunity to visit the **Pólo Cultural**.

José Borges Memorial

This memorial – actually a studio – honors 70-year-old Bezerros native José

Borges, the most famous of Bezerros' woodcut print artists. J. Borges still produces work, though at a slower pace than before due to his declining health and numerous trips abroad to lecture. When he is in town, the memorial is where he receives visitors, makes his pieces, and hands down his artistic knowledge to his children and grandson.
Avenida Major Aprígio da Fonseca, 420, tel. (81) 3728-0364. Mon – Fri, 8am – noon and 2pm – 4pm.

SERRA NEGRA CULTURAL CENTER
The Pólo Cultural is in the village of Serra Negra, 10 kilometers (6 miles) from downtown Bezerros. This imposing concrete structure stands in sharp contrast to its lush green surroundings and the Serra Negra mountain range. The view from atop the range is stunning, and the trails winding through the area are popular with locals and visitors alike. The center has a lovely open-air amphitheater that features regular music and theater productions.
Vila de Serra Negra, no #, Zona Rural (rural area), tel. (81) 3708-3004. Mon – Fri, 7am – 4:30pm; Sat, Sun and holidays, 10am – 2pm.

ARTS AND CRAFTS ASSOCIATION
The Associação dos Artesãos is one of the best places to buy the signature handicrafts of Bezerros. The association operates out of a building owned by City Hall, which allows the artists to sell their work at low prices. Traditional masks, like the paper mâché *papangu*, as well as others made of wood and fabric, are sold by many of the association's artists.
Rua Vigário Manuel Clemente, 123, Centro, tel. (81) 3728-6713. Mon – Fri, 7am – 5pm.

PERNAMBUCO ARTS AND CRAFTS CENTER
A combination museum, workshop, and store, the Centro de Artesanato de Pernambuco rivals similar centers found in the capitals and big cities of the Northeast. The museum and store exhibit items from practically every municipality that produces craftwork in the state of Pernambuco. Students at the workshop are taught woodcutting and mask-making.
Avenida Major Aprígio da Fonseca, 1.100, km 107, BR-232, tel. (81) 3728-2094. Tue – Sat, 9am – 6pm; Sun, 9am – 5pm.

THE PAPIER MÂCHÉ MASK TRADITION

Carnival celebrants in Bezerros first donned masks to parade through the streets in the early 20th century. These early masks were simple, made from wrapping paper or cardboard, and were dyed with natural ingredients (like bean leaves). It was a tradition in this era to give masked revelers gifts of fruit, eggs, *beiju* (sweet manioc starch cookies), and even chickens. Through the years these masks have become increasingly elaborate. The offerings given to the mask wearers have changed over time, as well. When residents of Bezerros began serving mask-wearers *angu* (cornmeal mash), the masks soon came to be known as *papangus* (literally, "those who eat *angu*"), an iconic symbol of Carnival in Bezerros. **Lula Vassoureiro** masks can be bought at his workshop, as well as other paper mâché artwork (like dolls).
Rua Otávia Bezerra Vila Nova, 64, Santo Amaro 1, tel. (81) 9102-0665. Daily, 8am – 5pm.

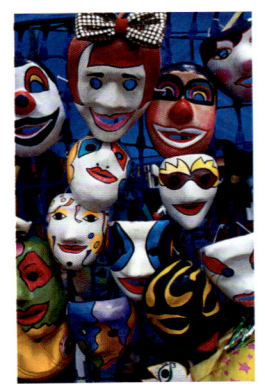

GRAVATÁ

Built at an altitude of 447 meters (1,470 feet), blessed with an average annual temperature of 21°C (70°F), and well supplied with fondue restaurants, Gravatá deserves the nickname "The Switzerland of the Northeast." The town is 80 kilometers (50 miles) west of Recife on the BR-232 highway. Its European climate complements its Brazilian traditional celebrations. June festivities attract crowds, as does the August **Festa da Estação**, which marks the end of the Circuito do Frio winter festival. Four other municipalities – Garanhuns, Pesqueira, Triunfo, and Taquaratinga – participate in the state government–supported August festival, which includes workshops, lectures, and musical presentations. (*Pátio de Eventos Chucre Mussa Zazar, Avenida Joaquim Didier, no #, Centro, tel. 81/3563-9047, Secretaria de Turismo.*) The industries that sustain Gravatá's economy – furniture, food, folk art, and flower cultivation – host the annual **Festival de Setembro**, featuring 1,500 square meters (16,100 square feet) of stands displaying the town's accomplishments.

ARTS AND CRAFTS STATION

A station in the most literal sense, the Estação do Artesão in the town's old railroad station displays the work of approximately 60 artisans. Gravatá's Artisan Association runs the space with support from City Hall. The Estação's two rooms showcase pieces in wood and fabric and canvases by local artists. *Rua João Pessoa, no #, Centro, tel. (81) 3563-9034. Mon – Sat, 9am – 5pm; Sun, 9am – 2pm.*

CRUZEIRO HILL

The replica of Cristo Redentor (Christ the Redeemer) with his arms stretched over the city, atop the Morro do Cruzeiro, is visible from all of Gravatá. Installed in July 1941, the monument is 7 meters (23 feet) tall and 8 meters (26 feet) wide at the base. It is a 5-minute drive from Igreja de Santana church or a 15-minute climb from the foot of the hill up the 365 steps of the Escadaria da Felicidade. The view from the the highest point in Gravatá is extraordinary, especially at sunset. A restaurant and a radio station also squat atop the hill.

FURNITURE CENTER

The 60 stores concentrated in the Pólo Moveleiro area sell furniture, wooden decorative items, and craftwork. Don't expect to find only local merchandise here: the stores sell pieces from all over the Northeast. *Rua Duarte Ceolho,. Tue – Sat and holidays, 9am – 6pm; Sun, 9am – 3pm.*

GARANHUNS

Though it is located in a hilly area 230 kilometers (143 miles) southwest of Recife, thus boasting an average annual temperature of 21° C (70° F), Garanhuns' claim to fame, is as a political hotspot: hometown of President Luiz Inácio Lula da Silva. But Garanhuns is more than just the self-proclaimed birthplace of the union leader who became president. It is the Northeast's largest mountain city and home to the popular Festival de Inverno. This event currently kicks off the Circuito do Frio festival and attracts visitors from all over

The picture-perfect flower clock in Tavares Corrêa Square, Garanhuns

Brazil. **Castainho**, a community descended from runaway slaves, is also part of Garanhuns. Some of its residents trace their families back to the fugitive slave community Quilombo dos Palmares. The top of **Colina do Cristo Magano** offers the best view of the city. While you're there, snap a photo of its 4-meter (13-foot) picture-postcard **flower clock** (*Praça Tavares Corrêa, at the beginning of Avenida Rui Barbosa*). To get from Recife to Garanhuns, take the BR-232 highway west to Km 150 (São Caetano), then go south on the BR-423 highway.

WINTER FESTIVAL

Garanhuns hosts the Festival de Inverno during July vacation. It's one of the main events on Pernambuco's tourist calendar. For ten days, various parts of the city host artistic presentations and workshops on visual arts, dance, literature, fashion, heritage, music, and theater. Festival de Inverno is organized by the Pernambuco State Department of Education and Culture (Fundarpe) in partnership with Garanhuns City Hall (*for more information call Fundarpe, tel. 81/3134-3077*).

FAZENDA NOVA

Since its so-called Nova Jerusalém theater complex opened 37 years ago, Fazenda Nova, 187 kilometers (116 miles) west of Recife, has gained international fame. The largest open-air theater in the world at 100,000 square meters (one million square feet), Nova Jerusalém has an area equivalent to one third of the walled area of the original city of Jerusalem. The sculptures in **Parque das Esculturas Monumentais Nilo Coelho** are another city attraction. (*Rua Antônio Lupe, no #, tel. 81/3732-1158; daily, 7am – 11am and 1pm – 5pm.*) The 60-hectare (148-acre) sculpture park contains 37 granite sculptures, some 2 meters (6.6 feet) tall. They represent religious, musical, folkloric, and other cultural aspects of the Northeast.

The Passion of Christ, staged in Nova Jerusalém

THE PASSION OF CHRIST IN NOVA JERUSALÉM

In 1951, entrepreneur Epaminondas Mendonça thought to stage the Passion of Christ in the streets of Fazenda Nova. Journalist Plínio Pacheco, who arrived in the city in 1956, expanded upon Mendonça's plan, with the vision of building a replica of Christ's Jerusalem. The first performance in the new theater, however, did not occur until 1968. Every year since then, from the day before Palm Sunday until Holy Saturday, an audience of around 8,000 has watched this performance of the best-known story in Western culture on nine enormous stages. Aided by the latest in special effects technology, 500 actors – including Brazilian television celebrities – perform for two and a half hours. The huge audience's members often become supporting actors in the interactive performance. The Good Friday show tends to be the week's most popular.

SERTÃO

SERRA TALHADA

Serra Talhada ("cut mountain range") takes its name from the large mountain range that rises in the north and ends abruptly in one clean cut (*talho*) of rockface. Approximately 430 kilometers (267 miles) west of Recife via the BR-232 highway, Serra Talhada is the birthplace of Virgulino Ferreira da Silva, the legendary *cangaceiro* Lampião. The city's main attraction is the small farm where the bandit was born in 1898. Serra Talhada is also known as the capital of *xaxado*, a rhythmic dance spread (but not invented) by Virgulino. On weekends the many *xaxado* groups rehearse throughout the city.

LAMPIÃO'S HOUSE

The small farm where the beloved bandit Lampião was born is 45 kilometers (28 miles) outside of town.

It became a museum in 2001 and features photographs, weapons, and possessions of the "*cangaceiros*' king." Getting there is an adventure, requiring travel along a hilly, poorly signed road full of stones, goats, cows, and flocks of hawks. Call in advance to ensure that the museum is open. Casa de Lampião – an informal organization set up by Anildomá Willians de Souza, an expert on Virgulino – often has guides available to accompany tourists to the museum. *45 kilometers (28 miles) from Fazenda São Miguel. 6 kilometers (4 miles) are on dirt roads. Estrada Virgulino Ferreira da Silva, tel. (87) 3831-2041 (Casa de Cultura). Daily, 7am – 4pm; arrange visits in advance.*

Xaxado

The triangle, *zabumba* drum, accordion, and tambourine accompany Lampião's favored dance. It's performed during June festivities and religious presentations and at the hour-long rehearsals held by *xaxado* groups on Saturday afternoons. The **Cabras de Lampião** and **Maria Bonita** groups rehearse at the Escola Estadual Methódio de Godoy Lima school (*Rua Manuel Antônio de Souza, 735, São Cristóvão*). The oldest of the groups, **Manuel Martins**, can be seen at the Faculdade de Formação de Professores de Serra Talhada college (*Avenida Afonso Magalhães, 380, Centro*), while **Cangaceiros da Vila Bela** rehearse at Colégio Antônio Timóteo school (*Rua Antônio Timóteo, no #, Bom Jesus*). Information on the groups and their rehearsals is available at the Fundação Casa de Cultura de Serra Talhada (*Praça Sérgio Magalhães, 868, Centro, tel. 87/3831-3454; Mon – Fri, 8am – noon and 1:30pm – 5:30pm; Sat, 8am – noon; Sun, 6pm – 10pm*).

Serra Talhada Municipal Market

The Mercado Municipal serves breakfast from 7am to 10am at communal counters scattered around the market. The one with the most customers tends to offer the best breakfast. Be sure to try *bolinho de caco*, a

Manuel Martins, the oldest *xaxado* group in Serra Talhada

kind of thick, sweet corn pancake. Lunch is served after 10am: *galinha capoeira* (the *sertão* version of *galinha caipira*, corn-fed backyard chicken), goat dishes, locally-grown red rice, and beef jerky with manioc. Pepper, manioc flour, water, and coffee are self-serve from the counters. Stall #26 offers choices beyond the local dishes – roast beef, lasagna, and grilled chicken. *Rua Deputado Afrânio Godoy, no #. Mon – Sat, 7am – 5pm.*

Triunfo

A few years of 1920s economic boom earned this town, 450 kilometers (280 miles) northwest of Recife, the nickname "Princess of the Sertão." Triunfo's sugarcane and coffee elite soon went bankrupt together, but not before leaving their mark architecturally. The old houses with well-preserved façades near the neo-Gothic church **Igreja Matriz Nossa Senhora das Dores** and around the lovely **Açude Borborema** reservoir in the town center are one attraction. The Teatro Guarany embodies the glory days of the 1920s and the Museu do Cangaço has an interesting collection of weapons and other possessions from the days when *cangaceiros* (bandits) controlled the Northeast. The highest point in Pernambuco – Pico do Papagaio – is within Triunfo's limits. Sugar mills such as São Pedro, which produces *rapadura* (brown sugar tablets) year-round, are plentiful on the road to Cachoeira do Pinga waterfall. **Biscoitos São Nicolau**, biscuits made with honey, cinnamon, and cloves, are a delicacy introduced by German nuns in 1939. Ivanilda Viana sells the homemade, heart-shaped *biscoitos* at her house. (*Rua José Nunes dos Santos, 74, Guanabara, tel. 87/3846-1432.*) To get to Triunfo from Recife, take the BR-232 highway west to Serra Talhada; from there, head north on the PE-365 state highway for 31 kilometers (19 miles).

Rapadura Mills
Triunfo is the backlands capital of *rapadura*. Between July and December,

Visitors can observe *rapadura* production in Triunfo's sugar mills

more than 60 small, traditional sugar mills produce the large tablets of brown sugar present on every table in the Northeast. These mills include the **Sítio Macaco** (*Zona Rural, 2 kilometers from the town center, tel. 87/3846-1239; Oct. – Dec., Tue – Fri, 4am – 4pm; visits must be arranged in advance*), **Sitio Timbaúba** (*PE-Triunfo-Flores, Zona Rural, 800 meters from the center; tel. 87/3846-1765; visits must be arranged in advance*), and **Sítio Serrinha** (*Zona Rural, 3 kilometers from the center, arrange visits with the Secretaria de Turismo, tel. 87/3846-1256*). **São Pedro** (*Sítio Bela Vista, Zona Rural, 500 meters from the center, next to Pousada Baixo Verde, tel. 87/3846-1229; daily, 7am – 4:30pm*) is the most organized of the mills and produces organic *cachaça* and liqueurs year-round. The road to the mills passes **Cachoeira do Pinga** waterfall, but you'll have to hire a guide to find it, as there are no signs. The waterfall has three cascades: the first has a pool, the second has a 50-meter (164-foot) drop, and the third, just a trickle in the dry season, earned the waterfall its name. ("Pingar" means "to trickle.") Locals often rappel down the waterfall. *Contact: The Secretaria de Turismo de Triunfo can recommend local guides. For information, call (87) 3846-1256.*

Cangaço Museum

Founded in 1971, this museum collects weapons, clothes, photographs, and possessions of famous *cangaceiros* (bandits) – from Corisco's knife to Lampião's old accordion and 1916 tray. The building also houses the Museu da Cidade (City Museum), featuring everyday objects from houses in Triunfo, and the Museu de Arte Sacra (Sacred Art Museum). The Sacred Art Museum exhibits the intriguing *roda dos enjeitados* (foundling wheel), where mothers placed their unwanted babies to be raised in convents and monasteries.
Praça Monsenhor Eliseu, no #, tel. (87) 3846-1124. Tue – Sun, 8am – noon and 2pm – 5pm.

Guarany Theater

Brothers and tradesmen Manuel and Carolino Siqueira Campos were inspired to build a large theater in Triunfo. Opened in 1922, the Teatro Guarany found its glory days short-lived. It fell into disuse that same decade, a result of Triunfo's political and economic decline. After several interior remodelings, the theater was repurposed as a bar, but it has since been restored to its original function. Teatro Guarany opens for shows on special dates, seating up to 180 people, though visits are possible all year.
Praça Carolino Campos, no #, Centro. Daily, 8am – noon and 2pm – 5pm.

Papagaio Peak

At an altitude of 1,260 meters (4,130 feet), Pico do Papagaio is the highest point in Pernambuco. Reaching the top involves an hour's drive over 9 kilometers (6 miles) of rough, rocky road, but the panoramas from the top are reward enough for the long ride.
Contact: The Secretaria de Turismo de Triunfo can recommend local guides. For information, call (87) 3846-1256.

Chico Santeiro

Francisco Pinheiro, known to many as Chico Santeiro, wandered the *sertão* at length before settling in Triunfo. Today he is considered the town's greatest artist. He is known for his distinctively styled wooden statues of saints with expressive features and beautiful finishes.
Avenida Getúlio Vargas, 206, Centro, tel. (87) 3846-1443. Daily, 9am – 9pm.

Petrolina

Petrolina, on the right bank of the São Francisco River in Pernambuco, connects to Juazeiro, Bahia, by bridge. Ferry boats also cross between the two cities (*see page 134*). The city embodies diversity and fusion, an identity embedded in its very name. "Petrolina" is a combination of "Pedro" (from Dom Pedro I) and "Leopoldina" (from Maria Leopoldina of Hapsburg, archduchess of Austria and empress of Brazil). The place used to be known as "Passagem de Joazeiro" (Joazeiro Walkway), a route for northeasterns heading towards the south of Brazil. Diversity exists not just in the city's name, but in its music – a rhythmic mix of *forró, pagode, axé,* rock, and *maracatu*. Planted in the middle of the *sertão*, 767 kilometers (477 miles) southwest of Recife, the city has defied drought to become Brazil's major fruit and flower exporter. It has also begun to perfect its production of wines, including Port, becoming the second major center in the country and the only one on northeastern soil. About five million boxes of grapes and twelve million boxes of mangos are sold annualy to Europe and Japan. Petrolina's highlights include the **Espaço Cultural Ana das Carrancas**, with its expressive figures, the **Museu do Sertão**, and the **Bodódromo**, a collection of restaurants which serve not goat (*bode*) as one might expect, but mutton. Heading west on the BR-232 highway from Recife will bring you to Petrolina, but passes an area with a high incidence of robberies. The stretch near Salgueiro is especially risky. A safer route approaches Petrolina from the south, via Juazeiro, Bahia. Petrolina airport greets regular flights from Recife and São Paulo.

Ana das Carrancas Cultural Center

Ana Leopoldina dos Santos, known as **Ana das Carrancas**, is one of the few women who make *carrancas* (grotesque gargoyle figures). Her work is notable not only for its material – clay rather than wood – but also for one specific detail: the empty eye sockets. She vowed years ago to make her *carrancas* eyeless if their sale would keep her blind husband from having to beg in the streets. Today, octogenarian Ana is extremely successful. Rock bands (the Carrancudos) and *maracatu* groups (Matingueiros) have honored her, the local journalist Emanuel de Andrade has written her biography (*Ana das Carrancas, a Dama do Barro*), and her work is available in Europe. The cultural center sells Ana's work and organizes workshops and courses for the community.
BR-407 highway, 500, Cohab Massangano, tel. (87) 3031-4399. Daily, 8am – 6pm. Call the Secretaria de Turismo before 1pm to schedule a visit.

Petrolina Cathedral

Community contributions helped build the neo-Gothic Catedral de Petrolina, which was finished in 1929 after four years of construction. The building's stones come from the banks of the São Francisco and the stained glass from Grenoble, France. The clock is a donation from Padre Cícero Romão Batista, a priest and politician from Ceará, recognized as a saint by northeasterners.
Praça Dom Malan, no #, Centro, tel. (87) 3861-3804. Mon – Fri, 6am – noon and 2:30pm – 5pm; Sat, 6am – noon; Sun, 9am – 10am and 4pm – 10pm.

Petrolina and its neo-Gothic cathedral

Sertão Museum

The Museu do Sertão's diverse collection encompasses the backlands universe. It features everything from Lampião's photographs and personal items to prehistoric fish fossils (proof that this region was once part of the ocean), from medicinal plants to a replica 18th-century backlands house. First opened in 1973, the museum was renovated and reopened in 1996.
Rua Esmelinda Brandão, no #, Centro, tel. (87) 3862-1943. Daily 8am – 6pm.

Bodódromo
Gastronomic Complex

In September 2000, City Hall donated land for a gastronomic complex specializing in goat meat. The complex opened with ten restaurants; now there are eight, none of which serve *bode* (goat). They've all switched to mutton for reasons of supply: sheep reproduce twice a year and can have up to four lambs while goats produce just one kid in the same period. Mutton is also more tender and has a milder smell than goat. The complex also includes a stage featuring musical shows, kiosks, and snack bars.
Avenida São Francisco, no #, Areia Branca. Daily, from 11am.

Wine in Petrolina

The phenomenon of São Francisco Valley wine production – the sun, northeastern soil, and river water allow the rare occurrence of biannual grape harvests – has already attracted the attention of European wine specialists. Unlike wines from the south of Brazil, this region's wines are young and produced in aluminum kegs rather than traditional wooden casks. **Vinícola Garziera**, built in 2003, is a tourist-friendly winery.
Fazenda Garibaldina, municipality of Lagoa Grande, 72 kilometers (45 miles) from Petrolina, towards Vermelhos. Tel. (87) 3869-9212. Arrange visits in advance, Mon – Sat, 9am – 4pm.

Paraíba

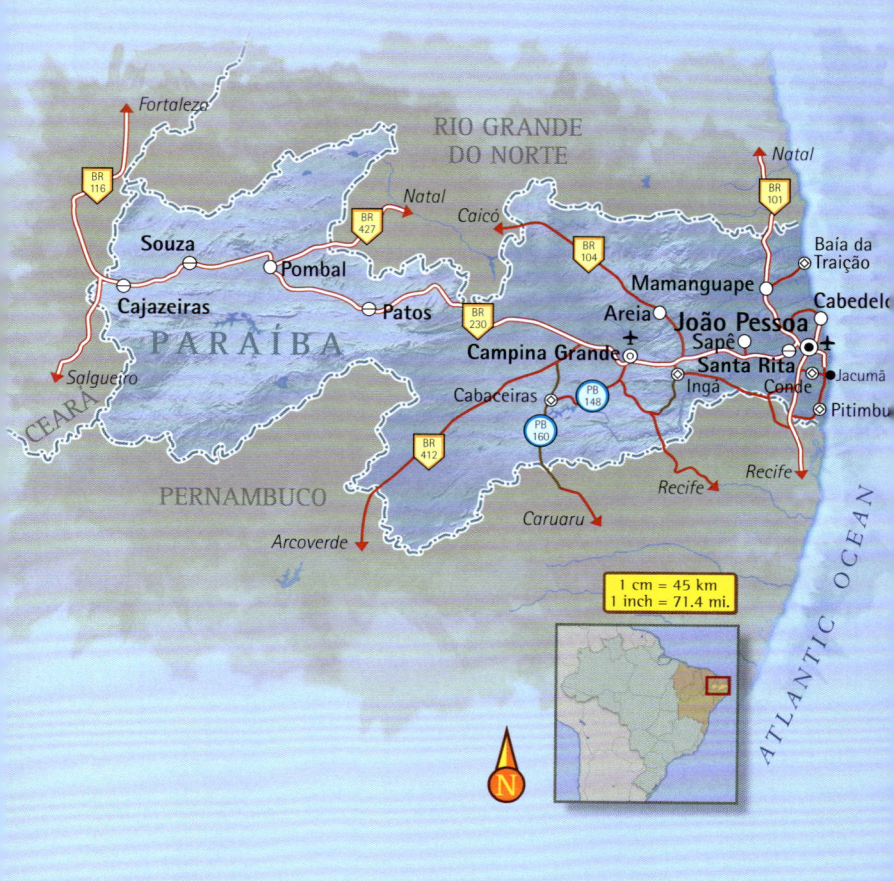

1 cm = 45 km
1 inch = 71.4 mi.

Highlights

- The urban beaches and historical buildings of **João Pessoa**.
- The easternmost point in South America – the Cabo Branco Lighthouse at **Ponta do Seixas**, in João Pessoa.
- The beaches and manatees at the Unesco Biosphere Reserve, **Barra de Mamanguape**.
- The granite expanse and boulders of Lajedo de Pai Mateus, in **Cabaceiras**, was the setting of the film *The Dog's Will* (*O Auto da Compadecida*).
- The prehistoric relics in the villages of **Ingá** and **Sousa**.

When to go

- In the busy **summer** (December to February), or in the low season if you want to relax in João Pessoa when it's quieter.
- **Any time of year** for the coast and inland towns like Areia, except during the rainy season, between May and July. Inland, in Cabaceiras, the sun shines year-round.
- During **Carnival**, visit a lively place like Jacumã, on the south coast.
- In **June**, sample some of the wildest festivities in Brazil, here in Campina Grande.
- Between **July and December**, in the dry season, for best viewing of the dinosaur tracks at Sousa village.

Paraíba's enchantment draws from both its history and its geography. In the early days of colonization, the Portuguese, French, and Dutch fought over the territory. Later, Paraíba played a significant role in political movements like the Revolução Pernambucana (1817) and the Confederation of the Equator (1824), in which the Carmelite Joaquim do Amor Divino, known as Frei Caneca, played an important role. In the 20th century, the assassination of governor João Pessoa, in Recife, ignited the 1930 revolution that ultimately turned Brazil into a populist dictatorship. Vestiges of these historical events are everywhere – starting with the capital's name. João Pessoa is one of the major tourist destinations in the state, and visitors flock here to see some of the country's most important architectural monuments, like the Redenção Palace (1586) and the São Francisco Church (1589). The region is also known for an important geographic feature: Ponta do Seixas, in João Pessoa, greets the dawn each morning as the easternmost tip of the South American continent. João Pessoa's lovely beaches are just a few of this coastline's many unforgettable landscapes of white sand, green seas, and coconut groves. In the developed state interior, Campina Grande's São João celebrations are the most popular in the country. The same region is home to other extraordinary attractions: the archeological site at Ingá, where stone inscriptions may be 25,000 years old, and the Vale dos Dinossauros (Dinosaur Valley), in Sousa, where researchers found a 50-meter (164-foot) stretch of dinosaur tracks, the longest such footprints in the world.

Ponta do Seixas, where the morning sun first shines on South America

JOÃO PESSOA

Sandwiched between the Sanhauá River and the Atlantic Ocean, this site's sunshine and reef-calmed seas are irresistible to visitors. A law prohibits the construction of waterfront buildings taller than four stories, enabling you to enjoy sunny beaches all day long. Besides its natural attractions, João Pessoa has enchanting baroque buildings and several excellent stores with regional handcrafts. Historically, the city has undergone several name changes. In 1585, it was founded as Nossa Senhora das Neves; in 1588, it was renamed Filipéia, to honor the reigning king of Portugal and Spain, Filipe I. With the Dutch invasion of 1634 came its new name, Frederica, an allusion to Prince Frederik of Orange. After the Dutch were expelled in 1654, the name was changed yet again to Paraíba, which means "arm of the sea" in Tupi-Guarani. In 1930 the assassination of the governor sparked such national fervor that the city was renamed for the final time in his name. This city of many names is 120 kilometers (75 miles) north of Recife and 180 kilometers (112 miles) south of Natal, along BR-101 highway.

BEACHES

The calm waters of João Pessoa – due in part to the barrier reef – are the backdrop to an increasingly popular tourist destination. Lively **Tambaú**, the city's central beach, has hotels, bars, kiosks, and street vendors. The wide strip of sand fills with walkers, joggers, and locals playing football and *frescobol,* a game for two played with wooden rackets and small rubber ball. In summer, the sea retreats to reveal the so-called "*picãozinho*" (little peak) coral formation. To the north, **Manaíra** and **Bessa**, two other city beaches, are not very different from Tambáu. The southern beach next to Tambáu, **Cabo Branco**, fills with people walking, running, and playing in the late afternoon. Between 5am and 8am the beach avenue closes to traffic; people walk, roller-skate, and work out along this pedestrian path. The Farol do Cabo Branco lighthouse is at **Ponta do Seixas**, the easternmost tip of South America. Be sure to catch the magnificent view of the city from the top of the lighthouse, but avoid the area at night – it becomes rather unsafe. Even further south is João Pessoa's very popular beach, **Penha**. Here you will find the famous church where the faithful approach on their knees.

SÃO FREI PEDRO GONÇALVES CHURCH AND SQUARE

The original Capela de São Frei Pedro Gonçalves was built in the 17th century and demolished in 1843 to make room for another church. Modifications of the new church, in 1916, created the structure that we see today. In 2002, restoration work uncovered the original foundations, which are now open to the public (*Largo São Frei Pedro Gonçalves, no #, Varadouro, tel. 83/3222-4777; Tue – Sun, 9am – noon and 2pm – 5pm*). To the left of the church square is another João Pessoa landmark, the **Hotel Globo**, built in 1929. This building, which today houses the Spanish consulate, features a style influenced by neo-classical and art deco periods. The best time to visit the square is in the late afternoon, as the sun spreads an orange glow over the buildings, painting everything in pastel shades. Try to visit here before 6pm, as the square becomes deserted and unsafe after that time.

The main beaches in João Pessoa attract sports fans

São Francisco Cultural Center

The Franciscans originally constructed this building – one of the best examples of Brazilian baroque – in 1589 as a wattle-and-daub convent. In 1602 they began construction on a limestone church, the **Igreja de São Francisco**. Construction on the frontispiece ended in 1779, with completion of the tower and the churchyard, in 1783 and 1788. The dates of construction are quickly forgotten, but no one forgets the interior of this old church: the nave, surrounded by a tiled mural depicting the story of Saint Joseph in Egypt, holds a beautifully carved pulpit. The ceiling painting depicts Saint Elias. To the left of the church is the Capela Dourada, a chapel with a statue of Saint Anthony and other gilded figures. The choir holds beautifully carved, jacaranda chairs and eight panels from the 18th century. The convent has functioned as a cultural center since 1990 and houses three museums. One museum features sacred art, another is dedicated to folk art, and the Galeria de Pedra, exhibits fragments of rocks from different eras, discovered during the church's restoration.

Praça de São Francisco, no #, tel. (83) 3218-4505. Tue – Sun, 9am – noon and 2pm – 5pm.

João Pessoa Square

State government buildings line Praça João Pessoa on all sides. The most imposing of these buildings is the **Palácio da Redenção**, the seat of government. The Jesuits built this palace in 1586, and today it houses the ashes of João Pessoa. It has undergone a series of alterations over time with the last in 1995 to remove a mosaic floor that contain displayed swastikas (*visits should be arranged by tel. 83/3216-8026*). Next to the palace is the **Faculdade de Direito da Paraíba**, a law school. The school operates out of the old Liceu Parahybano school building, which

Priceless tiles, paintings, and furniture fill São Francisco church

Palácio da Redenção, the seat of the Paraíba state government, contains João Pessoa's ashes

opened in 1745. On the opposite side of the square stands a state-protected building which was built in 1919 and houses the **Tribunal da Justiça**, the Justice Council. The crypt of former president Epitácio Pessoa can be found in the basement of this building. It is open in the morning for guided visits (tel. 83/3216-1515; Mon – Thu, 7am – 6pm; Fri, 7am – 1pm).

GUNPOWDER HOUSE
Sitting strategically on a rise, the small stone Casa da Pólvora fort built in 1710, used to be an arms store. Today it houses the **Museu Fotográfico Walfredo Rodrigues**, which has a small collection of photographs of the city. The biggest attraction, however, is the museum's view of the Sanhauá River.
Ladeira São Francisco, no #, Varadouro, tel. (83) 3222-8669 (Fundação Cultural de João Pessoa). Mon – Fri, 9am – noon and 2pm – 5pm.

SANTA ROSA THEATER
In the 36 years between the beginning of construction (1853) and opening day, this building was used as a military hospital. The neo-classical Teatro Santa Rosa finally opened its doors in 1889 to reveal its fine, imposing, German pine interior. After undergoing renovations 18 years ago, the theater now seats up to 418 people.
Praça Pedro Américo, no #, Centro, tel. (83) 3218-4383. Daily, 9am – noon, and 2pm – 6pm. On performance days, no fixed times.

ARTS AND CRAFTS

The Brazilian Agricultural Research Corporation developed colored cotton – which grows naturally in shades of beige – and produces it in the Campina Grande region. This raw material is used for hammocks, T-shirts, and other items sold at **Algodão de Cor** (Avenida Nego, 548, tel. 83/3247-6723; Mon – Sat, 9am – 7pm). The store also sells cotton rag dolls from Esperança, and work by the most important artisans in Paraíba. **Terra do Sol** (Rua Coração de Jesus, 145, tel. 83/3226-1940; Mon – Sat, 9am – 7pm), sells hand-woven cotton, sisal, wicker, and coconut fiber items, all produced by artisans in Gurinhém, in the interior of the state.

The neo-classical Santa Rosa Theater was once used as a military hospital

Tito Silva & Cia Winery

Inspired by French visitors to Paraíba, entrepreneur Tito Henrique da Silva established a winery in 1892. His wine, made from cashew fruit, won international acclaim at the beginning of the 20th century. Heavily in debt, the Fábrica de Vinhos Tito Silva & Cia closed down in the 1980s; however, the government's heritage institute declared the building, machinery, and equipment a National Heritage Site. Today, the three buildings house presses, casks, and other items. This is also the location of the **Oficina Escola de Revitalização do Patrimônio Cultural de João Pessoa,** a civic society dedicated to the revitalization of local culture. *Rua da Areia, 33, Varadouro. tel. (83) 3222-4302. Mon – Fri, 8am – 5pm.*

Literary Museums

Two of the greatest craftsmen of regional Brazilian literature, José Américo de Almeida (1887-1980) and José Lins do Rego (1901-1957), had their beginnings in Paraíba. The former was born in Areia and the latter in Pilar, and two cultural centers in the state capital bear their names. The **Fundação José Américo de Almeida** (*Avenida Cabo Branco, 3336, tel. 83/3214-8506; Mon – Fri, 9am – 5pm*) functions out of the house where the writer and politician (who governed Paraíba in 1950) lived from 1953 until his death. In addition to his personal affects, you can also see his small library – an extensive collection of books about the Northeast. The house, in the Cabo Branco neighborhood, stands right on the waterfront. It was the first building built when developers tackled that part of the shoreline. In addition to its responsibilities for the writer's collection, the foundation is also in charge of the heritage preservation projects occurring throughout the state. The **Fundação Espaço Cultural José Lins do Rego** (*Rua*

Abdias Gomes de Almeida, 800, Tambauzinho, tel. 83/3211-6270; Sat and Sun, 3pm – 7pm) is a cultural center housing a museum dedicated to the writer of *Menino do Engenho* (1932; published in English as *Plantation Boy*). José Lins do Rego spent part of his life in Pernambuco, although he died far away in Rio de Janeiro. Glass cases in the museum display manuscripts, books, and the author's old typewriter.

RELIGIOUS ARCHITECTURE

Aside from the São Francisco Church and Convent and São Frei Pedro Gonçalves Church, notable religious buildings include the Igreja de São Bento and Igreja de Nossa Senhora do Carmo. Both are distinguished by their ornate stone façades and rich interior carving. Built in the early 18th century, the government-protected **Igreja de São Bento** still retains its baroque façade, although the interior has lost many of its original features (*Rua General Osório, 60; the church stays open for one hour after mass, which occurs on Mon at noon and Tue – Sat at 7am; Thu, 6pm*).

Igreja de Nossa Senhora do Carmo is the other baroque church, annexed to the **Capela de Santa Teresa d'Ávila**. It is currently undergoing restoration (*Praça Dom Adauto, no #, tel. 83/3221-7817; Tue – Sat, 9m – 11am; mass: Sun, 10am*). The modest and largely unadorned **Igreja da Misericórdia** has stood since the 16th century. You can still see the emblem of the Portuguese Crown on the arch above the high altar (*Rua Duque de Caxias, no #, Centro*). Where the city's first chapel went up in 1585, the 19th century **Matriz de Nossa Senhora das Neves** now stands. Its eclectic façade is a product of extensive renovations that occurred between 1881 and 1884 (*Praça Dom Ulrico, no #, Centro, tel. 83/3221-2503; Mon – Fri, 2pm – 6pm; Sat, 5pm – 9pm; Sun, 6am – 11:30am and 5pm – 9pm*).

The restored façades of historical buildings in João Pessoa

The Coast

The north coast of Paraíba sharply contrasts with the south coast: **Jacumã**, in the south, is a district of Conde and a victim of chaotic urban sprawl; **Barra de Mamanguape**, in the north, is a Unesco Biosphere Reserve. Jacumã, accessible by the PB-008 highway, is lively and full of tourists. It draws the bulk of its tourist crowds from João Pessoa, 35 kilometers (22 miles) to the north. Carnival here is one of the busiest events in Paraíba; Jacumã serves as a base for neighboring Carapibus, Tabatingas and Coqueirinho during major festivals like Carnival. Jacumã is also home to **Tambaba**, one of the most famous nude beaches in Brazil. While Jacumã is an ideal tourist getaway, Barra do Mamanguape, 48 kilometers (30 miles) north of João Pessoa, has no hotels and thus would serve better as a day trip. The strong waves of **Praia Campina** and **Praia do Oiteiro** beaches are very popular with surfers. In Mamanguape, where the Rio Mamanguape meets the sea, the **Projeto Peixe-Boi**, an Ibama (Brazilian Institute of Environment and Renewable Natural Resources) project, plays a fundamental role in the protection of the manatee.

TAMBABA

The most famous beach in Jacumã is also a haven for nudists. Rules are strict: access is controlled and bathers have to keep their clothes in bags given out at the beach entrance. Cameras are forbidden (our photographer obtained an exception), and men are only allowed in if accompanied by women. Before you get to the nudist area, there is a

Charming Tambaba, a dedicated nude beach

RIO GRANDE DO NORTE

Baía da Traição
Calm waters and yellow sand, near an Indian reservation, where you can buy Indian-crafted artifacts.

Barra de Mamanguape
Virtually untouched, in an environmentally protected area. Headquarters of the Projeto Peixe-Boi manatee project. Reefs shield the beach, producing calm seas.

Tambaú
One of the liveliest beaches on the coast of Paraíba, with calm seas and powdery white sand. A paved promenade has bars, restaurants, and nightclubs.

Cabo Branco
A well-developed, urban beach, with coconut groves, cliffs, pale sand, and gentle seas.

Coqueirinho
Primarily isolated and quiet – one of the loveliest beaches on the coast, with freshwater springs and high, multi-hued cliffs.

Tambaba
A nude beach, with seas calmed by surrounding rocks. An area is reserved for people who prefer to remain clad.

Map labels:

- Natal
- Guaju
- da Baleia
- Barra de Camaratuba
- Mataraca
- do Giz Branco
- do Forte
- Baía da Traição
- Marcação
- Coqueirinho do Norte
- Rio Tinto
- Rio Mamanguape
- Mamanguape
- Guarabira
- Barra de Mamanguape
- Campina
- do Oiteiro
- Miriri
- Bonsucesso
- Rio Miriri
- Lucena
- Ponta de Lucena
- Gameleira
- Fagundes
- Costinha
- Cabedelo
- Ponta de Matos
- Ilha da Restinga
- Areia Dourada
- Camboinha
- do Poço
- Sapé
- Intermares
- do Bessa
- Rio Paraíba
- Santa Rita
- João Pessoa
- Manaíra
- Tambaú
- Bayeux
- Cabo Branco
- Ponta do Seixas
- Penha
- do Arraial
- BR 230
- Jacarapé
- Camurupim
- do Sol
- Campina Grande
- Rio Mamuaba
- Barra do Gramame
- Conde
- Jacumã
- Jacumã
- do Amor
- Carapibus
- Tabatinga
- Coqueirinho
- Tambaba
- Barra do Garaú
- Bela
- Pedras de Fogo
- Alhandra
- PERNAMBUCO
- 1 cm = 6,.5 km
- 1 inch = 10.3 mi.
- Pitimbu
- Pitimbu
- dos Mariscos
- Caaporã
- Acaú
- Acaú
- Recife

Inset: RN / PE / João Pessoa / PB

Highways: PB 065, BR 101, PB 041, PB 025, PB 019, PB 004, BR 230, BR 101, PB 018, PB 034, PB 008, PB 044

ATLANTIC OCEAN

N

200-meter (656-foot) stretch reserved for anyone who prefers to remain dressed.

BARRA DE MAMANGUAPE

One of those rare stretches of coast in Paraíba that has resisted the chaotic development, the Mamanguape Area of Environmental Protection includes a fishing village and some of the loveliest beaches in the state. **Praia Campina** attracts mostly surfers with its strong waves. At **Praia do Oiteiro**, the waves are equally good for surfing, but the scenery – dominated by red cliffs and coconut palms – is the main attraction. The **Projeto Peixe-Boi** (*Estrada da Barra de Mamanguape, no #, tel. 83/3228-3865; Tue – Sun, 10am – 4pm*), run by Ibama's Center for Aquatic Mammals, has been operating out of Barra de Mamanguape since 1985. This provides a rare opportunity to see manatees in their natural habitat. These animals usually reproduce in calm estuary waters, but as these areas are filled with silt, females give birth out at sea. The waves carry off the vulnerable calves and, if they are lucky, beaches them. At this stage the project's team goes into action, taking

---

CABEDELO

Soon after arriving in the area surrounding the Paraíba River, the Portuguese recognized the need to fortify the sea route to the new city of Nossa Senhora das Neves. They constructed Cabedelo, 18 kilometers (11 miles) north of Paraíba to protect the capital. Little remains from that construction, however, aside from the **Fortaleza de Santa Catarina** (*see photo*), a fort built in 1589 (*Rua Francisco Serafim, no #, tel. 83/3228-3959; daily, 8:30am – 5:30pm*). A daily spectacle occurring on **Praia Fluvial de Jacaré** has become famous beyond Cabedelo and the state itself. Every day Jurandy Félix, known as **Jurandy do Sax**, plays Ravel's *Bolero* on the banks of the river, as the setting sun reflects in the waters of the Sanhauá River. The event has become so popular that today many bars broadcast Jurandy's performance. Be sure to take the 15-minute ferry to **Costinha,** a district of Lucena. Don't be surprised if you see a bus traveling alongside the ferry: it's actually a bus frame mounted on a motorboat, which crosses the estuary at a more affordable price. Locals tend to favor the bus-motorboat crossing to the more expensive ferry. Whether you reach Costinha by ferry or by bus, don't miss the **Igreja de Nossa Senhora da Guia**. This enchanting church was built in the 16th century and reconstructed two centuries later. On the outside, its ornate stone façade depicts tropical fruit; inside, the mid-18th-century rococo altars are also carved from stone (*Estrada de Lucena, Km 4; daily, 7am – 4pm*).

Baía da Traição preserves its natural riches

the manatees to stay in an enclosure until they can be transferred to the manatee rehabilitation center on Itamaracá Island, in Pernambuco. In the Mamanguape base you can observe the manatees and the mangroves from a wooden lookout point (it's essential to take insect repellent). A nearby small gift shop sells locally crafted, plush manatee toys.

TRAIÇÃO BAY

The origin of the name Baía da Traição (Betrayal Bay) stretches back to the first Portuguese explorers: they are said to have named the bay in reference to an Indian ambush, or, according to another version, in reference to a sailors' mutiny. Although the memory of the actual incident has faded, the name has survived, just as the area's pristine landscape has remained untouched. This collection of beaches, many surrounded by high cliffs, is home to the Potiguar Indians. The Indians sell their handiwork in the 24 villages. Baía da Traição – 85 kilometers (53 miles) north of João Pessoa on the BR-101 highway – runs the **Centro de Cultura e Apoio ao Turista** (*Rua Ednílson de Medeiros, no #, tel. 83/3296-1385; daily, 8am – 11am and 2pm – 4pm*), an information center for tourists who want to visit these communities. There are plenty of other activities offered in the Baía da Traição: a catamaran trip up the Camaratuba River, a warm-water dive in the Lagoa Encantada lagoon, and a stop at Rio Tinto, an industrial, English-style village, which seems frozen in time.

INLAND

Paraíba's interior, which alternates mountain ranges with *sertão*, is one of the most prosperous inland areas in the Northeast. It is home to the second largest city in the state, **Campina Grande**. The area still has traces of the days when it was one of the greatest cotton producers in the world, but today it relies on the tourist industry by attracting large crowds to its grandiose folk celebrations. The Festa do Bode is a traditional event which takes place in the municipality of **Cabaceiras**; here you can also find the intriguing rock formations and drawings of the Lajedo de Pai Mateus. There are two other pre-historic treasures in the interior: the **Ingá** archeological site, with its millennia-old inscriptions, and the Vale dos Dinossauros (Dinosaur Valley), in the village of **Sousa**. One of the longest sections of dinosaur tracks was discovered in the village. Tiny **Areia**, on top of the Serra de Borborema range, is another historical must-see: Iphan declared this 19th-century town a National Heritage Site in 2005.

CAMPINA GRANDE

Sitting in the Serra da Borborema range, 125 kilometers (78 miles) west of João Pessoa, Campina Grande can be reached from the BR-232 highway. Founded in 1790 under the name Vila Nova da Rainha, Campina Grande took on its current name in 1864 when it officially became a city. Its brief moment of glory came in the mid-19th century, when the Civil War interrupted cotton production in the United States. That event elevated Brazil to the position of second major cotton producer in the world (England's Liverpool-based industry took first place). Alongside its historical traditions, the city zealously maintains its culture of music and folk festivals: this is the home of the original *forró*, called **pé-de-serra** – a dance accompanied by the triangle, *zabumba* drum, and accordion. The city's **São João festivities** are the most visited celebrations in the country. In June, approximately one million people show up for the festivities. On the night of June 23rd alone, the Parque do Povo – an enormous building in the center of the city that houses several artisans' stalls – admits 80,000 people to see *quadrilha* (quadrille) square-dances. Dancers perform about 300 such dances over the course of the month. In June and July, the fun extends during the weekend to the Trem Ferroviário, a train that brings a "traveling dance" to the district of Galante, 12 kilometers (7 miles) away. Each of the seven seat-less carriages has a trio of musicians. The *forró* train departs from the railroad station at 10am (*Praça Coronel Antônio Pessoa, 124, tel. 83/3341-1908*). The Parque do Povo in Campina Grande also holds the **Micarande**, the very popular out-of-season Carnival celebration in April.

COTTON MUSEUM
The Museu do Algodão, located in the old railroad station, keeps alive the memory of the time when cotton (known as "white gold") was the foundation of Campina Grande's

economy. The museum's collection includes apparatus – mostly rudimentary pieces made of wood – utensils, and photographs, as well as an authentic cotton bale weighing 100 kilos (220 pounds).
Rua Benjamin Constant, Largo da Estação Velha, no #, tel. (83) 3341-1039. Daily 8am – 11am and 1pm – 5pm.

CAMPINA GRANDE HISTORY MUSEUM

This building, from 1814, originally housed the city council and prison. Here, the government held captive the Carmelite friar Frei Caneca for his role in the Confederation of the Equator uprising. In 1897 the building held the Telagraph Company – the façade's inscription still reads "Telegráfo Nacional" (National Telegraph). The Museu Histórico de Campina Grande occupies the ground floor, featuring a collection of maps, photographs, and notes explaining the local history stretching from the first Indian villages, through to the sugarcane and cotton booms.
Rua Marechal Floriano Peixoto, 825, tel. (83) 3310-6182. Daily, 8am – noon and 1pm – 5pm.

ASSIS CHATEAUBRIAND MUSEUM OF ART

Founded in 1967 and run by the State University of Paraíba, the Museu de Arte Assis Chateaubriand has an important collection of 560 works, including paintings by artists Di Cavalcanti, Lasar Segall, and Tomie Ohtake. The collection, however, has currently been relocated; the museum features just one gallery of 54 works, but with canvasses by Brazilian painters Pedro Américo and Cândido Portinari, the visit is still worthwhile. Guided tours are available.
Avenica Marechal Floriano Peixoto, 718, Centro, tel. (83) 3310-9733.

A group dances the *quadrilha* in Campina Grande's São João festivities

Arts and Crafts

At **Dona Terra** (*Shopping Iguatemi, Avenida Severino Bezerra Cabral, no #, store #84, tel. 83/3337-6364; Mon – Sat, 10am – 10pm; Sun, 2pm – 8pm*), shoppers can browse Embrapa's famous items, which are made of naturally colored cotton. **Núcleo Familiar de Brinquedo Popular** (*BR-230 highway, Lagoa de Dentro, 4586, tel. 83/3334-8036; Mon – Sat, 8am – 9pm*) sells *piões* (spinning tops), wooden cars, yo-yos, *petecas* (shuttlecocks), and other classic, popular, and traditional Brazilian toys.

Cabaceiras

The quiet streets and simple, old houses of Cabaceiras served as the setting for the films *The Dog's Will* (*O Auto da Compadecida;* 2000) by Guel Arraes and *Cinema, Aspirins and Vultures* (Cinema, Aspirinas e Urubus; 2005) by Marcelo Gomes. Far away from the big screen, Cabaceiras, 69 kilometers (43 miles) southwest of Campina Grande and 193 kilometers (120 miles) southwest of João Pessoa, is the stage for the traditional **Festa do Bode** (Goat Fair). The fair takes place at the end of May and lasts for three days, completely occupying the town's interest for the duration. Here they sell or exchange the best-looking and fittest animals, buy and sell the latest goatskin items, and choose the year's "Goat King". The local reverence for this animal is well justified: tucked away in the semi-arid area known as Sertão do Cariri, Cabaceiras relies on goat breeding for economic survival. But life's not all about goats: with musical performances and other

Lajedo de Pai Mateus: boulders sit on an immense granite expanse

attractions, the fair also attracts those who are just looking for fun. The biggest attraction is a trip to the magnificent **Lajedo de Pai Mateus**, a huge flat granite formation – far bigger than a soccer field – peppered with enormous boulders. According to legend, the faith healer who gave his name to the place lived here in the 18th century, under the helmet-shaped boulder called **Pedra do Capacete**. The *lajedo* is located on property that belongs to Crysostomo Lucena de Almeida. If you wish to visit the area, ask his relative, Lucena de Almeida, for permission. It is easy to get lost among the stones, so be sure to ask Mrs. Almeida for a guide. The sun can be relentless on the flat granite – take a hat and water for protection. Since June 2004, more than 18,000 hectares (44,500 acres) of the region that includes Lajedo de Pai Mateus have come together to form the Cariri Area of Environmental Protection. Approaching the city from João Pessoa, take the BR-230 highway west to Campina Grande, then follow the PB-148 state highway south, toward Queimadas. Be doubly careful on the winding road from Boqueirão.

LEATHER CRAFTS
The small district of **Ribeira,** in Cabaceiras' rural zone, has the ten workshops known as **Arteza** (*tel. 83/3356-9001; Mon – Sat, 8am – noon and 1pm – 5pm*). This cooperative of leather curers and artisans makes shoes, bags, sandals, hats, and other items in the traditional way and sells the finely crafted items on site at attractive prices. Work produced at Arteza, which opened in 1998, can also be found in Campina Grande, Brasília, and São Paulo.

The inscriptions on Pedra de Ingá are thousands of years old

INGÁ

The **Sítio Arqueológico** makes this small town famous beyond the limits of Paraíba. The archeological site contains the **Pedra de Ingá**, also known as Itacoatiara de Ingá ("itacoatiara" means "stone inscriptions" in Tupi-Guarani). This 24-meter (79-feet)-long and 3.8-meter (12.5-foot)-high stone contains inscriptions that specialists figure may have been made 25,000 years ago, probably by groups who worshipped water. Tourists from all over the world visit the site. It escapes neglect thanks to the efforts of Cecília and Renato Alves da Silva, a local couple who receive no compensation for looking after this natural monument – it's "a labor of love". The famous Itacoatiara is accessible through the house that serves as an "archeological museum", with illustrations and maps.
Ingá is 109 kilometers (68 miles) southwest of João Pessoa, along the BR-230 highway.
Sítio Arqueológico de Ingá, no #. Daily 7am – 5pm.

AREIA

Tiny, enchanting Areia lacks good accommodations, but it is worth a visit, especially for anyone already in Campina Grande. Perched at the top of the Serra da Borborema range, the town is 49 kilometers (30 miles) northeast of Campina Grande and 130 kilometers (81 miles) west of João Pessoa on the BR-230 highway. Sugarcane plantations surrounded the town of Areia, since sugarcane used to thrive in its damp soil. Economic prosperity produced an intellectual, liberal elite, who became responsible for the lovely architecture that Iphan protects today. The same elite financed the building of the **Teatro Minerva** (*Rua Epitácio Pessoa, 102; Mon – Fri, 7am – 11am and 1pm – 5pm*) in

1859, which became the first theater in Paraíba. The Minerva, originally known as Recreio Dramático, owes its current name to the statue of the Roman goddess who stands atop the frontispiece. The small, gable-roofed theater stages plays by the town's drama groups. Novelist and politician José Américo de Almeida (1887-1980) was born in Areia, as was Pedro Américo (1843-1905), one of the most important 19th-century Brazilian painters. Known for the painting *Independência ou Morte* (Independence or Death), among others, Américo's work is featured in the Paulista Museum (also called the Ipiranga Museum) in São Paulo. At only nine years of age, Américo left Areia to draw for an expedition, led by a French naturalist, that traveled around the Northeast. His former house is known as **Museu Pedro Américo** (*Rua Pedro Américo, 66; daily, 8am – noon and 1pm – 5pm*), and even though it does not contain any original works by the artist (just black-and-white copies), art students often come here. Many visitors enjoy the **Museu do Brejo Paraibano**, also known as the **Museu da Cachaça e da Rapadura** (*Universidade Federal da Paraíba, Campus II, Areia, tel. 83/3362-2300, extension 216; Mon – Fri, 7am – 11am and 1pm – 5pm; Sat, Sun, and holidays, arrange visits in advance*). This Várzea sugarcane plantation *casa-grande* (master's big house) has a collection of furniture, utensils, and other items from the sugar boom. Located on the Areia campus of the Federal University of Paraíba and built around 1870, it is a typical Paraíba plantation – solid, simple, without ostentation, and very different from the luxurious constructions in other northeastern states.

Sousa

Sousa's 51 dinosaur footprints, spread out over 50 meters (164 feet) are among the world's longest stretches of dinosaur tracks. The footprints line the bottom of the Peixe River Valley, fittingly known as **Vale dos Dinossauros** (Dinosaur Valley). The passageway known as the Passagem das Pedras contains nine tracks, and the museum helps visitors understand the immense importance of this natural treasure. Try to visit the valley during the dry season, between July and December, when it's easiest to explore the Peixe River basin within two days. Visits must be arranged in advance. (*The tracks are just off the road to Uiraúna, 8 kilometers 5 miles/from Sousa, tel. 83/3522-3055; daily, 7am – 5pm.*) When visiting Sousa, you can also buy hand-made hammocks and bedcovers, which stores all over town sell. Sousa is located 436 kilometers (271 miles) west of João Pessoa along the BR-230 highway.

Prehistoric tracks line Dinosaur Valley

RIO GRANDE DO NORTE

HIGHLIGHTS

- The architecture and culture of Natal's **Cidade Alta** and **Ribeira** districts.
- The life and works of folklorist, historian, and ethnographer **Luís da Câmara Cascudo**, whose memorial and home are in Natal.
- Dune buggy trips to beaches near the Ceará border, including **Touros, São Miguel do Gostoso, Galinhos,** and **Ponta do Mel**.
- Pleasant **Pipa** beach, in Tibau do Sul, and the other highly developed beaches to the south.
- The festivities, food, and archeological sites of **Rio Grande do Norte's** *sertão*.

WHEN TO GO

- Any time of year for the excellent beaches, though prices and crowds peak in summer (December to February).
- In **June and July,** to square dance and savor local delicacies during the Seridó region's popular São João festivities.

Rio Grande do Norte

The Portuguese settlement of Rio Grande do Norte began just one year after the discovery of Brazil. In 1501, a squadron led by Gaspar Lemos landed on the coast of São Miguel do Gostoso (then known as Touros) and erected the Marco de Touros, the official emblem of the Portuguese crown. True occupation of the region, however, took another century, due to French invasions and the resistance of the native Potiguar Indians. ("Potiguar" means "shrimp-eater" in Tupi-Guarani.) With the help of troops from Pernambuco and Paraíba, Portugal finally seized control in 1598, beginning construction on the Forte dos Reis Magos. Its site would become the city of Natal.

The well-preserved fort is worth visiting, both for its historic value and for its excellent view of the city and the sunny, seductive coastline beyond. The state's natural scenery dazzles with shifting dunes in pink and beige, isolated beaches, and lakes of all sizes. Dune buggy trips are the most pleasant way to explore the coastal areas. Farther inland, find the rich folk culture of those who have braved arid conditions to preserve both Portuguese and native Indian traditions.

The city of Natal grew out of Forte dos Reis Magos, built at the end of the 16th century

NATAL

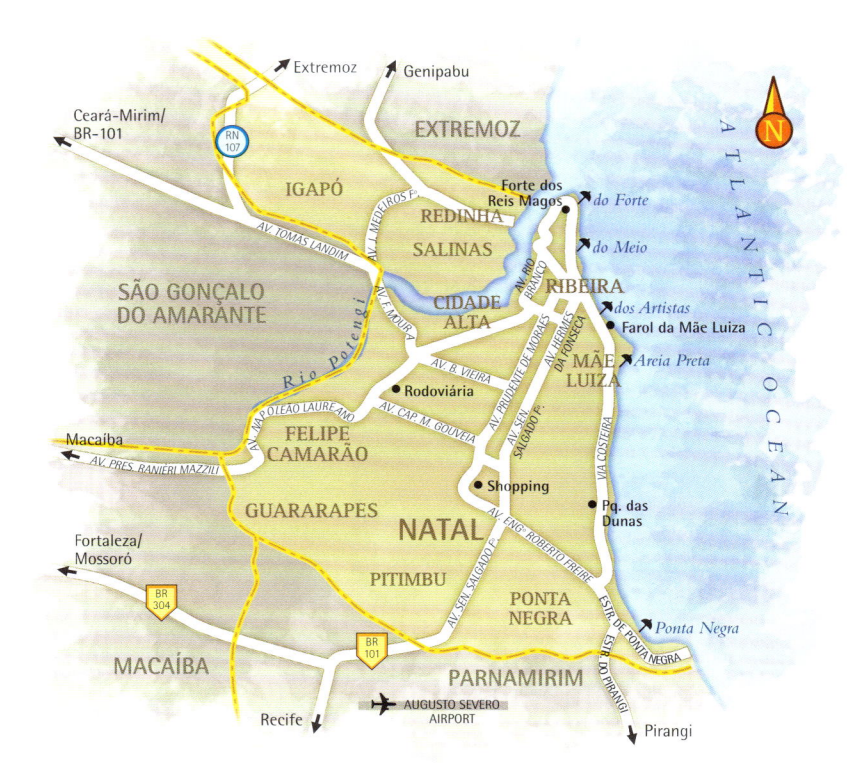

Nestled among endless rolling sand dunes, Natal occupies the scenic stretch of coast between the Atlantic and the Rio Potengi (formerly the Rio Grande do Norte). The left bank of the river was once inhabited by Potiguar Indians. On December 25, 1599, the Portuguese celebrated mass on the site of the original Potiguar settlement, naming it "Natal" ("Christmas") to commemorate the event. The state capital's year-round sunshine and friendly reputation earned it the nickname "Bride of the Sun" from folklorist Luís da Câmara Cascudo.

Via Costeira is the city's main drag and the site of most facilities for travelers. The coastal avenue links the city center, in the higher part of town, to Ponta Negra, Natal's nightlife hotspot. Natal is also the main departure point for dune buggy excursions to the famous Genipabu dunes (north of the Potengi River) and to the magnificent north and south coasts.

REIS MAGOS FORT

Built by the Portuguese as protection against the French, the five-pointed Forte dos Reis Magos is strategically positioned at the Potengi River's meeting with the ocean. The Portuguese broke ground for the fortress in 1598, on the day of the

Feast of the Epiphany (January 6). Since that feast celebrates the visit of the three Magi to see the baby Jesus, the star-shaped fort is called "Fort of the Magi." The wattle and daub walls were replaced with stone in 1628. Today visitors reach the well-preserved fort by an 800-meter walkway over marshland. The views of Natal, the ocean, and the river from the fort are unforgettable. An arms museum inside displays the Marco de Touros, a limestone block inscribed with the king of Portugal's cross and sword insignia. It originally stood on Praia do Marco, in São Miguel do Gostoso, signifying that the surrounding lands were Portuguese possessions. The fort's captain's quarters features a small exhibition of objects found during excavation work. More disturbing are the three torture chambers in the fort's underground dungeon. A particularly gruesome chamber features a deep hole that, when filled with sea water, drowned the prisoners held there. *Praia do Forte, no #, tel. (84) 3202-9006. Daily, 8am – 4pm.*

Mãe Luiza Lighthouse and Dune Park

One hundred fifty spiraling steps lead to the highest point in Natal, the Farol de Mãe Luiza, also called the Farol de Natal. (*Rua Camaragibe, no #, Mãe Luiza, tel. 84/3201-0477; Mon – Fri, 9am – 11am and 2pm – 4pm; Sun, 2pm – 5pm.*) Opened in 1951, the lighthouse is 37 meters high, but stands at 87 meters above sea level (with visibility of 39 nautical miles out to sea) because it was built on a sand dune. The 360-degree view from the top is one of Natal's finest, taking in parts of the Parque Estadual Dunas de Natal (also known as the Parque das Dunas, or Dune Park). The park was Rio Grande do Norte's first conservation area, created in 1977. Part of the Brazilian Atlantic Forest Biosphere Reserve since 1994, the park is a 1,172-hectare (2,896-acre) tree-covered dune. The park is well-cared for and has excellent signage. It offers hiking trails, a playground, an amphitheater, a picnic area, and a visitor's center, which arranges trips to the vivarium. The

The Farol de Mãe Luiza offers an unrivaled view of Natal

Enjoy the sunset from the deck on the River Potengi, in Ribeira

center also displays park photographs and offers restrooms and drinking water. Several guided walks are available: Perobinha (800 meters round-trip) is suitable for children. Beroba (2,800 meters round-trip) visits Barreira Roxa lookout point. Ubaia Doce (4,400 meters round-trip) is a difficult walk along steep slopes.
Avenida Alexandrino de Alencar, no #, tel. (84) 3201-3985. Tue – Sun, 8am – 6pm. Jogging: 4:30am – 6pm. Guided walks: between 8am – 8:30am and 2pm – 2:30pm.

Our Recommendation

🍽 The décor at **Manary Praia Hotel** features folk artifacts and craftwork from the Northeast – including cheese molds, *rapadura* crushers, and corn mills – as well as similar works from more than fifty other countries. The cozy rooms have hammocks on the balconies. Possibly Natal's best hotel, Manary Praia offers massages and a library focused on the architecture, craftwork, and natural beauty of Rio Grande do Norte.
Rua Francisco Gurgel, 9067, Ponta Negra, tel. 84/3204-2900).

Additional information on page 358.

Ponta Negra Nightlife

With the exception of the Ribeira neighborhood, the central areas of Natal are deserted at night. It's a striking contrast to the city's nighttime beach scene, where an active nightlife centers on the beach at Ponta Negra, near Morro do Careca hill (closed to traffic to protect the dune from erosion). On this stretch of coast, shops, restaurants, and live-music bars stay open late, attracting travelers, the *bugueiros* (dune buggy drivers) who accompany them, and local youth. For a quieter night, walk away from the hill along the pleasant stone promenade.

Upper City

Natal's residential neighborhoods are mostly in the upper part of the city, Cidade Alta. The lower part of the city is mostly historic. The rainwater that collected there drained to the Potengi River, earning the lower-district neighborhood the name Ribeira ("Floodplain"). These upper and lower parts of Natal are home to the city's oldest buildings and squares, often overlooked in favor of coastal attractions. The neo-classical **Instituto Histórico e Geográfico do Rio Grande do Norte** (*Rua da Conceição, 622, tel. 84/3232-9728; Mon – Fri, 8am – noon and 2pm – 5pm*) features everything from rare books to a baptismal font. The entrance to Cidade Alta is marked by the **Coluna Capitolina**, a gift of Benito Mussolini to reciprocate the warm welcome Natal gave to two Italian pilots who landed here in 1928. Don't miss the tiny **Museu Café Filho** (*Rua da Conceição, 601, Ribeira, tel. 84/3221-3333; Tue – Sun, 8am – 5pm*), which houses the personal effects of João Café Filho, a Rio Grande do Norte native who served as president of Brazil in 1954 and 1955 (in the aftermath of President Getúlio Vargas's suicide). Built between 1816 and 1820, the museum's Iphan-protected building is called the "bridal veil" because of its steeply sloped white roof. The **Teatro Alberto Maranhão** (*Praça Augusto Severo, no #, Ribeira, tel. 84/3222-3669, 3232-9702; Mon – Fri, 9am – 6pm; on performance days, no fixed times*) is Rio Grande do Norte's most important theater, founded in 1904 by the governor who gave it his name. In addition to its dazzling interior – patterned floor tiles, giant crystal mirrors, and handsome chandeliers – the theater features a small garden and café. The impressive auditorium has a unique, inlaid Belgian tile floor and two tiers of wooden seating for up to 642 people.

Ribeira

The historic Ribeira neighborhood is a highlight of Natal's lower city. Lovely cobblestone **Rua Chile** is the neighborhood's heart. During the day, the fish trade near the port is the main order of business, but after sunset, the city's life is in its nightclubs. A unique city sight is the **Pedra do Rosário**, also known as the **Paço da Pátria**, a deck on the Porengi River featuring a statue of the Virgin Mary. According to folklorist Câmara Cascudo, a box containing a statue of the Virgin Mary washed up on the site in 1753, on the feast day of the Presentation of the Blessed Virgin Mary. As a result, Nossa Senhora da Apresentação (Our Lady of the Presentation) became the patroness and protector of Natal. The original 1753 statue stands in the city's cathedral. Today the deck, surrounded by boats, is an ideal spot to enjoy the sunset. Nearby is the famous **Canto do Mangue**, a series of small quays where fishermen sell their fresh catches in the early morning hours.

Barreira do Inferno Launch Center

The Centro de Lançamento da Barreira do Inferno takes its name from the 28-meter red cliff named the *barreira do inferno* (barrier of hell) by local fishermen. The launch center is on a strip of coast between two beaches, Ponta Negra to the north and Pium to the south, in the municipality of Nova Parnamirim. The rocket launch site was created in 1965, though the main launchpad has since been transferred to Alcântara, in Maranhão *(see page 346)*. Today the center gathers meteorological information and exhibits replicas of launched rockets. Its two former launch pads are visible in the distance from a lookout point. Visits to the center must be pre-arranged and accompanied by a guide, since the area belongs to the Brazilian Army. A car is required, as there are long drives inside the complex. *RN-063 highway, Km 11, tel. (84) 3216-1270, 3216-1304. Mon – Fri, 8am – 5pm.*

Art Studios

Flávio Freitas and Dorian Gray are Natal's most prestigious artists. **Flávio Freitas** paints huge contemporary figurative works in acrylics and oils. He also does woodcut prints. His signature colors are red and ochre.

The 28-meter red cliffs of Barreira do Inferno

The Câmara Cascudo Memorial contains many of the folklorist's personal effects

(*Avenida Duque de Caxias, 182, Ribeira, tel. 84/3221-0070; Mon – Fri, 8am – 6pm; Sat, 8am – noon, arrange visits in advance.*) **Dorian Gray**, a painter, illustrator, engraver, poet, and author of more than thirty books, draws prolific inspiration from the land, folklore, and regional themes. His name comes from his father's passion for Oscar Wilde's book *The Portrait of Dorian Gray*. In 1955, Gray painted *O Cangaceiro* (*The Bandit*), a portrait of Lampião. The painting now stands at the entrance of the Casa de Câmara Cascudo, a museum dedicated to Gray's great friend and fellow writer Luís da Câmara Cascudo. (*Studio: Avenida Nascimento de Castro, 190 A, Lagoa Nova, tel. 84/3206-6380; Mon – Fri, 9am – 5pm*).

THE LIFE AND WORK OF CÂMARA CASCUDO

The folklorist, historian, and ethnographer Luís da Câmara Cascudo (1898–1986) was born at Chácara Tirol, a rural property that became the neighborhood of Tirol. The author of numerous works, he explained Brazilian folk culture with erudition and humor. Natal's favorite son is commemorated at two city sites. The **Casa de Câmara Cascudo** museum (*Avenida Câmara Cascudo, 377, tel. 84/3222-3293; Mon – Fri, 8am – 5pm; Sat, 8am ° noon*) is in the house where the scholar lived for forty years. The collection features messages from visitors and illustrious writer friends, as well as books and furniture. His table, desk, and typewriter are preserved exactly as he used them, covered by a Peruvian cloth. Dona Geralda da Silva Oliveira, who cares for the house, can tell stories about the writer. The **Memorial Câmara Cascudo** (*Praça André de Albuquerque, 30, Tirol, tel. 84/3201-6425; Tue – Sun, 8am – 5pm*) houses unique personal items (the agate basin in which he was first bathed and the cigars he smoked compulsively), as well as notebooks, newspaper clippings, and first and revised editions of his books. The second floor houses his 10,000-volume library. Note that the small Museu Câmara Cascudo is a natural history museum named for the scholar, but with no connection to him nor any historical items related to him.

Ponta Negra beach and the famous sand strip on Morro do Careca hill

Tourist Center

The Centro de Turismo comprises 38 stores (including a snack bar) surrounding a historic 19th-century building. The building was a shelter for the poor at the beginning of the 20th century, a girls' orphanage from 1920 to 1943, and a prison from 1945 to 1969. The stores sell clothes, toys, and souvenirs, including embroidery from Caicó, *carnaúba* palm straw boxes, and sisal items. At Store #2, the Cooperativa de Produtores Artesanais do Rio Grande do Norte (tel. 84/3222-3802) sells exquisite craftwork from the municipalities of Goianinha, Várzea, Espírito Santo, São Gonçalo do Amarantes, Apodi, Santo Antônio and Santa Cruz.
Rua Aderbal de Figueiredo, 980, Petrópolis, tel. (84) 3211-6149. Daily, 9am – 7pm.

City Beaches

Praia de Ponta Negra is a long beach met by rough seas, making some spots good for surfing. Small kiosks sell coconut juice to walkers and runners along the promenade in the early morning and late afternoon. Ponta Negra and the string of beaches that follow it are backed by the **Via Costeira**. This main coastal road is marked by nearly 13 kilometers of hotels, including Natal's biggest and most luxurious accommodations. Most of the beaches have rougher seas and are frequented mostly by travelers, who alternate between the ocean and hotel pools overlooking the beaches. The first beach after Ponta Negra is **Barreira d'Água**, followed by **Areia Preta**

Our Recommendation

Peixada da Comadre, one of Natal's oldest restaurants, opened in 1931 and is still managed by the same family. It is famed for serving fish caught fresh each day. The dish bearing the restaurant's name, fish cutlets in fish stock with whole vegetables, served with rice and thickened *pirão* sauce, is, of course, the specialty. *(Avenida Praia de Ponta Negra, 1.948, tel. 84/3219-3016; Tue –Sat, 11:30am – 4pm and 6:30pm – 11pm; Sun, 11:30am – 5 pm.)*

Additional information on page 358.

(which runs parallel to the Parque das Dunas). At the end of the Via Costeira is **Praia dos Artistas**, which is popular with young surfers (especially in the afternoon). With fewer tourist facilities than Ponta Negra, Artistas beach is more popular with locals. The next two beaches are **Praia do Meio** and **Praia do Forte**. Both have calm, shallow seas protected by reefs. A stretch near Praia do Forte, where the Potengi River empties into the sea, offers sports facilities as well as a wonderful view of the Reis Magos Fort.

BUGGY TRIPS ON THE DUNES

Dune buggy trips are enjoyable and exciting – *com emoção* (with emotion), as the buggy drivers say – but they are by no means always accident-free. Choose only drivers accredited by Setur, Natal's official tourism office (*Secretaria de Turismo de Natal, Rua Mossoró, 359, Petrópolis, tel. 84/3232-2500, 3232-2503; Mon – Fri, 7am – 1pm and 3pm – 6pm*). The driver's accreditation sticker must be visibly displayed on his vehicle, which should also have red license plates. Drivers should also always present a card showing their accreditation number. Higher-end hotels can recommend reputable agencies and drivers. There are numerous options for trips. The most common route departs from Natal heading for the dunes at Genipabu, the Pitangui lakes, and the golden dunes at Jacumã. Other trips terminate at Cabo de São Roque, Touros, Galinhos, or Pipa. The most extreme route goes from Natal to Fortaleza (one-way only). This route takes four days and requires overnight stops. Try to arrange meal breaks in advance, avoiding establishments that pay drivers commissions. On the north coast, we recommend **Mercado da Redinha**. The 13 kiosks at this Redinha neighborhood market feature such classic delicacies as tapioca with *ginga* (tiny fish caught with a fine net known as a *redinha*).

Dune buggy trips

Genipabu: Dunes, Lakes, and Ocean

Genipabu is most famous for its dunes. The town sits across the Rio Potengi from Natal, in the municipality of Estremoz. From Natal, drivers can reach Genipabu on the RN-302 and RN-304 highways; a ferry makes the 20-minute river crossing to Genipabu's Redinha district from the point known as the *rampa* in Natal. The dark color of the **Lagoa de Genipabu** lake (unsuitable for bathing) is a stark contrast to the dunes that surround it. This and other surrounding lakes are actually large pools of seawater stranded among the dunes. The local couple Cleide and Philippe was so struck by Genipabu's similarity to the Sahara desert that they imported one-humped camels. The 14 dromedaries are now a popular tourist attraction at a site known as **Dromedunas** (*Genipabu beach, tel. 84/3225-2053, 9991-9690, 3225-2324; daily 9am – 5pm*).

Despite being a state-protected environmental area, Genipabu Beach is cluttered with vacation homes, bars, and dune buggies. One of the more relaxing spots on the beach is **Bar 21**, a wooden deck amid the dunes. To reach the beaches beyond Genipabu, take a short ferry trip across the small river. The first beach you'll reach is quiet **Praia de Graçandu,** which opens onto the Pitangui dunes and the brown waters of the **Lagoa de Pitangui**. The tables and chairs at the water's edge by **Bar da Lagoa** are a great place to relax. Just beyond Graçandu are the vast **Dunas Douradas** (Golden Dunes), also known as the **Brazilian Marocco** dunes, which are covered in low-lying vegetation. The **Jacumã** dunes are the last stretch of sand after the Dunas Douradas. To reach nearby **Jacumã Lake**, take a ride on the ingenious homemade tram, a cloth chair rigged to a complex pulley system. A rope-pulled cart will convey you back.

Imported camels give Genipabu the look and feel of the Sahara desert

The dark waters of Genipabu Lake stand in stark contrast to the white dunes

Cabo de São Roque

Cabo de São Roque is Brazil's second-closest point to Africa, after Ponta do Seixas in Paraíba (*see page 245*). Known as the "Corner of Brazil," this 6-kilometer spit juts into the sea some 50 kilometers north of Natal, just after Barra de Maxaranguape beach. The terrain is largely dunes, coconut groves, rocks, and cliffs, punctuated by the famous *árvore do amor* (love tree) — two fig trees whose interlacing branches form a heart. Also of interest is the Farol de São Roque lighthouse. The very stony beach is not suitable for bathing. Like most of the north coast, Cabo de São Roque is easily visited by dune buggy or 4×4 vehicle from Genipabu.

Maracajaú

The main attraction of the tiny fishing village of Maracajaú (60 kilometers north of Natal) is its precious coral reefs, known locally as *parrachos*. The reefs occupy a 13 by 2.5 kilometer area some 7 kilometers out to sea. Boats head to the *parrachos* at low tide, when the warm waters are shallow enough (1 – 3 meters) to offer good visibility for snorkelers. Divers see fish, rays, and with luck, lobster and shrimp. Maracajaú beach, surrounded by dunes and coconut groves, features calm seas and natural pools. Restaurants cluster around **Farol Teresa Pança** lighthouse. Agencies in Natal can book one-day "package" trips to Maracajaú. Road conditions are extremely poor in the rainy season (June to August) and signage is inadequate; a guide is strongly recommended. Dune buggies also make the trip across the sand to the reefs, though these trips are limited by the extent of the tides.

Rio Grande do Norte

The South Coast

The Costa do Sul (South Coast) of Rio Grande do Norte offers travelers nearly uninterrupted views of the state's lush natural beauty: dunes, lakes, coconut groves, secluded beaches, stretches of coral, and natural pools. The region also boasts culture and history. The municipalities of Parnamirim and Nísia Floresta are known for their rich folk art tradition. Canguaretama is home to a 17th-century sugarcane plantation, and Vila Flor's quaint village architecture dates from the 1900s.

The most scenic route is the Rota do Sol (RN-063 state highway). The road hugs the coast from Natal to Pipa, passing all sorts of beaches – from built-up **Pirangi do Norte** and **Pirangi do Sul** to the quieter **Búzios**, **Barra de Tabatinga**, **Guaraíras**, **Tibau do Sul**, **Praia do Madeiro**, and **Praia do Curral** – en route. To reach famous **Praia da Pipa** beach as quickly as possible, however, take the BR-101 highway.

PIRANGI

Schooner trips to the beaches of Pirangi do Norte, Pirangi do Sul, Búzios, and Cotovelo are popular excursions. The typical two-and-a-half hour outing makes a snorkeling stop in the **Parrachos de Pirangi** reefs, where you can see the small fish that live in the coral (*Marina Badauê, tel. 84/3238-2066*). Pirangi do Norte beach is home to the famous **cajueiro de Pirangi**, a giant cashew tree said to be 110 years old. (The species can live up to 400 years.) The top of the tree covers an area of 8,400 square meters (90,420 square feet), and the tree produces nearly 80,000 cashew fruits between November and January each year. (*Avenida Deputado Márcio Marinho, no #, or Praça do Cajueiro, no #, tel. 84/3238-2684; daily, 7:30am – 5:30pm.*)

Madeiro, one of the South Coast's most beautiful beaches

Pirangi do Norte and Pirangi do Sul
These more popular beaches are packed with bars, restaurants, and residences. Reefs shelter their calm waters.

Búzios
Expansive and beautiful, with vacation homes scattered across the dunes. The rough sea and uneven ocean floor make it unsafe for swimming.

Barra de Tabatinga
Calm, reef-filled waters framed by cliffs alternate with rougher stretches ideal for surfing. The lookout point offers a view of Búzios.

Tibau do Sul
Imposing cliffs protect this beach also known as Praia do Giz or Cacimbinha. The lookout point is a great place to watch the sunset.

Guaraíras or Malembar
Also known as Malembar, this beach has no facilities and is nearly deserted. It's reachable only by a 10-minute ferry ride. The calm waters, particularly near Guaraíras lagoon, make it good for kayaking.

Praia do Madeiro
Tucked between 30-meter (98-foot) red cliffs, this is one of the region's most beautiful beaches. The walk to Baía dos Golfinhos starts here.

Praia do Curral
Sea turtles lay their eggs on the white, powdery sand surrounded by cliffs. The difficult walk to the beach covers extremely rocky terrain.

Pipa
The main beach in the Pipa district is very easy to reach and has plenty of barracas. Children enjoy the natural pools that form at low tide.

Barra de Cunhaú
Encircled by the Catu and Curimataú Rivers, with calm waters ideal for fishing. The surrounding area is dotted with summer homes.

Baía Formosa
A charming cove of fishermen's houses, cliffs, and swimmable waters. It is near the Mata Estrela, an important Atlantic forest reservation.

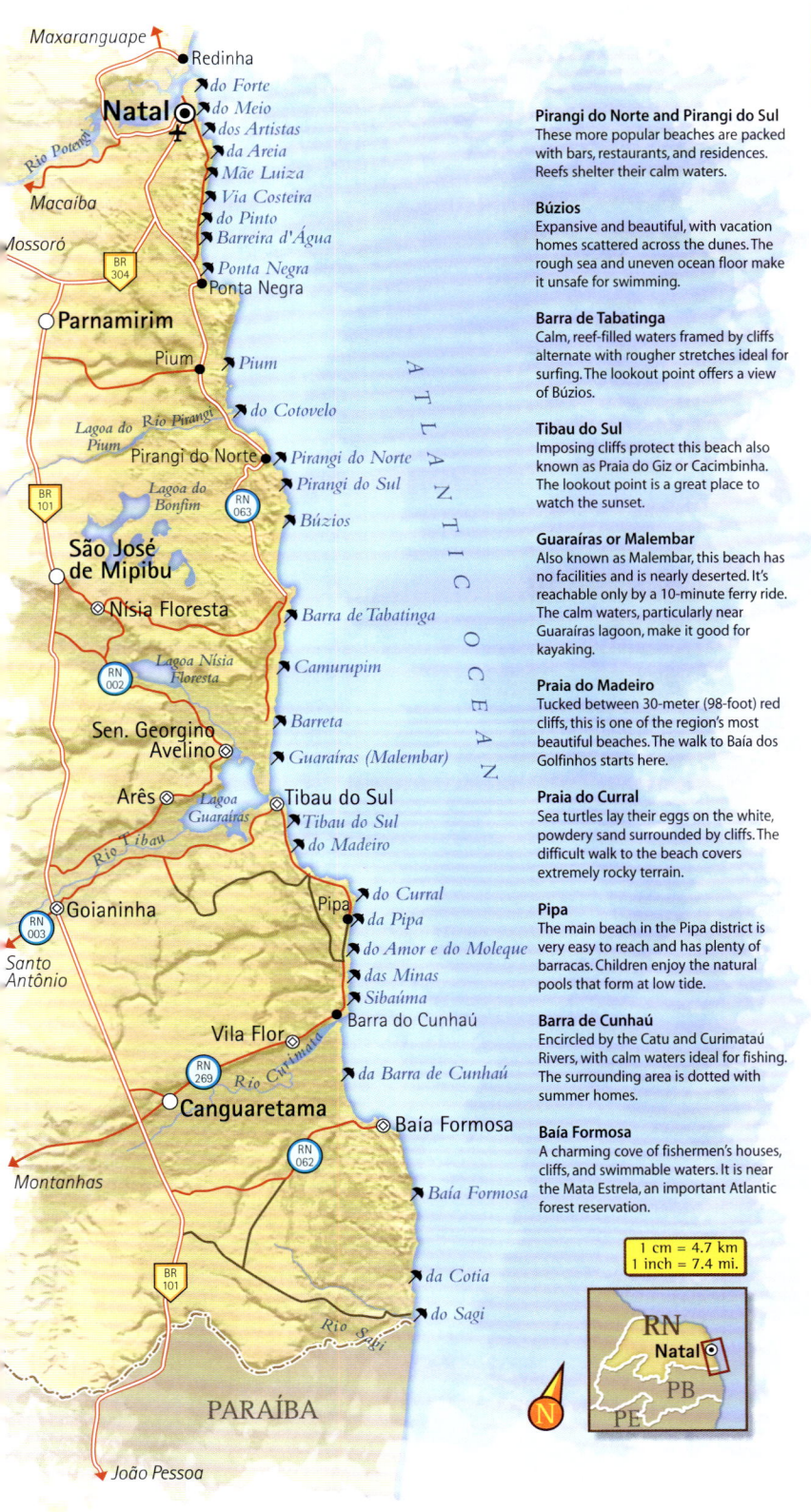

1 cm = 4.7 km
1 inch = 7.4 mi.

Craftwork in Nísia Floresta

The municipality of Nísia Floresta is famous for craftwork and for the large shrimp that inhabit its lake. Nísia Floresta is 43 kilometers (27 miles) south of Natal, accessible via either the RN-063 or BR-101 highways. The **Associação de Labirinteiras de Campo de Santana** (*Rua Deodécio Anselmo, 11, tel. 84/ 9967-8824; Mon – Sat, 8am – 5pm*) is comprised of 24 women who meet in the afternoon to produce *labirinto* (labyrinth), a famous style of Northeast lace. They work on wooden frames following traditional techniques. The women take orders for tablecloths, table runners, and entire dresses. The **Associação de Rendeiras de Alcaçuz** (*Rua Projetada, no #, tel. 84/ 9421-3562; Mon – Sat, 8am – 5pm*), is made up of 23 women who specialize in *renda de bilro* (bobbin lace). This form incorporates varied, often surprising, themes and elements, including pineapples, church doors, and raindrops. The artisan couple **Arlindo and Maria Barbosa** sell baskets, *covos* (shrimp traps), and *samburás* (fish baskets) of liana and *dendê* palm straw from a stall outside of their house (*Porto Vila São João, 43, tel. 84/3277-2533; daily, 6am – 11pm*). You can taste and buy *cachaça* at **Cachaça Artesanal de Alambique Papary**, a welcoming orange house with the ambiance of an old sugar plantation. The *cachaça* is produced 7 kilometers away at Fazenda Brasileira Augusta, a farm whose stills can be visited if you make prior arrangements. (*RN-063, tel. 84/3277-7011; Mon – Fri, 7am – 4pm; Sat – Sun, 10am – 4pm.*)

Artist José Pereira Barbosa's studio, **Inhepoan**, is next to the cashew tree. The studio sells ceramics and *cajuína*, white rum and cashew fruit, in charming clay bottles. (*Rua do Cajueiro, 100, Pirangi do Norte, tel. 84/3238-2958; daily, 7am – 6pm.*)

Dune Buggy Factory

This workshop lets visitors see the Selvagem dune buggies that carry them across the beaches being built, repaired, and restored. Marcos José de Oliveira das Neves, a pioneer in buggy production, presides over the shop. He sold one dune buggy a day in the 1980s, but sells just 60 per year now. His unusual vehicle collection includes a 1942 American Dodge and a WWII-era jeep from when U.S. forces kept seaplane bases in Natal. (*Avenida Doutor Carlos Mateus, 353, Monte Castelo, tel. 84/3272-2146; Mon – Fri, 8am – 11am and 1pm – 5:30pm; arrange visits in advance.*)

Pipa

This district of Tibau do Sul is a place of beautiful beaches and varied nightlife. Cliffs and clear seas impart natural beauty, and a lively social atmosphere is apparent in the variety of restaurants, bars, cafés, stores and guesthouses spread around this old fishing village. Pipa, which surfers discovered about two decades ago, is 82 kilometers (51 miles) south from Natal. The town wakes up late – stores don't open before 11am – and retires late, too – the bars stay open until the early hours of the morning. Not everything is busy, though. Right beside Pipa Beach and other crowded stretches, strips of deserted shoreline such as Praia das Minas offer blessed solitude. In high season (December to February), Mestre Geraldo Cosme's dance group performs the **coco-de-zambê**, a folklore dance accompanied by drumbeat. The group gives performances in hotels in Pipa and Timbau do Sol.

Beaches

Central **Praia da Pipa** is the beach with the best facilities. It usually gets quite crowded in high season. Large, warm, natural pools appear among the reefs at low tide. Nearby **Praia do Amor** got its name (meaning Love Beach) because it seems to be heart-shaped. On both Praia do Amor and the next beach to the south, **Praia do Moleque**, low tide creates shallow pools among the reefs and rocks. Fishes, octopi, and crustaceans often become visible. At high tide, there are good stretches for surfing. Visitors can reach these beaches from Praia da Pipa or by the steps embedded in the cliffs that frame them. Not many people frequent **Praia das Minas**, which is surrounded by high cliffs and untamed landscape. It has rougher seas and can only be reached by a rather precarious set of steps that are embedded in the cliffs.

Pipa Ecological Sanctuary

Set on 120 hectares (297 acres) of private, well-preserved Atlantic forest, the Santuário Ecológico de Pipa offers twelve short, well-signed trails of varying difficulty. The trail known as Caminho do Santuário passes by cashew and *murici* trees with labels identifying the species. You'll want insect repellent for the walks. The **Caminho dos Piratas** trail is one of the most difficult, with a descent by wooden steps to Praia do Madeiro. Start early if you want a full day in the sun. You'll need to leave the beach before 4pm, as the Sanctuary gates close at 5pm. The **Passeio da Peroba** walk skirts the cliffs of Ponta do Madeiro and leads to Mirante das Tartarugas, a lookout point. To the right, looking out from the point, gray tucuxi dolphins (*Sotalia fluviatilis*) sometimes cavort in the tranquil Baía dos Golfinhos bay. To the left, you'll spot Enseada do Madeiro cove.
Estrada Goianinha–Pipa, Praia da Pipa, km 23, Tibau do Sul, tel. (84) 3211-4559. Daily, 8am – 5pm.

Good facilities make Pipa the area's most popular beach

Amor beach offers surfing at high tide and shallow pools at low tide

Dune-Buggy Trips to Paraíba

Dune-buggy trips from Pipa to Sagi, a beach on the Paraíba border, offer wonderful views of the sea, Praia do Amor, Praia do Moleque and Praia das Minas. The buggies leave from Chapadão, on top of the cliffs. From Ponta do Cabo Verde, a piece of land that looks like a barrel (or a pipe, hence "pipa"), the route passes several beaches. The first is **Praia de Sibaúma**, a large beach fronted by calm seas. Next is a ferry crossing over the Catu River to the lovely **Praia de Barra de Cunhaú**.

Our Recommendation

🍽 In Tibau do Sul, the superb six-dish taster menu at **Camamo** restaurant begins with a tour of the kitchen and home of owner/chef Tadeu Lubambo. He chooses the day's dishes, generally fish or seafood, and cooks for no more than eight people a night. To enjoy the restaurant's candle-lit atmosphere and atmospheric jazz music, you'll have to book at least one month in advance during high season (*Fazenda Pernambuquinho, Pernambuquinho, Tibau do Sul, tel. 84/3246-4195; daily, 9:15pm – 2:30am*).

Additional information on page 358.

Another ferry over the Curimataú River takes you to **Praia dos Coqueiros**, a large expanse of white sand full of coconut trees, with calm seas. Approaching **Baía Formosa**, you again see stretches of white sand, this time surrounded by cliffs and rocks. This bay has calm waters protected by reefs, as well as rougher waters that are good for surfing. There's also a small port and lookout point with a view of the bay, its boats, and Praia dos Coqueiros. Baía Formosa is the gateway to Mata Estrela, the largest remaining stand of Atlantic forest in Rio Grande do Norte. Its 2,039 hectares (5,040 acres) include *restinga* vegetation, brazilwood trees, dunes and lakes, such as **Lagoa Coca-Cola**, which is named after its dark waters. Nearby is the Rio Sagi, a narrow river with dark waters, where you can swim amongst the mangroves. With luck you might see Xuxu, the manatee that has appeared here so often that it has been given a name. Baía da Traição, in Paraíba, is on the other side of the river.

Contact: *Pipatour, Avenica Baía dos Golfinhos, 767, Galeria das Cores, loja 3, Centro, tel. (84) 3246-2234.*

The North Coast

Touros
A fishing village with a quiet beach and calm seas, protected by reef barriers and a view of Farol do Calcanhar lighthouse.

São Miguel do Gostoso
Nearly deserted, this beach offers with calm seas and a promenade dotted with straw-thatch kiosks.

Tourinhos
Lovely, brown cliffs and unique, sea-sculpted rock formations that resemble old tree trunks provide interesting scenery.

Praia do Marco
A straight, deserted stretch of beach where turtles emerge from calm waters to lay their eggs. Accessible only from one of the neighboring beaches.

Galinhos
Low dunes, a river and sea that's good for swimming.

Ponta do Mel
An unspoiled beach in a lovely cove surrounded by red cliffs and dunes, with calm seas that make for ideal swimming.

Tibau
On the border with Ceará and frequented by summer vacationers from Mossoró. Dunes, coconut groves, cliffs, and calm, shallow waters make up the view. Barracas open on weekends and in the high season.

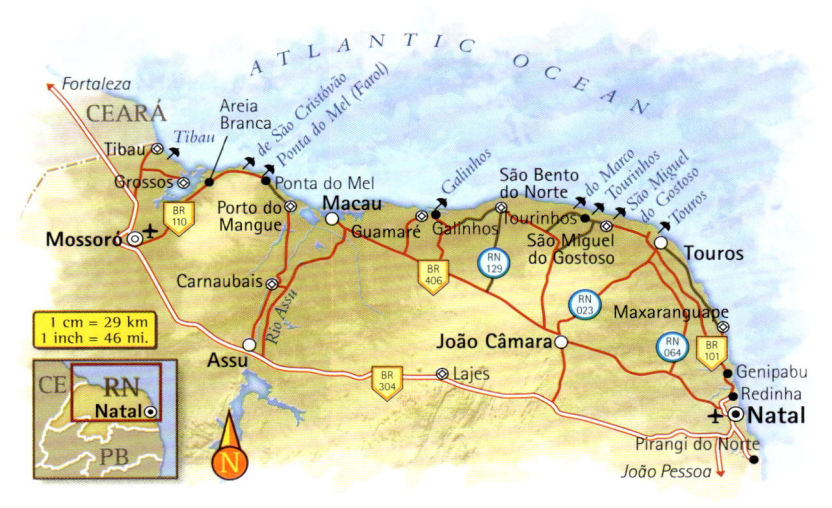

The unspoiled beauty of the north coast of Rio Grande do Norte is magnificent. A one- or two-day trip by dune buggy or 4×4 vehicle, up to the border with Ceará, is a perfect way to enjoy it. A series of fishing villages lie along the 250 or so kilometers (155 miles) of coastline. Each hamlet has semi-deserted beaches, dunes, cliffs, and calm seas dotted with *jangadas* (sailing rafts) or boats. Among these villages are such gems as Touros, São Miguel do Gostoso, Galinhos and Ponta do Mel. The last, which is nearly at the Ceará border, is on the so-called Costa do Sal (Salt Coast) or Pólo Costa Branca (White Coast Center). The monikers refer to the saltworks concentrated in the area, mostly around Mossoró, Macau and Areia Branca, where about 90% of Brazilian salt is produced.

Our Recommendation

🍽 **Pousada Sinos do Vento**, on the quiet Praia das Garças beach in Touros, has spacious rooms with guaranteed privacy and views of the ocean. Their farm's chickens provide fresh eggs for breakfast, and the on-site restaurant specializes in seafood dishes (*Estrada de Perobas, no #, 4 kilometers, 2.5 miles, from the center of Touros, tel. 84/3263-2353*).

Additional information on page 358.

Small but inviting, Touros knows how to welcome visitors

TOUROS

This town owes its name, which means "bulls," to a rocky formation on the beach that resembles a bull's head. Touros, 88 kilometers (55 miles) north from Natal along first the BR-101 and then RN-221 highways, has the best traveler-oriented facilities along the North Coast. It offers beaches – namely **Carnaubinha, Praia do Farol, Praia da Gameleira, Garças** and Perobas – that have calm seas, coconut groves and cliffs, quaint houses on the coast, and rafts dotting the water. **Perobas** is the place for diving on coral reefs. At low tide, motorboats makes two-hour runs for snorkeling on a long stretch of reef

OUR RECOMMENDATION

🍽 The menu at **Mar de Estrelas**, the restaurant in the eponymous guesthouse, in São Miguel do Gostoso, focuses on regional cuisine. The excellent house fish dish is cooked in coconut milk and served with rice, *pirão* (thickened sauce), and manioc fried cakes (*Avenida dos Arrecifes, 1120, tel. 84/3263-4168; daily, 7am – 11pm*).

Additional information on page 358.

(*contact: Pólo das Águas, tel. 84/3693-3000*). **Farol do Calcanhar**, a 65-meter-tall (213-foot) lighthouse built in 1943, is the tallest in Latin America. The base is 9 meters (30 feet) above sea level. The 298-step ascent is permissible only on Sundays, but those who time their visit right will enjoy a wonderfully contrasting view: on one side, deserted beaches, the town of Touros and the infinite ocean; on the other, towards Ceará, a stretch of untouched nature in shades of green and brown. In the latter direction, beyond a curve (the "*calcanhar*", ankle) of the Brazilian coastline, the climate and vegetation typical of the semi-arid Northeast begins.

SÃO MIGUEL DO GOSTOSO

According to a legend, perhaps apocryphal, this village, 105 kilometers (65 miles) north from Natal, took its name from a legendary local character, whose laughter was infectious and delightful (*gostoso*). Whatever the origin, it is a very pleasant village indeed. The flow of travelers from Natal, 105 kilometers (65 miles) to the south, has not changed the routine of fishing, *labirinto* lace making and manioc flour production. Sítio Caldeiro, the village's original dwelling and now a guesthouse, stands at the town center, along with tiny Praça dos Anjos square. Anyone visiting São Miguel do Gostoso between August and January, during the so-called "farinhada" (flour making process) period, can drop by the twenty-some *casas de farinha* (manioc flour mills). That of Dona Raimunda (*Avenida dos Arrecifes, 2263, Centro, tel. 84/3263-4020 (Dona Maria, a neighbor); Mon – Fri 7am – 6pm, from September to November*), for example, shows the traditional, small-scale production of coarse manioc meal (*farinha*) and of the starch used to make tapioca. The beaches on this part of the coast are still relatively unspoiled. They have calm waters, just a few summer homes and rafts, and fringes of sparse, low-lying vegetation. Dune buggies can be used to explore at low tide. **Praia de Ponta do Santo Cristo** is the best windsurfing beach, and the cliffs at **Praia de Tourinhos** are beautiful. At **Praia do Marco**, where the early Portuguese once erected a landmark called the Marco de Touros, you can now see a crude copy of that symbol of territorial possession. The original Marco de Touros is now in Natal. Take the BR-101 highway north from Natal, passing by Touros, and then the RN-221 state highway toward São Miguel do Gostoso to the turnoff onto a well-marked road to São Miguel do Gostoso.

Galinhos

Schools of *peixe-galo*, the fish after which this town is named, have no trouble finding their way to this riverside spot. But human visitors will find the trip to be something of a daring adventure. Tiny Galinhos is 175 kilometers (109 miles) north of Natal, and to reach it one has to drive first along the BR-406 highway and then down the RN-402 state highway. You'll need a dune buggy or 4×4 vehicle to navigate the roads' potholed stretches. Vehicles are not allowed into the village; drivers leave them parked on the banks of the Rio Pratagi, which they cross by boat. On the other side lies an enchanting, picturesque peninsula. Donkeys and

In Galinhos, simple guesthouses stand amid enchanting scenery

carts are the only vehicles to ply the sandy streets, locals run simple guesthouses, and a TV in the middle of the square plays all evening. The village beach, on a stretch of low-lying dunes, is relatively calm and good for swimming. During motorboat trips around the Pratagi, Aratuá, and Rio do Capim rivers, visitors can enjoy the botanical riches of the mangroves, the small freshwater island beaches and white mountains of locally mined salt. **Boteco da Nalvinha** (*Rua Candelária, 49, Galos, tel. 84/3552-2024*; daily, 8am – 9pm), a good spot to stop for lunch, serves a traditional dish of fish with tapioca. **Contact:** *Jairo Souza, tel. (84) 3552-0029; Gládston (Pimpinha), tel. (84) 9969-2782; Batista, tel. (84) 3552-0134, 9955-9509;*.

PONTA DO MEL

The houses of this simple village run from the top of some reddish cliffs down to a largely deserted beach. Anyone on top, where Farol da Ponta do Mel lighthouse sits, has a spectacular view of the cliffs, dunes, and ocean. The landscape here, 355 kilometers (220 miles) north of Natal, consists of *caatinga* vegetation, with cacti such as *mandacarus* and bromeliads such as *macambiras*. The town's name alludes to the production of wild honey (*mel*) in the Serra do Mel range, which is close by, but the most evident form of husbandry is raising goat and donkeys. It is well worth extending the trip to visit to watch the sunset from **Praia de São Cristóvão**, a wonderful and almost-deserted beach. A regular car can reach Ponta do Mel by driving northwest along the coast on BR-110, but a 4×4 vehicle can take BR-304 to Porto do Mangue, then cut across the dunes on a lovely stretch of sandy road. The second option demands care; there are no signs or gas stations. It's essential to fill up with gas before you set off. A little before Ponta do Mel, you can find **Praia do Rosado** (Rosy Beach), a name that refers to the pinkish shades of the dunes. Enjoy this spot as evening approaches, when the pink tones of the dunes mix with colors of the sky, in an unforgettable spectacle.

From Ponta do Mel, cliffs, dunes, and ocean stretch away as far as the eye can see

INLAND

Anyone wishing to penetrate the *sertão* of Rio Grande do Norte – the region known as the **Seridó** – will be surprised by the singular beauty of the semi-arid landscape and the rich culture of the area. From Natal, however, the trip is difficult by car. Historically engaged in cattle-husbandry, mining and cotton agriculture, the cities of the Seridó have geographical attractions (reservoirs and mountain ranges), culinary treasures (*queijo-manteiga* cream cheese and sun-dried beef), rich arts and crafts (embroidery and sculptures), and lively festivities (quadrille square-dance festivals), as well as archaeological sites, historically important mines, and pilgrimage sites. Despite a dearth of good services and facilities, the region's towns offer reasonable accommodations and food. The communities of **Acari** and **Caicó**, in particular, can serve as departure points for exploring neighboring towns on one-day trips.

ACARI

A chain of attractive mountains interspersed with reservoirs surrounds tiny Acari, which is 210 kilometers (130 miles) southwest of Natal and reachable by taking RN-226 to Currais Novos and then BR-427 westward. The sinuous character of the local geography has earned the town its nickname, "muse of the Seridó." Declared a municipality in 1833, the town's main attraction is the **Açude Gargalheiras**, in the Acauã River Basin, four kilometers (2.5 miles) from the center. That reservoir produces most of the fish that feed the local population and sits amid rocky, yellowish mountains. Two of the mountains are strangely pyramid-shaped, and all are covered in large cacti. The reservoir produces an enormous waterfall in winter. In addition, between February and March, when the river waters swell, the reservoir's waters spill down the dam wall in what is know as *sangria*. Local guides take visitors on hikes around the reservoir, on trails of medium difficulty, for about four hours. The trip can also be done by car. Another point of interest in Acari is the rock inscriptions that can be seen next to **Poço do Artur**. A pleasant dirt road leads cars to the site through a wild landscape of twisted trees, for fifteen minutes, followed by an easy five-minute walk. Nature lovers usually go up the **Serra do Bico da Arara** range between April and October, when the caves there are full of thousands of swifts that migrate across the ocean from Africa. The forty-minute ascent is only for those who aren't bothered that bird droppings mark the route. The best time to go up is around 5pm, when the

---

THE ARTISANS OF ACARI

Acari has four outstanding artisans: **Dimas Ferreira**, who sculpts stone in a shed on the banks of the Gargalheiras reservoir; **Dimauri Lima de Souza**, who creates dolls from old car parts; **Manoel Jerônimo Filho**, who makes very nicely finished wooden trucks; and **Ambrósio Córdula**, who is a master at sculpting wooden saints, angels and nativity scenes in detail. Their work can be found at the **Acari Artesanato** store (*Rua Tomás Araújo, 144, Centro, tel. 84/3433-2319; Mon – Sat, 8am – 11:30am and 2pm – 5:30pm; Sun, 8am – 11am*). The sales assistants will give the workshop addresses if visitors are interested in seeing the artists at work. Acari holds the **Feira de Artesanato e Comidas Típicas** (craft and food fair) on the second Sunday of August on Rua Otávio Lamartini street.

birds are flying back to the caves: It's a magnificent sight (*contact: Angelina, Bistrô Gargalheiras, tel. 84/9977-4150; Túlio Cortes, tel. 84/3433-2083, 9979-5812*). The **Museu Histórico de Acari** (*Rua Antônio Basílio, 11, tel. 84/3433-3988; Mon – Fri, 7:30am – 11:30am and 1:30pm – 5:30pm; Sat, 8am – 11am; Sun and holidays, to be arranged*), a museum installed in an imposing building built in 1887, tells the town's history through objects and photographs. A replica of a wattle and daub house and artifacts connected to fishing, leatherwork, and cotton planting paint a portrait of life in the Seridó. The **Igreja de Nossa Senhora do Rosário**, a church built in 1738, is also worth a visit for its fine statues dating from the 18th century.

CAICÓ

A municipality since 1868, Caicó offers good facilities and every imaginable service, including Internet access and lively nightlife. Locals flock to the squares to listen to music while eating snacks. Located 298 kilometers (185 miles) southwest from Natal, the town has several reservoirs, being **Itans** the most important of these. Its narrow banks are dangerous for drivers, especially at the curve leading to it. Apart from arts and crafts, Caicó's attraction is its cuisine, especially sun-dried beef, cheese (cream and curd), and homemade savory biscuits made with clarified butter. Created in 1973, the **Associação das Bordadeiras do Seridó** (*Avenida Seridó, no #, Centro, tel. 84/3417-3440; Mon – Fri, 7:30am – 11:30am and 1:30pm – 5pm; Sat, 7:30am – 11:30am*) sells hand-worked *richelieu* embroidery. The local sun-dried beef is sold at the **Açougue Público Augusto Frade** (*Avenida Seridó, no #, Centro, tel. 84/9962-6479; Mon – Fri,* *4am – 5pm; Sun and holidays, 4am – 11am*). If you do go to this meat market, look for "O Regional," At this stall, Hugo Régis de Medeiros, the main producer of sun-dried beef in the region and the ablest at butchering and salting process, gives information about his work. There are several small cheese makers who produce **queijo-manteiga** cream cheese. One of these is **Queijaria JD** (*Avenida Celso Dantas, 547, tel. 84/9962-3003; daily, 7am – 11:30am and 1pm – 6:30pm*). Owner Francisco Jardel Dantas prepares cheese in a huge pot on a wood-burning stove, as visitors look on. After the last batch of cheese is made, the cheese maker scrapes together the leftovers in the pot, which are eaten there and then, dusted with sugar and cinnamon. To reach the town from Natal, take BR-304 highway southwest to Macaíba, then BR-226 to Currais Novos, then BR-427 to Acari, and then RN-288 state highway.

CURRAIS NOVOS

A nice complement to a trip to Acari and Caicó, Currais Novos lies 187 kilometers (116 miles) southwest of Natal along BR-226 highway. Although it has some well-preserved old buildings, this settlement, which began as a corral and became a town in 1890, has already taken on a "modern" appearance in many respects. Its big attraction is the annual quadrille square dance festival, held in June; for four days *forró* music and dance holds sway in the central square, while stalls sell meat dishes, cheese, cakes and all kinds of *espetinhos* (meat cooked on skewers). After the fairly quiet children's quadrille performance, the competition between the many towns of the Seridó heats up, to the shouts of cheer groups of supporters and live broadcast on the

The rock paintings at Xique-Xique show impressive artistry

local TV channel. Competitors painstakingly and creative decorate their brightly colored clothes according to the year's theme – sometimes migrants, bandits, or butterflies. Groups and their leaders become regional celebrities. Also in Currais Novos, the disused **Brejuí** mine operated between 1943 and 1997 and was the largest scheelite (tungsten ore) mine in South America. During a visit here you can walk along a lengthy underground tunnel – there are more than 60 kilometers (37 miles) of excavations – and see the tracks once used to transport ore out of the mine, as well as the mining galleries and huge chambers. When guides turn the lights off, a special lantern detects and shows the presence of the mineral in the rock. The trip includes a tour of the mine's headquarters, which is now a museum of tools metal samples, and descriptions of the uses of scheelite.

Carnaúba dos Dantas

This small backlands town, founded in 1860, attracts researchers and tourists to its many archeological sites. Since it lacks accommodations and restaurants, the best place to stay in is neighboring Acari or Currais Novos. A day trip with a local guide, preferably in June or July, is the best way to see the sites scattered in the vicinity of the town. The nearest and most important site is at Xique-Xique, in the mountain range of the same name, at an altitude of 420 meters (1,380 feet). After about an hour's ascent, you arrive at a recess in the rocks where you can see paintings, mostly in shades of red. They show anthropomorphic figures in scenes of fighting, hunting, dancing and sex. The delicate drawings were executed with fine instruments, which allows us to see the technical accuracy of the lines (contact: Sidney, tel. 84/3479-2531, 9444-6816). Another local attraction is Monte do Galo, a cross with a statue of Christ placed at the top of a hill. According to tradition, cow herders who worked in the area were intrigued to hear a rooster crowing on top of the small Serrote do Galo (rooster) range. No one lived there, which generated a mystic about the location. It has since become a place of pilgrimage. Reach Carnaúba dos Dantas from Natal by driving RN-226 highway southwest to Currais Novos, then taking BR-427. The exit, at a fork in the road, is 12 kilometers (7 miles) after Acari.

CEARÁ

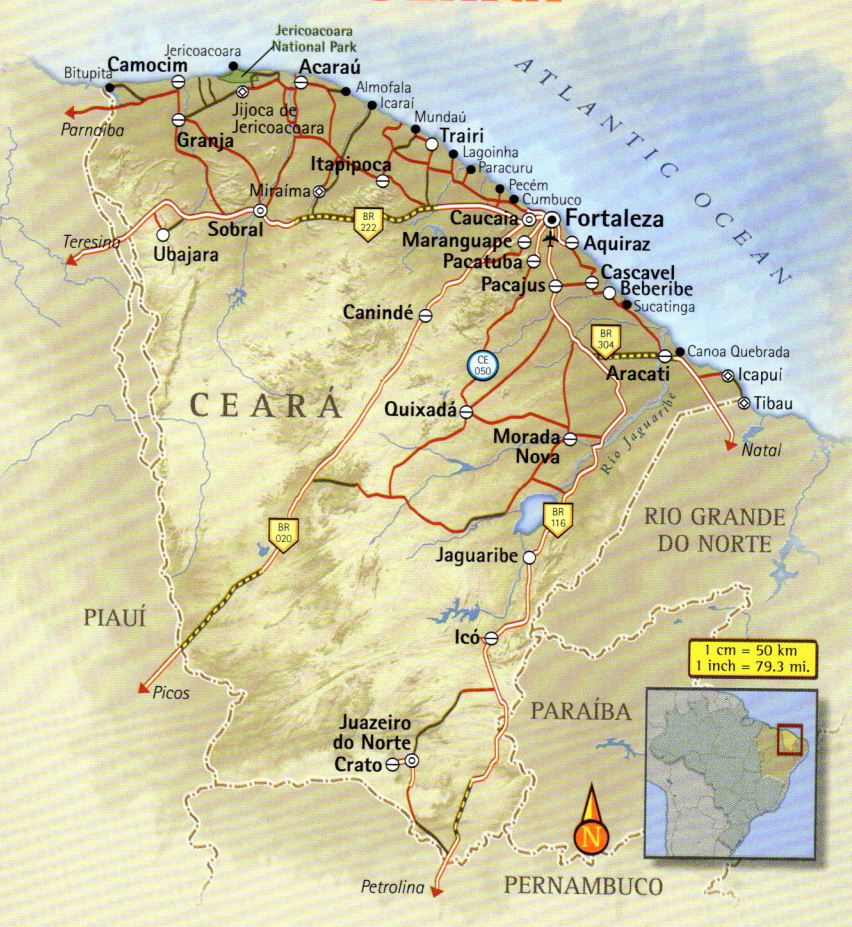

Highlights

- The historical and cultural attractions of **Fortaleza**.
- Unspoiled **Canoa Quebrada**, the jewel of the **Costa do Sol Nascente**.
- **Jericoacoara**, a cosmopolitan destination that still retains the charming simplicity of the **Costa do Sol Poente**.
- **Juazeiro do Norte**, in the *sertão* region of Ceará, site of the biggest pilgrimages in the Northeast.
- The historical architecture of **Sobral**.
- The limestone caves of **Ubajara National Park**.

When to Go

- From **July** to **December** to enjoy the beaches. Between **January** and **March**, the beaches are at their most crowded and prices at their highest.
- Between **December** and **May**, in the hot, rainy season, to enjoy the fuller lakes, the dunes, and the beaches.
- From **January** to **June**, when Sobral has milder weather.
- During the three great pilgrimages honoring Father Cícero: **September 15th**; from **October 30th** to **November 2nd**; and from **January 30th** to **February 2nd**.

CEARÁ

It is no accident that the symbol of Ceará is the *jangada* (sailing raft). The state has 573 kilometers (356 miles) of beaches, and many here still hold on to coastal fishing traditions. Ceará is sunny almost all year round, with a diverse landscape of dunes, lakes, and mangroves. The coast is one of the most popular tourist destinations in the entire country. Throughout its history, Ceará has been something of a frontrunner. The Spaniard Vicente Pinzón supposedly arrived on the coast of Mucuripe (now the state capital, Fortaleza) on February 2, 1500, long before Cabral made his first landing in Bahia. The story that locals take most pride in is that of *jangadeiro* (raftsman) Francisco José do Nascimento, known to many as Dragão do Mar (Sea Dragon). Born in Aracati, on the east coast of Ceará, he managed to prevent the unloading of slaves at Mucuripe – one of the country's most important abolitionist episodes. Indeed, Ceará was the fist province to free its slaves, doing so four years before the government passed the Lei Áurea (federal law freeing slaves).

A good example of the state's diversity of cultural treasures is its capital, Fortaleza. A busy metropolis with a vibrant cultural landscape, it is also the starting point for excursions to both the Costa do Sol Nascente (Sunrise Coast, to the east) and the Costa do Sol Poente (Sunset Coast, to the west). Visitors tend to venture inland from here to the *sertão*. In Fortaleza itself, a major attraction is Juazeiro do Norte, which is the center of public adoration to Father Cícero, a historical figure who is considered to be a saint throughout the Northeast. Sobral, the second-largest city in the state, was founded in 1841. Its well-maintained, rich architectural heritage has given it status as a national historical site. Unlike the rest of the state, where the heat reigns supreme, tiny Ubajara enjoys a mild climate. Sitting at an altitude of 847 meters (2,780 feet) in a mountainous section of Atlantic forest, the town is the gateway to a national park known for its spectacular limestone caves.

Jangadas (sailing rafts) rest on the sand at Beberibe, on the Costa do Sol Nascente

FORTALEZA

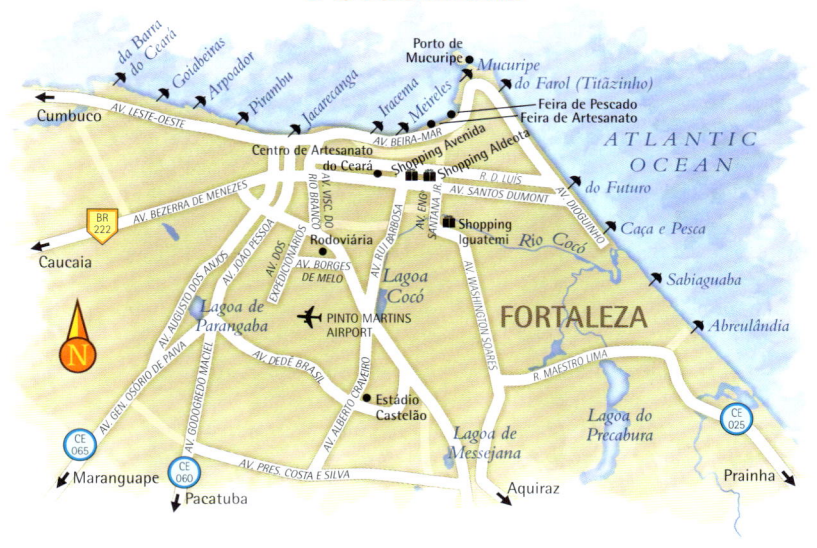

The fifth largest city in Brazil, sunny Fortaleza spreads out along a particularly scenic, emerald-green stretch of the Atlantic. The city beaches of Iracema, Meireles, and Mucuripe (connected by busy Avenida Beira-Mar) surround the city center. Within the center stand several 19th-century buildings, but outside of the center, little remains of the city's history. The city was founded in the 17th century when the Dutch built Schoonenborch Fort on the banks of the Pajeú River, later seized by the Portuguese and renamed **Fortaleza de Nossa Senhora da Assunção**, the building today is a major city landmark and an active regional headquarters for the Brazilian Army. Despite its lack of historical sights, the city is not without its attractions. Apart from the lovely beach scene, Fortaleza has modern art and cultural centers, a long tradition of fine regional craftwork, rich cuisine, and a buzzing nightlife. The city is particularly lively during **Fortal**, a raucous out-of-season Carnival held every July.

BEACH NEIGHBORHOODS

IRACEMA

The most famous beach neighborhood in Fortaleza, Iracema is named for the novel written by Ceará-born writer José de Alencar (1829-1877). Iracema, the novel's main character, is a Tabajara Indian woman described as a "maiden with lips of honey". She has become a symbol of the city, immortalized in statues at the beach, at Praia de Mucuripe, in the Palácio do Governo, and near Messejana Lake. Though the water is unsuitable for swimming, Iracema's promenade along Avenida Beira-Mar is always busy, particularly at sunset. The best lookout point here is at **Ponte Metálica** (also called Ponte dos Ingleses). This pier was built in 1906 when there was no port in the region and ships had to anchor far from shore.

Cultural life is particularly lively in the historical buildings in the neighborhood, particularly along **Rua dos Tabajaras**. One of the better options among the countless bars and restaurants lining this street is **Bar do Pirata** *(#325, tel. 85/4011-6161)*, famous for the lively *forró* dances held there every Sunday.

Meireles and Mucuripe

These adjacent beach neighborhoods could not be more different. Meireles is home to family-friendly hotels and luxury apartment buildings. It also holds Fortaleza's most traditional **craft market**, open daily at 6pm in front of the Clube Náutico Atlético Cearense. Located right in the middle of the urban center, Mucuripe is home to Fortaleza's fishing community. The **Mercado de Peixe** (Fish Market) is best visited in the late afternoon, when the market's 30 kiosks sell savory appetizers. The neighborhood first comes to life at 6am, when the rafts bring in their daily catches of fresh fish. The beaches at Mucuripe and at neighboring **Titanzinho** are both popular with surfers.

Statue of Iracema, at her namesake beach

Futuro Beach

Eight of Fortaleza's 25 kilometers of coastline are taken up by Praia do Futuro, the prettiest, cleanest beach in the city. *Barracas* (kiosks) line the promenade, offering freshwater showers, beach chairs and umbrellas, and drinks and food. Avenida Zezé Diogo offers the most traditional *barracas*. **Chico do Caranguejo** is a popular spot for crab-lovers *(#4930, tel. 85/3262-0108; daily, 8am – 6pm; Thu also 8pm – 2am)*; young people and sports enthusiasts favor **Cuca**

Seaside Pleasures

In the hustle and bustle along Praia de Meireles you can see everyone ranging from sports enthusiasts and street artists to artisans and tapioca vendors. A recommended stop is **Ponto do Guaraná**, which serves juices that mix the potent Amazonian fruit *guaraná* with limes, acerolas, plums, guavas, peanuts, or cashews *(on the promenade in front of Restaurante Geppo's, 7am –10pm)*. A team of massage therapists set up shop on a leafy corner of **Praça dos Estressados** (Stress Square, *on the promenade in front of Hotel Beira-Mar, tel. 85/8811-7577, Mon – Sat, 6pm – 10pm)*. **Sorveteria 50 Sabores** has been seducing passers-by for 30 years with tropical ice cream flavors like *murici*, *cajá*, and *graviola*, and exotic tapioca *(Avenida Beira-Mar, 4690; daily, 9am – 11pm)*. **Acarajé da Lúcia** has been offering the Bahian delicacy called acarajé for 22 years *(on the promenade in front of Clube Náutico; daily, 5pm – 11pm)*. Those who prefer a local specialty should try **X da Xica**. The restaurant serves Xiquito Cearense, a sun-dried beef and clarified butter sandwich with cheese, lettuce, tomato, and mayonnaise *(Rua Antônio Justa, 3455, tel. 85/3242-8514; Sun – Thu, 5pm – 1am; Fri and Sat, 5pm – 6am)*. **Real Sucos**, the main juice bar in the city, is a little farther away, in the Shopping Aldeota mall *(Avenida Dom Luís, 500, store #421, tel. 85/3458-1104; daily, 10am – 10pm)*. It serves several original northeastern fruit flavors.

Legal *(#3005, tel. 85/3265-1648; daily, 7am – 6pm; Thu, 7am – midnight)*. **Itaparicá** has facilities for children, including an on-duty life guard *(#6801, tel. 85/3265-1195; daily, 9am – 5pm; Thu also 7pm – 1am)*. From 4pm onward during the week (especially on Tuesdays and Thursdays) and all day on weekends, the promenade features live music and comedy acts. It should come as no surprise that Ceará is the birthplace of many of Brazil's best comedians, including Renato Aragão, Chico Anísio, and Tom Cavalcanti.

THE CITY CENTER

A trip around the historical center of Fortaleza should include a visit to the Museu do Ceará, near Praia de Iracema. Many consider it to be the most important museum in the city. Other important sights include the nearby historical **Praça dos Leões**, and the **Praça do Ferreira**, at the very heart of the city. The Praça dos Leões (Lion Square) is so named for the prominent life-sized bronze statues of the animal. Officially named **Praça General Tibúrcio Cavalcante**, it was built in 1914. Imposing 18th-century buildings ring the square, including the **Igreja de Nossa Senhora do Rosário**, and the **Palácio da Luz**. The church was built 1755 and the Ceará state government restored it to what is is today. The Palácio da Luz, once the seat of the government, is now home to the Academia Cearense de Letras (Ceará Academy of Letters).

CEARÁ MUSEUM

The ten-room Museu do Ceará has a collection of some 7,000 pieces. The collection includes items belonging to Father Cícero as well as original texts

1. Museu do Ceará
2. Praça do Ferreira
3. Cine São Luiz
4. Theatro José de Alencar
5. Centro Dragão do Mar de Arte e Cultura
6. Mercado Central
7. Mercado São Sebastião
8. Centro de Turismo
9. Praça Gal. Tibúrcio (Praça dos Leões)
10. Igreja do Rosário
11. Fortaleza de N. S. da Assunção
12. Ponte Metálica

The dazzling art nouveau stained-glass windows of the José de Alencar Theater

by the folk *cordel* poet Patativa do Assaré (1909-2002). The *Ceará, Serra e Mar* room highlights the geography of Ceará, while the *Escravidão e Abolicionismo* area examines Fortaleza's prominent role in Brazil's abolitionist history. The most notable part of this history involves the 1884 freeing of slaves, four years before the official prohibition of slavery.
Rua São Paulo, 51, tel. (85) 3101-2610. Tue – Sat, 8:30am – 5pm; Sun, 9am – 5pm.

Ferreira Square
Founded in 1825, Praça do Ferreira is the city's main square. The buildings that surround the square are rich in history. The **Cine São Luiz** (*tel. 85/3253-3332*) took 20 years to build (it was finished in 1958) and mixes neoclassical and art deco elements. The cinema has a fine Carrara marble staircase and three crystal chandeliers from the former Czechoslovakia. **Farmácia Osvaldo Cruz** has functioned as a pharmacy since 1932 in a building dating from 1890. The **Palacete Ceará**, built in 1914, headquartered the legendary Iracema Club, an old meeting place for high society. Photographs of the elite in early 20th-century eveningwear decorate **Pastelaria Leão do Sul**. This is a classic spot for anyone who wants to savor a wafer-thin *pastel* (deep-fried pastry) accompanied by sugarcane juice.

José de Alencar Theater
The most important architectural landmark in the city, the Teatro José de Alencar was built between 1908 and 1910. Its builders imported the metal structure from Scotland, and the building features many eclectic design elements, including stunning art nouveau stained-glass windows. Noted landscape artist Burle Marx designed the side garden. The unique stage inside can move forward, up, and down. Each theater box bears the name of a work by native novelist José de Alencar; a painting on the proscenium arch also honors the novelist. Declared a national heritage site in 1964, the theater offers guided

The Dragão do Mar has become an arts landmark

tours in English and Spanish.
Praça José de Alencar, no #, Centro, tel. (85) 3101-2583. Mon – Fri, 8am – 5pm; Sat, 8am – noon.

Dragão do Mar Art and Cultural Center

Opened in 1998 and installed in a modern, attention-grabbing building near the beach, the Centro Dragão do Mar de Arte e Cultura is the major cultural center in Fortaleza. Its calendar features diverse arts and entertainment programming for all tastes. In its 30,000 square meters (323,000 square feet) of space there are several art-house movie theaters, a traditional theater, a planetarium, a public library, and areas for temporary and permanent exhibitions. Dragão do Mar (Sea Dragon) was the nickname given to abolitionist icon Francisco José do Nascimento (1839-1914). A *jangadeiro* (raftsman) from nearby Aracati, he became famous in 1881 for refusing to transport slaves along the Ceará coast. Visitors can learn about the daily life of cowherds and other workers in the *sertão* region of Cariri at the **Memorial da Cultura Cearense**. The Museu de Arte Contemporânea do Ceará (*Tue - Thu, 9am – 9pm; Fri – Sun, 10am – 10pm*) focuses mainly on the work of local artist José Leonilson Bezerra Dias, known only as **Leonilson** (1957-1993). It also features experimental work by contemporary artists, from both Brazil and abroad.
Rua Dragão do Mar, 81, Iracema, tel. (85) 3488-8600. Tue – Sun, 2pm – 9pm.

Public Markets

The two large public markets in Fortaleza's center will satisfy anyone looking for insight into the local cultural scene. The 559 stores in the recently restored **Mercado Central** sell traditional food and regional items (*Avenida Alberto Nepomuceno, 199, Centro, tel. 85/3454-8586; Mon – Fri, 8am – 6pm; Sat, 8am – 4pm; Sun, 8am – noon*). Approximately 2000 shoppers frequent the non-touristy **Mercado São Sebastião** each day. It sells a combination of fish, kitchen utensils, and brightly colored northeastern fruits, including exotic varieties like *sapoti, pitomba,* and *cajarana* (*Rua Clarindo de Queirós, 1745, Centro, tel. 85/3468-1600; Mon – Sat, 5am – 5pm; Sun, 5am – noon*).

OFF THE BEATEN TRACK

JOSÉ DE ALENCAR'S HOUSE
The small farm Algadiço Novo houses the ruins of an old sugar mill. It also contains a preserved part of the 19th-century house where Cearense writer José de Alencar was born and lived. Though the house is not well maintained and serves better as an actual museum, it is well worth paying a visit. Local researcher José Ari gives guided tours in the mornings. *Avenida Washington Soares, 6055, Messejana, tel. (85) 3229-1898. Mon – Fri, 8am – 5pm; Sat, 8am – noon.*

SHOPPING
Shopping Iguatemi, in the Edson Queirós neighborhood (*Avenida Washington Soares, 85, Edson Queirós, tel. 3477-3577; daily, 10am – 10pm*), is the most sophisticated of Fortaleza's shopping malls. There are also decent shopping malls near Meireles Beach, including **Shopping Avenida** (*Avenida Dom Luís, 300, tel. 85/3264-9444; Mon – Sat, 9am – 10pm*) and **Shopping Aldeota** (*Avenida Dom Luís, 500, tel. 3458-1212; daily 10am – 10pm*). Nearby is the **Lino Villaventura** store. It is owned by the nationally recognized designer of the same name, a native of Pará who now lives in Fortaleza (*Avenida Senador Virgílio Távora, 304, store #316, Meireles, tel. 85/3261-2620; Mon – Fri, 10am – 7pm; Sat, 10am – 6pm*).

ART GALLERIES
Multiarte, run by art dealer Max Perlingeiro, has exhibited works by important Brazilian artists such as Cândido Portinari and Di Cavalcanti. Perlingeiro is the director of the Pinakotheke galleries in São Paulo and Rio de Janeiro (*Rua Barbosa de Freitas, 1727, Aldeota, tel. 85/3261-7724; Mon – Fri, 10am – 6pm*). The **Centro Cultural Oboé**, brainchild of art collector Newton Freitas, holds music and drama presentations, as well as book readings. The center has exhibited work by Aldemir Martins, Tarsila do Amaral, and Tomie Ohtake (*Rua Maria Tomásia, 531, Aldeota, tel. 85/3264-7038; Mon – Fri, noon – 8pm*).

Local writer José de Alencar's house at Algadiço Novo

TAPIOCA

Tapioca is a delicacy enjoyed throughout the Northeast, but it is only in Fortaleza that it has its own food court. This is the **Centro das Tapioqueiras**, a collection of 26 kiosks with outdoor tables and parking. It stands along local road CE-040 (Km 10 exit), en route to the east coast beaches in the direction of Messejana. The menu includes traditional tapioca as well as more unusual preparations filled with chicken, sun-dried beef, shrimp, banana, and chocolate (*Avenida Washington Soares, 10215, Messejana, tel. 85/3274-7566; daily, 5am – midnight*). At the junction of CE-040 and **Rua Barão de Aquiraz** you can find tapioca sellers who chose not to join the Center. Instead, they serve customers from the porches of their own homes.

CACHAÇA MUSEUM

The Museu da Cachaça, 25 kilometers (16 miles) southwest of Fortaleza in the municipality of Maranguape, recounts the history of *cachaça* production in Ceará. The farmhouse, which belongs to Fazenda Ypióca, and was built in 1846, is the main building of the museum. The old mill displays machinery, photographs, bottles, sugar crushers, and immense vats used in the production of *pinga* (another name for the potent liquor). Visitors can follow up their guided tour with a stop at the gift shop and bar.
Rua Senador Virgílio Távora, no #, tel. (85) 3341-0407; Tue – Sun, 8:30am – 5pm.

CRAFT STORES

The rich, varied craftwork of Ceará is on display in various neighborhoods throughout Fortaleza. The two mainstream options include the popular night market at Praia do Meireles and the city center's **Centro de Turismo**, which sells regional products from 99 separate stores. Market highlights include the fabric, wood, and leather craftwork as well as sweet treats (like brown-sugar *rapaduras*) and *cachaças*. The building housing the market dates from 1850, and served as the public jail until 1970. In addition to the market, the building features two modest museums, the **Museu de Arte e Cultura Popular** and the **Museu dos Minerais** (*Rua Senador Pompeu, 350, Centro, tel. 85/3101-5508;*

Well-preserved historic buildings in the city center

Several neighborhoods in Fortaleza showcase traditional Cearense craftwork

Mon – Fri, 9am – 4pm; Sat, 9am – 3pm; Sun and holidays, 9am – 11am). Visitors can find more interesting work at the four branches of the **Centro de Artesanato do Ceará** (**Ceart**), which receives government support. Here artisans sell hand-made work such as hammocks, ceramics, straw and *liana* basketwork, and *labirinto*, a painstakingly made lace of Arab origin (*branches: Aeroporto Pinto Martins; Shopping Iguatemi; Centro Dragão do Mar de Arte e Cultura; Avenida Santos Dumont, 1589, Aldeota, tel. 85/3101-1645; Mon – Fri, 9am – 8pm; Sat, 9am – 5pm*).

DUNE-BUGGGY AND 4×4 TRIPS

Visitors looking for dune buggy trips in Fortaleza should head to Praia do Meireles, near the Clube Náutico. Drivers offer day-long trips to the beaches just outside of Fortaleza, which include Morro Branco and Canoa Quebrada. Longer trips are also possible: the journey to Jericoacoara takes two days, while the trip to Natal (in Rio Grande do Norte), takes four. These longer trips can only carry two passengers and their luggage in the buggy; the buggies typically pick up passengers at their hotel (*contact: Cooperativa de Buggy de Fortaleza, tel. 9108-1504*). Trips over 300 kilometers (190 miles) can handle groups of up to six people in the comfort of an air-conditioned 4×4 vehicle, with overnight stops at hotels. Your choice of destinations includes Jericoacoara, Guaramiranga, Natal, Lençois Maranhenses, and São Luís do Maranhão.
Contact: Dunnas Expedições, tel. (85) 3264-2514.

OUR RECOMMENDATION

🍽 The creative menu at **Cantinho do Faustino** involves a fusion of wine, herbs, and traditional regional ingredients. This culinary alchemy results in such delicacies as lobster grilled in *caju azedo* (cashew vinegar, known locally as *mocororó*) and served with pumpkin purée. Desserts are a definite highlight, with standout options including *rapadura* (brown sugar) ice-cream and the unusual olive ice cream drizzled with olive oil (*Rua Delmiro Gouveia, 1520, Varjota, tel. 85/3267-5348; Tue – Fri, noon – 3pm and 7pm – midnight; Sat, noon – midnight; Sun, noon – 4pm*).

The East Coast

The stretch of coast between Aquiraz and Rio Grande do Norte is known as **Costa do Sol Nascente** (Sunrise Coast). Common morning sights include white sails on the horizon before sunrise and fishermen pushing their *jangadas* into the ocean. A visit to Ceará's coast reveals a culture rich in tradition, cast against a beautiful landscape of dunes and lively beaches. The CE-040 highway, which skirts the many beaches along this coast, leads the way to various pleasurable daytrips.

AQUIRAZ

Porto das Dunas
Hotels, guesthouses and condominiums complement the shore's white, powdery sands and surfer-friendly waves

Prainha
A popular tourist destination. Be prepared for intense harrassment from guides offering trips and accommodations

Presídio
The Salinas River runs along this stretch of white sand, famous for its beach Carnival

Iguape
The most built-up beach in Aquiraz attracts visitors with its white sands, calm seas, and a single lone sand dune

Barro Preto
Coconut groves line this stretch of dark sand. Dune buggies usually stop at Giovane Cavalcante's eponymous kiosk, decorated in scrap metal

Praia do Batoque
Cross the Barro Preto River to reach this isolated calm of pale sands, tranquil waters, and sun-kissed cliffs

Ceará

Porto das Dunas, at Aquiraz, offers beautiful sights and many tourist attractions

Cascavel

Caponga
This cove houses one of the biggest jangada ports on the coast of Ceará. Many of the beach's summer homes belong to denizens of Fortaleza

Águas Belas
The tranquil fishing community of Águas Belas begins at the end of Caponga cove. Dunes, coconut palms, the Malcozinhado River, and mangroves dominate the landscape

Barra Nova
Access to this small, often deserted beach is possible via a 4X4 vehicle or on foot from Águas Belas. A reef barrier rests just off the shoreline

Beberibe

Morro Branco
By far the most popular beach in Beberibe, with limitless bars and restaurants to prove it

Praia das Fontes and Praia do Diogo
Red cliffs face the coast of Praia das Fontes, a beach with calm seas and a shoreline of summer homes. Houses at Praia do Diogo sit atop cliffs

Praia de Uruaú and Lagoa de Uruaú
Also known as Praia de Marambaia, this stretch of white sand is an APA (Environmentally Protected Area). Water sports, but not certain other activities, are permitted in the lake.

Barra de Sucatinga
Red sand formations and a host of jangadas create a pleasant seascape here

Aracati

Majorlândia
A beach with bar, restaurant, and guesthouse facilities, framed by red and white cliffs

Quixaba
Coconut palms dot this cliffside fishing village

Porto Canoa
Fishermen dock their boats at the foot of this beach's red cliffs, hence the name ("canoe port")

Lagoa do Mato
A deserted, well-preserved beach that often serves as a stopover for roaming dune-buggies

Fontainha
The pale sands and colorful dunes of Fontainha may be visually tempting, but only fishermen brave the sea's strong waves

Retirinho
During high tide in the bay, the ocean waters reach the bottoms of the cliffs. Low tide reveals a reef barrier along the shore

Retiro Grande
A handful of houses overlook the dark sands and seaweed-capped water of this small fishing village

Icapuí

Ponta Grossa
Gentle waves make this small beach perfect for swimming. Catch a wonderful view of the sunset from the clifftops

Redondas
Admire the red cliffs but mind the strong waves on this beach, accessible on foot from Ponta Grossa

The gentle waves of Ponta Grossa are ideal for swimming

Aquiraz's swimming pools and the waterslides at Beach Park attract daytrippers from Fortaleza

AQUIRAZ

In 1713 the small settlement of Aquirás, once a stage for violent clashes between Europeans and Indians, became the capital of the Siará captaincy, and held the title until 1726. About 32 kilometers (20 miles) east of Fortaleza, the town still contains buildings from colonial times. Today the area attracts tourists for its wildly popular water park, Beach Park.

SÃO JOSÉ DE RIBAMAR CHURCH AND SACRED ART MUSEUM

Built in the mid-18th century, the Igreja Matriz de São José de Ribamar (*Praça Cônego Araripe, no #*) has undergone many renovations, resulting in a mix of neo-classical and baroque elements. The three great paneled doors at the main entrance date from the original construction, as do the carved wooden pulpit and the painted ceiling depicting scenes from the life of São José de Ribamar.

The Museu Sacro São José de Ribamar (*Praça Cônego Araripe, 22; Tue – Sat, 8am – 5pm; Sun, 8am – noon*), is a museum of sacred art. The collection of almost five hundred pieces from the 17th, 18th, and 19th centuries is housed in a well-preserved building from 1877, which once served as the council

---

MINIATURE *JANGADAS*

Seu Oliveira is a former fisherman from Prainha who transforms the native Timbaúba wood into small works of art. Oliveira learned his craft at the age of eight, and spends the better part of each day on his porch, carving small *jangadas* with a sharp knife. The high quality and wealth of details in his work (which feature fully-rendered sails, fish baskets, fishing lines, and other instruments) always catch the attention of travelers passing by on the beach (*Rua Damião Tavares, 349, Prainha, tel. 85/3361-5292; Mon – Sat, 7am – 6pm*). The Centro de Rendeiras da Prainha also sells his pieces.

chamber and prison. *Carnaúba*-wood structural beams in the upstairs portion of the museum are noteworthy. The most important piece in the museum is an 18th-century silver cross that the Jesuits took to Aquiraz.

Beach Park

This amusement park on the beach at Porto das Dunas offers a wide range of facilities for families, with 17 water rides and attractions. The complex also features snack bars, restaurants, and retail stores. There is no entrance fee, so you can enter just to enjoy the beach area or the bars and restaurants.
Rua Porto das Dunas, 2734, Porto das Dunas, tel. (85) 4012-3000. High season: daily, 11am – 5pm; low season: Fri – Tue and holidays, 11am – 5pm.

Lace Makers

The **Centro de Rendeiras da Prainha** (*Rua Damião Tavares, no #, Prainha, tel. 85/3361-5015; daily 9am – 5:30pm*) features seven kiosks of women making and selling *renda de bilro*, a bobbin lace made with either thick or thin thread (the finer thread can take several days to weave into lace). The **Centro de Rendeiras do Iguape** (*Avenida da Praia, no #, Iguape, tel. 85/3361-6447; daily 8am – 6pm*), near the dune and a shed used by local fishermen, sells *labirinto* and bobbin lace items, including table runners, beachwear, tray cloths, appliqués, and bags.

Crafts Market

The Mercado das Artes is a cultural center housed in an old 19th-century trading post and meat market, with art workshops, handicrafts stores, a restaurant, and library. The geometric harmony of the roof tiles and the technical precision of the construction, which utilizes *carnaúba* wood and adobe, are attractions in and of themselves.
Rua Santos Dumont, 76, Centro, tel. (85) 3361-2075. Daily, 6am – 6pm.

A lace maker braiding bobbins – delicate, painstaking work

Morro Branco is a popular destination on the east coast

CASCAVEL AND BEBERIBE

Lovely beaches and rich craftwork are the twin appeals of **Cascavel**, 64 kilometers (40 miles) east of Fortaleza on the CE-040 highway. **Beberibe** is a small town 83 kilometers (52 miles) east of Fortaleza and 20 kilometers (12 miles) northeast from Cascavel. This region boasts the two most famous beaches on the east coast: **Morro Branco** and **Praia das Fontes**.

CEARÁ LOBSTER

Ceará is responsible for more than half the lobster caught in Brazil. Naturally, the crustacean features in many of the most popular seafood dishes in Ceará. Unfortunately, this high demand threatens the lobster, which could face local extinction. The demand for lobster is so great that it is even fished illicitly during the *defeso* period, a span between January 1st and April 31st when catching lobsters is prohibited by law. In response to this, it is recommended that travelers not eat fresh lobster out of season and not accept small specimens (young lobsters) that have tails shorter than 13 centimeters (5 inches). That's the minimum size allowed by Brazilian law.

CRAFT CENTER

The Pólo Artesanal de Cascavel is at the entrance to town. Among the pieces on display are ceramics of Indian and Portuguese influence, made in the neighboring community of Moita Redonda, as well as furniture and other items made from liana.
CE-040, Km 56, entrance to Cascavel, tel. (85) 3334-0559. Mon – Fri, 8am – 5pm; Sat, 7am – 3pm; Sun, 8am – 3pm.

RAPADURA MILLS

The CE-040 state highway, between Aquiraz and Cascavel, is dotted with sugar mills that offer visitors the chance to watch the production of *rapadura*, *alfenim* (caramel candy), light molasses, *cachaça*, and brown sugar. Among the best places to visit are **Cana Dá** (*CE-040 highway, Km 37, tel. 85/9981-2897*), **Doces da Cana** (*CE-040 highway, Km 34, Centro, tel. 85/9602-0048; daily, 7am – 6pm*), and **Casa Grande** (*CE-040 highway, Km 37, tel. 85/9602-0048; Tue – Sun, 7am – 7pm*).

Garganta do Diabo offers access to the famous Canoa Quebrada beach

Canoa Quebrada

The most famous beach on the east coast of Ceará lies within the municipality of **Aracati**, about 161 kilometers (100 miles) outside Fortaleza. The town grew rich during the 18th century thanks to a brisk trade in dried beef. Today, it's known for its lively street Carnival, but accommodations remain scarce. A trip across town will reveal a handful of colonial-era buildings in unfortunate shape, though some remain preserved in their original Portuguese tiles. Follow the BR-304 highway for main access to Canoa Quebrada – by far the greatest local attraction. From Aracati you can also reach CE-261 highway, which extends from the Ceará coast to the border of Rio Grande do Norte. Since hippies discovered Canoa in the 1970s, the village has assumed an air of independence. This is best symbolized by the former name of the main street: Rua Dragão do Mar, after the nickname of a *jangadeiro* who gained fame through his anti-slavery militancy. Regrettably, the avenue today is called **Broadway**, where bars draw a loud and flashy crowd until the early morning hours.

Sand in a Bottle

Decorative glass bottles filled with layers of colored sand first gained popularity on **Majorlândia** beach, but can now be found in kiosks all along the Ceará coast, and sometimes in Fortaleza craft markets. The sands, often presented in 12 different shades, were originally collected from the dunes at Majorlândia. Today industrial dyes mimic the sands' natural spectrum of color. During a minutely detailed process achieved with the help of tiny spatulas, colored sand takes on the form of landscapes and sea scenes inside the bottles. It is impossible to leave Ceará without buying one.

The Coast by Dune Buggy

Two dune-buggy trips depart from Canoa Quebrada. One crosses the beaches of Porto Canoa, Majorlândia, Quixaba, Lagoa do Mato, Fontainha, Retirinho, and Retiro Grande, and ends with a spectacular sunset atop the dunes at Ponta Grossa. To make the most of the outing and escape the searing sun, start the three-hour-plus trek in the afternoon. The alternative journey is shorter – just over an hour – and follows a route from Porto Canoa to Quixaba. Buggy drivers can be hired at most Canoa Quebrada guesthouses and hotels, as well as in the village center. Be sure your driver is accredited by the Secretaria de Turismo do Ceará (*tel. 85/3101-4672; www.turismo.ce.gov.br*).

Regional Beaches

One can walk to **Porto Canoa** from neighboring Canoa Quebrada. The red cliffs here contrast with *jangada* sails at rest on the sand. **Majorlândia** is ideal for swimming and the trademark locale for collecting sand from multi-colored cliffs to fill the bottles sold throughout the state of Ceará. In October this beach serves as the starting point for the **Regata de Jangadas de Majorlândia** raft regatta. For those in search of peace and quiet, the white cliffs at **Quixaba** and the often deserted **Praia de Lagoa do Mato** are recommended. To reach the small lake that gives the latter beach its name, you must climb over the dunes. Though swimming at **Fontainha** beach does not come recommended, swing by just to see the colorful dunes similar to those at Majorlândia. Last but not least, it's important to mention the reef barrier at **Retirinho**, the seaweed-smothering **Retiro Grande** and **Ponta Grossa**, and tiny **Redondas**, a small fishing village perched atop beautiful cliffs.

Peace and quiet is the order of the day on the dunes of Canoa Quebrada

Ceará

THE WEST COAST

Known as the **Costa do Sol Poente** (Sunset Coast), the stretch of Ceará's coast that extends from Tabuba to the Piauí border ranges from rarely visited beaches (such as Bitupitá) to one of the most popular beach destinations in the Northeast, Jericoacoara. The beaches and villages along this coast have much in common, namely the hospitality they extend to visitors and the preservation of a cultural tradition, obviously connected to the sea. The dunes and wind play an important role here as well: One example is what happened to Tatajuba, a village that the dunes literally swallowed up; its residents have since relocated to **Nova Tatajuba**. The best way to reach the west coast from Fortaleza is by the Estruturante highway.

Tabuba
Seafront bars and natural pools are among the attractions on this beach, at the mouth of the Sapucaí River

Cumbuco and Lagoa do Banana
A favorite vacation destination for Fortalezans. Nearby attractions include Lagoa do Banana lake

PECÉM
Praia da Taíba
A large beach good for walking and cycling. Reefs protect the shoreline, popular with surfers and sailing enthusiasts

PARACURU
Munguba
A lively city beach where local fishermen build fish traps

Ronco do Mar
Surfers and young people favor this hotspot, also known as **Praia da Igreja Velha**

Pedra Rachada
Coconut palms and natural pools adorn this small cove

Praia da Bica
Visitors often stop over from neighboring beaches for the freshwater springs on this beach, which is also an anchor site for boats

Lagoinha
A beautiful cove featuring red dunes bursting with coconut palms. Crowds abound during peak season and on weekends.

Trairi
Embuaca
A fishing village with wattle and daub buildings beside its dunes and coconut palms. The sea draws its dark shade from the waters of the Mundaú River.

Guajiru
A quiet beach framed by coconut groves, with calm seas and natural pools

Flecheiras
A wide strip of compacted sand, ideal for swimming.

Mundaú
The nearby Mundaú River lends darkness to the seawater off this beach.

Jericoacoara
A national park since 1992, locals consider this one of the most beautiful beaches in Brazil. Dunes surround the bay, setting the scene for a great windsurfing spot.

Malhada
To the right of Jericoacoara village lies this beach, frequented almost exclusively by tourists en route to Pedra Furada.

Mangue Seco
Though dunes now occupy these grounds, formerly an old mangrove swamp, tree trunks still occasionally potrude from the sand. Frequented by residents of the Mangue Seco village.

Almofala
Tremembé Indians inhabit this area. Highlights include the 18th-century Igreja de Nossa Senhora da Conceição de Almofala.

Praia do Preá
A great walking beach, also popular with wind- and kite-surfers. Tourist facilities have begun to develop

Praia do Guriú
This picturesque scene comprises a river, fishing village, jangada port, coconut palms, mangrove, sailing canoes, and ferry boats. Locals from the nearby Guriú village relax here.

Camocim
Maceió
Gentle waves and shifting dunes nestle this beach, which features kiosks and two lakes, Cangalha and Boqueirão

Nova Tatajuba
A small, sleepy village with white-sand beaches, coconut palms, and dunes that can soar to heights of 50 meters (165 feet). Natural pools form among the dunes during the rainy season.

Bitupitá
Around this fishing community, you'll find fish traps, strong waves, and a wide strip of sand

CUMBUCO

Located 30 kilometers (19 miles) west of Fortaleza, Cumbuco is an ideal spot to spend a day outside the capital. Activities range from a relaxing sailing trip to a thrilling dune-buggy ride.

DUNE-BUGGY TRIPS

When it comes to choosing a dune-buggy tour, the question is: "With or without the thrills?" If your answer is the former, the driver will be more daring and travel at greater speeds. The standard trip lasts an hour, with stops at Lagoa do Parnamirim, Parque das Dunas, and Morro da Barriga hill. Alternatively, a 2-hour trip stops at **Lagoa do Banana**, where you can test jet-skis, banana boats, and motorboats or attempt water-skiing. **Barra do Cauípe** is worth a stop just to try *murici*, a regional fruit.
Contact: Cooperativa Cearense dos Proprietários e Condutores de Veículos para Passeios, tel. (85) 3318-7309.

SAILING-RAFT TRIPS

From Cumbuco, life-vest–equipped *jangadas* take up to six visitors out to sea for about 30 minutes.
Contact: Velas do Cumbuco, tel. (85) 3318-7555; Aldeia Brasil, tel. (85) 3318-7541.

JERICOACOARA

Once a little-known fishing village, Jericoacoara is now famous for its beach, considered by many one of the most beautiful beaches in Brazil, and the village is now frequented by tourists from all over the world. Nonetheless, Jeri (as it is known by locals and tourists alike) is still relatively isolated – only jeeps and dune buggies manage to cross the dunes that surround it, and its dirt streets have no public lighting. Visitors can eat in sophisticated restaurants, however, and guides and agencies offer every imaginable kind of trip. Give yourself at least four days to fully enjoy everything the area has to offer. With its calm waters and strong winds,

Boats on the beach at Jericoacoara

Pedra Furada: sculpted by nature

Jeri is a perfect destination for windsurfing and kite-surfing enthusiasts. The beach's long strip of compact sand is good for walking or playing soccer. In 2002, the village and surroundings were declared a national park – there are no restrictions on visits, but the environmental protection laws are rigorous.

From Jijoca de Jericoacoara, Jericoacoara is accessed by taking the CE-085 highway 280 kilometers (174 miles) west from Fortaleza, and 23 kilometers (14 miles) along a dirt road north from Jijoca to Jericoacoara beach. The trip is best made by dune buggy, truck, or *jardineira* (modified pick-up truck), as the road is sandy and full of pot holes.

Our Recommendation

🍽 Near Pôr-do-Sol dune, **Bar Sky** offers a wide variety of drinks. Visitors can enjoy the scenery while relaxing at the outdoor or 'indoor' tables of this bar without walls. (*Rua Principal, no #, tel. 88/3669-2048. High season: daily, 10am – until the last customer leaves; low season: daily, 10am – 3pm*).

Additional information on page 358.

Pedra Furada

A half hour's walk along Jericoacoara beach will bring you to Pedra Furada (Rock Hole), one of Jericoacoara's loveliest locations. A rock lying across the beach has a large hole in its center that resembles a sculpted gateway. Along the way, the calm waters of **Praia Malhada** beach are an excellent place to pause for a dive.

Head to Pedra Furada at low tide; at high tide you're forced to climb the steep dunes. It is also possible to reach the rock by dune buggy. The tours, which depart from the visitors' *pousada* or hotel (phone number below), include a stop at **Lagoa da Jijoca** lake.
Contact: *Dune buggy tours: Associação dos Bugueiros de Jericoacoara, tel. (88) 3669-2284, 9955-6046.*

Dune-Buggy Trips

The Associação de Bugueiros do Ceará offers two dune-buggy trips around Jericoacoara. The first travels 12 kilometers (7 miles) east along the coast and includes **Praia do Preá** beach and several miles of dunes. The other trip runs 20 kilometers (12 miles) west and includes the **Mangue Seco**, **Tatjuba Nova**, and **Guriú** beaches, as well as the villages of Tatjuba Nova and **Tatajuba Velha** – the latter village was abandoned twenty years ago and is slowly succumbing to advancing dunes. Both villages belong to the municipality of Camocim. Each trip is approximately five hours long.
Contact: *Associação de Bugueiros de Jericoacoara, tel. (88) 3669-2284, 9955-6046.*

Pôr-do-Sol Dune

Every evening, visitors and locals alike climb 40 meters (130 feet) up what is known as the *pôr-do-sol* dune to watch the sunset (*pôr-do-sol*). In a brilliant display of violet, red, yellow and orange, the sun sinks till it's a giant ball hovering over the sea. As it disappears beyond the horizon, the dunes turn yellow, gold, and finally, brown. The most enthusiastic spectators applaud, and the most adventurous slide down the dune. During the high season (Dec to Feb), it's often possible to catch a *capoeira* show on the dune.

Forró do Raimundo

Forró do Raimundo, a Jericoacoara tradition, began 25 years ago when passerby spontaneously began to dance the *forró* when they heard Mr. Raimundo playing vinyl records in the annex of his family's store. It became so famous that

Sweet Treats and Ice Cream

Friendly Tia Angelita, a locally-famous Jericoacoara native, delights customers with tapioca pudding, *cocadas* (a coconut dessert), and banana pie, all served with fresh coffee. While there is no shortage of stalls in the village and on the beach offering similar treats, none can match her delicious banana pie. Convince yourself at Tia's **Shopping da Tapioca** (*Rua Principal, no #, tel. 88/9962-3380; daily, 7am – 10pm*). On the same street, **Sorveteria Engenhoca** (*access road to Pôr-do-Sol dune; daily, 3pm – 1am*) uses homemade recipes for its ices. Try the Pedra Furada, raisin ice cream with cream, rum, and cashew nuts, or the Céu de Jeri, a mixture of bonbons and chocolate chips.

the street it is on has been renamed **Rua do Forró**. Today, Forró do Raimundo has moved from the sidewalks to a covered dance space with a large, well-waxed dance floor. Dancers quench their thirst at the **Bar do Forró** bar.
Rua do Forró, no #, tel. (88) 9931-0009. High season: Mon, Tue, Wed, Fri and Sat, 8pm – until the last customer leaves; low season: Tue, Wed, Fri and Sat, 8pm – until the last customer leaves. Live music starts at 11pm.

Jijoca de Jericoacoara

The municipal center of Jijoca de Jericoacoara, which is the name for this whole district, is 23 kilometers (14 miles) from Jericoacoara village and its beach. Among the center's attractions are **Lagoa Azul** and **Lagoa do Paraíso**, lakes that have become popular with windsurfers thanks to their reliable breezes. The green waters of both lakes are good for free-diving and sailing, and provide lovely, picturesque contrast to the dunes. For visitors who are planning to simply take in the landscape, the best time of year to visit is during the rainy season (March, April, and May), when the water levels are higher. Windsurfing is best July through November, when the winds are strongest. Equipment with engines is forbidden on both lakes.

Almofala

The tiny beach community of Almofala, nestled between the Aracati-Mirim and Aracati-Açu Rivers, guards a treasure: the **Igreja de Nossa Senhora da Conceição de Almofala** (*Praça Principal, no #; daily, 8am – 11am and 2pm – 5pm*). The church was built in 1712 on land belonging to the Tremembé Indians. By 1897, the structure was completely buried by dunes. Over 40 years later, the wind uncovered the church, revealing its lovely baroque lines. Igreja de Nossa Senhora da Conceição de Almofala has been protected by Iphan since 1980. During the first week of August locals celebrate the Feast of the Assumption in the church square, and in the first week of December they hold the festivities to honor Nossa Senhora da Conceição (Our Lady of the Immaculate Conception). To reach Almofala, which is 12 kilometers (7 miles) northeast of Itarema, take the BR-402 highway northeast to the CE-434 state highway.

Lagoa Azul: strong winds make this lagoon ideal for windsurfing

Camocim

Camocim sits at the confluence of the Coreaú River and the sea and has 60 kilometers (37 miles) of beaches. In the town center are hotels, guesthouses, restaurants, and bars. The landscape is dominated by the river beaches and hundreds of canoes and other boats on the water. Camocim lies 380 kilometers (236 miles) west of Fortaleza (via BR-085, a highway in good condition) and 100 kilometers (62 miles) west of Jericoacoara, following dirt roads. Alternatively, from Jericoacoara, you can drive more directly, if you go by dune buggy; it's 75 kilometers (47 miles) across the beaches. Camocim can also be reached via Sobral, a historic city 145 kilometers (90 miles) to the south, by driving north on the CE-362 highway.

Dune-Buggy Trips

The most enchanting day trip from Camocim is a dune-buggy tour highlighting the area's natural beauty. Buggies first cross the river by ferry boat (a five-minute ride), arriving on Ilha do Amor, an island with a beach of the same name. The beach is nothing more than a long, straight stretch of compacted sand. The trip becomes more interesting as the dune buggy passes through mangrove forest near Praia de Moréia, where mangroves encircle dunes and lakes. The tour stops at **Duna do Funil**, a series of enormous dunes next to lovely **Lagoa Verde** lake. From there, the buggies continue on to Tatajuba beach, Duna Encantada dune, and **Lagoa da Torta**, where you can swim and enjoy a snack from any one of a number of lunch kiosks. Visitors can choose to remain at Duna Encantada for the sunset or extend their trip to **Guriú** village, on the bank of the Guriú River. The mouth of the river is one of the most famous landscapes in Jericoacoara (although technically it is in Camocim). The scenery is dazzling, and alternating stretches of sand and water create warm fresh and saltwater pools. Anyone who wishes to extend his or her trip can take the ferryboat from Guriú to Jijoca de Jericoacoara. *Contact*: *Jegue Tur, tel. (88) 3621-7023.*

The dunes at Tatajuba, in Camocim, the last stretch of coast in Ceará

Wattle and daub houses and a chapel in Nova Tatajuba

BITUPITÁ

Bitupitá (pop. 6,000) sits on the border between Ceará and Piauí. The village is best visited on a day trip as tourist facilities are not available. Most residents live off the ocean, placing fish traps made from tree trunks covered by nets at a depth of about 8 meters (26 feet). Fish enter the tree-and-net labyrinth and are unable to find their way out again. At low tide, the fishermen haul their catch, fill their canoes, and head for the beach, where they sell their day's work. There are approximately ten traps near the shore at Praia de Bitupitá; others are placed about 10 kilometers (6 miles) off the coast. Visitors can watch the fishermen work while enjoying fresh, fried fish from beach kiosks.

To get to Bitupitá from Camocim, which is 40 kilometers (25 miles) to its east, take the BR-402 to Barroquinha. From there, a nameless but signposted dirt road, which should only be undertaken in a 4×4, leads 35 kilometers (22 miles) north to Bitupitá.

NOVA TATAJUBA

Nova Tatajuba is a small fishing village 32 kilometers (20 miles) west of Jericoacoara, in the municipality of Camocim. It was built in the 1980s, after the old village – Velha Tatjuba – was swallowed by dunes; the result of a slow, relentless process that began in the 1960s and ended when the last resident was forced out. Today you can see only the roofs of old Tatjuba's taller buildings and the chapel. Newer though it is, there is no electricity in Nova Tatajuba, the houses are wattle and daub, and the only vehicles on the narrow streets are the dune buggies that bring tourists from Jericoacoara and Camocim. The landscape is a simple tableau of coconut palms, pale sands, and high dunes. The most beautiful dune is **Duna Encantada**, which stands over 30 meters (100 feet) tall and is used as a landmark by fishermen returning from sea. Legend has it that there is an old ship buried beneath the dune's sands, and that the voices of the crew can still be heard in the still of night. Daytime dune-climbers will be rewarded, as well; Duna Encantada offers one of the most beautiful views in the entire region.

THE MOUNTAINS

SOBRAL

The neo-classical façade of the São João Theater

From its roots as a small, 18th-century village, Sobral has grown to become the second largest city in Ceará. Sobral sits at the foot of the Serra de Meruoca mountain range, on the left bank of the Aracaú River, along the BR-222, the road that connects Pernambuco to Piauí and Maranhão. Commercial development in the area began with the construction of a local railroad in 1882, which linked it to the port of Camocim and made the city the main commercial center in the north of the state. Houses, churches, museums, and theaters built around the turn of the 19th century are today national heritage sites, and lend the city a special brilliance. Highlights include **Praça São João** square, art nouveau-style **Praça João Pessoa** square, **Praça José Sabóia**, **Praça da Sé**, the **Arco de Triunfo** arch, **Rua Ernesto Deocleciano** street, and the street's two churches, **Igreja das Dores** and **Igreja do Rosário**. The Acaraú riverbank is a very pleasant place for a walk at daybreak or in the late afternoon, when the sun illuminates the bridges, making Sobral look even more beautiful.

The best time to visit is between January and June, when temperatures are mild as opposed to an average 30°C (86°F) the rest of the year. Sobral can be reached by taking the BR-222 highway northeast from Fortaleza, a 235 kilometer (146 mile) drive. This stretch of road is full of holes, and a significant number of trucks travel the highway through the Serra de Tainguá mountain range.

Sé Cathedral

The imposing grandeur of the Catedral da Sé, also known as Matriz de Nossa Senhora da Conceição is impressive and has been described by local writer, Domingos Olímpio (1850-1906). At night, the illuminated church forms a particularly beautiful tableau with the silhouette of the Serra da Meruoca rising darkly behind. The foundation stone dates to 1778 and construction was completed in 1783. The Portuguese limestone portico and high altar nave are exceptionally grand. In the main chapel, be sure to take a look at the beautiful wood tabernacle with Corinthian columns.
Praça da Sé, 100, Centro.

São João Square and Theater

Home to many lovely trees, Praça São João is the most pleasant square in the city. At night, when the square becomes a pedestrian-only zone, local university students sit around under the trees and talk. On the edge of the square you'll see the Casa de Cultura building (a cultural center that hosts workshops and exhibitions) and the Igreja Menino Deus church. It's the **Teatro São João** theater (*Praça São João, no #, Centro, tel. 88/3613-1906; Thu, 8am – noon and 2pm – 5pm*), however, that dominates the square. The theater's late 19th-century neo-classical façade is beautifully reflected in the lake of its well-tended gardens. Guided visits are available on Thursdays, though not necessarily in English, and should be arranged in advance with the Secretaria da Cultura (*Avenida Dom José, 881, Centro*).

DOM JOSÉ MUSEUM
Museu Dom José, the first museum of sacred art in Ceará, was founded in 1951 by Bishop Dom José Tupinambá da Frota, who is responsible for obtaining most of the collection's 30,000 pieces. In addition to religious items, the museum houses a vast collection of 18th- and 19th-century house wares, furniture, weapons, and clothes. The neo-classical building, built in 1844, is well maintained but lacks air-conditioning.
Avenida Dom José, 878, Centro, tel. (88) 3611-3525. Tue – Fri, 8am – 11am and 2pm – 5pm; Sat and Sun, 8am – noon.

UBAJARA

Surrounded by Atlantic forest, Ubajara sits atop the Serra da Ibiapaba mountain range at an altitude of 847 meters (2,780 feet). The town is 324 kilometers (201 miles) southwest of Fortaleza on the BR-222. In July, the best month to visit, the small, peaceful town is covered in the early hours by a beautiful early morning mist. (Bundle up, that month can be chilly.) Ubajara's main attraction is nearby Parque Nacional de Ubajara, a national park only 4 kilometers (2.5 miles) from the town center.

UBAJARA NATIONAL PARK
The Parque Nacional de Ubajara was created in 1959 and encompasses 6,288 hectares (15,538 acres) of Atlantic forest, mountain plateaus, and strips of *cerrado* and *caatinga* vegetation at lower elevations, where cacti are

Waterfalls dot the landscape in Ubajara National Park

Ubajara Cave: 420 meters of delicate limestone formations

abundant. Waterfalls slice through the intense green of the landscape. Trees like the jatoba, trumpet, *copaíbas*, and babassu palm thrive here. Native fauna include rock cavies, capuchins, marmosets, armadillos, snakes, lizards, agoutis, and anteaters. The park's trails and lookout points can be explored in one day; and several limestone caves are open to the more adventurous. Hikers should take insect repellent, snacks, and plenty of water.
Estrada do Teleférico, Km 4, tel. (88) 3634-1388 (IBAMA). Tue – Sun, 9am – 2pm.

UBAJARA CAVE
Portuguese prospectors in search of silver are said to have discovered Gruta de Ubajara cave in the 18th century. According to legend, it was inhabited by an old Indian who wandered the region's rivers in his canoe – the name "Ubajara" comes from the native Tupi-Guarani words *uba* ("canoe") and *jara* ("mister"). At the beginning of the 20th century, the cave attracted pilgrims devoted to Nossa Senhora de Lourdes (Our Lady of Lourdes), whose statue stands at the entrance. Gruta de Ubajara extends 1,120 meters (0.7 mile) into the mountain, but only 420 meters (1,380 feet) of this length are accessible. Visitors come here to admire the magnificent, delicate limestone formations, which include stalactites, stalagmites, columns, stone cascades, and curtains. The majestic Sala da Imagem (Statue Room) and the Corredor das Maravilhas (Corridor of Wonders) are particularly good places to see stalactites and stalagmites, while the Sala dos Brilhantes (Diamond Room) is full of shiny crystals. The cave entrance is accessed on foot by the Ubajara-Araticum trail, which takes three hours one-way, or by cable car, which takes only three minutes. The cable car is often closed for maintenance, so it's a good idea to call in advance to see if it's running on any given day (*tel. 88/3634-1219; Tue – Sun, 9am – 2:30pm*).

TRAILS AND WATERFALLS
The popular **Ubajara-Araticum** trail connects the visitors' center to the mouth of Gruta de Ubajara cave. Starting at the center, the trail is a three-hour downhill walk that passes through

Atlantic forest and includes several beautiful lookout points, natural pools, and roaring waterfalls, like the 50-meter (165-foot) **Cachoeira do Cafundó** (it is not safe to swim here). The trip back from the cave to the visitors' center can be made by cable car or on foot. The latter is uphill and takes approximately five hours. Travelers with small children may want to stick to the easier **Trilha das Samambaias** trail, instead. The trail passes by **Cachoeira da Gameleira** (another waterfall unsuitable for swimming), which can be reached in half an hour from the visitors' center. From the Cachoeira da Gameleira lookout point you can see Gruta de Ubajara, Cachoeira do Cafundó, and the Ubajara-Araticum trail. **Cachoeira do Gavião**, an 80 meter (260 foot) waterfall, is a difficult three-hour, round-trip hike; exhausted hikers sometimes refresh themselves in the cascades that precede the main waterfall.

GUARAMIRANGA

Guaramiranga, a mountain town in the Baturité nature reserve, is known for its mild climate. During the winter the average temperature dips to 15°C (59°F). Only 120 kilometers (75 miles) southwest of Fortaleza, the town is home to the last remaining patches of Atlantic forest in Ceará. The region attracts visitors who enjoy adventure sports, bird watching, and/or simply admiring nature. Its attractions include **Pico Alto**, one of the highest peaks in the state at a height of 1,115 meters (3,660 feet). The peak is 13 kilometers (8 miles) from the town center and can be reached by an unnamed but well-surfaced road. Guaramiranga is also home to several cultural events. During Carnival, the Festival de Jazz e Blues offers an alternative for tired partygoers looking to escape the beat of the *marchinhas* and *axé*. Local drama companies perform for the public during the Mostra de Teatro de Guaramiranga, in July, and again in September during the Festival Nordestino de Teatro. October sees the air come alive with delicious smells emanating from the Encontro de Gastronomia food festival, and you can wash it all down in November 2005 with a visit to the Festival de Vinhos (Wine Festival). Guaramiranga can be accessed from Fortaleza by taking the CE-060 highway southwest bound. Though longer, this is considered a safer route than state highway CE-065, which has some dangerous curves.

Sertão

Juazeiro do Norte

Juazeiro do Norte, the largest city in the Ceará backlands, was founded in 1911 by Father Cícero Romão Batista, a Christian monk known as "Padim Ciço" (Godfather Ciço) who was adored throughout the *sertão*. Today many consider him a saint. The city is home to many woodcut printers, a rich art and crafts scene, good hotels and restaurants, and confusing traffic signs. There are three great religious **pilgrimages** to Juazeiro that take place each year: one on September 15th, one between October 30th and November 2nd; and another from January 30th to February 2nd. In addition to these, the July 20th anniversary of Father Cícero's death attracts many faithful. During pilgrimage weeks Juazeiro buzzes with energy. Pilgrims come from all over the Northeast in trucks, buses, cars, and carts, and on donkeys, horses, motorcycles, and bikes. School is out and there are not enough hotels. Over a quarter million devoted pilgrims sing hymns in honor of Father Cícero, and some even dress as he did in a straw hat and black cassock – in fact, elderly people often dress like this on the 20th of every month, to honor the anniversary of his death. During pilgrimages, **Colina do Horto**, known locally as Morro do Padre Cícero (Father Cícero Hill), is lit up at night to guide new arrivals; stone steps lead to the top, where there is a church, museum, and a famous statue of the priest. From the top there is also a spectacular view of Juazeiro and its five churches: the Matriz de Nossa Senhora das Dores, the Santuário do Sagrado Coração de Jesus, the Capela de Nossa Senhora de Perpétuo Socorro, the Basílica de São Francisco, and the Paróquia de Nossa Senhora de Lourdes. Juazeiro do Norte is 495 kilometers (308 miles) south of Fortaleza on the BR-116 highway. The city is a good base from which to explore the nearby towns of Crato, Nova Olinda, and Santana do Cariri.

Father Cícero's statue, on top of Colina do Horto

Padre Cícero Statue

The imposing statue of Father Cícero stands on top of Colina do Horto hill, near the Museu Vivo. The monument is 25 meters (82 feet) high and 8 meters (26 feet) wide, and when added to the height of the hill itself, the statue is surpassed in height only by the statue of Cristo Redentor in Rio de Janeiro. On pilgrimage days the

Santuário do Sagrado Coração de Jesus, in Juazeiro do Norte

area around the statue is crowded with pilgrims, souvenir sellers, and boys who tell stories of the "*padim*" in exchange for a few coppers.
Colina do Horto, 8 kilometers (5 miles) from the center.

Padre Cícero Memorial
The house where Father Cícero lived has been turned into a museum. Visitors can view his kitchen, bedroom, bed, desk, clothes (including his vestments), and crockery. The memorial is also full of objects left behind by supplicants as thanks for blessings received – everything from soccer team banners and wedding photos to stuffed animals and plaques.
Praça do Socorro, tel. (88) 3511-2876. Mon – Fri, 8am – 6pm; Sat and Sun, 8am – noon.

Nossa Senhora do Perpétuo Socorro Chapel
Though it is the smallest and simplest of the churches in Juazeiro do Norte, the Capela de Nossa Senhora do Perpétuo Socorro has the honor of housing Father Cícero's tomb. During pilgrimages, the chapel is crowded with faithful who process from here to Matriz de Nossa Senhora das Dores church or Colina do Horto hill.
Praça do Cinqüentenário, no #, Socorro.

Padre Cícero Museum
A religious atmosphere dominates the Museu Vivo do Padre Cícero, an enormous house turned museum now full of votive offerings and plaster replicas of Father Cícero that have been left behind by thousands of his devotees. Notice all the books dedicated to him at the entrance.
Colina do Horto hill, 8 kilometers (5 miles) from the city center, tel. 88/3511-2876 Tue – Sun, 8am – 11am and 1pm – 5pm.

Mestre Noza Folk Culture Center
The Centro de Cultura Popular Mestre Noza, a large shed with a

> ### Padre Cícero
>
> Cícero Romão Batista was born in Crato on March 24th, 1844. In 1872, two years after his ordination, he is said to have had a dream in which Jesus Christ asked him to look after the poor backlands people of the settlement that would become Juazeiro. Cícero soon settled in there. The first miracle attributed to him was the transformation of wine into blood at the communion of a parishioner. News of the feat spread throughout the *sertão*. Soon after, Monsignor Francisco Monteiro, rector of Crato Seminary, publicly announced that Cícero could perform miracles and organized a pilgrimage of 3,000 faithful to Juazeiro. The Catholic Church reacted; back at the Vatican, the Holy Office wanted to excommunicate Cícero, but feared repercussions – the priest was popular among the people and connected to powerful landowners known as *coronéis*. Instead, Rome prevented him from saying mass. The priest eventually became mayor of Juazeiro do Norte, and the settlement grew as his devotees took up residence there. He died in 1934 at the age of ninety, but his mystic presence, and the city that thrives on it, survive to this day.

thatched roof housing dozens of artisans at work, is the main handicraft outlet in Juazeiro. Here you'll find innumerable wooden and plaster sculptures of the legendary bandit Lampião, *forró* musician Luís Gonzaga, and Father Cícero, as well as sculpted animals and dolls.
Rua São Luís, no #, Centro, tel. (88) 3511-3133. Mon – Fri, 8am – 6pm; Sat, 8am – 1pm.

LIRA NORDESTINA CORDEL LITERATURE PRINTING WORKS
The print works consists of a large room for printing (old typesetters and other machinery) and another room that houses a collection of *cordel* literature (*Folk Arts see page 40*).
Avenida Castelo Branco, 150, Rumerão, tel. (88) 3102-1150, 9201-1143. Mon – Fri, 7:30am – 11:30am and 1:30pm – 5:30pm; Sat, 7:30am – noon.

CRATO

Juazeiro do Norte's neighbor – only 10 kilometers (6 miles) to the west – sits near the Araripe Plateau and forest, and is full of hot springs. The woods and springs ensure agreeable temperatures year round, even though the climate is semi-arid. Crato (founded 1853) offers a variety of hotels, restaurants, and bars, making it a good alternative when Juazeiro do Norte is full (a frequent occurrence between September and February). Considered the cultural capital of Ceará's *sertão*, Crato is home to folklore groups, woodcut printers, literature clubs, and *cordel* (found at the Academia do Cordelista). The town also hosts dramatic dance performances, such as the *reisado*, and lively June festivities. The pleasant streets of Crato are lined with trees, and impressively large houses cluster along the paths that lead to the hills around the plateau. Hiking enthusiasts may want to take advantage of the local trail system. The path known as **Subida do Belmonte** climbs from 460 to 1,000 meters (1,500 to 3,300 feet) in just 50 minutes of walking. A more challenging possibility is the lovely 27-kilometer (17-mile) trail that connects the **Mirante da Cruz** and **Mirante da Coruja** lookout points. From Fortaleza, Crato is a 533 kilometer (331 mile) drive southwest. Take the BR-116 highway south to Icó, then, to avoid potholes, take the BR-230, which passes through the towns of Iguatu, Várzea Alegre, and Farias Brito on the way to Crato.

Around Crato

Patativa Do Assaré Memorial Foundation

Since 1999, tiny Assaré has preserved the memory of its most illustrious son, the folk poet Antônio Gonçalves da Silva, also known as Patativa do Assaré (1909-2002). Born into a family of small farmers, Patativa published six books in which he described the hardships of the Northeast and told vivid stories of backlands life. He became famous throughout the country after Luís Gonzaga set his poem, *A Triste Partida* (The Sad Departure), to music. The Fundação Memorial Patativa do Assaré exhibits manuscripts, personal objects, books by the writer, books of regional poetry, and various essays. In the audio-visual room you can view the poet reciting his verses and performing alongside the *forró* musician Luís Gonzaga.

Assaré is 60 kilometers (37 miles) northwest of Crato and 70 kilometers (43 miles) from Juazeiro do Norte on the CE-292 highway.

Rua Coronel Francisco Gomes, 82, Centro, Assaré, tel. (88) 3535-1742, 3535-1690. Mon – Sat, 8am – 5pm; Sun, 9am – noon.

Santana Do Cariri Palaeontology Museum

The Museu Paleontológico de Santana do Cariri sits in the center of the so-called Santana Formation, the most important fossil site in Brazil and the largest collection of fish fossils in the world. The museum belongs to the Regional University of Cariri, and it is a must-see for anyone staying in neighboring Crato, 50 kilometers (31 miles) to the east, or in Juazeiro do Norte, 65 kilometers (40 miles) to the west. The museum's exhibits display more than 750 fossils and fossil fragments from excavations, including a fossil of a pterosaur. The ground floor houses a model of the region, fossil replicas, and explanatory panels; upstairs, fossils are grouped by type and include dragonflies, fish, and plants. The ease with which great archaeological finds are made here has made it the target of international smugglers. Today, Santana do Cariri's policy is to encourage the manufacture of replicas, such as those sold in the museum. Guided tours with Professor Alexandre Magno can be arranged in advance. Cariri sits on the edge of an immense valley skirting the Chapada do Araripe plateau, and it's worth taking a break from fossils to admire the view and the town's old houses.

Rua Doutor José Augusto, 326, Santana do Cariri, tel. (88) 3545-1206. Tue – Sat, 8am – 4pm; Sun, 8am – 2pm.

Casa Grande Foundation

The Fundação Casa Grande foundation works to promote indigenous culture. The foundation is located in the town of **Nova Olinda**, 41 kilometers (25 miles) northwest of Crato and 51 kilometers (32 miles) northwest of Juazeiro do Norte via the CE-292 highway. The modest **Memorial do Homem Kariri** museum is also run by the foundation, and their collection includes utensils, polished stones, and ceramics that help illustrate the culture and traditions of the indigenous Cariris people. The foundation also houses the **Escola de Comunicação da Meninada do Sertão**, where local children receive schooling and make programs that are broadcast on local radio and TV.

Avenida Jeremias Pereira, 444, Centro, Nova Olinda, tel. (88) 3546-1333. Daily, 8am – 5pm.

PIAUÍ

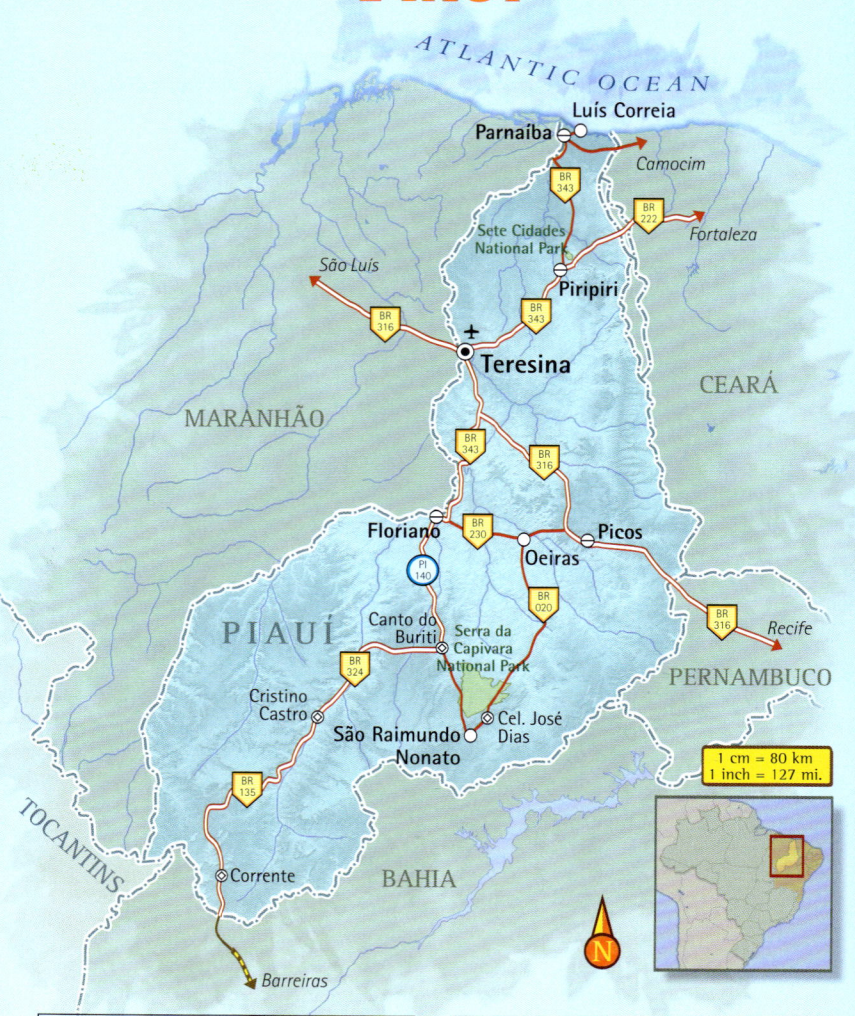

Highlights

- The cultural heritage of **Teresina**.
- The wind-carved rocks in the **Parque Nacional de Sete Cidades** reserve.
- The **Parque Nacional Serra da Capivara**, a reserve that holds the world's largest collection of petroglyphs, or rock paintings.
- The rock formations in the **Serra das Confusões** mountain range.
- The mangroves, dunes, and beaches of the **Parnaíba River Delta**.

When to Go

- Visit the Parnaíba River Delta any time during the year. There are more options for boat trips between **December and March**.
- The national parks are at their greenest between **December and May**, though rain can make the trails more difficult.
- From **May to November**, the *caatinga* vegetation loses its foliage and animals are easier to observe.

Piauí sets itself apart from Northeast's other states in many ways, and chief among them is that it is the least maritime of the bunch. It is the only northeastern state whose capital is not located by the sea. It has the shortest coastal strip in the region — stretching just 66 kilometers (41 miles). And, unlike the rest of the Northeast, settlement here began inland, in the *sertão*. The colonization of Piauí ("river of *piaus*" in Tupi-Guarani, a reference to the abundant fish in the state) began when pioneers left Bahia and Pernambuco in the 17th century, in search of new pastures. The city of Oeiras was the first to be colonized. Other towns sprang up quickly afterwards, and the Rio Parnaíba, the second largest river in the Northeast, linked them together. The river helped cities such as Floriano, Amarante, and Teresina, the state's capital since 1852, to flourish. The Rio Parnaíba known to locals as "Velho Monge" (Old Monk), begins in the Serra das Mangabeiras Range, on the border between Tocantins and Bahia; it flows 1,480 kilometers (920 miles) east to the Atlantic. At the mouth of the river is the Parnaíba Delta, the largest delta in the Americas and one of the most interesting stretches of Brazilian coastline. The hot, arid lands of Piauí's *sertão* reveal dazzling natural wonders like the rock formations in the Sete Cidades National Park and the rock faces in the Serra das Confusões National Park. The state's greatest treasure is the collection of rupestrian paintings in the Serra da Capivara National Park; Unesco declared the park to be a World Heritage Site in 1991. Charming Teresina is a main gateway to many of Piauí's attractions. Anyone heading to São Raimundo Nonato, a base for visitors to the Serra da Capivara and Serra das Confusões National Parks, should go through Petrolina, in Pernambuco. They are also be accessible from the Parnaíba Delta.

The Rio Parnaíba fans out where it meets the sea, creating an unusual delta

Teresina

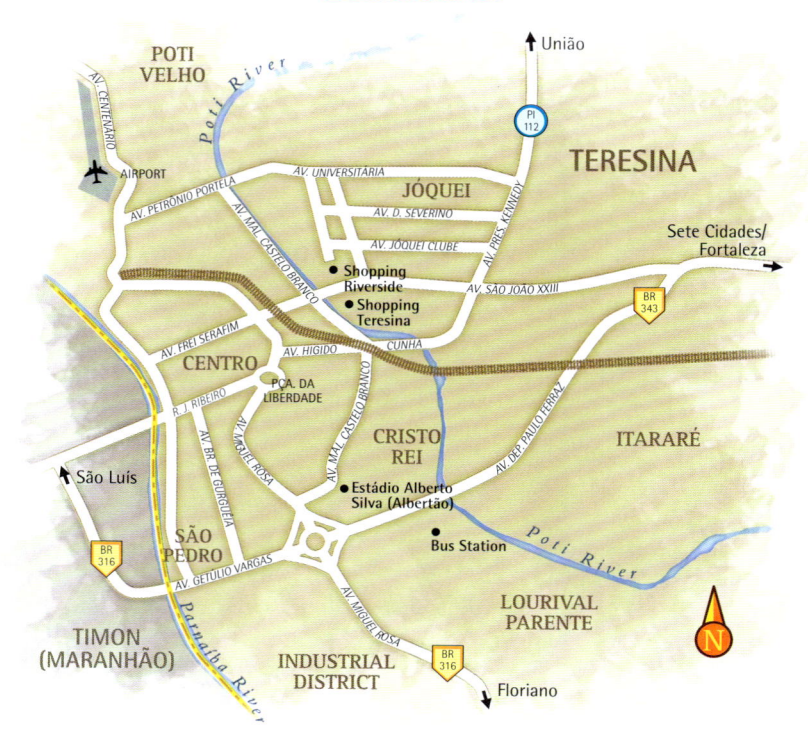

Teresina is 350 kilometers (217 miles) from the coast, but its two rivers, the **Poti** and **Parnaíba,** provide much-needed cool breezes in a city where the average annual temperature is 30°C (86°F). Founded in the 18th century, Teresina was initially called Vila do Poti; it was renamed in honor of Empress Teresa Cristina when it became the capital in 1852. The city is located in a region known as Chapada do Corisco (Flash Plateau) – named for the frequent flashes of lightning in the skies before a rainstorm. Teresina is flat, with a simple grid of streets. Unlike in other northeastern capitals, few tourists visit here. Those who do, however, have the privilege of enjoying over 30 city parks and a surprising variety of cultural events and lively nightlife. The schedule of cultural festivities is available at the city's Casa da Cultura.

Pedro II Square

Praça Pedro II is Teresina's cultural hot spot – the focus of the city's bohemian life, and a meeting place for artists. Here you'll find the **Teatro 4 de Setembro** (*Praça Pedro II, no #, tel. 86/3222-7100; Mon – Sat, 7:30am – 5:30pm*), a theater built in 1894, which opens its doors every week for affordable theatrical performances. The old **Cine Rex**, with its art deco façade, opened in 1939 and now functions as a live-music venue. The **Central do Artesanato** is a must-see (*tel. 86/3221-9502; Mon – Fri, 8am – 6pm; Sat, 8am – 3pm*). This crafts center sells folk art, with an emphasis on carved wood, hammocks, and opal items from the town of Pedro II. It also sells Abrahão Cavalcante's hand-crafted *buriti* wood furniture.

Cultural Center
The Casa da Cultura operates inside a well-maintained building built in 1870. It documents the city's history in seven rooms that feature a collection of photographs, paintings, coins, and other items. The center also contains pieces related to the lives of illustrious locals like journalist Carlos Castelo Branco (1920-1993) and photographer José de Medeiros (1921-1990). Branco donated his library, which is available for reference, to the center, and some of de Medeiros's beautiful pictures are also on display here.
Rua Rui Barbosa, 348, Centro, tel. (86) 3215-7849. Mon – Fri, 8am – 5:30pm; Sat, 9am – 1pm; Sun, noon – 5:30pm.

Piauí Museum
This former seat of government was erected in 1859 and restored in 2005. It houses a collection of religious art, canvases by significant local painters, including Gabriel Archanjo and

Our Recommendation
🍽 *Matrinxã* (a fish found in the Rio Parnaíba), goujons, fresh crab claws, and fresh shrimp in caper sauce: these are some of the tasty dishes served at **Camarão do Elias**. Friendly, chatty Elias owns this simple, welcoming restaurant (*Avenida Pedro Almeida, 457, São Cristóvão, tel. 86/3232-5025; Mon – Sat, 5pm – 2am; Sun, 11am – 4pm*).

Additional information on page 358.

Fernando Costa, as well as wood carvings by Mestre Dezinho and Nonato de Oliveira. The Museu do Piauí also features a miniature replica of a Parnaíba steamship and other 19th-century objects.
Praça Marechal Deodoro da Fonseca, no #, tel. (86) 3221-6027. Tue – Fri, 8am – 5:30pm; Sat and Sun, 8am – noon.

Karnak Palace
The seat of government since 1926, the sumptuous Palácio Karnak was built in classical style between 1874 and 1886. It now houses several art collections as well as lovely gardens designed by landscape artist Roberto

Teresina has multiple parks and a vigorous cultural life

Burle Marx. Visits inside need to be arranged in advance.
Avenida Antonino Freire, 1450, Centro, tel. (86) 3221-9820. Mon – Fri, 8am – 6pm.

DIÁRIOS CLUB CULTURAL CENTER
The Clube dos Diários hosted legendary Carnival balls in the 1960s. Today, it is a cultural center and meeting point for local writers, artists, singers, and journalists. It also houses the Torquato Neto cinema, which offers free showings at midday. A small store inside the club sells the locals' latest CDs and books.
Rua Álvaro Mendes, no #, Centro, tel. (86) 3222-7100. Mon – Fri, 7:30am – 7:30pm.

OFICINA DA PALAVRA CULTURAL CENTER
This center includes a library, auditorium, lecture room, and an art gallery, which exhibits works by regional artists. It also distributes the *Calendário Poético*, a free monthly publication showcasing the work of one poet and one artist. The "Encontros Inevitáveis" (Unavoidable Gatherings) take place here starting at 8pm on the last Wednesday of every month; these literary/musical gatherings focus on the work of local and international poets.
Rua Benjamin Constant, 1400, Centro, tel. (86) 3223-4441, 3223-6079. Mon – Fri, 8am – noon and 2pm – 6pm; Sat, 8am – noon.

ON THE BANKS OF THE POTI RIVER
At the end of every afternoon, people fill the **Avenida Raul Lopes**. This promenade along the banks of the Rio Poti is popular with runners, walkers, cyclists, and couples. At nightfall, kiosks attract a wide range of people, from businessmen to students, with happy hours that tend to extend well into the night. **Caneleiro** (*opposite the Shopping Riverside Mall; Mon – Wed, 7am – 11pm; Thu – Sun, 9am – 2am*) is a pleasant place to sample the city's classic meal: cold beer with tasty *paçoca* (beef jerky and manioc flour). The restaurant's name honors the *caneleiro*, a tree that is the symbol of Teresina. Visitors will find good facilities and stores at **Teresina Shopping** (*Avenida Raul Lopes, 1000, Bairro dos Noivos, tel. (86) 3230-2000; Mon – Sat, 10am – 10pm; Sun, 2pm – 8pm*).

ENCONTRO DOS RIOS PARK
The Parque Encontro dos Rios begins at the very point where the Rio Parnaíba meets the Rio Poti, just before the joined waters head toward the coast. A large statue of Fisherman Crispim stands in the park. The statue is informally known as "Cabeça de Cuia" (Gourd Head), in reference to a character of regional folklore who, according to legend, is condemned to wander along the river until he can devour seven virgins named Maria. Leafy trees line the Parnaíba, and you can see fishermen from the Poti Velho neighborhood casting their nets into the water from their brightly colored canoes.
Avenida Boa Esperança, no #, Poti Velho, tel. (86) 3217-5043. Daily, 8am – 6pm.

GUITAR PLAYERS
Guitar players (*violeiros*) usually play in Teresina's bars and restaurants at night, often going into the early morning. **Casa do Cantador** (*Rua Lúcia, 1419, Vermelha, tel. 86/3211-6833; daily, 2pm – 6pm*), a simple wooden bar surrounded by leafy mango trees, is a meeting place for the *violeiros*. They perform every night, but their Wednesday performances are the most popular.

Rock formation known as D. Pedro's Head, at the park

SETE CIDADES NATIONAL PARK

The Parque Nacional de Sete Cidades, 200 kilometers (124 miles) north of Teresina, has been a national park since 1961. Its 6,221 hectares (15,270 acres) reveal a wealth of geological monuments and a rare archaeological heritage. The area straddles the *cerrado* to *caatinga* landscapes, and the fauna and flora reflect the fact that they live in a transitional zone. The wildlife rely upon the park's 22 springs and several streams. The first attested references to this region date back to 1886: Jácome Avelino from Ceará stated that "on a huge plain the place called Seven Cities (Sete Cidades) can be found, which local people say is magical, and they tell many stories about it, which are nothing more than superstition". What is certain, however, is that the area consists of seven groups of sandstone, each of which has been carved by time and weather. From the Segunda Cidade lookout point, visitors can discern shapes that resemble roofs, chimneys, castles, forts, houses, as well as animals and human figures. At the end of the afternoon, when the rocks reflect the setting sun's gold tones, the area's aura is particularly mysterious. The curiously shaped rocks also bear **paintings**, ranging from 5,000 to 10,000 years old, that depict geometric symbols and animals in shades of red and yellow. The local fauna includes red broket deers, pacas, lesser anteaters, iguanas, rock cavies, nine-banded armadillos, agoutis, bush dogs, and more than 100 bird species. The verdant vegetation that grows between May and July, the period of light rains, becomes somewhat yellow during the dry summer season (between November and March). Large trees like the souari, bacuri, jatoba,

Brazil in silhouette at Terceira Cidade rock

springs you'll find palms such as carnauba, *tucum,* and *buriti.* You can drive through all 12 kilometers (7 miles) of the park in three hours, including stops at several small trails, or you can spend three to six hours exploring a smaller area on foot. Another option is to rent a bicycle in the park itself. However you choose to explore the park, go early in the day, before the sun gets too hot, and, if hiking, take along a hat, comfortable clothes, sneakers, sun screen, snacks, and water. Visitors must be accompanied by Ibama(Brazilian Institute of Environment and Renewable Natural Resources)-accredited guides. You can get to the park from Teresina by taking the BR-343 highway north to BR-222 north to the PI-111 state highway; follow this to the south gate. The park's north gate is accessible from Parnaíba by driving through **Piracuruca** (on BR-343 highway), which is 140 kilometers (87 miles) south of Parnaíba. Watch out for animals on the road on both routes. *Ibama offers information about the park, tel. (86) 3343-1342, daily, 8am – 5pm.*

trumpet angelim, *sambaíba,* and *cajuí* are everywhere. In the dry areas, typical *caatinga* species (like the spiny shrubs called *juazeiros),* the jurema tree, the Brazilian pepper tree, and several types of cacti grow. Near the

Pedro II

Perched on top of the Serra dos Matões Range, at an elevation of 600 meters (1,970 feet), the town of Pedro II is known for its old, brightly colored houses, quiet, tree-lined streets, and a fresh mountain climate. The town, named after the 19th-century Portuguese emperor of Brazil, is located 50 kilometers (31 miles) southeast of Piripiri on the BR-343 highway. The area contains the only opal mines in South America. Transparent or opaque, the opal is a rare stone which reflects light like a prism. Stores in every corner of the town sell this gem, with one of the best being **Opalas Pedro II** (*Avenida Coronel Cordeiro, 672, Centro, tel. 86/3271-1559; daily, 7:30am – 5pm*). Pedro II is not just known for mining; it also produces hammocks. The **Oficina do Artesanato** offers an up-close look at the entire process – from hand-weaving to embroidering and sewing (*Praça Domingos Mourão Filho, 329, Centro, tel. 86/3271-1402 (City Hall); Mon – Fri, 7:30am – 5:30pm; Sat, 7:30am – noon*). Also, the **Festival de Inverno**, held in June, on the Corpus Christi holiday, draws crowds with its jazz and blues performances. The **Morro do Gritador**, at 720 meters high, affords a stunning view of Pedro II and neighboring Piracuru. It was known as Coluna Prestes in the 1920s when it was on the path of the cross-country revolutionary march. A local guide can lead you to the summit (**contact**: Natureza Viva, *tel. 86/9422-8030*).

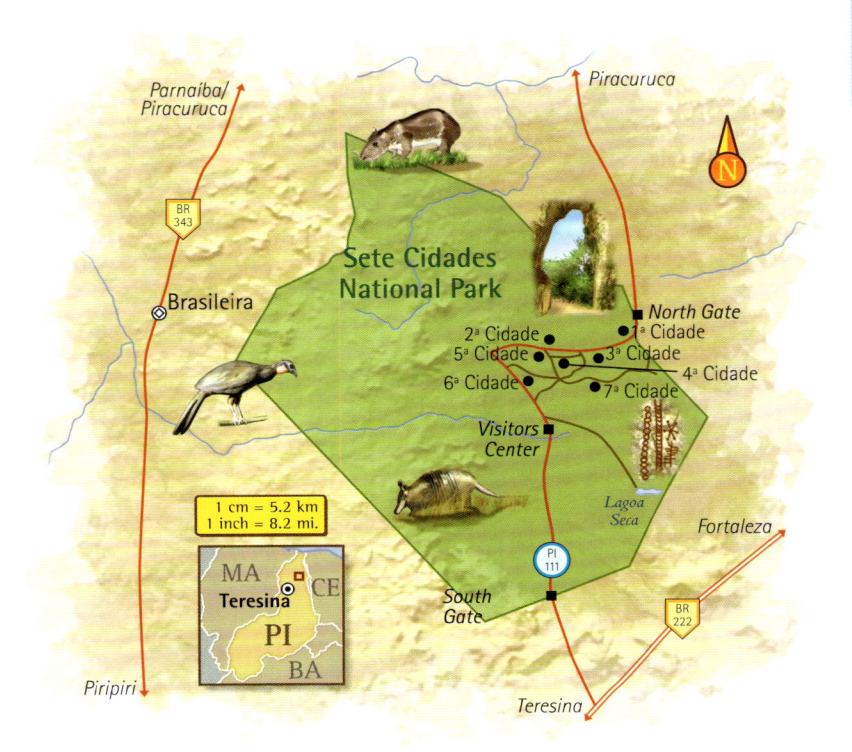

Primera Cidade: This is the site of Cachoeira do Riachão, a waterfall with a 21-meter (69-foot) drop. The rocks resemble twisted cannons.

Segunda Cidade: This area is rich in rock paintings. The Arco do Triunfo (Triumphal Arch) – also known as the Arco do Desejo (Arch of Desire) – is here. The iconic rock formation stands 18 meters (59 feet) high and is visible from a nearby lookout.

Terceira Cidade: The formations called Mapa do Brasil (the Map of Brazil) and Cabeça de Dom Pedro (Dom Pedro's Head) are here. You can access the Furo Solsticial trail from here, to see the winter (June) sun produce unusual lighting effects.

Quarta Cidade: Popular rock formations include the one that resembles two kissing lizards, and another one that looks like an apprentice's attempt at a map of Brazil.

Quinta Cidade: Rich in rock inscriptions and monuments, it has, among other formations, the Furna do Índio (Indian's Cave), Camelo (Camel), and Imperador (Emperor) rocks.

Sexta Cidade: The perfect polygons that comprise the Pedra da Tartaruga (Turtle Rock), Cachorro (Dog), and Elefante (Elephant) are the biggest attractions here. Note the elephant's "young" trailing behind it!

Sétima Cidade: This area has the clearest glyphic inscriptions, which are mostly marked in red. Of all the area's rock formations, the most impressive are Casario (Houses) and Gruta do Pajé Cave.

Strange rock formations cover Sexta Cidade

Oeiras

The colonizers were the first to make their way into the *sertão* region of the current state of Piauí. They settled on the banks of the **Rio do Mocha** and founded the village that would become Oeiras, 320 kilometers (199 miles) south of Teresina and 280 kilometers (174 miles) north of São Raimundo Nonato. They built a small wattle and daub chapel here in 1697, which the **Igreja de Nossa Senhora da Vitória** (finished in 1733) later replaced. This church, a national heritage site, still stands in tiny Oeiras, which has preserved many lovely old buildings on its narrow streets. The **Procissão de Bom Jesus dos Passos**, a traditional town procession, brings together thousands of the faithful during Holy Week. The town's traditional mandolin players stroll through the streets with their instruments during the procession. It's also possible to spot some of these musicians leisurely strumming their mandolins in the square on Saturday or Sunday evenings.

São Raimundo Nonato

Locals proudly call this town the "capital of prehistory." As a gateway to the Parque Nacional da Serra da Capivara, São Raimundo Nonato relies on tourism to the park and to the town's own natural attractions, which amount to an open-air prehistory museum. As in the rest of the state, the seasons are well defined here – in the dry season (May through November), the vegetation loses its leaves, and during the rainy season, December through early May, everything becomes green again. The most important local events take place when the rains stop. During the **Festa do Padroeiro** in August, the locals decorate the whole town with colorful flags in honor of the town's patron saint, Raymond Nonnatus. The **Serra da Capivara International Festival**, in September, showcases music, theater, and art from all over the world. Getting to São Raimundo Nonato is not easy: it is 540 kilometers (336 miles) south of Teresina, first along the BR-316 highway to the BR-343, then along the PI-140 state highway south to the BR-324 highway. If traveling from Petrolina, in Pernambuco, take BR-235 west to Remanso then take the BR-324 highway north. Stretches of road along this 300-kilometer (186-mile) portion of BR-324 are in poor condition.

Archaeological Museum
The Museu do Homem Americano opened in 1998 and offers a good introduction to Piauí's rich archaeological and geological heritage. Two floors exhibit panels, photographs, and rock samples that have been collected over the past 30 years. Highlights include the funeral urns and human fossils, especially **Zuzu**, a skeleton that's estimated to be around 10,000 years old. Archaeologists unearthed Zuzu at the Toca dos Coqueiros excavation site. The Fundação Museu do Homem Americano, which is also responsible for maintaining the National Park, runs the museum.
Centro Cultural Sérgio Motta, no #, Campestre, tel. (89) 3582-1612, fax 3582-1293. Tue – Sun, 9am – 5pm.

Serra da Capivara National Park

The world's largest collection of rock paintings is on perpetual exhibit in the 129,140 hectares (319,100 acres) of the Parque Nacional Serra da Capivara. Declared a Unesco World Heritage Site in 1991, the park is home to more than 800 archaeological sites, most of which are in sheltered areas of eroded rock known as *tocas*. The 128 sites that are open to visitors offer easy access, paths, and secure stairways that allow you see the paintings up close. Excavations have revealed polished stone artifacts, ceramics, and prehistoric fossils of animals such as sloths and giant armadillos. Archaeologist Niède Guidon, who runs the park, claims to have discovered signs of a settlement that could be up to 100,000 years old — this goes against the prevailing theory that man arrived in the Americas via the Bering Strait about 20,000 years ago. Controversy aside, the park is absolutely breathtaking: On all sides, you can see rough, hilly land, huge rocks covered in low-lying vegetation, and, on the plateaus, forests with trees up to 20 meters (66 feet) tall. The park's fauna includes more than 30 kinds of mammals and dozens of bird species, as well as lizards, toads, and snakes. While it's possible to explore the whole park by car, those who want to hike through the park have their choice of trails of varying difficulty levels. Adventure sports, such as hanggliding, are forbidden, and a guide must accompany you through the park (any local hotels or guide agencies in the city can recommend one). Comfortable clothes, sneakers, a hat, and sunscreen are essential for your visit.
Contact: Trilhas da Capivara, tel. (89) 3582-1294.

Pedra Furada Valley
A trip to Baixão da Pedra Furada can be done in one day. Start at the park's east entrance, which is just off the

Trails lead to the park's rock paintings

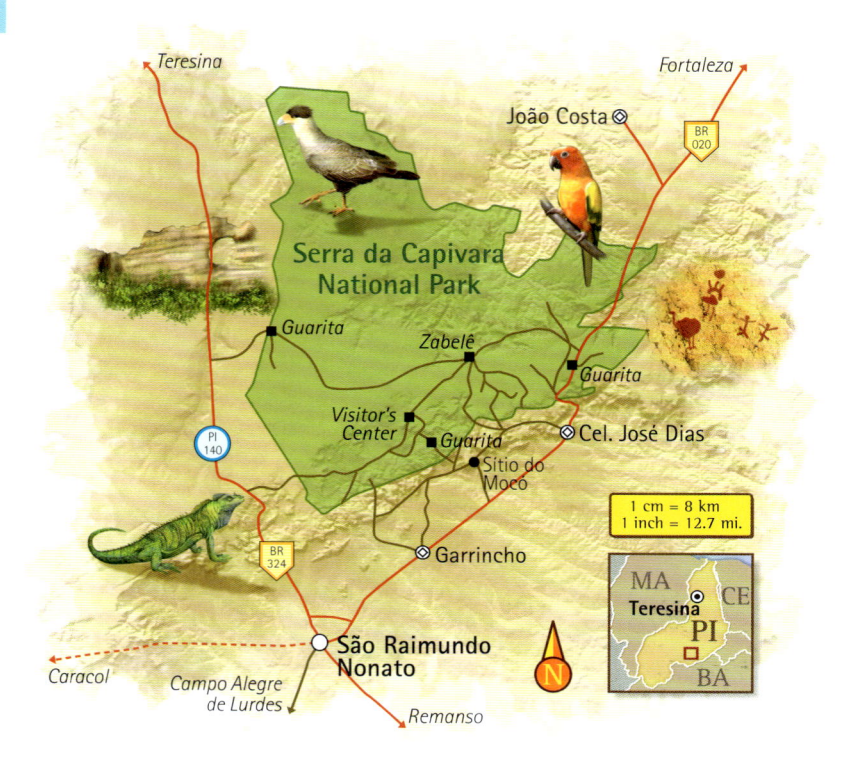

BR-020 highway, pass **Sítio do Mocó** (which offers facilities, a snack bar, and a campsite). A route from the east entrance also leads to the **Sítio do Meio**, which has ceramic fragments from over 8,900 years ago. The route passes by the **Toca do Cajueiro, Toca da Fumaça, Toca do Macário**, and **Toca do Fundo do Baixão** excavation sites. **Toca do Boqueirão da Pedra Furada** is the most important archaeological site in the Serra da Capivara. Here, archaeologists have discovered remains of a prehistoric bonfire that, according to Niède Guidon's team, proves that humans lived in the region 100,000 years ago. From the Baixão da Pedra Furada you can reach the **Circuito do Alto da Pedra Furada** trail, which passes through the **Baixão das Mulheres**, a 60-meter (197-foot) deep canyon with three archaeological sites, as well as **Alto do Caldeirão dos Rodrigues** and **Canoas**. Hale and hearty visitors can climb the 350 steps to the top of Pedra Furada; the route is not recommended for anyone with heart problems or limited physical fitness.

ALTO DOS CANOAS AND CALDEIRÃO DOS RODRIGUES TRAIL

From the Toca do Arame do Sansão excavation sites at the bottom of Baixão da Pedra Furada, an 800-meter (half-a-mile) trail takes visitors to a set of stone steps. These stairs lead to the top of the plateau and the rock paintings of the **Sítio dos Canoas** site. From here you can check out the *caldeirões* (cauldrons) – depressions in the rock that retain rainwater. From the

Serra das Confusões National Park

The name Serra das Confusões (Confusion Mountain Range) is well deserved: the mountains reflect light in several colors, which is disorienting to anyone who looks at the range from a distance. Since 1998, the unspoiled Parque Nacional Serra das Confusões has preserved about half a million hectares (1.2 million acres) of land. It's home to various little-known prehistoric sites, which are scattered among rocks and *caatinga* vegetation. The park's fauna includes the giant anteater, puma, jaguar, and the largest bat in the Americas, the spectral bat (*Vampyrum spectrum*), which has a wingspan of up to 1 meter (3.3 feet). The **Gruta do Riacho dos Bois**, a three-kilometer (two-mile) passage through the rocks, is the main attraction in the park. The park has no visitors' facilities To arrange a trip, visitors should contact the local Ibama branch, in Caracol (*Rua João Dias, 398, Centro, tel. 89/3589-1208; Mon – Fri, 8am – noon and 2pm – 6pm*), 100 kilometers (62 miles) west of São Raimundo Nonato on the PI-144 highway. The 10-kilometer road to the park begins in Caracol.

top of the plateau you can descend the iron steps to the bottom of the valley, called **Caldeirão dos Rodrigues ll**, where several rock paintings depict scenes from prehistoric life.

Desfiladeiro da Capivara Trail

Thousands of years ago, mountain dwellers used the trail and its many rock shelters as they passed through the Capivara Canyon. Today, the shelters are known as Toca da Entrada do Pajaú, Toca do Barro, Toca do Inferno, Toca da Entrada do Baixão da Vaca, Toca do Pajaú, and Toca do Paraguaio. A lookout point on the way into the canyon offers a panoramic view of the **Planície do São Francisco** plain. You can also hike to two other sites from this trail: the **Veadinhos Azuis**, a collection of blue-paint rock paintings (the first to be discovered in the world in this color), and **Boqueirão do Paraguaio**, a lone stand of Atlantic forest in the midst of *caatinga* vegetation, where prehistoric man left paintings of human figures and geometric shapes. The gate off the BR-020 highway, a bit

Caldeirão do Rodrigues II Valley, an archaeological site with important rock paintings

to the north of Coronel José Dias, leads to the Desfiladeiro da Capivara.

BAIXÃO DO PERNA AND ANDORINHAS TRAIL

On the edge of a canyon, the rock face of **Baixão do Perna** houses four archaeological sites. One of these sites contains the park's most famous rock painting, which depicts an orgy. From this canyon, you can reach the **Toca do Chico Coelho** and **Toca do Josué**, as well as the **Vila do Zabelê**, which leads to the sites on the **Alto da Chapada** – the top of the plateau. The trail is accessible through the Serra Vermelha gatehouse on the PI-140 state highway. The highway also leads to the Baixão das Andorinhas, a canyon known for the thousands of swallows that fly through every day around 5:30pm. The birds create a spectacular visual display.

A sandstone formation in Serra da Capivara

SERRA DA CAPIVARA CERAMICS

Nivaldo Coelho, a native of the region, was Nièdе Guidon's guide when the latter made his 1972 discovery of the archaeological sites in today's Parque Nacional da Serra da Capivara. Since 1992, the friendly, chatty Coelho has been in charge of a 20-person team that produces ceramic utensils inspired by the site's textures and drawings. Their studio is less than a kilometer from the park entrance in Barreirinho, and just three kilometers (two miles) from the center of Coronel José Dias (*Rua Projetada, no #, Barreirinho, tel. 89/3585-1204; daily, 8am – noon and 2pm – 4pm*).

THE HOMBU GUIDED NATURE TRAIL

The word *hombu* means "come and see with me" in the language of the indigenous people known as the Gê, who used to inhabit this region. The nine-kilometer (6-mile) hike along **Trilha Hombu** starts at Sítio do Mocó, on top of the range at **Toca de Invenção.** Keep an eye out here for the *lagartixas-da-serra*, a lizard species that's native to the Capivara region. The next stop, **Toca do Martiliano**, is a bird-watchers' paradise. Following along the rock face, in a landscape dominated by stone slabs and cacti, you will eventually reach **Boqueirão dos Caititus**. Here, there are two archaeological sites decorated with rock paintings and protected by high trees. The route passes by **Toca da Ema** and visits areas with large numbers of robust and the blond-crested woodpeckers are found. The trail ends at **Toca da Roça do Sítio do Brás I**, where the first colonizers lived. The remains of a wattle and daub building lean against the rock face, damaging the paintings.

Parnaíba River Delta

Between the coasts of Piauí and Maranhão, the Rio Parnaíba meets the sea to form the only open-sea delta in the Americas. As it nears the Atlantic, the Parnaíba branches out in five directions to create a set of ecosystems that sprawl over 2,700 square kilometers (1,040 square miles). Beaches, dunes, channels, and mangroves encircle more than 80 islands. Although 65% of the delta is located in the state of Maranhão, **Parnaíba**, a town in Piauí, is the main gateway to the region. Parnaíba, 354 kilometers (220 miles) north of Teresina and 19 kilometers (12 miles) southwest of Luís Correia, was a flourishing trading post for beef jerky in the 18th and 19th centuries. At the beginning of the 20th century, exported carnauba wax, used to polish furniture, shoes, and other items. Lovely buildings from these prosperous times still stand along the town's wide, tree-lined street. The nostalgic town of **Porto das Barcas** contains a small store, restaurant, and pizzeria among its beautiful old buildings. Oil lamps light this area on the banks of the Rio Igaraçu, which is a branch of the Rio Parnaíba. Six kilometers (4 miles) from Parnaíba, on the delta's largest island, **Ilha Grande de Santa Isabel**, the port of **Porto do Tatu** offers boats that run to local attractions, including towns that lie along the edge of the delta. The boats hold between 40 and 250 passengers. You can also rent a motorboat to get around. Some routes (*services Parnaíba, see page 409*) include a trip to Lençóis Maranhenses.

Baskets and Lace

The carnauba palm, which has supported the economy of the small delta communities for decades, is the raw material now used in a lot of the local craftwork. On Ilha Grande de

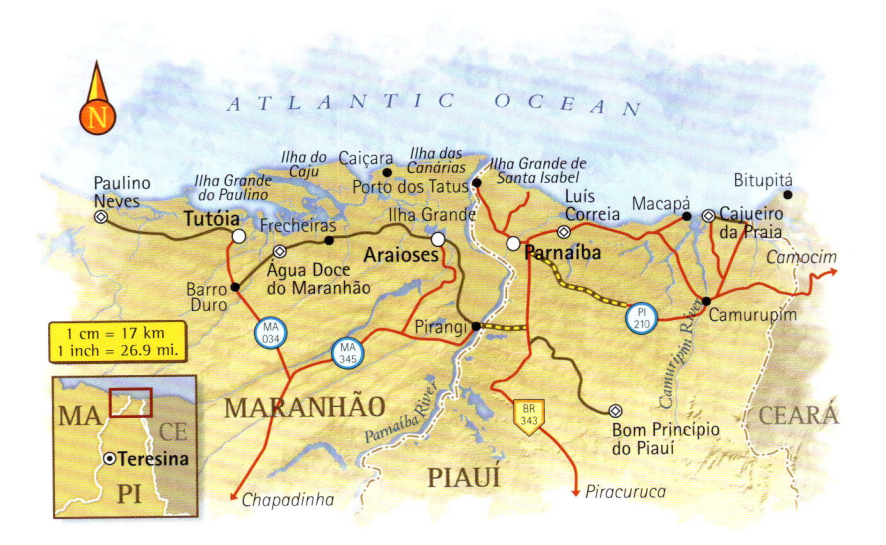

The Luís Correia dunes run along the Piauí coast

Santa Isabel, a consortium of 25 families called the **Associação de Trançados de Santa Isabel** (*Rua Evangelina Rosa, 548, Ilha Grande de Santa Isabel, tel. 86/3323-6581; daily, 8am – noon and 2pm – 5pm*) makes baskets, ornaments, table mats, and other items from this palm. In the **Morro da Mariana** neighborhood, on the same island, lace makers produce clothes and accessories that eventually end up in the sophisticated clothes stores of the south (*Rua Turiano Ribeiro, 380, Centro, tel. 86/3323-0187; Mon – Sat, 8am – 6pm*).

Boat Trips Through the Parnaíba Delta

There are two available boat trips that cross the labyrinthine mangroves of the Parnaíba Delta. On one, large boats holding up to 250 people cross in eight hours while serving fruit, lunch, and a *caranguejada* (crab feast). The boat stops at both **Praia de Ponta das Canárias**, a beach covered in carnauba palms, and at **Ilha de Poldros**, an island popular with kitesurfers. The other option involves going down the river on a *voadeira*, which is a simple motorboat that seats no more than four people. The four-hour trip takes in Ilha de Poldros as well as **Baía do Feijão Bravo**, a bay with rough seas. The bay is surrounded by mangroves, and natural salt-water pools form here at low tide. The best place to stay is on **Ilha das Canárias**, which has a small, friendly village where most people live by fishing and catching crabs; this island is the departure point for trips to Ilha do Caju.

Mangrove Crab

Every Wednesday and Saturday, for most of the year, a scene repeats itself at Porto dos Tatus, on Ilha Grande de Santa Isabel: Boxes teeming with crab – most of which are destined for the bars and restaurants of Fortaleza and the Ceará coast – fill myriad fishing boats. The *uçá* (known to science as *Ucides cordatus*), a large, blue crab, lives in the mangroves on the Brazilian coast. The delta has extensive mangrove swamps, so crab fishing here is particularly intense. Catching the crab involves a lot of hard work, and crab catchers spend the entire day wading among the mangrove roots, with their hands burrowing into the mud. Crab catching is prohibited between December and March, which is the breeding season. The rest of the year, local bars serve a traditional crab dish: four crabs strung together and boiled in broth that's flavored with onion, bell pepper, tomato, and parsley.

Contact: Eco Adventure Tour, tel. (86) 3323-9595; Natur Turismo, tel. 3323-0426, 9971-5143.

BEACHES

Piauí's 66 kilometers (41 miles) of coastline are a virtually unbroken string of dunes and calm seas. The fishing community of **Cajueiro da Praia** borders Ceará, which houses a research base for the **Projeto Peixe-Boi**. The *peixe-boi* (manatee) is an endangered species often spotted in these waters. **Praia de Barra Grande**, 8 kilometers (5 miles) west of Cajueiro, has strong waves and a strip of white sand. This beach leads to **Barra do Rio Camurupim** and its tiny fishing village. On the other side of the estuary, **Macapá** and **Maramar** beaches are popular for their calm waters and seafood kiosks. The two semi-deserted neighboring beaches, **Carnaubinhas** and **Itaqui**, have strong waves. **Praia dos Coqueiros** offers the best options for accommodations and restaurants. **Atalaia,** less than 10 kilometers (6 miles) from Luís Correia, also has kiosks and hotels. From here you can see the wild vegetation and the dunes of Ilha Grande de Santa Isabel. That island's beach, **Praia de Pedra do Sal**, has its kiosks and surfer-friendly waters.

CAJU ISLAND

Englishman James Frederick Clark settled in the delta region in 1847 in order to exploit the area's carnauba palms. He forbade hunting and deforestation on the 100-square-kilometer (39-square-mile) island, and this small paradise owes him much thanks for its existence. **Ilha do Caju**, 50 kilometers (31 miles) west of Parnaíba, actually lies in Maranhão. It contains six ecosystems and has 18 kilometers (11 miles) of beaches, four different types of marshland, flood lands, lakes, dunes, and forests. The island's wildlife includes coatis, foxes, armadillos, ocelots, as well as flocks of scarlet ibis – the symbol of the delta. Visits must be arranged in advance with the **Refúgio Ecológico Ilha do Caju** *(tel. 86/3321-1179)*, the island's only guesthouse. It provides boats and guides to those wishing to explore on foot, on horseback, or by jeep. Rubber boots, long-sleeves, sunscreen, and insect repellent are all recommended.

> ### FROM THE PARNAÍBA DELTA TO LENÇÓIS MARANHENSES
>
> There are two ways to travel from the Parnaíba Delta to Lençóis Maranhenses in the neighboring state of Maranhão. The first involves a three-hour drive that requires a 4×4 vehicle. On this route from Parnaíba toward Barreirinhas, gateway to the Parque Nacional dos Lençóis Maranhenses, consider stopping along the way to visit Paulino Neves. Better known as Rio Novo, this fishing village has dunes that extend all the way to the park. The other travel option is more tiring but more popular with the locals: It involves an uncomfortable eight-hour trip in a boat known as "*gaiola*" ("cage"). The boat travels from Porto das Barcas, in Parnaíba *(contact: Morais Brito Viagens, tel. 86/3321-1969)* to Tutóia, in Maranhão. It's best to take a hammock, water, snacks, and insect repellent. Trips to Rio Novo, Barreirinhas, and Caburé can be arranged, and leave from the center of Tutóia, where anyone who wants to visit Lençóis Maranhenses can find accommodations *(see page 350)*.

MARANHÃO

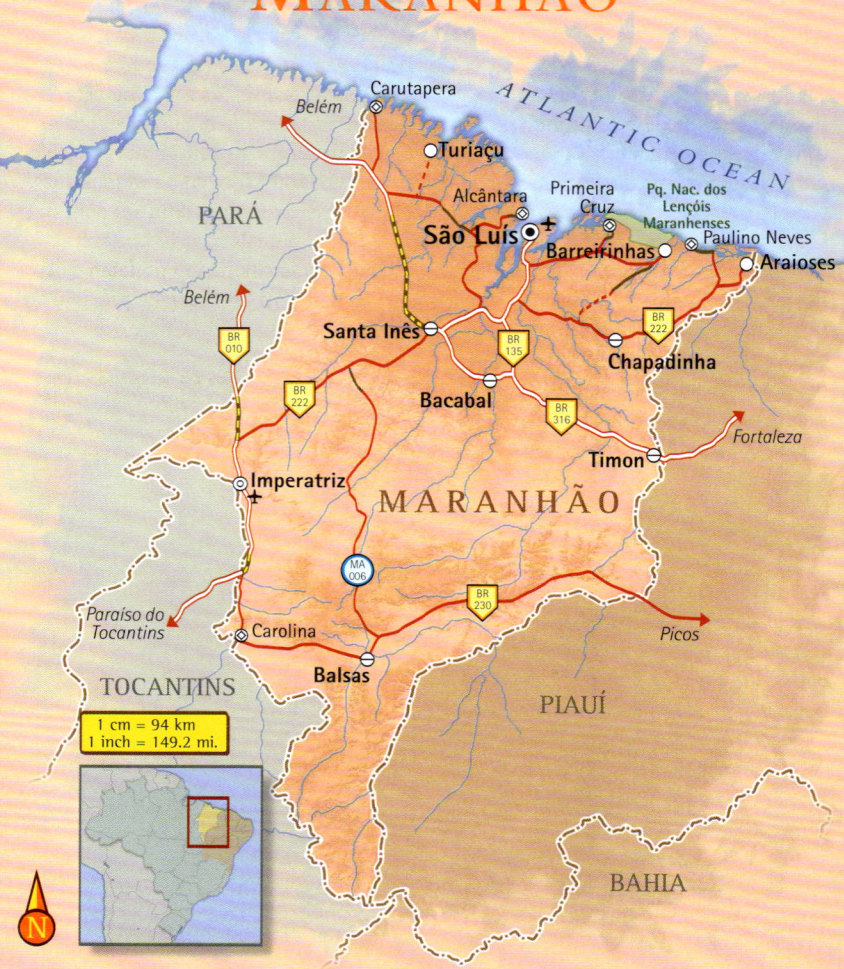

Scale: 1 cm = 94 km / 1 inch = 149.2 mi.

Highlights

- The Portuguese-tile façades of the buildings in the old part of **São Luís**, and the beaches, shopping malls, and good restaurants in the surrounding, modern new part of the city.
- The ruins of **Alcântara**'s churches.
- The lakes and the Preguiças River, in **Barreirinhas**.
- The virtually deserted **Lençóis Beach**, in the **Parque Nacional dos Lençóis Maranhenses** reserve.

When to Go

- From **March to July**, when the dune lakes in Lençóis Maranhenses are at their fullest.
- From **August to September**, when the sun reigns supreme in São Luís – but be prepared for the strong winds.
- In **May**, for the beautiful Festa do Divino Espírito Santo festivities in Alcântara.
- In **June**, for the São João festivities in São Luís and Barreirinhas, and particularly on **the June 23rd** to see the *bumba-meu-boi*.

Old and new walk hand-in-hand in Maranhão. Baroque tiles blend with space-age technology, centuries-old houses stand beside skyscrapers, and the music of the traditional *bumba-meu-boi* festival harmonizes with reggae. And though Maranhão is part of the Northeast, it is heavily influenced by the culture and traditions of Brazil's North, which themselves reflect a heavy indigenous influence.

The region has long been caught up in the sweep of foreign political strife. The Spanish arrived in Maranhão in 1500, the very year that Portuguese discovered Brazil. The Portuguese began struggling to consolidate their power over the region 35 years later. In 1612, the French, supported by indigenous groups, tried to establish their own France Équinoxiale, but the Portuguese expelled the French and regained the territory three years later. The Portuguese crown created the captaincy of Maranhão and Grão-Pará in 1624, but the Dutch invaded in 1641 and occupied the area until they were expelled in 1644. Maranhão separated from Pará in 1774 and prospered, producing sugar, spices, rice, and cotton.

In the 1970s, the government began restoring the capital's old buildings. In 1997, Unesco declared the historic center of São Luís a World Heritage Site. Its streets now offer visitors a chance to rediscover a piece of history. In Alcântara, the 17th-century ruins of Igreja de São Matias church grace every postcard and abut the modernity of the Brazilian Space Center. The Lençóis Maranhenses area boasts a dazzling natural heritage: snow-white dunes encircle shockingly blue lakes in the national reserve.

Rain-fed lakes nestle among the Lençóis Maranhenses dunes

São Luís

São Luís, a city on the west side of São Luís Island, was once called Saint Louis. The charming colonial town harbors a rich cultural mix. In 1612, the year of the French invasion, noblemen Daniel de La Touche, Lord of Ravardière, and François de Rasilly, Lord of Rasilly and Aunelles, landed here and named the settlement and its strategic river fort Louis XIII. But French colonization didn't last long: By 1615, São Luís was back in Portuguese hands. Its Portuguese legacy includes the original urban planning, by engineer Francisco Frias de Mesquita (1578-1645), and the tiled façades of the historic city center. São Luís has undergone a long and successful government-sponsored restoration, Projeto Reviver. More than 3,500 large *sobrado houses* and other buildings sport façades of old-fashioned Portuguese tiles called *azulejos* along with the limestone cobblestones of the curbs and sidewalks. The opening of the José Sarney Bridge in 1970 revitalized the city by connecting the historic center to modern buildings and luxury hotels in the new part of town. The crossing between the old and new parts of town, however, is complicated by poor signage and chaotic, heavy traffic. São Luís is 463 kilometers (288 miles) west of Teresina and accessible by the BR-135 highway.

There's plenty to see and do on Ponta d'Areia beach

New São Luís

The **Ponte José Sarney** bridge spans the Anil River and is the portal to Nova São Luís (New São Luís). The area is chock full of skyscrapers, luxury hotels, restaurants, and shopping malls. Three newer bridges also connect the old part of town to the new neighborhoods. The **Ponta d'Areia**, **São Francisco**, and **Renascença** neighborhoods are home to the capital's elite. While silt-laden waters and high tides limit the appeal of the city beaches, worthy sunbathing spots include **Ponta d'Areia**, **São Marcos**, **Calhau** (which is known for its sunsets), **Caolho**, **Olho d'Água**, **Praia do Meio**, and **Araçaji**. Kiosks dotting the beachfronts serve fresh fish and crab. Don't miss the *caranguejada* at **Base da Lenoca** (*base* is the local term for a restaurant that serves regional cuisine): eight steamed crabs with special seasonings and vinaigrette, served with rice and crispy bacon or *baião-de-dois* (rice and beans), and thickened *pirão* sauce. (*Avenida Litorânea, 9-B, São Marcos beach, tel. 98/3235-8971. Daily, 10am – 1am.*) The restaurant also has a branch in the historic center, but the original sets the standard.

Old São Luís

São Luís' historic center exemplifies colonial-era Portuguese urban planning and architecture. It's more than a living museum, however. The bustling old city preserves its heritage in a dynamic way, as people work and live there today. The area's museums, restaurants, bars, and stores cluster near the Praia Grande Market and the Terminal Hidroviário (River Terminal), along the old streets Rua do Trapiche, Rua do Giz, Rua da Estrela, and Rua Portugal. If possible, visit in the afternoon, when all the main attractions are open. Even when they're closed, though, the tiled colonial façades make a visit worthwhile.

① São Luís Building

The three-storey, 19th-century Edifício São Luís is said to be the largest tiled colonial building in Brazil. A fire destroyed the interior in 1969, but in 1976, the bank Caixa Econômica Federal restored the building and opened a branch office inside.
Rua de Nazaré, at the intersection with Rua do Egito.

Arroz-de-Cuxá

Cuxá, a sauce or paste made with sorrel leaves, dried shrimp, sesame seeds, and manioc flour, is very popular in Maranhão. In the famed local dish *arroz-de-cuxá*, the sauce is cooked with rice. Try it at **Base da Diquinha** *(Rua João Luís, 62, Diamante, no telephone)*, a simple restaurant that opened 40 years ago in the owner's backyard. The restaurant's other traditional dishes include sun-dried beef and crab claws.

---

② Portugal Street

These two blocks of tiled, colonial-style buildings, bars, and cafés are the focus of the city's nightlife. Rua Portugal becomes particularly crowded on Thursdays, when it hosts **Dia de Festa**, a celebration of varying musical styles that attracts some of Brazilian most famous musicians.

③ Casa do Maranhão Museum

This museum occupies the 1873 customs building and exhibits artifacts of the dance called *bumba-meu-boi*. The ground floor offers performances of the dramatized dance on a large screen, other televisions displaying Maranhão landscapes, and a gift shop. The first floor dedicates a room to each of *bumba-meu-boi*'s various rhythms (each is called a *sotaque*, or "accent") and its instruments and costumes. Other rooms explain the legend

behind the tradition, explore the rehearsals, and demonstrate how the costumes are made. A visit takes about an hour.
Rua do Trapiche, no #, Praia Grande, tel. (98) 3221-7001. Tue – Sun, 9am – 7pm.

4 CASA DE NHOZINHO MUSEUM
This museum, in a three-storey house with French-tiled eaves, explores day-to-day life in Maranhão. The first floor exhibits farm equipment, primarily used for cotton cultivation – wooden pestles, seed grinders, and looms – as well as products such as cotton bedspreads and rugs. Artifacts such as fish traps and a canoe carved from a tree trunk represent coastal life. The second floor houses works by the museum's namesake, the famous toymaker known as Nhozinho; Antonio Bruno Pinto Nogueira (1904-1974) was born in Curupu. The museum's third floor displays artifacts of indigenous culture, with items representing eight ethnic groups that still live in the state's interior. Outside, life-size replicas depict traditional Maranhão houses, including some of carnauba wood and wattle-and-daub. Visits can opt to take a guided tour.
Rua Portugal, 185, Centro, tel. (98) 3218-9951. Tue – Sun, 9am – 7pm.

5 DOMINGOS VIEIRA FILHO CULTURAL CENTER
Also known as Casa da Festa (Party House), the Centro de Cultura Popular Domingos Vieira Filho honors a local folklorist of that name and exhibits material relating to folk rites and traditions. The first floor is dedicated to religious practices in Maranhão. Its highlight is the section on Casa das Minas, a 19th-century *terreiro* (temple) where people practice Tambor-de-Mina, a religion of African origin. The second floor offers records of the Festa do Divino festivities, particularly those held in

Portugal Street has two blocks of tiled buildings and lively nightlife

Unesco protects the historic architecture of São Luís

Alcântara. It also has space dedicated to the *tambor-de-crioula*, a Afro-Brazilian circle dance accompanied by drums. Christmas ornaments and artifacts fill the third floor. Bilingual guided tours can be arranged.
Rua do Giz, 225, Centro, tel. (98) 3231-1557. Mon – Fri, 9am – 7pm.

❻ Mercês Convent
In 1654, a sermon by Portuguese writer and missionary Father Antônio Vieira inaugurated the Convento das Mercês, which subsequently housed members of the Spanish Mercedarian Order. Today the building is home to the **Fundação da Memória Republicana** (Republican Memory Foundation), which oversees the Memorial José Sarney, a collection of documents and objects belonging to the former president.
Rua da Palma, 502, Centro, tel. (98) 3231-0641. Tue – Fri, 9am – 6pm; Sat, 9am – noon.

❼ Sè Cathedral
Using an indigenous workforce for labor, Jesuits built the Catedral da Sé and inaugurated it in 1699 as the Igreja de Nossa Senhora da Vitória. On top of the

---

Afro-Brazilian Cults

African-derived religions find widespread expression in Maranhão. A prime example is Tambor-de-Mina. This religion is similar to Candomblé, from Bahia, and Xangô, from Pernambuco, but it has its own unique mythology. While the rituals and ceremonies vary from one temple to the next, they share a common feature: The practitioner invariably falls into a trance and becomes possessed by supernatural entities. The *orixás* (deities) are associated with elements of nature, flavored with traces of popular characters from local folklore. One such figure is King Sebastião, from Lençóis Island, who is said to have built a castle on the bottom of the ocean for his beloved Princess Ina. The largest and most traditional *terreiro* is **Casa das Minas** (*Rua de São Pantaleão, 857, Centro, tel. 98/3221-6856; daily, 9am – 6pm*), which was founded in the 19th century. Other temples are **Casa Fanti-Ashanti** (*Rua Militar, 1158, Cruzeiro do Anil, tel. 98/3225-1078, call ahead to schedule a visit*) and **Casa Nagô** (*Rua das Crioulas, 799, Centro, tel. 98/3232-1834; daily, 9am – 6pm*).

BUMBA-MEU-BOI

The *festas juninas* refers to a trio of popular celebrations, for the saints John, Anthony and Peter, all held in June. They take on a special flavor in Maranhão due to the richest expression of popular culture in the state. Maranhão celebrates the *bumba-meu-boi* more vibrantly than any other state. The tradition blends African, Portuguese, and indigenous influences in a ritual of theater, music and dance. The performance, inspided by the experiences of cattle-ranching slaves, tells the story of Catirina, a pregnant slave, who craves the tongue of a bull – particularly that of her master's favorite bull. Catirina summons her husband, called Pai Francisco, Nego Chico, or Preto Velho, to kill the bull and bring her the delicacy. He grants her wish, but, caught by his master, is ordered to revive the bull or die. A *pajé* (medicine man) comes to his aid and orders the bull to get up and dance, which the bull eventually does. Preparations for the performance begin in January; rehearsals begin in May. On June 23, the eve of Saint John's feast day, the *boi* (bull) gets symbolically baptized outside the church. The dances begin when performers present the bull – decorated with velvet, satin, beads, and sequins – to the public. Various *sotaques* (accents), or rhythms, are associated with the *bumba-meu-boi*. These include *matraca*, which is of indigenous origin; *zabumba*, which is predominantly African-inspired; and orchestra, which displays European influences. But Maranhão's folklore isn't limited to *bumba-meu-boi*. Other significant traces are the Festa do Divino Espírito Santo festivities and dances such as *tambor-de-crioula*, *dança-do-coco*, *dança-do-caroço*, and *dança-de-são-gonçalo* some of the most colorful festivals of its kind in Brazil.

subsequent name change, successive renovations have completely altered the original design. Today's façade dates from 1922, and the main chapel ceiling was painted in the 1950s by João de Deus. The altarpiece on the high altar, however, is a magnificent example of 18th-century baroque. Its detailed gilded carvings, restored in the 1990s, are considered the city's most beautiful. The Iphan institute

Bumba-meu-boi, a tradition with many rhythms

Arthur de Azevedo Theater, restored in 1991, displays its original splendor

has protected the church since 1954. *Avenida Dom Pedro II, no #, historic center, tel. (98) 3222-7380. Daily, 8am – noon; 2pm – 5:30pm.*

8 AND 9 OTHER CHURCHES

The Jesuits and other religious orders have built beautiful churches here since the founding of São Luís. After construction on the **Igreja da Nossa Senhora do Carmo** *(Praça João Lisboa, 350, Centro, tel. 98/3222-6104; Mon – Fri, 7am – 6pm; Sat, 7am – 11:30am and 3pm – 6pm; Sun, 6am – 9:30am and 3:30pm – 6pm)* began in 1627, the Dutch ransacked the structure in 1641. The Capuchins obtained it in 1894. Its impressive façade and main entrance preserve the original design. According to popular legend, **Igreja do Desterro** *(Largo do Desterro, no #; daily, 8am – 11:30am and 3pm – 6:30pm)* stands on the site of the city's first church, which got destroyed during the Dutch invasion. Donations from locals funded the current building in 1893.

10 AND 11 FOUNTAINS

Five jets of water spout from the mouths of gargoyles, fish, and deities in the **Fonte do Ribeirão** *(Largo do Ribeirão, no #, historic center)*, built in 1796. The water comes from a spring beneath the old city that once supplied houses in the city center and ships docked in São Luís. Legend has it that a giant snake sleeps beneath the spring and will one day awake to devour the city. A paved stone courtyard faces the fountain. The poorly preserved 17th-century **Fonte**

OUR RECOMMENDATION

🍽 **Bar Antigamente**'s greatest attraction is its ambiance – every detail recreates São Luís' past. The varied menu includes traditional fish, poultry, and meat dishes. Posters and pictures in the bar depict the city in the old days, while live music gives the setting an intimate feel. *(Rua da Estrela, 220, historic center, tel. 98/3232-3964; daily, 11am – midnight.)*

Additional information on page 358.

das Pedras (*Rua de São João, no #, historic center*), draws water from the springs that supplied Portuguese troops during their battle against the French. Surrounded by a walled square, this fountain's jets spurt from the mouths of imposing stone gargoyles.

12 ARTHUR DE AZEVEDO THEATER
Teatro União, later renamed Teatro São Luís, opened in 1817. Since the 1920s, it's been called Teatro Arthur de Azevedo. Closed in the 1960s, it lay in ruins until 1991, when a renovation restored its original splendor.
Rua do Sol, 180, historic center, tel. (98) 3232-0299. Daily, from 3pm.

13 LEÕES PALACE
Built by the French in 1612, the year the city was founded, Palácio dos Leões was originally called Fort Saint Louis. Today it is the seat of the state government. Of the original construction, just the São Cosme and São Damião bastions remain but all the architecture has been restored. A wing that's open to visitors exhibits artwork from the collection of local playwright Artur Azevedo (1855-1908), including important canvases by Vítor Meireles and some pieces of 18th-century furniture.
Avenida Dom Pedro II, no #, historic center, tel. (98) 3214-8638. Mon, Wed, Fri, 2pm – 5:30pm.

14 AND 15 CULTURAL CENTERS
Centro de Criatividade Odylo Costa Filho, a popular cultural center, offers European movies, drama classes, and art workshops. It also houses the Sala de Leitura Ferreira Gullar library (*Rampa do Comércio, 200, Praia Grande, tel. 98/3231-4058*). **Casa de Cultura Josué Montello** has an extensive collection of literature, history, and plays; it is open to the public and popular with researchers. (*Rua das Hortas, 327, Centro, tel. 98/3232-5906. Mon – Fri, 1pm – 7pm.*)

Palácio dos Leões, built in 1612, is the seat of the state government

⓰ Maranhão History and Art Museum

Dating from 1836, the Solar Gomes de Souza became the Museu Histórico e Artístico do Maranhão in 1973. Its collection of furniture, porcelain, and crystal recreates the splendor of the state's 19th-century residences.
Rua do Sol, 302, historic center, tel. (98) 3218-9920. Tue – Fri, 9am – 6:30pm; Sat – Sun, 9am – 5pm.

⓱ Sacred Art Museum

The townhouse known as Solar do Barão do Grajaú was built in the early 19th century. Since 1991, it has housed the Museu de Arte Sacra. The collections include religious statues and items used in religious plays, which were meant to spread the Catholic faith among indigenous people.
Rua 13 de Maio, 500, Centro, no telephone. Tue – Fri, 9am – 6pm.

⓲ Solar dos Vasconcelos Historical Center

The Centro Histórico Solar dos Vasconcelos illustrates São Luís' transformations through panels, photographs, and historical objects. The building is a typical example of colonial architecture. An exhibit of scale models includes examples of boats used in the state.
Rua da Estrela, 562, Praia Grande, tel. (98) 3231-9075. Mon – Fri, 8am – 7pm; Sat – Sun, 9am – noon.

⓳ Visual Art Museum

The Museu de Artes Visuais is a lesson on the European tiles that are a hallmark of São Luís. The 18th- and 19th-century tiles on the first floor are mostly Portuguese blue and white tiles, with some French, German, and English examples as well. The tiles on the second and third floors are the work of artists, including locals such as Cícero Dias, Tarsila do Amaral, and Alfredo Volpi. The third floor offers a fine view of the historic center, São Marcos Bay, and Praia Grande Market.
Rua Portugal, 293, Praia Grande, tel. (98) 3231-6766. Tue – Fri, 9am – 7pm; Sat, Sun, and holidays, 9am – 6pm.

⓴ Cafua das Mercês Museum

This museum, also known as Museu do Negro (Museum of the African), was built on the site of the city's slave market, and it was opened in 1975. The collection of statues, musical instruments, clothing, religious objects, and folk artifacts preserves Afro-Brazilian memories and culture. A replica of a whipping post stands in the inner courtyard.
Rua Jacinto Maia, 54, Praia Grande. Mon – Fri, 9am – 6pm.

Colonial tiles

㉑ and ㉒ Praia Grande Market and Arts and Crafts Center

Stores throughout old São Luís sell local products, particularly liquor, sweets, and handicrafts. Mercado Praia Grande (*Rua da Estrela, no #, historic center; daily, 9am – 7pm*), dating from 1820, is a market at the Casa das Tulhas which sells *tiquira* – a white manioc rum – and all sorts of fragrant grains and spices. Elderly men play cards or dominoes here, and on Friday nights the market is

The Praia Grande Market is full of liquor and fragrant comestibles

crowded. The arts and crafts market called Centro de Artesanato Ceprama (*Rua São Pantaleão, 1323, Madre de Deus, tel. 98/3232-2187; Mon – Sat, 9am – 7pm; Sun, 9am – 2pm*) sells hand-painted tiles, lace, and wood and fiber pieces from around the state.

Reggae and Radiolas

Jamaican reggae arrived in São Luís in the mid-1970s, and it came to stay. A constant presence on radio and TV, reggae also takes to the streets on *radiolas* – sound trucks that carry DJ equipment and play the likes of Bob Marley and Peter Tosh. In 2005, São Luís had more than fifty *radiolas*. Besides playing reggae classics, *radiola* owners also commission recordings by local musicians like Dub Brown, Henry Murvin, and Ronnie Green. Some of these artists, such as Célia Sampaio and Tribo de Jah, have gone on to achieve international success. Take the music home by buying a CD from the *radiolas*. You can dance to the beat – either alone, as the Jamaicans do, or in the *forró*-like manner the locals favor – at several local venues. **Roots Bar** (*Rua da Palma, 85, Centro; Wed – Sat, from 8pm*) collects true reggae fans and the most gifted dancers. **Bar do Nelson** (*Avenida Litorânea, no #, Calhau beach; Sat, from 9pm*) is frequented by upper- and middle-class locals, while **Bar do Porto** (*Rua do Trapiche, historic center; Wed and Fri, from 9pm*) is favored by tourists. **Bar do Léo** (*Mercado de Vinhaes, no #, Centro*) plays Brazilian music as well as reggae and often features live performances by artists such as Maranhão locals Zeca Baleiro and Rita Ribeiro.

Alcântara's ruins and historic buildings hark back to wealthier days

ALCÂNTARA

History pulses through the streets of Alcântara, 22 kilometers (14 miles) west of São Luís. Ruins and standing buildings are interspersed along these streets, as if reflecting the rise and fall of this town, which was born in the early 17th century. Alcântara grew through the following centuries, buoyed first by sugarcane and later by cotton. The town's historic dependence on an enslaved workforce is evident in the large number of residents who are of African descent.

> **COCONUT COOKIES**
>
> A Christmas tradition in Portugal, the sweets called *doce de espécie* have become a year-round specialty here. Children sell the treats on every corner in Alcântara. The original recipe, taken to the Iberian Peninsula by Arabs, relies on spices. In Maranhão, bakers use grated coconut, then add flour, sugar, cloves, and oil or butter. The cookies are usually served with coffee.

In the early 19th century, Alcântara was the area's third most important town in the northern region, after Belém and São Luís. The end of slavery, however, caused economic decline in Alcântara, as it did in São Luís and elsewhere, and many of Alcântara's buildings fell into ruin. In 1948, however, more than three hundred historic buildings remained, enough for the city to be declared a National Heritage Site. The peace and quiet of the old Alcântara contrasts with the modern bustle of the nearby space center, which opened in 1980. The **Centro de Lançamento** (Launch Center), 7 kilometers (4 miles) from the town center, is not open to visitors.

Alcântara has poor tourist facilities, including a dearth of good hotels and accredited guides, so it's best to visit on a daytrip from São Luís. On account of bad roads, a drive between the two towns can take up to two hours. So, even though Alcântara is on the mainland, the best way to get there is by taking a 75-minute motorboat trip from the capital. Motorboats depart from the river terminal in São Luís to Alcântara daily at 7am and 9am and return around 5pm, depending on the tide. After disembarking at Alcântara's Porto do Jacaré port, go up the steep street of the same name to admire the view of the ocean and of Ilha do Livramento and Ilha do Cajual islands. Scarlet ibises nest on the latter island.

HISTORY MUSEUM

This blue-and-white-tiled townhouse was nearly honored with a visit by Dom Pedro II. When the emperor's visit to Alcântara was announced, the Viveiros family, who lived here, prepared to receive him, as did the Ferreira family, who lived across the main square. But with the proclamation of the Republic, the trip was cancelled, and the townhouse became a footnote in history. The iron bed that was intended for the emperor's use is nevertheless on display at the Viveiros house, which became the Museu Histórico in 1977. The collection also includes a desk owned by jurist and former occupant Clóvis Beviláqua, as well as paintings, old photographs of the city, relics from Igreja de São Matias, and hollow wooden statues of saints once used to smuggle gold and precious stones.
Praça da Matriz, historic center. Daily, 9am – 2pm.

IPHAN MUSEUM

The Casa Histórica do Iphan exhibits items from the 17th to 19th centuries. Tiles, paintings, furniture, and porcelain are among the highlights.
Praça da Matriz, historic center. Mon – Fri, 10am – 4pm.

The colonial houses around Matriz Square are open to visitors

Churches

The **ruins of Igreja de São Matias** (*Praça da Matriz, historic center*) are Alcântara's most famous sight. A chapel dedicated to Saint Matthias is said to have stood on the site as early as 1662. The construction of the church began in 1648, but it was never finished, and after 1884 the building fell into disuse. **Igreja de Nossa Senhora do Carmo** (*Largo do Carmo, Rua Grande, historic center; Mon – Fri, 8am – 1pm and 2pm – 6pm; Sat, Sun, and holidays, 9am – 2pm*) dates from 1665 and had its interior recently restored. It boasts an exaggeratedly rococo high altar, sacristy, pulpit, tribune, and balcony. The Portuguese-tiled main nave contains old tombs. The main attraction of **Igreja de Nossa Senhora do Rosário dos Pretos** (*Largo do Rosário, Rua Doutor Silva Maia, Caravelas; Mon – Fri, 8am – 1pm and 2pm – 6pm; Sat, Sun, and holidays, 9am – 2pm*) is its high altar. The church's namesake, Our Lady of the Rosary, is the patron and protector of the black community in Maranhão (and throughout Brazil). The feast honoring Saint Benedict, a black saint, is held in front of the church on the first full moon in August.

Whipping Post

When the news reached Alcântara on May 13, 1888, that the Brazilian government had abolished slavery, people immediately tore down the whipping post in the central square, in front of São Matias Church. The hated symbol of slavery then vanished. When a team from the organization Projeto Rondon discovered and restored the object in 1948, the government declared the spot a national heritage site. The cylindrical stone column is almost 5 meters (16 feet) high and 40 centimeters (16 inches) wide.

The ruins of São Matias Church: construction began in the 17th century but was never finished

The Divino Espírito Santo festivities take over Alcântara for two weeks in May

Divino Espírito Santo Festival

The Festa do Divino Espírito Santo, honoring the Holy Spirit, is a Portuguese celebration that came to Maranhão from the Azores in the 17th century. Having incorporated various folk traditions, it has become one of Brazil's richest cultural events. The festivities mobilize all of Alcântara, particularly its residents of African descent, for two weeks each May.

The celebration begins on the Wednesday before Pentecost Sunday, with people carrying the 20-meter (66-foot) Mastro do Divino from the port to the main square. The pole, a banner flying atop it, remains there until the end of the festivities. On the following day, Ascension Thursday, the *mestre-sala* leads a colorful procession, complete with women called *caixeiras*, who play snare drums, as well as an orchestra and flag-bearers, to the Casa do Divino. This house is the home of the festival's reigning 'monarch,' who is an "Emperor" one year and an "Empress" the next. He or she joins the procession, which travels to the Igreja do Carmo church for mass and litanies. After a coronation ceremony, a dove, symbolizing the Holy Spirit, is released. The celebrants then return to Casa do Divino, where a feast awaits: liqueurs, hot cocoa, cake, and *doce de espécie*. These traditional cookies are made from a recipe that the town's bakers fiercely guard.

Throughout the celebration, various characters make appearances. On the first Saturday and Sunday, the *mordomo-régio* (royal butler) receives the royal court and revelers in his house. The next week, other "butlers" do the same. Flower-decked bulls parade along the streets on Friday and are sacrificed on Saturday morning. Also on Saturday, the Emperor or Empress and the butlers make donations to the poor. On Pentecost Sunday, after a celebratory mass and lunch at the Casa do Divino (the outgoing monarch's home), the crowd appoints the coming year's Emperor or Empress.

LENÇÓIS MARANHENSES

Lençóis Maranhenses (Maranhão Sheets), the name perfectly describes the dunes here, which look like enormous sheets billowing in the region's powerful wind. In fact, that very wind built these 50-meter (165-foot) dunes, which spread over 100 kilometers (62 miles) of coast and push 50 kilometers inland. The coastal beaches are wide and long, but the predominant inland terrain is the *morraria*, high dunes dotted with rain-fed lakes. The dunes span two desert areas: Grandes Lençóis Maranhenses, west of the Preguiças River, and Pequenos Lençóis, to the east. **Parque Nacional dos Lençóis Maranhenses** is a 155,000-hectare (383,000-acre) reserve inaugurated in 1981. Its 270-kilometer (168-mile) perimeter encloses the municipalities of Paulino Neves, Tutóia, Barreirinhas, Santo Amaro, Primeira Cruz, and Humberto de Campos. **Barreirinhas**, 265 kilometers (162 miles) east of São Luís, possesses the best tourist facilities and the local headquarters of the Brazilian Institute of Environment and Renewable Natural Resources (Ibama), which maintains the park. The town is also a departure point for trips to the Preguiças River and often features as a stop on trips to the Parnaíba River Delta in Piauí and Jericoacoara in Ceará. After Barreirinhas, the area's most popular destination is **Santo Amaro do Maranhão**, where the 2005 movie *The House of Sand (Casa de Areia)* was filmed.

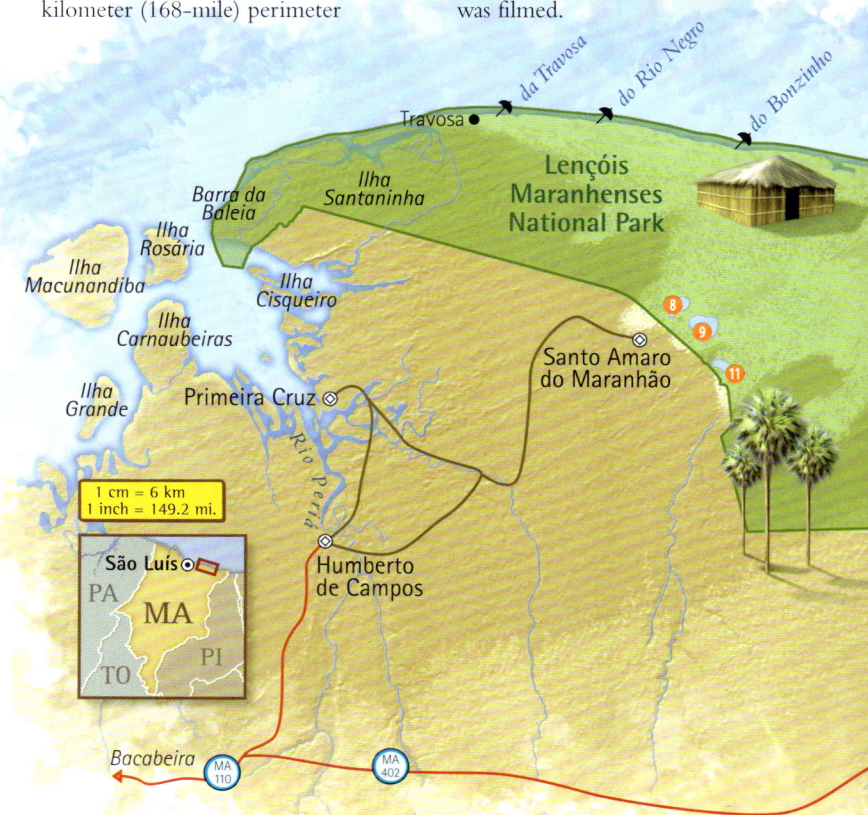

Barreirinhas

Founded on the banks of the Preguiças River in 1871, Barreirinhas has always been a base for visitors to the region. At first, it was an ideally located trading post for area fishermen and farmers; today, it thrives on tourism, offering hotels, guesthouses, restaurants, and visitor services. The Ibama headquarters *(Rua Principal, no #, Cantinho, tel. 98/3349-1155; Mon – Fri, 9am – noon and 2pm – 6pm)* hosts lectures, in Portuguese, on biodiversity in Lençóis Maranhenses National Park and on ways to enjoy the bounty in an ecological responsible way. Barreirinhas's main attraction is the dark, clean Preguiças River, which placidly winds through the town and the sprawl of disorderly development on its banks. A guide is necessary to explore the region, and the town's numerous agencies offer distinctly different experiences. **Tropical Adventure** *(Rua Anacleto de Carvalho, 260, Cruzeiro, tel. 98/3349-1987; Mon – Sat, 8am – 6pm)* offers customized trips in air-conditioned 4×4 vehicles. **Eco-Dunas** *(Rua Inácio Lins, 164, Centro, tel. 98/3349-0545; Mon – Sat, 7am – 7pm; Sun, 7am – 4pm)* specializes in adventure sports, flights over the park, tubing (*bóia-cross*), and trips to less-known parts of the park. **Rota das Trilhas** *(Avenida Joaquim Soeiro de Carvalho, 682-A, Centro, tel. 98/3349-0372; daily, 7:30am – 11:30am and 1:30pm – 6:30pm)* travels the best-known routes. The local **Secretaria de**

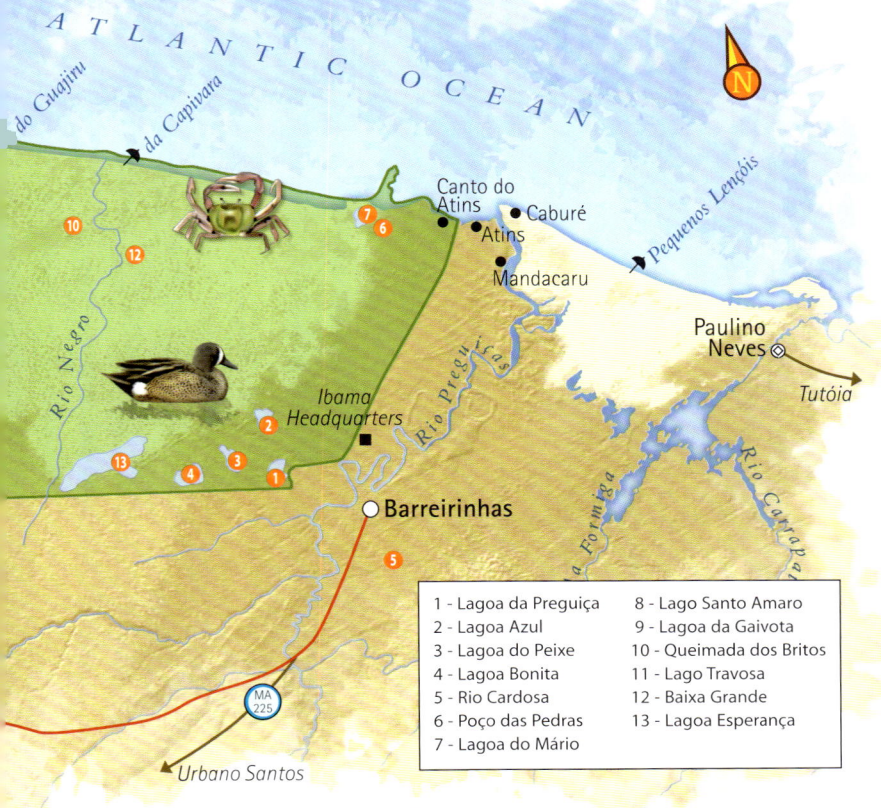

1 - Lagoa da Preguiça
2 - Lagoa Azul
3 - Lagoa do Peixe
4 - Lagoa Bonita
5 - Rio Cardosa
6 - Poço das Pedras
7 - Lagoa do Mário
8 - Lago Santo Amaro
9 - Lagoa da Gaivota
10 - Queimada dos Britos
11 - Lago Travosa
12 - Baixa Grande
13 - Lagoa Esperança

Turismo (*Avenida da Rodoviária, no #, Boa Fé; Mon – Fri, 8am – noon and 2pm – 6pm*) provides further information and can recommend agencies and services. Barreirinhas is 265 kilometers (165 miles) from São Luís, a 3-hour trip by the MA-402 highway (also called the Translitorânea).

PREGUIÇAS RIVER CRUISE

Trips on the Rio Preguiças, by motorboat or *voadeira* (a speedboat with an outboard engine), stop for numerous attractions along part of the area designated a national park covering 70 kilometers (43 miles) of beaches. Among them are the towering, 40-meter (130-foot) dunes in Vassouras, a fishing village 45 minutes from Barreirinhas, where visitors swim in the river or walk along the beach. The next stop, after passing native vegetation and mangroves, Espadarte, Morro do Boi, and Moitas, is Mandacaru village, home to the Preguiças lighthouse. The view of the village from 35 meters high (114 feet) is one of the most beautiful of the whole tour. Climb its 160 steps for the best view of the area. The lunch stop is in **Caburé**, near the river's mouth. The town's restaurants are its only attractions.

OUR RECOMMENDATION

🍴 **Pousada do Buna** offers ten simple, comfortable, and well-equipped chalets. The elegant bathrooms, in keeping with local tradition, offer cold showers only. The wood and brick building is charming, though, as are the hammocks everywhere. The guesthouse's greatest charm is its friendly owner, who cooks, tells stories, and arranges jeep or boat trips with local guides. (*Rua Principal, no #, Praia de Atins, 10, tel. 98/9616-9646.*)

Additional information on page 358.

LAKES

After crossing the Preguiças River by ferry, get into one of the waiting jeeps and head for the lakes at Lençóis Maranhenses National Park. The vehicles travel for 40 minutes on a winding road amid lakes and streams, with some flooded stretches. From where they stop, it's a 5-minute walk to turquoise **Lagoa da Preguiça**. Lovely **Lagoa Azul**, as blue as its name suggests, is 10 minutes farther on. The lagoon, surrounded by dunes with very fine sand, is one of the park's most popular spots and is usually crowded. For peace and quiet, walk 10 more minutes to the dark green **Lagoa do Peixe**, a tranquil lake which has waters darkened by the algae but nevertheless ideal for a refreshing swim, surrounded by vegetation. Lagoa do Peixe is one of the few lakes here that doesn't dry up in the summer; Lagoa Azul simply disappears toward the end of the year. Reaching **Lagoa Bonita**, surrounded by 40-meter (130-foot) dunes, requires driving along another winding road for about an hour.

DOWN THE CARDOSA RIVER

The Rio Cardosa is 90 minutes by car from the center of Barreirinhas. Its calm, crystal-clear waters are perfect for kayaking or floating down in an inner tube (*bóia-cross*). Take a snorkel mask to watch the fish. A trip down the river takes about 2 hours.
Contact: *Eco-Dunas, tel. (98) 3349-0545.*

FLYING OVER THE PARK

A twin-engine plane flies visitors over Lençóis Maranhenses National Park, taking off from Barreirinhas and traveling to the mouth of the Preguiças River in Atins. The 30-

Green waters lap against the powdery sand of the dunes

minute trip over the endless dunes and lakes is unforgettable.
Contact: Eco-Dunas, tel. (98) 3349-0545.

ATINS

The Preguiças River empties into the sea at Atins. The village marks the beginning of the Praia do Grandes Lençóis, a stretch of coast that ends 100 kilometers (62 miles) away in Travosa, at the other end of the national park. Arrange trips to Atins through the agencies in Barreirinhas. Electricity came to this small fishing village only recently, and the people here still earn their living from the sea. The sandy streets carry no cars, and one public telephone is the only connection to the rest of the world. The privileged location, between the river and the sea, accentuate Atins's magical atmosphere. The village abuts the park's dunes and its beach is dotted with natural pools at low tide. Attractions in town include **Poço das Pedras**, a turquoise pool amid the vast sands, and **Lagoa do Mário**, a dark lake decorated with floating white flowers. Dona Luzia serves incomparable shrimp at her kiosk next to the lake.

BURITI STRAW CRAFTS

The *buriti* palm is abundant around the Preguiças River and the region's lakes, and no part of the plant goes to waste. Starch is made from its core; oil, juice, ice cream, and candy from its fruit. Its leaves are used to thatch roofs, and its buds produce heart of palm and a fine fiber called *olhos* (eyes). The fiber is made into bags, purses, hats, and other items, which are on sale all over town, at kiosks on the banks of Lagoa Bonita, and on the ferries that cross the Preguiças.

The wind draws pictures in Lençóis's desert sands

Tutóia

Though it is surrounded by natural beauty, Tutóia, 400 kilometers (250 miles) northeast of Barreirinhas, has no attractions of its own. Its limited restaurants and guesthouses condemn it to be just a stop between Lençóis Maranhenses and the Parnaíba River Delta in Piauí, which can be seen in the distance from the port. No rentable motorboats are available for the crossing; regularly scheduled passenger boats depart every other day for the 8-hour trip. You can reach Parnaíba by car from Tutóia, via BR-402 east, but some stretches of the road are in poor condition.

Santo Amaro do Maranhão

Few visitors come to Santo Amaro do Maranhão, 232 kilometers (144 miles) east of São Luís, because reaching it is difficult. The trip here requires driving on a sandy, unpaved road for 35 of the 96 kilometers (60 miles) from Barreirinhas. During winter, heavy rains make a 4×4 vehicle the only possible means of arrival — and even then, you risk getting stuck. The 10,000-resident town sits on the banks of the yellow Rio Alegre and provides an alternative gateway to Lençóis Maranhenses National Park. This half-time desert, intersept with shape-changing lakes and dunes, has an etherial beauty that takes many visitors by surprise. Unlike Barreirinhas, which is an hour away from the dunes, Santo Amaro is tucked among them. Be careful, the dunes are surprising desorienting and lots of people get lost just wandering around. The sun and the heat — up to 40 C (104 F) — is always present in the region. Access to the town is by the MA-402 state highway, west to Vila de Sangue, but due to poor road conditions, it is best to hire a jeep and guide in Barreirinhas.

Lakes

Santo Amaro sits on the banks of the Alegre River and is surrounded by lakes, pools, and rivers that run through the vast, white dunes. One attraction is **Lago Santo Amaro**, a lake fed by a branch of the river. Teeming with fish, the lake provides a livelihood for many town residents. Rent a boat in the village and ride down the shallow river to the lake, passing small fishing communities on the way. Santo Amaro's postcard attraction is **Lagoa da Gaivota**, 6 kilometers (4 miles) from the town center. It takes an hour to get there on foot or half an hour by 4×4 vehicle. The lake's turquoise waters, kissed by snow-white dunes, are at their fullest during winter but never dry up even during the summer. The lake's edges are shallow and the center up to 2.5 meters (8 feet) deep, making the site irresistible to swimmers. Continue up and down the dunes for 20 minutes to reach the simple beauty of Cajueiro, a small house surrounded by leafy mango trees and the eponymous cashew trees (*cajueiros*). Some of the trees here are centuries old. The owner catches his lunch in the dark lake next to the house. Near Santo Amaro is also **Barreira das Pacas** pool.

Queimada dos Britos

One hundred people, their 5,000 goats, lovely dunes, and refreshing lakes characterize this village inside Lençóis Maranhenses National Park. Queimada dos Britos is a green oasis amid the surrounding sand, but its modest houses have thatched roofs and no electricity. You can reach the village in 2 hours by 4×4 vehicle or by a difficult 8-hour walk across the sand from the park's entrance. Near Queimada dos Britos is **Baixa Grande**, a luxuriant green patch among the dunes. The **Rio Negro**, which crosses the park from end to end, waters this oasis. At the river's mouth is lovely Lagoa Esperança lake.

Queimada dos Britos has natural beauty in spades — but no electricity

Simple Pleasures in Lençóis

The size and impressiveness of Lençóis Maranhenses is difficult to express in words. To understand it, you need to be there, to let your soul soar with the wind, to take in the relentless motion of sand carried inland from the beaches to form the dunes.

The landscape here offers unique natural gifts: sunsets over the river and the sea, flocks of scarlet ibises taking wing, long walks on deserted beaches, blue lakes punctuating the vast whiteness. Above all, Lençóis Maranhenses reminds us of simple pleasures lost: running, playing, swimming, sailing a canoe with improvised sails, breathing deeply, listening to the silence. And when the generators shut off at 10pm, just lie beneath the pitch-black sky streaked with shooting stars.

The dunes are divided into Pequenos Lençóis and Grandes Lençóis (Lesser and Greater Lençóis) by the charming, slow-flowing Preguiças River. The river's banks are dotted with small villages – Vassouras, Caburé, Mandacaru – that are quiet, undeveloped places, places very different from major tourist destinations. Barreirinhas, a base for trips around the region, is beginning to organize services for visitors. In high season, cars and jeeps take over the town's humble streets before shuttling visitors to the dunes around Lagoa Azul and Lagoa do Peixe, which are the area's most accessible lakes. If you are up for a little more walking, you will be rewarded with discovery of other lakes, deserted lakes. Any dune you climb may reveal another dune, a long stretch of white sand, or a warm, crystal-clear lake. Paradoxically, there is an almost

The ever-changing landscape of Lençóis

static quality to this ever-changing landscape, which plays stage to the perpetual dance of wind and sand. Its stasis is this: The landscape shows no trace of the 21st century, nor even the 20th. It has been shifting and reforming continually, and yet it has been the same for hundreds of years.

From Barreirinhas, you can take a trip along the Preguiças River, passing the villages that dot its banks. Its waters zigzag among sandy hills and flow into marshlands. Near the river's mouth, Caburé sits on a sandy peninsula. On one side lies the river, on the other, the ocean. Between them are a few simple buildings, some modest guesthouses, and you. Stand between river and sea, between the salt water and the fresh, and feel the wind on your face. From here you can see that Lençóis is not homogeneous. To the east, the dunes are yellowish, the lakes darker. From Caburé, you can take a *voadeira* (speedboat) to tiny Atins, and from there walk to Poço das Pedras, a deep, emerald pool. On your way, ask around for Luzia's shrimp, a taste of which will make for a most memorable trip.

In a world where even the most secluded spots often offer sophisticated hotels and impeccable service, Lençóis Maranhenses is a rare exception, a place of rustic charm. But with its rugged, unspoiled beauty, its modest facilities, and its friendly residents, it is nevertheless one of Brazil's most attractive destinations. If you know how to enjoy the experience, Lençóis Maranhenses can be the ultimate in luxury.

Robert Betenson
partner and director of the Matueté travel agency

Hotels, Restaurants and Services

The following pages describe services and amenities organized by town, in alphabetical order. The number of dollar signs next to an establishment indicates its price range (for price range definitions, see the footnotes). Quoted hotel prices are the daily rates for a couple. Restaurant prices were calculated based on the price of the most popular dish, plus a 10% service charge. Addresses, telephone numbers, hours, and prices were supplied by the establishments in question and checked by our team of field researchers. Nonetheless, there may be discrepancies or changes, and we recommend that information be confirmed beforehand whenever possible.

Some notes about the listings: In addition to having a main telephone number for incoming calls, some hotels have a separate reservations line (often one that doubles as a fax number). In these cases, the numbers are listed separately. Also, many beachfront hotels offer what they call a "beach service" (*serviços de praia*), which usually consists of staff providing a complimentary towel to each beachgoer and maintaining beachside restrooms, cold showers, and a small snack bar or kiosk that many have umbrella-shaded tables. Other hotels offer "recreation teams" (*equipe de recreação*), for which staff organize daytime games and activities for guests, often specifically for children.

In small towns with poor tourist facilities, travel agencies and tour companies may only operate on a part-time basis during the low season (March to June and August to November, with the exception of major public holidays). Where establishments have no numerical street addresses, it's indicated here by "no #".

Abrolhos – Bahia
(see Alcobaça and Caravelas)

Acari – Rio Grande do Norte

AREA CODE 84 POPULATION 11,303 DISTANCES Natal 210 kilometers (130 miles), Caicó 60 kilometers (37 miles), Campina Grande 168 kilometers (104 miles), Mossoró 236 kilometers (147 miles), João Pessoa 278 kilometers (173 miles) ACCESS From Natal, take the RN-226 highway to Currais Novos, then the BR-427 southwest to Acari BEST TIME TO VISIT February and March, to enjoy the Gargalheiras Reservoir at its fullest www.acari-rn.com.br

WHERE TO STAY

Bistrô Pousada e Restaurante $
Rooms here are simple and have few amenities, but are very pleasant. The owners also run a friendly restaurant (see *Where to Eat*). ACCOMMODATIONS 2 suites, 2 rooms, each with fan FACILITIES AND SERVICES parking, restaurant, guided walking tours, horseback riding, boat trips CREDIT CARDS not accepted

Açude Marechal Dutra, no #, Gargalheiras
TEL (84) 9977-4150

WHERE TO EAT

Bistrô $
Sauces made by Frenchman Christian create a winning combination when paired with fish prepared by local cook Angelina. The delicious *tucunaré* fish in wine sauce serves two. The atmosphere is relaxed, with outdoor seating in a well-tended garden that overlooks the reservoir. CUISINE Brazilian with French influences, fish CREDIT CARDS not accepted
Açude Marechal Dutra, no #, Gargalheiras
TEL (84) 9977-4150 OPEN Thu – Sun, noon – until the last customer leaves

Restaurante da Pousada do Gargalheiras $
The Pousada do Gargalheiras hotel restaurant serves generous regional dishes and appetizers. After lunch you can request a hammock and relax on the hotel veranda, which has a panoramic view of the reservoir. CUISINE regional, fish CREDIT CARDS not accepted
Açude Marechal Dutra, no #, Gargalheiras
TEL (84) 3504-4151 OPEN Daily, 7am – 10pm

PRICES	HOTELS (couple)	$ up to R$150	$$ from R$151 up to R$300	$$$ from R$301 up to R$500	$$$$ above R$500

HOTELS, RESTAURANTS AND SERVICES

SERVICES

Bus Station – Rodoviária
Rua Cantídia Galvão, 128, Ari de Pinho
TEL (84) 3433-2203, 3433-2236

Tourist Information – Posto de Informações Turísticas (Museu Histórico de Acari museum)
Rua Antônio Basílio, 11, Centro
TEL (84) 3433-3988 **OPEN** Mon – Fri, 7:30am – 11:30am and 1:30pm – 5:30pm; Sat, 8am – 11am; on Sun and holidays visits to the museum must be arranged in advance

Alcântara – Maranhão

AREA CODE 98 **POPULATION** 22,359 **DISTANCE** São Luís 22 kilometers (14 miles), by boat, across the water **ACCESS** one and a half hours by motorboat from São Luís **BEST TIME TO VISIT** May, for Festa do Divino celebrations

WHERE TO STAY

Pousada dos Guarás $
This guesthouse offers 10 basic chalets surrounded by a lovely tropical garden near Praia da Baronesa beach. The guesthouse restaurant serves seafood. **ACCOMMODATIONS** 10 chalets; 5 with veranda, air-conditioning, hot shower, TV; 5 with ceiling fan, cold shower **FACILITIES AND SERVICES** referrals to good restaurants and boat trips **CREDIT CARDS** Amex, Diners, MasterCard, Visa
Praia da Baronesa, no #, Caravelas
TEL (98) 3337-1339

WHERE TO EAT

Josefa $
Josefa's specialty is seafood, particularly shrimp, crab, and fish, but they also serve chicken and beef. The outdoor tables under the mango tree are a particularly pleasant place to eat. Be prepared to wait, the food takes a long time to prepare. **CUISINE** Brazilian, seafood **CREDIT CARDS** not accepted
Rua Direita 33, Centro
TEL (98) 3337-1109 **OPEN** Daily, 7am – 11pm

SERVICES

Alcântara–São Luís Boat Crossing – Navegações Pericumã
Porto do Jacaré (passenger terminal)
TEL (98) 3232-0692 **OPEN** Daily, 6am – 5:30pm

Alcobaça – Bahia

AREA CODE 73 **POPULATION** 23,858 **DISTANCES** Salvador 830 kilometers (516 miles), Vitória 420 kilometers (261 miles), Belo Horizonte 730 kilometers (454 miles), Rio de Janeiro 960 kilometers (597 miles) **ACCESS** From Salvador, take the BA-001 highway south, then the BA-240 east.

WHERE TO STAY

Brisa dos Abrolhos $
This simple, isolated hotel sits on Praia da Barra beach at the confluence of the river and the sea. Most rooms have a veranda with sea view. **ACCOMMODATIONS** 29 rooms, each with air-conditioning, minibar, telephone, TV **FACILITIES AND SERVICES** bar, restaurant, parking, pool, playground, restaurant, beach service **CREDIT CARDS** not accepted
Rua Fernando da Cunha, 1657, Praia da Barra
TEL and **FAX** (73) 3293-2022, 3293-2023
www.visanco.com.br/brisadosabrolhos

Paraíso Tropical $
One of the best hotels in Alcobaça, Paraíso Tropical provides its guests with a variety of leisure options including a professional pool table. Some suites have a veranda and sea view. **ACCOMMODATIONS** 35 rooms and 6 two-room suites, each with air-conditioning, minibar, telephone, TV; some rooms also have a veranda **FACILITIES AND SERVICES** bar, parking, laundry, convenience store, pool, playground, multi-sports court, restaurant, meeting room, game room, video-viewing room, sauna, guided tours and transportation to Abrolhos, beach service **CREDIT CARDS** Visa
Avenida Atlântica, 3711, Farol
TEL (73) 3293-2210 **FAX** 3293-9006
www.hotelparaisotropical.com.br

WHERE TO EAT

Maresias $
One of the oldest restaurants in town, Maresias' thirty years of business attest to its popularity. Patrons savor regional specialties, such as *moqueca de peixe ao molho de camarão* (fish with shrimp, coconut milk, and *dendê* palm oil), as well as dishes from Minas Gerais. **CUISINE** regional, Minas Gerais **CREDIT CARDS** Diners, MasterCard, Visa
Avenida Atlântica, 1041, Centro
TEL (73) 3293-2471 **OPEN** High season: daily, 8am – 6pm; low season: Tue – Sun, 8am – 6pm

SERVICES

Boat Rental – Abrolhos Embarcações
Cais Santo Antônio, 60, Centro
TEL (73) 3297-1172 **OPEN** Mon – Sat, 7am – noon and 3pm – 6pm. Affiliated with the Abrolhos Turismo Caravelas tour agency. www.abrolhosembarcacoes.com.br

Bus Station – Rodoviária
Avenida 7 de Setembro, 1915, Palmeiras
TEL (73) 3293-2212

Andaraí – Bahia

AREA CODE 75 **POPULATION** 13,633 **DISTANCES** Salvador 414 kilometers (257 miles), Lençóis 101 kilometers (63 miles) **ACCESS** BA-142 highway, exit at Km 50 or 53

WHERE TO STAY

Pousada Ecológica $
Its location on the banks of the Paraguaçu River allows guests to enjoy fishing, swimming, and sunbathing. The pousada's restaurant serves tasty fried *tucunaré* fish and other local dishes. **ACCOMMODATIONS** 31 suites, each with air-conditioning, minibar, TV **FACILITIES AND SERVICES** bar, parking, stores, pool, playground, indoor soccer court, restaurant, meeting room, game room, guided walking tours **CREDIT CARDS** MasterCard, Visa
Estrada Andaraí–Mucugê, Km 3, Vila da Passagem
TEL and **FAX** (75) 3335-2176, 3335-2207

Pousada Sincorá $
This pousada is one of the best places to stay in town. Friendly owners Elder and Ana Maria Madeira provide guests with an excellent breakfast and an insider's perspective on Chapada Diamantina. The Madeiras also own a small farm and campsite in the Marimbus wetlands, outside of

---

RESTAURANTS $ up to R$50 $$ from R$51 up to R$100 $$$ from R$101 up to R$150 $$$$ above R$150

town, where campers can rent canoes and enjoy guided tours of the area. ACCOMMODATIONS 5 suites, each with air-conditioning, minibar, TV FACILITIES AND SERVICES Internet access in communal areas, library, parking, store, guided walking tours CREDIT CARDS Diners, MasterCard, Visa
Avenida Paraguaçu, 120 (Igatu/Mucugê exit)
TEL (75) 3335-2210 FAX 3335-2486 www.sincora.com.br

SERVICES

Guides – Associação dos Condutores de Visitantes de Andaraí (ACVA)
Rua Doutor José Gonçalves Cincorá, no #
TEL (75) 3335-2255, 3335-2308 (ask to speak to Adriano or Herculano) OPEN High season: daily, 8am – noon and 2pm – 5pm; low season: Mon – Fri, 8am – noon and 2pm – 5pm

Aquiraz – Ceará

AREA CODE 85 POPULATION 69,343 DISTANCE Fortaleza 32 kilometers (20 miles) ACCESS From Fortaleza, take CE-040 east highway

WHERE TO STAY

Beach Park Suítes Resort $$$
The excellent facilities here make this resort ideal for families. The private beach in front of the hotel has calm, warm waters and is good for swimming. The suites, available for two or four people, each have a veranda facing the sea. ACCOMMODATIONS 175 suites, each with air-conditioning, private safe, minibar, telephone, cable TV, veranda; Internet access on some suites FACILITIES AND SERVICES Internet access in communal areas, bar, beauty salon, parking, convenience store, pool; courts for soccer, tennis, and volleyball; restaurant, meeting room, gym, game room, sauna, baby-sitting, 24-hour business center, valet parking, beach service CREDIT CARDS Amex, Diners, MasterCard, Visa
Rua Porto das Dunas, 2734, Praia Porto das Dunas
TEL (85) 4012-3084 FAX 4012-3040 www.beachpark.com.br

Laguna Blu $$
All rooms have a view of the ocean and are decorated with local handicrafts. The pool, with bar and waterfall, is a popular place to relax. Anyone traveling with children or elderly adults should ask for ground floor accommodation; the stairs of this three-story hotel are quite steep. ACCOMMODATIONS 22 suites and 17 rooms, each with air-conditioning, private safe, minibar, telephone, cable TV; the master suite has a hot tub FACILITIES AND SERVICES Internet access in communal areas, bar, parking, convenience store, pool, restaurant, meeting room, game room, massage room, sauna, business center CREDIT CARDS Diners, MasterCard, Visa
Avenida Damião Tavares, 902, Prainha
TEL (85) 3361-5543 FAX 3361-5368 www.lagunablu.com.br

Oceani Resort $$$
The Oceani Resort is located on a beach with natural pools that are ideal for swimming. Guests can take advantage of the hotel's business center and baby area (complete with minikitchen and toys), and frequently unwind at the end of each day with a relaxing massage or quiet nap in a garden hammock. Hotel décor is inspired by local art and crafts work, and the rotating menu is themed by region cuisines. ACCOMMODATIONS 133 suites, each with Internet access, air-conditioning, private safe, minibar, telephone, cable TV FACILITIES AND SERVICES Internet access in communal areas, bar, parking, convenience store, pool, restaurant, meeting room, massage room, sauna, travel agency, business center, currency exchange, 24-hour kitchen, recreational team for adults and children, guided walking tours, airport shuttle service, transportation to local attractions CREDIT CARDS Amex, Diners, MasterCard, Visa
Avenida dos Golfinhos, 455, Porto das Dunas
TEL (85) 3361-7777 FAX 3361-7799 www.oceaniresort.com.br

WHERE TO EAT

João Branco $
João Branco, a local chef, creates and prepares all the dishes himself. We recommend the fish stuffed with lobster and shrimp, served with white sauce and grated cheese, and accompanied by Milanese rice and gratin potatoes. Service is very attentive. CUISINE seafood CREDIT CARDS MasterCard, Visa
Rua Otonio Sá, 720, Gruta
TEL (85) 3361-2295 RESERVATIONS 9602-1113 OPEN Mon – Thu, 11am – 4pm; Fri and Sat, 11am – midnight; Sun, 11am – 6pm

SERVICES

Bus Station – Rodoviária
Avenida Torres de Melo, no #, Centro
TEL (85) 3361-1308

Tourism Department – Secretaria de Turismo
Rua Cônego Araripe, 76, Centro
TEL (85) 3361-1843, 3361-1830, 3361-1840 OPEN Tue – Fri, 8:30am – 5pm www.aquiraz.ce.gov.br

Aracaju – Sergipe

AREA CODE 79 POPULATION 498,619 DISTANCES Maceió 290 kilometers (180 miles), Salvador 330 kilometers (205 miles) ACCESS BR-101 highway, or the Linha Verde coastal highway. The latter is the best option from Bahia, since it has with fewer trucks BEST TIME TO VISIT In June, for forró music; the beaches are best December through March
www.aracaju.se.gov.br

WHERE TO STAY

Celi Praia $$$
Celi Praia's, on Atalaia beach offers comfortable, utilitarian rooms. The leisure facilities unfortunately leave a lot to be desired: the pool is small and the gym ill-equipped. ACCOMMODATIONS 78 rooms and 15 suites, each with Internet access, air-conditioning, private safe, minibar, telephone, cable TV; each suite also has a hot tub FACILITIES AND SERVICES Internet access in communal areas, bar, parking, snack bar, convenience store, small soccer field, pool, restaurant, meeting room, gym, game room, massage room, sauna, travel agency, recreational team for adults and children, business center, 24-hour kitchen, valet parking CREDIT CARDS Amex, Diners, MasterCard, Visa
Avenida Oceânica, 500, Praia de Atalaia
TEL (79) 2107-8000 FAX 2107-8001 www.celihotel.com.br

Del Mar $$$
The hotel sits on Atalaia beach and offers a great variety of recreational facilities. ACCOMMODATIONS 109 rooms and 4 suites, each with Internet access, air-conditioning, minibar, telephone, cable TV FACILITIES AND SERVICES Internet access in communal areas, bar, parking, snack bar, convenience store, pool, playground, tennis court, restaurant, meeting room, game room, beauty salon, sauna, gym, travel agency, business center, 24-hour kitchen, recreational team for adults

PRICES	HOTELS (couple)	$ up to R$150	$$ from R$151 up to R$300	$$$ from R$301 up to R$500	$$$$ above R$500

and children during the high season, valet parking CREDIT CARDS Amex, Diners, MasterCard, Visa
Avenida Santos Dumont, 1500, Praia de Atalaia
TEL (79) 2106-9100, 2106-9200 FAX 2106-9292 RESERVATIONS 2106-9142 www.delmarhotel.com.br

Quality Hotel Aracaju $$$
The hotel has smoking and non-smoking areas, two rooms for the disabled, and a wing exclusively for female guests. ACCOMMODATIONS 106 rooms and 3 suites, each with Internet access, air-conditioning, private safe, minibar, telephone, cable TV; luxury suites also have hot tubs FACILITIES AND SERVICES Internet access in communal areas, bar, parking, snack bar, pool, restaurant, meeting room, gym, sauna, business center, 24-hour kitchen CREDIT CARDS Amex, Diners, MasterCard, Visa
Avenida Delmiro Gouveia, 100, Coroa do Meio
TEL (79) 3234-7000 FAX 3234-7001
www.atlanticahotels.com.br

WHERE TO EAT

Bistrô do Twin $
This cozy, simple restaurant serves particularly tasty "*camarão* Twin," which is shrimp flambéed in cacao liqueur, and lamb with rosemary. Lobster in white wine or grilled salmon in mango sauce are also house specialties. Reservations are recommended. CUISINE varied CREDIT CARDS not accepted
Rua Doutor Bráulio Costa, 21, Atalaia
TEL (79) 3243-5322 OPEN Tue, noon – 3pm; Wed – Sat, noon – 3pm and 6pm – midnight; Sun, noon – 5pm

Cantina d'Italia $
This cantina is very pleasant. The restaurant's home-made shrimp and pasta dishes and its sauces (buttered shrimp, tomato, cream, and white wine) are culinary highlights. Other menu options include salad, poultry, fish, seafood, and other meat dishes. CUISINE varied, but with an Italian emphasis CREDIT CARDS AMEX, Diners, MasterCard, Visa
Avenida Santos Dumont, no #, kiosk #7, Atalaia
TEL (79) 3243-3184 OPEN Daily, 11am – 1am

Cariri $
Cariri is on the Passarela do Caranguejo walkway and shares a roof with a good, traditional *forró* music venue. The menu largely consists of seafood and traditional *sertão* dishes. House specialties include *camarão ao cariri* (shrimp and coconut milk served in a coconut shell with rice and seasoned manioc flour) and grilled goat. The restaurant also has a good selection of *cachaças* from Minas Gerais. Appetizers are particularly popular on busy *forró* music nights. CUISINE regional, seafood CREDIT CARDS Amex, Diners, MasterCard, Visa
Avenida Santos Dumont, no #, Passarela do Caranguejo, Atalaia
TEL (79) 3243-1379, 3243-5370 OPEN Daily, 10am – until the last customer leaves

Carne-de-sol do Ramiro $
Almost everything the restaurant serves is brought in from Picuí. The barbecue-grilled sun-dried beef is garnished with fried or roasted manioc, beans, flour, thickened cheese sauce, and pickled salad – a true feast. Goat is another specialty and can be enjoyed as an appetizer or main dish. CUISINE regional CREDIT CARDS MasterCard, Visa
Avenida Beira-Mar, 1250, 13 de Julho
TEL (79) 3246-1619, 3246-1007 OPEN Daily, 11am – 10pm

Gralha Azul Grill $
Gralha Azul Grill is a *rodízio* (all-you-can-eat) barbecue restaurant that serves twenty different meat options in a large, air-conditioned room. Classic beef cuts include rump and flank. Less common meats and cuts like quail and leg of mutton are available, and the buffet also includes salad, hot dishes (seafood, pasta), sushi, and sashimi. An à la carte menu is offered. Wines are stored in a temperature-controlled cellar. CUISINE varied, meats CREDIT CARDS Diners, MasterCard, Visa
Avenida Santos Dumont, no #, kiosk #G1, Atalaia
TEL (79) 3243-4204 RESERVATIONS (79) 3223-1471 OPEN Mon – Sat, 11:30am – 3:30pm and 6:30pm – 11pm; Sun, 11:30am – 5pm

O Miguel $
O Miguel is famous for its delicious sun-dried beef from Sergipe. The fillet of beef, seasoned with salt, can be grilled on the barbecue or cooked on a sizzling hotplate with clarified butter. Tasty and tender, the fillet is accompanied by milk-thickened sauce, seasoned manioc flour, pickled salad, and rice. Equally tasty is the grilled *surubim* (also known as *pintado*), a fish caught in the São Francisco River, that is drizzled with Portuguese olive oil. Try the feather-light, homemade *doce de leite* (caramelized milk) for dessert. Pizzas and pastas are served after 6pm. CUISINE regional CREDIT CARDS MasterCard, Visa
Avenida Antônio Alves, 340 (at the junction with Avenida Beira-Mar), Atalaia Velha
TEL (79) 3243-1444, 3243-4142 OPEN Mon, 11am – 4pm; Tue – Sun, 11am – 4pm and 6pm – 11:30pm

SERVICES

Airport – Aeroporto Santa Maria
Avenida Senador Júlio César Leite, no #, Atalaia Velha
TEL (79) 3212-8500, 3212-8557 OPEN Daily, 24 hours
www.infraero.gov.br

Bus Station – Rodoviária
Avenida Tancredo Neves, no #, Novo Paraíso
TEL (79) 3259-2848 www.socican.com.br

Tourist Information – Bureau de Informações Turísticas
Praça Olímpio Campos, no #, Centro
TEL (79) 3214-8848 OPEN Bureau: daily, 8am – 1am; Orla de Atalaia Branch (Centro de Cultura e Arte): daily, 9am – 6pm
www.turismosergipe.net

Tourist Information – Funcaju
Rua Santa Luzia, 602, São José
TEL (79) 3179-3679, 3179-3682, 3179-3681 OPEN Mon – Fri, 8am – 1pm and 3pm – 6pm www.aracaju.se.gov.br

Travel Agency – Agência de Turismo Propagtur
Avenida Ermes Fontes, 1109, São José
TEL (79) 3234-4444, 3234-4434 OPEN Mon – Fri, 8am – 6pm; Sat, 8am – noon
Airport Branch: TEL (79) 3179-4664 OPEN Daily, 5am – 8pm
www.propagtur.com.br

Travel Agency – Nozes Tour
Avenida Santos Dumont, 478 (annexed to Hotel Jatobá), Praia de Atalaia
TEL (79) 3243-7177, 3243-6891, 9977-6730 OPEN Daily, 7am – 9pm www.nozestur.com.br

---

RESTAURANTS | $ up to R$50 | $$ from R$51 up to R$100 | $$$ from R$101 up to R$150 | $$$$ above R$150

Areia – Paraíba

AREA CODE 83 **POPULATION** 24,879 **DISTANCES** João Pessoa 130 kilometers (81 miles), Campina Grande 49 kilometers (30 miles) **ACCESS** From João Pessoa, take the BR-230 highway west toward Alagoa Grande, then through the mountains to Areia (beware of sharp curves and animals on the road). From Campina Grande, the best route to Areia is east on BR-412 via Esperança town

SERVICES

Tourism Department – Secretaria de Turismo
Rua Epitácio Pessoa, no #, Centro
TEL (83) 8849-1342 **OPEN** Mon – Fri, 7:30am – 11:30am and 1:30pm – 5:30pm

Arembepe – Bahia

AREA CODE 71 Camaçari **DISTANCES** Salvador 40 kilometers (25 miles) north, Feira de Santana 120 kilometers (75 miles) east, Aracaju 220 kilometers (137 miles) south **ACCESS** Estrada do Coco (aka, the BA-099 highway)

WHERE TO STAY

Aldeia de Arembepe Refúgio Ecológico $$
Aldeia de Arembepe sits on a hill overlooking the sea near Lagoa de Arembepe lake. Bungalows can accommodate up to four people. The hotel organizes sight-seeing trips for guests. **ACCOMMODATIONS** 11 bungalows and 1 chalet, each with TV, ceiling fan and minibar **FACILITIES AND SERVICES** pool, playground, restaurant, bicycles, kayaks, beach service, airport shuttle service, transportation to local attractions **CREDIT CARDS** Amex, Diners, MasterCard, Visa
Estrada da Aldeia Hippie, no #, Projeto Tamar, Lotes #9 and 10, Praia de Arembepe
TEL (71) 3624-1031, 9153-5253
www.aldeiadearembepe.com.br

WHERE TO EAT

Mar Aberto $$
Mar Aberto operates out of a small house by the sea. Patrons come from as far as Salvador to try his delicacies (like the grilled lobster with buttered vegetables, rice, and mashed potatoes, which serves two). **CUISINE** Bahian, seafood **CREDIT CARDS** Amex, Diners, MasterCard, Visa
Largo de São Francisco, 43, Praia de Arembepe
TEL (71) 3624-1257, 3624-1623 **OPEN** Mon – Thu, 11am – 10pm; Fri and Sat, 11am – midnight; Sun, 11am – 7pm

SERVICES

Bus Station – Rodoviária
Rua da Rodoviária, no #, Centro, Camaçari
TEL (71) 3621-5056

Tourist Information – Posto de Informações Turísticas
Estrada do Coco, Km 11 (next to the tollbooth)
TEL (71) 3622-8233 **OPEN** Mon – Fri, 8am – 5pm

Arraial d'Ajuda – Bahia

AREA CODE 73 Porto Seguro **DISTANCES** Salvador 715 kilometers (444 miles), Porto Seguro 4 kilometers (2.5 miles, plus ten minutes by ferry), Ilhéus 324 kilometers (201 miles), Belo Horizonte 952 kilometers (592 miles) **ACCESS** From Porto Seguro, by ferry. Or by the BR-101 highway to Eunápolis, then the BR-367, and the BA-001.

WHERE TO STAY

Arraial d'Ajuda Eco Resort $$$$
The resort is casual, yet sophisticated. Guests enjoy access to the fitness center and a waterpark, the Arraial d'Ajuda EcoPark. The suites all have an adjoining sitting room and the master suites are more spacious than junior suites. **ACCOMMODATIONS** 157 rooms and 12 suites, each with air-conditioning, private safe, minibar, telephone, cable TV, ceiling fan, veranda with hammock; Internet access is available in 40 rooms; half the rooms have a sea view, the other half a river view; master suites also have hot tubs **FACILITIES AND SERVICES** Internet access in communal areas, bar, boat, nursery, kayaks, cinema, fishing equipment, parking, horseback riding, motorboats, convenience store, pool, jogging path, playground, tennis court, volleyball court, restaurant, meeting room, gym, game room, massage room, video room, beauty salon, sauna, travel agency, business center, currency exchange, 24-hour kitchen, recreational team for adults and children, guided walking tours, life guard for pool and beach, beach service, airport shuttle service, transportation to local attractions **CREDIT CARDS** Amex, Diners, MasterCard, Visa
Ponta de Apaga-Fogo, 60, Centro
TEL (73) 3575-8500 **FAX** 3575-1016 www.arraialresort.com.br

Atmosphera Pousada $$
The Atmosphera Pousada guesthouse offers a warm and welcoming atmosphere and sits on a nature reserve surrounded by lovely gardens only a few steps from the beach. The no-frills rooms can accommodate up to four people. First floor rooms have a partial sea view. **ACCOMMODATIONS** 14 rooms, each with air-conditioning, private safe, minibar, cable TV, veranda with hammock and chairs **FACILITIES AND SERVICES** bar, parking, pool, video room, airport shuttle service **CREDIT CARDS** MasterCard
Estrada do Mucugê, 735
TEL (73) 3575-1942, 3575-1954
www.atmospherapousada.com.br

Canto d'Alvorada Hotel Pousada $$
This charming hotel is a popular destination for foreigners and families. Rooms are simple and very cozy; the chalets are a bit more rustic. The ocean beach, dotted with natural pools, is ideal for children, and adult guests will enjoy a stroll in the gardens. The restaurant serves regional cuisine and Italian dishes. **ACCOMMODATIONS** 14 rooms and 7 chalets, each with air-conditioning, private safe, minibar, telephone, cable TV, veranda with hammock and garden view, ceiling fan **FACILITIES AND SERVICES** Internet access in communal areas, bar, kayaks, parking, pool, playground, beach volleyball, restaurant, game room, TV room, sauna, currency exchange, beach service, airport shuttle service **CREDIT CARDS** Amex, Diners, MasterCard, Visa
Estrada do Arraial d'Ajuda, 1993, Praia do Araçaípe
TEL and **FAX** (73) 3575-1218 www.cantodalvorada.com.br

Estação Santa Fé Hotel e Pousada $$$$
Décor is inspired by Mexican culture, and the suites are very pleasant, with large verandas overlooking the garden or pool. **ACCOMMODATIONS** 28 suites, each with air-conditioning, minibar, telephone, cable TV; one suite has a hot tub **FACILITIES AND SERVICES** Internet access in communal areas, bar, parking, convenience store, pool, volleyball court, meeting

PRICES	HOTELS (couple)	$ up to R$150	$$ from R$151 up to R$300	$$$ from R$301 up to R$500	$$$$ above R$500

room, game room, massage room, video room, beauty salon, sauna, recreational team for adults and children, airport shuttle service **CREDIT CARDS** Amex, MasterCard, Visa
Estrada do Arraial, 2020
TEL and **FAX** (73) 3575-2237   www.santafehotel.com.br

Hotel Pousada Beijo do Vento $$
Perched atop a cliff on Mucugê Beach and surrounded by greenery. All rooms have a view, though sometimes limited, of the sea. Children must be at least eight years old to stay here. **ACCOMMODATIONS** 10 rooms, each with air-conditioning, private safe, minibar, telephone, cable TV, private veranda with hammock **FACILITIES AND SERVICES** bar, parking, snack bar, pool, guided tours, beach service, airport shuttle service, transportation to local attractions **CREDIT CARDS** Amex, MasterCard, Visa
Travessa da Estrada do Mucugê, 730
TEL and **FAX** (73) 3575-1349   www.beijodovento.com.br

Hotel Pousada Caminho do Mar $$$
Caminho do Mar is located in the busiest part of town, in a popular shopping area. **ACCOMMODATIONS** 15 rooms, each with air-conditioning, private safe, minibar, TV, ceiling fan **FACILITIES AND SERVICES** bar, parking, pool with hot tub, travel agency, beach service, airport shuttle service **CREDIT CARDS** Amex, Diners, MasterCard, Visa
Estrada do Mucugê, 246
TEL and **FAX** (73) 3575-1099   www.caminhodomar.tur.br

Hotel Pousada Marambaia $$$
This quiet, charming guesthouse is within walking distance of the beach and the town center. Rooms are large and airy, with spacious verandas, and some can accommodate as many as four guests. **ACCOMMODATIONS** 33 suites, each with air-conditioning, minibar, telephone **FACILITIES AND SERVICES** bar, parking, pool, library, beach service **CREDIT CARDS** MasterCard, Visa
Alameda dos Flamboyants, 116
TEL and **FAX** (73) 3575-1275, 3575-1265
www.hotelmarambaia.com.br

Hotel Pousada Pitinga $$$$
Right next to the ocean and a mile from the town center. In the Cauim bar and restaurant, regional and contemporary dishes are served à la carte. **ACCOMMODATIONS** 10 suites and 11 rooms, each with air-conditioning, private safe, minibar, ambient music, veranda with hammock **FACILITIES AND SERVICES** Internet access in communal areas, bar, kayaks, parking, hot tub, pool, restaurant, meeting room, gym, game room, massage room, cable TV, video room, sauna, beach service, airport shuttle service **CREDIT CARDS** Amex, Diners, MasterCard, Visa
Praia de Pitinga, 1633
TEL (73) 3575-1067 **FAX** (73) 3575-3953, 3575-2007
www.pousadapitinga.com.br

Manacá Pousada Parque $$$
This simple guesthouse sits near the exit to the road that connects Arraial to Trancoso. Rooms have king-size beds, goose-feather pillows, veranda, and hammock with garden view. Guests can choose to have lunch delivered by the pool; the hotel restaurant serves regional and Italian cuisine. **ACCOMMODATIONS** 20 rooms, each with air-conditioning, private safe, minibar, telephone, cable TV **FACILITIES AND SERVICES** Internet access in communal areas, bar, parking, convenience store, jewelry store, pool, restaurant **CREDIT CARDS** Amex, Visa
Estrada Arraial–Trancoso, 500
TEL and **FAX** (73) 3575-1442   www.pousadamanaca.com.br

Paraíso do Morro $$$
Paraíso do Morro is located between Arraial and Praia de Mucugê. Rooms each have a veranda and panoramic sea view. **ACCOMMODATIONS** 13 rooms, air-conditioning, king-size beds, private safe, minibar, telephone, cable TV, veranda with hammock; three rooms also have two-person hot tubs **FACILITIES AND SERVICES** Internet access in communal areas, bar, parking, pool, laundry, airport shuttle service, transportation to local attractions, **CREDIT CARDS** not accepted
Estrada do Mucugê, 471, Centro
TEL and **FAX** (73) 3575-2423, 3575-3330
www.paraisodomorro.com.br

Privillage Hotel Pousada $$$
Rooms are well-equipped and nicely decorated but are not spacious. Some but not all can accommodate four people. The chalet has a kitchen and sitting room. **ACCOMMODATIONS** 15 rooms, 4 suites, and 1 chalet, each with Internet access, air-conditioning, private safe, minibar, telephone, TV; some rooms also have a veranda with hammock **FACILITIES AND SERVICES** kayaks, parking, pool, restaurant, beach service, transportation to local attractions **CREDIT CARDS** Amex, MasterCard, Visa
Estrada da Pitinga, 1800
TEL and **FAX** (73) 3575-1646   www.privillage.com.br

Saint-Tropez Praia Hotel $$$$
Rooms, chalets, and suites have a view of the garden. The hotel has ample recreational facilities, and children can play in a playroom under the watchful eye of a monitor. **ACCOMMODATIONS** 38 rooms, 12 suites, and 5 chalets, each with Internet access, air-conditioning, private safe, DVD, minibar, telephone, cable TV, veranda (hammocks in suites and chalets only); each master suite also has a hot tub **FACILITIES AND SERVICES** bar, horseback riding, parking, crafts and jewelry store, pool, playground, tennis court, volleyball court, restaurant, game room, massage room, sauna, video room, travel agency, currency exchange, recreational team for adults and children, valet parking, airport shuttle service, transportation to local attractions, and 24-hour kitchen and water aerobics classes (both December to February only) **CREDIT CARDS** Amex, Diners, MasterCard, Visa
Estrada da Pitinga, 100, Praia do Parracho
TEL (73) 3288-7700 **RESERVATIONS** 3288-7786 **FAX** 3288-7785, 3288-7794   www.saint-tropez.com.br

WHERE TO EAT

Boi nos Aires $
Boi nos Aires specializes in Argentinian cuts of beef prepared on a *parrilla* grill. The house specialty is beef *chorizo*, an Argentinian sirloin cut served with rice, beans, salad, herb sauce and bread. **CUISINE** Argentinian **CREDIT CARDS** Diners, MasterCard, Visa
Estrada do Mucugê, 200, Centro
TEL (73) 3575-2554. **OPEN** High season: daily, 5pm until the last customer leaves; low season: Mon – Sat, 5pm until the last customer leaves

Don Fabrizio $
Fabrizio Abbate serves customers personally, helping each select a meal from the ninety Mediterranean dishes offered. The seafood, pasta, and meat dishes are flavored with regional seasonings; we particularly recommend the spaghetti with seafood. The menu is printed in English. Fabrizio's wine list includes several international labels. **CUISINE** Mediterranean, seafood **CREDIT CARDS** Diners, MasterCard, Visa
Estrada do Mucugê, 402, Centro
TEL (73) 3575-1045 **RESERVATIONS** (73) 9979-4827 **OPEN** High season: daily, 1:30pm – midnight; low season: Wed – Mon, 4pm – 11:30pm

---

RESTAURANTS $ up to R$50 $$ from R$51 up to R$100 $$$ from R$101 up to R$150 $$$$ above R$150

HOTELS, RESTAURANTS AND SERVICES

Lotus Thai Mediterrasian Restaurante $
Lotus Thai's creations include *camarão fumegante* (smoking shrimp) and an ostrich fillet. Dishes are well-seasoned and accompanied by vegetables. There is an outdoor seating area covered by two tatami mats. CUISINE Mediterranean, Thai CREDIT CARDS Visa
Rua do Mucugê, 402-B
TEL (73) 3575-1106 OPEN High season: daily, 6pm – midnight; low season: Tue – Sun, 6pm – midnight

Manguti $
Manguti is best known for its signature gnocchi with beef fillet. They also serve pasta and fillet dishes with rice, beans, seasoned manioc flour, salad, and a potato side dish (french fries or mashed or sauted potatoes). According to tradition, eating gnocchi on the 29th of the month brings good fortune, and at Manguti they serve *nhoque da fortuna* gnocchi accompanied by live music and a free-dinner draw. CUISINE meat, pasta CREDIT CARDS not accepted
Rua do Mucugê, 99
TEL (73) 3575-2270 OPEN Daily, 1pm – midnight

Restaurante Paulo Pescador $
Two of the shrimp dishes, *bobó* (shrimp with creamy manioc) and stroganoff, are particularly tasty options. There is a long line at the door during the high season. CUISINE seafood, meats CREDIT CARDS not accepted
Praça São Braz, 116, Centro
TEL (73) 3575-1242 FAX 3575-2120 OPEN High season: daily, noon – 10pm; low season: Tue – Sun, noon – 10pm

Restaurante Portinha $
Enjoy home-made food cooked on a wood-burning stove and sold per kilo at the Portinha buffet. The buffet includes greens, vegetables, dishes from Minas Gerais, and Arab, Italian, and oriental food, all served hot and tasty. CUISINE varied CREDIT CARDS Diners, MasterCard, Visa
Rua do Campo, 1, Centro
TEL (73) 3575-1289 OPEN Daily, noon – 10pm

Restaurante São João $$
Located in the historic town center, it serves *bobó de camarão* (shrimp in manioc cream), mussels, *moqueca* (fish or shrimp in coconut milk), fish fillet in passion fruit sauce, and other dishes with authentic seasonings from Bahia. Dessert is included with your meal. CUISINE Bahian, seafood CREDIT CARDS not accepted
Praça Brigadeiro Eduardo Gomes, 41, Centro
TEL (73) 3575-1191 OPEN High season: daily, noon – midnight; low season: Mon – Sat, noon – midnight

Rosa dos Ventos $$
The extensive menu includes fish wrapped in a banana leaf, salads, pancakes, meat dishes (including suckling pig), and children's dishes. For dessert try walnut pancakes or *neguinho na camisola* (chocolate cake with almonds, chocolate topping, and ice cream). Some dishes, such as the lobster, chicken *caipira*, or young goat in one of several sauces should be ordered a day in advance. CUISINE varied, meats CREDIT CARDS not accepted
Alameda dos Flamboyants, 24, Centro
TEL (73) 3575-1271 OPEN High season: daily, 4pm – until the last customer leaves; low season: Thu – Tue, 5pm – midnight

SERVICES

Airport – Aeroporto Internacional de Porto Seguro
Estrada do Aeroporto, no #, Cidade Alta, Porto Seguro
TEL (73) 3288-1880, 3288-1877 OPEN Daily, 24 hours

Bus Station – Rodoviária (Porto Seguro)
Rodovia BR-367, Cidade Alta, Porto Seguro exit
TEL (73) 3288-1914

Diving Agency – Acqua Planet
Rua do Cais, 69, Centro, Porto Seguro
TEL (73) 3268-1499, 9993-1619, 9985-4996 OPEN Daily, 7am – 9pm.

Ferry-crossing – Rio Buranhém Navegação
Praça dos Pataxós, no #, Centro, Porto Seguro
TEL (73) 3288-2516 OPEN Daily, 24 hours

Tourist Information – Centro de Informações Turísticas de Porto Seguro
Praça Manoel Ribeiro Coelho, 10, Centro, Porto Seguro (near the ferry terminal)
TEL (73) 3268-1390 OPEN Mon – Sat, 9:30am – 11pm

Travel Agency – Arco-íris Turismo
Estrada do Mucugê, 199, Centro, Arraial
TEL (73) 3575-1672, 3575-2736 FAX (75) 3575-1580 OPEN Mon – Sat, 8am – 11pm; Sun, 4pm – 11pm

Travel Agency – Brasil 2000 Turismo
Estrada do Mucugê, 165, Centro, Arraial
TEL (73) 3575-1815, 3575-1627 OPEN High season: daily, 9am – midnight; low season: Mon – Sat, 9am – 10pm
www.brasil2000turismo.com.br

Travel Agency – Click Sul Bahia Viagens Turismo
Estrada do Mucugê, 96, room #8, Centro, Arraial
TEL (73) 3575-1294, 9122-3355 OPEN Mon – Sat, 9am – 5pm
www.clicksulbahia.com.br

Travel Agency – Paraíso Turismo
Estrada do Mucugê, 253, Centro, Arraial
TEL (73) 3575-2360, 3575-1844, 9198-6283 FAX 3575-1206 OPEN Mon – Fri, 9am – 6pm; Sat, 9am – noon; holidays, no fixed hours www.paraisoturismo.com.br

Travel Agency – Pataxó Turismo
Rua Oscar Oliveira, 4, Passarela do Álcool, Porto Seguro
TEL (73) 3288-1256, 3288-2507, 9979-5597 OPEN Mon – Sat, 8am – 7pm www.pataxoturismo.com.br

Travel Agency – Tropical Turismo
Estrada do Mucugê 125, store #3, Centro
TEL (73) 3575-2323 OPEN Mon – Sat, 9am – 8pm

Travel Agency, Car and Buggie Rental – Selvagem Adventure
Estrada da Balsa, 1446, Araçaípe
TEL (73) 3575-3031, 9985-4675 OPEN Daily, 9am – 7pm.
www.selvagemadventure.com.br

Baía Formosa – Rio Grande do Norte (see Pipa and Tibau do Sul)

Barra – Bahia

AREA CODE 74 POPULATION 46,958 DISTANCE Salvador 750 kilometers (466 miles) ACCESS BA-052 highway (Rodovia do Feijão) to Xique-Xique and then BA-160 to the ferry crossing to Barra. Another option is to take BR-242 near Ibotirama, followed by BA-161 BEST TIME TO VISIT June, for the traditional São João festivities

PRICES	HOTELS (couple)	$ up to R$150	$$ from R$151 up to R$300	$$$ from R$301 up to R$500	$$$$ above R$500

HOTELS, RESTAURANTS AND SERVICES

WHERE TO STAY

Barra Tropical Hotel $
Though simple, it has reasonably spacious rooms and an adequate breakfast. **ACCOMMODATIONS** 17 suites, air-conditioning, minibar, telephone, TV, ceiling fan **FACILITIES AND SERVICES** parking, video room **CREDIT CARDS** Visa
Alameda Plínio Mariano Guerreiro, no #
TEL (74) 3662-2699 **FAX** 3662-2315

SERVICES

Bus Station – Rodoviária
Praça Antônio Luís Camandaroba, no #, Centro
TEL (74) 3662-2131, 3662-2005

**Tourist Information –
Centro de Informações Turísticas**
Rua dos Mariani, no #, Centro
TEL (74) 3662-2307 **OPEN** Mon – Fri, 8am – noon and 2pm – 5pm; Holidays, 8am – noon and 2pm -10pm
www.barra.ba.gov.br

Barra de Cunhaú – Rio Grande do Norte (see Pipa)

Barra de Santo Antônio – Alagoas

AREA CODE 82 **POPULATION** 13,812 **DISTANCE** Maceió 44 kilometers (27 miles) **ACCESS** From Maceió, take Rodovia Litorânea (AL-101 highway) and then a ferryboat

WHERE TO STAY

Hotel Pousada Arco-Íris $$
This guesthouse has two floors; rooms on the upper floor have sea view. The restaurant serves both regional and international – mainly Swiss – dishes. **ACCOMMODATIONS** 12 rooms and 2 suites, air-conditioning, minibar, telephone, TV, veranda, ceiling fan **FACILITIES AND SERVICES** Internet access in communal areas, bikes and kayaks for rent, parking, pool, restaurant, games room, windsurfing, laundry **CREDIT CARDS** Amex, Diners, MasterCard, Visa
Rua 10, 6, Loteamento Tabuba
TEL (82) 3291-1250 **FAX** 3291-6000 www.tabuba.tk

WHERE TO EAT

Peixada da Rita $
On the banks of the Santo Antônio River, it has a lovely view and peaceful atmosphere that recalls the countryside. Everything is simple and homey. The handwritten menu offers fish dishes such as mackerel, amberjack, and *dourado*. Dona Rita uses coconut milk from the palms in her own garden. She also serves *galinha guisada ao molho pardo* (chicken in blood sauce) and crab. **CUISINE** fish and seafood **CREDIT CARDS** not accepted
Rua Pedro Cavalcanti, no #, Barra de Santo Antônio **OPEN** Daily, 8am – 7pm.

SERVICES

Bus Station – Rodoviária
Avenida Antônio Baltazar, no #
TEL (82) 3291-1166

Barra de São Miguel – Alagoas

AREA CODE 82 **POPULATION** 7,274 **DISTANCE** Maceió 34 kilometers (21 miles) **ACCESS** From Maceió, take Rodovia Litorânea (AL-101 highway) south

WHERE TO STAY

Brisamar Pousada $
This simple guesthouse stands just 50 meters (165 feet) from the sea. Five of the suites can accommodate up to 5 people each. **ACCOMMODATIONS** 17 suites, Internet access, air-conditioning, minibar, telephone, TV, ceiling fan **FACILITIES AND SERVICES** Internet access in communal areas, barbecue area, parking, pool, restaurant, games room **CREDIT CARDS** Diners, MasterCard
Rua Margarida Oiticica Lima, 38, Barra Mar
TEL and **FAX** (82) 3272-2030, 3272-2051
www.brisamarpousada.com.br

Pousada Dunas de Marapé $
Lunch is served on the other side of the Juquiá River in the Dunas de Marapé leisure complex, which contains, in addition to its restaurant, a craft shop and sport-fishing operation. Many guests spend the day in the complex, which is a free, five-minute ferry ride away from the rooms. The simple, cozy rooms can accommodate up to three people. **ACCOMMODATIONS** 12 rooms and 4 chalets, air-conditioning, minibar, telephone, TV, veranda with hammock **FACILITIES AND SERVICES** boats, parking, stores, restaurant, river, travel agency, currency exchange, 24-hour kitchen, recreational team for adults and children, guided walking tours, valet parking, lifeguard, beach service, shuttle service to airport and local attractions **CREDIT CARDS** Amex, Diners, MasterCard, Visa
Barra de Jequiá da Praia (45 kilometers, 28 miles, from Barra de São Miguel)
TEL (82) 3666-3349, 9308-2506 **FAX** 3272-1188
www.dunasdemarape.tur.br

Village Barra Hotel $$$
This is one of the best places to stay in Barra de São Miguel. There are 74 rooms (36 with a veranda) in a utilitarian building. Catamaran trips to Gunga beach and the mangroves, with trained guides, are among the attractions offered. **ACCOMMODATIONS** 74 rooms, air-conditioning, private safe, minibar, telephone, TV; veranda in luxury rooms **FACILITIES AND SERVICES** bar, parking, snack bar, pool, playground, soccer court, volleyball court, restaurant, convention room, games room, recreational team for children, catamaran trips, beach service, shuttle service to local attractions **CREDIT CARDS** Amex, Diners, MasterCard, Visa
Rua Senador Arnon de Melo, no #, Praia do Niquim
TEL and **FAX** (82) 3272-1000 www.villagebarrahotel.com.br

WHERE TO EAT

Bar e Restaurante do Tio $
Protected by a huge tree, the outdoor tables of this restaurant have a view of the quays where boats leave for Gunga beach. The menu includes fresh fish and seafood. The house specialty, *peixada* (fish stew), can be made to request with mackerel, amberjack or *dourado*. Also excellent is the seafood selection, which includes *peixada*, shrimp, *massunim* (a small mussel), *sururu* (shellfish) omelet, thickened sauce and rice. **CUISINE** fish and seafood, varied **CREDIT CARDS** not accepted
Rua Manoel Eleutério da Silva, no #, Praça São Pedro
TEL (82) 9381-7670 **OPEN** High season: daily, 9am – 5pm; low season: Tue – Sun, 9am – 4pm

Sauaçuhy $
This restaurant's name means "Monkey River" in Tupi-

RESTAURANTS | $ up to R$50 | $$ from R$51 up to R$100 | $$$ from R$101 up to R$150 | $$$$ above R$150

Guarani. Air-conditioned, it offers self-service per kilo or *rodízio* (all-you-can-eat). Lobster is prepared at the table, and there is also crispy shrimp, octopus, mussels, squid, and fish such as salmon. CUISINE fish and seafood, varied CREDIT CARDS Amex, Diners, MasterCard, Visa
AL-101 Sul, Km 21.3 (opposite Barra Mar gas station)
TEL (82) 3272-1248 OPEN Daily, 11am – 5pm

Barra Grande – Bahia

AREA CODE 73 DISTANCES Salvador 330 kilometers (205 miles; via ferryboat to Bom Despacho), Itacaré 60 kilometers (37 miles), Ubaitaba 66 kilometers (41 miles) ACCESS By boat, every hour from Camamu port (1.5 hours by regularly scheduled ferryboat or 30 minutes by chartered motorboat). By 4x4 vehicle, there are two options: from Itacaré, take the ferryboat across the Rio de Contas river (10 minutes) and then drive for around 50 kilometers (31 miles), or from Ubaitaba, take BR-030, a pot-holed stretch of road www.barragrande.net

WHERE TO STAY

Kiaroa Beach Resort $$$$
The eight bungalows have DVD players and private pools. The leisure area has a floodlit tennis court, a semi-Olympic pool, and a large pond. Scheduled shuttle service to the village is available. Children under fourteen are not allowed. ACCOMMODATIONS 16 rooms and 8 bungalows, air-conditioning, private safe, minibar, telephone, cable TV, private veranda with hammock, DVD and private pool in bungalows, Jacuzzi in 1 bungalow FACILITIES AND SERVICES Internet access in communal areas, bar, bicycles, parking, Jacuzzi, stores, tennis court, volleyball court, restaurant, gym, dry and steam sauna, travel agency, currency exchange, guided walking tours, landing strip, lifeguard, beach service, shuttle service to the village; 24-hour kitchen (high season only) CREDIT CARDS Amex, Diners, MasterCard, Visa
Praia da Bombaça, Loteamento da Costa, Área SD6 Quadra 3, Maraú
TEL (73) 3258-6215, 3258-6213 RESERVATIONS and FAX (71) 3272-1320 www.kiaroa.com.br

Pousada dos Tamarindos $$
One of the oldest and most charming guesthouses in Barra Grande. The Japanese-Brazilian owners give personalized service. Some rooms have futons ACCOMMODATIONS 18 suites, air-conditioning, minibar, telephone, TV, veranda with hammock FACILITIES AND SERVICES Internet access in communal areas, bar, parking, orchard, video room, restaurant (open only during holidays and high season); owners can recommend transportation to local attractions CREDIT CARDS not accepted
Rua José Melo Pirajá, 21, Praia de Barra Grande
TEL and FAX (73) 3258-6064
www.pousadadostamrindos.com.br

Pousada Fruta-Pão $
The guesthouse is 300 meters (0.2 mile) from the beach and is surrounded by breadfruit trees. ACCOMMODATIONS 7 rooms and 2 chalets, minibar, TV, private veranda, air-conditioning in 4 rooms, ceiling fan in chalets CREDIT CARDS Visa
Rua Maraú, no #, Centro
TEL and FAX (73) 3258-6083 www.barragrande.net

Pousada Lagoa do Cassange $$
This guesthouse sits on a narrow strip of land between the sea and Cassange Lagoon. The rooms are all equipped. It's rather far from the center of Barra Grande, but a shuttle runs to town at scheduled times. ACCOMMODATIONS 15 chalets, CD player, air-conditioning, minibar, hammock, telephone, ceiling fan FACILITIES AND SERVICES Internet access in communal areas, bar, boats, kayaks, parking, fishing lake, motorboat, stores, volleyball court, restaurant, reading room, video room, walking trails, travel agency, guided walking tours, beach service, shuttle service to airport and local attractions CREDIT CARDS Diners, MasterCard, Visa
Praia do Cassange, no #, Península de Maraú
TEL and FAX (73) 3255-2348 RESERVATIONS 3258-2166, 3258-2192 www.maris.com.br

Pousada Ponta do Mutá $$
This guesthouse is on the beachfront. It offers chalets and rooms, and the latter, while smaller, have the advantage of a sea view. The rooms are quite small, but comfortable, and the guesthouse's location makes for easy access to the village restaurants. ACCOMMODATIONS 8 suites and 2 chalets, air-conditioning, private safe, minibar, hairdryer, telephone, TV, veranda with hammock, ceiling fan FACILITIES AND SERVICES bar, bicycles, kayaks, parking, snack bar, volleyball court, outdoor massage room, beach volleyball, beach service CREDIT CARDS Visa
Rua do Anjo, no #, Ponta do Mutá
TEL and FAX (73) 3258-6028, 3258-6137, 3258-6202 www.pousadapontadomuta.com.br

Pousada Taipu de Fora $$
This pretty guesthouse offers comfortable, well-appointed rooms. It's on a *dendê* and coconut-palm plantation. The natural pools at Taipus de Fora beach are the main attraction here. The fact that Barra Grande village is so far away can be inconvenient, despite the availability of scheduled shuttle service. ACCOMMODATIONS 28 suites (2 adjoining), air-conditioning, minibar, telephone, TV, ceiling fan, veranda with hammock FACILITIES AND SERVICES Internet access in communal areas, bar, bicycles, kayaks, parking, fishing lake, stores, volleyball court, restaurant, river, games room, massage room, video room, walking trails, recreational team for adults and children, guided walking tours, heliport, landing strip, beach service CARDS Diners, MasterCard, Visa
Praia de Taipus de Fora, Península de Maraú
TEL (73) 3258-6278 RESERVATIONS 3258-6278, 3255-2276 FAX 3531-3376 www.taipudefora.com.br

WHERE TO EAT

Bar do Francês $
This simple bar sits in front of the popular natural pools of Taipus de Fora. It serves fish and seafood dishes. These comestibles are prepared with the freshest of ingredients. Suggestions include fried *agulhinha* fish and the large shrimp known as *camarão-pistola*. The fish *moqueca* (fish stew with coconut milk and *dendê* palm oil) serves two. CUISINE fish and seafood CREDIT CARDS Visa
Praia Bela, no #, Taipus de Fora
TEL (73) 3258-9036 OPEN High season: daily, 7am – midnight; low season: daily, 7am – 5pm

Café Latino $
Pasta and grilled entrees are the highlights here, as well as 18 types of coffee, which are available either piping hot or iced. CUISINE Italian, bar food CREDIT CARDS not accepted
Rua Doutor Chiquinho, 9, Centro
TEL (73) 3258-6188 OPEN Wed – Mon, and holidays, 6pm – until the last customer leaves; closed May – Jun

Matataúba $
Pizzas, which are the house specialty, are baked in an oven

| PRICES | HOTELS (couple) | $ up to R$150 | $$ from R$151 up to R$300 | $$$ from R$301 up to R$500 | $$$$ above R$500 |

beside the restaurant and are intended to be eaten with the hands; they're served up on wooden boards. Herbs from the garden go into the dishes. CUISINE Italian; pizza CREDIT CARDS not accepted
Rio Carapitangui, Ilha do Campinho, Barra Grande
TEL (73) 3258-6265 OPEN High season: daily, noon – 10pm; low season: advance reservations only

Restaurante do Jorge $
The tables and chairs are very rustic, but they are in pleasant surroundings, with a view of Goió Island. Suggestions include sumptuous grilled lobster (serves two) and the many different *moquecas* – stews made with octopus, lobster, and several varieties of crab or fish. While waiting for your meal, take the opportunity to visit tiny Sapinho Island. CUISINE Bahian, fish and seafood CREDIT CARDS not accepted
Ilha do Sapinho, Península de Maraú (access by boat from Barra Grande or Camamu quays)
TEL (73) 8107-7312 RESERVATIONS 3258-2309 OPEN Daily, 10am – 6pm

Restaurante e Bar das Meninas $
The main focus of this restaurant is regional food, as well as Mediterranean, with fresh fish and seafood. From the house specialties, try grilled seafood (serves two). Tatiana, one of the owners, speaks English, Italian, and French. CUISINE fish and seafood; regional. CARDS Amex, Visa
Loteamento Praia Bela de Taipus, Quadra U8, Lotes #21 and 22
TEL (73) 3258-9035 OPEN Daily, 8am – 6pm

Tubarão $
This restaurant, which is inside the guesthouse of the same name, faces the sea from a vantage point near the quays. The menu includes grilled fish, served with rice, salad, seasoned manioc flour, and beans (serves two); and octopus or shrimp and lobster risotto (both serve three). Try the delicious passion fruit juice made with fruit from the restaurant's own garden. CUISINE fish and seafood CREDIT CARDS Visa
Rua Vasco Neto, 92, Península de Maraú
TEL (73) 3258-6006 OPEN High season: daily, 8am – 10pm; low season: 8am – 7pm

Uai Bahia $
The owners are from Minas Gerais and they have brought a little of their cuisine to Barra Grande. The restaurant serves dishes such as beef jerky in pumpkin with cream cheese and herbs and *feijão-tropeiro* (beans with spicy sausage and manioc flour) served with rice, collard greens, pork crackling, pork ribs or pork loin. CUISINE Minas Gerais, Japanese, fish and seafood CREDIT CARDS Diners, MasterCard, Visa
Rua Desembargador Olny Silva, no #
TEL (73) 3258-6194 RESERVATIONS 3258-6336 OPEN High season: daily, noon – midnight; low season: Mon – Sat, 1pm – 10pm

SERVICES

Department of Tourism – Secretaria de Turismo
Avenida José Melo Pirajá, no #, Barra Grande
TEL (73) 3258-6167

Travel Agency – Camamu Adventure
Avenida Beira-Mar, no #, Camamu
TEL (73) 3255-2138, 3258-6236 OPEN Daily, 7am – 6pm
Boat rental, crossing from Camamu to Barra Grande and back
www.camamuadventure.com.br

Travel Agency – Natur e Mar Turismo
Avenida Beira-Mar, 8, Camamu
TEL (73) 3255-2343, 3258-6361 OPEN Mon – Fri, 8am – 6pm; Sat, 8am – 5pm
Boat rental, crossing from Camamu to Barra Grande and back, motorboat and 4x4 trips
www.naturemar.tur.br

Barreirinhas – Maranhão

AREA CODE 98 POPULATION 44,869 DISTANCES São Luís 265 kilometers (165 miles), Parnaíba 441 kilometers (274 miles), Teresina 593 kilometers (368 miles) ACCESS From São Luís, by Rodovia Translitorânea (MA-402 highway). By single or twin engine plane, about 50 minutes BEST TIME TO VISIT March to July, when the lakes are full, or on June 13 and 24, for the peak days of the São João festivals
www.barreirinhas.ma.gov.br

WHERE TO STAY

Hotel Pousada do Buriti $$
Rooms are fairly well equipped and spacious, with veranda and hammock, and breakfast is delicious. The small pool stays open at night, and the restaurant serves both guests and non-guests. ACCOMMODATIONS 29 rooms, air-conditioning, minibar, telephone, TV FACILITIES AND SERVICES Internet access in communal areas, bar, convenience store, pool, playground, restaurant, river, convention room, games room CREDIT CARDS Diners, MasterCard, Visa
Rua Inácio Lins, no #, Centro
TEL and FAX (98) 3349-1338 www.pousadadoburiti.com.br

Porto Preguiças Resort $$$
Possibly the most comfortable and charming hotel in Barreirinhas. The chalets have spacious suites, with top quality mattresses and bed linen. The huge pool has a sand bottom and is full of river water. ACCOMMODATIONS 30 suites, air-conditioning, minibar, cable TV, ceiling fan FACILITIES AND SERVICES Internet access in communal areas, wine cellar, bar, nursery, bicycles, parking, stores, natural pool, playground, volleyball court, restaurant, magazine reading area, river, games room, sauna, currency exchange, organized trips, airport shuttle CREDIT CARDS Diners, MasterCard, Visa
Estrada do Carnaubal, no #, right bank of the Preguiças River (2 kilometers of dirt road)
TEL (98) 3349-1220 RESERVATIONS 3349-1912 FAX 3349-0620
www.portopreguicas.com.br

Rancho do Buna $
This guesthouse is in Atins, near a fishing village, beach and dunes, in a lovely area. The no-frills rooms are comfortable enough, having orthopedic mattresses and good bed linens. The cold showers could be a problem for some guests, though. Buna, the owner, has a Toyota and boat for local guided trips (*see Where to Eat*). ACCOMMODATIONS 10 chalets, ceiling fan FACILITIES AND SERVICES bar, boat, pool, restaurant, river, walking trails, kayaks, horses, guided walking tours, motorboat, trimaran CREDIT CARDS MasterCard
Praia de Atins, 10
TEL (98) 9616-9646, 9132-7677
www.ranchodoslencois.multiply.com

WHERE TO EAT

Barlavento $
A good option for an informal, homemade lunch at a fixed,

RESTAURANTS $ up to R$50 $$ from R$51 up to R$100 $$$ from R$101 up to R$150 $$$$ above R$150

affordable price. **CUISINE** homemade, varied **CREDIT CARDS** MasterCard
Avenida Beira-Rio, no #, Centro
TEL (98) 3349-0627 **OPEN** Daily, 11am – until the last customer leaves

Paturi $

This is Caburé's best restaurant. The chef's specialty dish is a two-person feast of *moqueca de arraia* (stew of ray with coconut milk and *dendê* palm oil) served with rice and beans, seasoned manioc flour and pickled salad. Ask to try his wife Suzana's beans; almost fat-free and cooked only in the liquid from the vegetables that accompany them, they are simply delicious. **CUISINE** fish and seafood, regional **CREDIT CARDS** MasterCard
Praia do Caburé, no #
TEL (98) 9608-3032, 9126-8602, 8129-7430
RESERVATIONS 3246-7253 **OPEN** Daily, 6am – until the last customer leaves

Restaurante do Rancho do Buna $

Offering the same friendly service as the guesthouse, this restaurant serves sumptuous, delicious dishes, with an emphasis on fresh fish. The rice with *tarioba* (a kind of seafood) is the house specialty. Pizzas and pasta are also available. **CUISINE** fish and seafood, varied **CREDIT CARDS** not accepted
Praia de Atins, 10
TEL (98) 9616-9646, 9132-7677 **OPEN** Daily, 7am – 10pm

Terraço do Preguiças $

This restaurant serves simply cooked fish and seafood as well as more elaborate dishes such as fish fillet in mango sauce. **CUISINE** fish, seafood and meats **CREDIT CARDS** MasterCard, Visa
Avenida Beira-Rio, 307-A, Centro
TEL (98) 3349-0422 **OPEN** Daily, 11am – until the last customer leaves

SERVICES

Travel Agency – Agência de Turismo Eco-Dunas
Rua Inácio Lins, 164, Centro
TEL (98) 3349-0545 **OPEN** Daily, 7am – 7pm
www.ecodunas.com.br

Travel Agency – Agência de Turismo Rota das Trilhas
Avenida Joaquim Soeiro de Carvalho, 682-A, Centro
TEL (98) 3349-0372, 9116-0028 **OPEN** Daily, 7:30am – 6pm

Department of Tourism – Secretaria de Turismo
Avenida da Rodoviária, no #, Boa Fé
OPEN Mon – Fri, 8am – noon and 2pm – 6pm

Travel Agency – Tropical Adventure
Rua Anacleto de Carvalho, 260, Cruzeiro (above the boat gas station)
TEL (98) 3349-1987
www.tropical-adventure-expedicoes.com

Beberibe – Ceará

AREA CODE 85 **POPULATION** 45,815 **DISTANCE** Fortaleza 83 kilometers (52 miles) **ACCESS** From Fortaleza (Avenida Washington Soares), take the CE-040 highway to Cascavel, then continue east on that route for 20 kilometers (12 miles)

WHERE TO STAY

Bouganville $$

The rooms are well equipped and comfortable, with large verandas from which guests can admire the sunset. The charming snooker bar offers a good way to relax at the end of a busy day. **ACCOMMODATIONS** 32 rooms, Internet access, air-conditioning, private safe, minibar, telephone, cable TV **FACILITIES AND SERVICES** Internet access in communal areas, wine cellar, bar, soccer field, daycare center, parking, natural pool, playground, volleyball court, restaurant, convention room, gym, sauna, dune-buggy trips, shuttle service to airport and local attractions **CREDIT CARDS** Diners, MasterCard, Visa
Avenida A, Lotes #3 and 4, Quadra 20, Praia das Fontes
TEL and **FAX** (85) 3327-3037 www.hotelbouganville.com.br

Hotel Parque das Fontes $$

This hotel faces Praia das Fontes and is ideal for families with children, thanks to its water park with pools and three waterslides included in the daily rates. The simple rooms and overlook either the garden or water park. **ACOMMODATIONS** 211 rooms, air-conditioning, private safe, minibar, telephone, veranda with hammock **FACILITIES AND SERVICES** Internet access in communal areas, bar, parking, water park, children's pool, semi-Olympic pool, pool for playing *biribol* (an aquatic version of volleyball), playground, restaurant, convention room, games room, sauna, currency exchange, laundry, beach service **CREDIT CARDS** Amex, Diners, MasterCard, Visa
Avenida Coronel Antônio Teixeira Filho, no #, Praia das Fontes
TEL (85) 3327-3100 **FAX** 3327-3144
www.hotelparquedasfontes.com.br

Oásis Atlântico Praia das Fontes $$$

Here, at the only hotel on Ceará's east coast to adopt an all-inclusive system, food, domestic beverages, and sports activities are included in the daily rates. The hotel offers a wealth of leisure facilities. Entry to the neighboring water park in Hotel Parque das Fontes is free for guests here. **ACCOMMODATIONS** 148 chalets, 68 rooms, 34 suites, air-conditioning, private safe, minibar, telephone, cable TV **FACILITIES AND SERVICES** Internet access in communal areas, soccer field, nightclub, water sports, gym, fishing lake, convenience store, pool, playground, soccer court, squash court, tennis court, volleyball court, restaurant, convention room, sauna, dance lessons, business center, 24-hour kitchen, recreation team for adults and children, trips to the water park, treasure hunt, valet parking, beach service **CREDIT CARDS** Amex, Diners, MasterCard, Visa
Avenida Coronel Antônio Teixeira Filho, 3, Praia das Fontes
TEL (85) 3327-3000, 3327-3043 **RESERVATIONS** and **FAX** 4009-2900 www.hoteloasispraiadasfontes.com.br

WHERE TO EAT

Barraca do Sandro $$

This restaurant has a privileged location opposite the sailing-raft port. Owner Sandro has become famous for his grilled seafood: lobster served with rice and salad is the most popular dish. Dressed crab and fish goujons (snook, saw fish, or *dourado* fish) are other suggestions. **CUISINE** meats, fish and seafood **CREDIT CARDS** Amex, Diners, MasterCard, Visa
Avenida Beira-Mar, no #, Praia do Morro Branco
TEL (85) 3338-6484 **RESERVATIONS** 9957-1062 **OPEN** High season: daily, 8:30am – until the last customer leaves; low season: daily, 8:30am – 7pm

PRICES	HOTELS (couple)	$ up to R$150	$$ from R$151 up to R$300	$$$ from R$301 up to R$500	$$$$ above R$500

SERVICES

Department of Tourism – Secretaria de Turismo
Rua Maria Calado, no #, Centro
TEL (85) 3338-2333, 3338-2422, 3338-2420 OPEN Mon – Fri, 7:30am – 1:30pm www.beberibe.ce.gov.br

Bezerros – Pernambuco

AREA CODE 81 POPULATION 60,652 DISTANCE Recife 107 kilometers (66 miles) ACCESS From Recife, take the BR-232 highway

WHERE TO STAY

Brisa da Serra $
This is an establishment perfectly suited to the needs of Bezerros. This hotel offers attentive staff, cleanliness and a good pool. The restaurant is open to non-guests. ACCOMMODATIONS 25 rooms, air-conditioning, minibar, telephone, TV FACILITIES AND SERVICES Internet access in communal areas, parking, store, pool, restaurant CREDIT CARDS MasterCard, Visa
Avenida Major Aprígio da Fonseca, no #, BR-232, Km 102
TEL and FAX (81) 3728-1232

WHERE TO EAT

Churrascaria Rancho da Pamonha $
Originally specializing in corn-based foods, this restaurant's strong points are now meats and regional cuisine, as well as an innovative menu based on the palm heart, or *palma* (also called Indian Fig, or *opuntia*). This fruit is grown with the help of agronomist Paulo Suassuna, and served in a wide variety of sweet and savory dishes. CUISINE meats, regional CREDIT CARDS MasterCard
BR-232, Km 103 (near the Bezerros exit, towards Caruaru–Recife)
TEL (81) 3728-5498, 8857-0911 OPEN Daily, 7am – 6pm
www.ranchodapamonha.com

Cabaceiras – Paraíba

AREA CODE 83 POPULATION 4,259 DISTANCES João Pessoa 193 kilometers (120 miles), Campina Grande 69 kilometers (43 miles) ACCESS From João Pessoa, take the BR-230 highway to Campina Grande; from there, take the PB-148 toward Queimadas

WHERE TO STAY

Hotel Fazenda Pai Mateus $
This hotel, in the *sertão* of Paraíba, used to be a goat farm. So pleasant are its rooms, with king-size beds and veranda, that you won't even notice that there is neither telephone nor TV. On weekends and holidays they admit day guests, who disturb the peace and quiet a little. ACCOMMODATIONS 26 rooms, air-conditioning, minibar, veranda with hammock, ceiling fan FACILITIES AND SERVICES wine cellar, bar, bicycles, soccer field, horses, cart, parking, fishing lake and equipment, rappel, store, pool, hammocks, restaurant, convention room, video room, sauna, walking trails, 24-hour kitchen, guided walking tours, laundry, valet parking CREDIT CARDS Diners, MasterCard, Visa
Sítio Tapera, no #, Zona Rural (access by BR-412 highway to Boa Vista; turn left at the Ipiranga gas station and follow the dirt road for 21 kilometers, 13 miles)
TEL and FAX (83) 3356-1250 www.paimateus.com.br

Cabedelo – Paraíba (see João Pessoa)

Cabo de Santo Agostinho – Pernambuco

AREA CODE 81 POPULATION 169,229 DISTANCE Recife 37 kilometers (23 miles) ACCESS BR-101 and PE-60 highways
www.cabo.pe.gov.br

WHERE TO EAT

Bar do Artur $$
The restaurant steals the scene on Calhetas beach. Its tables are always full, and the seafood it serves is in high demand (though its meat dishes are nothing to scoff at). Fish stew or tile-cooked lobster fillet are excellent choices. CUISINE meats, fish, and seafood CREDIT CARDS Amex, Diners, MasterCard, Visa
Rua dos Carneiros, 17, Praia de Calhetas
TEL (81) 3522-6382 RESERVATIONS 3512-0940 OPEN Daily, 8am – 6pm

SERVICES

Department of Tourism – Secretaria de Turismo
Avenida Nossa Senhora do Bom Conselho, 852, Ponte dos Cardalhos
TEL (81) 3522-2755, 3522-2736 OPEN Mon – Fri, 8am – 5pm
www.cabo.pe.gov.br

Cachoeira – Bahia

AREA CODE 75 POPULATION 31,748 DISTANCES Salvador 116 kilometers (72 miles), São Félix 400 meters (0.2 mile), Santo Amaro da Purificação 54 kilometers (34 miles) ACCESS From Salvador, take the BR-234 highway to the access ramp to BA-420 at Km 52 (watch carefully, as vegetation conceals the signposts). BR-101 has two exits that lead into town: one runs 12 kilometers (7 miles) north–south from the Conceição de Feira intersection; the other starts at the Muritiba intersection

WHERE TO STAY

Hotel Fazenda Villa Rial $$
This farm has a nice, rural location between Cachoeira and Santo Amaro. Full board is included, and there are plenty of leisure options. The rather small and stuffy rooms are a weak point. Ask for the special suites, which have air-conditioning and TV. ACCOMMODATIONS 25 bungalows (with 4 or 5 rooms each), 11 suites, and 5 private rooms; minibar, telephone, veranda; ceiling fan, air-conditioning and TV on special suites FACILITIES AND SERVICES bar, waterfall, soccer field, horses, cart, parking, fishing lake and equipment, snack bar, store, pool, playground, orchard, tennis court, volleyball court, restaurant, river, games room, massage room, video room, walking trails, guided walking tours, recreational team for children (for large groups or by previous arrangement) CREDIT CARDS Amex, Diners, MasterCard, Visa
Ladeira do Padre Inácio, no #, Povoado da Murutuba
TEL and FAX (75) 3602-4600 www.villarial.com.br

Pousada do Convento $
Part of a Carmelite convent complex, this 18th-century convent has been restored and turned into a guesthouse. That attention to detail makes up for the simplicity – which verges on discomfort – of the rooms. Rooms on the ground

---

RESTAURANTS $ up to R$50 $$ from R$51 up to R$100 $$$ from R$101 up to R$150 $$$$ above R$150

floor have twin beds. Those on the upper floor have air-conditioning and are better bargains. For food options here, see *Where to Eat*, below. ACCOMMODATIONS 26 suites; air-conditioning, minibar, intercom and TV on special suites, ceiling fan on ground-floor suites FACILITIES AND SERVICES pool, playground, restaurant CREDIT CARDS Diners, MasterCard, Visa
Praça da Aclamação, no #, Centro
TEL and FAX (75) 3425-1716

WHERE TO EAT

A Confraria $
The Pousada do Convento's restaurant serves local dishes, such as *maniçoba* (cassava leaves with pork and sausage) and *xinxim de galinha* (well-seasoned chicken pieces, with shrimp, *dendê* oil, peanuts and cashew nuts) as well as fresh-caught fish. For dessert, try their homemade sweets and regional fruit. CUISINE regional, varied CREDIT CARDS Diners, MasterCard, Visa
Praça da Aclamação, no #, Centro
TEL (75) 3425-1716 OPEN Daily, 11am – 10pm

SERVICES

Tourist Information – Centro de Informações Turísticas
Rua Ana Nery, 7, Centro
TEL (75) 3425-1390, 3425-5225 (City Hall) OPEN Mon – Sun, 8am – 5pm

Caicó – Rio Grande do Norte

AREA CODE 84 POPULATION 60,988 DISTANCES Natal 269 kilometers (167 miles), Acari 73 kilometers (45 miles), Currais Novos 99 kilometers (62 miles) ACCESS From Natal, take the BR-304 to Macaíba, take the BR-226 turnoff toward Currais Novos. Then take BR-427 to Acari, and RN-288 to Caicó BEST TIME TO VISIT July, for the festivities in honor of the town's patron saint

WHERE TO STAY

Regente $
At this well-located hotel, the best rooms are on the upper floors. ACCOMMODATIONS 25 rooms and 6 suites, air-conditioning, TV, minibar and telephone in some rooms FACILITIES AND SERVICES parking, restaurant CREDIT CARDS Diners, MasterCard, Visa
Rua Doutor Pires Ferreira, 319, Centro
TEL and FAX (84) 3417-1333, 3417-1484

WHERE TO EAT

Galeteria Brilhante $
This reasonable eatery offers self-service with a cornucopia of regional dishes, salads, good juices, and low prices. Among the specialties are *mungunzá* (corn and milk pudding), locally grown red rice, fish stew, roasted goat, barbecue, three kinds of beans, seasoned manioc flour, *cuscuz* (tapioca and coconut cake), and typical desserts. CUISINE regional; varied CREDIT CARDS not accepted
Rua Joel Damasceno, 833, Centro
TEL (84) 3417-3866 OPEN Tue – Sun, 11am – 2:30pm and 5:30pm – until the last customer leaves

SERVICES

Bus Station – Rodoviária
Rua Renato Dantas, no #, Centro
TEL (84) 3421-2393, 3421-1256

Camamu – Bahia (see Barra Grande)

Camocim – Ceará

AREA CODE 88 POPULATION 58,213 DISTANCES Fortaleza 370 kilometers (230 miles), Jericoacoara 87 kilometers (54 miles), Sobral 124 kilometers (77 miles), Parnaíba 126 kilometers (78 miles) ACCESS From Fortaleza, BR-222 highway to Sobral, followed by CE-362 via Massapê. Another option is to take the Rodovia Estruturante (CE-085 highway) to Itapipoca, and then BR-402. You can reach Camocim from Jericoacoara by dune buggy, driving on the beach at low tide (a 2-hour trip that involves 3 ferry crossings) BEST TIME TO VISIT From January to May, for the dune lakes and mild weather. From July to December, for hot weather
www.camocim.ce.gov.br

WHERE TO STAY

Boa Vista Resort & Conference Centre $$$
Camocim's only resort has spacious rooms decorated with regional motifs, and *tucum* (a kind of sisal) hammocks on their verandas. There are three themed suites: tropical, African, and honeymoon. The horseshoe-shaped building has a large pool and bar in its center. ACCOMMODATIONS 120 rooms and 3 suites, air-conditioning, queen- or king-size beds, private safe, minibar, telephone, hairdryer, cable TV, veranda FACILITIES AND SERVICES Internet access in communal areas, bar, bicycles, nightclub, parking, kids club, pool, playground, soccer court, volleyball court, restaurant, river, convention room, gym, games room, beauty parlor, sauna, travel agency, recreational team for adults and children, guided walking tours, regular shuttle service to and from Fortaleza CREDIT CARDS Amex, Diners, MasterCard, Visa
Avenida Beira-Mar, no #, Praia das Barreiras (2 kilometers, 1.2 miles, from the center)
TEL (88) 3621-9888 FAX 3621-9889
www.boavistaresort.com.br

Pousada Verde Folha $
A very simple guesthouse, with chalets dotted among fruit trees and hammocks. The cold showers are not a big problem. See also *Where to Eat*. ACCOMMODATIONS 2 chalets with air-conditioning, 3 rooms with ceiling fan FACILITIES AND SERVICES kayaks, restaurant CREDIT CARDS not accepted
Praia de Tatajuba, no # (20 kilometers, 12 miles, from the center)
TEL (88) 3621-0950, 9962-8332 RESERVATIONS 9901-3754

WHERE TO EAT

El Mirador $
The most popular fish dish is cosmopolitan fillet à meunière, which is made with snook or porgy and comes with capers and rice. CUISINE fish and meats CREDIT CARDS Diners, MasterCard
Avenida Beira-Mar, no #, Praia das Barreiras (2.5 kilometers, 1.5 miles, from the center)
TEL (88) 3621-6011 OPEN Tue – Sun, 9am – until the last customer leaves

Fortim $
Don't be misled by the simplicity, the fried fish is nice and crispy, and the ingredients are always fresh. CUISINE homemade fish and seafood CREDIT CARDS not accepted
Avenida Beira-Mar, no #, São Pedro
TEL (88) 3621-1719 OPEN Daily, 10am – 11pm

PRICES	HOTELS (couple)	$ up to R$150	$$ from R$151 up to R$300	$$$ from R$301 up to R$500	$$$$ above R$500

Kiosks at Lagoa da Torta $$
Four *barracas* with a stunning view. Dishes such as grilled snook are simple and delicious. CUISINE fish and seafood CREDIT CARDS not accepted
Lagoa da Torta, Praia de Tatajuba
OPEN No fixed open hours, but some owners live in their kiosks

Leste Mar $
Our recommendation: fried mackerel with rice, beans, pasta, seasoned manioc flour and salad. Everything is simple but tasty. CUISINE homemade fish and seafood CREDIT CARDS not accepted
Praia de Bitupitá, no #
TEL (88) 3623-3126 OPEN Daily, 10am – 8pm

Restaurante da Pousada Verde Folha $
The food needs to be ordered at least one hour ahead. Generous portions of fish – porgy, snapper, or snook – please the hungriest patron. CUISINE fish and seafood CREDIT CARDS not accepted
Praia de Tatajuba, no # (20 kilometers, 12 miles, from the center)
TEL (88) 9962-8332 OPEN Daily, 10am –10pm

SERVICES

Bus Station – Rodoviária
Praça Sinhá Trévia, no #, Centro
TEL (88) 3621-0028 OPEN Daily, 6am – 10pm

Travel Agency – Jegue Tur
Rua Engenheiro Privat, 1927, Centro
TEL (88) 3621-7023 OPEN High season: Mon – Sat, 8am – 10pm; Sun, 8am – noon; low season: Mon – Sat, 8am – 6pm

Travel Agency – Koala Turismo
Avenida Beira-Mar, 1033, Esplanada do Porto
TEL (85) 8838-4115 OPEN Mon – Fri, 8am – 6 pm
www.koalapasseios.com.br

Campina Grande – Paraíba

AREA CODE 83 POPULATION 376,132 DISTANCE João Pessoa 125 kilometers (78 miles) ACCESS From João Pessoa, the BR-232 highway (after Sapé, the two-lane road is in poor condition, pot-holed and lacking signage up to Ingá)

WHERE TO STAY

Hotel Serrano $
The friendly, efficient service is the strong point. ACCOMMODATIONS 59 rooms, air-conditioning, private safe, minibar, telephone; Internet access in 8 rooms, cable TV in 10 rooms FACILITIES AND SERVICES Internet access in communal areas, bar, parking, pool, restaurant, convention room, games room, 24-hour kitchen, laundry, valet parking CREDIT CARDS Amex, Diners, MasterCard, Visa
Rua Tavares Cavalcanti, 27, Centro
TEL (83) 3341-3131 RESERVATIONS and FAX 3321-0635
www.hotelserranopb.com.br

Hotel Village $
The spacious, architecturally well-designed buildings that comprise Village are very welcoming. Good business and leisure facilities. ACCOMMODATIONS 60 rooms and 3 suites, Internet access, air-conditioning, private safe, minibar, telephone, cable TV FACILITIES AND SERVICES Internet access in communal areas, wine cellar, bar, parking, convenience store, pool, restaurant, convention room, gym, games room, business center, valet parking, airport shuttle CREDIT CARDS Amex, Diners, MasterCard, Visa
Rua Otacílio Nepomuceno, 1285, Catolé
TEL (83) 3310-8000 RESERVATIONS 3310-8001 FAX 3310-8002
www.hoteisvillage.com.br

WHERE TO EAT

Manoel da Carne-de-Sol $
The traditional but always-tasty sun-dried beef is the best option here. The atmosphere is rather cafeteria-like. CUISINE Brazilian, meats, regional CREDIT CARDS Diners, MasterCard, Visa
Rua Félix Araújo, 263, Centro
TEL (83) 3221-2877 OPEN Daily, 11am – until the last customer leaves

Tábua de Carne $
Portions are very generous – one main is enough for two people. The meat is barbecue grilled and served with boiled manioc, lima beans, seasoned manioc flour and pickled salad. CUISINE meats, regional CREDIT CARDS Amex, Diners, MasterCard, Visa
Avenida Manoel Tavares, 1040, Alto Branco
TEL (83) 3341-1008, 3341-1647 OPEN Mon – Sat, 11am – 10pm; Sun, 11am – 4pm

SERVICES

Bus Station – Terminal Rodoviário
Rua Eutécia Ribeiro, no #, Catolé
TEL (83) 3337-3001, 3337-3028 OPEN Daily, 6am – 10pm

Department of Tourism – Secretaria de Turismo
Rua 13 de Maio, 329, Centro
TEL (83) 3310-6100, 3310-6103 OPEN Mon – Fri, noon – 7pm
Tourist information: www.pcmg.pb.gov.br

Canavieiras – Bahia

AREA CODE 73 POPULATION 36,765 DISTANCES Salvador 560 kilometers (348 miles), Ilhéus 110 kilometers (68 miles) ACCESS From Ilhéus, take the BA-001 highway BEST TIME TO VISIT From October to March, for deep-sea fishing

WHERE TO STAY

Canes Porto Mar $$
Rooms can accommodate up to three people, and a single two-roomed suite for six is available. Two rooms are equipped for the disabled, with wide doors and specially designed bathrooms. ACCOMMODATIONS 46 rooms and 1 two-roomed suite; air-conditioning, minibar, telephone, TV FACILITIES AND SERVICES bar, parking, pool, playground CREDIT CARDS Diners, MasterCard, Visa
Avenida Beira-Mar, 601/631, Praia da Costa, Ilha de Atalaia, 2 kilometers (1.2 miles) from the center
TEL (73) 3284-1072 FAX 3284-4994
www.canesportomar.com.br

WHERE TO EAT

Cantinho da Zezé $
Dishes are simple (as is the ambience) but tasty and made from fresh ingredients. Seafood is the highlight of the menu. Top vote-getters include octopus risotto, fish in shrimp sauce, and shrimp risotto, all of which serve two. There are also typical dishes from Bahia. CUISINE Bahian, fish and seafood CREDIT CARDS not accepted

---

RESTAURANTS $ up to R$50 $$ from R$51 up to R$100 $$$ from R$101 up to R$150 $$$$ above R$150

Avenida Felinto Melo, 18, Centro
TEL (73) 3284-2885 OPEN Daily, 11am – 1am

Caravelas $

Codfish in coconut milk, fish in shrimp sauce, and mixed *moqueca* stew (fish, shrimp, crab) are house specialties. Rice, seasoned manioc flour, and pickled salad or rice and thickened sauce accompany all entrees. CUISINE bar food, meats, fish and seafood CREDIT CARDS Diners, MasterCard, Visa
Avenida Beira-Mar, 600, Praia da Costa, Ilha de Atalaia
TEL (73) 3284-2640 OPEN Daily, 9am – 11pm

SERVICES

Boat Rental – Artmarina
Rua Coronel Augusto Luiz Carvalho, 37, Centro
TEL (73) 3284-1262 OPEN Daily, 8am – 6pm
Boat rental, marina, yacht club, deep-sea fishing trips
www.artmarina.com.br

Boat Rental – Marina Canes
Alameda dos Periquitos, 85, Praia da Costa, Ilha de Atalaia (take the next left after Ponte ACM bridge)
TEL (73) 3284-3735, 9983-3140 OPEN Daily, 6am – 6pm
Boat rental, marina, yacht club

Bus Station – Rodoviária
Avenida Professor Assis Gonçalves, no # (at the entrance to the town)
TEL (73) 3284-1399 OPEN Daily, 6am – 9pm

Department of Tourism – Secretaria de Turismo
Praça da Bandeira, no #, Centro
TEL (73) 3284-1105, 8109-5699 OPEN Mon – Fri, 8am – 2pm

Travel Agency and Guides – FMS Turismo
Avenida Coronel Augusto Luiz de Carvalho, 35, Porto
TEL (73) 3284-3927, 9142-5059 FAX 3284-3928.
OPEN Daily, 9am – 6pm

Canoa Quebrada – Ceará

AREA CODE 88 Aracati DISTANCE Fortaleza 167 kilometers (104 miles) ACCESS From Fortaleza, take the CE-040 and BR-304 highways. The stretch of road after the bridge over the Jaguaribe River is in poor condition. 2.5 kilometers after the BR-304 gas station, turn left to Canoa Quebrada

WHERE TO STAY

Pousada Aruanã $
The guesthouse caters mostly to couples and families; anyone under 18 must be accompanied by an adult. 500 meters (0.3 mile) from Canoa Quebrada beach, its highlight is the large pool with bar, overlooking the sea. ACCOMMODATIONS 20 rooms, air-conditioning, private safe, minibar, cable TV, veranda with hammock FACILITIES AND SERVICES Internet access in communal areas, bar, parking, pool CREDIT CARDS MasterCard, Visa
Rua dos Bugueiros, no #, Praia de Canoa Quebrada
TEL and FAX (88) 3421-7154

Pousada Chataletta $
This rustic-style guesthouse has well-maintained and equipped, spacious chalets that can accommodate up to six. ACCOMMODATIONS 18 chalets, air-conditioning, minibar, TV, ceiling fan FACILITIES AND SERVICES parking, pool, gym CREDIT CARDS Visa
Descida da praia de Canoa Quebrada, no #

TEL (88) 3421-7200 FAX 3421-7169
www.pousadachataletta.com.br

Pousada La Dolce Vita $
The Pousada offers chalets for couples and families, but the rooms have a better view of the sea and sunset. The restaurant serves local and Italian food, and staff speak English and Italian. ACCOMMODATIONS 10 chalets, 4 rooms, and 2 suites; minibar, TV FACILITIES AND SERVICES Internet access in communal areas, bar, parking, pool, restaurant, guided walking tours, shuttle service to airport and local attractions CREDIT CARDS MasterCard, Visa
Descida da Praia de Canoa Quebrada, no #
TEL (88) 3421-7213 www.canoa-quebrada.it

Village Long Beach $$
The two-level chalets are large, with private terrace and hammock. All rooms have king-size beds and good linen. ACCOMMODATIONS 22 rooms and 20 chalets, air-conditioning, minibar, telephone, cable TV, ceiling fan FACILITIES AND SERVICES Internet access in communal areas, bar, parking, pool, restaurant, barbecue restaurant, massage room CREDIT CARDS Diners, MasterCard, Visa
Rua Quatro Ventos, no #
TEL (88) 3421-7404 FAX 3421-7407
www.longbeachvillage.com.br

SERVICES

Bus Station – Rodoviária
Rua Coronel Alexandrino, no # (at the entrance to the town), Aracati
TEL (88) 3421-6434 OPEN Daily, 5am – 9pm

Department of Tourism – Secretaria de Turismo
Rua Santos Dumont, 352, Centro, Aracati
TEL (88) 3421-2554, 3446-2451, 9922-9877 OPEN Mon – Fri, 8am – 2pm www.aracati.ce.gov.br

Canudos – Bahia (see Euclides da Cunha)

Caraíva – Bahia

AREA CODE 73 Porto Seguro DISTANCES Salvador 765 kilometers (475 miles), Porto Seguro 65 kilometers (40 miles) ACCESS From Trancoso, take a motorboat. If driving along the BR-101 highway, take the exit to Monte Pascoal, at Km 753, following 43 kilometers (27 miles) of dirt road to the Caraíva River; the crossing is by canoe

WHERE TO STAY

Pousada da Barra $$
The simple rooms have hot showers and ceiling fans, and either a river or sea view. Advance reservations are essential. ACCOMMODATIONS 4 rooms and 4 bungalows, private safe, veranda with hammock FACILITIES AND SERVICES bar, boat, horses, motorboat, river, horseback riding, boat trips (on both the river and the sea), guides CREDIT CARDS not accepted
Avenida dos Navegantes, no #, Praia da Barra
TEL (73) 9985-4302 RESERVATIONS (21) 2437-4273, 2437-1021
www.caraiva.com

Pousada Enseada do Espelho $$$
Surrounded by coconut palms and grass, this guesthouse on Curuípe beach offers a full beach service, with chairs,

| PRICES | HOTELS (couple) | $ up to R$150 | $$ from R$151 up to R$300 | $$$ from R$301 up to R$500 | $$$$ above R$500 |

beach mats, cushions and bar – even breakfast can be served on the beach! All rooms have hot showers and king-size beds. There is no television, nor are there any leisure facilities. The restaurant's à la carte menu has mainly seafood dishes. ACCOMMODATIONS 7 rooms; central water heating, air-conditioning, king-size beds, telephone, veranda with hammock, ceiling fan; Jacuzzi in 1 room FACILITIES AND SERVICES bar, parking, restaurant, guides, trips to local attractions, beach service; staff can recommend transportation to airport and attractions CREDIT CARDS Diners, MasterCard
Praia de Curuípe (10 meters, 33 feet, from the beach)
TEL (73) 3668-5091 RESERVATIONS 9985-4608
www.enseadadoespelho.com.br

Pousada Flor do Mar $$

This guesthouse has hot showers in only three rooms and lacks electricity, just like the rest of the village. All the lighting comes from flares, candles, and fires. ACCOMMODATIONS 5 rooms and 1 bungalow FACILITIES AND SERVICES reading area, beach service CREDIT CARDS not accepted
Rua da Praia, no #
TEL (73) 9985-1608 www.caraiva.tur.br/flordomar

Pousada Lagoa $

This guesthouse welcomes children and guests with pets. Apart from trees, the grounds include small lakes, and a river that flows within 50 meters (165 feet) of the restaurant, which specializes in pasta. Rustic in style and very colorful, it has rooms with veranda, lake view, and hammock. ACCOMMODATIONS 4 rooms (2 with hot shower) and 3 bungalows FACILITIES AND SERVICES bar, heliport, lake, restaurant, river, games room, currency exchange, laundry, boat trips, airport shuttle CREDIT CARDS not accepted
Beco da Lagoa, no #, Caraíva
TEL (73) 9985-6862 FAX and RESERVATIONS (31) 3225-5845
www.lagoacaraiva.com.br

Pousada Vila do Mar $$$

This guesthouse offers leisure facilities, and a restaurant and bar that open only in the high season. The rooms can accommodate three people and all have mosquito nets. ACCOMMODATIONS 5 rooms with veranda, 2 rooms with Jacuzzi; air-conditioning, minibar, cable TV, ceiling fan FACILITIES AND SERVICES bar, safe, pool, restaurant, video room, guide recommendation; motorboat and beach service (high season only) CREDIT CARDS MasterCard
Rua da Praia, no #
TEL and FAX (73) 3668-5111 www.pousadaviladomar.com.br

WHERE TO EAT

Boteco do Pará $

A friendly, riverside bar with tables both outdoors and indoors. Apart from moquecas made without dendê palm oil or coriander, he serves delicious pastéis (deep fried pastries) with fillings such as shrimp, cream cheese, cheese, and banana. CUISINE regional, seafood, appetizers CREDIT CARDS Diners, MasterCard
Rua Beira-Rio, Ponto dos Mentirosos (towards Barra)
TEL (73) 9991-9804 RESERVATIONS 9142-3659. OPEN High season: daily, 11am – until the last customer leaves; low season: Tue – Sun, 11am – 8pm

SERVICES

Airport – Aeroporto Internacional de Porto Seguro
Estrada do Aeroporto, no #, Cidade Alta, Porto Seguro
TEL (73) 3288-1880, 3268-1877 OPEN Daily, 24 hours

Tourist Information – Centro de Informações Turísticas de Porto Seguro
Praça Manoel Ribeiro Coelho, 10, Centro, Porto Seguro (near the ferry)
TEL (73) 3268-1390 OPEN Mon – Sat, 9:30am – 11pm

Caravelas – Bahia

AREA CODE 73 POPULATION 20,872 DISTANCES Salvador 886 kilometers (550 miles), Porto Seguro 210 kilometers (130 miles) ACCESS From Salvador, take BR-101, then BA-290 to Alcobaça, then BA-001 and BR-418
www.caravelas.ba.gov.br

WHERE TO STAY

Farol Abrolhos Hotel Iate Clube $

What makes this hotel different is its location, facing the Caravelas River, and the trips to Abrolhos offered here. (The hotel has its own pier and boats.) The à la carte restaurant is open to the public. ACCOMMODATIONS 15 rooms, air-conditioning, minibar, TV FACILITIES AND SERVICES bar, boat, bicycles, kayaks, parking, snack bar, stores, pool, volleyball court, restaurant, games room, video room, travel agency, laundry CREDIT CARDS Diners, MasterCard, Visa
Estrada Caravelas–Barra, Km 1, Kitongos
TEL (73) 3297-1002 FAX and RESERVATIONS 3297-1002, 3297-1173
www.farolabrolhos.com.br

Hotel Marina Porto Abrolhos $$

Humpback whales draw large groups of visitors from June to November. The restaurant serves seafood and meat dishes and is open to non-guests. ACCOMMODATIONS 9 rooms, 7 bungalows, 8 suites (2 adjoining); air-conditioning, minibar, cable TV, ceiling fan; veranda with hammock in the rooms FACILITIES AND SERVICES bar, bicycles, golf course, miniature golf, parking, convenience store, pool (children and adult); playground, volleyball court, restaurant, river, convention room, gym, games room, massage room, video room, sauna, 24-hour kitchen, beach service CREDIT CARDS Amex, Diners, MasterCard, Visa
Rua da Baleia, 333, Barra de Caravelas
TEL (73) 3674-1082, 3674-1059 FAX and RESERVATIONS 3674-1059
www.marinaportoabrolhos.com.br

WHERE TO EAT

Carenagem $

This simple restaurant specializes in seafood, though it also serves meat and poultry. The most popular dishes are fish moqueca, grilled fish, and sinfonia de peixe (snook, crab, oysters, and shrimp for two people). CUISINE regional, fish CREDIT CARDS Diners, MasterCard, Visa
Avenida das Palmeiras, 210, Centro
TEL (73) 3297-1280 RESERVATIONS 3297-1610 OPEN Daily, 10:30am – until the last customer leaves

SERVICES

Bus Station – Rodoviária
Praça Teófilo Otoni, no #, Centro
TEL (73) 3297-1422, 3297-1336, 3297-2101 OPEN Daily, 6am – 10:30pm

Department of Tourism – Secretaria de Turismo e Lazer
Praça Santo Antônio, 28, Centro

RESTAURANTS $ up to R$50 $$ from R$51 up to R$100 $$$ from R$101 up to R$150 $$$$ above R$150

TEL (73) 3297-1404, 3297-1113 OPEN Mon – Fri, 8am – noon and 2pm – 5pm

Tourist Information – Associação Costa das Baleias (ACB)
Praça Doutor Emílio Imbassahy, 46, Centro
TEL (73) 3297-2216, 3674-1060, 3674-1059 OPEN Mon – Fri, 8:30am – 5:30pm (closes for lunch)
www.costadasbaleiasabrolhos.com.br

Travel Agency – Abrolhos Turismo
Praça Doutor Emílio Imbassahy, 8, Centro
TEL (73) 3297-1149, 3297-1332 FAX 3297-1109 OPEN Mon – Sat, 7am – 7pm; Sun, 7am – 11:30am and 1pm – 7pm
www.abrolhosturismo.com.br

Travel Agency – Agência de Turismo Abrolhos Embarcações
Avenida Ministro Adalício Nogueira, 1294
TEL (73) 3297-1816, 3297-1172 OPEN Daily, 6:30am – 6pm
www.abrolhosembarcacoes.com.br

Travel Agency – Agência de Turismo Paradise Abrolhos
Avenida das Palmeiras, 313, Centro
TEL (73) 3297-1433, 8804-9534 OPEN Mon – Sat, 6am – 8pm
www.paradiseabrolhos.com.br

Carnaúba dos Dantas – Rio Grande do Norte (see Acari e Currais Novos)

Carpina – Pernambuco

AREA CODE 81 POPULATION 69,342 DISTANCE Recife 56 kilometers (35 miles) ACCESS BR-232 highway, towards Caruaru BEST TIME TO VISIT June, for the São João festivities. Early January, for the Festa de Reis celebrations

WHERE TO EAT

Panela Cheia $
This restaurant combines friendly service and a tasty mix of local food and that of Minas Gerais, such as lima beans and seasoned manioc flour become *feijão-tropeiro*. Steamed ribs, which serve two people, are the house specialty. Desserts include home-made fruit compotes, such as jackfruit compote. CUISINE Minas Gerais, barbecue, regional CREDIT CARDS Diners, MasterCard
Rodovia PE-90, Km 0
TEL (81) 3621-1278 OPEN Mon – Sat, 11am – 10pm; Sun, 11am – 4pm

SERVICES

Bus Station – Rodoviária
Avenida Ernesto Pompilho, no #, Centro
TEL (81) 3621-1332 OPEN Daily, 4am – 8pm

Caruaru – Pernambuco

AREA CODE 81 POPULATION 278,655 DISTANCES Recife 134 kilometers (83 miles), Campina Grande 145 kilometers (90 miles) ACCESS From Recife, BR-232 highway. From Campina Grande, BR-104

WHERE TO STAY

Caruaru Park Hotel $
The rooms are in colorful chalets, which are basic but well cared for. All have veranda and hammock. The restaurant serves regional food à la carte, as well as a very hearty breakfast, which is one of the hotel's attractions. ACCOMMODATIONS 68 rooms, Internet access, air-conditioning, private safe, telephone, cable TV; minibar (except for the 'standard' rooms) FACILITIES AND SERVICES convention rooms, bar, parking, snack bar, pool, restaurant, shuttle service to airport and local attractions CREDIT CARDS Amex, Diners, MasterCard, Visa
Rodovia BR-232, Km 128
TEL and FAX (81) 3722-9191
www.caruaruparkhotelonline.com.br

Hotel Village $
The hotel has comfortable rooms, a pleasant pool, good service, and a hearty breakfast that includes many regional dishes. Transportation to and from the bus station and airport can be arranged. ACCOMMODATIONS 56 rooms and 5 suites, Internet access, air-conditioning, private safe, minibar, telephone, cable TV FACILITIES AND SERVICES Internet access in communal areas, bar, parking, pool, playground, restaurant, convention room, gym, games room, video room, sauna, business center, airport shuttle CREDIT CARDS Amex, Diners, MasterCard, Visa
Rua Costa Carvalho, no #, Petrópolis (BR-232 highway, Km 135)
TEL (81) 3722-5544 FAX 3722-7033
www.hoteisvillage.com.br

WHERE TO EAT

Lengo Tengo $
A good choice for anyone visiting Alto do Moura, this restaurant serves goat (and goat sausage) cooked in the best local style, as well as other regional dishes, such as sundried beef. A trio plays live *forró* music. CUISINE regional CREDIT CARDS not accepted
Rua Mestre Vitalino, 450, Alto do Moura
TEL (81) 3722-4377 OPEN Daily, 11am – midnight

SERVICES

Bus Station – Rodoviária
Rua do Terminal Rodoviário, 12, Pinheirópolis
TEL (81) 3721-3869 OPEN Daily, 6am – 7pm

Department of Tourism – Secretaria de Turismo
Praça Coronel José de Vasconcelos, 100, Centro
TEL (81) 3722-2021, 3701-1533 OPEN Mon – Fri, 7:30am – 1pm
www.caruaru.pe.gov.br/pontosturisticos.asp

Cascavel – Ceará

AREA CODE 85 POPULATION 63,170 DISTANCE Fortaleza 64 kilometers (40 miles) ACCESS From Fortaleza, CE-040; exit at Km 64, on the left side of the road

WHERE TO EAT

Ravenga $
Visitors go there for the famous chicken dish *galinha cabidela*. Owner and cook Maria buys the free-range chickens at the local market, feeds them for a week on corn and leftovers (to get rid of any hormones or impurities) and, when the time comes to make the *cabidela* (a chicken-blood sauce), she uses pounded, sieved flour as a thickening agent. She takes the same care with the *paçoca*, which is beef jerky that has been fried in fat and then pounded with manioc flour. CUISINE regional CREDIT CARDS not accepted
Estrada da Caponga, no #, Sítio Tijucussu

| PRICES | HOTELS (couple) | $ up to R$150 | $$ from R$151 up to R$300 | $$$ from R$301 up to R$500 | $$$$ above R$500 |

HOTELS, RESTAURANTS AND SERVICES

TEL (85) 8833-0162, 8885-0523 OPEN Tue – Fri and Sun, 11am – 8pm; Sat, 11am – until the last customer leaves

SERVICES

Bus Station – Rodoviária
Rua Doutor Pedro de Queiróz, no #, Centro
TEL (85) 3334-1485, 3334-2146

Chapada Diamantina – Bahia
(see Andaraí, Ibicoara, Igatu, Lençóis, Mucugê and Vale do Capão (Caeté-Açu))

Coqueirinho – Paraíba (see Jacumã)

Coruripe – Alagoas

AREA CODE 82 POPULATION 44,272 DISTANCES Maceió 85 kilometers (53 miles) ACCESS From Maceió, the AL-101 highway
www.coruripe.al.gov.br

WHERE TO STAY

Surf Paradise $$
Mavericks, Bali, and Grajagan are the most comfortable rooms. The pool is floodlit, the chalets are dotted around a grassy area and a large screen shows films – about surfing of course. ACCOMMODATIONS 15 chalets and 4 rooms, air-conditioning, king-size beds, minibar, TV; Jacuzzi in one chalet, private thermal pool in 2 chalets FACILITIES AND SERVICES bar, soccer field, parking, convenience store, pool, thermal pool, playground, volleyball court, restaurant, games room, walking trails, recreational team for adults and children, beach service CREDIT CARDS Diners, MasterCard, Visa
Rua Projetada, 433, Pontal do Coruripe
TEL (82) 3273-7303, 9921-4182 www.surfparadise.com.br

WHERE TO EAT

Corais Massa Mar $
The highlight of the menu, the *moqueca* stews, can be made with fish, shrimp, different varieties of crab, or the shellfish known as *sururu*. Accompaniments are rice, thickened sauce, seasoned manioc flour and salad. CUISINE italian, fish and seafood, varied CREDIT CARDS Diners, MasterCard, Visa
Avenida Engenheiro Geraldo Magela de Carvalho Beltrão, 103, Pontal do Coruripe
TEL (82) 3273-7291 OPEN Tue – Sat, 10am – 10pm; Sun, 10am – 5pm

SERVICES

Bus Station – Rodoviária
Rua Boa Vista, no #, Centro
TEL (82) 3273-1447 OPEN Daily, 6am – 5:30pm

Tourist Information – Secretaria do Meio Ambiente, Turismo e Pesca
Rua da Alegria, 399, Centro
TEL (82) 3273-1142 OPEN Mon and Fri, 8am – 1pm; Tue – Thu, 8am – noon and 2pm – 5pm

Costa do Sauípe – Bahia

AREA CODE 71 Mata de São João DISTANCES Salvador 105 kilometers (65 miles), Praia do Forte 20 kilometers (12 miles) ACCESS From Salvador, BA-099 highway (Linha Verde)

Many of the hotels here belong to a group that share some of their facilities.

WHERE TO STAY

Marriott Resort & Spa $$$$
Rooms are comfortable, spacious, and very well equipped. As well as the on-site spa, guests can avail themselves of the facilities in the neighboring Renaissance Hotel. Guests under eighteen years of age must be accompanied by an adult or have their parents' authorization. ACCOMMODATIONS 256 rooms and 17 two-room suites, Internet access, air-conditioning, private safe, minibar, telephone, cable TV FACILITIES AND SERVICES Internet access in communal areas, bar, boat, soccer field, golf course, parking, horseback riding center, snack bar, stores, pool, playground, soccer court, tennis court, restaurant, convention room, gym, massage room, beauty parlor, sauna, spa, travel agency, business center, 24-hour kitchen, recreational team for adults and children, valet parking, lifeguard, beach service, shuttle service to airport and local attractions CREDIT CARDS Amex, Diners, MasterCard, Visa
Rodovia BA-99, Km 76, Linha Verde
TEL (71) 2104-7000 RESERVATIONS and FAX 0800-7031512
www.marriottbrasil.com

Pousada da Aldeia $$
This guesthouse is one of a group of six themed guesthouses (the others are Carnaval, Pousada do Agreste, Pousada da Torre, Gabriela and Pelourinho). The group collectively offers five sports centers, as well as restaurants, spa and cinema. ACCOMMODATIONS 20 rooms, air-conditioning, private safe, minibar, telephone, cable TV FACILITIES AND SERVICES Internet access in communal areas, bar, boat, kayaks, golf course, horses, parking, fishing lake and equipment, pool, squash court, tennis court CREDIT CARDS Amex, Diners, MasterCard, Visa
Rodovia BA-099, Km 76, Linha Verde
TEL (71) 2104-8200 RESERVATIONS 0800-7074004 FAX 2104-8239
www.costadosauipe.com.br

Pousada do Agreste $$
Guests here can enjoy leisure facilities that are shared by several guesthouses in this complex: multi-sports court, tennis court, golf, horses, and watersports. Rooms are simple but cozy, following the standard of all the guesthouses in Sauípe. ACCOMMODATIONS 20 rooms, air-conditioning, private safe, minibar, telephone, cable TV FACILITIES AND SERVICES Internet access in communal areas, bar, bicycles, kayaks, soccer field, golf course, miniature golf, horses, cart, parking, Jacuzzi, fishing lake and equipment, snack bar, stores, period furniture, pool, playground, pony, soccer court, squash court, tennis court, volleyball court, restaurant, reading area, convention room, gym, games room, massage room, video room, beauty parlor, sauna, spa, walking trails, business center, currency exchange, 24-hour kitchen, recreational team for adults and children, guided walking tours, lifeguard, beach service, shuttle service to airport and local attractions CREDIT CARDS Amex, Diners, MasterCard, Visa
Rodovia BA-99, Km 76, Linha Verde
TEL (71) 2104-8200 RESERVATIONS 2104-8241, 0800-707-4004 FAX 2104-8239 www.costadosauipe.com.br

Pousada Gabriela $$
Guests, as in the other guesthouses (see above and below), can use the shared sports centers. ACCOMMODATIONS 20 rooms, air-conditioning, private safe, minibar, telephone, cable TV FACILITIES AND SERVICES Internet access in communal ar-

---

RESTAURANTS $ up to R$50 $$ from R$51 up to R$100 $$$ from R$101 up to R$150 $$$$ above R$150

eas, bar, bicycles, kayaks; soccer field, golf course, miniature golf, horses, cart, parking, Jacuzzi, fishing lake and equipment, snack bar, stores, period furniture, pool, playground, pony, soccer court, squash court, tennis court, volleyball court, restaurant, magazine reading area, convention room, gym, games room, massage room, video room, beauty parlor, sauna, spa, walking trails, business center, currency exchange, 24-hour kitchen, recreational team for adults and children, guided walking tours, lifeguard, beach service, shuttle service to airport and local attractions CREDIT CARDS Amex, Diners, MasterCard, Visa
Rodovia BA-99, Km 76, Linha Verde
TEL (71) 2104-8200 RESERVATIONS 2104-8241, 0800-707-4004 FAX 2104-8239 www.costadosauipe.com.br

Pousada Pelourinho $$
Architecturally inspired by Salvador's historical district, this guesthouse is nearest to Vila Nova, which offers a cluster of stores, restaurants, and other establishments. The administrative center for the six guesthouses in the complex, it deals with check-in and check-out in all of them. ACCOMMODATIONS 40 rooms, air-conditioning, private safe, minibar, telephone, cable TV FACILITIES AND SERVICES Internet access in communal areas, bar, nursery, bicycles, kayaks, soccer field, golf course, miniature golf, horses, cart, parking, Jacuzzi, fishing lake and equipment, snack bar, stores, period furniture, pool, playground, pony, soccer court, squash court, tennis court, volleyball court, restaurant, magazine reading area, convention room, gym, games room, massage room, video room, beauty parlor, sauna, spa, walking trails, business center, currency exchange, 24-hour kitchen, recreational team for adults and children, guided walking tours, lifeguard, beach service, shuttle service to airport and local attractions CREDIT CARDS Amex, Diners, MasterCard, Visa
Rod. BA-99, km 76, Linha Verde
TEL (71) 2104-8200 RESERVATIONS 2104-8241, 0800-707-4004 FAX 2104-8239 www.costadosauipe.com.br

Renaissance Resort $$$$
The Renaissance is casual and attracts families with children, since it has good leisure facilities, including water aerobics, dance and gym classes. The restaurant serves Mediterranean food (pasta) and the Tequila Bar specializes in Mexican cuisine. ACCOMMODATIONS 195 rooms and 17 two-room suites, Internet access, air-conditioning, private safe, minibar, telephone, cable TV FACILITIES AND SERVICES Internet access in communal areas, bar, boat, soccer field, golf course, parking, horseback riding center, snack bar, stores, pool, playground, soccer court, tennis court, restaurant, convention room, gym, massage room, beauty parlor, sauna, spa, travel agency, business center, 24-hour kitchen, recreational team for adults and children, valet parking, lifeguard, beach service, shuttle service to airport and local attractions CREDIT CARDS Amex, Diners, MasterCard, Visa
Rodovia BA-99, Km 76, Linha Verde
TEL (71) 2104-7300 RESERVATIONS 0800-703-1512 FAX 2104-7301
www.marriottbrasil.com

Sofitel Costa do Sauípe $$$$
The very comfortable Sofitel has the largest pool and best convention facilities in Sauípe. The very pleasant rooms offer lovely views. ACCOMMODATIONS 392 rooms and 12 suites, Internet access, air-conditioning, private safe, minibar, telephone, cable TV, Jacuzzi in one suite FACILITIES AND SERVICES Internet access in communal areas, bar, kayaks, soccer field, golf course, water-sports center, horseback riding center, parking, snack bar, convenience store, pool, playground, soccer court, tennis court, restaurant, convention room, gym, games room, massage room, video room, sauna, recreational team for adults and children CREDIT CARDS Amex, Diners, MasterCard, Visa
Rodovia BA-099, Km 76, Linha Verde
TEL (71) 2104-7600 RESERVATIONS 2104-8080, 0800-703-7000 FAX 2104-8065 www.accorhotels.com.br

Sofitel Suites Costa do Sauípe $$$$
The suites are very comfortable and the service, professional. Guests use the leisure facilities in the other Sofitel, which is next door. ACCOMMODATIONS 198 suites, Internet access, air-conditioning, private safe, minibar, telephone, cable TV, Jacuzzi in the master suites FACILITIES AND SERVICES Internet access in communal areas, bar, soccer field, golf course, water-sports center, horseback riding center, parking, snack bar, pool, playground, soccer court, tennis court, volleyball court, restaurant, convention room, gym, games room, massage room, video room, beauty parlor, sauna, business center, 24-hour kitchen, recreational team for adults and children, valet parking CREDIT CARDS Amex, Diners, MasterCard, Visa
Rodovia BA-099, Km 76, Linha Verde
TEL (71) 2104-8000 RESERVATIONS 2104-8080, 0800-703-7000 FAX 2104-8065 www.accorhotels.com.br

Super Clubs Breezes Costa do Sauípe $$$$
This is the liveliest spot in the complex, with a wealth of daytime and nighttime activities. The daily rate includes food, drink, and all leisure activities. There is also a day-use system, from 10:30am to 5:30pm; during this time, non-guest visitors can use all the hotel's recreational and restaurant facilities for a fixed price. Rooms are all equally well equipped. There is no room service, but the recreational facilities are open 24 hours. ACCOMMODATIONS 167 luxury rooms, 140 premium rooms, 16 luxury and premium suites, and 1 residencial suite; air-conditioning, private safe, minibar, telephone, cable TV FACILITIES AND SERVICES bar, nursery, bicycles, parking, snack bar, stores, pool, tennis court, restaurant, convention room, recreational team for adults, valet parking, beach service CREDIT CARDS Amex, Diners, MasterCard, Visa
Rodovia BA-099, Km 76
TEL (71) 2104-8888 RESERVATIONS 0800-704-3210 FAX 2104-8810 www.superclubs.com.br

SERVICES

Tourist Information – Casa da Cultura
Praça Barão Açu da Torre, no # (Department of Culture and Tourism), Centro, Mata de São João
TEL (71) 3635-2409, 3635-2663
OPEN Mon – Fri, 8:30am – noon and 1pm – 4:30pm
www.pmsj.ba.gov.br

Crato – Ceará

AREA CODE 88 POPULATION 113,497 DISTANCES Fortaleza 533 kilometers (331 miles), Juazeiro do Norte 10 kilometers (6 miles) ACCESS From Juazeiro, 10 kilometers via Avenida Padre Cícero. From Fortaleza, take the BR-116 highway to Icó; to avoid the pot-holed stretches, continue via Iguatu, Várzea Alegre, and Farias Brito

WHERE TO STAY

Encosta da Serra $
This friendly hotel in the mountains has comfortable rooms. ACCOMMODATIONS 38 rooms and 2 suites, Internet access, air-conditioning, minibar, telephone, TV, Jacuzzi in the suites FACILITIES AND SERVICES Internet access in communal areas, bar, parking, convenience store, pool, soccer court, volleyball court; restaurant, convention room, games room, video

PRICES	HOTELS (couple)	$ up to R$150	$$ from R$151 up to R$300	$$$ from R$301 up to R$500	$$$$ above R$500

room, travel agency, valet parking, shuttle service to airport and local attractions CREDIT CARDS Amex, Diners, MasterCard, Visa
Avenida Pedro Felício Cavalcanti, 1898, Granjeiro
TEL and FAX (88) 3521-6515 www.encostadaserra.com.br

Pasárgada $
The hotel has friendly service and its leisure facilities are in the midst of well-tended gardens. ACCOMMODATIONS 20 chalets, 18 rooms, and 2 suites; air-conditioning, minibar, telephone, TV FACILITIES AND SERVICES Internet access in communal areas, bar, soccer field, parking, pool, jogging track, playground, restaurant, convention room, travel agency, recreational team for adults and children CREDIT CARDS MasterCard, Visa
Sítio Belmonte, no #, Lameiro
TEL and FAX (88) 3523-2323 www.pasargadahotel.com.br

SERVICES

Bus Station – Rodoviária
Avenida Perimetral, no #, São Miguel
TEL (88) 3523-1225, 3523-3258 (Viação Guanabara)

Department of Tourism – Secretaria de Turismo
Rua 13 de Setembro, 150, São Miguel
TEL (88) 3523-6473 OPEN Mon – Fri, 8am – 2pm
www.crato.ce.gov.br

Cumbuco – Ceará

AREA CODE 85 Caucaia DISTANCE Fortaleza 30 kilometers (19 miles) ACCESS Rodovia Estruturante (the CE-085 highway)

WHERE TO STAY

Chalés do Atlântico $
Chalets lie scattered around a green, tree-filled area on the oceanfront. The restaurant, which has a sea view, and the recreational facilities are open to non-guests. Recreational activities (available on weekends and holidays) make this a good spot for families with children. ACCOMMODATIONS 19 rooms, 5 suites, and 20 chalets, air-conditioning, minibar, telephone, TV FACILITIES AND SERVICES Internet access in communal areas, bar, soccer field, parking, pool, playground, restaurant, convention room, games room, water aerobics classes, recreational team for children, beach service CREDIT CARDS Amex, Diners, MasterCard, Visa
Quadra 22, Lote 1, Praia de Tabuba, Caucaia
TEL (85) 3318-8141 FAX 3318-8242
www.chalesdoatlantico.com.br

Golfinho $$
The comfortable rooms face a pool and have modern décor and equipment. The restaurant, which is open to non-guests, serves local, Portuguese and international dishes. ACCOMMODATIONS 23 rooms and 2 suites, air-conditioning, private safe, minibar, telephone, TV FACILITIES AND SERVICES parking, pool, restaurant, convention room, games room, sauna CREDIT CARDS Amex, Diners, MasterCard, Visa
Avenida dos Coqueiros, no #, Praia de Cumbuco
TEL (85) 3318-7444 FAX 3318-7429
www.hotelgolfinho.com.br

WHERE TO EAT

Velas do Cumbuco $$
This beach *barraca* has excellent facilities. It has several sections (sheds, kiosks, and dining room) and also three swimming pools (for adults, children, and babies), as well as stores and sports facilities. They can also arrange trips: by dune buggy, sailing raft, and on horseback. Their famous *caranguejada* (crab feast) is served on weekends. The most popular lunch dishes are sun-dried beef (sliced and served with *baião-de-dois*, fried manioc, and *paçoca*) and porgy (served with rice, French fries and seasoned manioc flour). CUISINE bar food, fish, regional CREDIT CARDS Amex, Diners, MasterCard, Visa
Avenida dos Coqueiros, no #, Praia do Cumbuco
TEL (85) 3318-7555 RESERVATIONS and FAX 3318-7562, 3318-7561 OPEN Daily, 9am – 5pm

Cumuruxatiba – Bahia

AREA CODE 73 Prado DISTANCES Salvador 844 kilometers (524 miles), Prado 42 kilometers (26 miles), Porto Seguro 70 kilometers (43 miles) ACCESS From Salvador, take the BR-101 highway to Itamaraju, and then BA-489 to the Cumuruxatiba exit (to the left). Follow this signposted dirt road for 18 kilometers (11 miles)

WHERE TO STAY

Hotel Cumuruxatiba – Costa das Baleias $
This hotel has well-equipped rooms. It offers good recreational facilities, including several sports courts. ACCOMMODATIONS 40 rooms, air-conditioning, minibar, telephone, cable TV, ceiling fan FACILITIES AND SERVICES Internet access in communal areas, bar, boat, bicycles, kayaks, parking, pool, playground, soccer field, volleyball court, beach volleyball, games room, travel agency, recreational team for adults and children, laundry, beach service CREDIT CARDS Diners, MasterCard, Visa
Avenida Beira-Mar, no #, Praia de Cumuruxatiba
TEL (73) 3573-1065 RESERVATIONS 3573-1065, (11) 5543-9444 FAX 3573-1045 www.cumuruxatiba.com.br

Pousada É $$
Surrounded by a vast green area, the rooms of this guesthouse each have a veranda and view of the sea. Hans Fritsch, the Swiss owner, has more than two hundred whiskies, for your tasting pleasure. The food in the restaurant is international, with an emphasis on Thai. ACCOMMODATIONS 8 rooms and 4 two-room suites, minibar, cable TV, ceiling fan FACILITIES AND SERVICES Internet access in communal areas, wine cellar, bar, library, bicycles, kayaks, parking, convenience store, pool, playground, volleyball court, restaurant, gym, games room, video room, beach service, recreational team for children (high season) CREDIT CARDS MasterCard
Alameda Roberto Pompeu, 8, Rio do Peixe Grande
TEL (73) 3573-1007 FAX 3573-1137 www.pousadae.com

Pousada Mandala $$
Impressive facilities – including a library and DVD/cable TV room. The restaurant serves seafood and vegetarian dishes. The staff speaks English, Spanish, Italian, and German. ACCOMMODATIONS 8 rooms and 1 suite, air-conditioning, minibar, TV, ceiling fan FACILITIES AND SERVICES Internet access in communal areas, bar, nursery, bicycles, kayaks, parking, pool, restaurant, massage room, video room, beach service, airport shuttle CREDIT CARDS Visa
Alameda Roberto Pompeu, 1, Praia do Rio do Peixe
TEL and FAX (73) 3573-1143, 3573-1145
www.pousadamandala.com.br

Pousada Rio do Peixe $
This guesthouse is on the beach and all rooms have sea

view, veranda, and hammock. The restaurant, which is light and airy but simple, serves local, home-cooked food, such as *moqueca*, *bobó*, and beef fillet. ACCOMMODATIONS 20 rooms, Internet access, air-conditioning, minibar, telephone, cable TV; king-size beds in 4 rooms FACILITIES AND SERVICES Internet access in communal areas, bar, parking, stores, pool, restaurant, games room, video room, beach service, airport shuttle service CREDIT CARDS Diners, MasterCard, Visa
Alameda Roberto Pompeu, 26, Praia do Rio de Peixe
TEL and FAX (73) 3573-1213 www.pousadariodopeixe.com.br

Uai Brasil Pousada $$
The rooms have king-size beds and verandas. The owner is an excellent chef and gives his guests personal attention (see *Where to Eat*). ACCOMMODATIONS 7 rooms, air-conditioning, minibar, cable TV, veranda with hammock, ceiling fan FACILITIES AND SERVICES Internet access in communal areas, wine cellar, bar, parking, pool, restaurant, beach service CREDIT CARDS Diners, MasterCard
Avenida Rio do Peixe, no #, Praia do Rio de Peixe
TEL and FAX (73) 3573-1130 RESERVATIONS 3573-1333 www.pousadauaibrasil.com.br

WHERE TO EAT

Asa Branca $
This centrally located restaurant opened in 1997 and has become very popular with Brazilian tourists from the state Minas Gerais. Owner/chef Rosa's specialty is sun-dried rump steak with milk-thickened sauce (serves two). Her very simple restaurant has wooden chairs and tables. CUISINE meats, regional CREDIT CARDS not accepted
Avenida 13 de Maio, no #, Centro
TEL (73) 3573-1205 OPEN Mon – Sat, 10am – 6pm

Catamarã $
Perched on top of a 45-meter (150-foot) high cliff, at the entrance to the town, this restaurant has a stunning view. The lookout point in front is good for whale-watching. Sated diners can walk down to the beach via steps and ramps. Among the dishes on offer are *moqueca*, octopus, octopus risotto, meat dishes, pasta, and *feijoada* on Sundays. CUISINE regional, meats, seafood, pasta CREDIT CARDS not accepted
Rua 1, Quadra 1, Areia Preta
TEL (73) 3573-1124 OPEN Daily, 10am – 1am and 10am – 9pm

Mama África $
In a relaxed atmosphere on the oceanfront, this restaurant serves vegetarian dishes, seafood, fish, excellent desserts, and a wide selection of *cachaça* liquor from Minas Gerais. The owner, Dolores Lameirão, is Angolan and her specialties are her codfish dishes, called *bacalhoadas*: They can be prepared *à portuguesa* (served with olive oil), *à moda da casa* (with plenty of vegetables), and *à florentina* (shredded codfish, served with spinach purée), which is the most popular. Or try something different: a typical Angolan *muamba*, which is a chicken *moqueca* made with *dendê* palm oil, eggplant, okra, and pumpkin. CUISINE fish and seafood, vegetarian CREDIT CARDS not accepted
Alameda Roberto Pompeu, 4, Rio do Peixe Grande
TEL (73) 3573-1274 OPEN High season: daily, 4pm – 11pm; low season, reservations must be made in advance

Restaurante da Pousada Uai Brasil $
The owner of Pousada Uai, Adriano, is also in charge of the kitchen. Non-guests need to make restaurant reservations in advance. The menu includes fish, meat, and seafood. We recommend steak in *jabuticaba* fruit sauce with gorgonzola potatoes, or shrimp risotto with plantain. CUISINE Brazilian with French influences, varied CREDIT CARDS MasterCard
Avenida Rio do Peixe, no #, Praia do Rio de Peixe
TEL (73) 3573-1130 RESERVATIONS 3573-1333 OPEN Daily, 10am – 10pm

Restaurante do Hermes $
This pleasant restaurant, which was once a mere kiosk, is in the center of Cumuruxatiba, right in front of the beach. Brothers Hermes and Geraldo refurbished the kiosk by adding lots of glass, a wooden deck, and outdoor seating to give it a sophisticated air. They serve meat, chicken, and seafood dishes such as pumpkin cream with shrimp. Their jambalaya (a risotto of chicken, shrimp, and sausage) is very spicy. CUISINE fish and seafood, varied CREDIT CARDS Diners, MasterCard, Visa
Avenida Beira-Mar, no #, Centro
TEL (73) 3573-1155 OPEN Daily, 11am – 11pm

SERVICES

Bus Station – Rodoviária
Avenida Itamaraju, no #, Centro
TEL (73) 3298-1273, 3298-1228

Tourist Information – Posto de Informações Turísticas
Rua Clarício Cardoso dos Santos, 100, Novo Prado (Pousada Barcaça)
TEL (73) 3298-1047 OPEN Mon – Fri, 8am – 2pm
www.prado.ba.gov.br

Travel Agency – Aquamar Ecoturismo Agência de Turismo
Avenida Beira-Mar, 7, Centro
TEL and FAX (73) 3573-1360 OPEN High season: daily, 7am – 8pm; low season: daily, 7am – 6pm
www.aquamarba.com.br

Currais Novos – Rio Grande do Norte

AREA CODE 84 POPULATION 41,144 DISTANCE Natal 187 kilometers (614 miles) ACCESS From Natal, BR-226 highway

WHERE TO STAY

Tungstênio $
Guests can opt for a room in the hotel itself, which deals with all guest services (including reservations), or stay in an annex that contains a block of apartments. Both have spacious rooms and are quite well-equipped. The restaurant opens for lunch only. ACCOMMODATIONS 33 rooms (18 with fan and communal bathrooms; the others offer air-conditioning and private baths) and 20 air-conditioned apartments; Internet access, minibar, telephone, cable TV FACILITIES AND SERVICES Internet access in communal areas, restaurant CREDIT CARDS Diners, MasterCard, Visa
Avenida Coronel José Bezerra, 25, Centro
TEL and FAX (84) 3431-1753, 3431-2475
www.minabrejui.com.br

WHERE TO EAT

Discot $
This large cafeteria-style restaurant serves breakfast, pizzas, regional dishes, ice cream, and snacks. CUISINE snacks, regional, varied CREDIT CARDS MasterCard, Visa
Praça Cristo Rei, 38, Centro
TEL (84) 3431-1601 OPEN Daily, 9am – 2am

PRICES	HOTELS (couple)	$ up to R$150	$$ from R$151 up to R$300	$$$ from R$301 up to R$500	$$$$ above R$500

Delta do Parnaíba – Piauí
(see Parnaíba)

Espelho and Curuípe – Bahia

AREA CODE 73 (Porto Seguro) **DISTANCES** Salvador 790 kilometers (491 miles), Trancoso 25 kilometers (16 miles) **ACCESS** From Trancoso, by hazardous dirt road, enter by driving through condominium complex. From Caraíva or Trancoso, by boat or motorboat.

WHERE TO STAY

Fazenda Calá $$$
The eight "house-suites" are built at a distance from each other and all within sight of the ocean. Most rooms have a veranda and hammock. The white rustic décor is complemented by king-size beds, cotton sheets and towels, and goose-feather pillows. **ACCOMMODATIONS** 8 suites **FACILITIES AND SERVICES** bar, kayaks, horses, parking, restaurant, beach service **CREDIT CARDS** not accepted
Estrada de Caraíva, no #, Praia do Espelho
TEL (73) 3668-5112 www.fazendacala.com.br

Pousada do Baiano $$$$
The rooms and bungalows are all the same standard, with super king-size beds. They offer outdoor massage, under the coconut trees. The restaurant is open to non-residents and guests can schedule their lunch and dinner. (See *Where to Eat*.) **ACCOMMODATIONS** 15 rooms and 3 bungalows, super king-size beds, private safe, minibar, *ofuro* tub, telephone, TV, ceiling fan **FACILITIES AND SERVICES** bar, woods, parking, restaurant, horses, 24-hour kitchen, walking-tour guides, beach service, airport shuttle **CREDIT CARDS** MasterCard
Praia do Espelho da Maravilha, no #
TEL and **FAX** (73) 3668-5020 www.pousadadobaiano.com

Pousada Porto Espelho $$$
All rooms have sea or garden view. Details such as silver cutlery, linen sheets, and crystal glasses show the level of refinement. They have a day-use system for a fixed price, which includes beach service and access to the restaurant. **ACCOMMODATIONS** 9 rooms and 2 suites, ceiling fan; air-conditioning in 3 rooms **FACILITIES AND SERVICES** Internet access in communal areas, wine cellar, bar, library, parking, restaurant, gym, beach service, airport shuttle **CREDIT CARDS** not accepted
Praia de Curuípe, no #
TEL and **FAX** (73) 3668-5031, 9985-4482
www.portoespelho.com.br

Pousada Pura Vida $$
The well-equipped rooms have king-size beds. It offers something different such as water-sports equipment, including kite-surfing. **ACCOMMODATIONS** 6 rooms; Internet access, DVD, and cable TV in luxury rooms; ceiling fan and veranda with hammock in standard rooms **FACILITIES AND SERVICES** bar, boat, horses, parking, motorboat, restaurant, walking trails, currency exchange, walking-tour guides, beach service, shuttle service to airport and local attractions **CREDIT CARDS** not accepted
Praia do Curuípe, no #
TEL and **FAX** (73) 3668-5038

WHERE TO EAT

Darley $
Darley operates as a bar all day. It is an à la carte restaurant in the afternoon, offering lasagnas, risottos, *moquecas,* and beef or chicken *parmigiana*. They serve pizza to order at night. In high season, they offer twelve pizza toppings, in low season, six. The *turim* pizza has mozzarella, Parmesan cheese, dried garlic, and dried red pepper. **CUISINE** pizza, varied **CREDIT CARDS** not accepted
Rua da Pousada, Condomínio Outeiro das Brisas
TEL (73) 3668-5059 **OPEN** Daily, 1pm – until the last customer leaves (restaurant) and 6pm – until the last customer leaves (pizzeria)

Restaurante do Baiano $$
The menu includes giant grilled shrimp and steak, as well as pasta, sun-dried beef, and fish goujons. We recommend the fresh tomato *bruschetta* as a starter. **CUISINE** regional, seafood **CREDIT CARDS** MasterCard
Praia do Espelho da Maravilha, no #
TEL (73) 3668-5020 **OPEN** Daily, 6am – 9pm

Restaurante Pura Vida $$
The specialty here is food from Bahia, and the seafood, served with salad and rice. We can recommend the lobster with caper sauce, and the seafood combination. **CUISINE** regional, seafood **CREDIT CARDS** not accepted
Praia do Curuípe/Espelho, no #
TEL (73) 3668-5038 **OPEN** Daily, 7am – 9pm

SERVICES (see Porto Seguro)

Euclides da Cunha – Bahia

AREA CODE 75 **POPULATION** 55,184 **DISTANCES** Salvador 321 kilometers (199 miles), Feira de Santana 210 kilometers (130 miles), Juazeiro 230 kilometers (143 miles) **ACCESS** From Salvador (northbound), BR-324 highway to Feira de Santana, then BR-116

WHERE TO STAY

Quirino $
The 19 rooms are all the same and there are no communal or leisure areas. You can negotiate a package that includes meals at nearby Churrascaria da Carminha. **ACCOMMODATIONS** 19 suites (8 with air-conditioning, 5 with air-conditioning and ceiling fan, 6 with ceiling fan), minibar, telephone, TV **FACILITIES AND SERVICES** parking **CREDIT CARDS** not accepted
Praça da Bandeira (Praça da Matriz), 378, Centro
TEL (75) 3271-4044 **RESERVATIONS** 3271-1013, 3271-1591

WHERE TO EAT

Churrascaria da Carminha $
Customers choose the meat, and it is cooked to order. The so-called *mistão* includes goat, rump steak, pork, and *calabresa* sausage. They also serve pork loin and chicken casseroles. Side dishes are pickled salad, rice, and seasoned manioc flour. **CUISINE** meats, barbecue **CREDIT CARDS** not accepted
Praça da Bandeira, 320, Centro
TEL (75) 3271-2521 **OPEN** Daily, noon – 10pm

SERVICES

Bus Station – Rodoviária
BR-116, 95 (at the entrance to the town)
TEL (75) 3271-1365

Fazenda Nova – Pernambuco

AREA CODE 81 Brejo da Madre de Deus **DISTANCES** Recife 187 kilometers (116 miles), Caruaru 50 kilometers (31 miles) **ACCESS** BR-232, BR-104 and PE-145 highways

---

RESTAURANTS $ up to R$50 $$ from R$51 up to R$100 $$$ from R$101 up to R$150 $$$$ above R$150

WHERE TO STAY

Pousada da Paixão $
Located inside the theater-city Nova Jerusalém. The rooms are not luxurious but are comfortable. The daily rate includes a hearty dinner. ACCOMMODATIONS 35 rooms, air-conditioning, minibar, TV FACILITIES AND SERVICES bar, bicycles, soccer field, horses, parking, fishing lake, store, pool, playground, tennis court, volleyball court, restaurant, games room, video room, sauna, walking trails CREDIT CARDS Diners, MasterCard, Visa
Teatro de Nova Jerusalém, no #, Fazenda Nova, Brejo da Madre de Deus
TEL (81) 3732-1602, 3732-1129 FAX 3732-1574
www.pousadadapaixao.com.br

Fernando de Noronha – Pernambuco

AREA CODE 81 POPULATION 2,280 DISTANCES Recife 545 kilometers (339 miles), Natal 360 kilometers (224 miles) ACCESS Daily flights from Natal or Recife

WHERE TO STAY

Pousada Beco de Noronha $$$
This welcoming guesthouse has comfortable beds, and solar-powered showers. The limited number of guests allows for more personal service. ACCOMMODATIONS 3 rooms, air-conditioning, minibar, telephone, TV, ceiling fan FACILITIES AND SERVICES garden, games room, music room, video room, guide recommendation, buggy rental, trips to local attractions, airport shuttle CREDIT CARDS MasterCard, Visa
Vila Floresta Nova, Quadra P, C 3
TEL (81) 3619-1285, 3619-1568, 3619-1569
www.becodenoronha.com.br

Dolphin $$$$
The rooms are simple, but cozy, all of the same standard. They can arrange trips with private operators and on Saturdays their restaurant, Marine, serves feijoada. ACCOMMODATIONS 11 rooms, Internet access, air-conditioning, minibar, telephone, cable TV FACILITIES AND SERVICES Internet access in communal areas, bar, parking, water gymnastic classes, pool, restaurant, magazine reading area, conference room, games room, video room, sauna, airport shuttle CREDIT CARDS Amex, Diners, MasterCard, Visa
Rodovia BR-363, no #, Vacaria
TEL (81) 3619-1100 RESERVATIONS 3465-7224 FAX 3619-1462
www.dolphinhotel.tur.br

Pousada da Morena $$$
The three bungalows (up to four people each) and two rooms (up to three people), all have a view of Conceição beach and Morro do Pico hill. ACCOMMODATIONS 3 bungalows and 2 rooms, Internet access, air-conditioning, minibar, telephone, TV FACILITIES AND SERVICES Internet access in communal areas, restaurant CREDIT CARDS MasterCard, Visa
Rua Nice Cordeiro, 2600, Vila Floresta Nova
TEL and FAX (81) 3619-1142 RESERVATIONS 3466-4300
www.noronha.com.br/morena

Pousada Maravilha $$$$
Designed by architect Sérgio Bernardes, this guesthouse blends in completely with the landscape. The detached bungalows, with Jacuzzi and a wonderful view of Sueste Bay, are for two people only. ACCOMMODATIONS 5 bungalows and 3 rooms, air-conditioning, private safe, minibar, telephone, cable TV; Jacuzzi in bungalows FACILITIES AND SERVICES Internet access in communal areas, wine cellar, bar, bicycles, parking, pool, restaurant, magazine reading area, massage room, sauna, airport shuttle CREDIT CARDS Amex, Diners, MasterCard, Visa
Rodovia BR-363, no #, Sueste
TEL (81) 3619-0028 RESERVATIONS 3619-1290 FAX 3619-0162
www.pousadamaravilha.com.br

Pousada Solar dos Ventos $$$
The cozy chalets are very airy and all have veranda, king-size beds with colorful cotton bedspreads from Paraíba, and sea view. ACCOMMODATIONS 8 chalets, air-conditioning, minibar, TV, veranda with hammock FACILITIES AND SERVICES Internet access in communal areas, airport shuttle; trips to local attractions can be arranged CREDIT CARDS Amex, Diners, MasterCard, Visa
Estrada do Sueste, no #, Sueste
TEL (81) 3619-1347 FAX 3619-1253
www.pousadasolardosventos.com.br

Pousada Zé Maria $$$$
The rooms have an unequalled view of Conceição beach. Three bungalows are special, with Jacuzzi. ACCOMMODATIONS 9 bungalows and 6 rooms, air-conditioning, private safe, minibar, telephone, cable TV; veranda/balcony with hammock in bungalows; Jacuzzi in 3 bungalows FACILITIES AND SERVICES wine cellar, bar, boat, fishing equipment, parking, hydroponic vegetable garden, motorboat, stores, pool, orchard, restaurant, gym, massage room, sauna, walking-tour guides, trips to local attractions, shuttle service to airport and local attractions; motorcycle, bicycle, buggy, and diving equipment rental CREDIT CARDS Amex, Diners, MasterCard, Visa
Rua Nice Cordeiro, 1, Floresta Velha
TEL and FAX (81) 3619-1258 www.pousadazemaria.com.br

WHERE TO EAT

Ecologiku's $$
Moqueca is the house specialty and they also serve octopus (the most popular dish), shrimp, mussels, and lobster, but no meat or poultry. The ingredients arrive by plane, which makes everything expensive. They serve lunch only to groups (a minimum of ten people) with advance reservations. CUISINE fish and seafood CREDIT CARDS Amex, Diners, MasterCard, Visa
Estrada Velha do Sueste (next to the airport)
TEL (81) 3619-1807 OPEN Daily, 7pm – 10:30pm (lunch: reservations only for party of 10)

Flamboyant $
This self-service restaurant serves good home-cooked food. Recommended for anyone who wants to try salads, meat, fish, pasta, and beans. CUISINE home-made CREDIT CARDS Amex, Diners, MasterCard, Visa
Bosque Flamboyant, Vila dos Remédios
TEL (81) 3619-1510 OPEN Daily, noon – 5pm and 7pm – 10:30pm

Museu Tubarões $
We recommend tubalhau (salted shark meat), which has a flavor similar to bacalhau (salted cod). Your main dish could be tubalhoada: alternate layers of tubalhau, tomatoes, onions, bell peppers, parsley and potatoes. CUISINE fish and seafood CREDIT CARDS Amex, Diners, MasterCard, Visa
Avenida Joaquim Ferreira Gomes, 40, Vila do Porto de Santo Antônio
TEL (81) 3619-1365 OPEN Mon – Sat, 8am – 6:30pm; Sun, noon – 6:30pm

PRICES	HOTELS (couple)	$ up to R$150	$$ from R$151 up to R$300	$$$ from R$301 up to R$500	$$$$ above R$500

Restaurante da Pousada Maravilha $$
The menu includes seafood, meats, and several different risottos, as well as regional delicacies, such as curd cheese and sweet *tapioca*. The mackerel involtini with lime risotto and *pitanga* fruit sauce is highly recommended. The menu served between 3pm and 8pm is much simpler. **CUISINE** contemporary **CREDIT CARDS** Amex, Diners, MasterCard, Visa
Rodovia BR-363, no #, Sueste
TEL (81) 3619-0028 **OPEN** Daily, noon – 11pm

Zé Maria $$
Wafer thin slices of *namorado* fish and flambéed shrimp are two of the special dishes. On Wednesdays and Saturdays, the food festival includes more than fifty options at a fixed price, including seafood, sushi, meats, and pasta. On these days you must make advance reservations. **CUISINE** Japanese, fish and seafood **CREDIT CARDS** Amex, Diners, MasterCard, Visa
Rua Nice Cordeiro, 1, Floresta Velha
TEL (81) 3619-1258 **OPEN** Daily, 11:30am – 11:30pm

SERVICES

Administrative Center – Sede da Administração
Palácio São Miguel, no #, Vila dos Remédios
TEL (81) 3619-1378 **OPEN** Mon – Fri, 8am – noon and 2pm – 7pm www.noronha.pe.gov.br

Buggy and Jeep Rental – Mulungu Locadora
Estrada da Alamoa, 211, Praia da Conceição
TEL (81) 3619-1755, 3619-1539 **FAX** 3619-1913 **OPEN** Daily, 24 hours

Buggy Rental – Loc Buggy
Avenida Major Costa, no #, Vila do Trinta
TEL (81) 3619-1490 **FAX** 3619-1284 **OPEN** Daily, 7:30am – 8pm
www.locbuggy.com.br

Buggy-taxis – Nortax
Rua São Miguel, 4, Vila dos Remédios
(next to the post office)
TEL (81) 3619-1314, 3619-1595 **OPEN** Daily, 24 hours

Tourist Information – Posto de Informações
Porto de Santo Antônio, Vila de Santo Antônio
TEL (81) 3619-1744 **OPEN** Mon – Sat, 8am –5pm; Sun, 8am – 2pm (closes at 6pm when cruise ships stop at the island)

Tourist Police Station – Delegacia de Turistas
Centro de Convivência, no #, Vila do Trinta
TEL (81) 3619-1179 **OPEN** Daily, 24 hours

Travel Agency – Agência de Turismo Atalaia Noronha
Rua Major Costa, 7, Vila do Trinta
TEL (81) 3619-1328, 3619-1991 **OPEN** Daily, 7:30am – 7:30pm
www.atalaia-noronha.com.br

Travel Agency – Yourway Habitat Noronha
Floresta Velha e Vila dos Remédios
TEL (81) 3619-1796, 9949-1087 **FAX** 3619-0238 **OPEN** Mon – Sat, 9am – 7pm www.yourway.com.br

Fortaleza – Ceará

AREA CODE 85 **POPULATION** 2,374,944 **DISTANCES** Natal 552 kilometers (343 miles), Teresina 637 kilometers (396 miles), João Pessoa 688 kilometers (428 miles), Recife 806 kilometers (501 miles) **ACCESS** BR-116, BR-222, and BR-020 highways
www.fortaleza.ce.gov.br

WHERE TO STAY

Casa Blanca $
The spacious lobby houses a video room, Internet café, store, bar, and reception. The leisure facilities are modest. **ACCOMMODATIONS** 62 rooms, Internet access, air-conditioning, private safe, minibar, telephone, cable TV, ceiling fan **FACILITIES AND SERVICES** Internet access in communal areas, bar, parking, convenience store, pool, restaurant, games room, 24-hour kitchen **CREDIT CARDS** MasterCard, Visa
Rua Joaquim Alves, 194, Praia de Iracema
TEL and **FAX** (85) 3219-0909 www.casablancahoteis.com.br

Golden Tulip late Plaza $$
Half of the rooms have sea view and despite being the most popular, they are the hottest rooms when the afternoon sun beats down. The pool, almost at sea level, with a view of the cove, is a great place to enjoy sunset. **ACCOMMODATIONS** 232 rooms, Internet access, air-conditioning, bathtub, hairdryer and intercom in bathrooms, private safe, minibar, mini-kitchen, telephone, cable TV **FACILITIES AND SERVICES** Internet access in communal areas, bar, parking, convenience store, pool, restaurant, conference room, gym, steam sauna, business center, valet parking **CREDIT CARDS** Amex, Diners, MasterCard, Visa
Avenida Beira-Mar, 4753, Praia do Mucuripe
TEL (85) 3466-4600 **FAX** (11) 3466-4660, 3466-4650
www.iateplazahotel.com.br

Gran Marquise $$$
The hotel has two restaurants: Marquise Grill (grills and salads) and Sumire (specializing in Japanese cuisine). All the rooms have king-size beds, and sea view. The pool bar has a marvelous view of the ocean. **ACCOMMODATIONS** 219 rooms and 16 suites (3 two-room suites), Internet access, air-conditioning, bathtub, private safe, minibar, telephone, cable TV; Jacuzzi in presidential suite **FACILITIES AND SERVICES** Internet access in communal areas, bar, parking, Jacuzzi, pool, restaurant, conference room, gym, massage room, sauna, business center, 24-hour kitchen, valet parking **CREDIT CARDS** Amex, Diners, MasterCard, Visa
Avenida Beira-Mar, 3980, Praia do Mucuripe
TEL (85) 4006-5000 **RESERVATIONS** (85) 4006-5222 **FAX** (85) 4006-5207 www.solmelia.com

Luzeiros $$
Well-located, this hotel is near the benches and food kiosks. The two restaurants offer varied menus and the rooms are well-equipped (3 telephones, armchair, work desk), offering sophistication and comfort. English, French, German, and Italian are spoken. **ACCOMMODATIONS** 200 rooms and 2 suites, Internet access, air-conditioning, private safe, minibar, telephone, cable TV; Jacuzzi in the suites **FACILITIES AND SERVICES** Internet access in communal areas, bar, parking, pool, restaurant, conference room, gym, massage room, sauna, business center, 24-hour kitchen, valet parking **CREDIT CARDS** Amex, Diners, MasterCard, Visa
Avenida Beira-Mar, 2600, Meireles
TEL (85) 4006-8585 **RESERVATIONS** 4006-8586 **FAX** 4006-8587
www.hotelluzeiros.com.br

Maredomus $$
Rooms, have city or sea view; we recommend those on higher floors. Service is friendly and the receptionists speak English, German, and Italian. **ACCOMMODATIONS** 80 rooms, In-

---

| RESTAURANTS | $ up to R$50 | $$ from R$51 up to R$100 | $$$ from R$101 up to R$150 | $$$$ above R$150 |

ternet access, air-conditioning, private safe, minibar, telephone, cable TV **FACILITIES AND SERVICES** Internet access in communal areas, bar, pool, conference room, gym, sauna **CREDIT CARDS** Amex, Diners, MasterCard, Visa
Avenida Almirante Barroso, 1030, Praia de Iracema
TEL (85) 4005-4500 **FAX** and **RESERVATIONS** 4005-4505
www.maredomushotel.com.br

Marina Park $$
Recommended for families, it offers excellent leisure facilities, especially the pool and marina. We recommend that you arrive and leave the hotel by car, rather than going anywhere on foot in this area. **ACCOMMODATIONS** 301 rooms and 14 suites, air-conditioning, private safe, minibar, telephone, cable TV; Internet access in some rooms **FACILITIES AND SERVICES** Internet access in communal areas, bar, parking, stores, marina, pool, playground, soccer court, tennis court, volleyball court, restaurant, magazine reading area, conference room, gym, games room, massage room, beauty parlor, sauna, business center, currency exchange, 24-hour kitchen, valet parking, shuttle service to local attractions (Praia do Futuro in the morning, tour along the coast in the afternoon) **CREDIT CARDS** Amex, Diners, MasterCard, Visa
Avenida Presidente Castelo Branco, 400, Praia de Iracema
TEL (85) 4006-9595 **FAX** 3253-1803 www.marinapark.com.br

Mercury Apartments Fortaleza Meireles $$
This hotel has rooms on 21 floors, all with a kitchen and electric stove. Rooms ending in the number 5 or 7 have the best view. Breakfast is charged extra. **ACCOMMODATIONS** 101 flats, Internet access, air-conditioning, private safe, open kitchen, minibar, telephone, cable TV **FACILITIES AND SERVICES** Internet access in communal areas, bar, parking, pool, restaurant, conference room, gym, sauna, business center **CREDIT CARDS** Amex, Diners, MasterCard, Visa
Rua Joaquim Nabuco, 166, Meireles
TEL (85) 3486-3000 **FAX** 3486-3003 www.accorhotels.com.br

Othon Palace Fortaleza $$$
The small lobby houses a piano bar and the La Terrazza Alfredo restaurant, which serves Italian and international cuisine. **ACCOMMODATIONS** 73 rooms and 10 suites, Internet access, air-conditioning, private safe, minibar, telephone, cable TV; Jacuzzi in suites **FACILITIES AND SERVICES** Internet access in communal areas, bar, parking, pool, restaurant, conference room, gym, massage room, sauna, business center, 24-hour kitchen, valet parking **CREDIT CARDS** Amex, Diners, MasterCard, Visa
Avenida Beira-Mar, 3470, Meireles
TEL (85) 3466-5500 **RESERVATIONS** 3466-5595 **FAX** 3466-5566
www.othon.com.br

WHERE TO EAT

Alfredo $
Open since 1958, this is the most traditional place to eat the fish dish known as *peixada*. They have kept the original recipe: fish cutlets cooked with vegetables, greens, eggs, coriander, and scallions, served with rice and thickened sauce. Dishes such as shrimp and lobster are also popular. **CUISINE** fish and seafood **CREDIT CARDS** Amex, Diners, MasterCard, Visa
Avenida Beira-Mar, 4616, Meireles
TEL (85) 3263-1803, 3263-1188 **OPEN** Sun – Thu, 10am – 1am; Fri and Sat, 10am – 4am

Boteco $
This is a reproduction of the classic *boteco* type of bar. The menu includes delicious bean broth and appetizers such as *coxinha de caranquejo* (crab cakes), served with a nice glass of draft beer if you wish. Main dishes include shredded beef jerky with manioc purée gratin, and *feijoada* on Saturdays. **CUISINE** bar food **CREDIT CARDS** Diners, MasterCard, Visa
Avenida Antônio Sales, 3177, Dionísio Torres
TEL (85) 3461-2872 **OPEN** Mon – Thu, 5pm – until the last customer leaves; Fri, 4pm – until the last customer leaves; Sat and Sun, noon – until the last customer leaves

Budega do Silva $
The excellent dishes include mutton risotto with pumpkin purée, and sun-dried beef with fried manioc, *baião-de-dois* (rice and beans), sweet potatoes, banana fritters, and *rapadura* (hard brown sugar). Arre Égua, a good place to dance to regional rhythms on Tuesday and Friday nights, is attached to Budega. **CUISINE** regional, varied **CREDIT CARDS** Diners, MasterCard, Visa
Rua Delmiro Gouveia, 420, Varjota
TEL (85) 3267-2325 **OPEN** Tue – Fri, 5pm – midnight; Sat and Sun, noon – midnight

Cantinho do Faustino $
Chef Faustino created the inventive menu of this simple restaurant, which focuses on regional ingredients mixed with herbs and wine. Note the shelled lobster grilled in cashew vinegar (known locally as *mocororó*), served with pumpkin purée, or the smooth, light tilapia (a freshwater fish) grilled in clarified butter. Recommended desserts are olive ice cream drizzled with olive oil and flambéed bananas with *rapadura* or basil ice cream. **CUISINE** contemporary, regional **CREDIT CARDS** Amex, Diners, MasterCard, Visa
Rua Delmiro Gouveia, 1520, Varjota
TEL (85) 3267-5348 **OPEN** Tue – Fri, noon – 3pm and 7pm – midnight; Sat, noon – midnight; Sun, noon – 4pm

Carneiro do Ordones $
This is a good place to eat a variety of mutton dishes. There are more than sixty options, such as rump, ribs, and *borrego* (lamb killed when it is fifty days old), which comes from the interior of Ceará and is cooked on a charcoal grill. **CUISINE** regional **CREDIT CARDS** Amex, Diners, MasterCard, Visa
Rua Azevedo Bolão, 571, Parque Araxá
TEL (85) 3281-5959 **OPEN** Daily, 9am – 2am

Cemoara $
The menu here concentrates on fish and seafood, all of excellent quality. Some dishes have a very local flavor, such as shrimp in aromatic *cajá* fruit sauce. They also serve *moqueca* and several types of fish, including salted cod. **CUISINE** fish and seafood **CREDIT CARDS** Amex, Diners, MasterCard, Visa
Avenida Abolição, 3340-A, Meireles
TEL (85) 3263-5001 **OPEN** Mon – Thu, noon – 3pm and 7pm – midnight; Fri and Sat, noon – 3pm and 7pm – 1am; Sun, noon – 5pm

Centro das Tapioqueiras $
On the avenue leading to the CE-040 highway, in the direction of the beaches east of Fortaleza, you will find this square of 22 exposed brick stalls. All of them have a good wood-burning stove delivering more than fifty *tapioca* options, for example beef jerky, curd cheese, chocolate with grated coconut, *romeu-e-julieta* (guava jelly and cheese), and banana with cinnamon. Try *cajuina*, a traditional drink made from cashew fruit, with your *tapioca*. **CUISINE** snack food, regional **CREDIT CARDS** Visa
Avenida Washington Soares, 10125 (CE-040), Messejana
TEL (85) 3474-1326 **OPEN** Daily, 5am – until the last customer leaves

Coco Bambu $
A self-service, per kilo system operates at lunchtime, with

dishes such as *sarapatel*, *buchada*, and *galinha de cabidela*. There are also generous salad and dessert buffets. At night, the menu includes pizzas, and Fortaleza's famous tapioca. An annex serves Japanese food. CUISINE regional, varied (lunch); crêpe, pizza and tapioca (dinner) CREDIT CARDS Diners, MasterCard, Visa
Rua Canuto de Aguiar, 1317, Meireles
TEL (85) 3242-7557 OPEN Sun – Thu, 11am – 3pm and 5pm – midnight; Fri and Sat, 11am – 3pm and 5pm – 2am

Colher de Pau $

A famous, traditional restaurant, Colher de Pau serves tender, tasty sun-dried beef – specially cut from the flank – accompanied by delights such as manioc fried in clarified butter, *baião-de-dois*, *paçoca*, and fried banana. They also offer mutton, fish, and seafood. Anyone wanting *buchada*, *rabada* (oxtail) or *panelada* (meat and vegetable stew) should order two days in advance. CUISINE regional CREDIT CARDS Amex, Diners, MasterCard, Visa
Varjota: Rua Frederico Borges, 206
TEL (85) 3267-3773 OPEN Daily, 11am – midnight
Iracema: Rua dos Tabajaras, 412
TEL (85) 3219-3605 OPEN Daily, 6pm – 12:30am

Itaparikà $

A typical Thursday night out in Fortaleza is a crab dinner in the kiosks along the beach on Praia do Futuro. The very busy Itaparikà is the one of the biggest of these. Totally informal, completely open-plan with the kitchen in full view, it serves innumerable crab appetizers (dressed crab in the shell, claws, pies and whole crab), as well as fish croquettes. CUISINE bar food, fish and seafood CREDIT CARDS Amex, Diners, MasterCard, Visa
Avenida Zezé Diogo, 6801, Praia do Futuro
TEL (85) 3265-3213 RESERVATIONS 3265-1195. OPEN Fri – Wed, 8am – 5pm; Thu, 8am – 5pm and 6:30pm – 1am

Juarez $

It is a simple spot, selling ice cream made on the premises. Regional fruits such as *sapoti*, *graviola*, and *cupuaçu*, as well as coconut and melon are some of the mouthwatering options. *Bacuri* – a kind of small coconut with creamy whitish-yellow pulp – ice cream is a good choice. CUISINE ice cream CREDIT CARDS not accepted
Avenida Barão de Studart, 2023, Aldeota
TEL (85) 3244-3848 OPEN Daily, 6:30am – 10:30pm

Lá na Roça $

Lá na Roça has a pleasingly rustic charm, family atmosphere, and well-cooked food. The flavors of the *sertão* are represented in the per kilo buffet, which includes *baião-de-dois*, *sarapatel*, *buchada*, manioc cakes, mutton risotto, among other dishes. The dessert buffet, prepared by Zil, the owner's mother is pure temptation. CUISINE regional CREDIT CARDS MasterCard, Visa
Avenida Eusébio de Queirós, 4425 (access by CE-040 highway), Eusébio
TEL (85) 3260-2464 OPEN Tue – Fri, 8am – 3pm; Sat and Sun, 8am – 4:30pm

Marcel $

Soufflés are the house specialty, including haddock, or shrimp, cheese, and mushroom. There are other successes too, like duck breast in pepper sauce. There is also a regional accent in the guinea fowl in herbs and ginger sauce, served with rice and chestnuts. The wine list covers a variety of nationalities. CUISINE French CREDIT CARDS Amex, Diners, MasterCard, Visa

Avenida Historiador Raimundo Girão, 800, Praia de Iracema
TEL (85) 3219-6767 RESERVATIONS 3219-7246. OPEN Mon – Thu, noon – 2:30pm and 7pm – midnight; Fri, noon – 2:30pm and 7pm – 1am; Sat, 7pm – 1am; Sun, noon – 4pm

Nostradamus $

The very competent French contemporary menu includes grilled snook with cashew nut crust served with Parmesan risotto and demonstrates the combination of imported techniques and regional ingredients. Choose a coffee, made on an Italian machine, from the special menu to accompany dessert. We recommend making a reservation. The dress code is "smart casual". CUISINE French, contemporary CREDIT CARDS Amex, Diners, MasterCard, Visa
Rua Joaquim Nabuco, 166 (Parthenon Meireles Hotel), Meireles
TEL (85) 3242-8500 OPEN Mon – Thu, 7pm – midnight; Fri and Sat, 7pm – 1am

Osmar do Camarão $

The limited menu, based on fish and seafood, includes the wonderfully fresh shrimp in oil and garlic. Try the lobster fried in clarified butter, with garlic. The atmosphere is very homely. CUISINE fish and seafood CREDIT CARDS Diners, MasterCard
Travessa São João, 147, Mucuripe
TEL (85) 3263-2812 OPEN High season: daily, noon – midnight; low season: Mon – Sat, noon – midnight

Pulcinella $

Their specialty is seafood spaghetti in fresh tomato sauce. Typical Italian antipasti are arranged buffet-style and charged per kilo. CUISINE Italian CREDIT CARDS Amex, Diners, MasterCard, Visa
Aldeota: Rua Osvaldo Cruz, 640
TEL (85) 3261-3411. Mon – Thu, noon – 3pm and 6pm – 1am; Fri – Sun, noon – 1am
Meireles: Avenida Senador Virgílio Távora, 600
TEL (85) 3244-0133 OPEN Daily, 4pm – 1am

Santa Grelha $

This is a good spot for meat lovers. Among other options, there are good Argentinian cuts such as *bife de tira* (sirloin steak) and *chorizo* beef, and American cuts like porterhouse and prime rib, all from the renowned Wessel meat supplier, in São Paulo. They also have some very uncommon salads, such as green leaves, grated carrot, grilled Brie, and honey. Drinks include special beers, for example organic Eisenbahn from Blumenau. CUISINE meats CREDIT CARDS Amex, Diners, MasterCard, Visa
Rua Vicente Leite, 1062, Aldeota
TEL (85) 3224-0249 OPEN Tue – Thu, 11:30am – midnight; Fri and Sat, 11:30am – 1am; Sun, 11:30am – 5pm

Sorveteria 50 Sabores $

Cajá, *graviola*, coconut, *bacuri*, and *sapoti* are all on offer. They also sell take away. The seating area is small but charming. CUISINE ice cream CREDIT CARDS not accepted
Avenida Beira-Mar, 4690, Mucuripe
TEL (85) 3263-1714 OPEN Daily, 9am – 11pm

SERVICES

Airport – Aeroporto Internacional Pinto Marins

Avenida Senador Carlos Jereissati, 3000, Serrinha
TEL (85) 3477-1200, 3477-1128 OPEN Daily, 24 hours
www.infraero.gov.br

| RESTAURANTS | $ up to R$50 | $$ from R$51 up to R$100 | $$$ from R$101 up to R$150 | $$$$ above R$150 |

Department of Tourism – Secretaria de Turismo
Rua Pereira Filgueiras, 4, Centro
TEL (85) 3252-1444 OPEN Mon – Fri, 8am – noon and 1pm – 5pm (phone enquiries until 9pm) www.fortaleza.ce.gov.br

Galinhos – Rio Grande do Norte

AREA CODE 84 POPULATION 2,082 DISTANCE Natal 175 kilometers (109 miles) ACCESS BR-406 highway, then RN-402 (25 kilometers of surfaced road, in terrible condition) and across the Pratagi River by boat

WHERE TO STAY

Brésil Aventure $
The rooms, which can accommodate up to four people, are very simple, and most of them have direct access to the beach. The modest décor is more than made up for by the wonderful view. ACCOMMODATIONS 13 chalets, minibar, TV, ceiling fan FACILITIES AND SERVICES Internet access in communal areas, parking, restaurant CREDIT CARDS not accepted
Rua Senador Dinape Mariz, 123, Centro
TEL (84) 3552-0085 FAX 3552-0120 www.bresil-aventure.com

SERVICES

Department of Tourism – Secretaria Municipal de Turismo
Praça dos Três Poderes, no #, Centro
TEL (84) 3552-0115. OPEN Mon – Fri, 8am – 1pm

Garanhuns – Pernambuco

AREA CODE 87 POPULATION 126,776 DISTANCES Recife 230 kilometers (143 miles), Caruaru 120 kilometers (75 miles), Maceió 155 kilometers (96 miles) ACCESS From Recife, take the BR-232 highway to the Km 150 marker (São Caetano), then take BR-423. Regular buses leave every hour from the bus station in Recife. More comfortable *executivo* buses leave in the morning and at night
www.garanhuns.pe.gov.br

WHERE TO STAY

Fazenda Brejo $
The daily rates include all meals, and the farm is open to day visitors. The dirt access road demands special care and attention in the rainy season (from April to July). ACCOMMODATIONS a dormitory accommodates 60 guests; 20 private rooms with minibar, hammock, and ceiling fan FACILITIES AND SERVICES bar, woods, waterfall, cascade, kayaks, mini-soccer field, horses, cart, fishing lake and equipment, snack bar, pool, natural pool, restaurant, games room, video room, walking trails, recreational team for adults and children, guided walking tours CREDIT CARDS MasterCard, Visa
Fazenda Brejo, Distrito de Iatecá, Saloá
TEL (87) 3926-2047 RESERVATIONS and FAX 3251-0756
www.fazendabrejo.com.br

Garanhuns Palace $
One of the best and most centrally located hotels in Garanhuns. The hotel can organize a city tour on request. ACCOMMODATIONS 44 rooms and 9 suites, Internet access, air-conditioning, minibar, telephone, TV, ceiling fan FACILITIES AND SERVICES Internet access in communal areas, bar, parking, pool, conference room, gym, games room CREDIT CARDS Amex, Diners, MasterCard, Visa
Rua Rui Barbosa, 626, Heliópolis
TEL (87) 3761-3550, 3761-1244

Sesc Garanhuns $
This is perhaps the best option for tourists. A spacious, tree-filled area and a well-tended garden offer numerous recreational options. ACCOMMODATIONS 60 rooms, minibar, telephone, TV, air-conditioning in luxury rooms, fan in standard rooms FACILITIES AND SERVICES Internet access in communal areas, bar, kids room, parking, snack bar, pool, thermal pool, playground, volleyball court, restaurant, games room, video room, recreational team for adults and children CREDIT CARDS Amex, Diners, MasterCard, Visa
Rua Manoel Clemente, 161 Centro
TEL (87) 3761-8300 FAX 3761-1227 RESERVATIONS (81) 3421-5054, 3421-2367 www.sesc-pe.com.br

Tavares Correia $
Set on extensive grounds, it has reasonably good recreational facilities, and guests can choose to stay in chalets, rooms, or suites. Non-smoking rooms are available. ACCOMMODATIONS 45 rooms, 36 suites, and 11 chalets; minibar, telephone, TV FACILITIES AND SERVICES Internet access in communal areas, wine cellar, bar, bicycles, soccer field, horses, cart, parking, snack bar, convenience store, pool, playground, tennis court, volleyball court, restaurant, conference room, games room, video room CREDIT CARDS Amex
Rua Rui Barbosa, 296, Heliópolis
TEL (87) 3762-0250 FAX 3763-1638 RESERVATIONS (81) 3464-0300
www.tavarescorreia.com

WHERE TO EAT

Buchada do Gago $
This restaurant is so no-frills that it doesn't even have a menu, but chef Gago's friendliness and the mild flavor of his *buchada* – among other goat dishes – have made this the most popular place in town. To get there, take the highway BR-423 and turn left after the Coca-Cola plant – everybody in town knows Gago's place. CUISINE regional CREDIT CARDS MasterCard
Rua Mariano Filho, 1, Vila do Quartel (exit Km 5, Rodovia José Cardoso)
TEL (87) 3761-3894 OPEN Daily, 10am – 6pm

Chez Pascal $
Once the most trendy restaurant in Garanhuns. Excellent service and a mastery of Swiss cuisine – cheese, beef, and shrimp fondues are among the menu basics. CUISINE Swiss, fondue CREDIT CARDS Amex, Diners, MasterCard, Visa
Avenida Rui Barbosa, 891, Heliópolis
TEL (87) 3762-0070 RESERVATIONS 8801-9210 OPEN Tue – Sun, noon – 3:30pm and 6pm – until the last customer leaves

SERVICES

Bus Station – Rodoviária
Avenida Caruaru, no #, São José
TEL (87) 3761-0537

Department of Tourism – Secretaria de Turismo
Rua Joaquim Távora, no #, Heliópolis
TEL (87) 3762-7000, 3762-7095, 3762-7096 OPEN Mon – Fri, 8am – 2pm www.garanhuns.pe.gov.br

Genipabu – Rio Grande do Norte

AREA CODE 84 Extremoz DISTANCE Natal 25 kilometers (16 miles) ACCESS From Natal, RN-304 highway

| PRICES | HOTELS (couple) | $ up to R$150 | $$ from R$151 up to R$300 | $$$ from R$301 up to R$500 | $$$$ above R$500 |

WHERE TO EAT

Bar 21 $
Among the picture-perfect dunes of Genipabu beach rests Bar 21, an informal eatery serving up generous portions and one of the most beautiful views of the Rio Grande de Norte coast. Fish dish *peixada* is the house specialty. **CUISINE** bar food, fish and seafood **CREDIT CARDS** Amex, Diners, MasterCard, Visa
Praia de Genipabu
TEL (84) 3224-2484 **OPEN** High season: daily, 9am – until the last customer leaves; low season: daily, 9am – 5pm

SERVICES

Bus Station – Rodoviária
Rua Principal, no # (next to the post office)
TEL (84) 3279-4912

Goiana – Pernambuco
AREA CODE 81 **POPULATION** 75,579 **DISTANCES** Recife 60 kilometers (37 miles), João Pessoa 52 kilometers (33 miles) **ACCESS** BR-101 highway

WHERE TO EAT

Buraco da Gia $
It all began five decades ago, when the owner opened a small bar with one item on the menu: crab. Photographs of illustrious visitors recall the good old days. **CUISINE** fish and seafood **CREDIT CARDS** MasterCard, Visa
Rua Padre Batalha, 100
TEL (81) 3626-0150 **OPEN** Daily, 8am – 9pm

SERVICES

Bus Station – Rodoviária
Rua Senador José Rabelo, no #, Vila Castelo Branco
TEL (81) 3626-1000

Gravatá – Pernambuco
AREA CODE 81 **POPULATION** 70,899 **DISTANCE** Recife 80 kilometers (50 miles) **ACCESS** From Recife, take the BR-232 highway

WHERE TO STAY

Highlander $$
Notable for its cozy mountain setting, the Highlander sits nestled in a calm of nature and quiet. To get there, drive 14 kilometers (9 miles) along the BR-232 highway, and continue along the dirt road for 5 kilometers. **ACCOMMODATIONS** 52 suites, air-conditioning, minibar, TV; veranda with hammock and lounger; fireplace in 4 suites **FACILITIES AND SERVICES** library, woods, horses, parking, fireplace, pool, playground, orchard, restaurant, conference room, games room, video room, sauna, walking trails, guided walking tours **CREDIT CARDS** MasterCard, Visa
Fazenda Água Fria, Chã Grande (take BR-232, Recife–Gravatá)
TEL and **FAX** (81) 3515-1517 **RESERVATIONS** 3424-3838
www.hotelhighlander.com.br

Hotel Casa Grande Gravatá $$$
The small water park, athletic courts, fishing lake and conference facilities make this hotel a tourist favorite. An on-site restaurant serves regional and international dishes. **ACCOMMODATIONS** 112 rooms and 7 chalets, air-conditioning, minibar, telephone, TV **FACILITIES AND SERVICES** Internet access in communal areas, bar, nightclub, woods, cascade, parking, Jacuzzi, fishing lake, snack bar, pool, thermal pool, playground, soccer court, tennis court, volleyball court, restaurant, games room, sauna, business center, recreational team for children, live music (weekends) **CREDIT CARDS** Amex, Diners, MasterCard, Visa
Rodovia BR-232, Km 82, no #
TEL (81) 3533-0920 **FAX** and **RESERVATIONS** 3465-3011
www.hotelcasagrandegravata.com.br

Hotel Fazenda Céu Aberto $
Horses, chickens, cows, birds, and even llamas add to the rural atmosphere of this hotel. Among the hotel's attractions are a fishing lake and three pools. The suites are rather small, though all have king-size beds. The driving route to the hotel is along 3 kilometers of dirt road, often difficult to navigate or inaccessible during the rainy season (April and July). **ACCOMMODATIONS** 30 suites, air-conditioning, minibar, cable TV, private veranda in premium suites **FACILITIES AND SERVICES** bar, woods, horses, cart, parking, fishing lake and equipment, snack bar, pool, ponies, multi-sports court, restaurant, gym, games room, walking trails, recreational team for adults and children, guided walking tours **CREDIT CARDS** not accepted
Estrada Velha de Chã Grande, Km 3 (exit Km 76 on the BR-232 highway)
TEL (81) 3228-8008, 9126-9600 **FAX** 3228-8010
www.hotelfazendaceuaberto.com.br

Hotel Fazenda Portal de Gravatá $$
With well-maintained facilities and a friendly staff, this is a great place to rest and relax. Rooms are spotless. In addition to the typical outdoor activities offered by area hotels, Portal de Gravatá gives guests the unique chance of hands-on experience with cattle ranching. A climbing wall and flying fox are among the leisure options. The hotel also accepts day visitors interested in the activities they offer. The restaurant serves well-cooked regional and international food. **ACCOMMODATIONS** 85 rooms and 3 suites, Internet access, air-conditioning, minibar, telephone, TV **FACILITIES AND SERVICES** bar, soccer field, horses, cart, parking, snack bar, convenience store, pool, pool bar, thermal pool, playground, ponies, restaurant, conference room, games room, sauna, recreational team for children, airport shuttle **CREDIT CARDS** Amex, Diners, MasterCard, Visa
Rodovia BR-232, Km 82
TEL (81) 3533-0288, 3533-1456 **RESERVATIONS** 3227-0345 **FAX** 3533-0610 www.portaldegravata.com.br

WHERE TO EAT

Buchadinha do Gordo $
Buchada (goat's or lamb's insides) may be an acquired taste, but this friendly eatery is the best place in town to taste the dish for yourself. The bilingual menu includes that and other regional dishes. **CUISINE** regional, varied **CREDIT CARDS** not accepted
Rua 7 de Setembro, 594, Centro
TEL (81) 3533-0995 **OPEN** Daily, 8am – 5pm

Pinheiros $
Chef Geraldo José da Silva cooks international specialties such as fondue, sliced lamb, and his specialty, steamed ribs. **CUISINE** regional, varied **CREDIT CARDS** Amex, Diners, MasterCard, Visa
Avenida Cícero Batista de Oliveira, 1778, Nossa Senhora das Graças
TEL (81) 3533-5217 **RESERVATIONS** 3533-5297 **OPEN** Wed and Thu, 10am – 10pm; Fri – Sun, 10am – 1am

---

RESTAURANTS $ up to R$50 $$ from R$51 up to R$100 $$$ from R$101 up to R$150 $$$$ above R$150

Tournée Delícias do Mundo $
The menu includes such globe-trotting delicacies as beef chateaubriand (serves two). The wine list includes Brazilian, Argentinean, and Italian vintages. CUISINE varied CREDIT CARDS Amex, Diners, MasterCard, Visa
Rua 15 de Novembro, 1175
TEL (81) 3533-0741, 9156-5806 OPEN Thu – Sun, noon – until the last customer leaves

SERVICES

Bus Station – Rodoviária
Avenida Padre Cícero Batista de Oliveira, no # (BR-232)
TEL (81) 3533-2031 OPEN Daily, 6am – 7pm

Department of Tourism – Secretaria de Turismo
Rua João Pessoa, 110, Centro
TEL (81) 3563-9047 OPEN Mon – Fri, 7am – 1pm; official holidays and events, also Sat and Sun, 7am – midnight
www.prefeituradegravata.com.br

Ibicoara – Bahia

AREA CODE 77 POPULATION 16,985 DISTANCES Salvador 460 kilometers (286 miles), Lençóis 202 kilometers (126 miles) ACCESS Take BA-142 and follow the Estrada de Ibicoara 18 kilometers (11 miles) further. (Watch out for potholes!) www.ibicoara.ba.gov.br

WHERE TO STAY

EcoPousada Buracão $
The rooms are simple, but have a view of the lovely mountains that surround Ibicoara. The service is good, and breakfast is hearty. ACCOMMODATIONS 15 suites, minibar, TV, ceiling fan FACILITIES AND SERVICES parking, natural pool, restaurant CREDIT CARDS not accepted
Estrada de Ibicoara, Km 12 off BR-142
TEL and FAX (77) 3413-2235, (71) 9962-6774

SERVICES

Department of Tourism – Secretaria de Turismo
Praça Américo Martins Jr., 120, Centro
TEL (77) 3413-2178 OPEN Mon – Fri, 8am – noon and 2pm – 5pm

Igarassu – Pernambuco

AREA CODE 81 POPULATION 90,904 DISTANCE Recife 28 kilometers (17 miles) ACCESS From Recife, take exit Km44 off BR-101 WHEN TO VISIT September, for the festivities in honor of the town's patron saints, Cosmas and Damian
www.igarassu.pe.gov.br

SERVICES

Bus Station – Rodoviária
BR-101, Km 41
TEL (81) 3543-3384

Department of Tourism – Secretaria Municipal de Turismo
Praça da Bandeira, 14
TEL (81) 3543-0435 (City Hall) FAX 3545-0494 OPEN Mon – Fri, 7am – 1pm

Igatu – Bahia

AREA CODE 75 Andaraí DISTANCES Salvador 414 kilometers (257 miles), Andaraí 14 kilometers (9 miles) ACCESS Take BA-142 from Salvador. One option is to take the exit at Km 52 and continue on 7 kilometers (4 miles) of stone-paved road until you reach Igatu. Another option is to take the exit at Km 82 and continue down 6 kilometers of dirt road (with some surfaced stretches)

WHERE TO STAY

Pousada Pedras de Igatu $
This is the only guesthouse in Igatu. Breakfast is excellent; other attractions are the restaurant, the gift shop selling regional items, and the small natural pool. ACCOMMODATIONS 14 rooms, ceiling fan FACILITIES AND SERVICES Internet access in communal areas, bar, stores, natural pool, restaurant, video room CREDIT CARDS not accepted
Rua São Sebastião, no #
TEL and FAX (75) 3335-2281 www.igatu.com.br

Ilha de Boipeba – Bahia

AREA CODE 75 Cairu DISTANCE Salvador 256 kilometers (159 miles); take BR-324 and BR-101, then continue 40 minutes by motorboat ACCESS From Salvador, take a catamaran (2 hours) or motorboat (2 hours, 10 minutes) to Morro de São Paulo. From there, take a 4x4 vehicle or motorboat (1 hour) to Boipeba. By car, take BR-324 and BR-101 from Salvador to Valença. From there, continue by boat (3 hours and 30 minutes) or motorboat (40 minutes) on to Boipeba. There are also direct flights from Salvador (35 minutes). From the village of Torrinhas, go to Cairu and continue by motorboat (30 minutes)

WHERE TO STAY

Pousada Luar das Águas $
Boipeba's first guesthouse was opened in 1988. Be sure to choose the bungalow, which is right in front of the sea. The restaurant serves seafood and meat dishes. ACCOMMODATIONS 8 rooms and 2 bungalow, minibar, ceiling fan; air-conditioning in 1 room FACILITIES AND SERVICES Internet access in communal areas, bar, kayaks, board games, restaurant, video room, walking trails, laundry, beach service; fishing and diving equipment (summer) CREDIT CARDS Visa
Praia Boca da Barra, no #
TEL (75) 3653-6015, 3641-2238, 9981-1012
www.luardasaguas.com.br

Pousada Maliale $
The rooms are more spacious and better-equipped than most in the region. The amenities include a pool with deck and waterfall, as well as two motorboats available for guests to use on trips to Boipeba. ACCOMMODATIONS 16 rooms, air-conditioning, minibar, TV, ceiling fan FACILITIES AND SERVICES bar, boat, kayaks, fishing equipment, waterskiing, motorboat, snack bar, pool, restaurant, games room, beach service CREDIT CARDS MasterCard
Ilha de São Miguel, Praia da Ilha de São Miguel
TEL (75) 3653-6134, 9981-3322 FAX (11) 4724-8577 RESERVATIONS (11) 4794-7474 www.pousadamaliale.com.br

Pousada Tassimirim $
Though simple like most other accommodations in Bioepba, this guesthouse sets itself apart by being charmingly rustic. We recommend the rooms near the beach, with their sea views. ACCOMMODATIONS 15 rooms; air-conditioning in some rooms, ceiling fan in others FACILITIES AND SERVICES Internet access in communal areas, bar, boat, board games, restaurant, walking trails, TV, boat trips CREDIT CARDS Diners, MasterCard, Visa

PRICES	HOTELS (couple)	$ up to R$150	$$ from R$151 up to R$300	$$$ from R$301 up to R$500	$$$$ above R$500

Praia Boca da Barra, no #, Vila Velha Boipeba
TEL and FAX (75) 3653-6030 RESERVATIONS 3653-6030, 9981-2378
www.ilhaboipeba.org.br/tassimirim.html

Pousada Vila Sereia $$
One of the most charming guesthouses in Boipeba. The stretch of Boca da Barra Beach where the bungalows are set up are good for bathing. Breakfast is served on the veranda. ACCOMMODATIONS 4 bungalows, minibar, veranda with hammock, ceiling fan. FACILITIES AND SERVICES garden with lounge chairs CREDIT CARDS MasterCard
Praia Boca da Barra, no #, Vila Velha Boipeba
TEL and FAX (75) 3653-6045 RESERVATIONS 9967-2878
www.ilhaboipeba.org.br/vilasereia.html

WHERE TO EAT

Mar e Coco $
This simple but very pleasant restaurant serves the best *moqueca* around. The house specialty is the delicious shrimp *moqueca* with plantain, but they also serve such delicacies as pickled octopus with crispbread and oven baked lobster with basil sauce (all dishes serve two). CUISINE regional, fish and seafood CREDIT CARDS not accepted
Praia de Morerê
TEL (75) 3653-6013 RESERVATIONS 9994-8816 OPEN Daily, 10am – 5pm

Santa Clara $
The restaurant is in the guesthouse of the same name, in a small but delightful thatch-roofed kiosk. Among the chef's suggestions are lobster ravioli (made on the premises), snapper in *cajá* fruit sauce, and the Vietnamese beef (grilled beef skewers served with a variety of sauces). Wash it all down with one of the fruit margaritas or the *bomba de maracujá* (passion fruit juice and liqueur mixed with *cachaça* or vodka). CUISINE regional, fish and seafood CREDIT CARDS Visa
Travessa da Praia, 5
TEL (75) 3653-6085 OPEN Tue – Sun, 8am – 10pm

Ilha de Itaparica – Bahia

AREA CODE 71 POPULATION 21,382 DISTANCE Salvador 280 kilometers (174 miles) by car, 45 minutes by ferry ACCESS From Salvador, take a ferry (more than one hour between each crossing) or a catamaran (the wait between crossings is even longer). Visitors can also hire private motorboats or planes, the latter landing at the Aeroclube da Bahia (highway BA-001, Km 15). Coming from Salvador by car, take BR-101 to Santo Antônio de Jesus, then BA-245 to Jacuruna. From there, take BA-001 until you cross the Ponte do Funil bridge, which connects the island to the mainland

WHERE TO STAY

Club Med Itaparica $$$
The recreational facilities will no doubt be the highlight of your stay, as adults and children alike are invited to join in numerous activities throughout the day. In addition to the standard all-inclusive stay, the resort offers a day-use pass for non-residents to enjoy a day at Club Med. ACCOMMODATIONS 330 rooms, Internet access, air-conditioning, private safe, minibar, telephone, cable TV FACILITIES AND SERVICES Internet access in communal areas, bar, windsurfing, sailboat, soccer field, golf course, parking, horseback riding center, stores, pool, jogging track, soccer court, tennis court, volleyball court, restaurant, beauty parlor, conference room, gym, games room, massage room, sauna, business center, 24-hour infirmary, recreational team for adults and children, guided walking tours, massage room, beach service, circus and silk-painting workshops CREDIT CARDS Amex, Diners, MasterCard, Visa
Rodovia Bom Despacho, Km 13, Nazaré
TEL (71) 3681-8800 RESERVATIONS 0800-707-3782 FAX 3681-7380
www.clubmed.com.br

Resort Sol e Mar $$$
The rooms are simple and rustic. The restaurant serves a varied menu, with an emphasis on local cuisine. ACCOMMODATIONS 7 chalets and 3 rooms, Internet access, air-conditioning, private safe, minibar, telephone, TV, ceiling fan; Jacuzzi in luxury chalets FACILITIES AND SERVICES Internet access in communal areas, parking, pool, restaurant, motorboat trips, valet parking, beach service, airport shuttle CREDIT CARDS Amex, Visa
Avenida Beira-Mar, 1650, Praia de Barra do Gil
TEL (71) 3633-1154 www.resortsolemar.com

SERVICES

Department of Tourism – Secretaria de Turismo
Avenida Monsenhor Flaviano, no #, Casarão Del-Rei, Centro
TEL (71) 3631-1778 OPEN Mon – Fri, 8am – 6pm

Ilha do Caju – Maranhão
(see Parnaíba)

Ilhéus – Bahia

AREA CODE 73 POPULATION 221,110 DISTANCES Salvador 462 kilometers (287 miles), Vitória da Conquista 270 kilometers (168 miles), Porto Seguro 318 kilometers (198 miles) ACCESS Take BA-001

WHERE TO STAY

Cana Brava Resort $$$$
This resort has excellent leisure facilities, with a variety of recreational activities. Though all the rooms are comfortable, the chalets are more spacious and private. ACCOMMODATIONS 92 rooms and 78 chalets, air-conditioning, private safe, minibar, telephone, cable TV FACILITIES AND SERVICES Internet access in communal areas, bar, bicycles, kayaks, soccer field, parking, snack bar, convenience store, pool, tennis court, volleyball court, restaurant, river, conference room, gym, games room, massage room, beauty parlor, sauna, walking trails, travel agency, car rental, recreational team for adults and children, guided walking tours, lifeguard, beach service, shuttle service to airport and local attractions CREDIT CARDS Amex, Diners, MasterCard, Visa
Rodovia Ilhéus–Canavieiras, Km 24
TEL (73) 3269-8000 www.canabravaresort.com.br

Ecoresort Tororomba $$$
The resort is ideal for children, featuring such facilities as a water trampoline and a small zoo. Opt for one of the VIP rooms, which are more comfortable and feature a lovely view of the beach. The Jairi River runs right by the hotel, forming a small magnesium spring open to guests. Facing the hotel across the highway is a replica of the main chapel of Engenho de Santana, the original colonial settlement in the area. ACCOMMODATIONS 61 rooms and 30 chalets, air-con-

---

RESTAURANTS $ up to R$50 $$ from R$51 up to R$100 $$$ from R$101 up to R$150 $$$$ above R$150

ditioning, private safe, minibar, telephone, cable TV **FACILITIES AND SERVICES** Internet access in communal areas, bar, bicycles, woods, waterfall, kayaks, soccer field, fishing equipment, parking, Jacuzzi, snack bar, stores, pool, natural pool, playground, soccer court, volleyball court, restaurant, river, conference room, games room, massage room, beauty parlor, sauna, walking trails, recreational team for adults and children, guided walking tours, lifeguard, beach service, airport shuttle **CREDIT CARDS** Amex, Diners, MasterCard, Visa
Rodovia Ilhéus–Comandatuba, Km 21
TEL (73) 3269-1200 **FAX** 3234-1409 www.tororomba.com.br

Hotel Fazenda da Lagoa $$$$
The bungalows are surrounded by greenery and come with either queen (in 4 rooms) or king beds (in 10 rooms). Chef Marc Le Dantec oversees the restaurant's contemporary menu. The hotel is only accessible by ferryboat from the Aliança River pier (300 meters). **ACCOMMODATIONS** 14 bungalows, air-conditioning, private safe, minibar, telephone, cable TV **FACILITIES AND SERVICES** bar, library, bicycles, kayaks, fishing lake, convenience store, pool, restaurant, massage room, games room, sauna, manicure salon, beach service, airport shuttle **CREDIT CARDS** MasterCard, Visa
Rodovia Una–Ilhéus, Km 18, Dependência
TEL (73) 3236-6046, 3236-6137 **RESERVATIONS** (21) 2259-8511 www.fazendadalagoa.com.br

La Dolce Vita $$$
The best room is the superior suite, which has a wonderful view, a separate living room, and a large veranda with its own shower. Leisure facilities are limited. **ACCOMMODATIONS** 42 rooms and 2 suites, air-conditioning, private safe, minibar, telephone, cable TV; Internet access in luxury rooms; Jacuzzi in suites **FACILITIES AND SERVICES** Internet access in communal areas, bar, parking, snack bar, convenience store, pool, volleyball court, restaurant, conference room, gym, video room, sauna **CREDIT CARDS** Amex, Diners, MasterCard, Visa
Rua A, 114, Jardim Paraíso (Rodovia Ilhéus–Canavieiras, Km 2.5)
TEL (73) 3234-1212 **FAX** 3234-1213 www.ladolcevita.com.br

Opaba $$
Guests are welcome to use the extensive leisure facilities at its sister resort, Cana Brava. Rooms vary only in terms of the view, either of the sea or of the airport. **ACCOMMODATIONS** 77 rooms and 2 suites, Internet access, air-conditioning, minibar, telephone, cable TV **FACILITIES AND SERVICES** Internet access in communal areas, bar, parking, pool, restaurant, conference room **CREDIT CARDS** Amex, Diners, MasterCard, Visa
Avenida Nossa Senhora Aparecida, 1, São Francisco (Km 0, Rodovia Ilhéus–Canavieiras)
TEL (73) 3234-8810 **FAX** 3632-1087 www.opaba.com.br

Transamérica Ilha de Comandatuba $$$$
This is one of the best resorts in all of Brazil. The resort offers a wide variety of leisure activities, including water sports, deep-sea fishing, archery, and golf, which is played on the resort's private golf course. The on-site spa is run by the French health and beauty company L'Occitane. Accommodation is in rooms, suites, or bungalows. **ACCOMMODATIONS** 239 rooms, 111 bungalows, and 13 suites; Internet access, air-conditioning, private safe, minibar, telephone, cable TV; Jacuzzi in luxury suites and bungalows **FACILITIES AND SERVICES** Internet access in communal areas, wine cellar, archery, bar, boat, bicycles, kayaks, soccer field, golf course, fishing equipment, waterskiing, parking, jet-ski, motorboat, snack bar, stores, marina, pool, playground, soccer field, squash court, tennis court, volleyball court, restaurant, reading room, river, cinema, conference room, gym, games room, massage room, beauty parlor, sauna, spa, babysitting, business center, currency exchange, 24-hour kitchen, recreational team for adults and children, guided walking tours, landing strip, lifeguard, beach service, shuttle service to airport and local attractions **CREDIT CARDS** Amex, Diners, MasterCard, Visa
Ilha de Comandatuba, no #
TEL (73) 3686-1122 **RESERVATIONS** 0800-126-060 **FAX** 3686-1457
www.transamerica.com.br

WHERE TO EAT

Boca du Mar $
The grilled sea bass with vegetables, the tasty octopus risotto, and the penne with salmon are all highly recommended. There is also a sushi and sashimi menu. The restaurant features live music daily. **CUISINE** fish and seafood, regional **CREDIT CARDS** Amex, Diners, MasterCard, Visa
Avenida Lomanto Jr., 15, Pontal
TEL (73) 3231-2822 **RESERVATIONS** 3231-3200 **OPEN** High season: Tue – Sat, noon – 2am; Sun, 11:30am – midnight; low season: Fri and Sat, 8am – 2am

Cabana Gabriela $
This is the largest of the *barracas* on Milionários Beach. The menu favors fish and seafood. The house specialties are *peixe à Gabriela* (whole fried fish with shrimp, garlic, and oil, served with seasoned manioc flour, french fries, and salad; serves three) and shrimp *moqueca* (served with rice and thickened sauce; serves two). **CUISINE** fish and seafood, regional **CREDIT CARDS** Amex, Diners, MasterCard, Visa
Rua Rui Penalva, 109, Centro
TEL (73) 3632-1836 **RESERVATIONS** 3231-7373 **OPEN** Daily, 8am – 8pm

Sheik $
The menu includes local, Italian, Portuguese, and Arabic dishes, the latter being the house specialty (the owner's family are of Arab origin). We recommend the Sheik special (a wide selection of Arabic dishes), *moqueca mariscada* (mussels served with rice and thickened sauce,) and *bacalhau portuga* (large salt cod cutlets with potatoes, bell pepper, eggs, olives, onion, and rice). **CUISINE** Arabic, regional, Italian, Portuguese **CREDIT CARDS** Amex, Diners, MasterCard, Visa
Oiteiro de São Sebastião, no #, Centro
TEL (73) 3634-1799 **OPEN** Mon – Sat, 6pm – until the last customer leaves

SERVICES

Aeroporto Jorge Amado
Rua Brig. Eduardo Gomes, no #, Pontal
TEL (73) 3234-4000 **OPEN** Daily, 6am – 11pm

Tourist Information – Bahiatursa
Rua Eustáquio Bastos, 308, Centro
TEL (73) 3231-2679 **OPEN** Mon – Fri, 7:30am – 5pm

Travel Agency – NV Turismo
Rua General Câmara, 27, Centro
TEL (73) 3634-4101, 3633-3331 **OPEN** Mon – Fri, 8:30am – 6pm; Sat, 8:30am – noon www.nvturismo.com.br

Tourist Information – Posto de Informações Turísticas
Praça da Catedral (kiosk)
OPEN Mon – Fri, 8am – 6pm

PRICES	HOTELS (couple)	$ up to R$150	$$ from R$151 up to R$300	$$$ from R$301 up to R$500	$$$$ above R$500

Imbassaí – Bahia

AREA CODE 71 Mata de São João **DISTANCES** Salvador 75 kilometers (47 miles), Costa do Sauípe 10 kilometers (6 miles), Praia do Forte 10 kilometers **ACCESS** Take BA-099 (Linha Verde)

WHERE TO STAY

Pousada Bichelenga $
The rooms have brightly colored walls and attractive wooden furniture. The covered veranda near the pool is particularly pleasant. **ACCOMMODATIONS** 21 rooms (4 double, 15 triple, 2 quads), air-conditioning, minibar, TV with satellite dish, veranda; bar in some rooms **FACILITIES AND SERVICES** bar, woods, parking, pool, playground, restaurant, conference room, home theater **CREDIT CARDS** Amex, Diners, MasterCard, Visa
Loteamento Miramar, no #, Lote 3
TEL and **FAX** (71) 3677-1122   www.bichelenga.com.br

Vilangelim Eco Pousada $$
The rooms, though simple, have nice balconies, and guarantee privacy as they are spread out quite spaciously on the property. The restaurant is the guesthouse's strong point, thanks to its carefully prepared selection of international dishes. **ACCOMMODATIONS** 20 chalets, air-conditioning, private safe, minibar, TV, ceiling fan, balcony **FACILITIES AND SERVICES** Internet access in communal areas, bar, woods, parking, stores, pool, restaurant, conference room, trip recommendations **CREDIT CARDS** Amex, Diners, MasterCard, Visa
Alameda dos Angelins, no #
TEL and **FAX** (71) 3677-1144, 3677-1224
www.vilangelim.com.br

WHERE TO EAT

Sombra da Mangueira $
The *dendê* palm oil used in the kitchen comes from the Sapiranga Reserve, where it is extracted from trees. The fish and coconut milk are always guaranteed fresh. Though not particularly unusual, the shrimp *moqueca* is very tasty, and well-cooked. For dessert, choose either Salvadorian ice cream or a coconut dessert made with very little sugar. **CUISINE** regional **CREDIT CARDS** Diners, MasterCard, Visa
Rua Diogo, no #, Mata de São João
TEL (71) 9133-4860 **OPEN** Daily, 10am – 6pm

Ingá – Paraíba (see Campina Grande)

Itacaré – Bahia

AREA CODE 73 **POPULATION** 17,925 **DISTANCES** Salvador 440 kilometers (273 miles), Ilhéus 65 kilometers (40 miles) **ACCESS** From Ilhéus, take Estrada Parque Ilhéus–Itacaré (BA-001 northbound) for 65 kilometers. From BR-101 southbound, take the road to Uruçuca and then the Estrada Parque Ilhéus–Itacaré for 30 kilometers. From BR-101 northbound, take the Itabuna exit, and follow the road to Ilhéus for 29 kilometers (18 miles)

WHERE TO STAY

Aldeia da Mata Eco Lodge $$$
Mata Eco Lodge sits on 15 hectares (37 acres) of Atlantic forest facing the sea. Built of bamboo, wood, and piassava palm, the bungalows spread across the property are charming and cozy, and can accommodate up to three people. The spa in the middle of the forest is a big draw. **ACCOMMODATIONS** 12 bungalows, private safe, minibar, telephone, TV, ceiling fan **FACILITIES AND SERVICES** Internet access in communal areas, bar, beach bar, stores, pool, restaurant, games room, massage room, video room, spa, 24-hour kitchen, beach service, airport shuttle **CREDIT CARDS** not accepted
Praia do Pé da Serra, Uruçuca (Rodovia Itacaré–Ilhéus, BA-001, Km 31.5)
TEL (73) 3086-2999   www.aldeiadamata.com.br

Aldeia do Mar Chalés $$$
These pleasant hillside chalets all face the sea. Rooms are spacious and comfortable. The on-site restaurant has a gorgeous sea view (*see Where to Eat*). **ACCOMMODATIONS** 13 chalets, air-conditioning, private safe, minibar, telephone, cable TV **FACILITIES AND SERVICES** Internet access in communal areas, bar, parking, snack bar, pool, restaurant, river, travel agency, beach service **CREDIT CARDS** Diners, MasterCard, Visa
Praia da Concha, Loteamento Conchas do Mar, 1ª Etapa, Rua D, Quadra E, Lote 8
TEL and **FAX** (73) 3251-2230 **RESERVATIONS** (71) 3356-4344
www.aldeiadomarchales.tur.br

Burundanga Pousada $$
This small guesthouse have very few suites. The leisure area has a small pool with hydro-massage. **ACCOMMODATIONS** 6 suites, air-conditioning, coffeemaker, private safe, minibar, telephone, cable TV, hair dryer, veranda/balcony, ceiling fan **FACILITIES AND SERVICES** Internet access in communal areas, bar, Jacuzzi, pool, travel agency **CREDIT CARDS** Diners, MasterCard
Condomínio Conchas do Mar, Quadra D, Lote 6, Praia da Concha
TEL and **FAX** (73) 3251-2543   www.burundanga.com.br

Itacaré Eco Resort $$$$
This resort shares leisure facilities with Itacaré Village, which is in the same condo complex. The private beach and on-site animal reserve (with capybaras and caimans) are major highlights. **ACCOMMODATIONS** 25 rooms, air-conditioning, private safe, minibar, telephone, cable TV, veranda Jacuzzi in 1 room **FACILITIES AND SERVICES** Internet access in communal areas, wine cellar, bar, woods, kayaks, soccer field, horses, parking, snack room, stores, pool, natural pool, restaurant, river, conference room, gym, games room, massage room, video room, sauna, walking trails, travel agency, business center, recreational team for adults and children, guided walking tours, lifeguard, beach service, shuttle service to airport and local attractions **CREDIT CARDS** Amex, Diners, MasterCard, Visa
Rodovia Ilhéus–Itacaré, BA-001, Km 65, Condomínio Vilas de São José
TEL (73) 3251-2151 **FAX** and **RESERVATIONS** 3251-3133
www.ier.com.br

Itacaré Village $$$$
The hotel has its own private beach in the Vilas de São José condominiums. Village 4 has the best rooms, with great views and a Jacuzzi. Ten rooms are available for long-term rental. The hotel shares a small leisure area with the neighboring Itacaré Eco Resort. **ACCOMMODATIONS** 24 rooms, 10 suites, and 10 bungalows, air-conditioning, private safe, minibar, telephone, cable TV, ceiling fan; Jacuzzi in some bungalows and suites **FACILITIES AND SERVICES** Internet access in communal areas, wine cellar, bar, boat, woods, kayaks, soccer field, horses, parking, snack bar, convenience store, pool, natural pool, playground, restaurant, games room, massage room, walking trails, recreational team for adults and children, guided walking tours, lifeguard, beach service, shuttle service to airport and local attractions **CREDIT CARDS** Amex, Diners, MasterCard, Visa

---

RESTAURANTS   **$** up to R$50   **$$** from R$51 up to R$100   **$$$** from R$101 up to R$150   **$$$$** above R$150

Rodovia Itacaré–Ilhéus, BA-001, Km 64, Condomínio Vilas de São José
TEL (73) 3251-2188 www.itacarevillage.com.br

Pousada Ilha Verde $

The outdoor communal areas are very welcoming, with an *ofuro* tub, massage tent, reading space with cushions, and a deck that hosts *capoeira* and African dance classes. ACCOMMODATIONS 8 rooms and 1 bungalow, air-conditioning, minibar, ceiling fan FACILITIES AND SERVICES *capoeira* and dance classes, reading area, *ofuro* tub, pool, conference room, massage room, laundry CREDIT CARDS MasterCard, Visa
Rua Ataíde Setúbal, 234, Centro
TEL (73) 3251-2056 www.ilhaverde.com.br

Pousada Sage Point $$$

This charming guesthouse has rooms stretched out along Tiririca Beach. The restaurant serves healthy snacks, almost all of which are made on-site. ACCOMMODATIONS 5 rooms, air-conditioning, private safe, minibar, ceiling fan; Jacuzzi in 3 rooms FACILITIES AND SERVICES bar, parking, snack bar, restaurant, airport shuttle CREDIT CARDS Diners, MasterCard, Visa
Praia da Tiririca, 65
TEL (73) 3251-2030 www.pousadasagepoint.com.br

Txai Resort $$$$

The charming bungalows offer an unrivaled view of Itacarezinho Beach. All the rooms are extremely comfortable. The communal areas, such as the lovely restaurant, reading space, and pool, are also pleasant, and quite spacious. The hotel offers guests therapeutic massage. ACCOMMODATIONS 26 bungalows and 14 rooms, air-conditioning, CD player, private safe, minibar, telephone; Jacuzzi in 4 bungalows FACILITIES AND SERVICES Internet access in communal areas, bar, bicycles, parking, stores, pool, tennis court, restaurant, games room, video room, sauna, spa, walking trails, travel agency, 24-hour kitchen, guided walking tours, lifeguard, beach service, shuttle service to airport and local attractions CREDIT CARDS Amex, Diners, MasterCard, Visa
Praia de Itacarezinho, Rodovia Itacaré–Ilhéus, Km 48
TEL and FAX (73) 2101-5000 RESERVATIONS 2101-5240, 2101-5241
www.txai.com.br

Vila de Ocaporan Hotel Village $$$$

Ocaporan is one of the best options near Itacaré, offering spacious rooms as well as flats with a sitting room, kitchen, and one or two bedrooms. The hotel's communal areas include a restaurant and an eight-meter-high lookout point with views of mangroves and Atlantic forest. Service is attentive. ACCOMMODATIONS 48 suites and 3 flats, air-conditioning, private safe, minibar, telephone, cable TV FACILITIES AND SERVICES bar, parking, lookout point, pool, restaurant, games room, travel agency, guided walking tours, shuttle service to airport and local attractions CREDIT CARDS Diners, MasterCard, Visa
Rua Jacarandá, no #, Condomínio Conchas do Mar
TEL (73) 3251-2470 FAX 3251-3116
www.viladeocaporan.com.br

Warapuru (due to open in October or November, 2007)

Despite the grand scale of the architecture, the décor tends towards minimalism. There are 40 bungalows and 21 private villas. Each lodging has an area of between 160 and 330 square meters (1,700 to 3,550 square feet) and features a private pool and deck. Warapuru also boasts 175 meters of private beach with two restaurants and a pool.
Praia da Engenhoca www.warapuru.com

WHERE TO EAT

Boca de Forno $

This informal eatery serves thin-crust pizzas on iron and stone hotplates. Among the pizza options are *boca de forno* (heart of palm, spicy sausage, mozzarella, crispy garlic, and dried tomatoes) and dried tomato (mozzarella, dried tomatoes, Parmesan, and black olives). They also serve delicious pies and other sweet items. CUISINE pizza CREDIT CARDS Amex, Diners, MasterCard, Visa
Rua Lodônio Almeida, 108, Beco das Flores, Centro
TEL (73) 3251-3121 OPEN Mon – Thu, 5pm – midnight; Fri, Sat, and Sun, 5pm – 1am

Casa Sapucaia $

This restaurant has a cozy atmosphere, with two tables at the entrance, a small dining area with a bar, and a lovely garden outside. Chef Gil Ribeiro's modern cuisine has Asian accents (particularly Thai) Among the suggested dishes are *camarão da ilha* (skewered shrimp grilled with ginger, caramel, and lime, served with sautéed vegetables and rice), Genghis Khan (a crispy potato basket filled with beef strips, shiitake mushrooms, bell peppers, red onions, green beans, and Swiss chard, flambéed in cognac), and fish carpaccio. CUISINE Asian, contemporary, Mediterranean CREDIT CARDS MasterCard, Visa
Rua Lodônio Almeida, 84, Centro
TEL (73) 3251-3091 OPEN Mon – Sat, 7pm – 11:30pm

Dedo de Moça $

The good selection of wines and *cachaças* complement chef Vagner Aguiar's delicious, creative dishes, such as *bobó de camarão*, fish with chestnuts, and beef medallions in red wine. CUISINE contemporary CREDIT CARDS Amex, Diners, MasterCard, Visa
Rua Plínio Soares, 26, Centro
TEL (73) 3251-3372 OPEN High season: daily, 4pm – midnight; low season: Mon – Sat, 7pm – 11pm

Estrela do Mar $

This restaurant is part of the Aldeia do Mar Chalés hotel. The menu created by Paulista chef Clodomiro Tavares focuses on seafood, in local and international preparations. We recommend the shrimp in passion fruit sauce, sea bass or *dourado* with caper sauce, and fish filet with tapioca and seafood. CUISINE regional, fish and seafood CREDIT CARDS Diners, MasterCard, Visa
Praia da Concha, no #, Aldeia do Mar Chalés
TEL (73) 3251-2492 OPEN Daily, 7am – 10pm

Itacarezinho $$

The only restaurant on Itacarezinho Beach resembles a *barraca*, with some tables arranged on a deck and others scattered around kiosks along the beach. They serve appetizers as well as main dishes such as *moqueca*, *mariscada* (mussels), and *camarão Itacarezinho* (grilled shrimp with capers, mushrooms, and hearts of palm). CUISINE regional, varied CREDIT CARDS not accepted
Estrada Parque Ilhéus–Itacaré, Km 50 (15 kilometers from Itacaré)
TEL (73) 3239-6154. OPEN High season: daily, 8am – 6pm; low season: daily, 10am – 6pm

SERVICES

Bus Station – Rodoviária

Rua Joaquim Vieira, no #, Centro
TEL (73) 3251-2200 OPEN Daily, 5am – 10pm

PRICES	HOTELS (couple)	$ up to R$150	$$ from R$151 up to R$300	$$$ from R$301 up to R$500	$$$$ above R$500

Hotels, Restaurants and Services

Surf School – Easy Drop Surf Camp
Rua João Coutinho, 140, Centro
TEL (73) 3251-3065 FAX (73) 3251-2078 OPEN Mon – Fri, 8am – noon and 2pm – 6pm; Sat, 8am – noon   www.easydrop.com

Travel Agency and Guides – Eco Trip Viagens and Turismo
Rua João Coutinho, 235, Centro
TEL (73) 3251-2191, 9975-1114 FAX (73) 3251-3646 OPEN Daily, 9am – noon and 4pm – 8pm   www.ecotrip.tur.br

Travel Agency and Guides – Itacaré Ecoturismo
Rua Lodônio Almeida, 117, Centro
TEL (73) 3251-3666, 9996-3890 OPEN Mon – Sat, 8am – noon and 2pm – 9pm; Sun, 8am – 10am and 6pm – 9pm
www.itacare-ecotur.com.br

Travel Agency and Guides – NV Turismo
Rua Pedro Longo, 520-A, Pituba
TEL (73) 3251-2039, 9199-2227 OPEN Mon – Fri, 8am – 6pm; Sat, 8am – noon   www.nvturismo.com.br

Travel Agency – São Miguel Aventuras
Guides and car rental
Avenida Castro Alves, 535 (BR gas station)
TEL (73) 3251-3109 FAX (73) 3251-2145 OPEN Daily, 7am – 10pm   www.saomiguelaventuras.com.br

Itacimirim – Bahia

AREA CODE 71 Camaçari DISTANCES Salvador 86 kilometers (53 miles), Praia do Forte 9 kilometers (6 miles) ACCESS Take Estrada do Coco (BA-099)

WHERE TO STAY

Pousada Jambo $$
This incredibly well-kept guesthouse has a garden with coconut trees, several beach kiosks, and a restaurant serving regional and international dishes. The simple, spacious rooms all have sea views. Owner Arno Dreschers also organizes excursions and water sports trips. ACCOMMODATIONS 20 rooms, Internet access, air-conditioning, minibar, telephone, cable TV, ceiling fan; veranda with hammock, table, and chairs FACILITIES AND SERVICES Internet access in communal areas, garden with loungers, store, pool, restaurant, beach service, shuttle service to airport and local attractions CREDIT CARDS Diners, MasterCard, Visa
Praia da Espera, Estrada do Coco
TEL (71) 3626-1091 FAX 3626-1697 www.pousadajambo.com.br

Jaboatão dos Guararapes – Pernambuco (see Recife)

Jacobina – Bahia

AREA CODE 74 POPULATION 76,476 DISTANCES Salvador 330 kilometers (205 miles), Feira de Santana 230 kilometers (143 miles), Lençóis 283 kilometers (176 miles) ACCESS From Feira de Santana or Salvador, take BR-324 highway (note that are 20 kilometers of poor, potholed roads between Porto Trevo and Tanquinho). From Morro do Chapéu, take BA-426
www.jacobina.ba.gov.br

WHERE TO STAY

Fiesta Park $
Everything in this hotel is spacious and spotless. The on-site restaurant serves a varied menu. The hotel also has a well-equipped water park (open to both guests and non-guests) that features a lazy river, wave pool, and water slide. ACCOMMODATIONS 50 rooms, Internet access, telephone, cable TV, veranda/balcony, ceiling fan; air-conditioning and minibar in luxury rooms FACILITIES AND SERVICES bar, soccer field, waterfall, parking, convenience store, water park, pool, playground, restaurant CREDIT CARDS Diners, MasterCard, Visa
Avenida Paulo Souto, 700, Nazaré
TEL (74) 3621-6916, 3621-5239, 3621-6184

Serra do Ouro $
Rooms are cozy and pleasant; those on the upper floors offer better views. The hotel's restaurant is among the city's best. ACCOMMODATIONS 30 rooms and 4 suites, air-conditioning, minibar, telephone, TV; Internet access in 8 rooms; balcony in some rooms FACILITIES AND SERVICES Internet access in communal areas, bar, parking, pool, soccer court, restaurant, conference room, games room, video room CREDIT CARDS MasterCard, Visa
Alto do Monte Tabor, no #, Caixa d'Água
TEL and FAX (74) 3621-3324, 3621-3325

SERVICES

Bus Station – Rodoviária
Rua Reinaldo Jacobina, 80, Peru
TEL (74) 3621-2666

Guides and Tourist Information – Grupo Ecológico Serra Verde
Condomínio Motinha, 95, Centro
TEL (74) 3621-1846, 8804-5497 OPEN Mon – Fri, 8am – noon and 2pm – 5:30pm   www.gruposerraverde.com.br

Tourist Information – Posto de Informações Turísticas
Praça do Garimpeiro, 34 (near the exit to Salvador)
TEL (74) 3621-6801 OPEN Mon – Fri, 7am – 8pm

Travel Agency Idéia 10 / Armat (Regional Guide Association)
Rua Rua Ulbaldino Mesquita Passos, 198, 1st floor, Caeira
TEL (74) 3621-6872 OPEN Daily, 24 hours

Jacumã – Paraíba

AREA CODE 83 Conde DISTANCES João Pessoa 29 kilometers (18 miles), Recife 121 kilometers (75 miles) ACCESS From João Pessoa or Pitimbu, take highway PB-008 WHEN TO VISIT Carnival, for anyone who likes fun and crowds

WHERE TO STAY

Hotel Pousada Conchas $
This small, friendly guesthouse features rooms and chalets facing a pool area, plus a bar and restaurant with a lovely view. Rooms are simple. ACCOMMODATIONS 17 rooms and 8 chalets, air-conditioning, minibar, TV FACILITIES AND SERVICES Internet access in communal areas, bar, parking, pool, playground, restaurant, games room, guided walking tours, beach service, shuttle service to airport and local attractions CREDIT CARDS not accepted
Rua Projetada, no #, Praia de Tabatinga
TEL (83) 3290-1303 FAX 3290-1401
www.conchashotel.com.br

Hotel Pousada Corais de Carapibus $
The regular rooms are fairly simple; however, the master

RESTAURANTS $ up to R$50 $$ from R$51 up to R$100 $$$ from R$101 up to R$150 $$$$ above R$150

suites have sea views and Jacuzzis. ACCOMMODATIONS 54 rooms and 2 suites, air-conditioning, minibar, TV, ceiling fan; Jacuzzi in suites FACILITIES AND SERVICES wine cellar, bar, boat, parking, Jacuzzi, pool, restaurant, conference room, games room, travel agency, shuttle service to airport and local attractions CREDIT CARDS Diners, MasterCard
Avenida Beira-Mar, no #
TEL and FAX (83) 3290-1900 RESERVATIONS 3290-1179
www.coraisdecarapibus.com.br

Pousada Enseada do Sol $

Its rooms have wooden beds and small windows, and paintings and beach-related items adorn the walls. The pool has a water slide that is ideal for children. ACCOMMODATIONS 30 rooms, air-conditioning, minibar, TV FACILITIES AND SERVICES bar, parking, pool with waterslide, playground, volleyball court, restaurant, conference room, games room CREDIT CARDS MasterCard
Avenida Beira-Mar, Quadra M1, Lote 9, Cidade Balneária Novo Mundo
TEL (83) 3290-1732, 9982-6389 FAX 3290-1935
www.enseadadosol.com.br

WHERE TO EAT

A Arca de Bilu $

This restaurant at the entrance to Tambaba Beach is a popular pit-stop for guided tours. The restaurant serves generous portions of simple, delightful food like *lenda de Tambaba* (seafood stew in a sizzling clay casserole dish, with rice, manioc flour, *dendê* palm oil, and thickened *pirão* sauce). They serve *cachaça* with herbs as an aperitif. CUISINE bar food, fish and seafood CREDIT CARDS not accepted
Rodovia Abelardo Jurema (PB-008 highway), Praia de Tambaba
TEL (83) 3298-1124 RESERVATIONS 9972-2369 OPEN Daily, 10am – 6pm

Canyon do Coqueirinho $

The sizzling octopus *moqueca*, made without *dendê* palm oil and thus wonderfully light, is delicious. Other good menu choices include *cajá* juice and jackfruit compote for dessert. The friendly service is the icing on the cake. CUISINE fish and seafood CREDIT CARDS not accepted
Praia de Coqueirinho, no #
TEL (83) 9309-9094 RESERVATIONS 9352-7927 OPEN Daily, 11am – 5pm

Tabatinga Arte Bar $

The bar menu features appetizers of fried manioc, codfish, and *frango a passarinho* (small pieces of deep fried chicken), as well as a delightful lobster casserole served with tapioca. In the season when lobster fishing is not allowed, this dish is replaced by fish broth. CUISINE fish and seafood, regional CREDIT CARDS not accepted
Praia de Tabatinga (in front of Pedra do Sal)
TEL (83) 8805-5406, 8859-3541 OPEN High season: daily, 8am – 5pm; low season: Fri – Sun and holidays, 8am – 5pm

Terraço Tropical $

This restaurant serves fish, seafood, and pasta. The main dish is *filé de peixe terraço tropical*, a delicacy of shrimp, grilled fruits, and white sauce. CUISINE pasta, fish and seafood CREDIT CARDS MasterCard
Praia de Carapibus, no # (near the PB-008)
TEL (83) 3290-1120 OPEN High season: daily, 11am – until the last customer leaves; low season: Thu – Sun, 11am – until the last customer leaves

SERVICES

Bus Station – Rodoviária (João Pessoa)

Rua Francisco Londres, no #, Varadouro
TEL (83) 3221-9611, 3222-8556 OPEN Mon – Fri, 8am – noon and 2pm – 6pm

Jericoacoara – Ceará

AREA CODE 88 Jijoca de Jericoacoara DISTANCE Fortaleza 300 kilometers (186 miles) ACCESS From Fortaleza, take Rodovia Estruturante (CE-085) to Jijoca, about 20 kilometers (12 miles) from Jericoacoara. The road from Jijoca is in very poor condition, and is recommended only for those in a bus, dune-buggy, or 4x4 pick-up.

WHERE TO STAY

Hannah Beach $$

This guesthouse has several great attractions aside from its ideal location – namely the homemade items served for breakfast, the pool and bar. The rooms are all equipped with a balcony featuring a hammock, tables, and a pool view. ACCOMMODATIONS 16 rooms, air-conditioning, private safe, minibar, cable TV, balcony FACILITIES AND SERVICES Internet access in communal areas, bar, parking, pool, laundry CREDIT CARDS Diners, MasterCard, Visa
Rua do Forró, no #
TEL (88) 3669-2325 www.hannahbeach.com.br

Hotel Mosquito Blue $$

Rooms are arranged around a garden and a pretty pool with a deck; "superior" level rooms are more private and have a better view. ACCOMMODATIONS 37 rooms and 6 suites, air-conditioning, private safe, minibar, telephone, cable TV FACILITIES AND SERVICES Internet access in communal areas, bar, Jacuzzi, pool, restaurant, gym, games room, sauna, beach service CREDIT CARDS Amex, Diners, MasterCard, Visa
Rua Ismael, no # (near the drugstore)
TEL (88) 3669-2203 FAX 3669-2204
www.mosquitoblue.com.br

Pousada Chez Loran $

This guesthouse offers guests private lakeside kiosks, with wonderful views. Guests are free to take all their meals by the lake, courtesy of the guesthouse's own bar and restaurant. Water sports enthusiasts will find good facilities. ACCOMMODATIONS 10 chalets and 3 two-room suites, air-conditioning, minibar, TV, ceiling fan FACILITIES AND SERVICES Internet access in communal areas, bar, kayaks, parking, volleyball court, restaurant, beach service CREDIT CARDS Diners, MasterCard, Visa
Córrego do Urubu, no #, Lagoa do Paraíso
TEL (88) 3669-1195, 9912-0232
www.paraisodejeri.com/pousadachezloran

Pousada Recanto do Barão $$

The rooms are small but comfortable and clean. Some rooms have a mezzanine and can sleep up to five. ACCOMMODATIONS 20 rooms, air-conditioning, private safe, minibar, TV FACILITIES AND SERVICES Internet access in communal areas, bar, parking, pool, reading room, laundry CREDIT CARDS Diners, MasterCard, Visa
Rua do Forró, 433, Centro
TEL (88) 3669-2149 FAX 3669-2136
www.recantodobarao.com

Pousada Sítio Verde $$

Water sports enthusiasts flock here as it has plenty of space

PRICES	HOTELS (couple)	$ up to R$150	$$ from R$151 up to R$300	$$$ from R$301 up to R$500	$$$$ above R$500

Hotels, Restaurants and Services

to store sports equipment. The La Távola restaurant on-site specializes in pasta made on the premises; meals are also served at the lakeside kiosks. Breakfast is not the standard communal buffet; guests can order whatever they want off the menu, and all of it will be made to order. **ACCOMMODATIONS** 5 chalets, air-conditioning, minibar **FACILITIES AND SERVICES** wine cellar, bar, parking, volleyball court, restaurant, gym, games room, beach service **CREDIT CARDS** MasterCard, Visa
Córrego do Urubu, no #, Lagoa do Paraíso
TEL (88) 3669-1151 www.jericoacoara.tur.br/sitioverde

Rancho do Peixe $$

Designed specifically to accommodate kite- and wind-surfers on Preá Beach. Eight of the bungalows have sea views. The hotel's restaurant restaurant is open to non-residents and overlooks the beach. Staff can organize dune-buggy trips to Jeri, Jijoca, or Tatajuba. **ACCOMMODATIONS** 16 bungalows, minibar, ceiling fan **FACILITIES AND SERVICES** Internet access in communal areas, bar, parking, pool, restaurant, wind- and kite-surfing lessons, beach service **CREDIT CARDS** Diners, MasterCard, Visa
Praia do Preá, Cruz (12 kilometers from Jericoacoara)
TEL (88) 3660-3118 www.ranchodopeixe.com.br

Surfing Jeri $$

Surfing Jeri is on the street where most bars, restaurants, and snack bars are concentrated in Jericoacoara. It's also within easy reach of the traditional *forró* venue that attracts crowds most nights, and is just 300 meters from the beach. **ACCOMMODATIONS** 18 rooms and 4 bungalows, air-conditioning, private safe, minibar, TV **FACILITIES AND SERVICES** Internet access in communal areas, pool, laundry **CREDIT CARDS** Diners, MasterCard, Visa
Rua São Francisco, 150
TEL and **FAX** (88) 3669-2260 www.jericoacoara.it

Vila Kalango $$

The bungalows and rooms all have beach access; some have mini-decks with hammocks, cushions, and beach mats, ideal for reading or just contemplating nature. The restaurant and bar serve residents only, and offer great views of the sunset. **ACCOMMODATIONS** 15 bungalows and 3 rooms, Internet access, minibar, ceiling fan **FACILITIES AND SERVICES** bar, library, parking, pool, restaurant, games room, massage room, video room, beach service **CREDIT CARDS** Diners, MasterCard, Visa
Rua das Dunas, 30, Centro
TEL (88) 3669-2290 **FAX** 3669-2291 www.vilakalango.com.br

WHERE TO EAT

Azul do Mar $

The generous portions are the main attraction of this restaurant. Highlights of the menu include the snook and the grilled shrimp, each served with seasoned manioc flour, rice, beans, salad, and fried manioc. **CUISINE** fish and seafood **CREDIT CARDS** MasterCard
Avenida Beira-Mar, no #, Vila Preá, Município de Cruz
TEL (88) 3660-3062 **OPEN** Daily, noon – 6pm

Carcará $$

Among the best main dishes are the shrimp or seafood *moqueca*, the sun-dried beef with *arroz de leite* (rice, milk, curd cheese, and butter), and *lagosta tropical* for two (griddled lobster served with fresh fruit). **CUISINE** seafood, regional **CREDIT CARDS** Diners, MasterCard, Visa
Rua do Forró, no #, Centro
TEL (88) 3669-2013 **OPEN** Mon – Sat, noon – 11pm; Sun, 8am – 11pm

Chocolate $

Good menu choices include the risottos, pastas, salads, and delicious desserts, such as the famous *petit gateau*. The restaurant has a great wine list. Reservations should be made in advance. **CUISINE** varied **CREDIT CARDS** Diners, MasterCard, Visa
Rua do Forró, 213, Centro
TEL (88) 3669-2190 **RESERVATIONS** 9611-2344 **OPEN** Daily, 2pm until the last customer leaves

Nômade $

Pizzas, salads, pasta, and risottos are served here. The wood-burning stove is on the upper floor, where the restaurant's 35 different pizzas (both deep dish and thin crust) are prepared in full view of customers. **CUISINE** Italian **CREDIT CARDS** Diners, MasterCard, Visa
Travessa Ismael, 90
TEL (88) 3669-2103 **OPEN** Daily, 8am – midnight (closed on Sundays occasionally during the low season)

Shopping Tapioca (Tia Angelita) $

The owner Angelina is a well-known character in Jeri. She used to sell her delicacies on the beach, where she became famous for her banana pie, made using the same pastry used for her savory pies. (The recipe was given to her more than 25 years ago by visitors from São Paulo.) Today Angelina's legendary banana pie is still sold at the many stalls that line the beach. At her main stall on Rua Principal, you'll find not only her famous delicacy but a coconut dessert and *tapioca*, served with fresh coffee. **CUISINE** bar food **CREDIT CARDS** MasterCard
Rua Principal, no #
OPEN Daily, 7am – 10pm

Sky Bar e Restaurante $

The bar presides over the stretch of beach that sees some of Jeri's liveliest nightlife, thanks largely to the excellent drinks and Mediterranean food (with a northeastern touch) that Sky serves. Regional musicians play daily. **CUISINE** bar food and seafood **CREDIT CARDS** Diners, MasterCard, Visa
Rua Principal, 1, Praia de Jericoacoara
TEL (88) 3669-2048 **OPEN** High season: daily, 10am – until the last customer leaves; low season: 10am – 3am

Sorveteria Engenhoca Doce $

All of Engenhoca Doce's ice creams are home-made; the more elaborate flavors are named for major attractions in Jeri, such as the Pedra Furada (cream and rum raisin ice cream with cashew nuts) and Lual das Dunas (ice-cream bonbon with sweet cashew nut topping). **CUISINE** ice cream **CREDIT CARDS** not accepted
Rua Principal, no # (access road to Pôr-do-Sol dune)
OPEN Daily, 10am – 1am

SERVICES

Tourist Information – Posto de Informações Turístic

Avenida Manoel Marques, no #
OPEN Daily, 7am – 5pm

Jijoca de Jericoacoara – Ceará
(see Jericoacoara)

João Pessoa – Paraíba

AREA CODE 83 **POPULATION** 660,798 **DISTANCES** Recife 120 kilometers (75 miles), Natal 180 kilometers (112 miles) **ACCESS** BR-101 highway
www.joaopessoa.pb.gov.br

RESTAURANTS $ up to R$50 $$ from R$51 up to R$100 $$$ from R$101 up to R$150 $$$$ above R$150

WHERE TO STAY

Hardman Praia $$
Originally designed as serviced apartments, all rooms have a kitchen and an eating area. ACCOMMODATIONS 75 rooms and 35 suites, Internet access, air-conditioning, private safe, minibar, telephone, cable TV FACILITIES AND SERVICES Internet access in communal areas, bar, parking, pool, playground, restaurant, conference room, gym, games room, sauna, travel agency, business center, 24-hour kitchen, valet parking, beach service CREDIT CARDS Amex, Diners, MasterCard, Visa
Avenida João Maurício, 1341, Praia de Manaíra
TEL (83) 3246-8811 www.hotelhardman.com.br

Hotel Pouso das Águas $
The charm of this hotel, which has the atmosphere of a guesthouse, is its simplicity. In the sitting room a framed drawing by Roberto Burle Marx welcomes visitors. ACCOMMODATIONS 20 rooms and 4 suites, air-conditioning, minibar, telephone, TV FACILITIES AND SERVICES parking, pool, shuttle service to airport and local attractions CREDIT CARDS Amex, Diners, MasterCard, Visa
Avenida Cabo Branco, 2348, Cabo Branco
TEL (83) 3226-5103 www.pousodasaguas.com.br

Igatu Praia $
This hotel has cozy suites with large beds. ACCOMMODATIONS 9 suites, Internet access, air-conditioning, minibar, telephone, cable TV FACILITIES AND SERVICES Internet access in communal areas, bar, parking, pool, restaurant, reading area, conference room, games room, sauna, business center, valet parking, beach service CREDIT CARDS Amex, Diners, MasterCard, Visa
Avenida Cabo Branco, 1984, Cabo Branco
TEL (83) 2106-8808 FAX 2106-8804 www.igatuhotel.com.br

Tropical Tambaú $$
The rooms occupy two circular floors; doors face inner courtyards, an oval pool, and children's playgrounds. Some rooms have sea views. ACCOMMODATIONS 169 rooms and 6 suites, air-conditioning, private safe, minibar, telephone, cable TV; Jacuzzi in suites FACILITIES AND SERVICES Internet access in communal areas, bar, parking, stores, pool, playground, garden, tennis court, restaurant, conference room, gym, games room, massage room, video room, beauty parlor, sauna, travel agency, car rental, business center, 24-hour kitchen, recreational team for adults and children, valet parking, beach service CREDIT CARDS Amex, Diners, MasterCard, Visa
Avenida Almirante Tamandaré, 229, Tambaú
TEL (83) 3218-1919 RESERVATIONS 0800-701-2670
FAX 3247-1070
www.tropicalhotel.com.br

WHERE TO EAT

Adega do Alfredo $
The house specialty – codfish with potatoes – reflects Portuguese cuisine, while other dishes, such as paella and pasta, reflect a Mediterranean influence. A children's menu is available. CUISINE fish and seafood, varied CREDIT CARDS Amex, Visa
Rua Coração de Jesus, no #, Tambaú
TEL (83) 3226-4346 RESERVATIONS 3226-3354 OPEN Tue – Sun, noon – 3pm and 7pm – midnight; Mon, 7pm – midnight

Badionaldo $
Badionaldo's simple menu relies on carefully prepared fish and seafood dishes. The tasty mackerel stew has been on the menu since the 1950s. CUISINE fish and seafood CREDIT CARDS MasterCard, Visa
Rua Vitorino Cardoso, no #, Praia do Poço, Cabedelo
TEL (83) 3250-1299 OPEN Mon, noon – 3pm; Tue – Sat, noon – 9:30pm; Sun, noon – 6pm

Bargaço $
Bargaço's forte is the fish and seafood cooked in the Bahia style, serving two or three people. Two shrimp dishes, *moqueca* and *bobó*, are particularly worth trying. CUISINE Regional, fish and seafood CREDIT CARDS Diners, MasterCard, Visa
Avenida Cabo Branco, 5160, Cabo Branco
TEL (83) 3247-1837, 3247-5100 FAX 3247-5220 OPEN Mon – Sat, noon – midnight; Sun, noon – 11pm

Mangai $
This restaurant serves more than seventy typical, self-service *sertão* dishes, including *rubacão* or *baião-de-dois* (rice, beans and beef jerky) and *sovaco-de-cobra* (sun-dried beef with corn). Tapioca, manioc bread, *canjica* (corn and milk pudding), and *cartola* (fried banana and cream cheese) are served for breakfast as well as à la carte. Alcohol is not served. The attached store features a variety pf items, including regional delicacies. CUISINE regional CREDIT CARDS MasterCard, Visa
Avenida Edson Ramalho, 696, Manaíra
TEL (83) 3226-1615 RESERVATIONS and FAX 3247-5840 OPEN Tue – Sun, 7am – 10pm

Porto Madero $
In addition to à la carte service featuring seafood, poultry, and meat dishes, Porto Madero boasts both a per kilo buffet and a pasta buffet that allows customers to handpick their dish's contents. Sushi and sashimi are also sold by weight. CUISINE international, varied CREDIT CARDS Amex, Diners, MasterCard, Visa
Rua Antônio Carlos Araújo, 60, Cabo Branco
TEL (83) 3247-1594 OPEN Tue – Fri, 11:30am – 4pm and 6:30pm – 1am; Sat, 6:30pm – 1am; Sun, 11:30am – 4pm

SERVICES

Airport – Aeroporto Internacional Presidente Castro Pinto
Aeroporto Internacional Presidente Castro Pinto, Bayeux
TEL (83) 3232-1200 OPEN Daily, 24 hours

Bus Station – Rodoviária
Rua Francisco Londres, no #, Varadouro
TEL (83) 3221-9611, 3222-8556

Tourist Information – Posto de Informações Turísticas
Largo de São Frei Pedro Gonçalves, no # (Instituto de Arquitetura Brasileira, IAB), Centro Histórico
OPEN Mon – Fri, 9am – noon and 2pm – 4:30pm; Sat, 2pm – 4:30pm

Tourist Information – Posto de Informações Turísticas
Avenida Almirante Tamandaré, 100, Tambaú
TEL 0800-281-9229, (83) 3214-8279, 3214-8270 OPEN Daily, 8am – 7pm www.paraiba.pb.gov.br/pbtur

Tourist Police Station – Delegacia do Turista
Avenida Almirante Tamandaré, 100, Tambaú
TEL (83) 3214-8022, 3214-8023 OPEN Daily, 24 hours

| PRICES | HOTELS (couple) | $ up to R$150 | $$ from R$151 up to R$300 | $$$ from R$301 up to R$500 | $$$$ above R$500 |

Juazeiro – Bahia

AREA CODE 74 POPULATION 203,261 DISTANCES Salvador 505 kilometers (314 miles), Feira de Santana 396 kilometers (246 miles) ACCESS From Petrolina, by Ponte Eurico Gaspar Dutra bridge or by boat. From Salvador, take the BR-324 highway northbound to Capim Grosso, then take BR-407
www.juazeiro.ba.gov.br

WHERE TO STAY

Grande Hotel de Juazeiro $$
Spacious rooms provide lovely views of the São Francisco River. The six conference rooms can accommodate 450 people. ACCOMMODATIONS 54 rooms and 2 suites, air-conditioning, minibar, telephone, cable TV; Jacuzzi in suites FACILITIES AND SERVICES Internet access in communal areas, bar, parking, snack bar, pool, restaurant, river, conference room, beauty parlor, business center, 24-hour kitchen CREDIT CARDS Amex, Diners, MasterCard, Visa
Rua José Petitinga, 466, Santo Antônio
TEL (74) 3612-3100 FAX 3612-7744 www.hoteislazar.com.br

WHERE TO EAT

Alpendre $
The restaurant's forte is lunch; try the barbecued mutton or grilled *surubim* (also known as *pintado* – a freshwater fish), served with vegetables or shrimp sauce. A strictly enforced dress code prohibits t-shirts and shorts. local artists perform live shows every weekend. CUISINE meats, regional, fish CREDIT CARDS MasterCard
Rua do Angari, no #, Orla Antiga
TEL (74) 3612-4655 OPEN Wed – Sat, 11am – midnight; Sun, 11am – 10pm

Maria do Peixe $
Over the past thirty years Maria José Silva has transformed her original gas station snack bar into an upscale restaurant. Silva's culinary standards remain high; she uses only lean *surubim* fillet from fish over 10 kilograms (22 pounds) in weight Other dishes prepared by Silva, include sun-dried beef and fillet steak. CUISINE fish, regional CREDIT CARDS MasterCard, Visa
Quadra C, 19, Castelo Branco
TEL (74) 3611-3043 OPEN Mon – Fri, 11am – 9pm; Sat – Sun, 11am – 4pm

SERVICES

Bus Station – Rodoviária
Rodovia Lomanto Jr., Km 3, Castelo Branco
TEL (74) 3611-7136 (Viação Gontijo)

Juazeiro do Norte – Ceará

AREA CODE 88 POPULATION 236,296 DISTANCES Fortaleza 495 kilometers (308 miles), Picos 290 kilometers (180 miles), Petrolina 373 kilometers (232 miles) ACCESS From Fortaleza, BR-116 highway toward Milagres WHEN TO VISIT September 15, January 30 to February 2, and October 30 to November 2, for the pilgrimages in honor of Father Cícero

WHERE TO STAY

Ingra Hotel $
This collection of chalets boast comfortable rooms, powerful showers, and an all-night pool among its top-notch facilities. ACCOMMODATIONS 74 rooms and 6 suites, air-conditioning, minibar, telephone, TV FACILITIES AND SERVICES Internet access in communal areas, bar, parking, pool, restaurant CREDIT CARDS Diners, MasterCard, Visa
Avenida Leão Sampaio, 1623, Lagoa Seca
TEL and FAX (88) 3571-2456

Panorama $
This eight-story building has a wonderful view of the entire city. Although Panorama's facilities are somewhat outdated, the rooms are comfortable. ACCOMMODATIONS 70 rooms and 5 suites, air-conditioning, minibar, telephone, TV FACILITIES AND SERVICES Internet access in communal areas, bar, nightclub, parking, pool, restaurant, conference room, games room CREDIT CARDS Amex, Diners, MasterCard, Visa
Rua Santo Agostinho, 58, Centro
TEL (88) 3512-3100 FAX 3512-3110
www.panoramahotel.com.br

Verdes Vales $$
Its airy rooms are very comfortable and well equipped. The attached waterpark is the resort's standout leisure facility. ACCOMMODATIONS 92 rooms and 5 suites, Internet access, air-conditioning, minibar, telephone, TV FACILITIES AND SERVICES Internet access in communal areas, bar, parking, convenience store, water park, pool, playground, soccer court, tennis court, volleyball court, restaurant, conference room, gym, games room, beauty parlor, sauna, walking trails, travel agency, business center, valet parking CREDIT CARDS Amex, Diners, MasterCard, Visa
Avenida Plácido Aderaldo Castelo, no #, Lagoa Seca
TEL (88) 3566-2544 FAX 3566-2500
www.hotelverdesvales.com.br

WHERE TO EAT

Coisas do Sertão $
Typical food from the *sertão* is served *per kilo* (by weight). *Baião de feijão-verde* (rice and lima beans), fava beans, corn-fed chicken, ribs, *buchada* (tripe), cream cheese, sun-dried beef, *paçoca* (jerked beef fried in fat and pounded with manioc flour), and pork crackling are some of the dishes available. *Mungunzá* (corn and milk pudding) and soup are available at night. CUISINE regional CREDIT CARDS not accepted
Avenida Padre Cícero, 3020, Triângulo
TEL (88) 3571-7676 OPEN Daily, 11am – 3pm and 6pm – 10pm

Giradouro $
This restaurant is famous for its lasagna dishes (particularly the chicken). Another, regional option is the *peixada cearense* (poached mackerel cutlets with vegetables, boiled egg, thickened *pirão* sauce, and rice). Appetizers are available at night. CUISINE regional, varied CREDIT CARDS Diners, MasterCard
Praça Feijó de Sá, no #, Triângulo
TEL (88) 3571-2181 RESERVATIONS 9965-0341 OPEN Tue – Sat, 4pm – midnight; Sun, 11am – 11pm

Mão de Vaca $
Families flock to the generous portions of regional food served in this meat-centric restaurant. Only available on Saturdays, *mão-de-vaca* consists of boiled beef heel, garnished with *cuscuz* (tapioca cake), rice, salad, and thickened *pirão* sauce. Other options include corn-fed chicken, sun-dried beef and beef flank. CUISINE meats, regional CREDIT CARDS MasterCard, Visa
Rua Rui Barbosa, 25, Santa Teresa
TEL (88) 3512-2543 OPEN Mon – Sat, 11am – 3pm and 5pm – midnight

---

RESTAURANTS $ up to R$50 $$ from R$51 up to R$100 $$$ from R$101 up to R$150 $$$$ above R$150

Trajubá Restô Jardim $

This restaurant serves international dishes adapted to the region's ingredients. One standout is *filé inglês*, seasoned fillet steak cooked in wine, with mango chutney and seasonal fruit salad. Also worth recommending are regional offerings such as corn-fed chicken with *pequi* fruit and tile-cooked *tucunaré* fish **CUISINE** international, regional **CREDIT CARDS** MasterCard, Visa
Avenida Leão Sampaio, 5460, Jardim Gonzaga (between Barbalha and Juazeiro)
TEL (88) 3571-7768 **OPEN** Wed – Mon, 11am – midnight

SERVICES

Aeroporto Regional do Cariri
Avenida Virgílio Távora, 4000 (6 kilometers from downtown)
TEL (88) 3572-0700, 3572-2118 **OPEN** Daily, 5am – 11pm

Lagoa do Carro – Pernambuco

AREA CODE 81 **POPULATION** 14,372 **DISTANCE** Recife 61 kilometers (38 miles) **ACCESS** After the Carpina intersection, follow the PE-090 highway **WHEN TO VISIT** At the end of the year, when rug-makers work together on the city sidewalks to complete a huge number of orders.

WHERE TO STAY

EcoResort Ruc – Fazenda Engenho Cordeiro $$
This is a friendly, welcoming option in the Carpina, Lagoa do Carro, Tracunhaém, and Passira region. Of the original sugar plantation only the simple church façade and mill remain. Although pleasant enough, the resort's main building is a replacement for the original plantation house. **ACCOMMODATIONS** 8 rooms, air-conditioning, minibar, TV **FACILITIES AND SERVICES** Internet access in communal areas, wine cellar, bar, boat, nursery, bicycles, woods, kayaks, soccer field, parking, horseback riding center, cart, fishing lake and equipment, snack bar, stores, period furniture, pool, orchard, restaurant, magazine reading area, river, games room, video room, flying fox, walking trails, 4x4 trails, 24-hour kitchen, guided walking tours, shuttle service to airport and local attractions **CREDIT CARDS** Diners, MasterCard, Visa
Rodovia PE-90, Km 10, Carpina
TEL (81) 3621-8188 www.ructurural.adm.br

Lagoinha – Ceará

AREA CODE 85 Paraipaba **DISTANCE** Fortaleza 130 kilometers (81 miles) **ACCESS** From Fortaleza, take Rodovia Estruturante (CE-085 highway). Turn right at the Paraipaba exit, cross the city; you'll reach Lagoinha after 12 kilometers (7 miles)

WHERE TO STAY

Vivamar Hotel Lagoinha $
The rooms are well equipped with balconies, hammocks, and sea views. The hotel's modestly-sized pool is located within view of tables in a public restaurant, evaporating any hope of privacy. **ACCOMMODATIONS** 20 rooms, air-conditioning, private safe, minibar, TV **FACILITIES AND SERVICES** pool, restaurant, beach service **CREDIT CARDS** Diners, MasterCard, Visa
Avenida Beira-Mar, 260, Lagoinha
TEL (85) 3363-5077, 3219-1981 **FAX** 3363-5168
www.vivamarhotel.com.br

WHERE TO EAT

Fullxico $
We can recommend *peixe ao Tasso* (grilled fish fillet with shrimp and eggplant served on a hot griddle) or spaghetti *à Verdes Mares* (pasta with octopus and shrimp cooked in olive oil, with capers, olives, and basil). At night, lamps made from quince wood (a typical tree in the region) contribute to a cozy atmosphere. **CUISINE** fish and seafood **CREDIT CARDS** not accepted
Rua Petrolina Barroso, no #
TEL (85) 9954-2754 **OPEN** Tue – Sun, 11am – until the last customer leaves

SERVICES

Travel Agency – Agência Pégoras
Rua Petronilha Barroso, 26, Praia de Lagoinha
TEL (85) 3363-5069 **OPEN** Daily, 6am – 8pm

Lençóis – Bahia

AREA CODE 75 **POPULATION** 9,741 **DISTANCE** Salvador 425 kilometers (264 miles) **ACCESS** By air or car. From Salvador, drive down BR-324 to Feira de Santana. Then, take BR-116 (Rio–Bahia) for 76 kilometers (47 miles), on a stretch full of trucks, and finally, BR-242 until you pass the airport intersection. There are no signs for this road at the highway junction, look for the exit on the right near the gas stations

WHERE TO STAY

Alcino Hostalage Atelier $
Some rooms don't come with ensuite bath. The lavish, multi-course breakfast includes delicious, home-grown fruit **ACCOMMODATIONS** 7 rooms, ceiling fan; bathroom in 4 rooms, air-conditioning in 3 of the rooms; **FACILITIES AND SERVICES** ceramic painting studio, library, parking, orchard, laundry **CREDIT CARDS** MasterCard
Rua Tomba Surrão, 139
TEL (75) 3334-1171 **FAX** 3334-1152

Canto das Águas $$$
This is a relaxing spot offering privacy and good food. Beautifully designed and remarkably well situated on the banks of the Lençóis River the meticulously landscaped facility is enveloped by the relaxing sound of the rapids; The pool area is particularly pleasant. The hearty breakfast is varied and includes regional dishes. The restaurant is one of the best in town. **ACCOMMODATIONS** 36 rooms and 8 suites, air-conditioning, minibar, telephone, TV, ceiling fan; Jacuzzi in the superior suite **FACILITIES AND SERVICES** bar, cascade, parking, pool, restaurant, river, games room, massage room, sauna **CREDIT CARDS** Amex, Diners, MasterCard, Visa
Avenida Senhor dos Passos, 1, Centro
TEL and **FAX** (75) 3334-1154 www.lencois.com.br

Hotel de Lençóis $$
This hotel is attractive, comfortable, well equipped and beautifully situated. Most of the hotel is in an old building that resembles a large old farmhouse. The hotel's excellent restaurant serves international cuisine, and has one of the best wine lists in town. **ACCOMMODATIONS** 50 rooms, private safe, minibar, telephone, TV, ceiling fan; air-conditioning in some rooms **FACILITIES AND SERVICES** Internet access in communal areas, wine cellar, bar, woods, parking, pool, playground, restaurant, conference room, games room **CREDIT CARDS** Amex, Diners, MasterCard, Visa
Rua Altina Alves, 747, Centro

| PRICES | HOTELS (couple) | $ up to R$150 | $$ from R$151 up to R$300 | $$$ from R$301 up to R$500 | $$$$ above R$500 |

TEL (75) 3334-1102 FAX 3334-1201 RESERVATIONS (71) 3369-5000
www.hoteldelencois.com

Portal Lençóis $$$
This high-standard hotel has a magnificent view of the mountains, Lençóis Canyon and River, and the city itself. The rooms are spacious, and the restaurant above par. Facilities are available for guests with physical disabilities. ACCOMMODATIONS 53 rooms, 16 chalets and 15 bungalows; air-conditioning, private safe, minibar, hairdryer, telephone, cable TV FACILITIES AND SERVICES Internet access in communal areas, bar, parking, store, pool, playground, restaurant, river, conference room, gym, games room, sauna, travel agency, 24-hour kitchen, shuttle service to the center of town CREDIT CARDS Amex, Diners, MasterCard, Visa
Rua Chácara Grota, no #, Altina Alves
TEL (75) 3334-1233 RESERVATIONS and FAX (71) 3450-7337, 3450-1090 www.portalhoteis.tur.br

Vila Serrano $
All rooms feature beautiful hand-made curtains, verandas and hammocks. The guesthouse's small size makes it a poor choice for anyone looking for privacy. Advance reservations are recommended. ACCOMMODATIONS 9 rooms, Internet access, minibar, balcony with hammock, ceiling fan; mezzanine and library in suite FACILITIES AND SERVICES parking, table tennis, video room with cable TV, laundry CREDIT CARDS MasterCard
Rua Alto do Bonfim, 8, Centro
TEL (75) 3334-1486 FAX 3334-1487
www.vilaserrano.com.br

WHERE TO EAT

Cozinha Aberta $
This restaurant has an open kitchen which blends in seamlessly with the two smalls rooms that make up the serving area. The chef offers painstakingly prepared dishes from several countries, including pasta and "real salads." CUISINE contemporary CREDIT CARDS not accepted
Rua da Baderna, 111, Centro
TEL (75) 3334-1066. OPEN Daily, 1pm – 11pm
www.cozinhaaberta.com.br

La Pergola $
In this restaurant, the fillet steak is served with a variety of sauces – green peppercorn, Dijon mustard, Roquefort, or wine. From the fish dishes, try one from the region – tucunaré – grilled, with herb sauce. CUISINE French, fish CREDIT CARDS Diners, MasterCard, Visa
Praça do Rosário, 70, Centro
TEL (75) 3334-1241 OPEN Daily, noon – 4pm and 6pm – 11pm

Neco's Bar $
Neco's Bar serves sun-dried beef, mutton, corn-fed chicken, and tucunaré fish with a variety of side dishes. One of the most popular dishes is godó, a typical Chapada recipe, consisting of green bananas, sun-dried beef, shrimp or codfish. CUISINE regional CREDIT CARDS not accepted
Praça Maestro Clarindo Pacheco, 15
TEL (75) 3334-1179 OPEN Daily, noon – 10pm

Restaurante do Hotel Canto das Águas $
This is one of the town's best restaurants, serving high-quality international dishes. Enjoy the view of the Lençóis River, which lies just below the balcony. CUISINE bar, international CREDIT CARDS Amex, Diners, MasterCard, Visa
Avenida Senhor dos Passos, 1
TEL (75) 3334-1154 OPEN Daily, noon – 4pm and 7pm – 10pm

Roda d'Água Gourmet (the Hotel de Lençóis restaurant) $
International cuisine with regional and contemporary touches. The most popular dish is fillet steak with rice, manioc purée (with basil, nutmeg, and cooked garlic) and tomato stuffed with curd cheese. He also has two original chicken recipes: Mexican (grilled breast in garlic, chocolate, and pepper sauce) and Thai (diced chicken in coconut milk, with ginger and pineapple). CUISINE contemporary, varied CREDIT CARDS MasterCard, Visa
Rua Altina Alves, 747, Centro
TEL (75) 3334-1102 OPEN Daily, noon – 3pm and 6pm – 10pm

SERVICES

Airport – Aeroporto Coronel Horácio de Matos
BR-242, Km 209 (25 kilometers, 16 miles, from the center), Coronel Otaviano Alves
TEL (75) 3625-8100 OPEN Daily, 24 hours

Bus Station – Rodoviária
Avenida Senhor dos Passos, no #, Centro
TEL (75) 3334-1112 (Viação Real Expresso bus company)

Guides – Associação dos Condutores de Visitantes de Lençóis (ACVL)
Rua 10 de Dezembro, 22, Centro
TEL (75) 3334-1425 OPEN High season: daily, 7:30am – 10pm; low season: 7:30am – noon and 2pm – 10pm

Travel Agency – Andrenalina
Rua das Pedras, 121, Centro
TEL (75) 3334-1689 OPEN Daily, 8:30am – noon and 3pm – 8pm

Travel Agency – Cirtur
Rua da Baderna, 41, Centro
TEL (75) 3334-1133, 3334-1464 OPEN Daily, 7:30am – 10pm

Travel Agency – Explorer Brasil
Praça Maestro Clarindo Pacheco, 5, Centro
TEL (75) 3334-1183, 9984-1661

Travel Agency – Lentur
Avenida 7 de Setembro, 10, Centro
TEL (75) 3334-1271 OPEN Daily, 7:30am – 10pm
www.lentur.com.br

Travel Agency – Marimbus Ecoturismo
Praça Otaviano Alves, no #, Centro
TEL (75) 3334-1292 OPEN Daily, 8am – noon and 5pm – 9pm
www.marimbus.com

Travel Agency – Nativos da Chapada
Rua Miguel Calmon, 29, Centro
TEL (75) 3334-1314, 9966-0131 OPEN Daily, 8am – noon and 4pm – 11pm

Travel Agency – Velozia Cicloturismo
Rua do Lagedo, 68, Centro
TEL (75) 3334-1700 OPEN Mon – Sat, 8am – noon and 2pm – 6pm www.ronybikes.com

Travel Agency – Zentur
Praça das Nagôs, 1, Centro
TEL (75) 3334-1397, 8101-1850 OPEN Daily, 7:30am – 10pm
www.zentur.tur.br

RESTAURANTS	$ up to R$50	$$ from R$51 up to R$100	$$$ from R$101 up to R$150	$$$$ above R$150

Lençóis Maranhenses – Maranhão
(see Barreirinhas and Santo Amaro do Maranhão)

Luís Correia – Piauí
AREA CODE 86 POPULATION 25,462 DISTANCES Teresina 348 kilometers (216 miles), Parnaíba 18 kilometers (11 miles), Sobral 257 kilometers (160 miles) ACCESS From Teresina, about 5 hours on TransPiauí Highway (BR-343). Be careful of animals on the road WHEN TO VISIT January, February and July, for the buzz of the high season; for peace and quiet, any other months

WHERE TO STAY

Islamar $$$
Nearly all the rooms have a sea view, with chalets scattered around that differ in size, décor, and price. ACCOMMODATIONS 19 rooms, 15 suites and 4 chalets; air-conditioning, minibar, telephone, TV FACILITIES AND SERVICES bar, bicycles, soccer field, parking, convenience store, pool, tennis court, gym, games room, massage room, video room, sauna, travel agency, buggy and mini-buggy rental, airport shuttle; 24-hour kitchen (high season) CREDIT CARDS Amex, MasterCard, Visa
Avenida Lagoa Doce, 315, Barro Preto, Praia do Coqueiro
TEL (86) 3366-1165, 3366-1208 FAX 3366-1132

Rio Poty $
This unpretentious hotel has a delightful pool in a very sunny spot, as well as a soccer field, and an airy restaurant that boasts good service and an equally good breakfast. The simple, well-equipped rooms face the pool. ACCOMMODATIONS 40 rooms, air-conditioning, minibar, telephone, cable TV FACILITIES AND SERVICES Internet access in communal areas, bar, soccer field, parking, pool, playground, restaurant, conference room CREDIT CARDS Diners, MasterCard, Visa
Avenida dos Magistrados, 2350, Praia de Atalaia
TEL and FAX (86) 3367-2200 www.riopoty.com.br

WHERE TO EAT

Chico e Izaura $
This restaurant on the banks of the Cumurupim River has a lovely view of the sea, dunes, and mangroves. The same scenery is the source of the fresh crab, fish, shrimp, and even the coconut juice. CUISINE fish and seafood CREDIT CARDS not accepted
Praia de Macapá, no #, 28 kilometers (17 miles) from the center
OPEN High season: daily, 8am – 9pm and 8am – 6pm

Dona Maria $
The most popular dish – peixada da Dona Maria – consists of six large shrimp, thickened pirão sauce, rice, and seasoned manioc flour. Other options are: baked fish with white sauce, cheese and ham, shrimp with sauce, and peixada brasileira. It stands on the beach, in an airy spot, supported by wooden pillars. CUISINE fish and seafood CREDIT CARDS MasterCard
Praia do Coqueiro, 10.425
TEL (86) 3366-1131 OPEN Daily, 10am – 8pm

Restaurante do Dedé $
The delicious shrimp moqueca arrives at the table steaming in a clay pot. The popular peixe à moda da casa consists of fish in a sauce of shrimp, vegetables and boiled eggs. CUISINE fish and seafood CREDIT CARDS not accepted
Praia do Coqueiro, no #
TEL (86) 3366-1115 OPEN Daily, 10am – 11pm

SERVICES

Bus Station – Rodoviária
Avenida José Maria de Lima, no #, Centro
TEL (86) 3367-1323 (Expresso Guanabara)

Maceió – Alagoas
AREA CODE 82 POPULATION 903,463 DISTANCES Aracaju 290 kilometers (180 miles), Recife 255 kilometers (158 miles) ACCESS BR-316 or BR-104 highway
www.maceio.al.gov.br

WHERE TO STAY

Matsubara $$$
With 110 rooms, it includes excellent leisure facilities, including one of the biggest pools in the region, two tennis courts, and a multi-sports court. Either dinner alone, or lunch and dinner, are included in the daily rates. The hotel has several types of suites. ACCOMMODATIONS 101 rooms and 9 suites, Internet access, air-conditioning, private safe, minibar, telephone, cable TV FACILITIES AND SERVICES Internet access in communal areas, bar, parking, stores, pool, playground, tennis court, multi-sports court, restaurant, magazine reading area, conference room, games room, reading room, massage room, beauty parlor, sauna, spa, currency exchange, 24-hour kitchen, valet parking, beach service; recreational team for children (high season) CREDIT CARDS Amex, Diners, MasterCard, Visa
Avenida Brig. Eduardo Gomes, 1551, Lagoa da Anta
TEL (82) 3214-3000 FAX 3235-1660
www.matsubarahotel.com.br

Jatiúca Resort $$$
This coconut palm-filled resort comprise a complex that includes a four-building hotel, seven floors of serviced apartments, a garden, and leisure facilities. The atmosphere is relaxed and the facilities are extensive, including a massage cabin on the beach, hammocks dotted throughout the resort and a natural pool. All meals are included in the daily rates. ACCOMMODATIONS 96 rooms and 83 apartments (16 facing the sea), Internet access, air-conditioning, private safe, minibar, radio, hairdryer, telephone, cable TV FACILITIES AND SERVICES Internet access in communal areas, bar, kids club, parking, stores, pools, playground, soccer court, tennis court, volleyball court, restaurants, conference room, gym, games room, massage room, beauty parlor, sauna, baby-sitting, room service, business center, currency exchange, 24-hour kitchen, recreational team for adults and children, laundry, valet parking, lifeguard, beach service CREDIT CARDS Amex, Diners, MasterCard, Visa
Rua Doutor Mário Nunes Vieira, 220, Mangabeiras
TEL (82) 2122-2000 RESERVATIONS 2122-2050, 2122-2040
FAX 2122-0107 www.hoteljatiuca.com.br

Maceió Mar $$
Other luxury hotels have sprung up in the city, but Maceió Mar continues to set the standard, with high-quality service, modern architecture, and comfortable rooms overlooking Ponta Verde beach. ACCOMMODATIONS 122 rooms (72 standard, 40 luxury, and 60 suites), Internet access, air-conditioning, private safe, minibar, telephone, cable TV; Jacuzzi in 3 suites; balcony in luxury rooms and suites FACILITIES AND SERVICES Internet access in communal areas, bar, parking, pool, playground, restaurant, conference room, gym, games room, sauna, business center, currency exchange, 24-hour kitchen, valet parking CREDIT CARDS Amex, Diners, Master-Card, Visa

| PRICES | HOTELS (couple) | $ up to R$150 | $$ from R$151 up to R$300 | $$$ from R$301 up to R$500 | $$$$ above R$500 |

Hotels, Restaurants and Services

Avenida Álvaro Otacílio, 2991, Ponta Verde
TEL (82) 2122-8000 **FAX** 3327-7026 www.maceiomar.com.br

Meliá Maceió $$$

A sophisticated beach-front hotel, the Meliá Maceió makes up for its lack of character with its excellent service and facilities. These include three pools set among the coconut trees and the 'plus' rooms with views overlooking the beach (the other rooms have only a side view). One of the restaurants serves Japanese food, the other regional cuisine. **ACCOMMODATIONS** 180 rooms (10 penthouse, 71 standard, 90 suites, and 9 plus), Internet access, air-conditioning, private safe, minibar, telephone, cable TV **FACILITIES AND SERVICES** Internet access in communal areas, bar, kids club, parking, drugstore, car rental, stores, pool, playground, tennis court, restaurants, magazine reading area, conference room, gym, games room, massage room, beauty parlor, sauna, travel agency, business center, currency exchange, 24-hour kitchen, recreational team for adults and children, valet parking **CREDIT CARDS** Amex, Diners, MasterCard, Visa
Avenida Álvaro Otacílio, 4065, Praia de Jatiúca
TEL (82) 2121-5656 **RESERVATIONS** 0800-703-3399
FAX 2121-5757
www.meliamcz.com.br

Ritz Lagoa da Anta $$$

The hotel has a spacious leisure area. Although it is near the sea, however, the beach here is not the best: a canal interferes with bathing and the sand is very powdery. **ACCOMMODATIONS** 196 rooms, air-conditioning, private safe, minibar, telephone, hairdryer, cable TV; *ofuro* tub in Bali suites **FACILITIES AND SERVICES** Internet access in communal areas, wine cellar, bar, parking, Jacuzzi, stores, pool, playground, tennis court, volleyball court, restaurant, beauty parlor, conference room, gym, games room, massage room, sauna, spa, business center, currency exchange, 24-hour kitchen, recreational team for adults and children, valet parking, laundry, beach service **CREDIT CARDS** Amex, Diners, MasterCard, Visa
Avenida Brigadeiro Eduardo Gomes, 546, Praia da Lagoa da Anta
TEL (82) 2121-4000, 2121-4120, 2121-4121 **FAX** 2121-4123
www.ritzlagoadaanta.com.br

Venta Club Pratagy $$$$

A little far from the most fashionable beaches, this hotel offers activities for adults at night, such as a theater and nightclub, and operates on an all-inclusive system (food and drinks are included in the daily rates, with the exception of lobster, shrimp, and imported drinks). **ACCOMMODATIONS** 178 rooms, air-conditioning, private safe, minibar, telephone, cable TV, ceiling fan; veranda/balcony in most rooms **FACILITIES AND SERVICES** archery, bar, bocce court, kayaks, soccer field, stores, pool, tennis court, restaurant, beauty parlor, conference room, gym, games room, massage room, sauna, recreational team for adults and children **CREDIT CARDS** Amex, Diners, MasterCard, Visa
Rodovia AL-101 Norte, Km 10, Pratagy
TEL (82) 2121-6200 **FAX** 2121-6201 www.pratagy.com

Verde Mar $

Wonderfully located near the craft fair and Pajuçara natural pools, this hotel has some rooms (14) with sea view. Daily rate includes either dinner or lunch and dinner. Up to one child under age five, per couple, is free. **ACCOMMODATIONS** 62 rooms, air-conditioning, private safe, minibar, telephone, cable TV **FACILITIES AND SERVICES** bar, parking, convenience store, pool, restaurant, conference room, games room, laundry **CREDIT CARDS** Amex, Diners, MasterCard, Visa
Avenida Doutor Antônio Gouveia, 81, Praia de Pajuçara

TEL (82) 2123-5700 **FAX** 2123-5799
www.hotelverdemar.com.br

WHERE TO EAT

Akuaba $

Akuaba means "welcome" in an old African dialect, and a mixture of influences from Africa and Bahia gave birth to the tasty dishes served in this restaurant run by a couple from Bahia. Their *acarajés* (black-eyed pea fritters) are made according to the traditional recipes of the "*baianas* (women) *do acarajé*" in Salvador. An example of the offerings: one dish combines large cooked shrimp, sliced okra, and smoked shrimp, seasoned with *dendê* palm oil, cashew nuts, peanuts, onion, and ginger. They serve twenty varieties of *moqueca*, as well as some northeastern dishes. **CUISINE** Afro-Bahian, fish and seafood **CREDIT CARDS** Amex, Diners, MasterCard, Visa
Avenida Álvaro Calheiros, 6, Mangabeiras
TEL (82) 3325-6199 **OPEN** Tue – Sun, 11am – until the last customer leaves

Associação das Doceiras de Massagueira $

At the entrance to the fishing village of Massagueira, 15 kilometers (9 miles) south of Maceió, is the row of 33 stalls that make up this association. Home-made delicacies sell at very reasonable prices. What's on offer is mostly *cocada* (coconut dessert), not only the traditional – white or with toasted coconut – but also with banana, guava, passion fruit, jackfruit, condensed milk and peanut. The meringues with grated lime peel are delicious. **CUISINE** desserts **CREDIT CARDS** not accepted
Rua Domina Barbosa, 185, Massagueira, Marechal Deodoro
TEL (82) 3260-7422 **OPEN** Daily, 8am – 6pm

Bar do Pato $

As you return from the beaches south of Maceió, make a lunch stop at this restaurant in Massagueira village, on the shores of Manguaba Lagoon. Opened in 1980 as a kiosk, this well cared for restaurant has a thatched roof and blue-painted wooden chairs as well as a wonderful view. It served delights such as crab, shrimp, and *agulhinha* fish, fried as a starter – everything is fresh and comes right from the lagoon itself. The name (Duck Bar) is justified by the duck, cooked in beer, with lima beans. **CUISINE** fish and seafood **CREDIT CARDS** MasterCard, Visa
Avenida Nossa Senhora da Conceição, 1308, Massagueira, Marechal Deodoro (15 kilometers, 9 miles, south of Maceió)
TEL (82) 3260-7048 **OPEN** Sun – Tue, 10am – 6pm; Wed – Sat, 10am – 2am

Canto da Boca $

Open for a decade, this restaurant's style has remained simple, even in the way the menu is presented. It serves several different versions of *moqueca* made with olive oil, coconut milk, and tomato sauce in a clay pot, which make the trip worthwhile. Also try the shrimp with octopus *moqueca*. They have classic *sertão* dishes, too, such as shredded, fried sun-dried beef served over manioc purée with coconut milk and covered in curd cheese gratin. Coconut mousse with guava syrup is a good suggestion for dessert. **CUISINE** fish and seafood, regional **CREDIT CARDS** Diners, MasterCard, Visa
Avenida Júlio Marques Luz, 654, Jatiúca
TEL (82) 3325-7346 **RESERVATIONS** 3325-7279 **OPEN** Mon, Wed and Thu, noon– midnight; Fri and Sat, noon – 1am; Sun, noon – 6pm

---

RESTAURANTS | $ up to R$50 | $$ from R$51 up to R$100 | $$$ from R$101 up to R$150 | $$$$ above R$150

HOTELS, RESTAURANTS AND SERVICES

Divina Gula $
At this restaurant, you can savor delicious food from Minas Gerais in an attractive, welcoming atmosphere. The menu, created by owner/chef André Generoso, covers all the classic dishes from Minas such as *tutu à mineira* (bean purée, homemade sausage, sliced leg of pork, collard greens, pork crackling, banana fritter, and rice), and André even gives a nod to the coast (shrimp with soy sauce). He grows his own organic produce, and makes *cachaças*, which are aged in *jequitibá-rosa* wood and European oak casks and can be bought in the adjoining shop. This restaurant belongs to the Associação dos Restaurantes da Boa Lembrança restaurant association. CUISINE Minas Gerais CREDIT CARDS Amex, Diners, MasterCard, Visa
Rua Engenheiro Paulo Brandão Nogueira, 85, Jatiúca
TEL (82) 3235-1016 RESERVATIONS and FAX 3235-1262 OPEN Tue – Sun, noon – until the last customer leaves

Lua Cheia $
The tables and chairs may be plastic, but the napkins are cloth, the service is first class, and the kitchen happily blends French cuisine with that of Brazil. One of the owners, Thierry Parra, is French, and his wife, Lúcia, lived in France for many years. In addition to the kitchen – which sends out fine dishes such as grilled fillet steak in Roquefort sauce, and shrimp in cream with herbs brought from Provence, in France – the couple shares another passion: music. Their rich collection of CDs harmonizes perfectly with the surroundings. CUISINE French-Brazilian CREDIT CARDS Amex, MasterCard
Rua General França Albuquerque, 250, Garça Torta
TEL (82) 3355-1186 OPEN Wed – Fri, 4pm – midnight; Sat, noon – midnight; Sun, noon – 5pm

Recanto do Picuí $
This humble restaurant serves quality regional food. The owners are from Picuí, in Paraíba, which produces excellent sun-dried beef – the highlight of the menu here. Barbecue grilled, tender, and succulent, it comes in several varieties: *gororoba*, for example, comes with onions, manioc purée, and grilled curd cheese. Other excellent choices are mutton, poultry, and rump steak. Round off your meal with a classic dessert from the *sertão*: curd cheese with molasses. CUISINE regional CREDIT CARDS Diners, MasterCard, Visa
Avenida Álvaro Calheiros, 110, Mangabeiras
TEL (82) 3325-7537 OPEN Mon – Thu, 11:30am– midnight; Fri and Sat, 11:30am – 1:30am

Sorveteria Bali $
Sixty flavors, some of which are nondairy, offer a good selection of regional fruits. They also have chocolate (white, milk, and dark) and alcoholic drinks like coffee with chocolate drops and whiskey. Milk shakes and banana splits also sell well, as do the savories sold. CUISINE ice cream CREDIT CARDS not accepted
Avenida Doutor Antônio de Gouveia, 451, Pajuçara
TEL (82) 3231-8833 OPEN Daily, 11am – until the last customer leaves

Wanchaco $
At this unique restaurant, you can try Peruvian cuisine and *nikkey* – a fusion between Japan and Peru. The restaurant's charm stems as much from the gastronomic intelligence of the rotating menu as from the friendliness of the owners and the laid-back sophistication of the surroundings (there are surf boards on the walls in honor of the beach in Peru that gives the restaurant its name). Three suggestions: ceviche (lime-marinated fish), grilled fish with shrimp in sweet and sour ginger sauce, and octopus and shrimp risotto.

Some items come directly from Peru, like the jellies made from Andean fruits. CUISINE Peruvian CREDIT CARDS Diners, MasterCard, Visa
Rua São Francisco de Assis, 93, Jatiúca
TEL (82) 3377-6114. RESERVATIONS 3377-6024 OPEN Mon – Thu, noon – 3pm and 7pm – 11:30pm; Fri, noon – 4pm and 7pm – 12:30am; Sat, 7pm – 2am

SERVICES

Bus Station – Rodoviária
Avenida Leste-Oeste, no #, Feitosa
TEL (82) 3221-4615

Tourist Information – Posto de Informações Turísticas
Avenida Dr. Antônio Gouveia, no #, Praia de Pajuçara (in front of Sueca restaurant)
TEL (82) 3315-1603 OPEN Daily, 8am – 6pm

Tourist Information – Posto de Informações Turísticas (Shopping Iguatemi)
Avenida Gustavo Paiva, 2990, Mangabeiras
TEL (82) 3357-1010 OPEN Mon – Sat, 10am – 10pm; Sun, 3pm – 10pm

Mangue Seco – Bahia

AREA CODE 75 Jandaíra DISTANCES Salvador 246 kilometers (153 miles), Aracaju 100 kilometers (62 miles), Sítio do Conde 77 kilometers (48 miles) ACCESS From Salvador, take the Linha Verde highway to the border with Sergipe. From there, take SE-318 to Indiaroba (15 kilometers, 9 miles), followed by the dirt road (12 kilometers) to the village of Pontal. Motorboats run from Pontal to Mangue Seco (15 minutes). From Aracaju, take SE-438 to Porto do Mato (73 kilometers, 45 miles), from where you can catch the Mosqueiro–Caueira ferryboat. From the ferry drop-off it is a further 25 minutes by motorboat.

WHERE TO STAY

Pousada Asa Branca $
This two-story guesthouse facing the Real River has a horseshoe shape, with a pool in the center. The superior rooms are the most pleasant and offer a fine view of the river. Though not the most comfortable option in Mangue Seco, Asa Branca does have some of the best facilities. For an additional fee, guests can arrange dune-buggy trips to the beach through the guesthouse. Tour groups frequent the on-site restaurant, which can get crowded. ACCOMMODATIONS 20 rooms, minibar, TV; air-conditioning in 15 rooms, fan in 5 rooms FACILITIES AND SERVICES Internet access in communal areas, bar, buggy, motorboat, pool, restaurant, river CREDIT CARDS Diners, MasterCard, Visa
Rua da Frente, 4, Praia de Mangue Seco
TEL (75) 3445-9054 FAX 3445-9053
www.infonet.com.br/asabranca

Pousada O Forte $
Frenchman Ives Niort has owned and run this guesthouse since 2004, undertaking several renovations on the property since his initial purchase. Simple and rustic in style, the guesthouse features 12 rooms and a garden, all facing the Real River Beach. We recommend the rooms with air-conditioning and sea views. The staff speaks French, English, Portuguese, and Spanish. ACCOMMODATIONS 12 rooms, air-conditioning, minibar, TV; ceiling fan in 3 rooms FACILITIES AND SERVICES Internet access in communal areas, bar, kayaks, mo-

| PRICES | HOTELS (couple) | $ up to R$150 | $$ from R$151 up to R$300 | $$$ from R$301 up to R$500 | $$$$ above R$500 |

torboat, pool, surf boards, restaurant, ecological trips **CREDIT CARDS** Diners, MasterCard, Visa
Praia da Costa, no #
TEL and **FAX** (75) 3445-9039 www.pousadaoforte.com

Village Mangue Seco $

Mangue Seco is just 800 meters from town along River Real Beach, situated on several acres of property facing a mangrove forest. Though modestly appointed (standard rooms only have cold showers), they offer lovely views of the river and easy access to the dunes right next door. **ACCOMMODATIONS** 19 rooms; ceiling fan, minibar, and cold shower in standard rooms; air-conditioning, minibar, and TV in others **FACILITIES AND SERVICES** pool, playground, restaurant **CREDIT CARDS** Diners, MasterCard
Praia da Costa, no #
TEL and **FAX** (75) 3445-9047
www.villagemangueseco.com.br

WHERE TO EAT

Frutos do Mar $

This simple restaurant sits at the point where the motorboats that cross the river usually stop. Fish with shrimp sauce is the most popular dish. Also recommended is *aratu* (a type of crab) available fried, in *moqueca*, and in *catado* – stewed in a sauce of tomatoes, bell peppers, onions, and coriander. All dishes are served with rice, beans, seasoned manioc flour, and salad. **CUISINE** homemade, fish, and seafood **CREDIT CARDS** Diners, MasterCard
Praça Santa Cruz, 58, Centro
TEL (75) 3445-9049 **OPEN** Daily, 8am – 9pm

Maracajaú – Rio Grande do Norte

AREA CODE 84 Maxaranguape **DISTANCE** Natal 61 kilometers (38 miles) **ACCESS** From Natal, take BR-101

WHERE TO STAY

Pousada Ponta dos Anéis $

The unique draw of this guesthouse is its location, on the calm, secluded bay of Ponta dos Anéis. In the rainy season, the bay is only accessible via the beach (either on foot or by dune buggy), but the trip is worth it for anyone in search of rest, relaxation, and calm surroundings. **ACCOMMODATIONS** 11 chalets, minibar in 6 rooms, TV, veranda, ceiling fan **FACILITIES AND SERVICES** parking, pool, volleyball court, restaurant, games room, dune-buggy trips, airport shuttle **CREDIT CARDS** not accepted
Avenida Enseada, no #
TEL (84) 9981-8121 **RESERVATIONS** and **FAX** 3206-1238
www.pousadapontadosaneis.com.br

Maragogi – Alagoas

AREA CODE 82 **POPULATION** 25,233 **DISTANCE** Maceió 130 kilometers (81 miles), Recife 130 kilometers (81 miles) **ACCESS** From Maceió, take Rodovia Litorânea (AL-101)

WHERE TO STAY

Bitingui Praia Hotel $$

Strategically situated right on the coast between Maceió and Recife, this hotel offers transportation to both capitals. The hotel has good recreational facilities, with four pools and a wooded area, among other attractions. **ACCOMMODATIONS** 42 rooms and 8 chalets, air-conditioning, private safe, minibar, telephone, cable TV **FACILITIES AND SERVICES** Internet access in communal areas, bicycles, woods, horses, parking, pool, playground, volleyball court, restaurant, games room, conference room, business center, recreational team for adults and children, dune-buggy trips, shuttle service to airport and local attractions **CREDIT CARDS** Amex, Diners, MasterCard, Visa
Sítio Bitingui, no #, Zona Rural, Japaratinga
TEL (82) 3297-1500, 3297-1283 **FAX** 3297-1293
www.bitingui.com.br

Hotel Praia Dourada $$

Combines elements of countryside and beachfront living. Peacocks, marmosets, and other animals roam the grounds. The hotel also organizes sightseeing trips on the walking trails in the surrounding area. They only offer two types of rooms (luxury or super luxury), both with sea views. **ACCOMMODATIONS** 117 rooms, air-conditioning, private safe, minibar, telephone, cable TV **FACILITIES AND SERVICES** Internet access in communal areas, parking, snack bar, stores, pool, restaurant, conference room, gym, games room, sauna, walking trails, business center **CREDIT CARDS** Amex, Diners, MasterCard, Visa
Rodovia AL-101 Norte, Km 130, Praia do Burgalhau (4 kilometers from the center)
TEL (82) 3296-6161 **RESERVATIONS** (81) 3424-4545 **FAX** (81) 3424-3840, 3424-6213 www.hotelpraiadourada.com.br

Marrecas Hotel Fazenda $$

Dating from 1817, this farm is a major attraction in Maragogi, thanks to its lovely restored main building, with guest rooms where the old slave quarters used to be. The on-site restaurant serves regional cuisine. **ACCOMMODATIONS** 25 rooms, air-conditioning, private safe, minibar, telephone, TV **FACILITIES AND SERVICES** bar, horses, cart, parking, fishing lake, paddleboats, pool, restaurant, games room, sauna, walking trails, recreational team for adults and children, guided walking tours **CREDIT CARDS** Diners, MasterCard
Rodovia AL-101, exit Km 130.9 (then follow a dirt road 4 kilometers to the farm)
TEL and **FAX** (82) 3666-1600 **RESERVATIONS** (81) 2123-5656
www.marrecas.com.br

Paraíso dos Coqueirais $

This guesthouse stands on an old farmstead, surrounded by greenery and coconut palms. The 35-hectare (86-acre) property boasts walking trails and a fishing lake, as well as a pool and a stable with horses. The guesthouse is also just 100 meters (330 feet) from a stretch of beach good for fishing, bathing, and water sports. **ACCOMMODATIONS** 32 rooms, air-conditioning, minibar, telephone, TV **FACILITIES AND SERVICES** Internet access in communal areas, horses, parking, fishing lake, pool, restaurant, walking trails, dune-buggy trips, shuttle service to airport and local attractions **CREDIT CARDS** Diners, MasterCard, Visa
Rodovia AL-101, Km 121, Sítio Nossa Senhora de Fátima
TEL (82) 3297-1125, 3297-1101
www.paraisodoscoqueirais.com.br

Pousada do Alto $$

This guesthouse sits atop a hill, meaning all the rooms have a wonderful view of the sea. The restaurant menu includes such tempting dishes as shrimp in cheese sauce with paprika-spiced manioc flour. **ACCOMMODATIONS** 10 rooms, air-conditioning, minibar, TV, DVD player in superior rooms **FACILITIES AND SERVICES** Internet access in communal areas, boats, bicycles and horses (outsourced service), parking, pool, restaurant **CREDIT CARDS** not accepted
Sítio Biquinha, no #, Centro, Japaratinga
TEL (82) 3297-1210 **FAX** 3297-1268
www.pousadadoalto.com.br

RESTAURANTS $ up to R$50 $$ from R$51 up to R$100 $$$ from R$101 up to R$150 $$$$ above R$150

Salinas do Maragogi Resort $$$$

The Maragogi River runs right through the coconut- and mangrove-dotted grounds of this seafront guesthouse. Rustic in style, with a friendly family atmosphere, the resort has plenty of activities for children as well as excellent facilities for adults, especially those interested in water sports. We recommend the therapeutic spa facilities. Dinner is included in the daily rate. Honeymoon packages are available. **ACCOMMODATIONS** 193 rooms and 10 suites, air-conditioning, private safe, minibar, telephone, cable TV **FACILITIES AND SERVICES** Internet access in communal areas, archery, bar, boat, woods, kayaks, soccer field, fishing equipment, waterskiing, parking, Jacuzzi, motorboat, snack bar, stores, pool, playground, orchard, soccer court, squash court, tennis court, volleyball court, restaurant, river, conference room, gym, games room, massage room, sauna, walking trails, travel agency, business center, recreational team for adults and children, guided walking tours, valet parking, lifeguard, beach service, shuttle service to airport and local attractions; beauty parlor **CREDIT CARDS** Amex, Diners, MasterCard, Visa
Rodovia AL-101 Norte, Km 124
TEL (82) 3296-3000 **RESERVATIONS** 3296-3030 **FAX** 3296-1158
www.salinas.com.br

WHERE TO EAT

Restaurante do Mano $

This restaurant is 2 kilometers from the center of town, on São Bento Beach. The dining area is completely open, with the kitchen in full view of customers. Chef Manoel Farias do Carmo (better known as Mano) specializes in fish and seafood, and though all his dishes are well-presented, the lobster and crab in coconut sauce is a definite highlight. For dessert Mano offers a variety of homemade compotes using jackfruit, guava, coconut, banana and even cashew fruit. **CUISINE** fish and seafood **CREDIT CARDS** not accepted
Rua Simeão Ribeiro de Albuquerque, no #, São Bento
TEL (82) 3296-7106 **OPEN** Daily, 8am – 10pm

Maraú – Bahia (see Barra Grande)

Marechal Deodoro – Alagoas
(see Praia do Francês)

Morro de São Paulo – Bahia

AREA CODE 75 Cairu **DISTANCES** Salvador 248 kilometers (154 miles) of driving, followed by 90 minutes by boat or 30 minutes by motorboat **ACCESS** By sea: Motorboats and catamarans leave from the pier at Salvador's Mercado Modelo for the 2-hour crossing. By land and sea: From Salvador, take BA-001 to Valença; boats (90-minute trip) and speedboats (30-minute trip) depart for Morro from there. By air: Two air-taxi services run flights from Salvador (20 minutes)

WHERE TO STAY

Catavento Praia Hotel $$

This hotel sits on extensive grounds in a quiet spot facing the natural pools of Quarta Praia Beach. Opened in 1989, the hotel has two wings of rooms, which are well-equipped but in need of some refurbishment. The eight luxury rooms are the best bet, since they face the sea. The hotel has plenty of amenities for children, including a toy room, games room, and a good, kid-friendly pool. The on-site gym is just one exercise bike and one treadmill. **ACCOMMODATIONS** 20 rooms, air-conditioning, private safe, minibar, telephone, cable TV **FACILITIES AND SERVICES** Internet access in communal areas, bar, toy room, kayaks, snack bar, mini-park, pool, playground, tennis court, restaurant, gym, games room, massage room, sauna, heliport, beach service, shuttle service to airport and local attractions **CREDIT CARDS** Amex, Diners, MasterCard, Visa
Quarta Praia, no #
TEL (75) 3652-2121, 3652-1052
www.cataventopraiahotel.com.br

Hotel Fazenda Vila Guaiamu $$

This laid-back, extremely pleasant hotel sits on 14 hectares (35 acres) in a nature reserve created to protect the *guaiamum* crab, which guests are sure to see crawling around as they walk through the garden. The property sits at the exact spot where the hubbub of Terceira Praia Beach ends, the packed crowds and scores of beach facilities giving way to deserted stretches of sand and relative peace and quiet. The rooms are simple, airy, and private, and built far apart from each other. Among the many amenities offered by the hotel are private ecological trails, particularly popular in summer. **ACCOMMODATIONS** 22 rooms, air-conditioning, private safe, minibar, TV, veranda with hammock **FACILITIES AND SERVICES** bar, soccer field, restaurant, river, games room, massage room, video room, walking trails, beach service **CREDIT CARDS** Amex, Diners, MasterCard, Visa
Terceira Praia, no #
TEL and **FAX** (75) 3652-1073, 3652-1035
www.vilaguaiamu.com.br

Patachocas Eco-Resort $$$

The spacious bungalows of this eco-resort are scattered among the coconut palms near the natural pools of Quarta Praia Beach. The communal areas include a lovely restaurant and pool with deck. Since the daily rate is the same for all rooms, be sure to ask for those nearest the beach, as they have good sea views. **ACCOMMODATIONS** 26 bungalows, air-conditioning, private safe, minibar, telephone, TV **FACILITIES AND SERVICES** Internet access in communal areas, bar, bicycles, snack bar, convenience store, stores, pool, restaurant, outdoors massage room, travel agency, recreational team for adults, guided walking tours, beach service, shuttle service to airport and local attractions **CREDIT CARDS** Amex, Diners, MasterCard, Visa
Quarta Praia, no #
TEL (75) 3652-2134 **RESERVATIONS** and **FAX** 3652-2129
www.patachocas.com.br

Hotel Portaló $$$

This is a good choice in Morro, conveniently located right in front of the Portaló, the arched gateway into town. The rooms are named after either books or writers, and each comes stocked with its namesake work or works. The chalets are preferable to the standard rooms as they are more spacious, comfortable, and private. The best attraction is definitely the massage deck, with its wonderful sea view. One disadvantage of Portaló's prominent location is its proximity to the quays, where boats loudly sound their horns as they approach. **ACCOMMODATIONS** 11 chalets, 8 rooms, and 4 suites; air-conditioning, private safe, minibar, hairdryer, telephone, cable TV; Jacuzzi in master chalets **FACILITIES AND SERVICES** Internet access in communal areas, bar, kayaks, cascade, fishing equipment, waterskiing, snack bar, pool, restaurant, wakeboarding **CREDIT CARDS** MasterCard, Visa
Ladeira da Igreja, no #
TEL (75) 3652-1373, 3652-1375 www.hotelportalo.com

Porto do Zimbo Small Resort $$$$

This charming hotel faces the natural pools of Quarta Praia Beach. Though all the rooms are comfortable, pleasant, and

well-equipped (ask for a room with a sea view), guests seeking true luxury should opt for the suite, with its *ofuro* tub, Jacuzzi, and 29"TV. The various wings of the hotel are connected by palm-thatched walkways. ACCOMMODATIONS 15 rooms and 1 suite (Jacuzzi and terrace with *ofuro* tub), air-conditioning, private safe, minibar, telephone, cable TV, ceiling fan; Jacuzzi in 7 rooms FACILITIES AND SERVICES Internet access in communal areas, bar, bicycles, kayaks, snack bar, pool with hydro-massage, restaurant, games room, massage room, video room, spa, travel agency, shuttle service to airport and local attractions CREDIT CARDS Amex, Diners, MasterCard, Visa
Quarta Praia, no #
TEL (75) 3652-2030 RESERVATIONS and FAX 3652-1278
www.hotelportodozimbro.com.br

Pousada Charme $$

This guesthouse is right in the middle of all the Morro action, which may be a disadvantage in the summer (which is high tourist season). The bar is the centerpiece of Charme, with rooms scattered all up the hillside, with side sea view. The best room is the one with a Jacuzzi on the balcony, highly recommended for couples without children. ACCOMMODATIONS 9 rooms, air-conditioning, private safe, minibar, telephone, cable TV; Jacuzzi in 1 room FACILITIES AND SERVICES bar, Jacuzzi, snack bar, pool, restaurant CREDIT CARDS Diners, MasterCard, Visa
Rua da Prainha, no #, Centro
TEL and FAX (75) 3652-1306 www.charmepousada.com.br

Pousada Solar do Morro $$

This guesthouse in Morro's central square has several different levels of rooms, from simple junior rooms up to a suite with a Jacuzzi and sea views. The ground floor features both a travel agency and a restaurant-cum-pizzeria (*see Where to Eat*). ACCOMMODATIONS 12 rooms and 1 suite, air-conditioning, private safe, minibar, telephone, cable TV; balcony with hammock in luxury rooms; Jacuzzi in 1 luxury room and in the suite, *ofuro* tub in 1 luxury room FACILITIES AND SERVICES bar, board games, pool with hydro-massage, restaurant, travel agency CREDIT CARDS Amex, Diners, MasterCard, Visa
Praça Aureliano de Lima, 155, Centro
TEL and FAX (75) 3652-1057
www.pousadasolardomorro.com.br

Pousada Villa das Pedras $$$

The rooms are simple in style; the best ones are the "superior" category rooms facing the beach. The guesthouse is right next door to a very popular square with stores, snack bars, and a *cahaçaria* (*cachaça* bar). ACCOMMODATIONS 24 rooms, air-conditioning, private safe, minibar, telephone, cable TV FACILITIES AND SERVICES Internet access in communal areas, bar, snack bar, stores, pool, restaurant, games room, massage room, video room, travel agency, beach service CREDIT CARDS Amex, Diners, MasterCard, Visa
Segunda Praia, no #
TEL (75) 3652-1075 FAX 3652-1122
www.villadaspedras.com.br

Praia do Encanto $$

Though the accommodations are simple, the nice chalets are both spacious and comfortable. There is a traditional still and an art studio on-site, as well as a restaurant serving Spanish cuisine. ACCOMMODATIONS 22 chalets, air-conditioning, private safe, minibar, telephone, cable TV FACILITIES AND SERVICES Internet access in communal areas, art studio, bar, boat, bicycles, kayaks, horses, convenience store, pool, playground, restaurant, games room, massage room, travel agency, landing strip, beach service, airport shuttle CREDIT CARDS Amex, Diners, MasterCard, Visa

Quarta Praia, no #
TEL and FAX (75) 3652-2000, 9981-3030
www.praiadoencanto.com.br

Villa dos Corais Pousada $$$

This guesthouse is on the border between Terceira and Quarta Praia Beaches. The rooms all face the sea, and are cozy, spacious, well equipped, and comfortable. The centerpiece of the property is a lovely Olympic-style pool and surrounding deck. Both the restaurant and reception desk sit poolside. ACCOMMODATIONS 40 rooms, air-conditioning, super king-size beds, private safe, minibar, telephone, cable TV, balcony/veranda with hammock FACILITIES AND SERVICES bar, pool, volleyball court, restaurant, gym, games room, sauna, travel agency, beach service CREDIT CARDS Amex, Diners, MasterCard, Visa
Terceira Praia, no #
TEL (75) 3652-1560 FAX 3652-1144
www.villadoscorais.com.br

WHERE TO EAT

Club do Balanço $

Balanço is a good lunchtime option as it is right on Segunda Praia, facing the sea. The *moqueca* is the highlight. Other good menu options are the shrimp *bobó* and tuna *à marinara*. CUISINE Espírito Santo, fish and seafood CREDIT CARDS Amex, Diners, MasterCard, Visa
Segunda Praia, no #
TEL (75) 3652-1110 OPEN High season: daily, 9am – midnight; low season: daily, 10am – 7pm

El Sítio $

Meat is the menu focus (though it also serves some seafood dishes). The most popular dish is steak filet served with a variety of Franco-Brazilian sauces, accompanied by rice, mashed potatoes, salad, and seasoned manioc flour. Live music is featured most evenings. CUISINE meat, fish, and seafood CREDIT CARDS Diners, MasterCard, Visa
Rua Porto de Cima, no #, Praia da Gamboa
TEL (75) 3652-1212. OPEN Daily, 10am – 10pm

Piscina $

This two-story restaurant is right on the waterfront at the edge of Quarta Praia Beach, near the border with Terceira Praia. The highlights of her menu include the shrimp and lobster casserole with thickened *pirão* sauce, accompanied by rice, salad, beans, and seasoned manioc flour (serves two). CUISINE regional, fish, and seafood CREDIT CARDS Diners, MasterCard, Visa
Quarta Praia, no #
TEL (75) 3652-1461 RESERVATIONS 3652-1117 OPEN Daily, 8am – 10pm

Via Brasil $

Via Brasil is on the ground floor of Pousada Solar do Morro. The atmosphere is relaxed, with live music almost every day. Though the menu is quite varied, the kitchen's forte is pizzas made in a wood-burning oven. Other good choices include the asparagus risotto and beef medallions. CUISINE pizza, varied CREDIT CARDS Diners, MasterCard, Visa
Praça Aureliano de Lima, 155 (Pousada Solar do Morro)
TEL (75) 3652-1443 OPEN Daily, 6pm – 11pm

SERVICES

Air-Taxi – Addey

Rua Caminho da Praia, no #
TEL (75) 3652-1242; in Salvador: (71) 3377-2451 OPEN Daily, 8am – midnight www.marlinstur.com

---

RESTAURANTS $ up to R$50 $$ from R$51 up to R$100 $$$ from R$101 up to R$150 $$$$ above R$150

Air-Taxi – Aero Star
Rua Caminho da Praia, no #
TEL (75) 3652-1535, 3652-1312 OPEN Daily, 7:30am – 10pm
www.aerostar.com.br

Diving Agency – Companhia do Mergulho
Primeira Praia, no # (Pousada Farol do Morro, ground floor)
TEL (75) 3652-1200, 9981-2110, 3653-7127 OPEN Daily, 8am – 7pm   www.ciadomergulho.com.br

Diving Agency – Tinharé Dive Club
Terceira Praia, 48
TEL (75) 3652-1573 OPEN High season: daily, 8:30am – 9pm; low season: daily, 8:30am – 8pm

Flying Fox – Tirolesa do Morro
Primeira Praia, no #
TEL (75) 3652-1219, 8805-9796, OPEN Daily, 10am – 6pm
www.tirolesadomorro.com.br

Tourist Information – Centro de Informações Turísticas
Travel agency and guides
Praça Aureliano Lima, no #
TEL (75) 3652-1083, 3652-1589 OPEN Daily, 8:30am – 10pm

Travel Agency – Agência de Turismo Itha do Mar
Rua da Prainha, no #
TEL (75) 3652-1104, 3652-1225 OPEN Daily, 8am – 9pm

Travel Agency – Madalena Tur
Segunda Praia, no #
TEL (75) 3652-1317, 3652-2076, 9148-3234 OPEN High season: daily, 8am – midnight; low season: daily, 8am – 10pm
www.madalenaturismo.com.br

Travel Agency – Marlins Ecotur
Rua Caminho da Praia, no #
TEL (75) 3652-1242, 3652-1222 OPEN Daily, 8am – midnight
www.marlinstur.com

Morro do Chapéu – Bahia

AREA CODE 74 POPULATION 36,203 DISTANCES Salvador 385 kilometers (239 miles), Feira de Santana 290 kilometers (180 miles), Lençóis 172 kilometers (107 miles) ACCESS Take Rodovia do Feijão (BA-052 highway) from Feira de Santana, or take BR-122 from BR-242. Alternatively, from Jacobina, take BA-346 or from Xique-Xique take BA-052 WHEN TO VISIT In the rainy season (November to March) for the waterfalls

WHERE TO STAY

Pousada Ecológica das Bromélias $
Though not very sophisticated, this guesthouse is clean and well run. A huge panel at reception displays photographs of regional natural attractions, topographical maps of the local state park, and sketches of Gruta dos Brejões cave. The rooms and bathrooms are spacious and spotless. Breakfast, however, could be better. ACCOMMODATIONS 4 rooms, telephone, TV FACILITIES AND SERVICES parking, pool, conference room, video room, guided walking tours CREDIT CARDS not accepted
Rua Caetano Dutra, no #
TEL (74) 3653-1314 FAX 3653-1468

WHERE TO EAT

Eusépio $
This restaurant, is famed for its pizzas. The menu also includes pastas and dishes such as steak fillet with onions or *à milanesa* (breaded). CUISINE Italian, pizza CREDIT CARDS Visa
Rua Antônio Balbino, 395
TEL (74) 3653-2205 OPEN Mon – Sat, 11am – 3pm and 6pm – 11pm

SERVICES

Guide – Gilmar Novaes Barbosa
Rua José Maria Tourinho, 70, Centro
TEL (74) 9991-6489 OPEN Telephone inquiries 24 hours

Tourist Information – Informações Turísticas
Praça Augusto Públio, Módulo Central, no #
TEL (74) 3653-1826 (Department of Tourism); 3653-1536 (City Hall) OPEN Mon – Fri, 8am – 7pm

Mossoró – Rio Grande do Norte

AREA CODE 84 POPULATION 227,357 DISTANCES Natal 283 kilometers (176 miles), Fortaleza 240 kilometers (149 miles) ACCESS From the coast take the BR-304 highway. From the *sertão*, take the hazardous BR-405 or RN-117

WHERE TO STAY

Thermas de Mossoró $$$
Its 200,000-square-meter (50-acre) grounds house Planeta Água, a water park with 12 pools, an artificial lake, playgrounds, restaurants, an events center, and many gardens. Eleven of the pools are filled by the thermal springs and boast temperatures between 28ºC and 50ºC (82ºF and 122ºF). The Moinhos restaurant, open to non-guests, serves regional cuisine. ACCOMMODATIONS 142 rooms and 2 suites, Internet access, air-conditioning, minibar, telephone, cable TV; Jacuzzi in suites FACILITIES AND SERVICES Internet access in communal areas, bar, parking, convenience store, natural pool, thermal pool, jogging track, playground, soccer field, squash court, tennis court, volleyball court, restaurant, conference room, gym, game room, 24-hour kitchen, recreational team for adults and children CREDIT CARDS Amex, Diners, MasterCard, Visa
Avenida Lauro Monte, 2001, Santo Antônio
TEL (84) 3422-1200 FAX 3422-1201
www.hotelthermas.com.br

Mucugê – Bahia

AREA CODE 75 POPULATION 15,780 DISTANCES Salvador 460 kilometers (286 miles), Lençóis 150 kilometers (93 miles) ACCESS Exits Km 96 and Km 99 on BA-142 highway

WHERE TO STAY

Alpina Resort $
Magnificent panoramas overlook mountains and hills. The pool offers a lovely view. ACCOMMODATIONS 32 rooms, minibar, TV, ceiling fan FACILITIES AND SERVICES Internet access in communal areas, bar, horses, parking, fireplace, shops, pool, soccer field, volleyball court, restaurant, conference room, game room, video room CREDIT CARDS Visa
Rodovia BA-142, Km 90, Alto do Capa-Bode
TEL (75) 3338-2150 RESERVATIONS and FAX (71) 3451-4900
www.alpinamucuge.com.br

Pousada Monte Azul $
The pleasantly situated guesthouse faces a picturesque mountain, home to Santa Isabel cemetery. Other draws are the excellent DVD collection and the restaurant's home-cooked food. ACCOMMODATIONS 11 rooms, minibar, tele-

| PRICES | HOTELS (couple) | $ up to R$150 | $$ from R$151 up to R$300 | $$$ from R$301 up to R$500 | $$$$ above R$500 |

phone, TV, fan **FACILITIES AND SERVICES** bar, parking, restaurant, video room **CREDIT CARDS** not accepted
Avenida Antonito Medrado, 5, Cidade Nova
TEL (75) 3338-2113, 3338-2195 **FAX** 3338-2195
www.pousadamonteazul.com.br

Pousada Mucugê $
Its attractive and well-maintained building is in the city center. The guesthouse resembles a hotel in style, offering formal service. Among the attractions are an excellent breakfast, a pool, and a restaurant serving Brazilian cuisine. **ACCOMMODATIONS** 30 rooms, minibar, telephone, TV, ceiling fan **FACILITIES AND SERVICES** parking, pool, restaurant, video room **CREDIT CARDS** Visa
Rua Doutor Rodrigues Lima, 30, Centro
TEL and **FAX** (75) 3338-2210 www.pousadamucuge.com.br

WHERE TO EAT

Dona Nena $
Try a *prato-feito* (meal served on a single plate) or a regular meal (served on a platters). The tables are next to Nena's kitchen. This very informal place has no fixed opening times. **CUISINE** regional, home-made **CREDIT CARDS** not accepted
Rua Direita do Comércio, 140
TEL (75) 3338-2123 **OPEN** no fixed time

Restaurante da Pousada Casa da Roça $
Artwork and odds and ends give the restaurant the air of a *casa da roça* (country cottage). Music adds to the atmosphere. Try the fried *tucunaré* fish with seasoned manioc flour, manioc, rice, and salad. **CUISINE** regional, bar food, pizza **CREDIT CARDS** not accepted
Rua Coronel Douca Medrado, no #, Centro
TEL (75) 3338-2431 **OPEN** Daily, noon – 3pm and 5pm – until the last customer leaves

SERVICES

Guides – Associação dos Condutores de Visitantes de Mucugê (ACVM)
Rua Coronel Douca Medrado, 71, Centro
TEL (75) 3338-2414 **OPEN** Daily, 8am – noon and 2pm – 8pm

Tourist Information – Centro de Atendimento ao Turista
Rua Coronel Douca Medrado, 71, Centro
TEL (75) 3338-2176 **OPEN** Daily, 8am – noon, 2pm – 5pm and 6pm – 10pm

Travel Agency – Km Viagens e Turismo
Praça Coronel Douca Medrado, 126, Centro
TEL (75) 3338-2152, 3338-2277 **OPEN** Daily, 8am – noon and 2pm – 10pm
Car and motorcycle rental, guides, tourist information, car-wash, Internet access, taxi

Travel Agency – Trilhas e Caminhos
Ecoturismo – Roberto Sapucaia (guide)
Guides and tourist information
Praça Quinze de Novembro, 12, Centro
TEL (75) 3338-2463 www.trilhasecaminhos.com.br

Natal – Rio Grande do Norte
AREA CODE 84 **POPULATION** 778,040 **DISTANCES** Fortaleza 552 kilometers (343 miles), João Pessoa 180 kilometers (112 miles) **ACCESS** BR-101, BR-226, or BR-406 highways
www.natal.rn.gov.br

WHERE TO STAY

Esmeralda $$$
Ideally located on buzzing Ponta Negra beach, Esmeralda opened in 2003. The European décor, in shades of brown, is at odds with the sunny climate, but the rooms are lighter than the rest of the hotel. Choose rooms overlooking the sea or Morro do Careca hill; avoid those with a view of the parking lot. **ACCOMMODATIONS** 100 rooms and 21 suites, Internet access, air-conditioning, private safe, minibar, hairdryer, telephone, cable TV **FACILITIES AND SERVICES** Internet access in communal areas, bar, bicycles, parking, pool, restaurant, conference room, massage room, video room, sauna, travel agency, currency exchange, guides, recreational team for adults and children, shuttle service **CREDIT CARDS** Amex, Diners, MasterCard, Visa
Rua Francisco Gurgel, 1160, Ponta Negra
TEL (84) 4005-0000 **FAX** 3219-5994
www.hotelesmeralda.com.br

Hotel-Escola Senac Barreira Roxa $
You can hear waves pounding against the rocks from the beach-facing rooms of this hotel. The view is magnificent, but the rough sea is not suitable for swimming. In the halls, charming Brennand-tiled floors look like floral carpets. Service is provided by occasionally over-attentive Senac hospitality students at this training hotel. Guests are mostly executives, but this hotel-school also accommodates families and tourists. **ACCOMMODATIONS** 50 rooms and 3 suites, Internet access, air-conditioning, private safe, minibar, telephone, cable TV **FACILITIES AND SERVICES** Internet access in communal areas, wine cellar, bar, parking, shops, pool, restaurant, conference room, video room, business center, 24-hour kitchen **CREDIT CARDS** Amex, Diners, MasterCard, Visa
Avenida Senador Dinarte Mariz, no #, Areias Pretas
TEL (84) 3209-4000 **FAX** 3209-4001 www.barreiraroxa.com.br

Manary Praia Hotel $$$
The welcoming and professional service is the first thing you notice at Manary Praia. The next is the rustic furniture, the northeastern cultural objects (traditional curd cheese moulds, a *rapadura* sugar press, and an old wooden corn mill), and the artwork from Africa, Mexico, and other countries. All have been collected by the owner, Eduardo Bugnoli. A small library contains works on the state of Rio Grande do Norte. The rooms have colorful hammocks on the verandas, beds with cotton canopies, and treats such as incense and candles. **ACCOMMODATIONS** 24 rooms, Internet access, air-conditioning, private safe, minibar, telephone, cable TV, ceiling fan **FACILITIES AND SERVICES** Internet access in communal areas, wine cellar, bar, parking, convenience store, pool, restaurant, magazine reading area, conference room, video room, business center, 24-hour kitchen, car rental, surfboard and bodyboard rental **CREDIT CARDS** Amex, Diners, MasterCard, Visa
Rua Francisco Gurgel, 9067, Ponta Negra
TEL (84) 3204-2900 **RESERVATIONS** 3204-2904 **FAX** 3204-2908
www.manary.com.br

Ocean Palace Hotel & Resort $$$$
This resort offers almost enough beds to be its own village. It sits on a calm stretch of beach, but guests seem to prefer the pool and deck bar. **ACCOMMODATIONS** 183 rooms, 23 suites, and 30 bungalows; Internet access, air-conditioning, private safe, minibar, telephone, cable TV **FACILITIES AND SERVICES** Internet access in communal areas, wine cellar, bar, nursery, bicycles, parking, pool, jogging track, playground, indoor soccer court, tennis court, volleyball court, restaurant, magazine reading area, conference room, gym, game

---

RESTAURANTS $ up to R$50 $$ from R$51 up to R$100 $$$ from R$101 up to R$150 $$$$ above R$150

room, massage room, video room, beauty parlor, sauna, spa, travel agency, business center, currency exchange, 24-hour kitchen, recreational team for adults and children, valet parking, lifeguard, beach service, airport shuttle **CREDIT CARDS** Amex, Diners, MasterCard, Visa
Via Costeira, Km 11, Ponta Negra
TEL (84) 3219-4144 **RESERVATIONS** 0800-84-4144
FAX 3219-3321
www.oceanpalace.com.br

Pestana Natal Beach Resort $$$$
One of Natal's best hotels, Pestana Natal accommodates a lot of foreign tourists and offers so many amenities that guests never need to leave the grounds. Leisure facilities include an enticing pool, a soccer field, shops, and a game room. The colorful modern décor in communal areas contrasts with the pale rooms and dark corridors. **ACCOMMODATIONS** 180 rooms and 4 suites, Internet access, air-conditioning, private safe, minibar, hairdryer, telephone with answering machine, cable TV **FACILITIES AND SERVICES** Internet access in communal areas, bar, bicycles, soccer field, parking, art gallery, Jacuzzi, shops, pool, playground, restaurant, magazine reading area, conference room, gym, game room, massage room, sauna, business center, currency exchange, 24-hour kitchen, recreational team for adults and children, guided walking tours, valet parking, lifeguard, beach service **CREDIT CARDS** Amex, Diners, MasterCard, Visa
Avenida Senador Dinarte Mariz (Via Costeira), 5525, Ponta Negra
TEL (84) 3220-8900 **RESERVATIONS** 3220-8923, 3220-8924
FAX 3220-8901 www.pestananatal.com.br

Pousada Flores Inn $$
The attentive service and laid-back atmosphere at Pousada Flores make guests feel at home. The rooms have bamboo furniture and the box-spring or king-size beds have locally made hand-woven spreads. A small pool at the entrance invites those returning from Ponta Negra beach to take a quick dip. **ACCOMMODATIONS** 11 rooms, Internet access, air-conditioning, minibar, telephone, TV, cable TV, ceiling fan; Jacuzzi in 2 rooms; balcony with hammock in 5 rooms **FACILITIES AND SERVICES** Internet access in communal areas, wine cellar, bar, deck, parking, Jacuzzi, mini-kitchen, pool, magazine reading area, travel agency, currency exchange, recommendations for trips to local attractions, manicures, massage room **CREDIT CARDS** Amex, Diners, MasterCard, Visa
Rua Francisco Gurgel, 9076, Ponta Negra
TEL and **FAX** (84) 3219-2457 www.dasfloresinn.com.br

WHERE TO EAT

Abade $$
At Abade, Portuguese and international cuisine meet a luxurious atmosphere and impeccable service. Norwegian codfish takes pride of place. Also try the rack of lamb in ginger sauce with mushroom risotto. The extensive wine list includes Portuguese Barca Velha and Pera Manca. Wines are offered to match menu dishes and the expert waiters can suggest novel combinations. **CUISINE** Portuguese, varied **CREDIT CARDS** Amex, Diners, MasterCard, Visa
Rua Hélio Galvão, 8828, Via Costeira, Ponta Negra
TEL (84) 3219-4469 **OPEN** Mon – Wed, noon – 3pm and 6:30pm– midnight; Thu, noon – 3pm and 6:30pm – 1am; Fri, noon – 3pm and 6:30pm – 2am; Sat, 6:30pm – 2am; Sun, noon – 3pm

Camarões $
Offering generous portions at good prices, Camarões is the place for shrimp lovers. The menu offers some twenty options, including popular giant breaded shrimp stuffed with cream cheese and shrimp grilled in butter and herbs. For a taste of regional cuisine, try shrimp grilled in country butter with pumpkin sauce and curd cheese gratin, served in the pumpkin shell. Waits for a table can be up to an hour. **CUISINE** fish and seafood **CREDIT CARDS** Amex, Diners, MasterCard, Visa
Avenida Engenheiro Roberto Freire, 2610, Ponta Negra
TEL (84) 3209-2424 **OPEN** Mon – Thu, 11:30am – 3:30pm and 6:30pm– midnight; Fri and Sat, 11:30am – 3:30pm and 6:30pm – 1am; Sun, 11:30am – 4pm and 6:30pm – 11pm

Lula $
This country-style restaurant serves excellent regional cuisine at fair prices. Good options include sun-dried beef and mutton – try the dishes served with *arroz-de-leite* (rice cooked in milk with curd cheese) and lima beans – and *galinha cabidela* (chicken in blood sauce). Homemade desserts include papaya compote with coconut and curd cheese with molasses. The restaurant is run by a former waiter who had been in the business for twenty years before opening Lula with his family, who live on the premises. **CUISINE** regional **CREDIT CARDS** not accepted
Avenida Xavier da Silveira, 1047, Morro Branco
TEL (84) 3206-3033 **RESERVATIONS** 3234-0224 **OPEN** Mon – Sat, 11am – midnight; Sun, 11am – 5pm

Mangai $
This restaurant serves the state's best regional cuisine at affordable prices. The spacious restaurant offers a friendly, country-style atmosphere. The lavish per-kilo buffet includes sun-dried beef with cream, freshwater *surubim* goujons, and goat leg. Fluffy manioc bread and innumerable tapioca items, among other options, can be ordered à la carte. Mangai is also an excellent spot for breakfast or a snack. Alcohol is not available, but the fruit juices are excellent. Most of the ingredients (milk, eggs, cheese, chicken, fruit, greens) are home-produced. The restaurant is usually crowded on Sundays. **CUISINE** regional **CREDIT CARDS** MasterCard, Visa
Avenida Amintas Barros, 3300, Lagoa Nova
TEL (84) 3206-3344 **OPEN** Tue – Sun, 7am – 10pm

Moqueca Capixaba $
Don't order anything except *moqueca* here. The many types are all light and mild. *Moqueca potiguar* ("shrimp eater" in Tupi-Guarani) is an invention of the owners, who have patented the name. The dish of shrimp in coconut milk dispenses with fish, the traditional basic ingredient of this dish; side dishes are rice in garlic and oil and a thickened *pirão* sauce of manioc and curd cheese. Owner Vera Lúcia cooks everything herself, and her husband, former soccer player Joel Ribeiro Pereira, buys the fish and seafood daily. All the cooking is done to order, meaning that the food takes a long time to be ready. **CUISINE** fish and seafood **CREDIT CARDS** Visa
Avenida Governador Sílvio Pedrosa, 266, Areia Preta
TEL (84) 3202-9673 **OPEN** Tue – Sat, 11am – 11:30pm; Sun, 11am – 2pm

Paçoca de Pilão $
This restaurant is worth the 25-kilometer (16-mile) trip from Natal. Try the signature dish: pounded sun-dried beef with banana, rice, lima beans, manioc, and curd cheese. Other delights include shrimp in a pumpkin shell and *galinha cabidela* (chicken in blood sauce). Stop here for lunch on the way back from the beach. **CUISINE** regional, fish and seafood **CREDIT CARDS** Diners, MasterCard
Rua Deputado Márcio Marinho, 5708, Pirangi do Norte

PRICES	HOTELS (couple)	$ up to R$150	$$ from R$151 up to R$300	$$$ from R$301 up to R$500	$$$$ above R$500

HOTELS, RESTAURANTS AND SERVICES

TEL (84) 3238-2088 OPEN Mon – Thu, 11am – 7pm; Fri – Sat, 11am – 11pm; Sun, 11am – 9pm

Peixada da Comadre $
The highlight is the mouthwatering Peixada da Comadre, fish cutlet poached in stock with vegetables, accompanied by rice and a famous thickened *pirão* sauce. CUISINE fish and seafood CREDIT CARDS Diners, MasterCard, Visa
Ponta Negra: Avenida Praia da Ponta Negra, 1948
TEL (84) 3219-3016
Praia do Meio (Praia dos Artistas): Rua José Augusto Bezerra de Menezes, 4 (near the street market)
TEL (84) 3202-3411 OPEN Wed – Mon, 11:30am – 3:30pm and 6:30pm – 10pm; Sun, 11:30am – 5pm

SERVICES

Bus Station – Rodoviária
Avenida Capitão-mor Gouveia, no #, Cidade da Esperança
TEL (84) 3232-7311

Tourist Police Station – Delegacia do Turista
Avenida Engenheiro Roberto Freire, 8790, Ponta Negra
TEL (84) 3232-7404, 3232-7402 OPEN Daily, 24 hours

Tourist Information – Posto de Informações Turísticas (Airport)
Aeroporto Internacional Augusto Severo, no #, Emaús, Parnamirim
OPEN Mon – Sat, 8am – noon and 1pm – 5pm

Tourist Information – Posto de Informações Turísticas (Praia Shopping)
Avenida Engenheiro Roberto Freire, no # (Central do Cidadão), Ponta Negra
TEL (84) 3232-7248 OPEN Tue – Fri, 10am – 10pm; Sat, 10am – 6pm

Travel Agency – Cariri Ecotours
Avenida Prudente de Morais, 4262, Store #3-B, Room #2, Lagoa Nova
TEL (84) 3606-0728, 3086-3601 FAX (84) 3206-4949 OPEN Mon – Fri, 8:30am – 6:30pm; Sat, 9am – noon
www.caririecotours.com.br

Nísia Floresta – Rio Grande do Norte

AREA CODE 84 POPULATION 22,239 DISTANCES Natal 43 kilometers (27 miles), João Pessoa 170 kilometers (106 miles) ACCESS From the south, take BR-101; from Natal, take RN-063

WHERE TO EAT

Camarão do Olavo $
Shrimp is served with *sertão* dishes, such as lima beans, fried or boiled manioc, and seasoned manioc flour, all of which usually accompany beef jerky or sun-dried beef. The restaurant's open layout includes outdoor seating. Live music (*forró* and MPB) enlivens Saturday nights. CUISINE fish and seafood, regional CREDIT CARDS MasterCard, Visa
Rua do Comércio, 5, Centro (3 kilometers from BR-101 highway)
TEL (84) 3277-2211 OPEN Daily, 11am – 7pm

Nova Jerusalém – Pernambuco
(see Fazenda Nova)

Nova Olinda – Ceará

AREA CODE 88 POPULATION 12,530 DISTANCES Fortaleza 492 kilometers (306 miles), Crato 41 kilometers (25 miles), Juazeiro 51 kilometers (32 miles) ACCESS From Crato, take CE-292

WHERE TO STAY

Pousadas Domiciliares $
These ten cottages were built in the backyards of the families whose children attend the The Cooperativa dos Pais e Amigos da Casa Grande association. Each room has two single beds. ACCOMMODATIONS 10 rooms, minibar, TV, ceiling fan FACILITIES AND SERVICES Memorial do Projeto Casa Grande museum CREDIT CARDS not accepted
Avenida Geremias Perreira, 444, Centro
TEL and FAX (88) 3546-1333

Oeiras – Piauí

AREA CODE 89 DISTANCES Teresina 310 kilometers (193 miles; by BR-316) and 320 kilometers (199 miles; by BR-343), Picos 87 kilometers (54 miles), São Raimundo Nonato 280 kilometers (174 miles) ACCESS From Teresina, take BR-316 or BR-343. From São Raimundo Nonato, take BR-020 and PI-143

WHERE TO STAY

Pousada do Cônego $
This simple and well-maintained guesthouse, opened in 1985, occupies a protected historic building. No leisure facilities, but the restaurant, open daily, offers meat dishes and pizza. Meals are served in a garden under the trees. ACCOMMODATIONS 19 rooms, air-conditioning, minibar, TV with satellite dish, ceiling fan FACILITIES AND SERVICES restaurant CREDIT CARDS not accepted
Praça das Vitórias, 18, Centro
TEL (89) 3462-1219

SERVICES

Bus Station – Rodoviária
Avenida Transamazônica, no #, Centro
TEL (89) 3462-2006

Olinda – Pernambuco

AREA CODE 81 POPULATION 384,510 DISTANCE Recife 7 kilometers (4 miles) ACCESS Less than 15 minutes north from Recife
www.olinda.pe.gov.br

WHERE TO STAY

Pousada do Amparo $$$
This guesthouse occupies an old building on buzzing Rua do Amparo, the center of what's happening in town. The rooms offer wooden furniture and views of the street or of Recife. Behind the guesthouse, a garden affords a magnificent view of the state capital. ACCOMMODATIONS 11 rooms, Internet access, air-conditioning, private safe, minibar, telephone, TV FACILITIES AND SERVICES bar, parking, pool, restaurant CREDIT CARDS Amex, Diners, MasterCard, Visa
Rua do Amparo, 191/199, Carmo
TEL and FAX (81) 3439-1749 www.pousadadoamparo.com.br

Sete Colinas $
Right on Ladeira de São Francisco, in the historic center of Olinda, this hotel stands among trees. The rooms have tiled floors, large box-spring beds, and understated, rustic décor.

RESTAURANTS $ up to R$50 $$ from R$51 up to R$100 $$$ from R$101 up to R$150 $$$$ above R$150

The lovely garden is a highlight. ACCOMMODATIONS 35 rooms and 4 suites, Internet access, air-conditioning, private safe, minibar, telephone, cable TV, ceiling fan, balcony FACILITIES AND SERVICES Internet access in communal areas, parking, pool, museum, restaurant, sauna CREDIT CARDS Amex, Diners, MasterCard, Visa
Ladeira de São Francisco, 307, Carmo
TEL and FAX (81) 3493-7766 www.hotel7colinas.com.br

WHERE TO EAT

Bodega de Véio $
Whether you like bars or not, you must stop here. Jam-packed with every imaginable item, this grocery store-cum-bar has been in business for more than a hundred years. Edval Hermínio da Silva, affectionately known as Véio, has been owner since 1981. Order a beer and some fresh-sliced cold cuts, then elbow yourself a space at the counter or settle on the busy sidewalk. On Saturday evenings, live forró-pé-de-serra is played at the house next door, a sort of annex. CUISINE bar food CREDIT CARDS Amex, Diners, MasterCard, Visa
Rua do Amparo, 212
TEL (81) 3429-0185 OPEN Mon – Sat, 8am – 11pm; Sun, 8am – 2pm

Goya $
Romantic Goya, opened in 1999, is a mixture of studio and restaurant. It's run by artists Petrucio Nazareno and Antônio Cabral. Cabral is in charge of the kitchen, where the menu focuses on fish and seafood. The house specialty is fish and shrimp parcels, which are wrapped in banana leaf and garnished with fried banana. Local ingredients come to the fore in the shrimp and coconut stew, served in a coconut shell with manioc purée and cream cheese gratin. Several dishes mix sweet and sour with great success. For dessert try the cajá mousse with cream cheese fried with ground nuts, covered in light molasses. CUISINE contemporary, fish and seafood CREDIT CARDS Diners, MasterCard, Visa
Rua do Amparo, 157, Carmo
TEL (81) 3439-4875 OPEN Mon, noon – 5pm and 6pm – midnight; Wed – Sat, 6pm – midnight; Sun, noon – 5pm and 6pm – 10pm

Kwetú $
Kwetú complements the cuisine of Belgian chef Brigitte Anckaerte with striking views of Olinda and the sea from outdoor tables. The dishes are predominately French, with Moroccan, Thai, and Vietnamese influences. Belgian specialties include rabbit in dark beer with prunes. The boned quail flambéed in cognac, served with fresh mushrooms and white wine, is recommended. Brigitte finds the time to chat with customers and her fluency in five languages makes it easy for her to make menu recommendations. CUISINE French, international CREDIT CARDS Diners, MasterCard, Visa
Avenida Manoel Borba, 338, Praça do Jacaré
TEL (81) 3439-8867 OPEN Mon, Wed – Thu, 6pm – midnight; Fri – Sun, noon – 4pm and 6pm – midnight

Maison do Bonfim $
French chef Jeff Colas offers franco-pernambucano cuisine, adapting French dishes to the local palate and ingredients. Mussels are served every Thursday, when they arrive fresh from Santa Catarina. In one version, they are served with home-baked bread, steamed in white wine with cream, garlic, parsley, and onions. Oysters live or au gratin are another option. CUISINE regional with French influences, fish and seafood CREDIT CARDS Diners, MasterCard, Visa
Rua do Bonfim, 115, Carmo
TEL (81) 3429-1674 OPEN Tue – Sat, noon – 4pm and 6pm – 1am; Sun, noon – 9pm

Oficina do Sabor $$
At Oficina do Sabor, chef César Santos is famous for his discernment in recreating the traditional cuisine of Pernambuco. Pumpkin, the star of the menu, is stuffed with tantalizing fillings, such as shrimp in pitanga fruit or mango sauce. It is also an ingredient of a simple farofa (seasoned manioc flour) and with manioc purée accompanies fried jerked beef. The view over Olinda and the background music – forró and other Brazilian rhythms – contributes to the ambiance. Oficina do Sabor belongs to the Associação dos Restaurantes da Boa Lembrança. CUISINE regional, fish and seafood CREDIT CARDS Amex, Diners, MasterCard, Visa
Rua do Amparo, 335, Carmo
TEL (81) 3429-3331 OPEN Tue – Thu, noon – 4pm and 6pm – midnight; Fri, noon – 4pm and 6pm – 1am, Sat, noon – 1am; Sun, noon – 5pm www.oficinadosabor.com

SERVICES

Guides – Cooperativa de Condutores Nativos de Olinda
Praça do Varadouro, no #, Mercado Eufrásio Barbosa, stall #7, Varadouro
TEL (81) 3493-5021 OPEN Mon – Fri, 8am – 5pm; Sat, 8am – 2pm

Guides – Projeto Guia Mirim
Avenida da Liberdade, 100, Carmo
TEL (81) 3305-1048 OPEN Mon – Fri, 8am – 5pm
www.olinda.pe.gov.br

Parnaíba – Piauí

AREA CODE 86 POPULATION 141,939 DISTANCES Teresina 354 kilometers (220 miles), Luís Correia 19 kilometers (12 miles), Piripiri 182 kilometers (113 miles), Sobral 248 kilometers (154 miles) ACCESS By land from Teresina, take the Transpiauí highway (BR-343) and then BR-222. From Fortaleza, take BR-222 to the junction with BR-343. From São Luís, take BR-402 and then BR-343. From Tutóia, take a boat; from Fortaleza or Teresina, take a plane (twice a week) WHEN TO VISIT In June, when the lakes are full, or between April and July for hiking and swimming

WHERE TO STAY

Cívico $
This hotel, opened in 1977 and now somewhat run down, is well located for visitors who don't have cars. The new wing has better facilities, especially the luxury rooms, which boast large, comfortable beds, good bathrooms, and balconies overlooking the pool. ACCOMMODATIONS 69 suites, air-conditioning, minibar, telephone, TV FACILITIES AND SERVICES bar, parking, pool, restaurant CREDIT CARDS Diners, MasterCard, Visa
Avenida Governador Chagas Rodrigues, 474, Centro
TEL (86) 3322-2470 FAX 3322-2028 www.hotelcivico.com.br

Pousada dos Ventos $
This guesthouse is well-maintained and pleasant, with fruit trees, a pool, and tasteful décor. A hearty breakfast is served beside the pool. The simple, cozy rooms could have better showers. As the guesthouse is 3 kilometers from town, it is difficult to access without a car. The service is excellent. ACCOMMODATIONS 48 rooms, air-conditioning, minibar, telephone, cable TV; 4 rooms with balcony FACILITIES AND SERVICES

| PRICES | HOTELS (couple) | $ up to R$150 | $$ from R$151 up to R$300 | $$$ from R$301 up to R$500 | $$$$ above R$500 |

bar, parking, pool, orchard, tennis court, restaurant, laundry **CREDIT CARDS** Amex, Diners, MasterCard, Visa
Avenida São Sebastião, 2586, Fátima
TEL (86) 3323-2555 **RESERVATIONS** 3322-2177 **FAX** 3323-2743
www.pousadadosventos.com.br

Refúgio Ecológico Ilha do Caju $$

On Ilha do Caju, 50 kilometers (31 miles) from Parnaíba, Refúgio Ecológico is the only place to eat and sleep on the island. Children under 15 are not permitted. Getting there requires a torturous hike. **ACCOMMODATIONS** come in three types: rooms in the main house, a four-bedroom house (*casa do vaqueiro*), and nine bungalows. The bungalows are the most expensive and the best, offering verandas and hammocks. The rooms have king-size beds, fluffy towels, mosquito nets, and bathrooms with cold water. Sadly, the guides are poorly trained, detracting from the otherwise pleasant stay. **ACCOMMODATIONS** 14 rooms, fan **FACILITIES AND SERVICES** bar, boat, kayaks, horses, restaurant, walking trails, guided walking tours **CREDIT CARDS** not accepted
Ilha do Caju (1 hour by speedboat or 3 hours by regular boat from Parnaíba)
TEL (86) 3321-3044 **RESERVATIONS** 3321-1179
www.ilhadocaju.com.br

WHERE TO EAT

Caranguejo Expresso $

This is where locals eat crab. Sit at one of the tables on the wooden sidewalk and savor the crabs, which come strung together in fours, in a no-frills atmosphere. **CUISINE** crab **CREDIT CARDS** not accepted
Rua Quetinha Pires, 64, Beira Rio
TEL (86) 3323-9653 **OPEN** Daily, 11am – 11pm

La Barca $

Details make the difference at this lovely restaurant: the wooden chairs and well-placed tables on the covered veranda, the air-conditioned room designed to look like a boat. Deliciously seasoned fish is served on a hot stone platter. The dishes serve two, but the hungry will be able to finish them off alone. Toca do Caranguejo restaurant, next door, shares an owner and is packed at night. The service is very fast. **CUISINE** fish and seafood **CREDIT CARDS** MasterCard
Avenida das Nações Unidas, 200, Beira-Rio
TEL (86) 3322-2825 **OPEN** Daily, 10am – midnight

Sabor e Arte $

This informal restaurant at the boat port is well decorated and offers a bilingual menu. The *galinha cabidela* (chicken with blood sauce) accompanied by rice and salad is delicious. Helpings are generous, though the food is generally mediocre. You can stroll around the port while waiting for your food or soak up the atmosphere at one of the outdoor tables. **CUISINE** regional, varied **CREDIT CARDS** not accepted
Avenida Presidente Vargas, 37, Porto das Barcas, Centro
TEL (86) 3322-1974 **OPEN** Mon – Sat, noon– midnight; Sun, 6pm – 11pm

SERVICES

Bus Station – Rodoviária (Expresso Guanabara)

Avenida Pinheiro Machado, no #
TEL (86) 3323-7300, 3323-7620 www.guanabara.com.br

Boat Trips – Morais Brito Viagens e Turismo

Porto das Barcas, 13, Centro
TEL (86) 3321-1969, 9412-0102 **OPEN** Daily, 7am – 8pm
www.deltadoparnaiba.com.br

Guide – Bal

Rua Manoel da Costa, conjunto Cândido de Oliveira, casa 10, Baixão
TEL (86) 3323-0145 (24-hour service), 3323-0100 **OPEN** Daily, 6am – noon and 2pm – 5pm

Guide – Mundinho

Rua Projetada 66, house #185, Tatus
TEL (86) 3323-0241 **OPEN** Daily, 24 hours (preferably 7am – 9am and after 7pm)

Tourist Information – PiemTur

Rua Dr. Oscar Clark, 575, Centro
TEL (86) 3321-1532, 3222-6202 (Teresina main office) **OPEN** Mon – Fri, 8am – 1pm www.piemtur.com.br

Travel Agency – Agência de Turismo Clip

Avenida Presidente Vargas, no #, Centro (Shopping Delta)
TEL (86) 3322-3129, 3323-9838, 9402-0171 **OPEN** Mon – Fri, 8am – noon and 2pm – 6pm www.clipecoturismo.com.br

Travel Agency – Eco Adventure Tour

Avenida Presidente Vargas, 26, Porto das Barcas, Centro
TEL (86) 3323-9595, 3323-9888, 3323-9515 **OPEN** Mon – Sat, 8am – 6pm www.ecoadventure.tur.br

Travel Agency – Natur Turismo Ecológico

Avenida Presidente Vargas, 18, Porto das Barcas, Centro
TEL (86) 3321-2505, 3323-0426, 9971-5143 **OPEN** Mon – Fri, 7am – 8pm; Sat, 7am – 6pm; Sun, 7am – 10am and 2pm – 6pm
www.naturturismo.com.br

Paulino Neves – Maranhão

AREA CODE 98 **POPULATION** 12,098 **DISTANCES** São Luís 501 kilometers (311 miles), Tutóia 36 kilometers (22 miles), Barreirinha 42 kilometers (26 miles) **ACCESS** By 4x4 vehicle along the beach from Caboré (20 kilometers, 12 miles). By the road that connects Tutóia to Paulino Neves (36 kilometers, 22 miles) **WHEN TO VISIT** From May to July, when the lakes are full and the temperatures mild

WHERE TO STAY

Pousada Oásis dos Lençóis $

Mazé's guesthouse on the riverbank has been in business since 1994. Hammocks swing beneath the leafy mango trees and sofas gather people from all over the world. Breakfast is delicious and hearty. The lobby and corridors are decorated with photographs of the region. The rooms are disappointing, though; the best ones have fans and mosquito nets, but are small and uncomfortable (*see Where to Eat*). **ACCOMMODATIONS** 8 suites and 2 rooms with communal bathroom; cold shower, fan **FACILITIES AND SERVICES** horses, parking, restaurant **CREDIT CARDS** not accepted
Avenida Rio Novo, no #, Centro
TEL (98) 3487-1012

WHERE TO EAT

Oásis dos Lençóis $

Mazé's restaurant is inside her guesthouse. The wooden tables are big and the room is airy. Order two hours in advance, perhaps before setting out on a trip. A *sururu* (shellfish) starter followed by mutton with pumpkin and finished

with coconut compote is difficult to beat. CUISINE seafood, regional CREDIT CARDS not accepted
Avenida Rio Novo, no #, Centro
TEL (98) 3487-1012 OPEN Daily, 7am – 8pm

SERVICES

Guides – Nilson and Kaka
Avenida Rio Novo, no #, Centro
TEL (98) 3487-1026 (best to call around 7am, noon, or 7pm), 3487-1139

Paulo Afonso – Bahia

AREA CODE 75 POPULATION 102,689 DISTANCES Salvador 471 kilometers (293 miles), Garanhuns 207 kilometers (129 miles), Alagoinhas 342 kilometers (213 miles) ACCESS Preferably by air from Salvador or São Paulo, as the roads are full of potholes and have no road signs, Highway Patrol support, or gas stations

WHERE TO STAY

Belvedere $
Opened in 1983, this city-center hotel caters mostly to business travelers. The small leisure area contains a pool and game room. Other amenities include a small clothes boutique and a craft shop. ACCOMMODATIONS 101 suites, air-conditioning, minibar, telephone, TV FACILITIES AND SERVICES parking, snack bar, shops, pool, game room; kitchen closes at 11pm CREDIT CARDS MasterCard, Visa
Avenida Apolônio Sales, 457, Centro
TEL (75) 3281-3814 RESERVATIONS and FAX 3281-4756
www.hotelbelvederepa.com.br

San Marino $
One of Paulo Afonso's best hotels, San Marino has four floors, with access by elevator. Tourists share the place with CHESF (São Francisco Hydroelectric Company) workers. At night the top-floor restaurant serves varied cuisine. Breakfast is a standard affair with no regional dishes at all. The hotel also has a small book and craft store. ACCOMMODATIONS 55 rooms and 10 suites, Internet access, air-conditioning, minibar, telephone, TV FACILITIES AND SERVICES Internet access in communal areas, bar, store, restaurant CREDIT CARDS Amex, Diners, MasterCard, Visa
Avenida Getúlio Vargas, 3, Centro
TEL and FAX (75) 3281-3026

WHERE TO EAT

Kaldinho e Cia $
A popular place to meet, Kaldinho e Cia is a restaurant until 4pm, when it becomes a crowded bar. As the name (a play on "caldo," which means "broth") indicates, the restaurant's forte is soup, and they serve eight varieties – bean is the most popular. Barbecued rump steak and roast goat are also on the menu. Tables on the sidewalk and good live music round out the pleasant vibe. CUISINE bar food, meats CREDIT CARDS Diners, MasterCard, Visa
Avenida Getúlio Vargas, 142, Centro
TEL (75) 3281-1103 OPEN Mon, 4pm – until the last customer leaves; Tue – Sun, 11am – until the last customer leaves

Visual $
Visual has an indoor area and outdoor seating offering live music. The kitchen sends out beef *parmigiana* with chili pepper, as well as dishes of chicken and rump steak. The service is good. CUISINE varied CREDIT CARDS Diners, MasterCard, Visa

Avenida Getúlio Vargas, no #, Centro
TEL (75) 3282-0555 OPEN Tue – Sun, 8am – 4pm

SERVICES

Guide – Edmilson Nascimento
Rua Otávio Drumont, 65, Centro
TEL (75) 9139-4520, 3281-4449 OPEN Daily, 24 hours
www.edtur.cjb.net

Guides – Associação de Guias de Turismo de Paulo Afonso
Avenida Apolônio Sales, no #, Centro
TEL (75) 3281-2757 OPEN Sat, Sun and holidays, 8am – 5pm; Mon – Fri, 8am – 11:30am and 2pm – 5pm

Tourist Information – Posto de Informações Turísticas
Avenida Getúlio Vargas, no #, Centro
TEL (75) 3281-3011 ext: 206 OPEN Mon – Fri, 7am – 6pm and Sat, 8am – 1pm

Pedro II – Piauí

AREA CODE 86 POPULATION 37,370 DISTANCES Teresina 205 kilometers (127 miles), Piripiri 45 kilometers (28 miles) ACCESS From Teresina, take the Transpiauí highway (BR-343) and then BR-404

WHERE TO STAY

Opala $
Opala is the only hotel in town. The rooms have TV and air-conditioning or a fan, but the mattresses are uncomfortable and the showers cold. ACCOMMODATIONS 19 suites, TV; air-conditioning in 9 suites, fan in 10; minibar in 2 suites FACILITIES AND SERVICES parking CREDIT CARDS MasterCard, Visa
Avenida José Lourenço Mourão, 813, Vila Operária
TEL (86) 3271-1160 FAX 3271-1387
www.opalaartesgemas.com

WHERE TO EAT

Estação Vila $
Estação Vila had been in business for a decade when it morphed from a bar to a restaurant at customer insistence. Zezé buys the meat, prepares the food, and greets the customers. The most popular dishes are beef fillet in *madeira* sauce and beef fillet *parmigiana*. For starters try the fried manioc – crispy perfection. CUISINE meats, home-made CREDIT CARDS not accepted
Avenida José Lourenço Mourão, 693, Centro
TEL (86) 3271-1963 OPEN Daily, 7am – 2pm and 5:30pm – midnight

SERVICES

Guides – Associação dos Condutores de Turistas nos Municípios da Comarca de Pedro II (Acontur)
Avenida José Lourenço Mourão, 949, room #3, Prodart (arts and crafts center)
TEL (86) 9422-1385 (Rogério), 9422-8030 (Ramiro) OPEN Mon – Sat, 8am – noon and 2pm – 4pm; Sun, 24 hours

Penedo – Alagoas

AREA CODE 82 POPULATION 59,968 DISTANCES Maceió 173 kilometers (107 miles), Aracaju 165 kilometers (103 miles) AC-

| PRICES | HOTELS (couple) | $ up to R$150 | $$ from R$151 up to R$300 | $$$ from R$301 up to R$500 | $$$$ above R$500 |

cess From Maceió, via AL-101 highway. From Aracaju, via BR-101 to the junction near Nascença village (there is a Highway Patrol post and road sign). Then SE-304 to Neópolis (35 kilometers, 22 miles), where the ferryboat departs for Penedo (departures every 30 minutes).

WHERE TO STAY

Hotel São Francisco $
Opened in 1963, this guesthouse is not as charming as Pousada Colonial, twenty years its junior, but the view of the São Francisco River is just as good. The superior luxury rooms have been refurbished and are by far the most comfortable. ACCOMMODATIONS 48 rooms and 4 suites, Internet access, air-conditioning, telephone, TV; minibar in some rooms FACILITIES AND SERVICES Internet access in communal areas, parking, snack bar, pool, restaurant, conference room, game room CREDIT CARDS Amex, Diners, MasterCard, Visa
Avenida Floriano Peixoto, 237, Centro
TEL (82) 3551-2273 FAX 3551-2274
www.hotelsaofrancisco.tur.br

Pousada Colonial $
A simple guesthouse in a 1754 building, very near Nossa Senhora da Corrente Church, Pousada Colonial steeps guests in Penedo's historic atmosphere. The rooms on the side are more spacious, but the rooms at the front have a better view of the São Francisco River. The service is adequate. ACCOMMODATIONS 12 suites, ceiling fan, telephone; air-conditioning in 10 rooms, minibar in 6 rooms, TV in 8 rooms FACILITIES AND SERVICES Internet access in communal areas, bar, snack bar, restaurant, game room, video room CREDIT CARDS not accepted
Praça 12 de Abril, 21, Centro
TEL and FAX (82) 3551-2355

WHERE TO EAT

Forte da Rocheira $
This restaurant at the foot of Rocheira, on the banks of the São Francisco, offers a lovely river view. The house specialty is alligator in coconut sauce. Other specialties are tilapia in white wine (accompanied by rice, beans, manioc purée, and seasoned manioc flour) and filé à Maurício de Nassau (steak, onions, onions, boiled potatoes, rice, beans, manioc purée, and seasoned manioc flour). The service is attentive and quick, even when the restaurant is full. CUISINE meats, varied CREDIT CARDS MasterCard, Visa
Rua da Rocheira, 2, Santo Antônio
TEL (82) 3551-3273 RESERVATIONS 3551-2578 OPEN Daily, 11am – 4pm and 6pm – 10pm

Petrolina – Pernambuco

AREA CODE 87 POPULATION 253,686 DISTANCES Recife 767 kilometers (477 miles), Salvador 517 kilometers (321 miles) ACCESS Take either the BR-232, BR-122, BR-407, or BR-235 highway
www.petrolina.pe.gov.br

WHERE TO STAY

Costa do Rio $
Opened in 2002, this hotel is small with narrow corridors. It overlooks the São Francisco River. The rooms are simple but comfortable; fifteen are doubles. Breakfast starts at 4am. ACCOMMODATIONS 34 rooms, Internet access, air-conditioning, minibar, telephone, cable TV FACILITIES AND SERVICES Internet access in communal areas, parking, snack bar, restaurant, walking trails, 24-hour kitchen CREDIT CARDS Amex, Diners, MasterCard, Visa
Rua Francisco Bosco Reis, 127-A, Orla Nova, Parque Brasil
TEL and FAX (87) 2101-1313 www.costadoriohotel.com.br

Petrolina Palace Hotel $$
One of Petrolina's best hotels, Petrolina Palace is a historic three-story building offering views of the São Francisco River. The spacious, airy rooms offer basic amenities. Its three conference rooms cater to executive visitors. ACCOMMODATIONS 47 rooms and 5 suites, air-conditioning, minibar, telephone, cable TV FACILITIES AND SERVICES Internet access in communal areas, bar, parking, snack bar, pool, restaurant, conference room, business center, 24-hour kitchen, shuttle service to local attractions CREDIT CARDS Amex, Diners, MasterCard, Visa
Avenida Cardoso de Sá, 845, Centro
TEL (87) 3862-1555 FAX 3861-4858
www.petrolinapalace.com.br

WHERE TO EAT

Barretu's Grill $
Though this informal restaurant hosts lots of mosquitoes in the afternoon, the owner always has repellent. Portions are generous and the beer is ice cold. Barbecue-grilled rump steak and surubim fish are popular menu items. The service is good and parking is available in front of the restaurant. Weekends offer live music. CUISINE regional, varied CREDIT CARDS Amex, Diners, MasterCard, Visa
Avenida Cardoso de Sá, 3, Orla
TEL (87) 3861-4277 OPEN Daily, 11am – until the last customer leaves

Bode Assado do Isaías $
Owner Isaías Rodrigues is the force behind the Bodódromo: he asked City Hall to donate the site. His restaurant alone serves 350 people a day, who eat up to fifty sheep a week. (Goat–bode–appear only in the name.) The spotless ambiance is kept lively by the shows on large screens. Don't miss a chat with friendly Isaías. CUISINE regional CREDIT CARDS Diners, MasterCard, Visa
Avenida São Francisco, 6, Lote 6, Bodódromo, Areia Branca
TEL (87) 3864-4249 OPEN Daily, 11am – 1am

Capivara $$
Named for Serra da Capivara National Park, Capivara is decorated with hand-made crockery from the park. Everything is cooked to order in clay dishes; it takes an average of 25 minutes for the food to be served. The house specialty is grilled surubim fish in caper or passion fruit sauce, but also try the dressed crab in the shell as a starter. The wine list features regional labels. An air-conditioned section overlooks the São Francisco River. The service is good. CUISINE fish and seafood, regional CREDIT CARDS Diners, MasterCard, Visa
Avenida Cardoso de Sá, 429, Orla Velha
TEL (87) 3862-2585 RESERVATIONS 3862-2715 OPEN Tue – Fri, noon – 3:30pm and 6:30pm – 11pm; Sat, noon – midnight; Sun, noon – 6pm

SERVICES

Airport – Aeroporto Senador Nilo Coelho
BR-235, Km 11 (10 kilometers, 6 miles, from the center)
TEL (87) 3863-3366 FAX 3863-3699 OPEN Mon – Fri, 8am – noon and 1pm – 5pm (administration office)
www.infraero.gov.br

| RESTAURANTS | $ up to R$50 | $$ from R$51 up to R$100 | $$$ from R$101 up to R$150 | $$$$ above R$150 |

Tourist Information – Agência de Desenvolvimento Econômico, Turismo, Ciência and Tecnologia
Avenida 31 de Março, no #, Centro de Convenções Senador Nilo Coelho
TEL (87) 3862-9261 OPEN Mon – Fri, 7:30am – 1pm
www.petrolina.pe.gov.br

Tourist Information – Associação Interestadual de Turismo
Avenida Tancredo Neves, no #, Centro de Convenções Nilo Coelho
TEL (87) 3862-1616 OPEN Mon – Fri, 8am – 1pm and 6pm – 8pm
Travel agency and guides www.valedosaofrancisco.tur

Travel Agency – GTUR Guimarães Turismo
Avenida Doutor Fernando Góes, 87, Centro
TEL (87) 3861-2630, 3861-0234 OPEN Mon – Fri, 8am – noon and 2pm – 6pm; Sat, 8am – noon

Travel Agency – Opção Turismo
Avenida Joaquim Nabuco, 505, Centro
TEL (87) 3862-1616, 3862-1886, 8802-9615 (Nivaldo)
OPEN Mon – Fri, 8am – noon and 2pm – 6pm; Sat, 9am – 1pm

Piaçabuçu – Alagoas

AREA CODE 82 POPULATION 16,688 DISTANCES Maceió 138 kilometers (86 miles), Penedo 26 kilometers (16 miles) ACCESS From Maceió, take the AL-101 highway.

WHERE TO STAY

Pousada Chez Julie $
This unpretentious and friendly guesthouse opened in 1998 and is run by Belgian-born Roeland Eniel, a naturalized Brazilian. He also owns an agency that organizes river trips. The guesthouse is 18 kilometers (11 miles) from Piaçabuçu and accessible by car along the river beach. ACCOMMODATIONS 10 rooms, air-conditioning, TV FACILITIES AND SERVICES Internet access in communal areas, bar, pool, restaurant, shuttle service to airport and local attractions CREDIT CARDS MasterCard, Visa
Avenida Beira-Mar, 53, Praia de Pontal do Peba
TEL (82) 3557-1217

WHERE TO EAT

Beira-Rio – Alô Alô $
Owner Marijorge Beltrão's love of chatting earned him the nickname Alô Alô. His simple restaurant seats up to seventy; in December and January there aren't enough tables. Guests savor shrimp or fish in shrimp sauce on the banks of the São Francisco. All dishes serve two. Sun-dried beef, beef stew, and chicken stew round out the menu. CUISINE fish and seafood, varied CREDIT CARDS not accepted
Rua Tamandaré, 272, Centro
TEL (82) 3552-1837 RESERVATIONS 9961-4456 OPEN Daily, 7am – 8pm

Pipa and Tibau do Sul – Rio Grande do Norte

AREA CODE 84 (Tibau do Sul) DISTANCES Natal 82 kilometers (51 miles) ACCESS Take BR-101 into Goianinha, then take RN-03 for 16 kilometers (10 miles). Watch out for pedestrians

WHERE TO STAY

Blue Dream Resort $$
The resort's location, facing the calm seas of Barra de Cunhaú, is a dream. Opened in 2004, it has spacious suites; the first floor offers better views and more privacy. The Swedish owners attract numerous Swedish visitors. ACCOMMODATIONS 18 suites, air-conditioning, minibar, telephone, cable TV FACILITIES AND SERVICES Internet access in communal areas, bar, boat, bicycles, pool, volleyball court, beach volleyball, restaurant, magazine reading area, conference room, massage room, currency exchange, guided walking tours, beauty parlor, shuttle service to airport and local attractions CREDIT CARDS Amex, Visa
Avenida do Pontal, 6, Barra de Cunhaú
TEL (84) 3241-4200 www.bluedreamresort.com.br

Hotel Casablanca Resort $$
A good choice if you'd like to be as far as possible from busy Pipa, this resort offers spacious chalets with closets, verandas, brick walls, and ceramic-tiled floors. The privileged cliff-top location offers wonderful sea views. Children are accepted, but the hotel prefers not to host very young ones. ACCOMMODATIONS 14 chalets, air-conditioning, tub, minibar, telephone, cable TV, ceiling fan FACILITIES AND SERVICES Internet access in communal areas, bar, parking, dune buggy trips, pool, tennis court, gym, sauna, beach service, shuttle service to airport and local attractions CREDIT CARDS Visa
Rua da Praia, no #, Centro, Tibau do Sul
TEL (84) 3246-4164, 3502-2331, 3246-4165 FAX 3246-4242
www.pipacasablanca.com.br

Hotel Marinas Tibau do Sul $$$
Charming chalets with verandas face the point where Guaraíras Lagoon meets the sea. The delightful rooms have rustic décor, wooden ceilings, and clay-tiled floors, but limited privacy. ACCOMMODATIONS 33 chalets, air-conditioning, private safe, minibar, telephone, cable TV, ceiling fan FACILITIES AND SERVICES wine cellar, bar, boat, kayaks, horses, parking, fishing lake and equipment, motorboat, snack bar, convenience store, marina, pool, playground, tennis court, volleyball court, restaurant, magazine reading area, massage room, walking trails, beach service, shuttle service to airport and local attractions. CREDIT CARDS Diners, MasterCard, Visa
Rua Governador Aluísio Alves, no # (beach front), Tibau do Sul
TEL (84) 3246-4111 RESERVATIONS 3221-5548 FAX 3246-4228
www.hotelmarinas.com.br

Hotel Ponta do Madeiro $$$
The chalets here are set in quiet corners, away from the noise of the pool and scattered along a path with a marvelous view of Ponta do Madeiro. The almost two hundred steps down to the beach are worth the effort. The rooms are decorated with regional materials, such as the liana light fittings made by a local artisan. An inviting pool and a restaurant with sea view complete the picture. ACCOMMODATIONS 16 chalets and 10 rooms, air-conditioning, private safe, minibar, telephone, cable TV; Jacuzzi in master room FACILITIES AND SERVICES wine cellar, bar, parking, pool, restaurant, 24-hour kitchen, airport shuttle CREDIT CARDS Amex, Diners, MasterCard, Visa
Rota do Sol, Km 3, Tibau do Sul
TEL (84) 3246-4220 RESERVATIONS 3246-4220, 3502-2377 FAX 3502-2377 www.pontadomadeiro.com.br

Hotel Village Natureza Beach Resort $$$
Make reservations at this popular hotel in advance. The charming wooden bungalows have verandas and sea-fac-

| PRICES | HOTELS (couple) | $ up to R$150 | $$ from R$151 up to R$300 | $$$ from R$301 up to R$500 | $$$$ above R$500 |

ing hammocks. Try the large pool if you're not in the mood to descend the more than one hundred steps to Golfinhos Bay. The staff struggles to keep up with the many guests. **ACCOMMODATIONS** 14 chalets, 12 rooms, and 5 suites; air-conditioning, private safe, minibar, telephone, TV, ceiling fan **FACILITIES AND SERVICES** Internet access in communal areas, bar, beach bar, parking, pool, restaurant, magazine reading area, game room, video room, currency exchange, valet parking, beach service, shuttle service to airport and local attractions **CREDIT CARDS** MasterCard, Visa
Avenida Antônio Florêncio, 3647, Baía dos Golfinhos, Tibau do Sul
TEL (84) 3246-4200 **RESERVATIONS** 3246-4910 **FAX** 3246-4203
www.villagenatureza.com.br

Pousada da Mata $$

Small wooden chalets are hidden in 110,000 square meters (27 acres) of Atlantic forest. At night the only sounds are those of unseen toads and cicadas. The bed linens are cotton and the bedspreads and curtains hand-woven. The place is popular with families, young people, and tennis enthusiasts. **ACCOMMODATIONS** 8 chalets and 6 rooms, air-conditioning, private safe, minibar, telephone, TV; Jacuzzi and cable TV in 2 chalets **FACILITIES AND SERVICES** Internet access in communal areas, bar, woods, waterfall, parking, convenience store, natural pool, orchard, tennis court, restaurant, game room, walking trails, shuttle service to airport and local attractions **CREDIT CARDS** Amex, Diners, MasterCard, Visa
Rua Sucupira, 680, Pipa
TEL (84) 3246-2217 **RESERVATIONS** and **FAX** 3502-2304
www.pousadadamata.com.br

Pousada Vila Bonita $$

This small welcoming guesthouse stands on a cliff top. The rooms – chalets and suites set at different levels– have sea views. Some of the chalets look like small houses from the northeastern *sertão*; the suites are glass-fronted and have wonderful views. The floors are stone and cement and the curtains are hand-woven cotton. The attentive Portuguese owners, Nelson and Cristina, offer goose-feather pillows and soft cotton bed linen. Liana and wicker are featured in the décor, the light fittings, and the reception desk. **ACCOMMODATIONS** 9 rooms, 4 suites, and 3 chalets; air-conditioning, minibar, cable TV; ceiling fan in chalets; telephone in rooms and suites **FACILITIES AND SERVICES** bar, parking, Jacuzzi, pool, restaurant, walking trails, guided walking tours, shuttle service to airport and local attractions **CREDIT CARDS** Diners, MasterCard, Visa
Rua Francisco Fernandes Freire, 361, Baía Formosa
TEL (84) 3244-2056 www.vilabonita.com.br

Sombra e Água Fresca $$$$

On Pipa's highest point, this hotel has a panoramic view of Praia do Amor beach. The rooms have high ceilings, large windows, and king-size beds facing a balcony. One of the pools is surrounded by a dark-tiled deck, which contrasts with the blue sky. The other pool also has a lovely view and offers a 24-hour bar for the lively younger guests. **ACCOMMODATIONS** 11 suites and 8 rooms, air-conditioning, CD player, private safe, minibar, hairdryer, telephone, cable TV, ceiling fan; private pool in suites **FACILITIES AND SERVICES** Internet access in communal areas, bar, kayaks, parking, pool, restaurant, magazine reading area, 24-hour kitchen, airport shuttle **CREDIT CARDS** Diners, MasterCard, Visa
Rua Praia do Amor, 1000, Pipa
TEL and **FAX** (84) 3246-2376, 3246-2258, 3246-2144
www.sombraeaguafrescaresort.com.br

Toca da Coruja Pousada $$$

The rooms are scattered around a manicured garden and amid fruit trees in a 25,000-square-meter (6-acre) area. At night the lighting is warm and romantic. Flares guide guests to the entrance, which is set back from the road. The pool water is ozone treated and the shower is solar powered. Breakfast is fresh tapioca pancakes cooked on a wood-burning stove. **ACCOMMODATIONS** 9 chalets and 6 rooms, Internet access in communal areas, air-conditioning, private safe, minibar, telephone, cable TV, ceiling fan; Jacuzzi in luxury chalets **FACILITIES AND SERVICES** bar, boat, parking, shops, hammocks, restaurant, gym, game room, sauna, airport shuttle **CREDIT CARDS** Amex, Diners, MasterCard, Visa
Avenida Baía dos Golfinhos, 464, Pipa
TEL and **FAX** (84) 3246-2226 www.tocadacoruja.com.br

WHERE TO EAT

Camamo $$$$

A visit to Camamo is a story to be told over and over again. Tadeu Lubambo, the cook and host, greets guests on the veranda with subtle background jazz. The candle-lit "gastronomic ritual" starts every evening at 9:15 with a tour of the kitchen and other corners of the house. The tasting menu of six dishes is chosen by the chef daily (guests are asked about dietary restrictions when they make reservations). While excellent polyglot waiters serve, Tadeu talks about the menu. He accommodates four couples per night at most; the majority are foreigners. He does not take single reservations. A second visit can be made only after an interval of six months. In the high season, make reservations about one month in advance. **CUISINE** contemporary, fusion **CREDIT CARDS** not accepted
Fazenda Pernambuquinho, no #, Estrada Tibau–Goianinha, Tibau do Sul
TEL (84) 3246-4195 **OPEN** Daily, at 9:15pm – 2:30am

Casarão $

One of Pipa's oldest restaurants, sea-front Casarão offers a lovely view of Pescadores village and the sea of fishing boats. The laid-back restaurant serves customers in swimwear, before or après-beach. The menu is based on fish and seafood, focusing on the stews called *moquecas*. Northeastern dishes include sun-dried beef with fried manioc, lima beans, and seasoned manioc flour. The cooks have been there since the place opened in the late 1980s. **CUISINE** regional, fish and seafood **CREDIT CARDS** Amex, Diners, MasterCard, Visa
Largo São Sebastião, no #, Pipa
TEL (84) 3246-2274 **OPEN** High season: daily, 11am – 11pm; low season: 11am – 6pm

Cruzeiro do Pescador $

This charming restaurant has flowers on the tables, attentive service, and a hand-written menu of fish and seafood. Owner Daniel Rios creates dishes with tastes of Portugal and India, countries he has lived in. The *arroz do mar* – rice with generous helpings of octopus, shrimp, squid, *sururu* (shellfish), and oysters – is the highlight. Another option is curried shrimp with ginger and cardamom, served with grilled fruits in season. **CUISINE** fish and seafood **CREDIT CARDS** not accepted
Rua do Concris, 1, Chapadão
TEL (84) 3246-2026 **OPEN** Tue – Sun, 11am – midnight

La Provence $$

French cuisine is not merely a label here. The beautifully presented dishes are inspired by the flavors of Provence, home of French chef Jean Louis Ferrari. Frog is featured. At night, flares create a relaxed, cozy atmosphere. A good wine list is available. **CUISINE** French **CREDIT CARDS** MasterCard
Rua da Gameleira, 111

| RESTAURANTS | $ up to R$50 | $$ from R$51 up to R$100 | $$$ from R$101 up to R$150 | $$$$ above R$150 |

TEL (84) 3246-2280 OPEN High season: daily, noon – 3pm and 7pm – 11pm; low season: Wed – Mon, noon – 3pm and 7pm – 11pm. Closed in June.

Ombak $
Jovino Soares opened Ombak as a bar offering good *cachaça* and snacks. Lack of options on Sagi beach, on the dune buggy route from Pipa and Tibau do Sul, have led him to expand his business. It's now an often busy bar-restaurant. Seating is available indoors or outdoors under umbrellas. Oak barrels are part of the décor. *Cachaças* from several parts of Brazil are served. CUISINE bar food, fish and seafood CREDIT CARDS Amex, Diners, MasterCard, Visa
Rua da Praia, 70, Praia do Sagi, Baía Formosa
TEL (84) 3244-5008, 3244-5024 OPEN Daily, 9am – 6pm

Panela de Barro $
Moquecas in the tradition of the state of Espírito Santo (without *dendê* palm oil or coconut milk) are this restaurant's forte. Generous portions arrive at the table in the famous clay dishes of Vale do Mulembá in Espírito Santo. The dazzling hilltop view unfolds the sea majestically before you. The background music is MPB and *bossa-nova*. Entertaining marmosets often make an appearance. CUISINE Espírito Santo, fish and seafood CREDIT CARDS Amex, Diners, MasterCard
Rua do Cruzeiro, 56, Pipa
TEL (84) 3246-2611 OPEN Daily, noon – 11pm

Ponta do Pirambu $
The restaurant in this day spa serves a simple, varied menu. The highlight is the tapioca lasagna with manioc purée, crab, organic shrimp, and coconut milk. A rustic panoramic elevator takes you down the cliff. The sea-facing pool offers kiosks and a snack bar. CUISINE bar food, varied CREDIT CARDS Diners, MasterCard
Rua Sem Pescoço, 252, Tibau do Sul
TEL (84) 3246-4333 OPEN Daily, 9am – 5pm

Rancho da Pipa $
Rancho da Pipa is a great spot for meat lovers. The house specialty is Argentinean rump, which arrives tender and well seasoned. It's prepared on a sloping grill that collects the fat in channels, preventing smoking and preserving the flavor of the meat. The generous side dishes include rice, black beans, fried manioc, pickled salad, onions, and seasoned manioc flour. Even individual dishes are ample. CUISINE meats CREDIT CARDS not accepted
Rua da Gameleira, 47, Pipa
TEL (84) 3246-2282 OPEN Daily, 5pm – 11pm

Solimar $
This restaurant on bustling Barra do Cunhaú beach consists of several open areas like large kiosks and an inner room with wooden tables and chairs. The area nearest to the sea allows you to enjoy the view away from the noise. Grilled shrimp are a house specialty. CUISINE fish and seafood CREDIT CARDS Visa
Rua Gilberto Rodrigues, no #, Barra do Cunhaú
TEL (84) 3241-4242 OPEN Daily, 10am – 5pm

SERVICES

Tourist Information – Posto de Informações Turísticas
Praia de Barra do Cunhaú, near the multi-sports court
OPEN Mon – Fri, 8am – 5pm (Jan and Feb only)

Piranhas – Alagoas
AREA CODE 82 POPULATION 23,483 DISTANCE Maceió 327 kilometers (203 miles) ACCESS From Maceió, take BR-316 highway to Pilar, then BR-101 to São Sebastião, then AL-110 to Arapiraca, then AL-220 to Olho d'Água do Casado, and finally AL-225. From Aracaju, take BR-101 and then SE-206

WHERE TO STAY

Guesthouses $
Piranhas has no hotels, only guesthouses. Some, like Lírio do Vale and Lampião, are simply family homes that rent out individual rooms. These types of guesthouses charge a high price for offering so little – the rooms are extremely simple and there are barely any facilities. The room price does include breakfast. The town is small, so you can, and should, visit all the guesthouses before making a decision. The guesthouses don't have addresses: if you can't find one, just ask a local.
Lampião TEL (82) 3686-3335. Lírio do Vale TEL 3686-3145. Maria Bonita TEL 3686-1777. Marihá TEL 3686-1326. Nosso Lar TEL 3686-3406. Remanso TEL 3686-1157. Pousada da Trilha TEL 3686-1172

WHERE TO EAT

Flor de Cáctus $
Atop a lookout point built at the end of the 19th century, this restaurant offers views of the Rio São Francisco and the colorful houses of Piranhas. You'll find the best views while climbing the steps (more than 300) up the side of the hill. The restaurant has a bistro-like atmosphere, and the menu includes meat, fish, and soup dishes. The delicious house specialty fish dishes such as *surubim* or tilapia, are baked to order and brought whole to the table. The restaurant opens for breakfast, but only for tourist groups with advance reservations. The owners are former CHESF (São Francisco Hydroelectrical Company) employees who cater to tourists and offer quality service. CUISINE meats, fish CREDIT CARDS Diners, MasterCard, Visa
Mirante Secular, 1600, Centro
TEL (82) 3686-1365 RESERVATIONS 8835-1162 OPEN Mon – Sat, 8am – 10pm; Sun, 8am – 8pm

SERVICES

Travel Agency – Agência de Turismo Angico Tour
Rua Martiniano Vasco, 210, Centro
TEL (82) 3686-1782, 9965-1104 OPEN High season, daily, 8am – 10pm; low season, 8am – 6pm

Travel Agency – Xingó Turismo Receptivo
Rua São Sebastião, 23, Xingó
TEL (82) 3686-1775, 9961-1138 OPEN Daily, 8am – 5pm

Piripiri – Piauí
AREA CODE 86 POPULATION 61,965 DISTANCES Sete Cidades National Park 25 kilometers (16 miles), Teresina 183 kilometers (114 miles) ACCESS From Teresina, take the BR-343 highway towards Fortaleza

WHERE TO STAY

Hotel Fazenda Sete Cidades $
Most rooms are large but basic; the communal areas are cheerfully decorated. The hotel offers a swimming pool, and

a children's play area, and is located 8 kilometers (5 miles) from the park visitors' center. ACCOMMODATIONS 37 rooms, air-conditioning, minibar, cable TV FACILITIES AND SERVICES bar, horses, parking, pool, playground, restaurant, game room CREDIT CARDS not accepted
Parque Nacional de Sete Cidades (exit Km 63, BR-222 highway towards Fortaleza)
TEL and FAX (86) 3276-2222

Parque Hotel Sete Cidades $
The hotel sits within the national park, and features a beautiful setting with a delightful natural pool. Unfortunately, the setting does not make up for the hotel's other disappointments: the rooms are very simple, the shower has no hot water, the service is poor, and the restaurant, the only option around, serves mediocre home-style food. Visitors have to go to Piripiri, 25 kilometers (16 miles) away, to find something better. ACCOMMODATIONS 12 rooms, air-conditioning, minibar FACILITIES AND SERVICES parking, natural pool, restaurant, game room, video room, walking trails CREDIT CARDS MasterCard
Parque Nacional de Sete Cidades (exit Km 63, BR-222 highway towards Fortaleza)
TEL (86) 3223-3366   www.hotelsetecidades.com.br

Ponta do Corumbau – Bahia

AREA CODE 73 Prado DISTANCES Salvador 844 Kilometers (524 miles), Porto Seguro 220 Kilometers (137 miles) ACCESS Take the BR-101 highway to Itamaraju and BA-489 (15 kilometers, 9 miles), then travel 57 kilometers (35 miles) along a dirt road. By sea, take a motorboat or boat from Cumuruxatiba

WHERE TO STAY

Fazenda São Francisco $$$$
This sea-side coconut plantation has an exclusive, sophisticated air, and only eight, airy, well-decorated rooms, each designed by Roberto Migotto. In addition to the plantation's 1,000 meters (3,300 feet) of private beach, there is also a river out back with mangroves and islands. After the plantation changed hands, it accepts children as guests, but only when accompanied by a full-time nanny. The hotel holds *pataxó* dance presentations. ACCOMMODATIONS 6 bungalows and 2 rooms, air-conditioning, private safe, minibar, telephone, ceiling fan, veranda/balcony FACILITIES AND SERVICES Internet access in communal areas, bar, boat, bicycles, woods, horses, parking, swimming pool, orchard, ponies, restaurant, magazine reading area, river, game room, video room, walking trails, guided walking tours, heliport, beach service, shuttle service to airport and local attractions CREDIT CARDS Amex, MasterCard
Praia de Ponta do Corumbau, no #
TEL and FAX (73) 3294-2250 RESERVATIONS (11) 3078-4411
www.corumbau.com.br

Jocotoka Eco Resort $$$
With 700 meters (2,300 feet) of beach, a branch of the river out back, and several walking trails, this sea-side coconut plantation is another charming option. Open since 1987, it offers spacious, rustic chalets, and excellent water-sports facilities. The boats at the plantation often transport guests to and from the Porto Seguro airport. In the high season, dinner is included in the daily rate. ACCOMMODATIONS 20 chalets, air-conditioning, private safe, minibar, ceiling fan FACILITIES AND SERVICES Internet access in communal areas, wine cellar, bar, boat, kayaks, horses, cart, fishing equipment, parking, motorboat, stores, swimming pool, volleyball court, beach volleyball, restaurant, game room, massage room, video room, travel agency, currency exchange, recreational team for adults and children, guided walking tours, beach service, shuttle service to airport and local attractions CREDIT CARDS MasterCard
Praia de Ponta de Corumbau, no #
TEL (73) 3294-1244, 3288-2291 FAX 3288-2540
www.jocotoka.com.br

Vila Naiá $$$$
Opened in 2004, this hotel is on a private national nature reserve with trails. In addition to a semi-private beach, this old coconut plantation encompasses a preserved area with *restinga* vegetation and mangroves. The rooms have been constructed based on studies of old local wooden dwellings and have been built by local artisans without the use of nails. ACCOMMODATIONS 4 rooms and 3 bungalows, private safe, minibar, telephone, TV, ceiling fan FACILITIES AND SERVICES Internet access in communal areas, wine cellar, bar, boat, kayaks, bicycles, woods, soccer field, parking, convenience store, period furniture, swimming pool, restaurant, gym, massage room, video room, walking trails, recreational team for adults and children, guided walking tours, beach service, shuttle service to airport and local attractions, horses, motorboat. CREDIT CARDS Amex, Diners, MasterCard, Visa
Estrada Guarani–Corumbau, no #, Ponta do Corumbau
TEL and FAX (73) 3573-1006   www.vilanaia.com.br

SERVICES

Tourist Information and Travel Agency – Aquamar Agência de Turismo
Avenida Beira-Mar, 7, Centro, Cumuruxatiba
TEL and FAX (73) 3573-1360 OPEN High season: daily, 7am – 8pm high season; low season: 7am – 6pm low season
www.aquamarba.com.br

Travel Agency – Agência de Turismo Prado Aventuras
Avenida 2 de Julho, 229, Centro, Prado
TEL (73) 3021-0349, 9987-4045 OPEN High season: daily, 9am – 10pm; low season: Mon – Fri, 9am – 4:30pm; Sat, 9am – 2pm
www.pradoaventuras.com.br

Ponta do Mel – Rio Grande do Norte

AREA CODE 84 Areia Branca DISTANCES Natal 355 kilometers (221 miles) ACCESS If traveling by car, take the BR-110 highway. If traveling by a 4x4 vehicle, take BR-304 to Porto do Mangue, then go along a stretch of dunes where there are no road signs or gas stations.

WHERE TO STAY

Costa Branca Eco Resort $$
The beach is only a pleasant 10-minute walk away from this guesthouse. The chalets are simple, but cozy. The communal areas offer a beautiful view of Ponta do Mel and the sea. Park benches scattered around the garden, the swimming pools, the bar and restaurant all offer lovely sea-views. ACCOMMODATIONS 17 chalets, air-conditioning, minibar, telephone, cable TV, veranda/balcony FACILITIES AND SERVICES wine cellar, bar, safe, parking, swimming pool, restaurant, reading room, walking trails, airport shuttle; pub with a large-screen TV CREDIT CARDS Visa
Rua Projetada, no #, Praia de Ponta do Mel
TEL (84) 3332-7062 FAX 3332-7075   www.costabranca.com.br

RESTAURANTS $ up to R$50 $$ from R$51 up to R$100 $$$ from R$101 up to R$150 $$$$ above R$150

Porto de Galinhas – Pernambuco

AREA CODE 81 Ipojuca **DISTANCE** Recife 60 kilometers (37 miles) **ACCESS** From Recife, take BR-101 highway towards the south coast. From there, take PE-060 to Ipojuca followed by PE-038 to Nossa Senhora do Ó. Finally, PE-09 leads to the town

WHERE TO STAY

Nannai Beach Resort $$$$
This charming resort on Muro Alto beach is ideal for swimming, thanks to the reef barrier. Its wooden, understated Polynesian-style bungalows, each with a private pool, DVD player, and 29" TV, are popular with honeymoon couples. The swimming pool in the communal area is 6,000 square meters (65,000 square feet) and stretches to the doors of the guests' rooms. **ACCOMMODATIONS** 49 bungalows and 42 suites, Internet access, air-conditioning, private safe, minibar, telephone, cable TV, DVD player (in bungalows), jacuzzi (in master bungalow) **FACILITIES AND SERVICES** Internet access in communal areas, bar, parking, heliport, stores, swimming pool, playground, soccer, tennis, and volleyball courts, restaurant, gym, game room, massage room, beauty parlor, sauna, recreational team for adults and children, guided walking tours, valet parking, beach service, shuttle service to airport and local attractions **CREDIT CARDS** Amex, Diners, MasterCard, Visa
Rodovia PE-09, Km 3 (exit to Muro Alto)
TEL (81) 3552-0100 **FAX** 3552-1474, 3552-5097
www.nannai.com.br

Pousada Porto Verde $
Surrounded by trees, the comfortable suites of this guesthouse are only 100 meters (330 feet) from the natural pools in Porto de Galinhas. Owners Fernando and Ana Regina Soares offer useful tips about what's happening in Porto de Galinhas and arrange trips, as well. **ACCOMMODATIONS** 14 suites, air-conditioning, minibar, TV **FACILITIES AND SERVICES** swimming pool, restaurant, game room, cable TV **CREDIT CARDS** Diners, MasterCard, Visa
Loteamento Recanto Porto de Galinhas, Praça 1, Lote J
TEL and **FAX** (81) 3552-1410
www.pousadaportoverde.com.br

Pousada Tabajuba $$
On the sea-front at Praia do Cupe, this spotlessly clean rooms of this sophisticated guesthouse are tastefully decorated with rustic furniture and local craftwork. The communal areas face the garden courtyard. Very popular with honeymoon couples, the guesthouse doesn't accept children under the age of 12. The staff provides very efficient service. **ACCOMMODATIONS** 24 rooms, air-conditioning, minibar, telephone, TV, ceiling fan **FACILITIES AND SERVICES** bar, parking, snack bar, stores, swimming pool, restaurant, shuttle service to airport and local attractions **CREDIT CARDS** Amex, Diners, MasterCard, Visa
Praia do Cupe, Loteamento Merepe II, Quadra I, Lote 6 (exit Km 6.5, PE-09 highway)
TEL (81) 3552-1049 **FAX** 3552-1006 www.tabajuba.com

Summerville Beach Resort $$$$
A true leisure and entertainment complex, it offers facilities including a 2,300 square meter (25,000 square foot) pool that stretches over a large part of the grounds, and a well-equipped gym. The activity schedule changes constantly. Guests are free to choose from among ten different kinds of pillows, each containing a different blend of herbs. There is a self-serve restaurant, as well as an à la carte restaurant. **ACCOMMODATIONS** 65 suites and 36 bungalows, Internet access, air-conditioning, private safe, minibar, telephone, cable TV, Jacuzzi (in 2 bungalows) **FACILITIES AND SERVICES** Internet access in communal areas, wine cellar, archery, bar, nursery, bicycles, kayaks, soccer field, waterskiing, parking, jacuzzi, jet-ski, snack bar, stores, pool, playground, tennis court, volleyball court, restaurant, conference room, gym, game room, massage room, sauna, spa, travel agency, business center, currency exchange, recreational team for adults and children, valet parking, lifeguard, beach service, shuttle service to airport and local attractions **CREDIT CARDS** Amex, Diners, MasterCard, Visa
Rodovia PE-09, Km 2 (exit to Muro Alto)
TEL (81) 3302-5555 **FAX** 3302-5577
www.summervilleresort.com.br

WHERE TO EAT

Beijupirá $
Charming in many ways, Beijupirá has become a tradition in Porto de Galinhas. The kitchen prepares typical regional dishes, but adds its own twist with new ingredients. The *Maracatu Imperial*, for example is shredded beef jerky cooked with butter, tabbouleh made with rice, cracked wheat, and northeastern *cuscuz*, colored bell pepper and honey vinaigrette. Tempting desserts include the delicious *aussuba* (sweet crepes with tapioca ice cream and light molasses); the word *aussuba* means "love" in Tupi-Gurani. **CUISINE** fish and seafood, regional **CREDIT CARDS** Amex, Diners, MasterCard, Visa
Rua Beijupirá, no #
TEL (81) 3552-2354, 3552-2758 **OPEN** Daily, noon – midnight

Peixe na Telha $$
This restaurant has a sophisticated but casual beach style and serves recipes with a touch of flair. Fish is their forte, but they also serve up salads and meat dishes. The tile-cooked fish in shrimp sauce arrives at the table, as tradition dictates, steaming, and garnished with saffron rice and golden-brown potatoes. For dessert, try the traditional *cartola* (curd cheese with banana and cinnamon). The restaurant is located on the beach-front; on sunny days at low tide outdoor seating is available. **CUISINE** fish and seafood **CREDIT CARDS** Amex, Diners, MasterCard, Visa
Avenida Beira-Mar, 40-B
TEL (81) 3552-1323 **RESERVATIONS** 3552-1851 **OPEN** Daily, 10am until the last customer leaves

Porto Seguro – Bahia

AREA CODE 73 **POPULATION** 133,976 **DISTANCES** Salvador 723 kilometers (449 miles), Itabuna 250 kilometers (155 miles), Vitória 600 kilometers (373 miles) **ACCESS** Take the BR-101 and BR-367 highways from Salvador **WHEN TO VISIT** Summer, for anyone who enjoys lively beaches, parties, and *axé* music. The rest of the year for quiet beaches and cultural sightseeing

WHERE TO STAY

Brisa da Praia $$$$
This modern building on the beach-front has large glazed windows overlooking the sea, spacious rooms, and hallways designed to maximize the natural light. The communal areas are decorated with local craftwork and offer several leisure options. **ACCOMMODATIONS** 152 rooms and 1 suite, Internet access, air-conditioning, private safe, minibar, background music, telephone, cable TV, Jacuzzi (in the suite) **FACILITIES AND SERVICES** Internet access in communal areas, wine cellar, bar, soccer field, parking, Jacuzzi, convenience store,

PRICES	HOTELS (couple)	$ up to R$150	$$ from R$151 up to R$300	$$$ from R$301 up to R$500	$$$$ above R$500

swimming pool, playground, soccer court, squash court, restaurant, conference room, gym, game room, massage room, video room, beauty parlor, sauna, business center, 24-hour kitchen, recreational team for adults and children, airport shuttle CREDIT CARDS Amex, Diners, MasterCard, Visa
Avenida Beira-Mar, 1860, Praia de Taperapuan
TEL (73) 3288-8600 RESERVATIONS 3288-8611 FAX 3288-8636
www.brisadapraia.com.br

Hotel Villagio Arcobaleno $$

The high quality services and facilities, make this beach avenue hotel one of the best places to stay in Porto Seguro. It has spacious rooms and the communal building stops the noise from nearby barraca Axé Moi from reaching them. The hotel has its own barraca. ACCOMMODATIONS 163 suites, Internet access, air-conditioning, private safe, minibar, telephone, cable TV FACILITIES AND SERVICES Internet access in communal areas, bar, parking, Jacuzzi, stores, swimming pool, playground, tennis court, restaurant, conference room, gym, game room, massage room, video room, beauty parlor, sauna, 24-hour kitchen, recreational team for adults and children, airport shuttle CREDIT CARDS Amex, Diners, MasterCard
Rodovia BR-367, Km 67, Praia de Taperapuan
TEL (73) 3679-2000, 0800-2845222 RESERVATIONS 3679-1284 FAX 3679-1269   www.hotelarcobaleno.tur.br

La Torre $$

Opened in 2001, just 30 meters (100 feet) from the beach, this hotel has a pleasant atmosphere, with a courtyard garden, and a small lake. All areas are wheelchair accessible. The hotel's beach barraca has a massage kiosk. ACCOMMODATIONS 54 rooms and 34 suites, Internet access, air-conditioning, private safe, minibar, telephone, TV FACILITIES AND SERVICES Internet access in communal areas, bar, parking, Jacuzzi, convenience store, swimming pool, playground, restaurant, gym, massage room, conference room, video room, sauna, currency exchange, guided walking tours, valet parking, shuttle service to airport and local attractions CREDIT CARDS Amex, Diners, MasterCard, Visa
Avenida Beira-Mar, 9999, Praia do Mutá
TEL (73) 2105-1700 FAX 2105-1800
www.latorreaparthotel.com.br

Monte Pascoal Praia $$

This hotel faces the Axé Moi barraca complex and offers a variety of services like ticket sales for night events and trip arrangements. Guests can order in-room massages. The bedrooms – with tiled floors and colorful bedspreads and curtains – are spacious, but basic. ACCOMMODATIONS 77 rooms and 3 two-room suites, Internet access, air-conditioning, crib, private safe, minibar, telephone, TV, Jacuzzi (in suites) FACILITIES AND SERVICES Internet access in communal areas, bar, cascade, parking, Jacuzzi, convenience store, swimming pool, playground, restaurant, card-playing tables, conference room, gym, game room, beauty parlor, sauna, recreational team for adults and children, laundry, beach service CREDIT CARDS Diners, MasterCard, Visa
Avenida Beira-Mar, 5959, Praia de Taperapuan
TEL (73) 3679-3055 FAX 3679-3057
www.montepascoal.com.br

Porto Seguro Praia Hotel $$

Set along 50,000 square meters (12 acres) of beautiful woods and gardens on the beach avenue, this hotel has spacious, well-equipped rooms, with understated décor and balconies. Suites have an unparalleled sea view. ACCOMMODATIONS 145 rooms and 5 suites, air-conditioning, private safe, minibar, telephone, cable TV, balcony, jacuzzi (in suites) FACILITIES AND SERVICES Internet access in communal areas, bar, beach kiosk, chapel, parking, stores, swimming pool with waterslide, playground, tennis court, volleyball court, restaurant, gym, game room, massage room, video room, sauna, background music, business center, currency exchange, 24-hour kitchen, recreational team for adults and children, valet parking CREDIT CARDS Amex, Diners, MasterCard, Visa
Avenida Beira-Mar, no #, Praia de Curuípe
TEL (73) 3288-9393 RESERVATIONS 3288-9321 FAX 3288-2069
www.psph.com.br

PortoBello Resort $$$

This hotel is located next to the popular beach barraca Axé Moi. Its extensive grounds, contain a forest, gardens, and coconut palms, as well as a small lake and deck, both of which face the sea. The rooms, complete with veranda and hammock, overlook the garden, but, other than the view, they lack charm. Three restaurants serve regional and varied cuisine. ACCOMMODATIONS 96 rooms and 1 suite, Internet access, air-conditioning, private safe, minibar, telephone, cable TV, veranda, Jacuzzi (in the suite) FACILITIES AND SERVICES Internet access in communal areas, bar, soccer field, miniature golf, parking, jacuzzi, stores, swimming pool, playground, tennis court, volleyball court, restaurant, conference room, gym, game room, massage room, video room, beauty parlor, sauna, business center, 24-hour kitchen, recreational team for adults and children, car rental, beach service CREDIT CARDS Amex, Diners, MasterCard, Visa
Avenida Beira-Mar, 6111, Praia de Taperapuã
TEL (73) 2105-6000 RESERVATIONS 2105-6110 FAX 2105-6123
www.portobellohoteis.com.br

Vela Branca Resort Hotel $$

This resort comprises 120,000 square meters (30 acres) of gardens and lawns on Cidade Alta cliff, next to the historical city. It offers a magnificent view of the coastline and excellent facilities and services. ACCOMMODATIONS 110 rooms and 10 suites, air-conditioning, private safe, minibar, telephone, cable TV FACILITIES AND SERVICES Internet access in communal areas, bar, soccer field, parking, convenience store, swimming pool, tennis court, restaurant, gym, massage room, beauty parlor, sauna, business center, recreational team for children, taxi CREDIT CARDS Amex, Diners, MasterCard, Visa
Rua Antônio Ricaldi, 177, Cidade Histórica
TEL (73) 3288-2318 RESERVATIONS and FAX 3288-2316
www.velabranca.com.br

WHERE TO EAT

Anti$caro $$

The house specialty here is the lobster, which serves two. Or, try the whole fish in champagne sauce, served with mashed potatoes and oriental rice; filé à Oswaldo Aranha (fillet steak topped with fried garlic and served with rice and seasoned manioc flour); trio elétrico (vatapá, bobó, and caruru), and shrimp in pineapple. Located in a historic building, it has a wine list and cellar. CUISINE fish and seafood, varied CREDIT CARDS Amex, Diners, MasterCard, Visa
Travessa Assis Chateaubriand, 26, Centro
TEL (73) 3288-2683 OPEN High season: daily, 1pm – 4pm and 6pm – midnight; low season: 6pm – midnight

Bistrô da Helô $

Owner Heloísa Leal Lima, known to all as Helô, prepares creative, tasty dishes such as lambreta (a type of shellfish) gratin, fish carpaccio, and fillet steak with capers and vermouth. Her restaurant, located in a historic building, attracts

| RESTAURANTS | $ up to R$50 | $$ from R$51 up to R$100 | $$$ from R$101 up to R$150 | $$$$ above R$150 |

a varied clientele with its informal atmosphere, and has a wine list, outdoor tables, and live music. CUISINE fish and seafood, varied CREDIT CARDS Diners, MasterCard
Travessa Assis Chateaubriand, 29, Centro
TEL (73) 3288-3940 RESERVATIONS 9141-4999 OPEN Mon – Sat, 6:30pm – midnight

Cabana Recanto do Sossego $$

On the sea front, chef Ettore Dertoni, resident in Porto Seguro for more than 15 years, specializes in fish with an Italian touch. We highly recommend the *grelhado sossego* (shrimp, lobster, squid and fish fillet), and *moqueca Italiana* (with the same ingredients as the previous dish, but with the addition of clams). Both dishes serve two and are accompanied by salad and rice. The restaurant offers a wine list and cellar, a bilingual menu, and outdoor tables. CUISINE fish and seafood CREDIT CARDS MasterCard, Visa
Avenida Beira-Mar, 10130, Praia do Mutá
TEL (73) 3677-1266 OPEN Daily, 8am – 5pm

Colher de Pau $$

A culinary tradition in Porto Seguro, this restaurant serves a variety of meat and fish dishes. House specialties are the rump steak, served with *feijão-tropeiro* (beans, spicy sausage, and manioc flour) pickled salad, and rice, and *mariscada* (mussels served with rice and thickened *pirão* sauce). Popular with locals, it has outdoor tables and live music. CUISINE meats, fish and seafood CREDIT CARDS MasterCard, Visa
Travessa Augusto Borges, 28, Centro
TEL (73) 3268-4124 OPEN Daily, noon until the last customer leaves

Restaurante da Japonesa $$

In business for 20 years, this restaurant is near the ferryboat terminal and is always bustling. The menu includes fish, seafood, meat dishes, sandwiches, pasta, snacks, and Asian dishes, such as sushi and temaki. Among the house specialties are teppan-yaki (shrimp with vegetables) and yakisoba (fried noodles with strips of beef and vegetables). They also have a good selection of drinks and desserts. CUISINE Asian, varied CREDIT CARDS Amex, Diners, MasterCard, Visa
Praça dos Pataxós, 38 (near the ferryboat terminal)
TEL (73) 3288-2592 OPEN Daily, 7am – 11pm

Tia Nenzinha $

One of the first restaurants in Porto Seguro, Tia Nenzinha is installed inside a historic building. It serves a wide variety of simple fish, lobster, and meat dishes. We recommend the fish *moqueca* with shrimp, served with rice *pirão*, and tile-cooked fish with rice, potato salad, and seasoned manioc flour. CUISINE meats, fish and seafood, regional CREDIT CARDS Diners, MasterCard, Visa
Avenida Portugal, 170 (Passarela do Álcool, Centro
TEL (73) 3288-1846 RESERVATIONS 9141-9812 (ask for Fernanda) OPEN Daily, 11am – midnight

SERVICES

Airport – Aeroporto Internacional de Porto Seguro

Estrada do Aeroporto, no #, Cidade Alta
TEL (73) 3288-1877 OPEN Daily, 24 hours

Tourist Information – Posto de Informações Turísticas

Praça Manoel Ribeiro Coelho, 10 (Passarela do Álcool), Centro
TEL (73) 3268-1390 OPEN Mon – Fri, 9am – 11pm

Travel Agency – Agência de Turismo Brasil Travel

Avenida 22 de Abril, 186, store #13/14
TEL (73) 3288-3513, 3288-1824 OPEN Mon – Fri, 9am – 6pm; Sat, 9am – 1pm www.braziltravel.com.br

Travel Agency – Agência de Turismo Porto Mondo Adventure

Passarela do Álcool, 344, store #101
TEL (73) 3288-0040, 9985-4974 OPEN High season: Mon – Sat, 8:30am – 10pm; low season: 8:30am – 8pm
www.portomondo.com

Travel Agency – Agência de Turismo Yes Tour Receptivo

Rua Rui Barbosa, 15, room #4, Centro
TEL (73) 3288-3363, 3288-1644 FAX 3288-3664 OPEN Mon – Fri, 8am – 6pm www.yestours.tour.br

Travel Agency – Pataxó Turismo

Rua Oscar Oliveira, 4 (Passarela do Álcool), Centro
TEL (73) 3288-1256, 3288-2507, 9979-5597 (24 hours) OPEN High season: daily, 8am – 11:30pm; low season: Mon – Fri, 8am – 7pm www.pataxoturismo.com.br

Prado – Bahia

AREA CODE 73 POPULATION 28,920 DISTANCES Salvador 812 kilometers (505 miles), Vitória 450 kilometers (280 miles) ACCESS From both the BR-101 and the BA-489 WHEN TO VISIT From July to November, for whale-watching

WHERE TO STAY

Pousada Ponta de Areia $$

On the beach, away from the center of town, this guesthouse is accessible only by sand road. It is well-maintained and rustic in style with charmingly decorated rooms and leisure facilities. It also has a beach kiosk and walking trails. ACCOMMODATIONS 18 rooms and 2 suites, air-conditioning, minibar, TV, ceiling fan, Jacuzzi (in suites) FACILITIES AND SERVICES Internet access in communal areas, bar, parking, pool, volleyball court, sand volleyball court, massage kiosk, sauna, walking trails, guided walking tours, beach service, shuttle service to local attractions CREDIT CARDS MasterCard
Avenida Beira-Mar, 300, Coqueiral
TEL (73) 3298-1313 FAX 3298-2941
www.pousadapontadeareia.com.br

Praia da Paixão $$

Located on a beach bearing the same name, this hotel has a cliff-top lookout point, with kiosks and barbecue facilities. Goats, sheep, and cows can be seen wandering around the fruit trees of the 50,000-square-meter (12-acre) grounds. Apart from the view, the rooms could do with a touch of charm. ACCOMMODATIONS 25 rooms, air-conditioning, minibar, TV, ceiling fan FACILITIES AND SERVICES bar, parking, swimming pool, playground, sand soccer court, volleyball court, restaurant, conference room, gym, game room, video room, sauna, walking trails, guided walking tours, beach service, shuttle service to airport and local attractions CREDIT CARDS Diners, MasterCard, Visa
Estrada Prado–Cumuruxatiba, Km 12
TEL (73) 3298-1316 RESERVATIONS 3021-1316
www.praiadapaixao.com.br

Villaggio Guaratiba Resort $$

Between Caravelas and Prado, this resort is inside a condo with 24-hour security. The complex also contains houses to

| PRICES | HOTELS (couple) | $ up to R$150 | $$ from R$151 up to R$300 | $$$ from R$301 up to R$500 | $$$$ above R$500 |

rent, stores, restaurant, beach kiosk, and full leisure facilities. **ACCOMMODATIONS** 50 chalets, air-conditioning, refrigerator, TV, ceiling fan, Jacuzzi and cable TV (in some rooms) **FACILITIES AND SERVICES** Internet access in communal areas, bar, bicycles, soccer field, horses, parking, fishing lake, stores, pool, soccer court, tennis court, volleyball court, restaurant, sauna, telephone, walking trails, travel agency, currency exchange, guided walking tours, beach service, shuttle service to airport and local attractions; lifeguard (high season) **CREDIT CARDS** not accepted
Rodovia Prado – Alcobaça, Km 10, Balneário Praia de Guaratiba, no #
TEL (73) 3021-0675 **FAX** 3021-0677
www.praiadeguaratiba.com.br

WHERE TO EAT

Jubiabá $
This restaurant on Beco das Garrafas, the street with the main restaurants in Prado, serves good regional food à la carte. Try the *budião* fish fillet in shrimp sauce (served with heart of palm rice), or grilled salted cod cutlet in garlic sauce (served with potatoes, onions, boiled eggs, and garlic rice). The menu also features poultry, meat, and pasta dishes. **CUISINE** Portuguese, fish and seafood **CREDIT CARDS** Amex, Diners, MasterCard, Visa
Beco das Garrafas, 140, Centro
TEL (73) 3298-2180 **OPEN** High season: daily, 11am until the last customer leaves; low season: 11am – 11pm

SERVICES

Guide – Pradinho
Rua 6, #25, Novo Prado (Pousada Guaratiba)
TEL (73) 8811-3886, 3298-1514 **OPEN** Daily, 24 hours

Guide – Prev Tur – Turismo e Lazer
Rua São Benedito, no #, Cais da Ilha
TEL (73) 3021-0346, 9966-8126 (ask for Bila) **OPEN** Daily, 7am – 6pm

Travel Agency – Agência de Turismo Prado Aventuras
Avenida 2 de Julho, 229, Centro
TEL (73) 3021-0349, 9987-4045 **OPEN** High season: daily, 9am – 10pm; low season: Mon – Fri, 9am – 4:30pm; Sat, 9am – 2pm
www.pradoaventuras.com.br

Praia do Forte – Bahia

AREA CODE 71 Mata de São João **DISTANCES** Salvador 91 kilometers (57 miles), Itacimirim 9 kilometers (5.5 miles), Imbassaí 10 kilometers (6 miles), Costa do Sauípe 20 kilometers (12 miles) **ACCESS** From Salvador, take the Estrada do Coco highway; from Aracaju, take the Linha Verde

WHERE TO STAY

Porto Zarpa $$
This pretty guesthouse has direct access to the beach. Rooms are comfortable and well equipped, and decorated with regional craftwork. The wide range of leisure facilities includes a lookout point and video room. **ACCOMMODATIONS** 31 rooms, air-conditioning, private safe, minibar, telephone, TV, balcony with hammock **FACILITIES AND SERVICES** Internet access in communal areas, bar, parking, massage, lookout point, pool, playground, restaurant, conference room, video room, reading room, travel agency, business center **CREDIT CARDS** Amex, Diners, MasterCard, Visa
Rua da Aurora, Quadra 21, Aldeia dos Pescadores
TEL (71) 3676-1414 **RESERVATIONS** 3676-1056
www.portozarpa.com.br

Praia do Forte Eco Resort & Thalasso Spa $$$$
This is one of the oldest resorts in Brazil. Though it's situated on one of the area's best beaches for bathing, some guests never make it any farther than the excellent on-site pools. The spa (open daily to guests) will surely be a highlight of your stay; it is a relaxation spa, with sea-water based treatments. The gym, saunas, and other attractions are all included in the daily rate. **ACCOMMODATIONS** 250 rooms and 2 suites, Internet access, air-conditioning, private safe, minibar, telephone, cable TV, private veranda/balcony **FACILITIES AND SERVICES** Internet access in communal areas, bar, soccer field, parking, Jacuzzi, motorboat, stores, pool, jogging track, soccer court, tennis court, volleyball court, restaurant, conference room, gym, games room, massage room, video room, beauty parlor, business center, 24-hour kitchen, recreational team for children, beach service, shuttle service to airport and local attractions **CREDIT CARDS** Amex, Diners, MasterCard, Visa
Avenida do Farol, no #
TEL (71) 3676-4000 **RESERVATIONS** 0800-118-289
www.ecoresort.com.br

Vila dos Corais $$
Opened in 2004, this hotel has rustic décor, featuring mosaics and wood furnishings. The rooms are spacious, and centered on a very pleasant veranda. The hotel also has rooms adapted for the physically disabled. **ACCOMMODATIONS** 50 rooms, air-conditioning, minibar, telephone, cable TV **FACILITIES AND SERVICES** Internet access in communal areas, bar, bicycles, parking, pool with hydro-massage, restaurant, gym, massage room, beauty parlor, sauna, business center; kitchen closes at 10pm **CREDIT CARDS** Diners, MasterCard, Visa
Rua do Dourado, no #, Aldeia dos Pescadores
TEL (71) 3676-8000 www.viladoscorais.com.br

WHERE TO EAT

Caramuru e Catarina $
Decorated in a rustic style with wooden furniture and a veranda, this restaurant specializes in regional food and has a per-kilo buffet, which includes dessert. There is a small à la carte menu offering just shrimp, fish, or mixed *moqueca* (all for two people). Groups of thirteen or more people should call in advance. **CUISINE** regional, fish and seafood **CREDIT CARDS** Diners, MasterCard, Visa
Alameda da Felicidade, no #
TEL (71) 3676-1343 **OPEN** Thu – Tue, noon – 4pm

Sabor da Vila $
This restaurant is better known as "Restaurante do Zequinha" after the owner, a former carpenter who opened the place with his wife, Rai. The couple specializes in *moquecas* and stews, of which the *moqueca mista* (with octopus, shrimp, and fish) and sea bass in shrimp sauce are highlights. For starters, try the small fish cakes. All dishes serve two. **CUISINE** regional, fish and seafood **CREDIT CARDS** Diners, MasterCard, Visa
Avenida ACM, no #
TEL 3676-1156 **OPEN** Daily, 10am – 10pm

Souza $
In business for almost twenty-five years, Souza serves the best fish cakes in the area. Based on Souza's mother's orig-

---

RESTAURANTS $ up to R$50 $$ from R$51 up to R$100 $$$ from R$101 up to R$150 $$$$ above R$150

inal recipe, the cakes are delicate and well seasoned. The menu also features a variety of *moquecas*, soups, and stews, as well as fruit-based drinks. The restaurant is simple, on a lovely property with plenty of trees shading the outdoor tables. CUISINE regional, bar food, fish and seafood CREDIT CARDS Diners, MasterCard, Visa
Avenida ACM, no #
TEL (71) 3676-1386 RESERVATIONS 3676-1129 OPEN Daily, 10am until the last customer leaves

Tango Café $

Argentinians Vito and Graziela have lived in Praia do Forte for many years. Graziela still oversees the kitchen, and the recipes are all her own. This is a good place for sandwiches and savories, as well as pies, truffles, and other sweets, best enjoyed while sipping a coffee and enjoying the great background music. Tango offers Internet access at the back of the café. CUISINE Café, snack food CREDIT CARDS Amex, Diners, MasterCard, Visa
Alameda do Sol, no #
TEL (71) 3676-1637 OPEN Daily, 10am until the last customer leaves

Praia do Francês – Alagoas

AREA CODE 82 Marechal Deodoro DISTANCE Maceió 20 kilometers (12 miles), Marechal Deodoro 8 kilometers (5 miles) ACCESS From Maceió, take the AL-101

WHERE TO STAY

Casa de Esportes Hotel $

Barely 100 meters from the beach, Casa de Esportes was opened in 2004 by Swiss-born Guido Schnell and his Brazilian wife Heloísa. The spacious rooms are decorated and furnished in wood, with verandas overlooking an interior garden. The owners speak English, French, German, Italian, and Portuguese, and work with travel agencies in Switzerland and Italy. ACCOMMODATIONS 14 rooms, air-conditioning, private safe, minibar, telephone, cable TV, ceiling fan, balcony FACILITIES AND SERVICES Internet access in communal areas, bar, barbecue facilities, parking, snack bar, pool, tennis court, volleyball court, restaurant, games room, travel agency, beach service, shuttle service to airport and local attractions CREDIT CARDS Visa
Rua Mexilhão, 32, Praia do Francês
TEL (82) 3260-1303 FAX 3260-1621
www.hotelcasadeesportes.com.br

Pousada Hotel Mahon-Mar $

This guesthouse is 200 meters from the beach. It is run very professionally and offers a high level of service. The well-kept, cozy rooms have wooden furniture and sea-themed décor. The restaurant, open only to guests, serves fish, meat dishes, and snacks. ACCOMMODATIONS 30 rooms, air-conditioning, minibar, telephone, TV, balcony FACILITIES AND SERVICES bar, parking, snack bar, pool, playground, tennis court, volleyball court, restaurant, games room, laundry, beach service CREDIT CARDS Amex, Diners, MasterCard, Visa
Avenida Caravela, no #, Praia do Francês
TEL (82) 3260-1223 FAX 3260-1133
www.hotelmahonmar.com.br

WHERE TO EAT

Chez Patrick $

Decorated with paintings by local artists, this cozy restaurant has just ten tables. Among the highlights of the meny created by French owner Patrick Bertin are *camarão à jangadeiro* (shrimp in cheese sauce with rice) and delicious steak in gorgonzola sauce. The wine list features varietals from Chile, Argentina, Italy, and Brazil. The restaurant is just 200 meters from the beach, on a dead-end street. CUISINE French, seafood CREDIT CARDS Amex, MasterCard, Visa
Rua Maresia, 15
TEL (82) 3260-1377 OPEN High season: Mon – Sat, noon – 10pm; Sun, noon – 5pm; low season: Tue – Sat, noon – 10pm; Sun, noon – 5pm

Parada de Taipas $

This simple, agreeable restaurant features wattle and daub walls in the kitchen and an open eating area with wooden pillars. The owner Wilson chats with customers while also overseeing the kitchen. He claims to be the creator of *chiclete de camarão* (fried shrimp with garlic, bell pepper, tomato sauce, cream cheese, and mozzarella), a dish that is served (and widely imitated) throughout the area. Fried fish is also a menu highlight. CUISINE fish and seafood CREDIT CARDS Diners, MasterCard, Visa
Avenida Caravelas, no #
TEL (82) 3260-1609 OPEN Daily, noon – 10pm

Praia dos Carneiros – Pernambuco
(see Tamandaré)

Recife – Pernambuco

AREA CODE 81 POPULATION 1,501,008 DISTANCES João Pessoa 100 kilometers (62 miles), Maceió 255 kilometers (158 miles) ACCESS Coming from the north or south, take BR-101; coming from the east or west, take BR-232 WHEN TO VISIT February, to enjoy Carnival; June, for the São João festivities

WHERE TO STAY

Atlante Plaza $$$

This is a modern hotel catering to executives, with three panoramic elevators looking out onto the beach. The Atlante equals the luxurious Dorisol Grande Hotel in comfort and efficiency, but offers the added benefit of a better location. The hotel offers several different classes of regular rooms (some with side sea view and some facing the sea) as well as first-class rooms that occupy an entire floor and feature better quality furnishings. ACCOMMODATIONS 197 rooms and 44 suites, Internet access, air-conditioning, private safe, minibar, hairdryer, telephone, cable TV FACILITIES AND SERVICES Internet access in communal areas, bar, parking, stores, thermal pool, restaurant, conference room, gym, games room, massage room, beauty parlor, convention center, sauna, travel agency, 24-hour kitchen and bar, business center, laundry, valet parking, shuttle service to airport and local attractions CREDIT CARDS Amex, Diners, MasterCard, Visa
Avenida Boa Viagem, 5426, Boa Viagem
TEL (81) 3302-3333 RESERVATIONS 3302-4446 FAX 3302-4445
www.atlanteplaza.com.br

Blue Tree Towers $$

Opened in 1994, this modern, twenty-story hotel offers attentive service, good equipment, and an excellent location facing Piedade Beach. The rooms all feature small balconies and pleasant sea views (full view in the luxury rooms and junior suites; partial view in the standard and superior rooms and duplex suites). The duplex suites have private pools and saunas. The on-site restaurant serves varied cuisine. ACCOMMODATIONS 116 rooms and 9 suites, air-conditioning, private safe, minibar, telephone, cable TV, balcony; Internet access in some rooms FACILITIES AND SERVICES Internet

PRICES	HOTELS (couple)	$ up to R$150	$$ from R$151 up to R$300	$$$ from R$301 up to R$500	$$$$ above R$500

access in communal areas, bar, parking, convenience store, pool, restaurant, conference room, gym, massage room, sauna, business center, 24-hour kitchen, valet parking, beach service **CREDIT CARDS** Amex, Diners, MasterCard, Visa
Avenida Bernardo Vieira de Melo, 550, Piedade, Jaboatão dos Guararapes
TEL (81) 2123-4567 **RESERVATIONS** 2123-4550 **FAX** 2123-4568
www.bluetree.com.br

Boa Viagem Praia $
Opened in 2004, this hotel has both business and leisure facilities. Since the rooms are all equal in terms of facilities and furnishings, with wood furniture and very little décor, they are classified as either luxury (facing the sea) or standard (side view of the building) based on their sea view. The suites are more spacious and can accommodate families. **ACCOMMODATIONS** 93 rooms and 2 suites, air-conditioning, private safe, minibar, telephone, cable TV **FACILITIES AND SERVICES** Internet access in communal areas, parking, convenience store, pool, conference room, gym, business center, laundry, room service, airport shuttle **CREDIT CARDS** Amex, Diners, MasterCard, Visa
Avenida Boa Viagem, 5576, Boa Viagem
TEL (81) 3462-6454   www.boaviagempraia.com.br

Dorisol Recife Grande Hotel $$
Right on the sea front, this former Sheraton Hotel offers very professional service. The understated décor features wicker furniture, though most rooms (excepting the luxury suites) have just a side sea view. Check with the security guards first for access to the private beach. The restaurant has a good wine list and is run by Miguel, a chef from Madeira. **ACCOMMODATIONS** 177 rooms and 21 suites, Internet access, air-conditioning, tub, private safe, minibar, telephone, cable TV **FACILITIES AND SERVICES** Internet access in communal areas, bar, parking, florist, convenience store, pool, playground, volleyball court, restaurant, conference room, gym, games room, massage room, video room, beauty parlor, sauna, business center, currency exchange, 24-hour kitchen, recreational team for adults, guided walking tours, laundry, lifeguard, airport shuttle **CREDIT CARDS** Amex, Diners, MasterCard, Visa
Avenida Bernardo Vieira de Melo, 1624, Piedade, Jaboatão dos Guararapes
TEL and **FAX** (81) 2122-2700 **RESERVATIONS** 2122-2712
www.dorisol.com.br

Mar Hotel Recife $$$$
About 200 meters (660 feet) from fashionable Boa Viagem Beach, this hotel has good business and leisure facilities as well as a large pool. The property is spacious and open, with clean lines and a tiled floor. Rooms overlook either the airport or the pool. The water park was landscaped by noted designer Roberto Burle Marx. **ACCOMMODATIONS** 175 rooms and 32 suites, air-conditioning, tub, private safe, minibar, telephone, cable TV, balcony; Internet access in executive rooms **FACILITIES AND SERVICES** Internet access in communal areas, bar, parking, stores, pool, tennis court, restaurant, conference room, gym, games room, massage room, beauty parlor, sauna, travel agency, car rental, baby-sitting, business center, infirmary, kids club, laundry, travel agency, room service, airport shuttle **CREDIT CARDS** Amex, Diners, MasterCard, Visa
Rua Barão de Souza Leão, 451, Boa Viagem
TEL (81) 3302-4446   www.marhotel.com.br

Pousada Casuarinas $
There is nothing too luxurious or gaudy about this airy but pleasant guesthouse, decorated with regional folk art. It is actually the former private home of its owner, Patrícia Moreira Fontelles, who built the house in 1960 and turned it into a guesthouse in 1994. Patrícia offers personal service and works with local tour operators, and speaks English, French, German, and Portuguese. Rooms overlook the guesthouse grounds. **ACCOMMODATIONS** 14 rooms, air-conditioning, private safe, minibar, cable TV; balcony in 7 rooms; ceiling fan in some rooms **FACILITIES AND SERVICES** Internet access in communal areas, bar, pool, orchard **CREDIT CARDS** not accepted
Rua Antônio Pedro Figueiredo, 151, Boa Viagem
TEL (81) 3325-4708 **FAX** 3465-2061
www.pousadacasuarinas.com.br

Pousada Villa Boa Vista $
Opened in 2002, this guesthouse is decorated with historical photographs of Recife as well as poems about the city by famous writers. There are three levels of rooms; all are named after streets in Boa Vista. Though there is an on-site restaurant, recreational facilities for guests are modest. **ACCOMMODATIONS** 18 rooms, air-conditioning, minibar, telephone, cable TV; balcony in 4 rooms **FACILITIES AND SERVICES** Internet access in communal areas, parking, restaurant **CREDIT CARDS** Amex, Diners, MasterCard, Visa
Rua Miguel Couto, 81, Boa Vista
TEL and **FAX** (81) 3223-0666
www.pousadavillaboavista.com.br

Shelton Hotel Inn $
This seafront hotel has good facilities for businessmen and leisure travelers. The communal areas are spacious and sophisticated, with rustic décor and wooden, wicker, and straw furniture. The comfortable rooms are much simpler and more traditionally decorated, with ceramic-tiled floors and Formica furnishings. The superior class of rooms have sea view. The hotel pool has a great beach-facing view. **ACCOMMODATIONS** 98 rooms, Internet access, air-conditioning, private safe, minibar, telephone, cable TV **FACILITIES AND SERVICES** Internet access in communal areas, bar, parking, pool, restaurant, conference room, gym, sauna, business center, 24-hour kitchen, valet parking, shuttle service to airport and local attractions **CREDIT CARDS** Amex, Dinners, MasterCard, Visa
Avenida Bernardo Vieira de Melo, 694, Piedade, Jaboatão dos Guararapes
TEL (81) 2123-4343 **FAX** 2123-4344

WHERE TO EAT

Anjo Solto $
This *creperie* in the Galeria Joana d'Arc mall serves a variety of well-made crêpes. The wine list, though short, is adequate and reasonably priced. Originally popular just with local artists, today it draws a more diversified adult clientele. Despite its trendy atmosphere (including high-quality electronica playing in the background), this is still a cozy spot for couples. **CUISINE** crêpes, salads **CREDIT CARDS** Diners, MasterCard
Avenida Herculano Bandeira, 513, Galeria Joana d'Arc, Pina
TEL (81) 3325-0862 **OPEN** Sun – Thu, 6pm – until the last customer leaves; Fri and Sat, 7pm – until the last customer leaves

Boratcho $
Tucked away in a corner of the Galeria Joana d'Arc, this is a great place for casual groups. The stylish Mexican dishes are all great, and varied. Owner Valdelio de Carvalho is a tattoo artist (who also works in medical tattooing and re-pigmentation); he runs the restaurant with his wife, Renata, and pays special attention to the background music. On Thursday nights in summer, the restaurant's *Sem Noção* project

| **RESTAURANTS** | **$** up to R$50 | **$$** from R$51 up to R$100 | **$$$** from R$101 up to R$150 | **$$$$** above R$150 |

brings in DJs spinning all types of music. CUISINE Mexican CREDIT CARDS Amex, Visa
Avenida Herculano Bandeira, 513, Galeria Joana d'Arc, Pina
TEL (81) 3327-1168 OPEN Tue – Sun, 7pm – until the last customer leaves

Buongustaio Famiglia Giuliano $

This is the place to go to enjoy pasta in a sophisticated atmosphere. The restaurant has several signature dishes, including the spaghetti with fresh tomatoes, basil, fine herbs, and white wine, which is cooked and brought to the table covered in aluminum foil, so that none of the delicious herbal aromas are lost. CUISINE Italian CREDIT CARDS Diners, MasterCard, Visa
Avenida Engenheiro Domingos Ferreira, 3.980, Boa Viagem
TEL (81) 3465-9922 OPEN Mon – Thu, noon – 3pm and 7pm – midnight; Fri and Sat, noon – 4pm and 7pm – midnight; Sun, noon – 4pm and 7pm – 11pm

O Buraquinho $

Visitors to the historic Pátio de São Pedro building (opened in 1984) may initially be disappointed by the lack of activities or attractions at this protected site. Luckily for them, the building is home to the excellent restaurant O Buraquinho, with its authentic informality, delicious regional cuisine, and ridiculously cheap prices. The perfect homemade flavors go well with the friendly service. All the menu options are good, though the choice is limited to galinha cabidela (chicken in blood-enriched sauce), sun-dried beef, and a variety of omelets (including crab, beef jerky, and shrimp). The courtyard features nightly music performances at night, when locals pack the restaurant. Those seeking a quieter dining experience should visit in the day. CUISINE regional CREDIT CARDS not accepted
Pátio de São Pedro, no 3, São José
TEL (81) 3224-3765 OPEN Mon – Sat, 11am – until the last customer leaves

Cafeteria do Instituto Ricardo Brennand $

Visitors to the Institute should be sure to stop by this enchanting café run by Rosa Didier, the woman who makes one of the best bolos-de-rolo (jelly rolls) in Recife. The few tables and comfortable chairs face the beautiful sculpture garden. Highlights of the snack menu include buttered tapioca with Parmesan, manioc cake, sweet corn canjica (sweet corn and milk pudding), and pastel de festa – a sweet and savory deep-fried pasty, filled with ground beef and dusted with sugar. CUISINE café CREDIT CARDS not accepted
Alameda Antônio Brennand, no #, Várzea
TEL (81) 2121-0371 FAX 2121-0370 OPEN Tue – Sun, 1pm – 5pm

Casa de Banhos $

Resembling a large, grand veranda built on a dyke, Casa de Banhos (which means "Bathhouse") is much more notable for its building and location than for its food. Between 1887 and the mid-1920s, the building was a popular bathing spot for the local elite, who thought the surrounding waters had medicinal properties. The highlights of the simple menu are the traditional northeastern broth of either sururu (a local shellfish) or mussels and the peixada, prepared with amberjack or white marlin. The restaurant is accessible by car or by a ten-minute boat crossing from Marco Zero. CUISINE fish and seafood CREDIT CARDS Diners, MasterCard
Arrecifes do Porto do Recife, Km 1, Brasília Teimosa
TEL (81) 3075-8776 RESERVATIONS 3467-9951 OPEN Wed and Thu, 11am – 5pm; Fri – Sun, 11am – 7pm

Casa dos Frios $

This small, refined restaurant inside a traditional delicatessen seats just forty people. Customers reach the restaurant by walking through a magnificent air-conditioned wine cellar stocked with nearly 1,000 bottles – making it no surprise that the wine list is one of Casa dos Frios's great attractions. The best items on the menu are those that show a Portuguese influence (particularly the salted cod dishes), though there are also good meat, pasta, and seafood options. The staff is polite and well trained. There is a branch of this delicatessen in the Graças neighborhood, though it has no restaurant. CUISINE contemporary, fish and seafood CREDIT CARDS Diners, MasterCard, Visa
Avenida Engenheiro Domingos Ferreira, 1920, Boa Viagem
TEL (81) 3327-0612 OPEN Tue and Wed, noon – 3:30pm and 6pm – 11pm; Thu – Sat, noon – 3:30pm and 6pm – midnight

Central $

Opened in 2004, this charmingly decorated restaurant with a retro air has become the favored haunt of local journalists, artists, musicians, and filmmakers. It serves breakfast, lunch, and dinner in a casual setting, open from 8am to "round about midnight" as owner André Rosemberg explains. The menu features interesting sandwiches and a variety of dishes, some with Asian and traditional Jewish influences. Special drinks complete the picture. Customers get to choose the background music courtesy of the beautiful token-operated jukebox, which is stocked with many CDs. It's best to visit at night, when the café takes on the air of a bar. CUISINE Bar food, sandwiches CREDIT CARDS Diners, MasterCard, Visa
Rua Mamede Simões, 144, Boa Vista
TEL (81) 3222-7622 OPEN Mon – Fri, 11am – until the last customer leaves; Sat, 5pm – until the last customer leaves

Cuba do Capibaribe $

Occupying the top floor of the Shopping Paço Alfândega mall, this restaurant has a lovely view of the Capibaribe River and a décor inspired by Cuba, which is also the main influence on the menu. Among the most popular dishes are the delicious roast beef filet, flambéed in rum and served with linguini, as well as the chicken risotto with peas and saffron. The service could be a little more professional, but the dishes are prepared with care and sophistication. The place takes on the air of a nightclub in the evening, with live music and a dance floor. The restaurant also sells top-quality Cuban cigars like Montecristo and Cohiba. CUISINE Cuban CREDIT CARDS Diners, MasterCard, Visa
Shopping Paço Alfândega, Rua da Alfândega, 35, store #P306, Recife Antigo
TEL (81) 3419-7502 OPEN Mon and Tue, noon – 4pm; Wed – Sat, noon – until the last customer leaves; Sun, noon – midnight

Entre Amigos – O Bode $

Scorned by "true" Brazilian haute cuisine chefs, goat meat (bode) earns its rightful place on the menu in this welcoming restaurant-cum-bar. Among the ten goat dishes on offer are stew, tripe, leg, and grilled rump. Grilled goat is served with lima beans, rice, fried manioc, paçoca (fried beef jerky with manioc flour), cheese-thickened pirão sauce, seasoned manioc flour with butter, and pickled salad. The meat is shipped in by exclusive suppliers from the owners' home state of Paraíba. Another major attraction of the menu are the appetizing snacks and ice-old beers, which reinforce the bar-like atmosphere the place takes on in the late afternoon. There is another branch in Espinheiro. CUISINE regional CREDIT CARDS Amex, Diners, MasterCard, Visa

| PRICES | HOTELS (couple) | $ up to R$150 | $$ from R$151 up to R$300 | $$$ from R$301 up to R$500 | $$$$ above R$500 |

Rua Marquês de Valença, 50, Boa Viagem
TEL (81) 3466-2023, for delivery 3466-8282 OPEN Mon – Thu, 11am – 1am; Fri and Sat, 11am – 3am; Sun, 11am – midnight

La Cuisine Bistrô $

This restaurant serves classic French cuisine as well as simpler dishes such as stylish salads and sandwiches. One of the best sandwiches is the leg of lamb in pita bread with mint-marinated onions, crispy lettuce, and mozzarella gratin. The steak in Roquefort sauce with peeled tomato and basil risotto is another good choice; the meat is cooked to order and is beautifully complemented by the risotto. For dessert, try the delicious apple pie, with caramel syrup and cinnamon ice cream. CUISINE French, snack food CREDIT CARDS Diners, MasterCard
Avenida Boa Viagem, 560, Pina
TEL (81) 3327-4073 RESERVATIONS 3466-0555 OPEN Mon – Wed, noon – 11pm; Thu, noon – midnight; Fri, noon – 1am; Sat, 1pm – 1am; Sun, 1pm – 11pm

Leite $

Opened by a Portuguese transplant at the end of the empire era, in 1882, this absolute classic in the heart of Recife is one of the oldest restaurants in the country. Leite is still run by a Portuguese family, which accounts for the strong Portuguese influence on the extensive menu (which also has some Brazilian regional dishes). The hallmarks of the menu are quality ingredients and culinary competence, as seen in recipes like *bacalhau à moda do chef* (salted cod grilled with onions, boiled potatoes, olives, olive oil, and garlic). You must save room for dessert; the *cartola do Leite* (grilled banana and cream cheese, covered in sugar and cinnamon) is legendary. CUISINE Portuguese, international CREDIT CARDS Amex, Diners, MasterCard, Visa
Praça Joaquim Nabuco, 147, Santo Antônio
TEL (81) 3224-7977 OPEN Sun – Fri, 11am – 4pm

Parraxaxá $

"*Parraxaxá!*" is the legendary cry of marauding *cangaceiro* bandits – so it should come as no surprise that this restaurant honors the culture of the *sertão*, not only with its menu but with its music, décor, and waiters' costumes (modeled on typical *bandito* outfits). The dishes served in the buffet are all regional specialties, including sun-dried beef, *baião-de-dois* (the so-called manioc lasagna), baby goat (kid), corn-fed chicken, and *paçoca* (ground sun-dried beef, clarified butter, manioc flour, and onions). Although the restaurant is not on the waterfront, the sea breeze reaches the open-plan eating area. There is a small store at the entrance selling manioc bread, homemade sweets, and typical *sertanejo* craftwork. The original branch of this restaurant is in Casa Forte. CUISINE regional CREDIT CARDS MasterCard, Visa
Rua Baltazar Pereira, 32, Boa Viagem
TEL (81) 3463-7874 OPEN Mon – Thu, 11:30am – 10pm; Fri, 11:30am – 11pm; Sat, 6am – 11pm; Sun, 6am – 10pm

Portoferreiro $

This restaurant is named for a village in northern Portugal that is known for preserving the country's gastronomic tradition. Understated and elegant, inside a beautiful old building, Portoferreiro the restaurant is equally distinguished, with its excellent wine list and wonderful menu showing Italian, French, and Portuguese influences. Lamb filet with mushroom risotto and fresh asparagus is very popular, as is one of the house suggestions: rondelli with mozzarella and spinach in an Emmentaler cheese sauce. The menu offers more unusual dishes such as duckling in white wine with caramelized pear and apple purée. A piano, flute, and violin trio plays live music during dinner on Thursdays, Fridays, and Saturdays. CUISINE varied, international CREDIT CARDS Amex, Diners, MasterCard, Visa
Avenida Rui Barbosa, 458, Graças
TEL (81) 3423-2795 RESERVATIONS 3423-0854 OPEN Mon – Thu, noon – 3:30pm and 7pm – midnight; Fri and Sat, noon – 2am; Sun, noon – 4:30pm

Restaurante da Mira $

Eccentric is the best word for this hospital-themed restaurant inside the house of its owners, a mother and her five children. It was son Edmilson ("The Menu Man") who invented the curious terminology that makes a visit to Mira so memorable. To get to the tables, you first pass through the "surgical center" (kitchen), where 65 year-old Almira will allow you help with her expert preparations. After your meal, you are welcome to take a nap in the "UTI" room (Portuguese for ICU). The menu itself features "*galinha indexada* ("operated-on chicken"), really *galinha ao molho pardo* (chicken in blood sauce). The jokes may be entertaining, but it is the flavor of this impeccably prepared homemade regional cuisine that leaves its mark on the memory, prepared as it has always been since the restaurant opened almost thirty years ago. CUISINE regional CREDIT CARDS not accepted
Rua Eurico Chaves, 916, Casa Amarela
TEL (81) 3268-6241 RESERVATIONS 9973-3274 OPEN Daily, noon – 6pm

Tasca $

This restaurant serves carefully prepared traditional Portuguese cuisine in a very pleasant atmosphere. The big attraction is the rare Norwegian codfish Porto Imperial, which is available in several main dish preparations and also used in the restaurant's signature fish cakes. One of the most popular dishes is the thick codfish cutlet, sprinkled with garlic and baked with onions, potatoes, Portuguese olives, parsley, and olive oil. Tasca serves an excellent stew on Sundays, with thirteen types of meat, sausage, and smoked meat, as well as vegetables served *al dente* and thickened *pirão* sauce. The two owners are always there, circulating among the customers and also supervising the kitchen. CUISINE Portuguese, international CREDIT CARDS Amex, Diners, MasterCard
Rua Dom José Lopes, 165, Boa Viagem
TEL (81) 3326-6309 OPEN Tue – Thu, 6:30pm – midnight; Fri and Sat, 6:30pm – 2am; Sun, noon – 4pm

Wiella Bistrô $

Chef Claudemir Barros has developed his extraordinary talent at traditional restaurants throughout Recife, as well as while training in São Paulo with chef Alex Atala. The menu features intelligently-prepared international cuisine that makes good use of local ingredients. For starters, try deep-fried *pastéis* with beef jerky, cream cheese, and pumpkin filling. The snoqk in grape sauce is particularly delicious, as are other highly recommended main dishes such as duck *confit* with polenta purée and penne with shrimp in coconut sauce. Some of the recipes come from the family of the owners, the Wiethaeuper bothers. Among the best of these is the crunchy cashew nut *pavê*, a layered cream dessert. CUISINE international CREDIT CARDS Amex, Diners, MasterCard, Visa
Shopping Decoração, Avenida Domingos Ferreira, 1274, Boa Viagem
TEL (81) 3463-3108 OPEN Tue – Thu, noon – midnight; Fri and Sat, noon – 1am

SERVICES

Airport – Aeroporto Internacional dos Guararapes
Praça Ministro Salgado Filho, no #, Imbiribeira
TEL (81) 3464-4353

| RESTAURANTS | $ up to R$50 | $$ from R$51 up to R$100 | $$$ from R$101 up to R$150 | $$$$ above R$150 |

Bus Station – Rodoviária
Rodovia BR-232, Km 16
TEL (81) 3452-1103

Tourist Information – Centro de Informações Turísticas (Airport)
Praça Ministro Salgado Filho, no #, Imbiribeira
TEL (81) 3341-6090 OPEN Daily, 24 hours

Tourist Information – Centro de Informações Turísticas (Bus Station)
Rodovia BR-232, Km 16
TEL (81) 3452-1892 OPEN Daily, 7am – 7pm

Rio de Contas – Bahia

AREA CODE 77 POPULATION 13,695 DISTANCE Salvador 673 kilometers (418 miles), Lençóis 225 kilometers (140 miles) ACCESS From Salvador take BA-142 and then BA-148

WHERE TO STAY

Pousada Rio de Contas $
This guesthouse, housed in a very old building, is among the better options in the city. The main lobby has an interesting collection of objects, paintings, and period photographs. In addition to the the comfortable, airy, and well-lit rooms, there is also a pretty garden, a circular pool, and hammocks slung on the large veranda out front. ACCOMMODATIONS 11 rooms and 2 suites, minibar, TV, ceiling fan FACILITIES AND SERVICES parking, pool CREDIT CARDS not accepted
Rua Doutor Basílio Rocha, 40, Centro
TEL and FAX (77) 3475-2090, 3248-6999
www.pousadariodecontas.com.br

Raposo Chalé $
This very pleasant, quiet guesthouse (and accompanying campsite) is surrounded by woodlands. Some rooms have a lovely view of the valley and the mountains, as the building is right at the foot of the range. The rooms are spacious; be sure to reserve one with valley view. Owner Luiz Carlos Ribeiro Farias makes beautiful wood sculptures, which are on display all over the guesthouse. The small gift-shop sells cachaça, crafts, and T-shirts. The restaurant served good regional cuisine (see Where to Eat) – some of the ingredients come from the organic vegetable garden on the property. ACCOMMODATIONS 14 rooms and 7 chalets, minibar, telephone, TV, ceiling fan; hammock in some rooms FACILITIES AND SERVICES bar, soccer field, parking, fishing lake, stores, pool, orchard, volleyball court, restaurant, walking trails CREDIT CARDS Visa
Rodovia BA-148 (Estrada Rio de Contas–Livramento), Km 8
TEL and FAX (77) 3475-2111 www.raposochale.com.br

WHERE TO EAT

Café Colonial $
Just behind the Igreja Matriz church, this café serves delicious savory pies and a selection of sweet cakes in a relaxed atmosphere, complete with pleasant background music. CUISINE snack food CREDIT CARDS not accepted
Travessa São Bento, no #
OPEN Daily, 5pm – 10pm

Frango na Brasa $
This restaurant with outdoor tables offers a pleasant, simple atmosphere facing the square. The dish of the day could be any variety of grilled meats or even the more elaborate sundried beef with rice, feijão tropeiro (beans with spicy sausage), cortadinho de palma (diced and braised prickly pear), salad, and seasoned manioc flour. The homemade food is always cooked with care. CUISINE bar food, homemade, barbecue, regional CREDIT CARDS not accepted
Praça da Matriz, 433
OPEN Daily, 11am – 8pm

Orquidarium $
Rio de Janeiro-born owner Antonio Toscano is not only a botanist but an avid orchid lover, which explains why beautiful speciments of the flower decorate his restaurant. Customers can leaf through books on flowers and plants while listening to good music at the bar. The menu features excellent Italian pasta as well as traditional Portuguese dishes like salted cod and vegetables, baked in a wood-burning oven and drizzled with olive oil (serves two). CUISINE Italian, Portuguese, bar food CREDIT CARDS Visa
Largo do Rosário, 89
TEL (77) 3475-2251 OPEN Thu – Sat, 7pm – 11:30pm; Sun, noon – 4:30pm

Restaurante do Raposo Chalé $
This is one of the best places in the area to savor dishes from the sertão, including roast mutton, pirão de parida (corn-fed chicken with manioc flour), and quenga (corn-fed chicken with grated sweet corn). The typical accompaniments and side dishes like fried manioc are also delicious. The restaurant is inside the Raposo Chalé guesthouse, which is on the way down the mountain range, between Rio de Contas and Livramento. There is a lovely view of the garden and mountains in the distance. The owner produces and serves an organic cachaça aged in oak barrels. CUISINE bar food, regional CREDIT CARDS Visa
Rodovia BA-148 (Estrada Rio de Contas–Livramento), Km 8
TEL (77) 3475-2111 OPEN High season: daily, 11:30am – 9pm; low season: daily, 11:30am – 3pm www.raposochale.com.br

Salvador – Bahia

AREA CODE 71 POPULATION 2,673,560 DISTANCES Aracaju 337 kilometers (209 miles), Maceió 617 kilometers (383 miles), Rio de Janeiro 1726 kilometers (1072 miles), São Paulo 2025 kilometers (1258 miles) ACCESS Take BR-101, BR-324 or BA-099 (the Linha Verde highway) WHEN TO VISIT January and February, for festivities in honor of Nosso Senhor do Bonfim and Iemanjá; Carnival; June, for the São João festivities
www.salvador.ba.gov.br

WHERE TO STAY

Atlantic Tower $$
Usually occupied by executives, this hotel houses tourists in the high season. The rooms are spacious and well-equipped, but communal areas lack charm and are not so well kept. From the fifth floor up, some rooms have a sea view. ACCOMMODATIONS 79 apartments, Internet access in communal areas, air-conditioning, private safe, minibar, telephone, cable TV FACILITIES AND SERVICES parking, pool, restaurant, conference room, sauna, travel agency, business center, 24-hour kitchen, valet parking CREDIT CARDS Amex, Diners, MasterCard, Visa
Avenida Oceânica, 1545, Ondina
TEL (71) 2203-3000 RESERVATIONS 0800-701-1009
FAX 3237-4668

A Casa das Portas Velhas $$$
Five minutes from Pelourinho, this sophisticated hotel occupies a 230-year-old building, with décor including an-

tique doors. All the rooms are individually decorated and offer numerous amenities including personal care items sound equipment and a DVD player. There is no pool, but the outer area has a Jacuzzi. If you wish to have lunch, order one day in advance. English and German are spoken. **ACCOMMODATIONS** 14 rooms and 1 suite, Internet access, air-conditioning, private safe, minibar, telephone, cable TV, ceiling fan **FACILITIES AND SERVICES** Internet access in communal areas, bar, parking, Jacuzzi, reading room, guide recommendation, shuttle service to local attractions **CREDIT CARDS** Amex, Diners, MasterCard, Visa
Largo da Palma, 6, Santana
TEL (71) 3324-8400 **FAX** 3321-5677
www.acasadasportasvelhas.com.br

Convento do Carmo Hotel $$$$

One of the largest historic luxury hotels in Brazil, the Convento do Carmo served as the Dutch military headquarters in 1624 and later housed 98 Carmelite monks. Renovations and refurbishments have blended refinement with historical and architectural features from the 17th and 18th centuries. The hotel is comprised of two cloisters housing 79 suites, with luxuries such as Egyptian cotton bed linen. The larger cloister houses the restaurant, which specializes in Portuguese cuisine and is open to non-residents. The museum and sacristy are closed for renovations until 2008. English, French, and Spanish are spoken. **ACCOMMODATIONS** 79 suites, Internet access, air-conditioning, private safe, minibar, telephone, cable TV; tub in 5 rooms **FACILITIES AND SERVICES** bar, Jacuzzi, pool, restaurant, gym, massage room, sauna, spa, laundry, pillow menu, champagne upon check-in; butler (master suite) **CREDIT CARDS** Amex, Diners, MasterCard, Visa
Rua do Carmo, 1, Santo Antônio
TEL (71) 3327-8400 **RESERVATIONS** 3327-8410 **FAX** 3327-8401

Hotel Catharina Paraguaçu $$

Location is this hotel's forte: in the Rio Vermelho neighborhood a short hop from the historical center, it's located near busy nightlife and only two blocks from the beach. The historical building has been completely renovated and refurbished with tiles painted by local artists and craftwork from Maragogipinho. The delicious breakfast includes tapioca *cuscuz* and an irresistible *bolo de estudante*. **ACCOMMODATIONS** 25 rooms and 7 suites, air-conditioning, private safe, minibar, cable TV **FACILITIES AND SERVICES** Internet access in communal areas, parking, restaurant; kitchen closes at 10:30pm **CREDIT CARDS** Amex, Diners, MasterCard, Visa
Rua João Gomes, 128, Rio Vermelho
TEL (71) 3334-0089 **RESERVATIONS** and **FAX** 3334-0089, 3334-2414
www.hotelcatharinaparaguacu.com.br

Hotel Sofitel Salvador $$$

Sited atop a hill with a wonderful view of the sea at Itapuã, on the way to the fashionable beaches of Stella Maris and Flamengo, this is an excellently located hotel for anyone wanting to enjoy the city's beaches. Elegant and luxurious, it offers impeccable service. Facilities include an enormous pool and plenty of leisure options. The hotel has gone "green" with a garbage collection system, energy-saving light sensors, and water treatment system that reflect concern for the environment. **ACCOMMODATIONS** 204 rooms and 2 suites, Internet access, air-conditioning, private safe, minibar, cable TV **FACILITIES AND SERVICES** Internet access in communal areas, bar, soccer field, golf course, parking, crafts store, pool, playground, soccer court, tennis court, restaurant, conference room, gym, games room, massage room, gallery, sauna, 24-hour kitchen, recreational team for adults and children, guided walking tours, valet parking, beach service, airport shuttle **CREDIT CARDS** Amex, Diners, MasterCard, Visa
Rua da Passárgada, no #, Itapuã
TEL (71) 2106-8500 **FAX** 2106-8536 www.accorhotels.com.br

Pestana Bahia $$$$

Formerly the Meridien Hotel, this hotel was renovated by 2001 and now caters mostly to business travelers, but also attracts honeymoon couples. The pool offers a sea view, as do the 23 floors of rooms, which are divided into seven categories differing by floor, décor, and size. The beach, however, is rocky and not suitable for swimming. **ACCOMMODATIONS** 430 rooms, air-conditioning, private safe, minibar, telephone, cable TV, balcony; Jacuzzi in presidential suites; Internet access in some rooms **FACILITIES AND SERVICES** bar, convenience store, pool, restaurant, conference room, gym, massage room, beauty parlor, sauna, travel agency, business center, currency exchange, recreational team for children (pool), 24-hous room service, beach service, airport shuttle **CREDIT CARDS** Amex, Diners, MasterCard, Visa
Rua Fonte do Boi, 216, Rio Vermelho
TEL (71) 2103-8000 **RESERVATIONS** 0800-266-332
FAX 2103-8001, 2103-8066. www.pestanahotels.com.br

Pousada do Boqueirão $$

This guesthouse caters to foreign travelers (the staff speak Italian, Spanish, and English). Located in the upper part of the city in a tastefully decorated historical building, it commands a magnificent view of Todos os Santos Bay. Opened in 1993, the hotel offers limited leisure facilities restricted to a cable TV room and a bar. Rooms offer a view of the sea or the historical center. There are also five dormitories with communal bathroom. Italian owner Fernanda Cabrini knows Salvador like the back of his hand. **ACCOMMODATIONS** 10 rooms, Internet access, air-conditioning, private safe, minibar, telephone, ceiling fan; 5 dormitories with communal bathroom **FACILITIES AND SERVICES** bar, cable TV **CREDIT CARDS** Amex, Visa
Rua Direita do Santo Antônio, 48, Santo Antônio
TEL (71) 3241-2262 **FAX** 3241-8064
www.pousadaboqueirão.com.br

Redfish $$

This colonial-style guesthouse with rustic décor, in operation near Pelourinho since 2003, has a lovely view of Todos os Santos Bay. The hotel employs staff who can speak English and is very popular with foreign visitors. With only eight rooms, it's a very pleasant spot and a good choice for those who want to be near the historical center. **ACCOMMODATIONS** 8 rooms, air-conditioning, private safe, minibar, telephone, ceiling fan **FACILITIES AND SERVICES** Internet access in communal areas, laundry **CREDIT CARDS** Visa
Ladeira do Boqueirão, 1, Santo Antônio
TEL (71) 3241-0639 **RESERVATIONS** 3243-8473 **FAX** 3326-2544
www.hotelredfish.com

Sol Victoria Marina $$

Excellently located on the avenue locally known as Corredor da Vitória, this hotel offers a wonderful view of Todos os Santos Bay from some rooms. A great attraction here is the cable car down to a pier with pool and Thai restaurant/bar. **ACCOMMODATIONS** 155 rooms and 5 suites, Internet access, air-conditioning, private safe, minibar, telephone, cable TV **FACILITIES AND SERVICES** Internet access in communal areas, bar, nightclub, parking, convenience store, pier, pool, restaurant, conference room, equipment rental **CREDIT CARDS** Amex, Diners, MasterCard, Visa
Avenida 7 de Setembro, 2068, Vitória
TEL (71) 3336-7736 **FAX** 3336-0507 www.solexpress.com.br

RESTAURANTS	$ up to R$50	$$ from R$51 up to R$100	$$$ from R$101 up to R$150	$$$$ above R$150

Solar Santo Antônio $$

This 18th-century building has only two rooms, but guests staying here find themselves immersed in the culture of Bahia. The house's owner, Dimitri, is of one of the city's most fervent disciples. Born in Morocco, Dimitri lived in Portugal for many years and before settling in Salvador, which he is passionate about. English, Spanish, Italian and French are spoken. **ACCOMMODATIONS** 2 rooms, minibar, ceiling fan, airport shuttle **CREDIT CARDS** not accepted
Rua Direita de Santo Antônio, 177, Santo Antônio
TEL (71) 3242-6455 www.salvadorcultural.com.br

Tropical da Bahia $$

Formerly the Hotel Bahia, this 1940s hotel was one of the first modernist buildings in the city. Time, however, has left its mark on the building, evident in the faded carpet and other deterioration. The décor includes murals by Carybé. Business facilities are available and most guests are there on business. The Cravo e Canela restaurant, also open to non-guests, serves regional and international food. **ACCOMMODATIONS** 244 rooms and 9 suites, private safe, minibar, hairdryer, telephone, cable TV; air-conditioning in some rooms, tub in superior rooms **FACILITIES AND SERVICES** Internet access in communal areas, bar, parking, snack bar, stores, pool, natural pool, restaurant, gym, games room, reading room, beauty parlor, travel agency, business center, currency exchange, 24-hour kitchen **CREDIT CARDS** Amex, Diners, MasterCard, Visa
Avenida Sete de Setembro, 1537, Campo Grande
TEL (71) 2105-2000 **RESERVATIONS** 0800-7012670
FAX 2105-2035 www.tropicalhotel.com.br

Vila Galé Salvador $$

This hotel, opened in 2003, sits next to museums, the historical center, and the bustle of Barra and Rio Vermelho. The highlight here is the exceptional sea view. **ACCOMMODATIONS** 200 rooms and 24 suites, Internet access, air-conditioning, private safe, minibar, hairdryer, telephone, cable TV; Jacuzzi in suites **FACILITIES AND SERVICES** Internet access in communal areas, bar, parking, Jacuzzi, convenience store, pool, playground, restaurant, conference room, gym, sauna, travel agency, business center, 24-hour kitchen, laundry **CREDIT CARDS** Amex, Diners, MasterCard, Visa
Rua Morro do Escravo Miguel, 320, Ondina
TEL (71) 3263-8888 **RESERVATIONS** 0800-284-8818
FAX 3263-8800
www.vilagale.pt/hoteis/bahia/salvador

WHERE TO EAT

Acarajé da Cira $

In business for more than four decades, this restaurant is owned by Jaciara de Jesus Santos, known as Cira. Cira took over the *tabuleiro* at the age of twelve, after learning the tricks of the trade from her mother. To this day, she gets up at 4am to supervise a team of thirty employees. Most raw ingredients are bought at the São Joaquim market; the smoked shrimp and *dendê* palm oil have come from the same supplier for years. The restaurant also serves *abará*, fried fish, tamarind compote, and other delicacies. The branch in Mariquita is run by one of Cira's daughters. **CUISINE** regional **CREDIT CARDS** not accepted
Rua Aristides Milton, no #, Itapuã (in front of Posto 12 bar)
TEL (71) 3249-4170 **OPEN** Daily, 10:30am – 11pm

Acarajé da Dinha $

Run by the same family for more than sixty years, this *tabuleiro* serves some of the most famous *acarajés* in Salvador, prepared with quality ingredients. They also serve such delights as *passarinha* (cow spleen), *bolinho-de-estudante*, and *cocada preta* (coconut dessert) made with *rapadura* (hard brown sugar). Cláudia de Assis helps runs the restaurant, once owned by her great-grandmother and named after her mother. **CUISINE** regional **CREDIT CARDS** not accepted
Largo de Santana, no #, Rio Vermelho
TEL (71) 3334-1703, 3334-9715 **OPEN** Mon – Fri, 4:30pm – midnight; Sat and Sun, 11am – midnight

Acarajé da Loura $

First, the backstory: Deny Costa Ramos, known as Loura, started out as a surfer and only prepared her first *acarajé* after a bet with a friend. She became good at it, and, after testing out her fare at a party, she opened a restaurant. Fifteen years later, she has eleven employees. Always packed, the restaurant serves other food such as *abará*, *passarinha*, and on Fridays, *sarapatel*. **CUISINE** regional **CREDIT CARDS** not accepted
Avenida Santa Luzia, no #, Horto Florestal (near the park's exit)
TEL (71) 3232-6805, 9937-5814 **OPEN** Mon – Fri, 4pm – until the last customer leaves

Acarajé da Regina $

Regina dos Santos Conceição opened her first restaurant in Graça 25 years ago. Then came one in Rio Vermelho – the only one that opens seven days a week – and another in the Parque Metropolitano de Pituaçu park. She still makes the bean mass for the *acarajés*, which she sends out to the restaurants run by her children, nieces, and nephews. They also serve *abará*, *cocada*, and *bolinho-de-estudante*. **CUISINE** regional **CREDIT CARDS** not accepted
Largo de Santana, no #, Rio Vermelho
TEL (71) 3232-7542, 8115-3842 **OPEN** Mon – Fri, 3pm – 10pm; Sat, Sun and holidays, 10am – 10pm

Agdá $

This restaurant has been serving reasonably priced, generous helpings of well-seasoned fish and seafood for some four decades. The crab *moqueca* arrives bubbling at the tableamid a mouthwatering aroma. For the health-conscious, there's a version made without *dendê* palm oil. The restaurant is a simple, rather unkempt, but friendly spot. The waitresses wear the typical white local dresses and seem to enjoy their work. The restaurant's reliable supplier (in Valença) has been delivering pre-cleaned, sliced fish and seafood for around fifteen years. **CUISINE** regional **CREDIT CARDS** Diners, MasterCard, Visa
Rua Orlando Moscoso, 1, Praia dos Artistas, Boca do Rio
TEL (71) 3461-3375 **OPEN** Tue – Sun, 11:30am– midnight

Amado $$

Chef Edinho Engel brings to Salvador the ingenuity and art he showed while in charge at the impeccable Manacá restaurant in Camburi, on the north coast of São Paulo. The menu consists of contemporary cuisine with an emphasis on Brazilian, especially Bahian, flavors. It overlooks Todos os Santos Bay. **CUISINE** Contemporary **CREDIT CARDS** Diners, MasterCard, Visa
Avenida do Contorno, 660
TEL (71) 3322-3520 **OPEN** Mon – Thu, noon – 3pm and 7pm – midnight; Fri – Sat, noon – 4pm and 7pm – 1am; Sun, noon – 4pm

Bar da Ponta $

This bar-restaurant is as modern as its clientele and shares ownership with the trendy Trapiche Adelaide, both overlooking Todos os Santos Bay. Large windows stay open to let in the breeze. At the end of the day you can admire the sunset; after dark, candle-lit tables provide subdued light-

| PRICES | HOTELS (couple) | $ up to R$150 | $$ from R$151 up to R$300 | $$$ from R$301 up to R$500 | $$$$ above R$500 |

ing. The menu includes appetizers and grilled dishes. Skewers of curd cheese and pineapple or shrimp with fresh heart of palm in ginger sauce are very popular, as is the fillet steak in Dijon mustard sauce. CUISINE bar food CREDIT CARDS Diners, MasterCard, Visa
Praça dos Tupinambás, 2 (Avenida do Contorno), Comércio
TEL (71) 3326-2211 OPEN Mon – Sat, 5:30pm – 1am

Bate-Boca $
This restaurant offers traditional local supper every Sunday starting at 6pm. Cooked by the owner's mother, the meal consists of two kinds of soup, pasta, and a wide variety of savory and sweet dishes, as well as hot drinks (chocolate, coffee, tea) and natural juices. The bean soup is exceptional, as are the desserts. During the week, the restaurant offers an à la carte menu featuring simple dishes like Jorge Amado (fillet steak in Madeira sauce, served with French fries, rice, seasoned manioc flour, and fried banana). CUISINE Brazilian, regional, varied CREDIT CARDS Diners, MasterCard, Visa
Alameda Antunes, 56, Barra Avenida
TEL (71) 3264-3821 OPEN Daily, noon – 11pm

Boteco do França $
This is a good place to have fun at night in Rio Vermelho, though it also serves lunch and dinner. Music including genres such as MPB, rock, and jazz forms a good accompaniment to the appetizers and ice-cold beer. Besides the outdoor seating, there are two indoor rooms, one of which is air-conditioned. The dishes are well cooked, but the service is rather slow and ca'nt always cope at busy times. CUISINE Brazilian, bar food CREDIT CARDS Amex, Diners, MasterCard, Visa
Rua Borges dos Reis, 24-A, Rio Vermelho
TEL (71) 3334-2734 OPEN Tue – Sun, noon – until the last customer leaves

Cantina Cortile $
This typical Italian trattoria operates alongside two other restaurants in a large complex that even has a playground for children. Divided into four areas, the complex has a warm atmosphere despite its size. Most of the pasta is made on the premises. The wine list has about four hundred bottles of several nationalities, stored in a beautiful, spacious, air-conditioned cellar – well worth a visit. CUISINE Italian CREDIT CARDS Amex, Diners, MasterCard, Visa
Rua Adelaide Fernandes da Costa, no #, Parque Costa Azul
TEL (71) 3341-3572 RESERVATIONS 3341-0959 OPEN Daily, noon until the last customer leaves

Cien Fuegos $
Excellent Mexican food is served on pretty clay platters in this welcoming restaurant that also functions as a bar. Four brothers, sons of Cubans, opened the business in 1998. The restaurant' comprises several small rooms, one with tiled benches and an interesting mirror mosaic mural. Papier maché dolls and other delicate items decorate the walls. Chicken, beef, or shredded beef jerky fill the excellent tacos, which come with refried beans, Mexican salsa, grated cheese, and shredded lettuce. CUISINE Mexican, bar food CREDIT CARDS Amex, Diners, MasterCard, Visa
Rua Alexandre Gusmão, 60, Rio Vermelho
TEL (71) 3334-7711 RESERVATIONS 3334-7915 OPEN Mon – Sat, 7pm – 2am

Jardim das Delícias $
This well-kept old building in Pelourinho really does feel like a garden (jardim), with its trees, cobblestones, small tables decorated with flowers, and live music – chorinho and MPB

at lunchtime and jazz and blues during dinner. The menu features dishes from the northeastern interior and coast, with a contemporary touch. The sun-dried beef Gabriela, grilled with a sprinkling of olive oil and sugar, stands out with its special flavor. Attentive service adds to the experience. CUISINE regional, varied CREDIT CARDS Amex, Diners, MasterCard, Visa
Rua João de Deus, 12 (Largo Rosa de Oxalá), Pelourinho
TEL (71) 3321-1449 FAX and RESERVATIONS 3322-7086 OPEN Daily, noon – 1am

Juarez $
This restaurant inside the Mercado do Ouro is best known for its filé do Juarez– a thick cut of fillet steak, crispy outside and bloody inside, with a dark onion sauce that is a house secret: it contains wine. Served with beans, manioc flour, and salad, the dish serves two. The restaurant, which is clean and simple, has been in operation for more than thirty years and filé do Juarez remains the most popular dish to this day. If you enjoy good meat and want to visit a rather chaotic place frequented by locals, you'll enjoy Juarez. CUISINE Brazilian CREDIT CARDS not accepted
Avenida Jequitaia, 804, Mercado do Ouro, Comércio
TEL (71) 9922-3378 OPEN Mon – Sat, 11:30am – 3:30pm

Maria Mata Mouro $$
This restaurant offers refined charm, appetizing contemporary cuisine and – its forte – an excellent wine cellar housing two hundred wines from different countries. Indoor seating is available, as well as outdoor tables in a small courtyard sheltered by trees and plants. The menu features well-presented, delicately flavored dishes such as fresh sea bass in caper sauce, served with potatoes. The restaurant also offers good meat dishes and some regional cuisine. CUISINE contemporary CREDIT CARDS Amex, Diners, MasterCard, Visa
Rua da Ordem Terceira de São Francisco (former Rua Inácio Acioly), 8, Pelourinho
TEL (71) 3321-3929 OPEN Daily, 11:50am – until the last customer leaves

Mercado do Rio Vermelho $
This round-the-clock market known as Mercadão comprises a collection of thirty kiosks (or boxes) to the left of Largo da Mariquita and has a very unsophisticated atmosphere. Go at the end of a long evening for a straightforward meal – moqueca, feijoada, and sarapatel – and a beer.
Largo da Mariquita, no #, Rio Vermelho
TEL (71) 3172-4268 OPEN Daily, 24 hours

Mistura Fina $
This pleasant old building near the Itapuã lighthouse offers a fun beach atmosphere, well-arranged tables, and a menu combining Mediterranean and local food. We recommend the seafood pasta dishes, such as spaghetti cooked al dente with shrimp, fresh tomato sauce and shrimp bisque (shrimp shells simmered in white wine and seasonings). The restaurant serves a good antipasti and salad buffet, charged per kilo. A sommelier helps customers choose wine. CUISINE Italian, regional, seafood CREDIT CARDS Amex, Diners, MasterCard, Visa
Rua Sousa Brito, 41, Itapuã
TEL (71) 3375-2623, 3285-0291 OPEN Mon – Thu, 11:30am – midnight; Fri and Sat, 11:30am – 1am; Sun, 11:30am – 11pm

Paraíso Tropical $$
At of the best restaurants in Salvador chef/owner Beto Pimental cooks local food in a new fashion. Dendê palm oil for example, is replaced by dendê fruit juice, and lime leaves are

| RESTAURANTS | $ up to R$50 | $$ from R$51 up to R$100 | $$$ from R$101 up to R$150 | $$$$ above R$150 |

used instead of coriander, resulting in a more delicate flavor. The restaurant is located on the grounds of a small farm in the middle of the city, yielding particularly pleasant surroundings. Tables are arranged on a suspended veranda at tree-top height. The orchard has more than 4,000 fruit trees, planted and tended by Pimental, who is also an agronomist. An exuberant fruit basket accompanies most dishes (complete with a bag to take home any leftovers). CUISINE regional CREDIT CARDS Amex, Diners, MasterCard, Visa
Rua Edgar Loureiro, 98-B, Cabula
TEL (71) 3384-7464 OPEN Mon – Sat, 11am – 11pm; Sun, 11am – 10pm

Pereira $$

This lovely restaurant offers sophisticated architecture, a sea view, and an outdoor area. The menu features dishes like a rack of lamb in red wine, served with fresh mushroom risotto, and a shrimp and octopus risotto. The *millefeuille* of fillet steak and *foie gras* is the most popular dish. The draft beer, drinks, appetizers, and the excellent *feijoada* on Saturdays are also favorites. CUISINE bar food, contemporary CREDIT CARDS Amex, Diners, MasterCard, Visa
Avenida 7 de Setembro, 3959, Porto da Barra
TEL (71) 3264-6464 OPEN Daily, 6pm – 2am

Ponte Aérea 2 $

Locals fill the tables at Ponte Aérea in the late afternoon, when they take over the sidewalk and invade the tree-lined, dead-end street in Pituba. The bar atmosphere is very agreeable, and there's no shortage of ice-cold beer. The house specialty is rump steak served on a hotplate and cooked to your liking. Appetizing snacks, such as *caldinho de sururu* (shellfish broth) and small codfish cakes, are also served. Take note of the address as there is no name outside the restaurant. The main branch is at the corner of São Paulo and Rio de Janeiro streets, which explains the restaurant's name: *ponte aérea* means "air shuttle", a reference to the regular flights between São Paulo and Rio. CUISINE bar food, meats CREDIT CARDS Diners, MasterCard, Visa
Rua Mato Grosso, 510, Pituba
TEL (71) 3346-3583 OPEN Mon – Fri, 5pm – midnight; Sat and holidays, 11am – midnight

Porto do Moreira $

This popular, traditional restaurant has been at this location in Largo do Mucambinho square since 1966. Once a haunt of celebrated local journalists and artists like Jorge Amado and Glauber Rocha, it serves very generous helpings. One highlight is meat *moqueca*, made with beef, jerked beef, dried shrimp, eggs, and seasonings. Their *sarapatel* (stewed pig's tripe and liver enriched with thickened blood), served on weekends, is a sensation. For dessert, try home-made compotes, made with guava, coconut, pineapple, tamarind, or genipap fruit. CUISINE Brazilian, regional CREDIT CARDS Amex, Diners, MasterCard, Visa
Largo do Mucambinho, 488, Centro
TEL (71) 3322-4112 RESERVATIONS 3322-2814 OPEN Daily, 11:30am – 4pm

Senac $

Visitors to Pelourinho flock to this restaurant-school, which serves good examples of typical local food – some forty daily options including *moquecas* made with salted cod, *surubim* (a freshwater fish), ray and shrimp. The team of cooks, all teachers at the SENAC school, has been led by almost three decades by chef Nivaldo Galdino, who also develops the menu. This practical and economical self-service restaurant has an atmosphere that's somehow simultaneously simple and formal. CUISINE regional CREDIT CARDS Amex, Diners, MasterCard, Visa
Praça José de Alencar, 13–19, Pelourinho
TEL (71) 3324-4550, 3324-4552 OPEN Mon – Sun, 11:30am – 3:30pm and 6:30pm – 10pm

Soho $$

This is the best place for Japanese food in Salvador. With its clean lines and lovely view of Todos os Santos Bay, it offers a beautiful but un-intimidating atmosphere, a polite welcome and efficient service. Chefs prepare sushi and *robatas* at two counters in view of customers. We recommend classic salmon sashimi (with fresh fish from Chile). The sushi rolls have a North American influence, with cream cheese an ingredient in most of them. Local cuisine makes an appearance in some of the *robatas*, such as those made with sun-dried beef, and in some desserts, like banana roll with tapioca and coconut ice cream. CUISINE Japanese CREDIT CARDS Amex, Diners, MasterCard, Visa
Avenida do Contorno, 1010, Pier D, Bahia Marina, Comércio
TEL (71) 3322-4554 RESERVATIONS 3322-8150 OPEN Sun – Thu, noon – 3pm and 7pm – midnight; Fri and Sat, noon – 4pm and 7pm – 1am

Trapiche Adelaide $$

This highly professional restaurant has light, modern décor and a view of Todos os Santos Bay. The contemporary international menu balances meat dishes, pasta, fish, and seafood. We recommend the fillet steak gratin with cheese fondue, surrounded by Parma ham and saffron risotto, or the tagliatelle with shrimp, lime cream and green pepper. Desserts includes small, deep-fried pastries filled with chocolate and hazelnut crunch, served with flambéed bananas. CUISINE contemporary, international CREDIT CARDS Amex, Diners, MasterCard, Visa
Praça dos Tupinambás, 2 (Avenida do Contorno), Comércio
TEL (71) 3326-2211 RESERVATIONS 3326-0443 OPEN Mon – Thu, noon – 3pm and 7pm – 1am; Fri and Sat, noon – 1am; Sun, noon – 5pm

Uauá $

This restaurant's owner, Joana Loiola, specializes in northeastern country cuisine, opening her first restaurant in Itapuã in 1979 and moving to Pelourinho in 1993. The restaurant is named after Uauá, the small town in the *sertão* region of Bahia where she was born. Try the delicious *paçoca*: sun-dried beef pounded in a mortar and then shredded, cooked with onion, coriander, parsley, and manioc flour, then served with banana *farofa* (seasoned manioc flour) and rice. The mutton stew with chayote and pumpkin is also excellent. The restaurant offers both indoor seating and outdoor tables that overlook the calm, diligent work that goes on in the kitchen. CUISINE regional, varied CREDIT CARDS Amex, Diners, MasterCard, Visa
Rua Gregório de Matos, 36, 1st floor, Pelourinho
TEL (71) 3322-1778 OPEN Tue – Sun, 11am – 3pm and 7pm – 11pm

Vida $

This unpretentious, friendly restaurant serves tasty health food, offering vegetarian and white meat dishes, fish, and mussels. The salmon in caper or passion fruit sauce is a tasty choice. During the day, meals are priced per kilo; at night, . in keeping with local custom, the restaurant offers thirty varieties of soup, including traditional recipes like *canja* (chick-

---

PRICES | HOTELS (couple) | $ up to R$150 | $$ from R$151 up to R$300 | $$$ from R$301 up to R$500 | $$$$ above R$500

en broth with rice). CUISINE Brazilian, health food CREDIT CARDS Amex, Diners, MasterCard, Visa
Travessa Macapá, 66, Ondina
TEL (71) 3263-1086. OPEN Daily, 11:30am – 3:30pm and 5:30pm – 9:30pm

Yemanjá $
Overlooking Armação beach and opened almost fifty years ago, this is one of the city's most traditional restaurants. Waitresses dressed in traditional local costume offer friendly service. The twelve varieties of *moquecas*, served in generous portions, are legendary in Salvador, with .and can be prepared with olive oil and low-sodium salt for the health-conscious. At dessert time a waitress circulates with the cart full of delights. Expect long lines on weekends. The restaurant has a branch in Ipanema, Rio de Janeiro. CUISINE regional CREDIT CARDS Amex, Diners, MasterCard, Visa
Avenida Otávio Mangabeira, 4655, Jardim Armação
TEL (71) 3461-9010. Sun – Thu, 11:30am– midnight; Fri and Sat, 11:30am – 1am

SERVICES

Airport – Aeroporto Internacional de Salvador Deputado Luís Eduardo Magalhães
Praça Gago Coutinho, no #, São Cristóvão
TEL (71) 3204-1010 OPEN Daily, 24 hours
www.infraero.com.br

Tourist Information – Bahiatursa
Rua das Laranjeiras, 12, Pelourinho
TEL (71) 3321-2133, 3321-2463, 3370-8694 (main office). Mon, Wed – Sat, 8:30am – 9pm; Tue and Sun, 8:30am – 8pm
Praça Gago Coutinho, no #, São Cristóvão (Airport)
TEL (71) 3204-1244 OPEN Daily, 10am – 11pm
www.bahiatursa.ba.gov.br

Tourist Police Station – Delegacia de Proteção ao Turista
Largo Cruzeiro de São Francisco, 14, Pelourinho
TEL (71) 3322-1188, 3322-7155 OPEN Daily, 24 hours

Tourist Information – Emtursa
Elevador Lacerda, Praça Municipal, no #
TEL (71) 3321-2697, 3322-2598, 3176-4200 OPEN Mon – Fri, 9am – 6pm www.salvadordabahia.ba.gov.br

Santa Cruz Cabrália – Bahia

AREA CODE 73 POPULATION 34,760 DISTANCES Salvador 727 kilometers (452 miles), Porto Seguro 22 kilometers (14 miles), Eunápolis 85 kilometers (53 miles), Vitória 622 kilometers (386 miles) ACCESS From Porto Seguro, take the BR-367 highway for 22 kilometers (14 miles)

WHERE TO STAY

Baía Cabrália $
This hotel, opened in 1987, offers well-equipped rooms and plenty of leisure facilities, including a nightclub and children's playground. The rooms accommodate up to four and sport a beach-inspired déco, including ceramic floors and wooden furniture. ACCOMMODATIONS 116 rooms, air-conditioning, private safe, minibar, telephone, TV, balcony; Internet access in some rooms; Jacuzzi in luxury rooms FACILITIES AND SERVICES Internet access in communal areas, bar, nightclub, parking, hot tubs in 5 rooms, stores, pool, playground, soccer court, tennis court, volleyball court, restaurant, conference room, gym, games room, massage room, video room, beauty parlor, sauna, travel agency, currency exchange, recreational team for adults and children, 24-hour room service, airport shuttle CREDIT CARDS Amex, Diners, MasterCard, Visa
Rua Sidrack Carvalho, 141, Centro
TEL and FAX (73) 3282-8000 www.baiacabralia.com.br

WHERE TO EAT

Maria Nilza $
Maria Nilza cooks for customers in a palm-thatched beach kiosk, serving them herself. Her friendly personal service is famous in the south of Bahia. *Moquecas*, fish, *vatapá*, risottos, and appetizers all feature in her menu. CUISINE regional, fish and seafood CREDIT CARDS not accepted
Rua da Praia, 380, Guaiú
OPEN Daily, 9:30am – 5pm and 6pm – 10pm

Restaurante da Vanda $$
One of best eateries in Cabrália, this twenty-year-old restaurant serves such dishes as sea bass in octopus or shrimp sauce, *moquecas*, and lobster. The dressed crab served in its shell is one of the most popular items. CUISINE fish and seafood CREDIT CARDS not accepted
Rua Frei Henrique de Coimbra, 75, Centro
TEL (73) 3282-1384 OPEN High season: daily, 11am – 1am; low season: 11am – 10pm

Tião Belmonte $
For twenty years, this restaurant has offered a varied menu to suit all tastes: fish, seafood, *moquecas*, lobster, poultry and meat dishes, as well as appetizers. *Caruru* and *vatapá* must be ordered in advance. CUISINE regional, fish and seafood CREDIT CARDS not accepted
Rua Campos Tourinho, 349, Centro
OPEN High season: daily, 11am – 10pm; low season:11am – 8pm

SERVICES

Boat Trips – Navegação Cabrália
Rua do Sossego, no # (near the ferryboat terminal)
OPEN Daily, 7:30am – 5pm

Santo Amaro da Purificação – Bahia

AREA CODE 75 POPULATION 61,079 DISTANCES Salvador 70 kilometers (43 miles) ACCESS From Salvador, take highway BR-234 to the junction with BA-026, then drive along BA-026 and follow the signs for Santo Amaro

WHERE TO STAY

Enseada do Caeiro Eco Resort $$
Tucked deep inside Todos os Santos Bay, 18 kilometers (11 miles) from the city on Itapema beach, this is an excellent place to stay near Santo Amaro. Some rooms overlook the sea, which on this stretch is not suitable for bathing. At a small pottery, guests can learn to work with clay. ACCOMMODATIONS 32 rooms, air-conditioning, minibar, intercom, TV, veranda/balcony with hammock FACILITIES AND SERVICES bar, kayaks, dollhouse, horses, cart, parking, snack bar, stores, pottery, pool, playground, ponies, volleyball court, restaurant, conference room, games room, video room, walking trails CREDIT CARDS MasterCard
Rodovia BA-878, Km 14, Praia de Itapema
TEL (75) 9999-1872 RESERVATIONS and FAX 3264-3000
www.enseadadocaeiro.com.br

RESTAURANTS	$ up to R$50	$$ from R$51 up to R$100	$$$ from R$101 up to R$150	$$$$ above R$150

WHERE TO EAT

Frutos do Mar $

Located in São Brás village on the road to Santo Amaro's beaches, this tiny restaurant perches on the second floor and has just a few tables in the dining room and on the terrace. It offers a view of the mangroves which dominate the backdrop of Todos os Santos Bay. The stews, shrimp, lobster or crab *moquecas* (all serving two) are menu highlights. *Mariscada* (fish, shrimp, crab, and mussels) is a bigger dish and serves four. The family owners do all the cooking and serving. CUISINE regional, fish and seafood CREDIT CARDS Visa
Praça João Damasceno Borges, 10, São Brás
(8 kilometers from Santo Amaro)
TEL (75) 3216-1064, 9929-4812 OPEN Daily, 11:30am – 9pm

Santo Amaro do Maranhão – Maranhão

AREA CODE 98 POPULATION 9,705 DISTANCES São Luís 232 kilometers (144 miles), Barreirinhas 100 kilometers (62 miles) ACCESS The road from Sangue. It best to hire a 4x4 vehicle and hire a guide in Barreirinhas, as the route is confusing WHEN TO VISIT From February to July, when the lakes are full and the dune winds are less strong

WHERE TO STAY

Pousada Água Doce $

This guesthouse, with exposed brick and a huge veranda, stands on the banks of a river (suitable for bathing). The room windows and doors open straight onto the veranda, where breakfast and meals are served. This setup interferes with privacy but forces the guests together, providing a community feel. The staff is very friendly. The air-conditioned rooms have good bathrooms with electric shower (see *Where to Eat*, below). ACCOMMODATIONS 8 rooms, air-conditioning FACILITIES AND SERVICES bar, parking, restaurant, river, TV CREDIT CARDS Visa
Rua Osvaldo Cruz, 27, Centro
TEL and FAX (98) 3369-1105

Solar das Gaivotas $

The large rooms here, all on the second floor, have double windows and river view. A pavilion with carnauba thatched roof affords a lovely view of the river, which flows close to the guesthouse and is good for bathing. The setting makes it one of the best places to stay in the area, but the breakfast and service are poor. ACCOMMODATIONS 9 rooms, air-conditioning FACILITIES AND SERVICES parking, river CREDIT CARDS MasterCard
Rua Osvaldo Cruz, 33, Centro
TEL and FAX (98) 3369-1064

WHERE TO EAT

Restaurante da Pousada Água Doce $

This large carnauba-wood kiosk, belonging to the guesthouse of the same name, faces the Alegre River and is surrounded by leafy mango trees. The manager greets customers personally and serves the freshly cooked food; order ahead to avoid the lines. It's common for some dishes to be off the menu. The home-style food is well cooked and comprises meat, poultry and fish. The highlight of the menu is griddled fish. CUISINE meats, fish, home-made CREDIT CARDS Visa
Rua Osvaldo Cruz, 27, Centro
TEL (98) 3369-1105 OPEN Daily, 7am – 11pm

Santo André – Bahia

AREA CODE 73 Santa Cruz Cabrália DISTANCES Salvador 660 kilometers (410 miles), ACCESS From Porto Seguro, 30 kilometers (19 miles) via BR-367 highway to Santa Cruz Cabrália plus 10 minutes by ferryboat

WHERE TO STAY

Gaili Pousada Restaurante $

This quiet guesthouse is surrounded by 80,000 square meters (20 acres) of gardens and wood. The chalets and rooms are simple and pleasant. Beck, the multilingual (including English) Swiss owner, makes the bread, cakes, and pies served at breakfast. ACCOMMODATIONS 6 chalets, 2 rooms, and 2 suites; air-conditioning, minibar, TV, ceiling fan FACILITIES AND SERVICES Internet access in communal areas, bar, boat, nursery, bicycles, woods, kayaks, parking, horseback riding center, fishing lake, motorboat, pool, jogging track, orchard, tennis court, restaurant, river, massage room, walking trails, travel agency, currency exchange, guided walking tours, beach service, airport shuttle CREDIT CARDS MasterCard, Visa
Avenida Beira-Rio, 1820, Praia de Santo André
TEL (73) 3671-4060 www.gaili.com

Resort Costa Brasilis $$$

This sea-front resort, with lovely gardens and woods, offers spacious rooms with colonial touches. The Premium suite is decorated in Balinese style and has a Jacuzzi. The leisure program, including many water sports, is a big attraction. The hotel also has a spa. ACCOMMODATIONS 92 rooms, 19 bungalows, and 11 suites; Internet access, air-conditioning, private safe, minibar, telephone, cable TV, ceiling fan; Jacuzzi in some rooms FACILITIES AND SERVICES Internet access in communal areas, bar, boat, bicycles, kayaks, fishing equipment, parking, motorboat, stores, period furniture, pool, thermal pool, playground, soccer court, tennis court, volleyball court, sand volleyball court, restaurant, conference room, gym, games room, massage room, beauty parlor, sauna, business center, 24-hour kitchen, recreational team for adults and children, guided walking tours, lifeguard, beach service, airport shuttle CREDIT CARDS Amex, Diners, MasterCard, Visa
Avenida Beira-Mar, 2000, Praia de Santo André
TEL (73) 3282-8200 RESERVATIONS 0800-703-8201, 0800-701-1413 FAX 3282-8219 www.costabrasilis.com.br

Toca do Marlin $$$$

This hotel offers suites with a sea view, Swiss position-control beds and 29" flat-screen TVs. The beach is ideal for walking. Completely built in *ipê* wood, the sumptuous building boasts high ceilings, an Italian floor in the reception and a Spanish floor in communal areas and suites. Works of art and antiques feature in the décor, such as a sofa that belonged to the Javanese Royal Family. The bread and desserts are made in the hotel's own bakery. Inclusive packages are available. Privacy is guaranteed; they don't even have a sign at the entrance. ACCOMMODATIONS 11 suites, Internet access, air-conditioning, position-control beds, private safe, minibar, telephone, cable TV FACILITIES AND SERVICES Internet access in communal areas, wine cellar, bar, boat, bicycles, kayaks, fishing equipment, waterskiing, parking, horseback riding center, motorboat, stores, period furniture, pool, orchard, restaurant, river, conference room, gym, games room, massage room, currency exchange, 24-hour kitchen, recreational team for adults and children, valet parking, beach service, shuttle service to airport and local attractions. CREDIT CARDS Amex, MasterCard, Visa
Rodovia BA-001, Km 40.5, Estrada Santo André–Belmonte
TEL (73) 3671-5009 RESERVATIONS 9985-0380
www.tocadomarlin.com.br

PRICES	HOTELS (couple)	$ up to R$150	$$ from R$151 up to R$300	$$$ from R$301 up to R$500	$$$$ above R$500

São Cristóvão – Sergipe

AREA CODE 79 POPULATION 75,353 DISTANCES Aracaju 23 kilometers (14 miles), Salvador 330 kilometers (205 miles) ACCESS From Aracaju, take Rodovia João Bebe-Água (SE-004 highway)

WHERE TO EAT

Casa da Queijada $
A pleasant surprise in São Cristóvão, this simple sweet shop is run by sisters Givalda and Marieta, who learned their recipes from their mother, the founder of the business. For more than thirty years their *queijadinhas* (coconut cakes), baked *cocada* (coconut dessert), and *caju ameixa* (cashew fruit cooked for so long that they look like prunes) have enjoyed success. They have another store, for sweets, at Praça da Rodoviária, 87. The restaurant also sells tapioca cookies and typical fruit liqueurs, for example genipap and *mangaba*. CUISINE desserts CREDIT CARDS not accepted
Praça da Matriz, 36, Cidade Alta
TEL (79) 3261-1376 OPEN Daily, 8am – noon and 2pm – 6pm

São Luís – Maranhão

AREA CODE 98 POPULATION 978,824 DISTANCES Teresina 463 kilometers (288 miles), Belém 803 kilometers (499 miles) ACCESS BR-135 highway WHEN TO VISIT May for the *bumba-meu-boi* rehearsals, and June for the performances. June and July for the São João festivities
www.saoluis.ma.gov.br

WHERE TO STAY

Brisamar $$
This inexpensive yet comfortable three-story hotel has a pool, some trees, and a breakfast restaurant. It offers large, soft beds, good pillows and showers. The best rooms by far are in the "A" wing, with sea views. ACCOMMODATIONS 109 rooms and 4 suites, Internet access, air-conditioning, minibar, telephone, cable TV FACILITIES AND SERVICES Internet access in communal areas, bar, parking, stores, pool, restaurant, conference room, gym, games room, beauty parlor, 24-hour kitchen, beach service CREDIT CARDS Amex, Diners, MasterCard, Visa
Avenida São Marcos, 12, Ponta d'Areia, (5 kilometers from the center)
TEL (98) 2106-0606 RESERVATIONS 3212-1171 FAX 3212-1153
www.brisamar.com.br

Pousada do Francês $
One of the best places to stay in the center, this lovely three-story building has been completely restored. It doesn't have an elevator, but the best rooms are on the top floor: they have a small mezzanine and view of the sea and city center. The beds are large and comfortable, with good pillows. One weak point is the lighting, which is white and cold. A good breakfast is served daily. ACCOMMODATIONS 29 rooms, Internet access, air-conditioning, minibar, telephone, TV FACILITIES AND SERVICES bar, period furniture, restaurant CREDIT CARDS Amex, Diners, MasterCard, Visa
Rua da Saavedra, 160, Centro
TEL (98) 3232-0879

Pousada Portas da Amazônia $
A good option in the historical center, this guesthouse is near the main attractions. The restored, 1835 building has a cozy, charming atmosphere and décor that respects the original design. The ground-floor communal areas have stone floors, brought from Portugal and typical of houses in São Luís. Rooms are equipped with silent, remote-controlled air-conditioning and have spacious bathrooms. ACCOMMODATIONS 28 suites, air-conditioning, minibar, telephone, TV FACILITIES AND SERVICES Internet access in communal areas, bar, snack bar, travel agency, airport shuttle CREDIT CARDS MasterCard, Visa
Rua do Giz, 129, Centro
TEL (98) 3222-9937 FAX 3221-4193
www.portasdaamazonia.com.br

Rio Poty $$
This large building on Avenida dos Holandeses opened in 2002. Spacious rooms with understated décor overlook Ponta d'Areia, a unswimmable beach with good facilities for landlubbers. Large double beds, small sofas, and fittings such as TV, air-conditioning, minibar, and telephone guarantee guests' comfort in each room. ACCOMMODATIONS 133 rooms and 9 suites, air-conditioning, private safe, minibar, telephone, cable TV; Internet access in luxury rooms FACILITIES AND SERVICES Internet access in communal areas, bar, parking, pool, restaurant, conference room, gym, travel agency, 24-hour kitchen, airport shuttle CREDIT CARDS Amex, Diners, MasterCard, Visa
Avenida dos Holandeses, no #, Quadra 32, Lote 2/5, Praia Ponta d'Areia
TEL (98) 3215-1500 RESERVATIONS 3215-1507 FAX 3227-6576
www.riopotysaoluis.com.br

São Luís Park $$$
Standing near Praia do Calhau, this is one of the city's most luxurious hotels. The imposing lobby is decorated with statues, oil lamps, and replicas of the city's stone fountains. The rooms on the second floor are less damp and smell nicer. They have a double and single bed, wardrobe with drawers, pleasant lighting and marble-topped desk. The bathrooms are spacious and comfortable. A small balcony overlooks the pool. ACCOMMODATIONS 109 suites, Internet access, air-conditioning, private safe, minibar, telephone, cable TV FACILITIES AND SERVICES Internet access in communal areas, bar, woods, soccer field, parking, convenience store, stores, pool, playground, tennis court, volleyball court, restaurant, conference room, gym, games room, sauna, travel agency, 24-hour kitchen, massage room, airport shuttle CREDIT CARDS Amex, Diners, MasterCard, Visa
Avenida Avicênia, no #, Praia do Calhau
TEL (98) 2106-0505 FAX 3235-4921
www.saoluisparkhotel.com.br

WHERE TO EAT

Amendoeira $
This restaurant's specialty is mutton, stewed in coconut milk or served as a barbecued fillet. Another highlight, the sun-dried beef, comes with generous helpings of *baião-de-dois* (rice and beans), banana fritters, fried manioc, and *paçoca* (dried beef pounded with manioc flour). The restaurant also serves examples of Arab cuisine, such as dolma, kibbeh, and kofta. The surroundings are simple and airy, with palm-thatched roof and children's play area. The main branch, opened in the early 1990s in the Olho d'Água neighborhood, is more like a bar, busier and serving more appetizers. CUISINE meats, regional CREDIT CARDS Diners, MasterCard, Visa
Rua dos Tucanos, 18, Parque Atlântico, Calhau
TEL (98) 3248-0228 OPEN Daily, 11am – midnight

Antigamente
A great find right in the middle of the São Luís historical center, Antigamente opened in 1989. It's styled as a traditional bar from the old days, with wooden tables, tablemats, a Portuguese-stone floor and a huge colored mural depicting protected houses in the area. The restaurant offers both

a self-service system and à la carte options. The menu offers local delicacies cooked with care and attention. Try the regional tasting menu: small portions of *arroz de cuxá*, and rice with crab, *cuxá*, shrimp pie, dressed crab served in the shell and crab claws, *vatapá*, and pumpkin purée. At night, customers spill out onto the corner sidewalks, listening to live local and MPB music. Service could be better. CUISINE bar food, regional CREDIT CARDS Amex, Diners, MasterCard, Visa
Rua da Estrela, 220, Centro
TEL (98) 3232-3964 OPEN Mon – Sat, 10am – until the last customer leaves

Armazém da Estrela $$

Next to the cultural center, this complex comprises several different sections in two floors. The bar and sandwich area, which serves a good espresso, are on the lower floor, with neon signs on the old stone walls. A book store and Internet café are also found here. Upstairs, the restaurant itself combines local cuisine with French and Italian elements, serving dishes like sorrel and shrimp risotto or fried fish fillet with buttered vegetables and tapenade (extra-virgin olive oil, dried tomatoes, capers, and olives). CUISINE regional, sandwiches CREDIT CARDS Amex, Diners, MasterCard, Visa
Rua da Estrela, 401, Centro
TEL (98) 3254-1274 RESERVATIONS 3254-1281 OPEN Mon – Fri, noon – 1am; Sat, 6pm – 2am

Auguri $

Quite unlike other city restaurants in terms of atmosphere, this small restaurant is decorated with stills from Fellini films, mirrors, and miniature cars. It serves good pasta dishes, for example ricotta and walnut ravioli in cheese sauce, or seafood spaghetti, both chef's recommendations. A friendly café operates next door, serving a selection of pies, sandwiches and savories. Another branch of the café is located near the Lagoa da Jansen park. CUISINE Italian CREDIT CARDS Amex, Diners, MasterCard, Visa
Avenida dos Holandeses, 6, Quadra 9, Calhau
TEL (98) 3227-5050 OPEN Daily, noon – midnight

Base da Lenoca $

Typical restaurants in Maranhão are called "base". One of the most famous in São Luís is Base da Lenoca, which prepares the widest variety of crab dishes. The most popular dish in this sea-front kiosk on São Marcos beach is crab salad – so generous that it serves two as a main course – served with chopped tomatoes, onion and coriander. CUISINE regional, fish and seafood CREDIT CARDS Amex, Diners, MasterCard, Visa
Avenida Litorânea, 9-B, Praia de São Marcos
TEL (98) 3235-8971 OPEN Daily, 10am – 1am

Cabana do Sol $

This high-ceiling, open-walled restaurant serves generous portions of excellent sun-dried beef, accompanied by a banquet: *baião-de-dois*, lima beans, *paçoca*, boiled manioc, manioc purée, banana fritters, and clarified butter. Other interesting options and appetizers, such as fried fish cutlets with *arroz-de-cuxá*, feature on the menu To round off your meal, try *cupuaçu* fruit cream. Tables with checked tablecloths and wood and straw chairs help create a pleasant atmosphere. Service is efficient. CUISINE regional, fish and seafood CREDIT CARDS Amex, Diners, MasterCard, Visa
Rua João Damasceno, 24-A, Farol de São Marcos
TEL (98) 3235-2586 OPEN Daily, 11am – midnight

Cheiro Verde $

This spacious, airy restaurant, with children's play area and a very popular small fishing lake, is one of the best places in town to enjoy fish and seafood. Owner Filomena Castelo Branco has run this restaurant successfully for about twenty years. The grilled fish fillet with shrimp sauce (very nicely cooked with tomato and chopped onions), served with *vatapá* and *arroz-de-cuxá*, does not disappoint. Shrimp stew and several pies, such as shellfish and crab, are also served. CUISINE fish and seafood CREDIT CARDS Amex, Diners, MasterCard, Visa
Avenida São Luís Rei de França, 131, Olho d'Água
TEL (98) 3248-1641 OPEN Daily, 11am – midnight

A Diquinha $

At this restaurant, you can try one of the most famous *cuxás* (sorrel leaves, dried shrimp, sesame seeds, and manioc flour) in Maranhão. It accompanies every dish. Be prepared for simplicity – the place is actually owner Diquinha's front yard. The delicious *pescada amarela* (sea trout) fillet is fried to perfection and served without a hint of fat. Other northeastern dishes complete the menu: sun-dried beef, crab claws, and fried pig's tripe served as an appetizer. CUISINE regional CREDIT CARDS not accepted
Rua João Luís, 62, Diamante

Maracangalha $

Painted in blue and orange, with sea view, this restaurant has a very lively atmosphere. As a starter, try the crispy *pastéis* (deep-fried pastries) filled with meat, shrimp, eggplant, chicken, or salted cod, all served with the restaurant's own chili pepper jelly – a big success here. The main courses are based on Brazilian cuisine with touches of Maranhão, such as grilled fish fillet with *arroz-de-cuxá*. Owner/chef Dantas recommends the sweet and sour shrimp served in a pineapple shell. The place gets crowded on weekends, and the service can be rather slow. CUISINE regional, fish and seafood CREDIT CARDS Visa
Rua Mearin, Quadra 3, casa 13
TEL (98) 3235-9305 OPEN Daily, 11:30am – 1am

Papagaio Amarelo $

Next to Antigamente, and close enough to hear the live music played there, this restaurant specializes in well-seasoned, thin-crust pizzas. On the outside, it's a typical historical building. The inside is more subdued, with air-conditioning, and comfortable chairs, but is less charming. CUISINE regional, pizza CREDIT CARDS Diners, MasterCard, Visa
Rua da Estrela, 210, Centro
TEL (98) 3221-3855 OPEN Tue – Sat, 5pm – until the last customer leaves; Sun, 11am – until the last customer leaves

A Varanda $

The welcoming atmosphere and food make this place unforgettable. It stands in the backyard of the owner Maria Castelo, an enchanting lady who makes fish and seafood dishes. The tables are reached up a flight of stairsand down corridor full of plants, sheltering under a majestic cashew fruit tree. Fresh raw ingredients come directly from the Central Market. Leave room for a dessert made from local fruits. Be patient: the food takes a while to arrive. CUISINE regional, fish and seafood CREDIT CARDS MasterCard
Rua Genésio Rego, 185, Monte Castelo
TEL (98) 3232-8428 RESERVATIONS 3232-7291 OPEN Mon – Sat, noon – until the last customer leaves

SERVICES

Airport – Aeroporto Marechal da Cunha Machado

Avenida dos Libaneses, no #, Tiriricaì
TEL (98) 3217-6133 OPEN Daily, 24 hours www.infraero.gov.br

| PRICES | HOTELS (couple) | $ up to R$150 | $$ from R$151 up to R$300 | $$$ from R$301 up to R$500 | $$$$ above R$500 |

HOTELS, RESTAURANTS AND SERVICES

Boats to Alcântara
Terminal Hidroviário, no #, Rampa Campos Melo
TEL (98) 3322-6092. Departures from São Luís at 7am, 9:30am and 3pm; from Alcântara at 3pm and 5pm

Bus Station – Rodoviária
Avenida dos Franceses, no #, São Cristóvão
TEL (98) 3249-2488

Tourist Information – Central de Serviços Turísticos
Praça Benedito Leite, no #, Centro
TEL (98) 3212-6211 OPEN Mon – Fri, 8am – 7pm; Sat and Sun, 8am – 2pm

Tourist Police Station – Delegacia de Turismo
Rua da Estrela, 427, Centro
TEL (98) 3214-8682 OPEN Mon – Fri, 8am – 6pm

Travel Agency – Lótus Turismo e Aventura
Travessa Marcelino Almeida, 85, Centro
TEL (98) 3221-0942 OPEN Mon – Fri, 9am – 8pm; Sat, 9am – 1pm www.lotusturismo.com.br

Travel Agency – Maranhão Turismo
Avenida Avicênia, no # (Hotel São Luís Park), Calhau
TEL (98) 3227-2136 OPEN Mon – Fri, 8am – 6pm; Sat, 8am – noon www.maranhaoturismo.com.br

São Miguel do Gostoso – Rio Grande do Norte

AREA CODE 84 POPULATION 8,680 DISTANCES Natal 105 kilometers (65 miles) ACCESS Start off on the BR-101 highway, then take RN-221 WHEN TO VISIT Summer, when you can reach the neighboring beaches via dirt road

WHERE TO STAY

Pousada Arraial do Marco $
This simple but special guesthouse, rests on a deserted stretch of Praia do Marco beach. Fifteen rooms face the sea, decorated in white with space on the veranda for a hammock. During the rainy season, reaching the guesthouse involves going via the beach, 18 kilometers (11 miles) from São Miguel do Gostoso. ACCOMMODATIONS 9 chalets and 6 suites, air-conditioning, ceiling fan FACILITIES AND SERVICES bar, horses, parking, pool, playground, restaurant, games room, TV, guided walking tours, shuttle service to airport and local attractions CREDIT CARDS not accepted
Praia do Marco, no #
TEL (84) 9984-6662 FAX 3202-9095
www.pousadaarraialdomarco.com.br

Pousada do Gostoso $
Santo Cristo beach boasts this cozy guesthouse catering to wind- and kite-surfers on this stretch of the coast. Things may be a bit on the small side, but good taste remains intact from the restaurant to the TV room. Rooms have large fans, indirect lighting, and a hammock on the veranda. ACCOMMODATIONS 10 chalets, ceiling fan FACILITIES AND SERVICES bar, boat, kayaks, basketball hoop, pool, restaurant, reading area, game room, TV CREDIT CARDS MasterCard
Rua dos Corais, 2, Praia do Santo Cristo
TEL (84) 3263-4087 www.pousadadogostoso.com.br

Pousada dos Ponteiros $
Colorful chalets fill this spacious guesthouse, some overlooking a calm stretch of sand and sea. Rooms at the back, though they lack beachfront views, are bigger. A mini-spa invites guests to spoil themselves with a massage or soak in an *ofuro* tub. Waxing services are also available. The inn's restaurant features a cozy interior with indirect lighting and wooden tables and chairs. Service is very friendly. ACCOMMODATIONS 14 chalets, air-conditioning, minibar, cable TV, ceiling fan FACILITIES AND SERVICES bar, library, bicycles, parking, crafts store, *ofuro* tub, pool, restaurant, conference room, sitting room, game room, massage room, video room, spa, beach service, shuttle service to airport and local attractions CREDIT CARDS MasterCard, Visa
Rua Enseada das Baleias, 1000, Centro
TEL (84) 3263-4007 FAX 3263-4008
www.pousadadosponteiros.com.br

Pousada e Restaurante Mar de Estrelas $
Owners Maristela and Torres opened this guesthouse upon mastering the fine art of hospitality. Chalets are sprinkled a short distance apart across the fruit tree-filled grounds. The traditional breakfast is delicious: cake, tapioca, *cuscuz*, roasted cheese, and even ground beef. Decor and presentation here are very modest, except for one important feature: the restaurant, which, in Maristela's golden hands, serves a menu focused on regional cuisine. Her forte is *peixe à moda da casa* – fish cooked in coconut milk (served with rice, thickened *pirão* sauce, and small manioc cakes). The hostess' generosity is enchanting, exemplified best on pizza evenings when guests pay only for drinks. The festivals in June here are wonderful. ACCOMMODATIONS 14 chalets, minibar, cable TV; ceiling fan in 8 chalets, air-conditioning in 6 FACILITIES AND SERVICES library, horses, parking, orchard, restaurant, game room, guided walking tours CREDIT CARDS MasterCard, Visa
Avenida dos Arrecifes, 1120, Centro
TEL (84) 3263-4168, 3263-4232
www.pousadamardeestrelas.com

São Miguel dos Milagres – Alagoas

AREA CODE 82 POPULATION 6,463 DISTANCE Maceió 100 kilometers (62 miles) ACCESS From Maceió, take the AL-101 highway

WHERE TO STAY

Aldeia Beijupirá $$$
The unqualifiable good taste of Joaquim dos Santos, from Portugal, and Adriana, from Pernambuco, are present here in every touch of the hotel. The two own a restaurant of the same name in Porto de Galinhas. Local artisans have fashioned furniture to match a mostly white motif. Three of the chalets have Jacuzzis, and each come equipped with a DVD player. ACCOMMODATIONS 9 chalets, air-conditioning, DVD player, minibar, telephone, TV; Jacuzzi in 3 chalets FACILITIES AND SERVICES bar, parking, pool, restaurant, shuttle service to airport and local attractions CREDIT CARDS Visa
Sítio Roteio, no #, Praia da Lage
TEL (82) 3298-6520 FAX and RESERVATIONS 3298-6549
www.aldeiabeijupira.com.br

Pousada Côte Sud $$
Though most visitors to this charming guesthouse are European backpackers, owners of Roger Luypaert, from Belgium, and Corine, from France, guarantee a private stay. Chalets are scattered amidst an area of mangrove trees. ACCOMMODATIONS 9 chalets, air-conditioning, minibar, TV FACILITIES AND SERVICES Internet access in communal areas, bicycles, horses, parking, restaurant, walking trails, guided

RESTAURANTS $ up to R$50 $$ from R$51 up to R$100 $$$ from R$101 up to R$150 $$$$ above R$150

walking tours, beach service, shuttle service to airport and local attractions **CREDIT CARDS** not accepted
Rua Pedro Calu, no #, Porto da Rua
TEL and **FAX** (82) 3295-1283 www.pousadacotesud.com.br

Pousada do Caju $
About 200 meters (660 feet) in from Praia do Toque beach lies this guesthouse run by partners Antônio "Dudu" Cavalcanti and Jérôme Perez. A wraparound veranda complements the colonial-style building, whose décor has been left in the hands of Perez, a French antiques expert. Rooms bear the names of animals, such as *tatu* (armadillo), *tamanduá* (anteater), and *jacaré* (caiman). Homemade touches are visible even in the smallest of details: The bread is baked onsite from a mixture of flour and cashew nuts. **ACCOMMODATIONS** 6 rooms, air-conditioning, private safe, minibar, telephone, TV, DVD player in 3 rooms **FACILITIES AND SERVICES** Internet access in communal areas, bicycles, soccer field, horses, fishing equipment, parking, period furniture, natural pool, restaurant, walking trails, guided walking tours, beach service, airport shuttle, shuttle service to local attractions **CREDIT CARDS** not accepted
Praia do Toque, no # (access via Toque village)
TEL (82) 3295-1103 www.pousadadocaju-al.com.br

Pousada do Toque $$$
This guesthouse sits just off the beaten path (literally, you'll follow two kilometers of dirt road to get here) but possesses a happy, fun atmosphere, with the generous hospitality of owners Gilda and Nilo Burgarelli. The chalets have king-size beds, flat-screen TVs, and CD and DVD players (there are 1,300 films, at the guest's disposal). Some feature private pools and *ofuro* tubs. Access is by two kilometers of dirt road. **ACCOMMODATIONS** 12 chalets, air-conditioning, private safe, minibar, Jacuzzi, telephone, cable TV, ceiling fan **FACILITIES AND SERVICES** Internet access in communal areas, wine cellar, bar, bicycles, kayaks, DVD library, parking, chlorine-free pool, clay tennis court, restaurant, beach service, airport shuttle **CREDIT CARDS** Diners, MasterCard
Rua Felisberto de Ataíde, no #, Praia do Toque, Povoado do Toque
TEL and **FAX** (82) 3295-1127, 9991-2168

Pousada Um Milhão de Estrelas $$
The Portuguese owners of this guesthouse take pride in their well-tended gardens and tastefully decorated restaurant.. The spacious chalets are equipped with DVD players. But take caution when driving here: A dirt road leads from the highway with no signs for anyone traveling from Maceió to Maragogi. **ACCOMMODATIONS** 15 chalets, air-conditioning, minibar, TV, ceiling fan **FACILITIES AND SERVICES** Internet access in communal areas, bar, boat, bicycles, kayaks, horses, parking, pool, restaurant, baby-sitting, beach service, airport shuttle **CREDIT CARDS** Amex, Diners, MasterCard, Visa
Praia de Tatuamunha, no #
TEL (82) 3298-6223 **RESERVATIONS** 9987-1626 **FAX** 3298-6239
www.pousadaummilhaodeestrelas.com.br

WHERE TO EAT

Cantinho de Nanã $
This simple beachfront restaurant sits so close to the water's edge at Porta da Ruat hat high tide the sea will sometimes lap against the front entrance. Loving prepared food is exemplified best with the house specials, shrimp *à moda alagoana* (in coconut sauce, served in a coconut shell), and shrimp *thermidor* (in white sauce). Décor includes items fashioned from coconut shells. **CUISINE** fish and seafood **CREDIT CARDS** not accepted

Rua Ana Marinho Braga, no #, Praia Porto da Rua
TEL (82) 3295-1573 **OPEN** Daily, 8am – 8pm

São Raimundo Nonato – Piauí

AREA CODE 89 **POPULATION** 28,993 **DISTANCES** Teresina 530 kilometers (329 miles), Canto do Buriti 113 kilometers (70 miles), Picos 339 kilometers (211 miles) **ACCESS** Transpiauí (BR-324 highway)

WHERE TO STAY

Hotel Serra da Capivara $
Though the building belongs to the government, the hotel is privately managed. Capivara operates as an informal park headquarters, and often considered the best hotel in town. A spacious outdoor area features a pool and pleasant restaurant serving good home-cooked food. Rooms are spacious and service is good, but the showers leave much to be desired. **ACCOMMODATIONS** 18 rooms (12 double, 3 triple and 3 for up to 5 people) and 1 suite, air-conditioning, minibar, TV **FACILITIES AND SERVICES** bar, parking, snack bar, restaurant, pool **CREDIT CARDS** MasterCard, Visa
Rodovia PI-140, Km 0, Santa Luzia
TEL (89) 3582-1389 **FAX** 3582-1798

Lelinha Pousada $
This guesthouse, opened in 2002, is one of the best in São Raimundo Nonato. Simple but well kept, the Pousada houses surprisingly spacious rooms, some of them fitting up to five beds. A smorgasbord of a breakfast includes *pão de queijo* (cheesy bread rolls), *sertão*-style yoghurt (made with *umbu* fruit), two kinds of cake, and coffee. **ACCOMMODATIONS** 19 rooms, air-conditioning, minibar, telephone, TV **FACILITIES AND SERVICES** snack bar **CREDIT CARDS** Diners, MasterCard
Rua Doutor Barroso, 249, Aldeia
TEL and **FAX** (89) 3582-2993 www.lelinhapousada.com.br

WHERE TO EAT

Bode Assado do Tango $
This restaurant serves two specialties: griddled goat and mutton, accompanied by rice, *feijão-tropeiro* (beans with spicy sausage and manioc flour), tapioca, and fried manioc. Live *forró pé-de-serra* music and dancing spices things up Thursdays. Indoor and outdoor seating is available. It's worth noting about 70 kilos (150 pounds) of meat are consumed here per week. **CUISINE** meats, regional **CREDIT CARDS** not accepted
Rua Francisco Antunes de Macedo, 449, Santa Fé
TEL (89) 3582-2128 **RESERVATIONS** 9405-6347 **OPEN** Daily, 4pm – midnight

Soares $
In business for two decades, this restaurant operates out of the owner's backyard serving one main dish, always cooked to order: *galinha caipira ao molho pardo* (corn-fed chicken in blood-enriched sauce). Rice, thickened *pirão* sauce, and salad, accompany the entrée, which feeds up to four. Soares' wife, Osmarina, also takes orders for *galinha-d'Angola de cabidela* (guinea fowl in blood-enriched sauce). **CUISINE** home-made, regional **CREDIT CARDS** not accepted
Rua Bartolomeu Ribeiro de Castro, 175, Santa Fé
TEL (89) 3582-1347 **OPEN** Daily, 11am – 10pm

SERVICES

Travel Agency – Agência de Turismo Trilhas da Capivara
Rua Moisés de França, 22, Santa Luzia
TEL (89) 3582-1294 **OPEN** Daily, 8am – 6pm

PRICES	HOTELS (couple)	$ up to R$150	$$ from R$151 up to R$300	$$$ from R$301 up to R$500	$$$$ above R$500

Serra da Capivara (National Park) – Piauí (see São Raimundo Nonato)

Serra Talhada – Pernambuco

AREA CODE 87 POPULATION 70,017 DISTANCES Recife 430 kilometers (267 miles) ACCESS From Recife, take the BR-232 highway. From Teresina, follow BR-316 then BR-232
www.serratalhada.pe.gov.br

WHERE TO STAY

Hotel das Palmeiras $
Despite the simple rooms and service, this is one of the best hotels in town. Vacancy is often limited, especially in July. Pillows are thin and the bedspreads a bit hard to the touch. Each room contains two beds, a small TV…and a noisy atmosphere. The lack of window screens means you may be bothered by mosquitoes overnight. Still, breakfast has an intact regional touch: curd cheese (roasted by guests on-site), typical cakes, *cuscuz*, fruits, bread, and juices. ACCOMMODATIONS 19 suites, Internet access, air-conditioning, minibar, telephone, TV, veranda FACILITIES AND SERVICES bar, parking, pool, playground, restaurant CREDIT CARDS MasterCard
Rodovia BR-232, Km 416
TEL and FAX (87) 3831-1625

WHERE TO EAT

Bode na Brasa $
It's near the bus station and resembles a big kiosk, but the roast goat, served with boiled manioc and seasoned manioc flour with pickled salad, is crispy and delicious. Service is friendly but slow, so it's best to order everything at once.. CUISINE regional CREDIT CARDS not accepted
Avenida Miguel Nunes de Souza, 684
TEL (87) 3831-7321 OPEN Tue – Sat, 11am – 11pm; Sun and Mon, 11am – 4pm

Sete Cidades (National Park) – Piauí (see Piripiri)

Sítio do Conde – Bahia

AREA CODE 75 Conde DISTANCE Salvador 202 kilometers (126 miles) ACCESS From Salvador, follow the Estrada do Coco highway, then take Linha Verde to the Conde exit. Continue for 6 kilometers (4 miles)

WHERE TO STAY

Coco Beach $
Facilities at Coco Beach may be among the best in Sítio do Conde. The hotel is located on the road to Barra do Itariri, facing a semi-deserted stretch of Praia do Conde beach. Rooms and chalets are comfortable but basic, and lacking in charm. Be sure to request a room with a (beachfront) view. ACCOMMODATIONS 12 rooms and 10 chalets, air-conditioning, minibar, TV FACILITIES AND SERVICES Internet access in communal areas, bar, bicycles, horses, parking, convenience store, pool, playground, volleyball court, restaurant, games room, airport shuttle CREDIT CARDS Diners, MasterCard, Visa
Estrada para Barra do Itariri, Km 2 (road to Barra do Itariri)
TEL and FAX (75) 3449-1171, 3449-1300 www.cocobeach.ch

Itariri Resort $$
One of the best resorts in the area. beach Accoutrements may be old, but the rooms are spacious and comfortable. The lake beside the hotel offers a lovely view of the nearby Praia do Itariri beach. During low season, the resort caters to business and school groups. If you're looking for privacy, choose a chalet. ACCOMMODATIONS 18 rooms, 10 chalets, and 2 suites; air-conditioning, minibar, radiotelephone, TV; fan in chalets FACILITIES AND SERVICES bar, boat, bicycles, kayaks, horses, cart, parking, fishing lake, paddleboat, pool, playground, volleyball court, restaurant, river, game room, flying fox, recreational team for adults and children; beach service (during high season) CREDIT CARDS Amex, Diners, MasterCard, Visa
Fazenda Ribeiro, no # (Km 131, Linha Verde),
Barra do Itariri
TEL and FAX (75) 3449-1142 www.itariri-resort.com

Sobral – Ceará

AREA CODE 88 POPULATION 172,685 DISTANCES Fortaleza 235 kilometers (146 miles), Jericoacara 152 kilometers (94 miles) ACCESS From Teresina or Fortaleza, take the BR-222 highway (Note: From Teresina, there is a terrible stretch of road in the Tainguá Mountain Range) WHEN TO VISIT From January to July, when rain takes the edge off the heat
www.sobral.ce.gov.br

WHERE TO STAY

Hotel Vila Real $
Just five minutes from the city center, Vila Real offers pleasant, clean rooms in a quiet neighborhood. Be sure to make reservations well in advance! ACCOMMODATIONS 13 rooms and 8 flats, Internet access, air-conditioning, minibar, telephone, TV FACILITIES AND SERVICES Internet access in communal areas, parking, pool, restaurant, conference room CREDIT CARDS Diners, MasterCard, Visa
Rua Bélgica, 297, Parque das Nações, Cofeco
TEL and FAX (88) 3614-2530 www.hvr.com.br

Visconde Hotel $
A good option for travelers on foot who wish to stay in the heart of the city. Rooms at Visconde get booked up quickly, because good service and spotless rooms are a sure thing year-round. ACCOMMODATIONS 36 rooms and 12 suites, air-conditioning, minibar, telephone, TV FACILITIES AND SERVICES Internet access in communal areas, parking, restaurant, conference room, video room CREDIT CARDS Amex, Diners, MasterCard, Visa
Avenida Lúcia Sabóia, 473, Centro
TEL (88) 3611-5800 FAX 3613-1887

WHERE TO EAT

Aragão $
The most popular dish here is the generously served sun-dried meat, which owner-operated Aragão has perfected over nearly two decades. Set just outside the center of town, Aragão's serves local politicians, tourists, and business executives against a backdrop of antique wall clocks. CUISINE regional CREDIT CARDS not accepted
Avenida Hélio Arruda Coelho, 42, Sinhá Sabóia
TEL (88) 3614-4004 RESERVATIONS 3614-4003 OPEN Daily, 11am – 10pm

Doce Cultura $
Aluminum tables and chairs and wall photographs of old Sobral complete the charm of this snack bar. The local newspaper is always available for browsing, and straightforward

menu features sweet items, savories, juices, and sandwiches. CUISINE sweets and cakes CREDIT CARDS Diners, MasterCard, Visa
Rua Menino Deus, 169, Centro
TEL (88) 3611-4917 OPEN Daily, 7am – 11pm

SERVICES

Airport – Aeroporto Coronel Virgílio Távora
Avenida Geraldo Rangel, no #, Betânia
TEL (88) 3613-1477, 9961-4919 OPEN Daily, 24 hours

Bus Station – Rodoviária
Rua Deputado Emanoel Rodrigues, no #, Tamarino
TEL (88) 3611-1554 www.guanabaraexpress.com.br

Sousa – Paraíba

AREA CODE 83 POPULATION 63,358 DISTANCES João Pessoa 436 kilometers (271 miles), Campina Grande 311 kilometers (193 miles) ACCESS From João Pessoa and Campina Grande, take the BR-230 highway; from Natal, BR-226 to Currais Novos / BR-427 to Pombal / BR-230. As an alternative, try BR-116 to Felizardo, then transfer to BR-230 WHEN TO VISIT From July to December, when the drier river beds provide easier access to and better views of the dinosaur tracks

WHERE TO STAY

Estância Termal Brejo das Freiras $
An ideal spot to relax, ride horses, walk a little, and eat a lot – the homemade food is well-flavored and the *doce de leite* (caramelized milk dessert) is delicious. Rooms are very simple but spacious. The medicinal-waters complex is enticing, but bathtubs in some of the bedrooms are rather uninviting. ACCOMMODATIONS 45 rooms and 15 chalets, air-conditioning, minibar, telephone, TV FACILITIES AND SERVICES Internet access in communal areas, bar, soccer field, horses, parking, Jacuzzi, convenience store, pool, jogging track, playground, landing strip for small planes, volleyball court, restaurant, conference room, game room; kitchen closes at 9pm CREDIT CARDS Amex, MasterCard, Visa
São João do Rio do Peixe, 8 kilometers (5 miles) from the center; 32 kilometers (20 miles) from Cajazeiras
TEL and FAX (83) 3522-1515, 3552-1517

Jardins Plaza $
This new hotel boasts comfortable rooms equipped with TV, fluffy pillows, and spacious "power showers." It's a pity, though, how the tiled building clashes with the atmosphere of the *sertão*. ACCOMMODATIONS 36 rooms, Internet access, air-conditioning, minibar, telephone, TV FACILITIES AND SERVICES bar, convenience store, pool, restaurant, travel agency CREDIT CARDS Amex, Diners, MasterCard, Visa
Rua João Bosco Marques de Sousa, no # (exit to Patos), Gato Preto
TEL (83) 3522-4212 FAX 3522-4214
www.newline.com.br/jardins

WHERE TO EAT

O Mirante $
Dine on crispy fried fish (*tucunaré*) with pickled salad while admiring views of the reservoir and its forested island. Note sauces are not the forte here, and many of the stews drown out the flavor of the fish. CUISINE fish, regional CREDIT CARDS MasterCard, Visa
Alto da Gruta, no #, São Gonçalo
TEL (83) 3556-1101 OPEN Fri – Sun, 10am – 6pm

Taíba – Ceará

AREA CODE 85 São Gonçalo do Amarante DISTANCES Fortaleza 75 kilometers (47 miles), Praia de Pecém 18 kilometers (11 miles by road) or 6 kilometers (4 miles via the beach), São Gonçalo do Amarante 27 kilometers (17 miles), Paracuru 56 kilometers (35 miles) ACCESS From Fortaleza, take the Rodovia Estruturante (CE-085 highway); from São Gonçalo do Amarante, follow the CE-065; from Paracuru, take the CE-065 and connect to CE-341

WHERE TO STAY

Isca do Sol $
This pleasant guesthouse offers direct access to a beach of pale, powdery sand, so quiet it seems private. A pool and bar liven the grounds of the hotel. Breakfast includes pancakes and *tapioca* made to order. ACCOMMODATIONS 17 suites, 3 chalets, and 1 flat; Internet access, private safe, minibar, cable TV; air-conditioning in some rooms FACILITIES AND SERVICES Internet access in communal areas, bar, bicycles, parking, pool, playground, quadricycle, restaurant CREDIT CARDS Amex, Diners, MasterCard, Visa
Rua Atlântico Sul, 350, Praia da Colônia, Colônia de Férias Pecém
TEL (85) 3315-2020 FAX 3315-2021 www.pecem.tur.br

Taíma Beach Lodge $
This hotel, opened in 2004, features the best facilities in Taíba and is only 100 meters (330 feet) from the beach. Each of the four suites caters to a different decorative taste. All include a veranda, fan, and minibar. A lovely garden surrounds the pool and bar. ACCOMMODATIONS 4 suites, minibar, ceiling fan, veranda FACILITIES AND SERVICES bar, parking, pool CREDIT CARDS not accepted
Rua Capitão Inácio Prata, 73, Praia da Taíba
TEL (85) 3315-6384, 8828-6251 FAX 3315-6222

WHERE TO EAT

Le Petit $
French Claudine has been cooking for Pecém visitors since 1995. Hers is a small, simple eatery – just eight wooden tables, most set up on the veranda. The house special is a variety of fish fillets served with French sauces, ranging from curry to French mustard or *taíba* (a mix of ground cashew nuts and butter). Claudine carries mostly cobia, snook, and *galo-do-alto* fish. She also serves shrimp or lobster and crêpes with a variety of fillings. CUISINE fish and seafood CREDIT CARDS Diners, MasterCard
Rua Capitão Inácio Prata, no #, Praia da Taíba
TEL (85) 3315-6016 OPEN High season: Thu – Sat, 11am – 5pm and 7pm – 11pm; Sun, 11am – 5pm; low season: Fri and Sat, 11am – 5pm and 7pm – 11pm; Sun, 11am – 5pm

Volta ao Mundo $
Jean-Luc and Nadia Cristofari opened this restaurant following a stint at a guesthouse in Jijoca. The French couple cooks and serves the food themselves in a dining room decorated with items purchased during their travels. Entrée suggestions include duck fillet in green peppercorn sauce or porgy fillet *marseille* (fish cooked in the house tomato sauce, with shrimp and olive oil). CUISINE French CREDIT CARDS Diners, MasterCard, Visa
Rua Capitão Inácio Prata, 8, Praia da Taíba
TEL (85) 3315-6053 OPEN High season: Mon – Fri, 11am – 10pm; Sat, 11am – until the last customer leaves; low season: Wed – Mon, 11am – 10pm (closed on Tue)

PRICES	HOTELS (couple)	$ up to R$150	$$ from R$151 up to R$300	$$$ from R$301 up to R$500	$$$$ above R$500

Tamandaré – Pernambuco

AREA CODE 81 POPULATION 18,831 DISTANCE Recife 89 kilometers (55 miles) ACCESS Take BR-101, PE-060, and then PE-073

WHERE TO STAY

Pontal dos Carneiros Beach Bungalows $$$$
Each bungalow sleeps up to six people, with three bedrooms, two bathrooms, sitting room and fully-equipped kitchen, arranged on the ground floor and mezzanine. ACCOMMODATIONS are very comfortable (massage services are available to guarantee it) and sit only 60 meters (200 feet) from the beach, separated from each other by lawns and surrounded by hammocks, beach mats, cushions, and wicker sofas. Breakfast is served in the bungalow, as are other meals, per guest request. Each cottage includes its own barbecue facilities. ACCOMMODATIONS 8 bungalows, air-conditioning, private safe, kitchen, minibar, stereo, DVD player, telephone, TV, veranda with hammock FACILITIES AND SERVICES Internet access in communal areas, parking, playground, volleyball court, restaurant, game room, motorboat trips, jet-ski, waterskiing, beach service, shuttle service to airport and local attractions CREDIT CARDS MasterCard, Visa
Sítio dos Manguinhos (access by the road to Carneiros, Km 5)
TEL (81) 3676-2365 www.pontaldoscarneiros.com.br

Pousada do Farol $
Opened in 2004, this guesthouse owes its name to the 15-meter (50-foot) high lighthouse (*farol*) in the middle of the pool, which is 17 meters (56 feet) long and features a bridge connecting the two sides. Each bungalow includes a bedroom that can sleep up to five people, with king-size beds, two verandas, and spacious bathroom – 40 square meters (430 square feet) in all! All verandas are equipped with a hammock, lounger, and small table. The rustic building features exposed brick, stone, and wood accents. ACCOMMODATIONS 10 bungalows, air-conditioning, minibar, cable TV FACILITIES AND SERVICES pool with hydro-massage, boat and horse trips, restaurant CREDIT CARDS not accepted
Praia dos Carneiros, no # (accessible from the road to Carneiros)
TEL and FAX (81) 3676-2054 www.pousadadofarol.com

Resort Praia dos Carneiros $$
Fantastic hilltop views of the mouth of Rio Formoso and its mangroves can be had here, as well as catamaran access to Praia dos Carneiros (included in the daily rate). All rooms feature exposed brick, ceramic flooring, wooden artifacts, and said panoramas. ACCOMMODATIONS 26 bungalows, 4 rooms, and 2 suites; air-conditioning, private safe, minibar, telephone, cable TV FACILITIES AND SERVICES Internet access in communal areas, boat, horses, waterskiing, parking, snack bar, stores, pool, playground, restaurant, recreational team for adults and children, valet parking, lifeguard, beach service, shuttle service to airport and local attractions CREDIT CARDS Diners, MasterCard, Visa
Granja Havaí, no #, Zona Rural, Rio Formoso
TEL and FAX (81) 3678-1221
www.hotelpraiadoscarneiros.com.br

WHERE TO EAT

Frente de Quintal $
Located on a small, quiet street, about 700 meters (0.4 mile) from the center of Tamandaré, this family-run restaurant serves grilled fish, lobster, and shrimp, as well as the house special, *arroz de polvo* (rice with octopus). We recommend the well-portioned *peixada* (fish cooked in coconut milk, served with rice, thickened *pirão* sauce, and vegetables), which serves up to three people. CUISINE fish CREDIT CARDS not accepted
Rua José Paulo Lins, no #
TEL (81) 3676-1863 OPEN Daily, 10am – 10pm

O Pescador $
Opened in 2004 only 150 meters (500 feet) from the shoreline, this restaurant serves *peixada* (rice with octopus and fish in shrimp sauce) as the house special. Patrons can watch cooks at work while they await their food. A small bar inside the restaurant plays Brazilian popular music. CUISINE fish and seafood CREDIT CARDS Amex, Diners, MasterCard, Visa
Rua Raul de Pompéia, no #, Loteamento Brigite
TEL (81) 3676-1345 RESERVATIONS 9658-2802 OPEN Daily, 11am – 11pm

Tambaba – Paraíba (see Jacumã)

Teresina – Piauí

AREA CODE 86 POPULATION 788,773 DISTANCES São Luís 463 kilometers (288 miles), Parnaíba 348 kilometers (216 miles), Fortaleza 634 kilometers (394 miles) ACCESS Take BR-343 highway (Transpiauí), then BR-316 WHEN TO VISIT January and February (summer) and June (for the São João festivities) are the liveliest months
www.teresina.pi.gov.br

WHERE TO STAY

Luxor Piauí $
Luxor Piauí, which opened in 2001, is a good choice if you want to stay in the city center without spending a lot. The rooms, which nearly all accommodate two, are modern and well equipped. The service is good. ACCOMMODATIONS 83 rooms, Internet access, air-conditioning, minibar, telephone, cable TV FACILITIES AND SERVICES Internet access in communal areas, bar, parking, pool, restaurant, conference room, gym, travel agency, business center, 24-hour kitchen, valet parking CREDIT CARDS Amex, Diners, MasterCard, Visa
Praça Marechal Deodoro, 310, Centro
TEL (86) 3131-3000 FAX 3221-5171 www.luxor-hotels.com

Metropolitan Hotel $$$
One of Teresina's best hotels, Metropolitan is well preserved and very well located. Its tenth-floor bar offers an excellent view of the heart of the city. Even non-guests should go up to enjoy the sight. ACCOMMODATIONS 124 rooms and 5 suites, Internet access, air-conditioning, private safe, minibar, telephone, cable TV; Jacuzzi in 2 suites FACILITIES AND SERVICES Internet access in communal areas, 3 bars, parking, pool, restaurant, conference room, gym, sauna, travel agency, business center, 24-hour kitchen, valet parking, VIP lounge at the airport CREDIT CARDS Amex, Diners, MasterCard, Visa
Avenida Frei Serafim, 1696, Centro
TEL and FAX (86) 3216-8000 www.metropolitanhotel.com.br

Rio Poty $$$
Though it's a bit unkept, this hotel offers fine views. The family-friendly pool has a waterfall and a children's area. ACCOMMODATIONS 112 rooms and 8 suites, Internet access, air-conditioning, private safe, minibar, telephone, cable TV; Jacuzzi in suites FACILITIES AND SERVICES Internet access in communal areas, bar, waterfall, parking, pool, restaurant, conference

RESTAURANTS	$ up to R$50	$$ from R$51 up to R$100	$$$ from R$101 up to R$150	$$$$ above R$150

room, gym, game room, massage room, video room, beauty parlor, sauna, business center, 24-hour kitchen, car rental, valet parking. CREDIT CARDS Amex, Diners, MasterCard, Visa
Avenida Marechal Castelo Branco, 555, Ilhotas
TEL (86) 4009-4009 RESERVATIONS 4009-4300 FAX 4009-4001
www.riopoty.com

WHERE TO EAT

Camarão do Elias $
Elias was born in Parnaíba, of white, Indian, French, and Portuguese descent. He knows where to buy good ingredients and can please even the most demanding palate. His *vatapá* is very good, as is the shrimp with capers fried on a clay hotplate. The plump, succulent crab claws in vinaigrette sauce are also worth trying. Although the restaurant is 400 kilometers from the ocean, it gives off an air of the sea. The simple setting offers tables arranged on a pleasant veranda.
CUISINE fish and seafood, varied CREDIT CARDS Diners, MasterCard, Visa
Avenida Pedro Almeida, 457, São Cristóvão
TEL (86) 3232-5025 OPEN Mon – Sat, 5pm – 2am; Sun, 11am – 4pm

Carnaúba $
As the menu warns, your food here will take thirty minutes to prepare, as all the dishes are cooked to order. The compensation is tasty sun-dried beef, cooked to perfection and served with *paçoca*, *feijão-tropeiro* (beans with spicy sausage and manioc flour), and *maria-isabel* (chopped sun-dried beef fried with rice). Also try *baião-de-dois* (rice and beans) and the corn-fed chicken. CUISINE regional CREDIT CARDS MasterCard, Visa
Avenida Jóquei Clube, 1662, Jóquei
TEL (86) 3233-6829 OPEN Mon, 6pm – 12:30am ; Tue – Sat, 11am – 4pm and 6pm – 12:30am; Sun, 11am – 4pm

Longá $$$
Specializing in regional cuisine, this restaurant is an oasis of air-conditioning and comfortable chairs. Frequented by executives from the city and surroundings, it offers professional service and good food. Try *capote* (guinea fowl) cooked in various manners. The corn-fed chicken is also famous. As everything is cooked to order, be prepared to wait. CUISINE regional CREDIT CARDS Diners, MasterCard, Visa
Avenida Ininga, 1245, Fátima
TEL (86) 3232-6868 OPEN Daily, 11am – until the last customer leaves

Theresina Grill $$
Young people, executives, and families make up the eclectic clientele of this restaurant in one of the city's best neighborhoods. The menu features pasta, sushi, fish, and other options. The outdoor tables are the most pleasant, especially at night. A playground and videogame area keep the children busy. CUISINE varied CREDIT CARDS Diners, MasterCard, Visa
Rua Tulipas, 330, Jóquei
TEL (86) 3233-9555 OPEN Daily, 11am – 2am

SERVICES

Airport – Aeroporto Senador Petrônio Portella
Avenida Centenário, no #, Aeroporto
TEL (86) 3225-2947, 3225-2600, 3225-2535 OPEN Mon – Fri, 8am – noon and 1pm – 5pm

Tourist Information – Piemtur (Piauí Turismo)
Rua Acre, no #, Centro de Convenções, Cabral
TEL (86) 3222-6202, 3222-6254 OPEN Mon – Fri, 8am – 1:30pm

Bus Station – Rodoviária
BR-343 (towards Campo Maior), Km 3, Redenção
TEL (86) 3218-2037, 3218-1514

Touros – Rio Grande do Norte

AREA CODE 84 POPULATION 32,052 DISTANCE Natal 88 kilometers (55 miles) ACCESS Take the BR-101 and then RN-221 highways

WHERE TO STAY

Sinos do Vento $$$
The four accommodation blocks and the communal areas are separate, arranged at different levels around the grounds. All the rooms overlook the calm sea and deserted beach. The rustic décor features furniture inspired by Minas Gerais. White canopies over the beds contrast with the blue ceilings. The red floor tiles create a warm, relaxing atmosphere. The chickens guarantee fresh eggs for breakfast; there are also horses. ACCOMMODATIONS 12 rooms and 2 suites, Internet access, air-conditioning, minibar, telephone; cable TV in master suite FACILITIES AND SERVICES Internet access in communal areas, wine cellar, bar, horses, parking, convenience store, pool, playground, orchard, restaurant, magazine reading area, game room, massage room, valet parking, shuttle service to airport and local attractions CREDIT CARDS Amex, Diners, MasterCard, Visa
Estrada de Perobas, no #
TEL (84) 3263-2353, 3263-2020 FAX 3263-2021
www.sinosdovento.com.br

Siri Resort $$$
Refined, yet rustic, this Portuguese-owned resort is popular with European visitors. The cozy wooden chalets sit on Praia de Perobas. They are equipped with microwaves, sitting rooms, and verandas with hammocks. In the low season this is an excellent spot for peace and quiet. ACCOMMODATIONS 23 chalets, Internet access, air-conditioning, minibar, TV, veranda FACILITIES AND SERVICES bar, parking, pool, playground, restaurant, game room, massage room, manicures, trips to local attractions, beach service CREDIT CARDS Visa
Estrada de Carnaubinha, no #, Praia de Perobas
TEL (84) 3693-3035, 3693-3036 RESERVATIONS 3263-2353, 9953-0198

Trairi – Ceará

AREA CODE 85 POPULATION 49,654 DISTANCE Fortaleza 125 kilometers (78 miles) ACCESS From Fortaleza, Rodovia Estruturante (CE-085 highway), toward Triângulo do Ipu and Gualdrapas

WHERE TO STAY

Orixás Art $$$$
This hotel opened in late 2004. The architecture harmonizes with the surrounding nature, which is protected for the most part. The wood, stone, and soapstone sculptures throughout the hotel are from a gallery one of the owners used to run. The suites have private pools and excellent sea views. Beach access is by stairs, which are unsafe for children and the elderly. The service is personalized and attentive. ACCOMMODATIONS 10 suites, Internet access, air-conditioning, private safe, minibar, private pool, telephone, TV FACILITIES AND SERVICES Internet access in communal areas, bar, parking, shops, pool, restaurant, game room, massage room, video room CREDIT CARDS Visa
Rua da Praia, no #, Flecheiras
TEL (85) 3351-3114 FAX 3351-3144 www.orixasclub.com

PRICES	HOTELS (couple)	$ up to R$150	$$ from R$151 up to R$300	$$$ from R$301 up to R$500	$$$$ above R$500

HOTELS, RESTAURANTS AND SERVICES

Pousada das Marés $
One kilometer from the center of Mundaú, Trairi's neighbor, this guesthouse offers courteous service and the expected leisure facilities. Rustic, but with sophisticated touches, the guesthouse offers cozy rooms with exposed brick walls. Natural pools form right in front. Guests vary in age and nationality. ACCOMMODATIONS 22 rooms and 2 adjoining suites, air-conditioning, private safe, minibar, cable TV; Jacuzzi in 4 rooms FACILITIES AND SERVICES bar, parking, convenience store, pool, playground, volleyball court, restaurant, catamaran trips, beach service CREDIT CARDS MasterCard
Estrada Barra Estrela Mundaú, no #
TEL (85) 9969-7489 FAX 3351-9092
www.pousadadasmares.com.br

Trancoso – Bahia

AREA CODE 73 (Porto Seguro) DISTANCES Salvador 735 kilometers (457 miles), Porto Seguro 25 kilometers (16 miles); by road and ferryboat) ACCESS From Porto Seguro, take a ferry to Arraial d'Ajuda, then follow a stretch of road, or go direct via BA-001 (47 kilometers, or 29 miles, of road with hazardous stretches)

WHERE TO STAY

Capim Santo $$
This guesthouse sits amid woods and gardens, with an outdoor *ofuro* tub and massage kiosk, 700 meters (0.4 mile) from the beach. The atmosphere is rustic, but emphasizes comfort. The small rooms are charming, and the spacious suites have mezzanines. The beauty salon on Beco da Flor offers all kinds of treatments. There is also a restaurant (see *Where to Eat*). ACCOMMODATIONS 12 suites and 3 rooms, Internet access, air-conditioning, minibar, telephone, TV; Jacuzzi in 1 suite FACILITIES AND SERVICES wine cellar, bar, parking, *ofuro* tub, pool, restaurant, massage room, video room, airport shuttle, babysitting CREDIT CARDS Amex, MasterCard, Visa
Rua do Beco, 55, Quadrado
TEL and FAX (73) 3668-1122 www.capimsanto.com.br

Club Med Village Trancoso $$$$
This cliff-top resort offers beautiful views of the surrounding rivers and beaches from its communal areas. The multi-colored blocks of spacious rooms recall the architecture of Trancoso's main square, the Quadrado. Wooden fittings and murals from the Oficina de Agosto craft workshop in Minas Gerais round out the rustic décor. Shows are included among the daily events. The G-Os (*gentis organizadors*, friendly organizers), who live in the club, welcome and entertain guests. ACCOMMODATIONS 168 rooms and 82 suites (26 adjoining), air-conditioning, private safe, minibar, telephone, cable TV FACILITIES AND SERVICES Internet access in communal areas, wine cellar, archery, bar, boat, sailboat, kayaks, soccer field, golf course, horses, parking, Jacuzzi, shops, kids club (for children over 4), pool, playground, tennis court, volleyball court, restaurant, magazine reading area, conference room, gym, massage room, beauty parlor, sauna, spa, walking trails, travel agency, business center, currency exchange, recreational team for adults and children, guided walking tours, valet parking, lifeguard, beach service, shuttle service to airport and local attractions CREDIT CARDS Amex, Diners, MasterCard, Visa
Fazenda Itaípe, no #, Estrada Arraial–Trancoso, Km 18
TEL (73) 3575-8400 RESERVATIONS 0800-7073-782 FAX 3575-8484
www.clubmed.com

Etnia Pousada $$$
This boutique guesthouse is set among trees. The themed rooms have interior gardens and verandas, Italian bed linen of Egyptian cotton, goose-feather pillows, and spacious bathrooms. Art, antiques, and furniture designed by the owners complete the experience. ACCOMMODATIONS 8 suites, air-conditioning, private safe, minibar, telephone; cable TV in master suites FACILITIES AND SERVICES Internet access in communal areas, bar, woods, parking, shops, pool, restaurant, therapeutic center, massage room, travel agency, airport shuttle CREDIT CARDS Amex, MasterCard, Visa
Avenida Principal, no #, Centro
TEL and FAX (73) 3668-1137 www.etniabrasil.com.br

Hotel da Praça $$$
This charming guesthouse is about 700 meters (0.4 mile) from the beach and set in spacious gardens dotted with sofas, tables, and loungers. Architect Sig Bergamin is responsible for the rustic-sophisticated décor. Each room has its own color and ambiance. In high season a fashionable restaurant operates in the breakfast area (see *Where to Eat*). ACCOMMODATIONS 11 rooms, air-conditioning, private safe, minibar, cable TV; telephone (except in standard rooms) FACILITIES AND SERVICES wine cellar, bar, horses, parking, video room, airport shuttle; restaurant (open December to March) CREDIT CARDS Visa
Praça São João, 1, Quadrado
TEL (73) 3668-2121, 3668-1493
www.pousadadoquadrado.com.br

Mata N'ativa Pousada $$
This charming little guesthouse harmonizes perfectly with its natural surroundings. The rustic main house and accommodation blocks have wooden benches, pillars, doors, and windows. The rooms are spread around three separate blocks. The restaurant is open only in high season and offers residents a varied dinner menu. The guesthouse is 5 minutes from Praia dos Nativos and from the Quadrado. It does not have a sea view, but the Trancoso River flows through the grounds. ACCOMMODATIONS 8 rooms, minibar, TV, veranda with hammock; air-conditioning in 6 rooms, ceiling fan in 2; flat-screen TV with satellite dish in 2 rooms FACILITIES AND SERVICES bar, kayaks, parking, restaurant, gym, massage room, video room, laundry, organized trips to local attractions, shuttle service to airport and local attractions CREDIT CARDS MasterCard
Estrada do Arraial, no #, Praia dos Nativos
TEL and FAX (73) 3668-1830
www.matanativapousada.com.br

Pousada El Gordo $$$
This cozy guesthouse next to the church in the Quadrado offers a picturesque view of the surroundings. The restaurant, which specializes in Portuguese and international cuisine, is open late (see *Where to Eat*). The simple leisure area includes a bar, a pool, a gym, and a massage room. ACCOMMODATIONS 8 rooms, Internet access, air-conditioning, private safe, minibar, telephone, cable TV FACILITIES AND SERVICES bar, pool, restaurant, gym, massage room, sauna, valet parking, shuttle service to airport and local attractions CREDIT CARDS Amex, Diners, MasterCard, Visa
Praça São João, 7, Quadrado
TEL and FAX (73) 3668-1193, 3668-2041 www.elgordo.com.br

Pousada Estrela d'Água $$$$
Once the home of singer Gal Costa, this guesthouse faces the sea, but is far from the city center. It is separated from the beach by a wooden walkway over the river. It also offers pools and charming communal areas with sea views. The atmosphere is mostly rustic, but includes antiques. Less-common amenities include therapeutic massages, physical activities (Pilates, stretching, walks), and organic food. ACCOMMODATIONS 22 rooms and 5 suites, air-conditioning, private safe, minibar, telephone, cable TV; private pool and Jacuzzi in master suites FACILITIES AND SERVICES Internet access in communal areas, bar, bicycles, horses, parking, motorboat,

| RESTAURANTS | $ up to R$50 | $$ from R$51 up to R$100 | $$$ from R$101 up to R$150 | $$$$ above R$150 |

shops, pool, restaurant, gym, game room, massage room, video room, walking trails, currency exchange, guided walking tours, valet parking, beach service, shuttle service to local attractions CREDIT CARDS Amex, Diners, MasterCard, Visa
Estrada do Arraial, no #, Praia dos Nativos
TEL (73) 3668-1030 FAX 3668-1485
www.estreladagua.com.br

Pousada Porto Bananas $$
This charming, friendly guesthouse is on the Quadrado, next to the church, and offers spacious, well-ventilated rooms. The décor mixes wood and greenery – a true tropical garden – in a rustic style that combines sophistication and charm. French, English, Italian, and Spanish are spoken. ACCOMMODATIONS 10 rooms and 2 chalets, air-conditioning, private safe, minibar, telephone, ceiling fan; cable TV in chalets and 2 rooms FACILITIES AND SERVICES bar CREDIT CARDS Visa
Praça São João, 234, Quadrado
TEL (73) 3668-1017 FAX 3668-1475
www.portobananas.com.br

Villas de Trancoso $$
The five spacious bungalows making up one of Trancoso's best guesthouses breathe exclusivity. Opened in 2002, the guesthouse has excellent beach facilities and a spacious leisure area. Everything from the washbasins to the ceilings is wood, matched to the bed linens and towels, which creates a warm, refined atmosphere. ACCOMMODATIONS 5 bungalows, Internet access, air-conditioning, private safe, minibar, telephone, cable TV, ceiling fan FACILITIES AND SERVICES Internet access in communal areas, wine cellar, bar, boat, kayaks, horses, bicycles, parking, pool, restaurant, magazine reading area, gym, massage room, video room, recreational team for adults, beach service CREDIT CARDS Amex, Diners, MasterCard, Visa
Estrada Arraial d'Ajuda–Trancoso, no 192, Km 23, Praia dos Nativos
TEL (73) 3668-1151 FAX 3668-1460
www.mybrazilianbeach.com

WHERE TO EAT

O Cacau $$
This restaurant in the city's historic center has been in business since 1998. It is simply decorated with wood and offers good ventilation. The *camarão nativo* (shrimp in coconut sauce, with coconut rice, toasted coconut shavings, and pink peppercorns) and the *peixe tropical* (grilled sea bass fillet in pineapple sauce, with arracacha purée and saffron raisin rice) come recommended. All dishes serve one. A wine list, a cellar, and outdoor tables are available. CUISINE varied CREDIT CARDS MasterCard
Praça São João, 96, Quadrado
TEL (73) 3668-1266 RESERVATIONS 3668-1144 OPEN Tue – Sun, 6pm – 11:30pm

Capim Santo $$
Trancoso's first restaurant, Capim Santo arrived in 1986 and became so successful that a branch was opened in São Paulo. The restaurant is inside the guesthouse of the same name. Its relaxed atmosphere emanates from the surrounding coconut palms and gardens. Wood is prominent in the furnishings; the tables are ceramic. Fish and seafood are served. The lobster gratin in pineapple, the grilled tuna in soy sauce, and the shrimp flambéed in vodka are worth special mention. CUISINE contemporary, fish and seafood CREDIT CARDS Amex, MasterCard
Rua do Beco, 55, Quadrado
TEL (73) 3668-1122 OPEN Mon – Sat, 5pm – 11pm

El Gordo $$
Portuguese food is the specialty here. Salted cod is available *bacalhau ao murro* (with potatoes), *com natas* (with cream), and *bacalhoada* (baked with vegetables). All dishes are à la carte and do not come with side dishes. The chef, S. Shain, is from India and previously worked in other Portuguese restaurants owned by the proprietor of El Gordo. Indian, Chinese, and other cuisines are also available. The menu is in English, Portuguese, and French. Small outdoor tables, near the pool, allow views of the sea at Trancoso. CUISINE Chinese, Indian, Portuguese CREDIT CARDS MasterCard, Visa
Praça São João, 7, Quadrado
TEL (73) 3668-1193, 3668-2041 OPEN Daily, 1pm – midnight

Japaiano $$
This restaurant in the charming Pousada do Quadrado opens only in the high season and only at night. The atmosphere is laid back, with tables scattered on the veranda and in the gardens. The cuisine is varied, the chef is Felipe Bronze. The restaurant tends to get very busy, with crowds coming for the DJ and music. CUISINE varied, a mixture of japonese and Bahian food. CREDIT CARDS Visa
Praça São João, 1, Quadrado
TEL (73) 3668-2121, 3668-1493 OPEN High season: daily, 7pm – until the last customer leaves; low season: 7pm – 11pm

Maritaka $
Pizzas with a variety of toppings are this restaurant's forte – try one with asparagus and Brie. Maritaka also serves sandwiches and *rolos* (rolled pizza filled with grilled meats). Large cushions and sofas complement the rustic décor. The restaurant is at the entrance to the Quadrado. CUISINE pizza, sandwiches CREDIT CARDS not accepted
Rua do Telégrafo, no #
TEL (73) 3668-1702 RESERVATIONS 3668-1258 OPEN High season: Thu – Tue, 7pm – 2:30am; low season: Thu – Tue, 7pm – midnight

Portinha $
Customers come for the piping hot dishes made on a wood-burning stove. The food is self-service, per kilo. The buffet includes dishes from regional (Minas Gerais), Arab, Italian, and Asian cuisine, with a good selection of greens and vegetables as well. CUISINE varied CREDIT CARDS Visa
Praça do Quadrado, 324
TEL (73) 3668-1054 OPEN Daily, noon – 10pm

Silvana & Cia $
A 10-minute walk from Praia dos Coqueiros, this restaurant has been in business for more than twenty years. Owner/cook Silvana serves up fish, octopus and fish with shrimp *moquecas*, and fish baked in banana leaf as the main dishes. All serve two people generously. A less fancy option is grilled or breaded chicken, with rice, salad, and potatoes. This is a simple, rustic restaurant. CUISINE fish and seafood, varied CREDIT CARDS Amex, Diners, MasterCard, Visa
Praça São João, no #, Quadrado
TEL (73) 3668-1049 OPEN Daily, noon – 11pm

SERVICES

Travel Agency – Brasil 2000 Turismo
Estrada do Mucugê, 165, Centro, Arraial
TEL (73) 3575-1815, 3575-1627 OPEN High season: daily, 9am – midnight; low season: Mon – Sat, 9am – 10pm
www.brasil2000turismo.com.br

PRICES	HOTELS (couple)	$ up to R$250	$$ from R$151 up to R$300	$$$ from R$301 up to R$600	$$$$ above R$500

Travel Agency – Candeias Turismo
Rua Carlos Alberto Parracho, 100, Trancoso
TEL (73) 3668-1168, 8813-1490 OPEN Mon – Fri, 8am – noon and 1:30pm – 6pm; Sat, 8am – 1pm

Travel Agency – Trancoso Receptivo
Rua Carlos Alberto Parracho, no #
TEL (73) 3668-1333, 3668-1183 OPEN High season: daily, 9am – 11:30pm; low season: Mon – Fri, 9am – 7:30pm; Sat, 9am – 1pm
www.trancosoreceptivo.com

Triunfo – Pernambuco

AREA CODE 87 POPULATION 14,846 DISTANCES Recife 450 kilometers (280 miles), Serra Talhada 31 kilometers (19 miles) ACCESS From Recife, take the BR-232 highway to Serra Talhada, then PE-365 (31 kilometers, 19 miles) WHEN TO VISIT June and July, for the milder weather and São João festivities

WHERE TO STAY

Pousada Baixa Verde $
Although near the town center, this guesthouse stands at the bottom of a slope and is quiet. The attractions are the two-level pool with water slide and the restaurant. All rooms are spacious; some overlook the pool and garden. The small store sells products from Engenho de São Pedro mill, including *cachaças*, liqueurs, and *rapadura* (brown sugar tablets). ACCOMMODATIONS 15 rooms and 2 chalets, minibar, telephone, TV, fan FACILITIES AND SERVICES Internet access in communal areas, bar, waterfall, sugar mill, parking, convenience store, pool, playground, skating, restaurant, conference room, guided walking tours CREDIT CARDS Amex, Diners, MasterCard, Visa
Rua Manoel Paiva dos Santos, 114, Centro
TEL (87) 3846-1103 FAX 3846-1410
www.baixaverdetriunfo.hpg.ig.com.br

Pousada Café do Brejo $
This guesthouse near the town entrance, after the lookout point, offers friendly service. Though it takes courage to go down the slope from the roadside, doing so pays dividends in peace and quiet. Teca (Maria Teresa Althoff) and Bel (José Alberto Pires) started their business serving afternoon tea, which became famous for its more than thirty items (cakes, juices, breads, and cheeses) all you can eat. In 1999 they began to take reservations, and soon after they built a small chalet. Today they have six rooms. Teca breeds peacocks, which sleep in the top of a tree (see *Where to Eat*). ACCOMMODATIONS 6 rooms, air-conditioning, minibar, telephone, TV FACILITIES AND SERVICES parking, orchard, restaurant CREDIT CARDS MasterCard
Rodovia PE-365, Chácara Kelé, no #, Sítio Bom Jesus
TEL (87) 3846-1621, 3846-1623, (81) 9609-4453

WHERE TO EAT

Baixa Verde $
This self-service restaurant has an à la carte menu, but not all dishes are always available (they run out of ingredients or run into a "delay" in preparing a particular dish). The buffet includes chopped sun-dried beef and potato soufflé. The unusual goat fondue is prepared with fillet from Serra Talhada. Other specialties are salted cod and fillet steak with mushrooms, both flambéed in *cachaça*. Some dishes are made to order: roast leg of kid, goat stew, and corn-fed chicken with *guandu* (a pulse, similar to peas), rice, seasoned manioc flour, salad, and manioc. CUISINE regional CREDIT CARDS Diners, MasterCard, Visa
Rua Manoel Paiva dos Santos, 114, Centro
TEL (87) 3846-1103 RESERVATIONS/FAX 3846-1410 OPEN Daily, 7am – 11pm

Café do Brejo $
This is a refuge deep in the mountain ranges of Pernambuco. After crossing a tree-filled yard, you reach a large veranda. You're greeted by Brazilian music from loudspeakers. The dinner set menu includes homemade bread and pâtés, soup, beef, chicken, locally grown red rice, seasoned manioc flour, and salad, as well as desserts, coffee, and homemade liqueurs. Some dishes are made to order, including roast leg of mutton, codfish and rice gratin, and eggplant gratin. Afternoon tea includes more than thirty items. Those not staying at the guesthouse need to make reservations. CUISINE regional CREDIT CARDS MasterCard
Rodovia PE-365, Chácara Kelé, Sítio Bom Jesus
TEL (87) 3846-1621, 3846-1623, (81) 9609-4453 OPEN Daily, 7:30am – 9:30am (breakfast); noon – 2:30pm (lunch); 4:30pm – 6:30pm (tea); 7:30pm – 9:30pm (dinner)

Ubajara – Ceará

AREA CODE 88 POPULATION 29,426 DISTANCES Fortaleza 324 kilometers (201 miles), Tianguá 18 kilometers (11 miles), Sobral 81 kilometers (50 miles), Piripiri 138 kilometers (86 miles), Teresina 314 kilometers (195 miles) ACCESS From Teresina, take BR-222 WHEN TO VISIT July offers the most pleasant weather
www.ubajara.ce.gov.br

WHERE TO STAY

Neblina Parque Hotel $
This guesthouse is adjacent to the park and surrounded by Atlantic forest, with well-tended gardens on-site. Despite its fairly simple amenities – including very basic room set-ups and barely adequate pillows and sheets – it is one of the best options for those who want to enjoy the park but still stay in town. ACCOMMODATIONS 39 rooms, minibar, TV FACILITIES AND SERVICES Internet access in communal areas, bar, woods, soccer field, parking, snack bar, pool, restaurant, walking trails CREDIT CARDS Diners, MasterCard, Visa
Avenida Governador César Cals, no #, Teleférico
TEL and FAX (88) 3634-1270 www.pousadaneblina.com.br

WHERE TO EAT

Nevoar $
This restaurant has the air of a bar, with a TV blaring all the time in the background. The most popular dishes on the bilingual menu are steak filet *parmigiana* and the fish dish *peixada*. Wash down your meal with a glass of the excellent *graviola* juice. CUISINE pizza, varied CREDIT CARDS not accepted
Avenida Monsenhor Gonçalo Eufrásio, 171, Centro
TEL (88) 3634-1312 OPEN Daily, 9am – 11pm

SERVICES

Department of Tourism – Secretaria de Turismo
Avenida dos Constituintes, no #, Domício Pereira (Engenheiro José Ribamar Cavalcante Bus Station)
TEL (88) 3634-2365 OPEN Mon – Fri, 8am – noon and 1:30pm – 5pm

União dos Palmares – Alagoas

AREA CODE 82 POPULATION 59,369 DISTANCE Maceió 70 kilometers (43 miles)
ACCESS From Maceió, take BR-101 and BR-104

RESTAURANTS	$ up to R$50	$$ from R$51 up to R$100	$$$ from R$101 up to R$150	$$$$ above R$150

WHERE TO STAY

Quilombo Park $

This hotel is on a small farm 5 kilometers (3 miles) off the highway. The comfortable amenities available to guests include two pools, a sauna, a games room, trails, fishing facilities, and 33 ACCOMMODATIONS, either chalets or rooms. The road to the farm is very precarious, particularly when it rains. ACCOMMODATIONS 20 rooms and 13 chalets, air-conditioning, minibar, telephone, TV FACILITIES AND SERVICES Internet access in communal areas, bar, woods, waterfall, soccer field, horses, cart, parking, fishing lake, pool, playground, restaurant, conference room, games room, sauna, walking trails, guided walking tours CREDIT CARDS Diners, MasterCard, Visa
Rodovia BR-104, Km 35 (towards Recife), Sítio Jaqueira
TEL and FAX (82) 3281-1135 www.hotelquilombo.com

Vale do Capão (Caeté-Açu) – Bahia

AREA CODE 75 Palmeiras DISTANCE Lençóis 70 kilometers (43 miles) ACCESS From Palmeiras, follow a precarious road for 18 kilometers (11 miles). In the rainy season, it is imperative that you get information on road conditions before attempting the drive

WHERE TO STAY

Pousada Candombá $

Rustic, with simple rooms, Candombá is a very pleasant, quiet spot. ACCOMMODATIONS 7 chalets, ceiling fan; minibar in luxury chalets FACILITIES AND SERVICES Internet access in communal areas, wine cellar, parking, orchard, restaurant, sauna, walking trails CREDIT CARDS MasterCard, Visa
Rua das Mangas, no #, Vale do Capão, Caeté-Açu
TEL and FAX (75) 3344-1102 www.infochapada.com

Pousada do Capão $

This guesthouse has great views of the surrounding mountainside, including Morro Branco do Capão (Morrão) and the path up to Cachoeira da Fumaça waterfall. Unfortunately, though the setting is lovely, some of the finishing touches on the guesthouse are lacking. The rooms on the second floor are the ones with the spectacular views. The chalets are very private and excellent for anyone looking for peace and quiet. There is also a hot-stone sauna in the shape of an igloo, as well as a craft store. ACCOMMODATIONS 12 rooms, minibar, ceiling fan FACILITIES AND SERVICES Internet access in communal areas, bar, woods, parking, stores, natural pool, orchard, restaurant, river, games room, reading room with fireplace, massage room, video room, sauna, walking trails CREDIT CARDS Diners, MasterCard
Rua do Chamego, no #, Vale do Capão, Caeté-Açu
TEL and FAX (75) 3344-1034 www.pousadadocapao.com.br

Pousada Lendas do Capão $

This guesthouse has a lovely garden and orchard, as well as a top-floor tower with a panoramic view of Morro Branco, the Serra do Candombá mountains, and Cachoeira da Fumaça waterfall. The rooms are simple and come equipped with hammocks; opt for the more spacious and airier superior class. Other amenities include a restaurant serving traditional local food and a large TV room with a fireplace. ACCOMMODATIONS 13 rooms and 4 chalets, minibar; fireplace in chalets and 2 rooms FACILITIES AND SERVICES Internet access in communal areas, canopy climbing, bar, woods, parking, stores, orchard, rappel, restaurant, river, video room, sauna, flying fox CREDIT CARDS Visa
Rua dos Gatos, 201, Vale do Capão, Caeté-Açu
TEL and FAX (75) 3344-1141 www.valedocapao.com.br

Pousada Pé no Mato $

The three special-class rooms have a beautiful view of the mountains. The restaurant is open to the public and serves snacks and regional dishes like sun-dried beef. The hiking store on-site can also hire guides and organize trips in the area. ACCOMMODATIONS 7 rooms; veranda with hammock in special rooms FACILITIES AND SERVICES bar, parking, snack bar, stores, restaurant, walking trails, travel agency, guided walking tours CREDIT CARDS MasterCard, Visa
Ladeira da Vila, no #, Centro, Vale do Capão, Caeté-Açu
TEL and FAX (75) 3344-1105 www.penomato.com.br

Vila Esperança $

Owners Celso (from São Paulo) and Paloma (from Spain) are known for the care and attention they lavish on their guests. All the rooms are spacious and airy, with verandas and hammocks. The chalets are particularly comfortable, with beautiful mosquito nets made by an artisan in Lençóis, good-quality towels, paintings on the walls, and careful attention paid to every last detail. The breakfast is also excellent. ACCOMMODATIONS 4 rooms and 2 chalets, minibar, mosquito nets FACILITIES AND SERVICES parking, walking trails CREDIT CARDS not accepted
Rua dos Gatos, no #, Vale do Capão, Caeté-Açu
TEL and FAX (75) 3344-1384

WHERE TO EAT

Casa das Fadas $

This is one of the coziest and best-maintained eateries in Vale do Capão. Italian dishes stand out. The restaurant is a few kilometers before the village, with signs pointing the way and its stone wall visible from the road. CUISINE Italian CREDIT CARDS not accepted
Estrada Palmeiras–Capão, Km 12, Riachinho, Caeté-Açu
TEL (75) 3344-1166 OPEN Thu – Tue, 1pm – 9pm. Closed November 20 to December 20

Dona Beli $

Dona Beli serves tasty homemade food in her own home. There is no menu, just a list of daily dishes served with either *palma* (prickly pear), banana *godó* (a thick broth), or *pepino de jaca* (peeled, fried, and seasoned jackfruit), typical accompaniments in Chapada Diamantina. CUISINE homemade, regional CREDIT CARDS not accepted
Rua do Folga, no #, Vale do Capão, Caeté-Açu
TEL (75) 3344-1085 OPEN Daily, noon – 9pm

Pizza Integral do Capão $

This pizzeria right in the central square in town is known for its whole wheat crust pies. CUISINE pizza CREDIT CARDS not accepted
Praça São Sebastião, no #, Vale do Capão, Caeté-Açu
TEL (75) 3344-1138 OPEN Mon – Fri, 4pm – 10pm; Sat, 4pm – 11pm; Sun, noon – 10pm

SERVICES

Guides – Associação dos Condutores de Visitantes do Vale do Capão (ACVVC)

Rua Campos, no # (on the way up to Fumaça Waterfall), Vale do Capão, Caeté-Açu
TEL (75) 3344-1087 OPEN Daily, 8am – 6pm

Travel Agency – Pé no Mato

Tourist information and guides
Ladeira da Vila, no #, Centro, Vale do Capão, Caeté-Açu
TEL (75) 3344-1105 OPEN Daily, 7am – 10pm
www.penomato.com

| PRICES | HOTELS (couple) | $ up to R$150 | $$ from R$151 up to R$300 | $$$ from R$301 up to R$500 | $$$$ above R$500 |

HOTELS, RESTAURANTS AND SERVICES

Travel Agency – Tatu na Trilha
Tourist information and guides
Rua da Vila, no #
TEL (75) 3344-1124 OPEN Mon – Fri, 8:30am – noon and 2pm – 6:30pm; Sat, 8:30am – noon. Closed in May
www.infochapada.com

Travel Agency – Terra Chapada
Tourist information and guides
Vila do Capão, no #
TEL (75) 3334-1227, 3334-1304 OPEN High season: daily, 8am – noon and 5pm – 10pm; low season: 8am – noon
www.terrachapada.com.br

Valença – Bahia

AREA CODE 75 POPULATION 84,136 DISTANCES Salvador 120 kilometers (75 miles) via ferry from Itaparica Island or 271 kilometers (168 miles) driving overland, Nazaré 32 kilometers (20 miles) ACCESS Take BA-001

WHERE TO STAY

Portal Rio Una $$
This hotel is right on the banks of the River Una. There are good leisure facilities on-site, especially the tennis courts. An agency in the hotel organizes trips to Morro de São Paulo and Boipeba, and the hotel has its own pier for private boat excursions. ACCOMMODATIONS 33 rooms and 3 suites, Internet access, air-conditioning, minibar, telephone, TV; Jacuzzi in suites FACILITIES AND SERVICES bar, parking, snack bar, pool, playground, tennis court, volleyball court, restaurant, conference room, gym, games room, video room, sauna, 24-hour kitchen, recreational team for children CREDIT CARDS Amex, Diners, MasterCard, Visa
Rua Maestro Barrinha, no #, Graça
TEL (75) 3641-5050 FAX 3641-5051 RESERVATIONS (71) 3450-7337
www.portalhoteis.tur.br

Village Hotel Águas do Guaibim $$
These accommodations consist of several two-story houses, each with two suites that share a fully-equipped kitchen. Amenities include a restaurant, pool, small soccer court, and beach volleyball area. ACCOMMODATIONS 10 rooms, air-conditioning, minibar, telephone, TV FACILITIES AND SERVICES bar, soccer field, parking, snack bar, pool, volleyball court, restaurant, games room, sauna, travel agency, beach service, airport shuttle CREDIT CARDS Diners, MasterCard, Visa
Avenida Taquary, no #, Guaibim
TEL and FAX (75) 3646-1047
www.aguasdoguaibim.com

USEFUL INFORMATION

Airports

ALAGOAS
Maceió
Zumbi dos Palmares International Airport
BR-104, Km 91, Tabuleiro
TEL (82) 3214-4000

BAHIA
Ilhéus
Jorge Amado Airport
Rua Brigadeiro Eduardo Gomes, no #, Pontal
TEL (73) 3234-4000

Lençóis
Coronel Horácio de Mattos Airport
BR-242, Km 209, Coronel Otaviano Alves
TEL (75) 3625-8100, 3625-8697

Porto Seguro
Porto Seguro International Airport
Estrada do Aeroporto, no #, Cidade Alta
TEL (73) 3288-1877, 3288-1880

Salvador
Deputado Luís Eduardo Magalhães International Airport
Praça Gago Coutinho, no #, São Cristóvão
TEL (71) 3204-1010

CEARÁ
Fortaleza
Pinto Martins International Airport
Avenida Senador Carlos Jereissati, 3000, Serrinha
TEL (85) 3477-1200

Juazeiro do Norte
Cariri Regional Airport
Avenida Virgílio Távora, 4000
TEL (88) 3572-0700, 3572-2118

Sobral
Coronel Virgílio Távora Airport
Avenida Gerardo Rangel, no #, Cidao
TEL (88) 3613-1477

MARANHÃO
São Luís
Marechal Cunha Machado Airport
Avenida dos Libaneses, no #, Tirirical
TEL (98) 3217-6133

PARAÍBA
João Pessoa
Presidente Castro Pinto International Airport
BR-101, Km 11, Bayeux
TEL (83) 3232-1200

PERNAMBUCO
Petrolina
Senador Nilo Coelho Airport
BR-235, Km 11
TEL (87) 3863-3366

Recife
Guararapes/Gilberto Freyre International Airport
Praça Ministro Salgado Filho, no #, Imbiribeira
TEL (81) 3464-4353, 3464-4180

PIAUÍ
Teresina
Senador Petrônio Portella Airport
Avenida Centenário, no #, Aeroporto
TEL (86) 3225-2600, 3225-2535, 3225-2947

RIO GRANDE DO NORTE
Natal
Augusto Severo International Airport
Avenida Torquato Tapajós, no #, Parnamirim
TEL (84) 3644-1000, 3644-1070, 3644-1110

SERGIPE
Aracaju
Santa Maria Airport
Avenida Senador Júlio César Leite, no #, Aeroporto
TEL (79) 3212-8500, 3212-8557

Airlines
BRA – (11) 3017-5454
GOL – 0800-280-0465
OCEAN AIR – 0300-789-8160
TAM – 0800-570-5700
TRIP – (19) 3743-3100, 0800-558-747
VARIG – 4003-7000

Highways

State Highway Patrol
Alagoas (82) 3231-8026, 3375-4303, 3375-3342
Bahia (71) 3301-9868
Ceará (85) 3383-1674, 3383-2444
Paraíba (83) 3231-3366
Pernambuco (81) 3303-8008
Rio Grande do Norte (84) 3318-3440
Sergipe (79) 3259-3099

Federal Highway Patrol

Alagoas (82) 3324-1135
Bahia (71) 2101-2201, 2101-2250
Ceará (85) 3295-3591
Maranhão (98) 3244-5390
Paraíba (83) 3231-3366
Pernambuco (81) 3464-0707
Piauí (86) 3233-1011
Rio Grande do Norte (84) 3203-1550
Sergipe (79) 3261-1495

Car Rental

Avis
0800-725-2847 www.avis.com.br

Hertz
0800-701-7300 www.hertz.com.br

Localiza
0800-979-2000 www.localiza.com

Mobility
0800-160-525 www.mobility.com.br

Road Safety

When driving in the Northeast, get information on road conditions before setting out, either from the Highway Patrol, your hotel, or both. The roads in even the most developed areas can have hazardous stretches, and gas stations and services can be scarce or even non-existent. Always start a long drive with a full tank of gas, light snacks, and plenty of water available. Some regions should only be driven during the day because of highway maintenance or safety issues.

Tourist Police

Aracaju (79) 3255-2155
Fortaleza (85) 3101-2488
João Pessoa (83) 3214-8022
Maceió (82) 3326-5533, 3241-9401
Natal (84) 3232-7404
Recife (81) 3464-4088
Salvador (71) 3322-1188
São Luís (98) 3214-8682
Teresina (86) 3216-5233

Health

The Northeast's high temperatures dictate that travelers take particular care with their health. Drink plenty of fluids and wear sunscreen, a hat, and lightweight cotton clothes. If daytime temperatures are excessively high, opt for light food rather than overindulging in heavy regional dishes – which may be hard to do when the food is so delicious and tempting. Sneakers or hiking boots are essential for long walks. For hikes in national parks or forested areas, use insect repellent as a precaution against insect-borne diseases such as dengue fever, malaria, and leishmaniasis. Travelers headed to areas with a risk of yellow fever (which is transmitted by mosquitoes and confined to the western half of the Northeast; see www.cdc.gov) should get a vaccination ten days before traveling.

Climate

The climate in the Northeast is predominantly hot, with little temperature variation during the year. On average, temperatures range from 18°C (64°F) in the morning to 34°C (93°F) in the afternoon. The exception to this are the areas that are more than 200 meters (660 feet) above sea level, including Chapada Diamantina and Planalto da Borborema. These mountainous areas have a more temperate climate and average annual temperatures of less than 20°C (68°F). In the Northeast, the seasons are defined less by temperature than by rainfall. The dry season is in summer, from December to February, while the rainy season is in winter, from June to August. There is some locale-by-locate variation to this pattern – for example, during the winter the northeast coast gets much more rain than the south coast. Note that the semi-arid *sertão* region sees very little rain.

Time Zones

The Northeast is in the same time zone as Brasília, Rio de Janeiro, and São Paulo (3 hours behind GMT). The exception to this is Fernando de Noronha Island, which is one hour ahead of Brasília. Between October and February, some states implement Daylight Saving

Time, which puts them one hour ahead (just 2 hours behind GMT). Since the Northeast region have recently abandoned the practice of Daylight Saving, however, it's advisable to confirm details such as flight times in advance during this period.

Emergency Numbers

MILITARY POLICE – 190
FEDERAL HIGHWAY PATROL – 191
AMBULANCE – 192
FIRE DEPARTMENT – 193
FEDERAL POLICE – 194
CIVIL POLICE – 197
STATE HIGHWAY PATROL – 198
CIVIL DEFENSE – 199
PUBLIC HEALTH, DRUG AND FOOD ADMINISTRATION – 150
PROCON (consumer protection) – 151
IBAMA (Brazilian Institute for the Environment and Renewable Natural Resources) – 0800-618080
Department of Transport – 154

Holidays

Carnival and Easter are widely celebrated throughout the Northeast. Some lesser-known religious celebrations have also become major secular holidays, such as the Festas Juninas (June Festivities), during which several municipalities declare a holiday on the following Saints' Feast Days in June: 13th (Santo Antônio/Saint Anthony), 24th (São João/Saint John), and 29th (São Pedro/Saint Peter). The following is a short list of the important festivities and holidays celebrated in the nine states of the Northeast:

Alagoas
APRIL – Festival de Tradições Populares de Penedo (folk festiva; variable date)
JUNE – Floriano Peixoto Day (29th)
AUGUST – Nossa Senhora dos Prazeres, patron saint of Maceió (27th)
SEPTEMBER – Political Emancipation of Alagoas (16th)
NOVEMBER – Maceió Fest (out-of-season Carnival, held the last week of the month)
DECEMBER – Anniversary of the city of Maceió (5th)

Bahia
JANUARY – Lavagem do Bonfim, in Salvador (stair-washing ceremony, held on the second Thursday after the Epiphany)
Nossa Senhora da Purificação, in Salvador (29th)
FEBRUARY – Iemanjá festivities, in Salvador (2nd)
MARCH – Anniversary of the city of Salvador (29th)
MAY – Bembé do Mercado, in Santo Amaro da Purificação (folk festival, held during the first two weeks of the month)
JUNE – Feast Day of the Holy Spirit (variable date)
JULY – Bahia Independence day (2nd)
AUGUST – Nossa Senhora da Boa Morte, in Cachoeira (13th to 15th)
Nossa Senhora d'Ajuda (15th)
DECEMBER – Saint Barbara (4th)
Nossa Senhora da Conceição (Our Lady of the Immaculate Conception), patron saint of Salvador (8th)

Ceará
MARCH – São José (Saint Joseph), patron saint of Ceará (19th)
APRIL – Anniversary of the city of Fortaleza (13th)
AUGUST – Nossa Senhora da Assunção (Our Lady of the Assumption), patron saint of Fortaleza (15th)
SEPTEMBER – Nossa Senhora das Dores (Our Lady of Sorrows), patron saint of Juazeiro do Norte (15th)
OCTOBER – Dia do Romeiro (Pilgrims' Day; 29th)

Maranhão
MAY – Festa do Divino (Festival for the Holy Spirit), in Alcântara (Wednesday on the week before Pentecost Sunday)
Santa Rita de Cássia (Saint Rita of Cascia; 22nd)
JUNE – Bumba-Meu-Boi (folk festival; 23rd)
JULY – Adherence Day (Maranhão's acceptance of Brazilian independence; 28th)
SEPTEMBER – Anniversary of the founding of São Luís (8th)
São José do Ribamar, patron saint of Maranhão (first full moon)
NOVEMBER – Nossa Senhora da Vitória (Our Lady of Victory), patron saint of São Luís (21st)

Paraíba
APRIL – Micarande, in Campina Grande (out-of-season Carnival, second week of the month)
AUGUST – Nossa Senhora das Neves (Our Lady of the Snows), patron saint of João Pessoa (5th)
Anniversary of the city of João Pessoa (5th)
OCTOBER – Anniversary of the city of Campina Grande (11th)

Pernambuco
MARCH – Anniversary of the city of Recife (12th)
JULY – Nossa Senhora do Carmo (Our Lady of Mount Carmel), patron saint of Recife (16th)
AUGUST – Feast of the Transfiguration, in Olinda (6th)
NOVEMBER – Encontro de Maracatus, in Nazaré da Mata (folk festival; variable date)

Piauí
JUNE – Encontro Nacional de Folguedos (folk festival; during the second half of the month)
JULY – Planeta Micarina, in Teresina (out-of-season Carnival, first week of the month)
AUGUST – Anniversary of the city of Teresina (16th)
OCTOBER – Emancipation of Piauí (19th)

Rio Grande do Norte
NOVEMBER – Nossa Senhora da Apresentação (Presentation of the Blessed Virgin Mary), patron saint of Natal (21st)
DECEMBER – Carnatal, in Natal (out-of-season Carnival, first weekend of the month)
Birthday of the city of Natal (25th)

Sergipe
MARCH – Anniversary of the city of Aracaju (17th)
JUNE – Forró Caju, in Aracaju (third week of the month)
JULY – State Independence Day (8th)
DECEMBER – Nossa Senhora da Conceição (Our Lady of the Immaculate Conception), patron saint of Aracaju (8th)

USEFUL INFORMATION

CONSULATES IN THE NORTHEAST

ARGENTINA
Recife – PE
Tel: (81) 3327-1451
Salvador – BA
Tel: (71) 3241-4863

CHILE
Recife – PE
Tel: (81) 3224-3740
Salvador – BA
Tel: (71) 3345-4141

FRANCE
Natal – RN
Tel: (84) 217-4558, 9407-5123
Porto Seguro – BA
Tel: (73) 3668-1661
Recife – PE
Tel: (81) 3465-3290
Salvador – BA
Tel: (71) 3241-0168

GERMANY
Fortaleza – CE
Tel: (85) 3246-2833/2091
Recife – PE
Tel: (81) 3463-5350

ITALY
Recife – PE
Tel: (81) 3466-4200

JAPAN
Recife – PE
Tel: (81) 3465-9115

MEXICO
São Luís – MA
Tel: (98) 3232-6732/6232

PARAGUAY
Recife – PE
Tel: (81) 3459-1277

PORTUGAL
Fortaleza – CE
Tel: (85) 3261-7420
João Pessoa – PB
Tel: (83) 226-2120
Maceió – AL
Tel: (82) 336-4564
Recife – PE
Tel: (81) 3327-2073/1514

SWITZERLAND
Fortaleza – CE
Tel: (85) 3226-9444
Recife – PE
Tel: (81) 3439-4545
Salvador – BA
Tel: (71) 3341-5827

TURKEY
Salvador – BA
Tel: (71) 3335-1064

UNITED KINGDOM
Recife – PE
Tel: (81) 3465-0230

UNITED STATES
Fortaleza – CE
Tel: (85) 3252-1539
Recife – PE
Tel: (81) 3421-2441
Salvador – BA
Tel: (71) 3113-2091

URUGUAY
Salvador – BA
Tel: (71) 3322-7093

EMBASSIES IN BRASÍLIA

Algeria
Tel: (61) 3248-4039
Fax: (61) 3248-4691
Angola
www.angola.org.br
Tel: (61) 3248-4489
Fax: (61) 3248-1567
Argentina
www.embarg.org.br
Tel: (61) 3364-7600
Fax: (61) 3364-7666
Australia
www.brazil.embassy.gov.au
Tel: (61) 3226-3111
Fax: (61) 3226-1112
Austria
www.austria.org.br
Tel: (61) 3443-3111
Fax: (61) 3443-5233
Belgium
www.belgica.org.br
Tel: (61) 3443-1133
Fax: (61) 3443-1219
Bolivia
Tel: (61) 3366-3432
Fax: (61) 3366-3136
Bulgaria
Tel: (61) 3223-6193/3223-9849
Fax: (61) 3323-3285
Cameroon
www.embcameroun.org.br
Tel: (61) 3248-2400
Fax: (61) 3248-0443
Canada
www.dfait-maeci.gc.ca/brazil
Tel: (61) 3424-5400
Fax: (61) 3424-5490
Cape Verde
Tel: (61) 3364-3472

Fax: (61) 3364-4059
Chile
www.eta.com.br/chile
Tel: (61) 2103-5151
Fax: (61) 3322-0714
China
www.embchina.org.br
Tel: (61) 3346-4436
Fax: (61) 3346-3299
Colombia
www.embcol.org.br
Tel: (61) 3226-8997
Fax: (61) 3224-4732
Costa Rica
Tel: (61) 3328-2219/3328-2485
Fax: (61) 3328-2243
Croatia
Tel: (61) 3248-0610
Fax: (61) 3248-1708
Cuba
www.embaixadacuba.org.br
Tel: (61) 3248-4710/3248-4130
Fax: (61) 3248-6778
Czech Republic
www.mzv.cz/brasilia
Tel: (61) 3242-7785/3242-7905
Fax: (61) 3242-7833
Democratic Republic of Congo
Tel: (61) 3365-4822/3365-4823
Fax: (61) 3365-4822
Denmark
Tel: (61) 3445-3443
Fax: (61) 3445-3509
Dominican Republic
Tel: (61) 3248-1405
Fax: (61) 3364-3214
Ecuador
www.embequador.org.br
Tel: (61) 3248-5360

Fax: (61) 3248-5560
Egypt
www.opengate.com.br/embegito
Tel: (61) 3323-8800
Fax: (61) 3323-1039
El Salvador
Tel: (61) 3364-4141
Fax: (61) 3364-2459
Finland
www.finlandia.org.br
Tel: (61) 3443-7151
Fax: (61) 3443-3315
France
www.ambafrance.org.br
Tel: (61) 3312-9100
Fax: (61) 3312-9108
Gabon
Tel: (61) 3248-3536/248-3533
Fax: (61) 3248-2241
Germany
www.alemanha.org.br
Tel: (61) 3442-7000
Fax: (61) 3443-7508
Ghana
Tel: (61) 3248-6047/3248-6049
Fax: (61) 3248-7913
Greece
www.emb-grecia.org.br
Tel: (61) 3443-6573
Fax: (61) 3443-6902
Guatemala
Tel: (61) 3365-1908/3365-1909
Fax: (61) 3365-1906
Guyana
Tel: (61) 3248-0874
Fax: (61) 3248-0886
Haiti
Tel: (61) 3248-6860/3248-1337
Fax: (61) 3248-7472

Honduras
Tel: (61) 3366-4082
Fax: (61) 3366-4618
Hungary
www.hungria.org.br
Tel: (61) 3443-0822
Fax: (61) 3443-3434
India
www.indianembassy.org.br
Tel: (61) 3364-4195/3248-4006
Fax: (61) 3248-7849
Indonesia
www.indonesia-brasil.org.br
Tel: (61) 3443-8800
Fax: (61) 3443-6732
Iran
www.webiran.org.br
Tel: (61) 3242-5733
Fax: (61) 3244-9640
Iraq
Tel: (61) 3346-2822
Fax: (61) 3346-7442
Ireland
Tel: (61) 3248-8800
Fax: (61) 3248-8816
Israel
brasilia.mfa.gov.il
Tel: (61) 2105-0500
Fax: (61) 2105-0555
Italy
www.embitalia.org.br
Tel: (61) 3442-9900
Fax: (61) 3443-1231
Japan
www.japao.org.br
Tel: (61) 3442-4200
Fax: (61) 3242-0738
Jordan
Tel: (61) 3248-5407/3248-5414
Fax: (61) 3248-1698
Kuwait
www.embaixadadokuwait.org.br
Tel: (61) 3213-2333
Fax: (61) 3248-0969
Lebanon
www.libano.org.br
Tel: (61) 3443-3808
Fax: (61) 3443-8574
Libya
Tel: (61) 3248-6710/248-6716
Fax: (61) 3248-0598
Malaysia
Tel: (61) 3248-5008/3248-6215
Fax: (61) 3248-6307
Malta
Tel: (61) 3272-0402
Fax: (61) 3347-4940
Mexico
www.mexico.org.br
Tel: (61) 3244-1011
Fax: (61) 3244-1755
Morocco
Tel: (61) 3321-4487
Fax: (61) 3321-0745
Mozambique
Tel: (61) 3248-4222/3248-5319
Fax: (61) 3248-3917
Namibia
Tel: (61) 3248-7621
Fax: (61) 3248-7135
Netherlands
www.embaixada-holanda.org.br
Tel: (61) 3321-4769

Fax: (61) 3321-1518
New Zealand
Tel: (61) 3248-9900
Fax: (61) 3248-9916
Nicaragua
Tel: (61) 3248-1115/3248-7902
Fax: (61) 3248-1120
Nigeria
Tel: (61) 3226-1717/3226-1870
Fax: (61) 3226-5192
North Korea
Tel: (61) 3367-1940
Fax: (61) 3367-3177
Norway
www.noruega.org.br
Tel: (61) 3443-8720
Fax: (61) 3443-2942
Pakistan
Tel: (61) 3364-1632
Fax: (61) 3248-0246
Panama
Tel: (61) 3248-7309
Fax: (61) 3248-2834
Paraguay
Tel: (61) 3242-3732
Fax: (61) 3242-4605
Peru
www.embperu.org.br
Tel: (61) 3242-9933/3242-9435
Fax: (61) 3244-9344
Philippines
Tel: (61) 3224-8694
Fax: (61) 3226-7411
Poland
www.polonia.org.br
Tel: (61) 3212-8000
Fax: (61) 3242-8543
Portugal
www.embaixadadeportugal.org.br
Tel: (61) 3032-9600
Fax: (61) 3032-9642
Romania
www.romenia.org.br
Tel: (61) 3226-0746
Fax: (61) 3226-6629
Russia
www.brazil.mid.ru
Tel: (61) 3223-3094/3223-4094
Fax: (61) 3226-7319
Saudi Arabia
Tel: (61) 3248-3525/3248-2201
Fax: (61) 3248-1142
Senegal
Tel: (61) 3223-6110/3321-5866
Fax: (61) 3322-7822
Serbia and Montenegro
Tel: (61) 3223-7272
Fax: (61) 3223-8462
Slovakia
Tel: (61) 3443-1263
Fax: (61) 3443-1267
South Africa
www.africadosulemb.org.br
Tel: (61) 3312-9500
Fax: (61) 3322-8491
South Korea
www.korea.net
Tel: (61) 3321-2500/3321-2506
Fax: (61) 3321-2508
Spain
Tel: (61) 3244-2776/3244-2023/3244-2145
Fax: (61) 3242-1781

Sri Lanka
Tel:(61) 3248-2701
Fax:(61) 3364-5430
Syria
Tel: (61) 3226-1260/3226-0970
Fax: (61) 3223-2595
Sudan
www.sudanbrasilia.org
Tel: (61) 3248-4834/3248-4835
Fax: (61) 3248-4833
Suriname
Tel: (61) 3248-3595/3248-6706
Fax: (61) 3248-3791
Sweden
Tel: (61) 3442-5200
Fax: (61) 3443-1187
Switzerland
www.eda.admin.ch/brasilia_emb
Tel: (61) 3443-5500
Fax: (61) 3443-5711
Thailand
www.thaiembassy.org/brasilia
Tel: (61) 3224-6943/3224-6849
Fax: (61) 3223-7502
Trinidad and Tobago
Tel: (61) 3365-1132/3365-3466
Fax: (61) 3365-1733
Tunisia
Tel: (61) 3248-7277/3248-7366
Fax: (61) 3248-7355
Turkey
www.turquia.org.br
Tel: (61) 3242-4563
 Fax: (61) 3244-4257
Ukraine
Tel: (61) 3365-1457
Fax: (61) 3365- 2127
United Arab Emirates
www.uae.org.br
Tel: (61) 3248-0717/3248-0591
Fax: (61) 3248-7543
United Kingdom
www.uk.org.br
 Tel: (61) 3329-2300
 Fax: (61) 3329-2369
United States
www.embaixada-americana.org.br
Tel: (61) 3312-7000
Fax: (61) 3312-7676
Uruguay
www.emburuguai.org.br
Tel: (61) 3322-1200
Fax: (61) 3322-6534
Vatican
Tel: (61) 3223-0794
Fax: (61) 3224-9365
Venezuela
Tel: (61) 3322-1011/3322-9324
Fax: (61) 3226-5633
Vietnam
Tel: (61) 3364-5876/3364-0694
Fax: (61) 3364-5836
Zimbabwe
Tel: (61) 3365-4801/3365-4802
Fax: (61) 3365-4803

Additional information

MINISTRY OF FOREIGN RELATIONS
www.mre.gov.br
Tel: (61) 3411-6161/3411-6456

Acknowledgements

Adriano Gambarini, Ana Verena Almeida Mendes, Andrea Ciacchi, André Magalhães, André Sá, Arair Pinto Paiva, Augusto Coelho, Beatriz Fonseca Corrêa do Lago, Benedito Ramos, Bettina Orrico, Bruno Albertim, Carlos Arthur Ortenblad, Cristiana Viana Garcia, Cristiano Mascaro, Eliana Dumet, Fersen Lamas Lambranho, Francisco L. da Silva Neto, Francisco Senna, Gilberto Sá, Isaura Ramos, Jean Boghici, Joana Câmara, João Martins de Oliveira Filho, João Ricardo Barbosa Coelho, Joaquim Falcão, José Carlos Bôa Nova, Katia Rejane de Oliveira, Lélia Coelho Frota, Leo Caldas, Leonardo Dantas, Lourdes Brennand, Lúcia Coli Badini, Luís Tadeu Mantovani Sassi, Pe. Manoel de Oliveira Filho, Marcos Guerra, Marcos Aguinis, Maria Afonsina Braga Barbosa Lima, Maria Alice Coelho, Marisa Vianna, Mario José Estabelini, Mazzô França Pinto, Max Perlingeiro, Melquíades Pinto Paiva, Moema Cavalcanti, Nième Guidon, Norma Lacerda, Paloma Paiva Lamas Lambranho, Pedro Corrêa do Lago, Reinaldo Azevedo, Rogério Braga, Rosa Trakalo, Samira Leal, Sylvia Athayde, Tereza Torres, Zenir Campos Reis, Vivian Laneand, and Walter Carvalho

Photo Credits

Adriano Gambarini, 37 (cacau), 40, 90, 122, 129, 137, 153, 161, 178, 205, 304, 325, 330, 332
Alexandre Belém/Titular, 230, 255, 283
Andréa D'Amato, 29, 305, 309, 349
André Arruda/Press release, 46
André Seale/Pulsar, 59
Antonio Gauderio/Folha Imagem, 80
Arnaldo Carvalho/Agência Lumiar, 250
Ben Batchelder, 12 (turrets), 228, 323
Carlos Goldgrub/Editora Abril, 293, 295
Carol Riva, 310, 344
Cícero Viegas/Isuzu Imagens, 12 (Fernando de Noronha), 13 (Lençóis), 26, 32 (acarajé, beiju, caruru, moqueca, baião-de-dois), 34, 39 (cocada, caranguejada), 57 (king vulture) 65, 71, 72, 125, 144, 149, 216, 311, 312, 319, 324, 327, 329, 347, 353, 355, 356
Cristiano Mascaro, 50, 52, 68, 69, 96, 168, 191, 195, 197, 198, 209, 210, 289, 342
Daniel Cymbalista/Pulsar, 104
Daniel Katz/Fotoarkivo, 252
Delfim Martins/Pulsar, 77, 86, 115, 117, 134, 185, 211, 267, 290, 291, 292, 321, 339, 343, 345
D. M. Images/Fotoarkivo, 155
Eduardo Queiroga/Agência Lumiar, 35, 233, 236, 270, 307
Eugênio Sávio, 82, 187
Fabio Colombini, 36 (jambo, açaí), 37 (pitanga), 57 (bromeliad), 118,

120, 126, 156, 231, 246, 248, 256, 287, 300
Fabio Paradise/Pulsar, 36 (serigüela), 99, 177
Fernando Vivas/Editora Abril, 93
Flávio de Barros/Instituto Moreira Salles, 23
Foto divulgação/Francisco Brennand, 190
Foto divulgação/João Câmara, 48
Foto divulgação/Instituto Mauá, 79
Geyson Magno/Agência Lumiar, 36 (dendê)
Gilvan Barreto/Agência Lumiar, 103, 179
Imago Fotografias/acervo Ricardo Brennand, 19
J. L. Bulcão/Pulsar, 128
João Thibes/Fotoarkivo, 39 (sururu)
José Rosael/acervo Museu Paulista da USP, 17
Juca Martins/Pulsar, 64, 278, 285, 296, 297, 337, 340
Leo Caldas/Titular, 32 (buchada), 36 (mangaba, graviola), 37 (juá, cajá, cashew fruit), 57 (mandacaru),157, 166, 200, 206, 235, 237, 238, 241, 249, 258, 259
Luciano Candisani, 57 (manatee)
Manoel Novaes/Pulsar, 158
Marcelo Delduque, 140, 146
Marisa Moreira Salles, 36 (araçá)
Mauricio Simonetti/Pulsar, 83, 84, 139
Milton Shirata/Editora Abril, 247
Milton Shirata/Isuzu Imagens, 12 (Jericoacoara), 174, 176, 299, 301
Moacyr Lopes/Folha Imagem, 81
Pacífico Medeiros/Fotoarkivo, 280

Paolo Curto/Isuzu Imagens, 131
Patrick Altman/Isuzu Imagens, 263, 264, 266, 268, 272, 279
Paulo Pereira/Folha Imagem, 87
Pipo Gialluisi/Isuzu Imagens, 13 (Chapada), 98, 180
Pierre Verger/Fundação Pierre Verger, 15
Ricardo Azoury/Pulsar, 61, 132, 183, 298
Rogério Reis/Pulsar, 109, 335, 346, 354
Rubens Chaves/Isuzu Imagens, 94, 102, 113, 192, 220
Salomon Cytrynowicz/Pulsar, 243
Sergio Dutti/Editora Abril, 315
Sérgio Carvalho, 37 (pinha), 57 (coral crab, brown booby), 39 (bolo-de-rolo), 43, 73, 203, 226, 232, 245, 253
Sérgio Jorge/Isuzu Imagens, 57 (palm groves), 219, 271
Solange A. Barreira, 57 (mangrove swamo)
Stefan Kolumban/Pulsar, 163, 165, 169, 218, 261, 269, 308, 341, 348
Valdemir Cunha/Agência Peixes, 275, 276
Valdemir Cunha/Editora Abril, 314
Valéria Simões/Isuzu Imagens, 223
Zig Koch, 58, 147

Every effort was made to contact the copyright holders for the images reproduced in this guide. For further information, please write to: fotografia@bei.com.br